Basics of International Business

T0330708

Basics of International Business

James P. Neelankavil and Anoop Rai

Routledge
Taylor & Francis Group

LONDON AND NEW YORK

To
Angel, Prince, Erica, and Salve
and
Justin, Sonali, and Pat
with our love

First published 2009 by M.E. Sharpe

Published 2015 by Routledge
2 Park Square, Milton Park, Abingdon, Oxon OX14 4RN
711 Third Avenue, New York, NY 10017, USA

Routledge is an imprint of the Taylor & Francis Group, an informa business

Library of Congress Cataloging-in-Publication Data

Neelankavil, James P.
  Basics of international business / by James P. Neelankavil and Anoop Rai.
    p. cm.
  Includes bibliographical references and index.
  ISBN 978-0-7656-2392-8 (pbk. : alk. paper)
  1. International business enterprises. 2. International finance. I. Rai, Anoop, 1955– II. Title.

HD2755.5.N44 2009
658'.049—dc22   2008049003

ISBN 13: 9780765623928 (pbk)

Contents

Preface and Acknowledgments

This textbook is aimed at students who wish to learn and work in the field of international business. International business consists of the activities of commercial organizations across borders. Over the past 50 years, international business has grown rapidly, and it is now fair to say that it makes up a large portion of the business activities around the world. Moreover, the globalization of markets—that is, the trend toward borderless markets—has further enhanced the growth in activities of international companies.

The field of international business is dynamic, complex, and challenging. Daily worldwide events such as changes in governments, economic shifts, political turmoil, and natural disasters all affect the operations of international companies. To function under these challenging conditions, international business executives need to understand the complexities of their external environments; furthermore, they need to have a sound knowledge of business practices that can help them develop viable strategies to manage their operations. With this in mind, the objectives of this introductory textbook are to familiarize students with the external environments that affect international businesses, to show students how to recognize the processes in identifying potential foreign markets, and to help students understand the functional strategies that can be developed to succeed in this highly competitive environment. Every student of international business should be familiar with this process.

The concepts, theories, and techniques presented here are organized around seven major topical areas:

1. An introduction and overview of international business
2. Environmental variables and in-depth discussion of the key variables

    a. Culture and its effects on businesses and customers
    b. Political and legal environment
    c. Economic and competitive environment

3. Discussion of entry strategies
4. International trade and foreign direct investments
5. Integration of functional areas
6. Discussion of specific functional areas

        a. Production and operations management
        b. International marketing
        c. Human resources management and organizational structures
        d. International financial decisions
        e. Managing foreign exchange
        f. International accounting

7. Global outsourcing and its role in international operations

In writing this book, we have drawn from our collective experiences in teaching international business courses. Our philosophy in developing this textbook has been shaped by many authors, who over the years have influenced our thinking.

Many people assisted us in the preparation of this book by contributing their time and efforts in suggesting revisions, compiling data, writing programs, and being cheerleaders. To them we owe a great debt of gratitude. Of the many individuals who helped in the development of this text, the following went out of their way to see this work to its completion: our colleagues Mauritz Blonder, Claudia Caffereli, Debra Comer, Songpol Kulviwat, Keun Sok Lee, Rusty Mae Moore, Shawn Thelen, Rick Wilson, and Yong Zhang; our graduate assistants Eugene Dotsenko, Daniel Novello, and Sila Saylak; and Eileen G. Chetti for her editorial work.

ACKNOWLEDGMENTS

We appreciate the helpful suggestions of our peers who took time out from their busy schedules to read individual chapters and suggest changes that have considerably improved the material in the text:

Dr. Sandip Dutta, Southern Connecticut University
Dr. Tao Gao, Northeastern University
Dr. Jing Hu, California State Polytechnic University
Dr. M. P. Narayanan, University of Michigan
Dr. Sam Rabino, Northeastern University
Dr. Gladys Torres-Baumgarten, Kean University
Dr. Ashok Vora, Baruch College
Dr. Erik Devos, University of Texas—El Paso

We would like to extend a special thanks to Harry M. Briggs, executive editor of M.E. Sharpe, for his interest in and wholehearted support of this project. Also, thanks to all the staff at M.E. Sharpe, especially Stacey Victor, Production Editor, and Elizabeth Granda, Associate Editor for their help during the production process.

Finally, we would like to thank our families—Angel, Prince, Erica, and Salve, and Justin, Sonali, and Pat—for being there for us throughout this process and encouraging us during times of frustrations and setbacks; to them, we are eternally indebted.

Basics of International Business

1 Introduction and Overview

International business involves understanding the external environment, conducting country risk analysis, deciding on an entry strategy, managing the strategic functions, understanding the effects of foreign exchange transactions, and recognizing the value of global outsourcing.

LEARNING OBJECTIVES

- To understand the growth and importance of international business
- To understand the scope of international business
- To recognize the differences among various international organizations
- To understand the importance of international business research
- To understand the ethical considerations in international operations
- To understand stakeholder theory and corporate social responsibility in an international setting
- To understand the causes and effects of corruption

Businesses have engaged in international trade for thousands of years. In fact, international business has played a major role in shaping world history, from nations' attempts to control trading routes to their colonization of countries. International trade (exports and imports) has grown from US$50 billion just 50 years ago to US$12 trillion in 2006.[1] Between 2000 and 2006, international trade grew at an annual rate of 13 percent for a total growth rate of 87 percent over the course of just six years. The following sections discuss some of the critical activities involved in international companies' business operations, including (1) the reasons for pursuing overseas markets, (2) the various forms of entry into foreign markets, (3) the types of organizations that are involved in international operations, (4) the need for information and functional strategies among international companies, and (5) the ethical and corporate social responsibility considerations in international operations.

In the new world order, Chinese, European, Japanese, South Korean, and U.S. companies will not only be competing with each other; they will also be competing with highly competitive companies from many parts of the world, including companies from other Asian countries, Latin American countries, and central European countries.

Because of these changes, the World Economic Forum's Global Competitiveness Index (GCI) will reflect the emergence of many countries that were not on the previous lists. For example, Brazil and Russia have both moved up to the top half of the list. One surprising element is that the United States—even with its recent economic turmoil due to the 2008 credit crisis—is still ranked number one on the index.

International business management is a complex, multidimensional field. The intense competition for world markets, global expansion, and dramatic changes in technology have made the task of managing an international firm very challenging. Phenomenal growth in many Asian and Latin American countries is shifting the world economic order from the West to other parts of the world. Singapore, which a few years ago was labeled a newly industrialized country (NIC), is now a fully industrialized country. China has been experiencing double-digit economic growth rates for nearly a decade and projections point to a sustained growth rate of greater than 8 percent for the coming decade. India's real gross domestic product (GDP) grew by 7.5 percent in 2005, by 8.1 percent in 2006, and by an estimated 8.5 percent in 2007.[2] China and India are expected to be major economic powers of the twenty-first century. On a macroeconomic level, these countries pursue different strategies: China follows a state-driven export-oriented economy; India, however, follows a market-oriented consumption-driven economy. Both countries have been successful in their pursuit of economic growth.

The emergence of China and India as major forces in international trade is not an isolated random occurrence. Countries such as Brazil, South Korea, and Taiwan are leading exporters of high value goods, including automobiles, commercial airplanes, and computer hardware. South Korea is one of the world's leading shipbuilders. These countries present a vast and untapped market for goods and services. Such growth, coupled with stagnant and saturated markets in most of the industrialized nations, is forcing many companies to seek their own growth in these emerging markets. For example, Hewlett-Packard (HP) has weathered the softening of demand for its computers through its expanding international operations. HP generates approximately 65 percent of its revenues from overseas markets.[3] Similarly, domestic sales for Power Curbers, a U.S.-based machinery manufacturer, are expected to decline by 10 percent, but this decline is offset by the firm's foreign sales, which are growing at a much higher rate.[4] Hence, the foreign expansion of U.S. companies into overseas markets is driven by both large and small to medium-sized companies, and most U.S. companies have recognized the immense potential for growth in foreign markets. According to the Standard & Poor's 500 stock index (S&P 500), more than half of these companies' sales are expected to come from abroad.[5]

Rising input costs in industrialized countries are another motivation for companies to expand their operations into overseas markets. An assembly line worker in the Volkswagen plant in Wolfsburg, Germany, earns $25 an hour and works 33 to 35 hours per week compared to a factory worker in China who earns $2 to $3 a day and works 45 to 48 hours per week. (Minimum wage standards in China vary from province to province. For example, in Shenzhen the minimum wage is $101.25 per month, in Shanghai it is $86.25 per month, and in Fujian it is $53.75 per month.)[6] The availability of low-cost resources such as labor and raw materials in foreign markets

Table 1.1

Average Hourly, Weekly, and Monthly Wage Rates in the Manufacturing Sector for Selected Countries (US$), 2006

#	Country	Hourly Wage Rate	Weekly Wage Rate	Monthly Wage Rate
1	Austria	19.38	—	—
2	Australia	—	870.00	—
3	Canada	17.76	—	—
4	Czech Republic	—	—	884.32
5	China	—	—	102.00[a]
6	Ireland	19.04	758.10	—
7	Japan	—	—	3,569.10
8	Netherlands	—	1,082.72	—
9	Philippines	5.32	—	—
10	Romania	—	—	383.83
11	Singapore	—	—	2,364.70
12	South Korea	—	—	2,799.35
13	Spain	16.97	—	2,382.50
14	Taiwan	—	—	1,298.40
15	United Kingdom	19.25[b]	—	—
16	United States	16.50–25.00[c]	—	—

Source: ILO Statistics and Database, available at http://www.ilo.org/ (accessed June 19, 2007).

Notes: The International Labor Organization (ILO) reports labor rates in hourly, weekly, and monthly rates depending on how each country reports the data. The ILO reports rates in local currency. Rates have been translated in U.S. dollars using the average exchange rate for the year.

[a]As reported by *China Labor Watch,* July 2006, pp. 1–4.

[b]UK Statitistics Authority, "Wage Rates." Available at http://www.statistics.gov.uk/ (accessed June 19, 2007).

[c]U.S. Bureau of Labor Statistics, available at http://www.bls.gove/oes (accessed June 19, 2007).

makes global expansion attractive to international firms. For example, Motorola, a U.S.-based electronics company, has set up two large manufacturing plants in China to tap into the low-cost but highly trained workforce. Motorola has invested more than $3 billion in China and is the largest foreign investor in China's electronics industry. It employs 9,000 Chinese workers and has committed itself to improving China's technological base. Similarly, Intel is building a chip manufacturing facility at Dalian at a cost of $2.5 billion. Table 1.1 presents hourly, weekly, or monthly labor costs for 16 selected countries.

As shown in Table 1.1, wage rates range widely from country to country. China's monthly wage rate, one of the lowest at $102.00, is one-thirty-fifth of Japan's monthly rate of $3,569.10. It is no wonder, then, that international companies seek out countries where they can benefit from these low wage rates, provided the skill and productivity levels of the workers from the low-wage-rate countries are comparable to those of higher-wage-rate countries.

Businesses are adapting to a more global philosophy, as well. Globalization implies that the countries of the world are more interdependent on each other and that the people in these countries are affected by events and conditions outside their own country. Take for example the 2008 credit crisis. The mess caused by fast-and-loose

Table 1.2

The World's Ten Largest International Corporations Ranked by Revenues, 2007

Rank	Company	Country	Revenues (000,000,000)	Net Earnings (000,000,000)	Total Assets (000,000,000)	Employees (000)	In # of Countries
1	Wal-Mart	U.S.	351.1	11.2	151.2	1,900.0	15
2	ExxonMobil	U.S.	347.2	39.5	235.3	108.0	130
3	Royal Dutch Shell	Netherlands	318.8	25.4	192.8	114.0	145
4	British Petroleum	U.K.	274.3	22.0	217.6	96.0	100
5	General Motors	U.S.	207.3	(2.0)	284.0	186.2	150
6	Toyota	Japan	204.7	4.1	244.6	299.4	170
7	Chevron	U.S.	200.6	17.1	125.8	62.5	180
8	DaimlerChrysler	Germany	190.2	3.2	201.6	360.4	Over 100
9	ConocoPhillips	U.S.	172.5	15.6	164.8	32.7	40
10	Total	France	168.4	14.8	126.3	96.4	130

Source: "Global Five Hundred," *Fortune,* July 24, 2008, pp. 89–98; *Fortune Global 500,* July 23, 2008, pp. 130–139, and company financial reports, December 2007.

mortgage lending in the United States escalated into a perilous global crisis of confidence that revealed both the scale and the limitations of globalization. The credit crisis worsened and became a global problem because of the interdependence of the countries of the world. Tied together in an increasingly tattered web of loans, banks around the world dragged one another down.

Globalization proposes that companies view the world as one single market to assemble, produce, and market goods and services. Globalization is defined as *sourcing, manufacturing, and marketing goods and services that consciously address global customers, markets, and competition in formulating a business strategy.* According to John Zeglis, CEO and president of AT&T, in the future, there will be two kinds of companies: those companies that go global and those companies that go bankrupt.[7] From simple across-the-border transactions a few decades ago, international business has grown to encompass a vast network of countries, installations, individuals, resources, and organizations. Table 1.2 presents the world's ten largest international corporations ranked by revenues for the year 2007.

The dynamic changes affecting the economic, political, and social climate in many countries represent a new challenge to businesses. Western Europe has dismantled the internal barriers to form a unified region with a single currency and a vast market made up of 500 million consumers. The former Soviet Union has spawned 18 new countries. Eastern Europe and Russia have acknowledged the failure of centrally managed economies and have adapted free market economic structures and privatization. Indeed, the world has changed profoundly over the past decade. Some perceive these dynamic shifts as problem areas, but these changes also provide some rare opportunities that never existed before. Higher economic growth among emerging economies, coupled with stagnant economic growth in Europe and Japan in the past decade, has shifted the balance of and direction in investments. Since the 1950s, growth in international investments has been substantially larger than the growth in the U.S. economy. Large multinational companies derive more than half of their revenues and profits from international operations. Examples of such companies and their percentage of international earnings include Siemens (77 percent), Philips (73 percent), Sony (71 percent), Coca-Cola (70 percent), Toyota (66 percent), Procter & Gamble (51 percent), and Unilever (50 percent).

REASONS FOR GROWTH IN INTERNATIONAL BUSINESS

We have mentioned many reasons for the growth in international business. Some are related to the internal workings of a company; others are market-related factors; and still others are related to the external environment. The following list includes some of the main reasons for international business growth over the last 20 years.

- *Saturation of domestic markets.* In many of the industrialized countries, market penetration of most goods and services has reached saturation levels. For example, penetration of appliances, telephones, and televisions in Europe, Japan, and the United States is over 95 percent. Therefore, further growth potential in these countries is nonexistent.
- *Sales and profit opportunities in foreign markets.* As the markets in industrialized countries attain saturation levels, consumers in countries that are just attaining economic growth are demanding goods and services at unprecedented levels—levels that most often only international companies can meet. For instance, the number of cars sold in Asia is growing rapidly, with sales in China alone expected to reach more than 6 million by the year 2008.[8]
- *Availability of low-cost labor.* As show in Table 1.1, labor rates in industrialized countries are high, driving production costs higher. To counter this increased cost, international companies shift production facilities to countries with lower labor costs. For example, 90 percent of the clothes bought by Americans come from places like China, Mexico, Bangladesh, Honduras, Indonesia, and Vietnam.[9]
- *Phenomenal economic growth in many emerging economies.* The economic growth occurring in Brazil, China, the Czech Republic, India, South Korea, Tunisia, and Taiwan, for example, has created a large middle-class consumer base that is in a position to acquire high-priced quality goods and services from global brand-name producers.
- *Competitive reasons.* Either to stem the increased presence of foreign companies in their own domestic markets or to counter the expansion of their domestic competitors into foreign markets, international companies have used overseas market entry as a countermeasure to increased competition. Both these actions are defensive measures that prevent domestic and foreign competitors from gaining undue advantage.
- *Pent-up demand for goods and services among the population of the emerging economies.* Consumers in countries that did not have the purchasing power to acquire high-quality goods and services are now able to buy them due to improved economic conditions.

- *Diversification attempts by international companies to reduce risk.* One benefit of the international expansion of businesses is that international companies are able to counter the cyclical patterns of growth observed in different parts of the world. For example, if Asian countries are undergoing a downturn in their economies that affects profitability, the robust economies of Latin America will provide opportunities for substantial profits.
- *Progressive reduction of trade barriers among nations through cooperation.* This shift has stimulated cross-border trade between countries and opened markets that were previously unavailable for international companies due to tariff and nontariff barriers.
- *Cultural convergence in tastes and values.* Due to advances in telecommunication technology, the world is well informed about events, product offerings, and sites (McDonalds, Starbucks, and MTV) that offer goods and services online. This has led consumers from all over the world to buy goods and services made in different countries through Web sites such as Amazon.com, eBay, and the like.
- *The spread of economic integration among nations facilitating trade and the barrier-free flow of resources from country to country (expanded European Union, NAFTA, and other bilateral arrangements).* In addition, the integration of countries has created vast domestic markets that open up investments in capital-intensive industries.
- *Advances in technology in such areas as computers, telecommunications, and travel.* Technological advances have reduced the costs of transportation and logistics and have also produced improvements in supply-chain management, significantly reducing the costs of coordinating production among globally distributed suppliers.

As international companies venture into foreign markets, these companies will need managers and other personnel who understand and are exposed to the concepts and practices that govern international companies. Therefore, the study of international business may be essential to work in a global environment.

TYPES OF INTERNATIONAL OPERATIONS

Businesses can get involved in international operations in many different ways. The most common and perhaps the easiest way for companies to venture into international operations is through exports and/or imports of goods and services. Other types of international operations include licensing agreements such as franchising; direct investments; and portfolio investments. Chapter 6 discusses these operations in detail as part of the entry strategies available for an international company.

EXPORTS/IMPORTS

Trading through exporting and importing is a good way for companies to enter and establish a presence in foreign markets. It may serve as a stepping stone for greater commitment in the market at a later date. This is especially true for larger international companies. In most countries, smaller firms are in the business of exporting or importing (or both) goods and services. These operations require minimal capital and very few staff. Typically, exports are the easiest means of generating foreign-currency reserves, provided the country imports fewer goods and services than it exports. For example, China's trade surplus for 2007 was estimated to be more than US$200 billion. Chinese and foreign companies operating in China exported US$350 billion worth of goods, while their imports for the year were valued at US$150 billion. Through exports, an international company can sell any type of goods from slippers to large commercial airplanes.

Services too, can be exported. Service exports may be in the form of travel, tourism, financial services (banking, insurance, investment banking, and the like), and other services such as accounting, education, engineering, and management consulting. Many Caribbean countries earn a major share of their foreign-currency reserves through tourism. As people travel to these islands for vacations, they exchange their currencies for local currency, which they then use for food, lodging, and sightseeing.

LICENSING AND FRANCHISING AGREEMENTS

Licensing agreements allow a local company to use a copyright, patent, or a trademark that is owned by a foreign company for a preset fee. Franchising is a specific type of licensing agreement in which the foreign company (the franchisor) sells to a local company or independent party (the franchise) the use of a brand name or trademark, which is considered an important business asset. For example, many McDonald's outlets in overseas markets are set up as franchise agreements.

FOREIGN DIRECT INVESTMENTS

A foreign direct investment (FDI) is the acquisition of plant, machinery, and other assets in foreign countries. These investments may be through joint venture partnerships or through a wholly owned subsidiary in a foreign country. Through direct investments, management has partial or full control of its operations. For example, when Intel invests US$2 billion in Leixlip Ireland to manufacture chips, it is involved in FDI operations.[10] Intel assumes that its investments will generate sufficient cash flows to justify this investment. In recent years, China has been the world's biggest recipient of FDI: in 2006 alone its FDI inflows were nearly US$70 billion. Table 1.3 presents the FDI flows of ten selected countries for 2006.

PORTFOLIO INVESTMENTS

Portfolio investments are purchases of financial assets with a maturity greater than one year (as opposed to short-term investments, which mature in less than one year). As companies go global, so do increasing numbers of investors. Investors are buying foreign stocks and bonds as part of their financial portfolios. The total return on an investment is made up of dividend or interest income, capital gains

Table 1.3

FDI Flows to a Few Selected Countries, 2006

#	Country	FDI flows (US$ hundred millions)
1	Australia	24.0
2	Brazil	18.2
3	Canada	69.0
4	China	69.5
5	Czech Republic	5.9
6	India	16.9
7	Mexico	19.0
8	New Zealand	8.0
9	Philippines	2.3
10	United States	175.3

Source: United Nations Conference on Trade and Development, World Investment Report, 2007.

and losses, and currency gains and losses. International investing diversifies an investor's portfolio, which helps reduce risk and provides greater opportunities than domestic investing.

ORGANIZATIONAL LABELS FOR INTERNATIONAL COMPANIES

International companies are given different names depending on who labels them, that is, government agencies, international organizations, the business press, or academicians. Though they have similar meanings, these labels are quite often confusing. The following is a list of labels that apply to international companies.

- International company—a company of any size that participates in any form of business operation (export/import, licensing/franchising, strategic alliances, and FDI) outside its national boundaries (cross-border activity).
- Multinational corporation (MNC)—a large international company that has extensive involvement in international operations through direct investments and control of operations.
- Multinational enterprise (MNE)—similar to an MNC; a large, well-organized international company that operates in overseas locations and has considerable resources invested abroad.
- Transnational corporation (TNC)—an international company owned and managed by nationals from different countries. For example, Unilever is a joint holding of British and Dutch nationals. The term "transnational" is also used by the United Nations in reference to international companies.
- Global company—an international company with a network of worldwide integrative activities that attempts to standardize its products and service offerings. A global company might have its manufacturing in one country, technology from another country, capital from a third country, and distribution covering many countries. For example, Canon Inc. manufactures its products in China, uses

Japanese technology, gets financing from outside Japan, and sells its finished goods worldwide.

INTERNATIONAL BUSINESS RESEARCH AND THE NEED FOR INFORMATION

As businesses venture outside their own countries, the need to understand the market conditions in foreign countries becomes more and more critical. Business research, like all business activity, has become increasingly global. Companies that have operations in foreign countries must understand the unique features of these markets and determine whether they need to develop customized strategies to be successful. For example, to tap into the vast Chinese market, international companies are dispatching legions of researchers to China in order to get a sense of consumers' tastes.[11] Before 1990 there was only one professional marketing research firm in the whole of China; today there are more than 300 professional firms.[12] From the first quarter of 2000 to the second quarter of 2002, requests for market research proposals in China increased dramatically, from 22 percent to 42 percent.[13] Most of the world's large research suppliers now have offices in China. It is no longer sufficient to try to determine what Chinese consumers want simply by accessing lists of how much individuals earn and what they own. Companies need to understand what motivates Chinese consumers and what products they want and can use.

Information about environments, customers, market forces, and competition is essential in planning entry into an overseas market. Generally, business executives lack detailed knowledge of overseas market conditions. Compounding the problem is the unpredictability of the foreign markets compared to markets in many of the industrialized countries, which are more stable and predictable. For instance, the economic turmoil experienced in countries such as Indonesia, Malaysia, and Thailand in July 1997 came as a surprise to most business leaders and economists, as these countries had been projected to continue their strong growth into the twenty-first century. The home market presents a known environment for business executives, whereas a foreign market appears to be a black hole for many of these same executives. The availability of accurate information is most often the equalizer in this equation, which is why large international companies spend millions of dollars on information acquisition. For example, Hitachi Corporation of Japan spends a major portion of its $4 billion research and development (R&D) budget on understanding its target customers.[14]

Information is essential to business decision making. Information gathered through research is useful in defining problems, resolving critical issues, identifying opportunities, and fundamentally improving the strategic decision-making process in an organization. Specifically, in international business, research may be used to identify countries with the greatest growth potential, to predict changes in the political environment of a country, to decide on a location for a manufacturing plant, to identify sources of capital, or to select a target market. In addition, information may be used to evaluate the effectiveness of a business plan.

Access to current, high-quality information is essential for businesses, whether they operate domestically or internationally; for international companies, however, the need for useful information is much greater because of the uncertainties of the international markets. As mentioned earlier, international business operates in an unknown and more volatile environment than domestic business. Many of the external variables that have little effect on businesses in domestic markets play a critical role in international operations. For example, changes in political stability, exchange-rate volatility, and sudden surges in inflation do not ordinarily take place in Japan, the United States, and other industrialized countries. For companies and their executives operating in these countries, managing such environments is much easier than, say, running a subsidiary in Bolivia, Ghana, or Indonesia, where inflation sometimes reaches double and triple digits. In addition, some developing countries can present serious problems such as the sudden collapse of governments, the unpredicted devaluation of local currencies, or unexplained changes in business regulations. Outside of the industrialized group of countries, the business environment tends to be unpredictable.

Many international business failures result from executives neglecting to recognize cultural and market-related differences. Consider the following examples, which show how research would have helped the international company avoid an embarrassing situation while preventing the loss of market share and/or profits. When a furniture polish company introduced its aerosol spray polish and advertised its timesaving attribute in Portugal, the product failed miserably; the housewives in Portugal were reluctant to buy such a labor-saving device for their maids. A comprehensive consumer study might have revealed the cleaning habits of Portuguese households and helped the company avoid this costly mistake. In a similar case, when General Mills introduced one of its breakfast cereals in the United Kingdom, its package showed a grinning freckle-faced redheaded kid with a crew cut saying, "See, kids, it's great." The campaign failed to recognize that in the United Kingdom, the family is not as child oriented as it is in the United States; hence, mothers seldom turn over the decision of which foods to buy to their kids. Also, depicting a so-called typical American kid on the package was not very helpful either. Again, some research on food-buying habits in the United Kingdom could have saved General Mills some time and money without significantly delaying their cereal entry into the UK market.[15]

Most international executives recognize the need for and usefulness of reliable information, but quite often time and competitive pressures force them to act quickly, without doing adequate research. A systematic approach to business research is a critical first step in exploring international markets. Gathering information through research is not just confined to the marketing function anymore; more and more financial institutions, manufacturing firms, and even human resource departments of international companies are using business research to be more efficient and effective in their decision making. For example, as the competitive landscape for financial services became crowded, investment companies and brokerage houses rushed to grab consumer deposits. This meant that these institutions needed information. Today, financial service companies in many parts of the world use an array of qualitative and quantitative research techniques to guide their decisions, both strategic and tactical.[16] Similarly, sophisticated new techniques in cognitive mapping are now being used by the human resources departments of international companies to assess managers' mental models.[17]

Conducting international research is challenging, expensive, and time-consuming. There are many factors that affect international research. Key factors that need to be addressed include the cost of research, the availability of secondary data, the quality of data, time pressures, lead time (time that it takes to complete an international research study), the complexity of the study, whether a multicountry study is necessary, and how the research is ultimately used.

COSTS

International research is expensive, and the cost of conducting research varies considerably from country to country. However, information is essential in reducing operational costs through improved decision making, and research should be viewed as an investment, not an expense. One of the reasons for the higher costs in international research is the inability to find uniformly qualified staff to execute research studies. A lack of well-qualified research staff implies that the people hired to conduct the research need to be trained, which adds to the overall cost of the research. In addition, many developing countries lack a research infrastructure (focus-group facilities, training facilities, computing skills, and so on). Therefore, international companies have to either not use the local research setup or develop the necessary infrastructure on their own. Choosing the latter means these companies have to train staff, establish research facilities, and develop the needed computing systems. Such efforts add costs far and beyond the normal costs associated with conducting research. In some industrialized countries, the costs of conducting research are higher due to higher personnel wages. Even among industrialized countries, however, costs vary considerably. For example, a focus group study may cost as little as $5,000 in the United States, and the same focus group might cost about $10,000 in Japan.

AVAILABILITY OF SECONDARY DATA

Secondary data is the backbone of international research. It is cost efficient and easily gathered. Secondary data is sometimes the only information available for international executives facing critical decisions. In many countries, though, secondary data is sparse or nonexistent. Local governments do not have the resources or personnel to collect data; therefore, economic, financial, and other relevant information at the macro level is often outdated or unavailable. Researchers in the United States, Japan, and other industrialized countries who are accustomed to an abundance of government-provided secondary data find their forays into other countries shockingly disappointing.

In some instances when secondary data is available, it is often inaccurate or unreliable. In Middle Eastern and African countries where there are large nomadic tribes, the size of the population might vary depending on the season. Similarly, population figures would be less accurate where estimates are drawn from village elders, who sometimes exaggerate the number of villagers residing in a village. In countries where national income statistics are compiled from tax returns, population figures tend to be notoriously understated.

QUALITY OF DATA

International research suffers from inconsistency in quality. In some countries, such as Germany, Japan, the Netherlands, and the United States, the quality and the reliability of the data collected are high. In other countries, however, especially among less-developed countries, the quality and reliability of data collected may be questionable. Quality problems apply to both secondary data and primary data. In many countries of Africa, Asia, and Latin America, commonly used secondary data such as the population census, industrial output, and national incomes are often two to three years old, and in some cases are not available at all.

TIME PRESSURES

Quite often the decision to enter an overseas market is made under considerable time pressure. Decisions have to be made fast in order for a firm to be the first in a new country and attain certain competitive advantages. In some instances competitors are already in the market, and there is an urgency to follow. At other times the necessary negotiations with host-government agencies dictate the need for quick action. These conditions lead to a very small window of opportunity for an international company, forcing executives to arrive at a decision under less-than-ideal time constraints and leading to actions based on very little information.

LEAD TIME

Generally, it takes more time to obtain information from overseas markets than from domestic ones. Some of the problems associated with data collection abroad have already been identified. In addition, an international executive's lack of knowledge of the overseas markets makes the task of compiling data even harder. Sometimes, to overcome its lack of knowledge in the target country, an international company will rely on local research suppliers or local staff to collect and process data. Other factors that contribute to the need for longer lead time in international research are the lack of sophistication in data-collection techniques, the unavailability of databases to gather up-to-date information, and the lack of single-source data (scanners that read bar codes off packaged items).

COMPLEXITY OF INTERNATIONAL RESEARCH

Conducting a successful research project in one's own country is challenging in itself. When the project is international in scope, the dynamics are even more complex. In an international setting, even the basic research steps have their own twists. Schedules tend to be longer, vendor selection is more difficult, and depth of analysis can be weak. Even more difficult is controlling the exact design and methodology for each country in a multicountry study.[18] Among the factors that contribute to the complexity in international research are different levels of market development, the vast differences in government policies toward foreign firms, unique sets of external variables present in foreign markets, and the unfamiliarity of international managers with consumers and markets in foreign countries.

COORDINATING MULTICOUNTRY RESEARCH

By definition, international research is conducted across many countries. The differences in languages, cultures, business practices, and customs make the coordination of research activities across these markets all the more difficult. Difficulties in establishing the comparability and equivalency in data collection and analysis can make research across countries difficult and unusable.

International operations encompass a multitude of activities from a simple export operation to management of a wholly owned subsidiary. The information requirements for decision makers vary from situation to situation, depending on a firm's level of international activity.

By nature, the operations of international companies are far-flung. Diverse activities located, in some instances, thousands of miles away from the home office complicate the management of an international company. For instance, it is much easier for a Japanese multinational to manage one of its subsidiaries in Guangdong province in China, just three hours away by air, than to manage one of its operations in Munich, Germany, which is more than 12 hours and several time zones away.

The issues discussed in the previous section reinforce the importance of research in international business. At the same time, they highlight the difficulties of conducting international research, especially considering how the extent and the method of international research vary from situation to situation. In other words, the information required to develop an export strategy is quite different and less involved than that needed to set up a wholly owned subsidiary.

An early decision that many international companies have to make is the choice of a country in which to expand their operations. Companies choose different approaches in selecting which markets to enter. Larger companies tend to do their own (internal) country risk analysis. For medium-sized companies, outside research suppliers provide this type of research. For smaller companies, secondary data through government publications or through periodic reports published by the business press can be used to assess country risk. There are a few research studies available for free or at a reasonable cost for companies that do not have the personnel or capabilities to conduct a country risk analysis; Euromoney's *Country Risk Analysis* is one such study.

USES OF RESEARCH

International companies use research to identify market potential, to make financial decisions, to select locations for manufacturing plants, and to develop strategies.

Determining Market Potential

As domestic markets become saturated, companies branch out into foreign countries to seek newer, untapped markets and maintain a steady flow of revenues and profits.

Market potential, which is defined as the upper limit of market demand, is the basis for selecting a country for entry. In estimating market potential, companies consider factors such as total demand, the size of the target market, overall sales potential, the size of the subsegment, the buying power of the target segment, frequency of purchase, volume of purchase per shopping trip, and individual competitors' share of market. Information on these and other related areas can make the decision simpler for international executives.

Financial Decisions

Financial decisions in the international field are complex and risky. Exchange-rate fluctuations, different accounting systems, and government intervention often complicate financial decisions. Timely, high-quality information assists financial planners in making objective financing and investment choices. As technology and computers play a key role in financial decisions, the need for a fast information turnaround becomes a necessity. Thus, to compete in a complex global financial market, international companies need to invest in information systems. International companies, which have more options for acquiring funds than domestic companies, can borrow euro-based currencies, make use of offshore banking facilities, and borrow from financial institutions in the countries where they have operations. Because of the number of choices available for acquiring funds, information becomes crucial in selecting the most cost-efficient funding source.

The many options available to international companies also force them to obtain the most current information to minimize their cost of capital and remain efficient in the management of their funds. Some of the factors that affect financial decisions are unpredictable and may undergo dynamic shifts. A case in point is the recent exchange-rate volatility observed in Latin America, Russia, and Southeast Asian countries. Exchange-rate fluctuations, along with a rise in inflation, increase both the cost and the risk associated with financial decisions.

Manufacturing Plant Location Decisions

Production facilities are located to take advantage of such factors as inexpensive and technically qualified labor forces, abundant supplies of raw materials, qualified supplier sources, efficient transportation systems, and proximity to markets. If raw materials and adequate parts suppliers are available near major markets, then a production facility can be located closer to both the source and the market, completing the value chain. However, for many multinational firms, inputs come from around the world, and markets may or may not be located near supply sources.

In addition to location of the production facility, international companies must decide on the size of the plant, or the capacity, for each of its manufacturing facilities. Some companies adopt a concentrated production approach, that is, a small number of large plants in a few locations. Other companies have set up a dispersed strategy, that is, a large number of small plants in many locations. Matsushita of Japan has just a few manufacturing facilities, most of them concentrated around Asia and servicing the entire world market. On the other hand, Philips of the Netherlands has hundreds of plants located in many countries and servicing one or two markets each.

As international companies develop their manufacturing strategies, they need to be aware of the highly competitive environment in which they operate. Many factors affect manufacturing strategies. Some, like costs, are relatively easy to control, while others, such as quality, are affected by a combination of variables and tend to be difficult to manage. Efficiency, reliability, and flexibility are the other factors that international firms need to manage well to gain a competitive advantage in global operations. Competitive reports and information on sources of materials and suppliers can help companies create an effective manufacturing strategy. As the globalization process continues, the need for information on business-related areas also grows.

Formalizing Strategies

High-quality information is essential for developing strategies. By understanding competitors' strengths and weaknesses and taking that information through a thorough internal analysis, firms are better able to develop both functional and corporate winning strategies in the marketplace. Functional strategies focus on individual functions such as manufacturing and marketing. Corporate strategies guide the company's overall efforts in all its functional areas. For example, Sharp, the large consumer electronics company based in Japan, was able to use market research information called "Town Watching" to increase its operating income by 25 percent in fiscal year 1994 alone.[19]

Most companies realize that going global is more important than ever before and something they can no longer avoid. In developing a global strategy these companies must assess global opportunities and establish a tracking system to evaluate their efforts. International research is the key to the development of a global strategy.[20] International business research has definitely increased since the late 1990s. Many large international companies make use of research to chart their strategies. In cases where resources are scarce, global companies typically concentrate on the data that is most important in conducting their overseas operations.[21] The size of the non-U.S. market for research is now larger than it was in the past. Additionally, some small exporters are using research to explore foreign markets. These exporters do not make use of traditional research approaches but rely on personal contact with distributors, agents, customers, and even competitors to gather information concerning the markets they serve.[22]

ETHICAL CONSIDERATIONS IN INTERNATIONAL BUSINESS

Ethical behavior in general relates to actions that affect people and their well being. Whereas the need for ethical behavior at the corporate level applies both to domestic and international firms and their management, our discussion focuses on international companies and their managers.

In business, the wrongful actions of managers and their companies can have drastic effects on their employees, their customers, their suppliers, the general public, and the environment. When companies disregard safety standards, employees risk injury or death due to dangerous working conditions, customers may be harmed by unsafe products, the lives of the general public may be endangered due to dumping of chemicals in residential neighborhoods, and the environment may be harmed due to the emission of pollutants into air and water. A firm's disregard of legal and financial rules—using corrupt bookkeeping practices, for instance—may result in suppliers incurring losses or, in a worst case scenario, a company going bankrupt.

It is generally accepted that beyond their normal profit maximization goals, businesses have a responsibility to society at large, referred to as "corporate social responsibility," or CSR. CSR involves the ethical consequences of companies' actions, policies, and procedures and is defined as *"the social responsibility of business, [which] encompasses the economic, legal, ethical, and discretionary expectations that society has of organizations at a given point in time."*[23] Mark S. Schwartz and Archie B. Carroll advanced the three-domain model of CSR, stressing that economic, legal, and ethical responsibilities are equally important and that managers need to find a balance among the three in developing their strategies.[24] The definition implies that social responsibility requires companies not only to strive for economic gains, but also to address the moral issues that they face.

Companies seek economic gains to enhance the value of their investors (U.S. model of business). Accordingly, the primary duty of managers is to maximize shareholder returns. Some argue, however, that management's responsibility is to balance shareholders' financial interests against the interests of others, including employees, customers, and the local community, even if it reduces shareholders' returns. Advocates of this opinion feel that employees, customers, and the general community (called the stakeholders) contribute either voluntarily or involuntarily to a company's wealth, creating capacity and activity, and are therefore its potential beneficiaries and/ or risk bearers.[25] The principle of social responsibility means that companies need to be concerned as much about the wider group of stakeholders as about the typical company stockholders. The issue of satisfying the shareholders versus satisfying the stakeholders is not as simple as it appears. In a competitive global environment, executives who wish to make their organizations better "corporate citizens" face significant obstacles. If they undertake costly initiatives that their rivals do not embrace, they risk eroding their competitive position.[26]

Companies are often held responsible for behavior that in some way affects the society in which they operate; clearly, businesses must consider the welfare of the people and their environs. International companies have made major shifts in their CSR policies and actions in recent years. Initiatives such as investing in organic products, sustainable energy, and environmentally sound practices are becoming part of international companies' standard business operations; such practices now are considered mainstream.[27] For example, in its efforts to improve its CSR, Royal Dutch Shell, the large Anglo-Dutch oil company, has initiated a three-step process in dealing with stakeholders' concerns: after soliciting input from stakeholders, the company develops an organizational language so that CSR is uniformly understood by every member of the organization, and finally it takes actions that resolve some of its stakeholders' concerns.[28] Shareholders are increasingly pressuring companies to ensure that their investments are morally and ethically justified, showing the close relationship between business ethics and social responsibility. Some of the initiatives taken by international companies in the area of CSR include donating money for improving neighborhoods, providing grants to improve agricultural practices, setting up medical clinics, and sponsoring educational programs.[29]

For international managers and their companies, these issues are complicated, as they are foreigners in the countries where they operate. As a result, their behavior is scrutinized more closely than that of local businesses and their managers. Furthermore, because of cultural differences and unique business customs, there may be differences in what is considered harmful. Depending on the country, the extent to which unethical behavior is tolerated might vary, as well. For example, under the banner of economic development, logging has reached new heights in countries with vast tracts of forest. Logging in the Amazon forests of Brazil and the jungles of Borneo has helped efforts to increase arable land and add to housing stocks. At the same time, indiscriminate logging has created vast tracts of barren land that have changed the weather patterns, increased soil erosion, decreased the land's fertility, and created devastating mudslides. The governments of developing countries such as Bangladesh, Mexico, and Nigeria may set a premium on employment to the detriment of the environment, making them unintended supporters of environmental hazards. Hence, international managers constantly face ethical issue that they may not be equipped to deal with.

In a dynamic global community, potential conflicts in ethical business behavior become inevitable due to differences in values and business practices across cultures. Global business ethics is the application of moral values and principles to complex cross-cultural situations.[30] The question is, Which country's moral values should be applied? That is, should business executives adopt the moral values of their home country, called "absolutism," or the moral values of the host country, called "relativism"? Absolutism theorists suggest that the home country's ethical values must be applied everywhere the multinational corporation operates. In contrast, relativism theorists follow the adage "when in Rome, do as the Romans do." In practice, however, companies do not tend to adopt one of these two extreme positions when faced with cross-cultural ethical questions, but consider a middle range of ethical responses that might be less controversial.[31] The case of Levi Strauss & Co. illustrates this issue very clearly. Levi Strauss & Co.'s contractors in Bangladesh employ young children, a legal practice in Bangladesh, but one contrary to U.S. laws and the company's own policy. The fact that these children were often the sole providers— or supplied a significant source—of their family's income did not change the fact that Levi Strauss was using child labor. The company's response to the problem was to send the children to school and at the same time pay the families their children's wages as if they were working.

Local cultures and customs also affect business ethics in other ways. Research has shown that dimensions of national cultures could serve as predictors of the ethical standards desired in a specific society.[32] It has been suggested that in some countries societal norms and local institutions may unwittingly encourage people to behave unethically. For example, cultures that value high achievement and are highly individualistic societies are likely to pursue achievement at any cost, even if it means

Table 1.4

International Companies: Areas of Ethical and Social Responsibility Concerns

Affected Stakeholder	Ethical/CSR Issues	Situations
Customers	• Product safety • Fair price • Labels	• Should a company delete safety features to make a product more affordable for people in poorer countries? • Should a sole supplier of goods or services take advantage of its monopoly? • Should a company assume the cost of translating all its product information into other languages?
Stockholders	• Fair return on investment • Fair wages • Safety and working conditions	• If a product is banned because it is unsafe in one country, should it be sold in other countries where it is not banned to maintain profit margins? • What should a company do if it is found that its executives have been involved in accounting scandals? • How much should CEOs be paid? Should shareholders ignore extremely generous severance packages? • Should company pay more than market wages when such wages result in people living in poverty? • Should a company be responsible for the working conditions at its own facilities as well as those of its suppliers? • Should an international company use transfer pricing and other internal accounting measures to reduce its actual tax base in a foreign country?
Employees	• Child labor • Discrimination • Impact on local economies	• Should an international company use child labor if it is legal in the host country? • Should a company assign a woman to a country where women are expected to remain separate from men in public?
Host country	• Following local laws • Impact on local social situations • Environment	• Should an international company follow local laws that violate home-country laws? • Should an international company require its workers to work on local religious holidays? • Is an international company obligated to control its hazardous waste to a degree higher than local laws require?
Society in general	• Raw-material depletion	• Should an international company deplete natural resources in countries that are willing to let them do so?

Source: John B. Cullen and K. Praveen Parboteeah, *Multinational Management: A Strategic Approach,* 4th ed. (Mason, OH: Thomson Publishing), p. 138.

taking unethical actions.[33] Therefore, it is more likely that international managers from the United States—a nation that values high achievement and is an individualistic society—will engage in unethical behavior than will Japanese managers, who belong to a collectivistic society in which high achievement is not pursued as vigorously as it is in the United States. Table 1.4 summarizes the ethical and social responsibility concerns of international companies.

ETHICAL THEORIES

From a philosophical point of view, business ethics can be discussed from three different perspectives: the utilitarian (also called teleological), the deontological, and the moral language philosophies. Utilitarian philosophy suggests that "what is good and moral comes from acts that produce the greatest good for the greatest number of people."[34] Many international companies operate under this philosophy, especially when establishing offices or plants in developing countries. It would be morally justifiable, then, to operate plants that fail to comply fully with home-country environmental laws as long as they meet the host-country standards. Although the plant's operation would most probably pollute the environment, it would likely result in higher employment, as well, thus aiding in the host country's economic growth and providing the nation's people with an opportunity to use modern technology.

Deontological philosophy focuses on actions by themselves, regardless of the consequences that factor into utilitarian philosophy. Deontology philosophy is also called the theory of obligation: it postulates that rightness or wrongness resides in the action itself.[35] Therefore, actions themselves are morally good or bad. Hence, in the previous example, the international company that pollutes the environment is doing something morally wrong in spite of the positive benefits that are accrued due to higher employment or improvement in the economy.

The moral language approach builds on the utilitarian and deontological theories and focuses on international business ethics. First proposed by Thomas Donaldson, it suggests that the moral code of international corporations can be explained through the "language of international business ethics."[36] The key questions raised by this philosophy are: "In what ways do people think about ethical decisions, and how do they view their choices?" The moral language that is based on *rights* and *duties, avoidance of harm,* and *social contracts* is more appropriate for understanding international corporate ethics than those based on *virtues, self-control,* or *the maximization of human happiness.* Each one of these variables is entrenched in human behavior and results in how managers act in international business situations. For example, *rights* and *duties* imply that each individual has certain responsibilities that bestow on the individual certain rights. Similarly, *avoidance of harm* focuses on the consequences of behavior, but unlike the utilitarian principle, it stresses avoiding unpleasant consequences; therefore, actions by managers that do not harm people or the environment are considered acceptable behavior.

REGULATIONS AND SELF-REGULATIONS TO COMBAT ETHICAL BEHAVIOR

Today, there are different management standards, codes of conduct, and certification requirements at the international level. These standards and codes are meant to reduce or correct unethical corporate behavior and promote adherence to CSR by international companies. Most international regulations are aimed at transnational corporations, but business regulations can be created by governments or by nongovernmental organizations. When the regulations are established by a particular industry—known as self-regulation—individual industries or firms establish their own rules of behavior and codes of conduct.[37] Similarly, the European Union has developed policies to ensure that international companies operating within its boundaries follow certain accepted behavior in terms of CSR and have become part of the European regulation process.[38] In self-regulation, certification is a system by which a firm's products and services comply with basic management or output standards agreed upon by the industry group. For example, the International Advertising Association monitors and certifies the actions of its members.

To assist their managers in avoiding unethical behavior, international companies often develop programs that help these managers to behave ethically. Such programs have a definite country bias. For example, international companies in France rely on ethical codes; in the United Kingdom and the United States, international managers depend on a set of written procedures; and in Germany, international companies rely on training as a means to foster ethical behavior.[39]

STAKEHOLDER THEORY AND CORPORATE SOCIAL RESPONSIBILITY

From the earliest of times, safeguarding shareholders' and/or owners' interests has been the paramount goal of corporate executives; taking responsibility for the concerns of and interests of stakeholders, on the other hand, is a relatively new concept, probably less than a hundred years old. The earliest recorded reference to stakeholders was made by E. Merrick Dodd, Jr., a Harvard law professor, in the 1930s. Based on information from General Electric (GE) executives, Dodd referred to shareholders, employees, customers, and the general public as the stakeholders of a company.[40] The only current major stakeholder missing from Dodd's original grouping is the suppliers. This implies that GE and probably a few other American companies may have considered the stakeholder concept even before the 1930s. Since Dodd embraced the stakeholder concept, about a dozen books and more than a hundred articles focusing on stakeholder issues have been published.[41]

The formal introduction of the stakeholders concept into management literature, though not by that name, is credited to William R. Dill based on a 1958 Scandinavian field study that referred to many of the present groups considered stakeholders.[42] Other equally important figures in the evolution of the stakeholder concept and general stakeholder theory are Edward R. Freeman, who traced the term "stakeholder" to a 1963 CRI internal memo,[43] and James D. Thompson,[44] who along with Freeman formalized the stakeholders' principles and wrote extensively about them.

WHO ARE STAKEHOLDERS?

A stakeholder *"is an individual or group, inside or outside the organization that has a stake in and can influence an organization's performance."*[45] Among the many definitions that are used to describe stakeholders, this one seems to capture the essence of the group. Using this definition, we can identify a number of stakeholders, including shareholders/owners, employees, customers, suppliers, the community at large, the government, banks, other service providers (accounting firms, consultants, and so on), trade unions, and even competitors. Although the potential list of stakeholders can number into the double digits, in most research studies related to stakeholders, the commonly identified groups are the shareholders/owners, employees, customers, suppliers, and the community.

STAKEHOLDER THEORY

According to the stakeholder theory, every company should identify individuals or groups whose involvement is critical to a company's success and make every attempt to satisfy each one's needs and interests. Moreover, the company must be seen through numerous interactions with its stakeholders.[46] The theory implies that as a company strives to create shareholder wealth, it should also meet the expectations of its employees, customers, suppliers, the community in which it operates, and any other individual or group that it affects. The theory does not imply that any one stakeholder is more important than the others; hence, it assumes that a company and its managers should strive to satisfy the interests and concerns of all. From a practical standpoint, the level of satisfaction that needs to be delivered to the stakeholders is not defined, and herein lies the conundrum for executives, practitioners, academicians, and community representatives. Is it possible to satisfy the needs and interests of all concerned parties? Some believe it is, but others view this notion as impractical.

INTERESTS AND CONCERNS OF VARIOUS STAKEHOLDERS

To simplify the discussion of the issues concerning the stakeholders, only the major stakeholders are addressed here. As noted earlier, researchers have identified the major stakeholders of a company as the shareholders/owners, the employees, the customers, the suppliers, and the general community.[47,48] Each of these stakeholder groups has varied concerns and interests, and they may not all fit into one neat package. Some of the concerns of the community may be part of CSR. Table 1.5 offers a brief listing of the interests, needs, and concerns of the major stakeholders.

As seen in the table, the interests, needs, and concerns of the major stakeholders seem diverse and sometimes conflicting. For example, one way to increase profits and create shareholder wealth, at least in the short run, would be to offer acceptable quality products at the highest possible prices and pay employees low salaries and wages. This strategy may help the shareholders achieve their goals, but it goes against the interests and concerns of employees and customers.

STAKEHOLDERS' DYADIC VS. SYMBIOTIC RELATIONSHIP WITH THE COMPANY

One of the controversial discussions in regard to the stakeholder theory has been whether the relationship between a company and its stakeholders is dyadic or symbiotic. In the dyadic mode, each company establishes a relationship with and meets the interests and needs of each stakeholder on a one-to-one basis (see Figure 1.1). This model is simple and presumably easy to maintain, but it does not take into account the interrelationships among the stakeholders. For example, employees and customers

Table 1.5

Interests, Needs, and Concerns of Major Stakeholders

#	Stakeholder	Interest, Need, and Concerns	Major Driving Force in Achieving the Goals
1	Shareholder/owner	• Wealth • Capital gains • Dividends	• Costs • Efficiency • Effective management • Core competency • Competitive advantage
2	Employees	• Job satisfaction • Salaries/wages • Fringe benefits • Working conditions • Opportunities • Fair treatment	• Recruiting • Competitive salaries and benefits • Training • Motivation • Fair evaluations
3	Customers	• Quality products/services • Satisfaction • Value • Reasonably priced • After-sales service	• Reasonable quality • Effective communication • Extensive distribution • Customer relationship • Dependability
4	Suppliers	• Fair prices • Good accounts payable policy • Strong commitment • Long-term relationships • Flexible	• Competitive prices • Good quality • Flexible • Innovative • Financially sound • Prompt
5	The community	• Safe environment • Employment • Funds for community development • Socially responsible	• Setting up plants and facilities with fewest affects on the environment • Hiring locally • Funding projects for schools, hospitals, the arts etc.

not only are in direct contact with the company, but also happen to be members of a larger community in which the company operates.

Proponents of the symbiotic relationship acknowledge a wider network of relationships between the stakeholders and the company (see Figure 1.2). According to this theory, the stakeholders are dependent on one another for their success and well being; hence, managers must acknowledge interdependence among employees, customers, suppliers, shareholders, and the community.[49] Furthermore, this type of relationship is not simply a contractual exchange between parties: it involves interaction and network effects, as well.[50] It also means that in order to solve core strategic problems associated with the stakeholders, one must understand the firm's entire set of relationships with all entities.

Once the symbiotic relationship is accepted, the task of providing above-minimum levels of satisfaction to each member of the stakeholder group becomes difficult and complex. The interconnectivity among the groups assumes that each stakeholder is in contact with all the others and understands their needs. Therefore, the company's employees not only want good wages and benefits, they also want the company to spend money on improving the community in which they live.

Figure 1.1 **Dyadic Relationship between the Company and the Stakeholder**

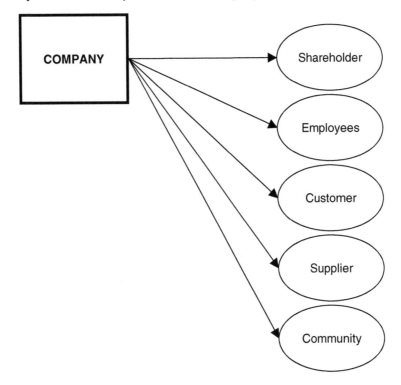

Figure 1.2 **The Symbiotic Relationship between the Company and Its Stakeholders**

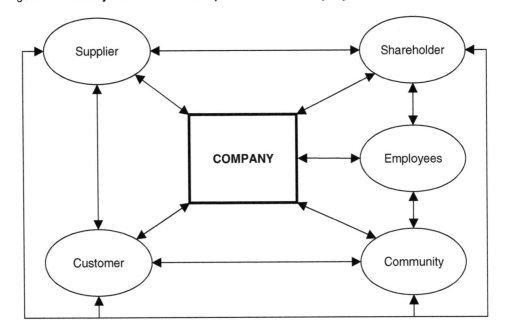

Complexity and Problems with Achieving Success within a Symbiotic Model

The symbiotic relationship believes in the importance of the interactions and interconnectivity between the stakeholder groups and the company. Therefore, it suggests that the company be knowledgeable about each stakeholder's interests, needs, and concerns and develop a strategic action plan to deliver the desired results. Based on current research, some companies have at least partially accomplished this. For example, Sears has successfully provided a high level of employee satisfaction and customer satisfaction, and at the same time has delivered very good financial results.[51] In a study of some Australian companies, Jeremy Galbreath found that corporate governance and employee management are positively associated with corporate performance.[52] In a similar vein, DuPont has decided to widen its sustainable goals for 2015 to include a commitment to expand its reach by addressing safety, environment, energy, and climate change, according to its CEO Charles Holliday.[53]

Though the evidence suggests that companies can meet multiple concerns through their symbiotic relationships with the stakeholders group, in reality this ideal has not yet been reached. For starters, not everyone believes that the various primary stakeholders are equally important for the company. According to this view, the needs of the most important stakeholders must be met first; only then should the needs of others be addressed. In the traditional American corporate model, the most important stakeholders are the shareholders, and satisfying their needs overrides the interests of all others. This may seem contrary to the proposed direction advocated by the stakeholder theorists, but a surprising amount of influential individuals are staunch supporters of the idea that increasing the value of the shareholders is the most critical goal for corporate executives. People like the late economist Milton Friedman have always stressed this point; according to Friedman, "Corporations exist entirely for the benefit of their shareholders."[54] Similarly, Robert Lutz, former vice chairman of Chrysler Corporation and now a top executive with General Motors, once stated that "we are here to serve the shareholder and create shareholder value."

From a theoretical standpoint, it seems easy to fulfill the needs and concerns of all stakeholders equally. But, based on current research, it appears that meeting the expectations of all stakeholders is bound to create some imbalances. Hence, many suggest a proportionate approach to satisfying the needs of the stakeholders by finding a balance among the diverse and potentially competing interests.

Reasons for a Balanced Approach to Satisfying Stakeholders' Interests

Stakeholder groups are connected through dynamic relationships. The question is how to create an acceptable level of satisfaction for each group. Ideally, a company would like to create a high level of employee satisfaction, which leads to greater employee effort, which leads to higher-quality products and services, which results in customer satisfaction, which leads to more repeat business, which generates higher revenues and profits, which leads to investor satisfaction and more investment in the company, which then provides additional funds for community development projects, which leads to a satisfied community and general public.[55]

It is difficult to present a case for treating all stakeholders equally. Who is more critical to the company: the investors who supply the funds; the employees who labor to deliver goods and services; the customers who provide the main source of revenue for the company; the suppliers who provide the necessary materials for assembling goods and services; or the community, which to a large extent supports the company, its employees, and its customers? Strong arguments can be made for considering the investors most important, and in many quarters they still are. A strong case could also be made for either the employees or the customers.

It is not easy for corporate executives to devote equal amounts of energy and time to shareholders' expectations and community concerns. Moreover, in each company there may be specialists who are responsible for dealing with different stakeholder groups. For example, the marketing group may have the primary responsibility for satisfying customer's needs and developing programs to maintain a core group of loyal customers. Similarly, the purchasing group may be responsible for maintaining supplier relationships. In some companies, there may even be a group responsible for community activity. But, the question remains, if the shareholders clamor for higher dividends and at the same time the community wants a school playground, which group will get the most attention?

Added to the aforementioned concerns are modern global corporations' problems. These companies operate in several countries with equally large numbers of stakeholders whose interests and concerns may not be homogenous. How should these companies proceed when local laws differ and internal policies may not necessarily meet the expectations of all the diverse stakeholders?

WHAT IS A BALANCED APPROACH TO DEALING WITH STAKEHOLDER'S INTERESTS?

Assuming a symbiotic relationship among the various stakeholders, a company needs to develop programs and procedures to meet those stakeholders' diverse needs. Stakeholders' concerns are a part of the business environment, and there is no escaping the effects of poorly planned strategies to meet their needs. This implies that companies must to some extent satisfy some or all of the stakeholders' needs. The results of ineffective stakeholder relationships may be a decline in sales, a boycott of the company and its products by the general public, or even government sanctions. Following are suggested steps to deal with growing stakeholder concerns.

- The first step in developing a comprehensive stakeholder strategy is to develop a communication link between the company and its stakeholders. This link should be used for understanding the concerns of the various stakeholders, determining priorities, and preempting problems. The keys are, "informing," "responding," and "involving."[56] It is important that managers build legitimacy and a positive reputation.
- The next step in the process is ranking the effects and consequences of not meeting the needs of each stakeholder and setting priorities accordingly. For

example, the shareholders are expecting their stock prices to go up; at the same time, the employees are seeking substantial pay raises. Which is more critical? Each company must have a system for addressing these competing demands.
- Reevaluate stakeholder relationships periodically to see whether any of the dynamics have changed. If they have changed, then the priorities need to be reconfigured.
- In all dealings with the various stakeholders, it is important to make sure that the treatment of each is perceived to be fair. For example, a community will not demand a major water-treatment plant from a company if it is losing money.

ADDITIONAL RECOMMENDATIONS AND CONCLUSIONS

Based on our review of the literature, it is apparent that all the concerns of all stakeholders cannot be met all the time. As one gets its wishes, others may lose. Hence, this process may be viewed as a zero-sum game. But is there an approach by which the losses of one party could be reduced without significantly compromising the gains of the others?

Corporate executives are often driven to satisfy the interests of the most critical member(s) of their stakeholder group. This drive is based on their fundamental business training and their mindset that every action has a cost-benefit trade-off relationship attached to it. In making decisions, these executives must decide which of their actions returns the highest reward or has the lowest cost. In such a decision-making environment, corporate executives aim to meet the minimum expectations (threshold) of each stakeholder group; at the same time, they try to deliver satisfaction levels above the minimum for different stakeholders. Usually, a company might aim to satisfy its customers, perform well for its employees, and deliver a threshold level of satisfaction to the general public. In setting these levels, the executives must be careful not to violate the various stakeholder groups' sense of fairness about the relative treatment they are getting.[57]

CORRUPTION

International business corruption affects adversely national economies as well as the international business environment. Some attempts have been made in the past two decades to resolve this complex problem. Although some success has been achieved, the problem is far from being totally eradicated.

Corruption is not a new phenomenon: incidents of bribing and seeking illicit favors have been recorded for centuries and existed in early Chinese, Egyptian, Greek, and Indian civilizations. Mankind, with its proclivity for power and wealth, has always succumbed to corruption in one form or another.

Corruption is found in all walks of life. Naturally, it is endemic to the business world. Internationally, it is even more pervasive, and it affects many aspects of business from cost of operations to business relationships and even government-to-government relationships. Understanding corruption in the international environment is made more difficult because international business transcends many countries and cultures. How

Table 1.6

Types of Corruption

#	Type of Corruption	Examples	Predominantly found in
1	Business corruption	• Bribing officials • Accounting irregularities • Tax evasion • Insider trading • Money laundering • Embezzlement • Falsifying documents (research data)	Most countries
2	Political corruption	• Voting irregularities • Holding on to power against the will of the people • Nepotism and cronyism • Rule of the few	Mostly in developing and less developed countries

should international companies with one set of rules and codes of conduct in their home country operate in countries that may have different sets of rules, especially if the host-country rules are less stringent than the ones in their home country?

TYPES OF CORRUPTION

Corruption involves many types of misdeeds. The extent to which people abuse their position for personal gain is virtually limitless. At one end of the spectrum we have a local low-level official taking small sums of money to expedite routine approvals or transactions, called *petty corruption;* in the middle we have defense contractors paying millions of dollars to lawmakers for awarding them major defense or transportation projects, called *grand corruption;* at the far end of the spectrum are the huge campaign contributions by lobbyists to politicians, called *influence peddling.*[58] Corruption is also classified by sphere—business corruption and political corruption—as shown in Table 1.6.

DEFINITION OF CORRUPTION

Corruption implies some form of illicit and criminal behavior for personal enrichment. Any definition of corruption starts with the premise of "abuse of power." In the international business context, there are three key players who are part of the corruption problem: the *principal* or the receiver, the entity that has the authority to grant and approve projects (for example, a government agency such as the ministry of industry); the *agent* or the intermediary who represents the principal and is actually responsible for granting permission on behalf of the principal (for example, a civil servant); and the *client* or the solicitor, a company or an individual who seeks a favor such as a permit for projects or investments (for example, a business entity).[59] See Figure 1.3.

Figure 1.3 **Key Actors in International Business Corruption**

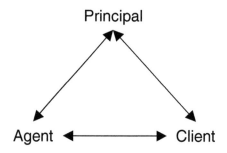

In this model, corruption occurs when the agent betrays the interests of the principal and accepts gifts or monies from the client to grant a favor to the client; the agent acts without any thought for the fairness of such an exchange. Corruption could also stem from the principal going directly to the client. Therefore, in defining corruption all three actors must be included in this triumvirate. Over the years various agencies have tried to define corruption. Table 1.7 presents the five most commonly used definitions of corruption.[60]

CORRUPTION PERCEPTION INDEX

In light of the ongoing problem with international business corruption, Transparency International (TI) has developed a scale called the corruption perception index (CPI) to measure the level of corruption among different countries. Each year using various factors and survey methods, TI classifies countries on a ten-point scale, with $10 =$ least corrupt and $0 =$ the most corrupt. The CPI uses seven different sources to assemble its ranking, including the World Competitiveness Yearbook, Gallup International, and DRI/McGraw-Hill Global Risk Service. Table 1.8 presents the ten least corrupt countries listed by TI among the 179 that it surveyed in 2007.

Countries like Finland and Denmark that rank very high on the CPI list have a relatively stable political system, very efficient government agencies, and a high level of trust between politicians and the populace.

The ten most corrupt countries in the world for 2007, according TI's corruption perception index, are presented in Table 1.9 (p. 32).

According to TI, Somalia and Myanmar rank as the worst two countries in terms of corruption. Over the years TI has successfully publicized the problem of international business corruption. Hence, more and more people are becoming aware of this issue.

EFFECTS OF CORRUPTION

Corruption can have adverse economic/monetary, social, and political effects.

- *Economic effects.* Corrupt systems do not provide open and equal market opportunities to all the firms. Payments and/or bribes do not have a market value,

Table 1.7

Definition of Corruption as Defined by a Particular International Organization

#	International organization that defines it	Definition of corruption
1	The United Nations (UN)	"Commission or Omission of an act in the performance of or in connection with one's duties, in response to gifts, promises or incentives demanded or accepted, or the wrongful receipt of these once the act has been committed or omitted."
2	Organisation for Economic Co-operation and Development (OECD)	"The offering, giving, receiving, or soliciting of any thing of value to influence the action of a public official in the procurement process or in contract execution."
3	Transparency International (TI)	"The misuse of entrusted power for private gain." Transparency International further differentiates corruption "according to rule' or "against the rule." In the first instance, the definition covers all the areas in which the receiver is required by law to receive some form of compensation (bribe), and in the second instance, the receiver is prohibited from providing some of these services and therefore is not entitled to any compensation (bribe).
4	World Bank and Asian Development Bank (ADB)	"Corruption involves behavior on the part of officials in the public and private sectors, in which they improperly and unlawfully enrich themselves and/or those close to them, or induce others to do so, by misusing the position in which they are placed."

Table 1.8

The Ten Least Corrupt Countries of the World, 2007

Rank	Country	Corruption Perception Index (CPI)*
1	Denmark	9.4
1	Finland	9.4
1	New Zealand	9.4
4	Singapore	9.3
4	Sweden	9.3
6	Iceland	9.2
7	Netherlands	9.0
7	Switzerland	9.0
9	Canada	8.7
9	Norway	8.7

Source: Transparency International, "Corruption Perception Index." Available at http://www.transparency.org/ (accessed June 5, 2008).
*CPI Scale: 10 = Clean; 0 = Corrupt.

so they raise the overall cost of operations. Many international companies try to avoid investing in countries that appear to be corrupt. A lack of foreign direct investment (FDI) flows to a country increases financing costs for both private and public projects. The limited capital within the country forces local investors to pay higher rates for borrowings. For example, a study done by the Milken

Table 1.9

Ten Most Corrupt Countries of the World, 2007

Rank	Country	Corruption Perception Index (CPI)*
179	Somalia	1.4
179	Myanmar	1.4
178	Iraq	1.5
177	Haiti	1.6
175	Uzbekistan	1.7
175	Tonga	1.7
172	Sudan	1.8
172	Chad	1.8
168	Laos	1.9
168	Guinea	1.9

Source: Transparency International, "Corruption Perception Index." Available at http://www.transparency.org/ (accessed June 5, 2008).
*CPI Scale: 10 = Clean; 0 = Corrupt.

Institute[61] found that in comparing sovereign bond issues, countries with a higher corruption index had to pay much higher premiums than those with a lower corruption index. In comparing Sweden and Brazil with a similar amount of bond issuance for 1997 and 1998 ($23 billion versus $22 billion, respectively), Brazil's financing costs were about 25 times greater than that of Sweden ($38,157 billion versus $1,531 billion) because of graft and corruption.

- *Social effects.* Besides the monetary costs, corruption leads to some social costs that could be detrimental to a country's overall economic growth. Some of the social costs associated with higher corruption levels are seen in the areas of health, education, and hygiene. Because of corruption, the amount spent on public services is considerably lower than the spending in other comparable countries with lower corruption levels.[62] Using regression analysis, Paulo Mauro demonstrated that a country that improves its corruption perception index (CPI) by 2 points ends up increasing its education budget at least by 1 percent of its GDP.[63]
- *Political effects.* Politically, corruption strengthens the power of corrupt, self-serving leaders. They amass wealth for themselves, allocate very low levels of funds for projects that could benefit the country, perpetuate the rule of a few, and suppress the rights and voices of the majority of the population. To continue in power, these leaders need funds, and most often the monies come from bribes.

PRESCRIPTION TO REDUCE INTERNATIONAL BUSINESS CORRUPTION

Efforts to curb corruption in the past three decades have had somewhat less than stellar results. Some improvements have come with the actions of individual governments like the United States, international organizations such as the Organisation for Economic Co-operation and Development (OECD) and TI, and individual companies.[64] Because of globalization, many more companies operate internationally compared to 20 years ago. All indications are that the number of cases of corruption is on the rise. In order to reduce worldwide corruption that affects businesses, there has to be a concerted and well-coordinated effort on the part of all concerned. The parties that must take an active role in this effort are listed below.

Individual Country Governments

Any attempt to curb corruption has to start at the country level. Governments in the most corrupt countries must introduce programs to root out the offenders. Since many highly corrupt countries are economically poor, the incentives for these countries to get rid of corruption must be economic in nature. Through greater FDI flows, transfer of technology from industrialized countries, and reduction in unemployment, these countries can attain an unprecedented level of economic growth. Some specific steps that countries with high levels of corruption should undertake to curb corruption are listed below.

1. *Enact anticorruption regulations.* Most of the countries with high levels of corruption either do not have anticorruption laws or have them but do not enforce them.
2. *Set up monitoring systems.* Laws and regulations will be observed only if there is a mechanism to monitor and enforce them.
3. *Penalties.* Anticorruption laws will not be obeyed unless there are severe penalties meted out to law breakers.
4. *Codes of conduct for government employees.* It is imperative that codes of conduct for government employees be developed and then enforced.
5. *Incentive systems for government employees.* Most social scientists agree that individuals are more likely to obey rules if compliance is reinforced with a reward system. Rewarding employees who are honest and obey the codes of conduct lowers the temptation to take bribes.
6. *Better salary structure for government employees.* In many developing countries, taking bribes is almost a necessity for some government employees because of poor wages.

International Organizations

Because of lack of funds and technical knowledge, attempts by individual countries to reduce corruption would not work without outside help. To assist the countries in curbing corruption, some of the international agencies must get involved with necessary financing and training. Corruption is a worldwide problem that funnels productive funds out of the economic system and into the hands of a few who then use it for personal gains without contributing to the developments efforts of the country.

Some specific steps that these agencies could undertake include:

1. *Providing knowledge and training.* Organizations such as the World Bank, the International Monetary Fund (IMF), TI, and the United Nations could provide

technical help to those countries suffering from high corruption. Initiatives might include formulating laws, developing codes of conduct for government employees, and helping in the development of monitoring systems to track the violators of these corruption codes.

2. *Providing funding.* In order to curb corruption in developing countries, funding is needed to carry out some of the prescriptions/steps outlined earlier. The countries with highest level of corruption are those that are economically poor; therefore, it is imperative that some of the international organizations that have developmental funds at their disposal—for example, the IMF and the Asian Development Bank—provide some of these funds.

3. *Harmonizing the codes.* At present countries (especially the industrialized countries) set their own standards for business behavior. The process of curbing corruption would go a long way, if anticorruption codes could be standardized so that there is no confusion, especially when an international firm operating in two different countries has to follow two different sets of rule.

International Firms

Among the key participants in the corruption process are the international firms who try to use influence, gifts, and bribes to get better deals from host nations. It is important that international firms collectively follow uniform codes of conduct in dealing with host countries for the benefit of the consumers, the economic growth of the host country, and for their own profit objectives. To help in the fight against corruption, international firms could:

1. *Set up internal codes of conduct.* Typically, international firms have their own internal codes of conduct for conducting business with host nations and vendors. For example, in many companies, the specific amount of gift that one can accept from vendors is limited to a very small amount. Similarly, there are written rules banning bribes to host-country officials and also an explanation of what constitutes a bribe. Firms need to improve the way they monitor and enforce these rules and policies.

2. *Employee training.* Employee training programs can help employees understand the rationale for the good behavior rules.

3. *Provide funding.* For the worldwide anticorruption program to succeed, it needs developmental funds that could be used at the country level for establishing various programs. The countries themselves are poor and do not have the funds to set up anticorruption programs. Some of the international organization may provide some funding, but it appears that this is not adequate. To augment the existing budgets, international firms could step in and fill the need. The funds that are provided by the international firms should not go to individual countries, but to the international agencies who then can distribute these funds.

Figure 1.4 presents a summary of the key issues of international business corruption.

Figure 1.4 **Framework of Corruption: Summary of Causes and Prescriptions**

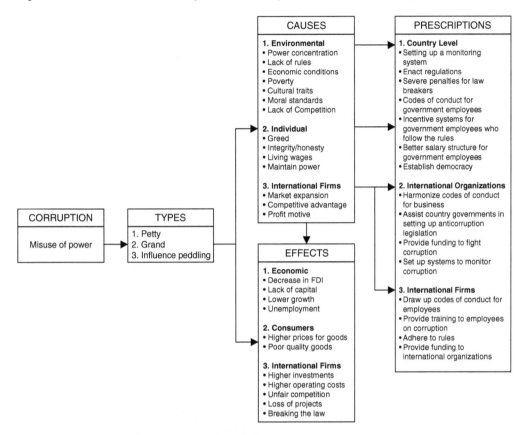

Source: James P. Neelankavil, "International Business Corruption: A Framework of Causes, Effects, and Prescriptions," Conference Presentation, Academy of European International Business, Athens, Greece, December 8–10, 2002.

CHAPTER SUMMARY

International business management is a complex, multidimensional field. The intense competition for world markets, global expansion, and dramatic changes in technology have made the task of managing an international firm challenging. Phenomenal growth in many Asian and Latin American countries is shifting the world economic order from the West to other parts of the world.

As a result, businesses are adapting to a more global philosophy. Globalization proposes that companies view the world as one single market to assemble, produce, and market goods and services. Globalization is defined as sourcing, manufacturing, and marketing goods and services that consciously address global customers, markets, and competition in formulating a business strategy.

The dynamic changes occurring in the economic, political, and social climate in many countries represent a new challenge to businesses. Western Europe has dismantled its internal barriers to form a unified region with a single currency and a vast market made up of 500 million consumers. The Soviet Union does not exist anymore, but instead has spawned 18 new countries. Among the many reasons for the growth in international business are those that are related to the internal workings of a company, others that are market-related factors, and still others that are related to the external environment.

Businesses can get involved in international operations in many different ways. The most common and probably the easiest way companies get involved in international operations is through exports and/or imports of goods and services. Other types of international operations include licensing agreements and franchising, direct investments, and portfolio investments.

As businesses venture outside their own countries, the need to understand that the market conditions in foreign countries is becoming more and more critical. Business research, like all business activity, has become increasingly global. Firms that conduct business in overseas markets must understand the unique features of these markets and determine whether they need to develop customized strategies to be successful.

Information is essential to business decision making. Information gathered through research is useful in defining problems, resolving critical issues, identifying opportunities, and fundamentally improving an organization's strategic decision-making processes. Conducting international research is challenging, expensive, and time-consuming. Many factors affect its outcome, including the cost of conducting the research, the availability of secondary data, the quality of the data collected, time pressures, lead time (the time it takes to complete an international research study), the complexity of the study, and whether a multicountry study is necessary.

Ethical behavior in general relates to actions that affect people and their well-being. In business, the actions of managers and their companies may have drastic effects on their employees, customers, suppliers, the general public, and the environment. The need for ethical behavior among managers and their companies is not restricted to international companies, but extends to domestic firms as well. In a dynamic global community, potential conflicts in ethical business behavior due to differences in values and business practices across cultures are inevitable. Global business ethics is the application of moral values and principles to complex cross-cultural situations.

It is generally accepted that beyond their normal profit-maximization goals, referred to as corporate social responsibility (CSR), businesses have a responsibility to society at large. CSR is generally defined as the ethical consequences of companies' actions, policies, and procedures.

Companies seek economic gains chiefly to enhance the value for their investors. Accordingly, managers have a duty primarily to maximize shareholder returns. Some argue, though, that a manager's duty is to balance the financial interests of the shareholders against the interests of others such as employees, customers, and the local community, even if it reduces shareholder returns. In their opinion, these individuals, called the stakeholders, contribute either voluntarily or involuntarily to a company's wealth, creating capacity and activity, and are therefore its potential beneficiaries and/ or risk bearers. The principle of social responsibility means that companies need to be concerned about the wider group of company stakeholders, not just the typical company stockholders.

A large number of stakeholders exist, including shareholders/owners, employees, customers, suppliers, the community at large, the government, banks, other service providers (accounting firms, consultants, and so on), trade unions, and even competitors. Although the potential list of stakeholders can number into the double digits, in most research studies related to stakeholders, the commonly identified groups are the shareholders/owners, employees, customers, suppliers, and the community.

International business corruption is a worldwide phenomenon with no end in sight. Its effects on local economies are very damaging. A few industrialized nations and international organizations such as the OECD and Transparency International have introduced new initiatives to curb the problem of corruption. The collective efforts of these groups have succeeded to some extent in publicizing the problem and forcing countries to take action.

The three main actors in the corruption equation are: the *principal,* the *agent,* and the *client.* Any attempt to curb corruption has to bring order into all three parties; attempting to solve the problem from one entity alone will definitely fail. To truly reduce corruption, the efforts of the countries involved, the international firms who participate in corruption, and international watchdog organizations must all work together. The main focus of their efforts must be in developing codes of conduct, harmonizing those codes, providing training, establishing monitoring systems, and setting up a judicial process to hear corruption cases.

KEY CONCEPTS

Globalization
Reasons for International Expansion
International Business Ethics
Corporate Social Responsibility

DISCUSSION QUESTIONS

1. Identify and explain the reasons why companies seek foreign markets.
2. Define globalization. What are the implications of globalization for companies?
3. How do companies get involved in international business?
4. Identify and distinguish among the various types of international organizations.
5. Why is international research important?
6. What are some of the complexities and difficulties inherent in conducting international research?
7. How do international companies use research?
8. What is corporate social responsibility (CSR)?
9. Why is corporate social responsibility important?
10. Enumerate and explain the various ethical theories of international business.
11. How does corruption affect international business?
12. What is the corruption perception index (CPI)?

2 International Business Environment: Culture

> Culture, because it is learned, constitutes the major method that people use to adapt to a changing environment, whether the changes happen through traditional means or through technological advances.

LEARNING OBJECTIVES

- To understand the importance of the international business environment
- To understand the cultural environment
- To understand cultural components
- To understand the various dimensions of culture
- To understand cross-cultural differences
- To learn about cultural clusters
- To understand the differences between cultural convergence, culture shock, and cultural orientation

Every business operates in an environment that is outside its control. This environment is external to the firm and influences its actions. Therefore, the external environment in which a business operates is the sum of all forces surrounding and affecting its operations. Each factor plays a critical role in a firm's decisions, whether these decisions include entering a particular market or how to behave once a firm enters this market.

The external environment in which a firm operates includes:

- The cultural environment
- Economic factors
- The political system
- Technological development
- The banking and financial systems
- Infrastructural capabilities
- The competitive environment
- Regulatory developments
- Social systems
- Supplier networks

These external factors confront all companies—both domestic and international—though dealing with the environmental factors is easier in the domestic market than in international markets. The external environment of international markets is more complex and unpredictable, making it difficult to analyze. Take, for example, the issue of foreign exchange. The costs, prices, revenues, and profits for a domestic firm such as Toshiba, operating in Japan, are expressed in the local currency, the yen, and so Toshiba's domestic division is not subject to the exchange-rate risks that its international division faces. Exchange rates can make costs rise and profits disappear. Tracking and predicting exchange-rate movements are important for international companies, but at the same time it is difficult to forecast exact rate changes. In contrast, for a purely domestic firm, this is less of a problem (unless that firm imports all its raw materials and supplies). Similarly, culture plays an important role in business strategy, but for domestic firms operating under a single cultural environment, this is not a major issue. On the other hand, international firms often operate in countries with cultures that are very different from those of their home countries, and in many instances the firms have little familiarity with these cultural distinctions.

All of the above-mentioned external factors are collectively very important and dictate how an international firm operates. Depending on the industry and product category, some factors are more important than others; for example, in the computer and software industry, technological development may be more important than social systems.

Analysis of the external environment is useful in the selection of foreign countries/markets, as well as for developing viable strategies once a firm enters a particular market. Most environmental analysis is done using secondary sources, that is, using existing information that is available through government sources, journal and newspaper publications, and databases, and utilizing internal information that was previously collected for other purposes.

For international companies, the most critical external variables are *culture, the economy, political stability, the banking and financial systems,* and *the competitive environment.* Culture is important because a majority of international business blunders can be traced to a lack of understanding of the host country's cultural values and business customs. Economy is important because economic factors contribute to the firm's overall financial viability. Political systems are important because it is difficult for an international firm to succeed when the host country's political systems are unstable. A sound banking and financial system helps international companies avail themselves of operating capital, manage export transactions through letters of credit and other instruments, and repatriate profits to the home country. Finally, the competitive environment is critical because competitive forces dictate strategic actions and ultimately influence performance in the marketplace.

CULTURAL ENVIRONMENT

International companies have to deal with different cultures in different countries. Companies such as Coca-Cola that operate in many countries (about 197 in Coke's case) have to learn, understand, and use these cultural differences in their strategic action plans. Learning new cultures does not mean just mastering a few of the "hidden languages" of the host country; it also means learning to bridge the differences between cultures to create successful interactions. Culture operates on the unconscious level, and its effects are subtle. For example, the French are very proud of their culture and language and therefore are sensitive to issues that deal with the cultural environment, especially in business transactions. The Japanese run their meetings not with a set agenda, but with a flexible one, which sometimes unnerves Western business executives. And one has to be aware when dealing with German executives that they are sensitive about titles and are very formal in their business negotiations.[1]

In fact, as cultures tend to be more societal in nature (each society has its own culture), international companies sometimes have to deal with more than one culture in a single country. For instance, culturally, northern Italians are different from southern Italians in their behavior and tastes. Similarly, the various regions of China are made up of multiple cultures with contrasting cultural differences. Hence, different layers of culture exist at the national, regional, societal, gender, social class, and corporate levels.[2] At the country level, research has shown that cultural values have significant effects on a country's economic development, regulatory policies, and levels of corruption.[3] At the regional level, studies indicate that cultural settings create opportunities and limitations for people that vary from country to country within the same region.[4] Similarly, at the corporate level, research reveals that culture affects not only the strategic level, but also the area of management and its market orientation.[5] In the discussions on culture that follow, the terms "country" and "society" are used interchangeably.

Cultural changes take place very slowly, and their influence endures for centuries. Even with the technological advances in travel and communications, cultural traits within societies have remained virtually unchanged. The static nature of culture is often a mechanism whereby a society can preserve its values and guard against outside influences.

The impact of culture on international business is real and far-reaching. The effects of culture can be seen as a firm selects a country for market entry and determines what mode of entry it will use. For example, researchers have found that for international companies the choice between licensing and establishing a wholly owned subsidiary depended to a large extent on cultural differences between the host and home countries. Specifically, differences in levels of trust impact perceptions of transaction costs and thereby influence a firm's choice of entry mode into a foreign market.[6] Culture also affects international companies' strategic actions. For example, the relationship between culture and brand image has been found to be very strong and is often a key consideration in developing brand image in foreign markets.[7] For international companies, culture might be a key variable to consider in their efforts to standardize their international strategies or develop global brands. In a study that examined transferring advertising strategies across countries, researchers found that the consumers in the host markets did not always understand the focus of the advertising campaign and therefore did not buy the product.[8] Finally, culture also plays a role in how an international company is organized in foreign markets.[9] In many collectivistic societies, organizational structures need to consider the effect of a particular design on the group as a whole rather than on the individual.

The student of international business must recognize that culture does not fit into a neat, compact, and manageable model. Each society and its culture is a unique and complex system of values, norms, folklore, mores, codes of conduct, standards of behavior, and relationships. Hence, most definitions of culture tend to be descriptive ones that identify a culture's individual elements.

CULTURE DEFINED

A good working definition of culture is *the knowledge, beliefs, art, law, morals, customs, and other capabilities of one group distinguishing it from other groups.* In other words, culture is the way of life of a society. From a practical standpoint, culture includes behavior, symbols, skills, heroes, knowledge, superstitions, motives, traditional ideas, artifacts, and achievements that are learned and perpetuated through a society's institutions to enhance its chances for survival. Since culture contains so many elements, it is no wonder that businesses find it very difficult to fully understand its influence on a society. It also explains international business failures that can be traced to ignoring and/or not understanding the basic cultural patterns of a country.

Culture is mostly an internalized phenomenon. Cultural behaviors evolve over time; they are learned and tend to be passed down from generation to generation. Few if any books are prescribed by a society to understand its own culture. Most individuals are hard-pressed to explain these natural values, customs, attitudes, and behavior patterns, and practice them without a second thought.

CULTURAL PROCESS AND CULTURAL COMPONENTS

As a learned behavior, culture is influenced by and learned through experiences. Some of the institutions that play a critical role in learning a particular culture include *family, religious institutions, schools,* and social groups such as *friends, neighbors,* and *the general society.* These institutions, through their dominant role in many societies, shape the value systems of that society.

The key components of culture are:

- Language and communication
- Social structure
- Religion
- Values
- Attitudes
- Customs
- Aesthetics
- Artifacts

These components also form the core of the definition of culture.

Language and Communication

Language is one of the defining expressions of culture. It is used for communicating ideas, thoughts, emotions, and decisions. Language includes spoken thoughts (vocal), signs, gestures, and other nonspoken means that people use to communicate with one another. It is the means by which a society transfers its value systems to others and how norms and customs are expressed and communicated. To understand another culture, one first has to learn the language of that culture.

In the Internet age, English is becoming the lingua franca of the business world. Though English is the official language of only about 500 million people (less than 8 percent of the world's total population), it is universally accepted as the language of business because of its extensive business-related vocabulary.[10] In a borderless global marketplace, the importance of communication is forcing the emergence of one business language that can be understood by all. This does not mean that communication among people and businesses is simple. Even if people use the same language, it does not necessarily mean that the language is equally understood by people who come from different backgrounds. Words and expressions in the same language differ from society to society. English in the United States is not the same as English spoken in the United Kingdom, especially in the use of slang words. For example, *truck* in the United States is *lorry* in England, and *gas* is *petrol.* If the Americans and the British have problems understanding each other, one can imagine the difficulties that arise in business negotiations if participants come from different parts of the world, even if they all speak English.

Nonverbal language, which includes hand gestures and body language, is unique to each society, as well. In fact, in some cultures the nonverbal language may be more important than the spoken language. Italians, for example, are known to be animated in their conversations, with hand gestures that demonstrate the feelings behind their spoken words. Nonverbal language is also an area that leads many international companies to embarrassing blunders. For example, the A-OK sign used by Americans (closing of the thumb and index figure to form an O) implies zero for the French, money or change for the Japanese, and an obscene symbol for Brazilians and Greeks.

For international companies, knowing the nuances of languages, understanding the differences in dialects, and recognizing the usage of slang is very important. To succeed in international business, it is important to respect different languages and gain knowledge of host cultures.[11] Language blunders by international companies are common. Calling one of its automobile models Nova in Puerto Rico, General Motors virtually killed the car's launch. Though the literal translation of *nova* is "star," when spoken, it sounds like *no va,* which in Spanish means "it doesn't go." Similarly, the now-defunct Braniff, an American airline that proudly advertised "rendez-vous lounges" on its newest jets, may have wished that its advertisements had never reached Brazil. In Portuguese, *rendez-vous* means "a room rented out for prostitution." Braniff also inadvertently exhorted Mexican airline passengers to "fly naked for major comfort," when they actually meant to promote the comfort of their leather seats. Other examples of language blunders include Pepsi-Cola's advertisement "comes alive," which translated into Chinese as "brings your ancestors from their burial place," and a hair product, Mist Stick, which unintentionally conjured up thoughts of "manure" in Germany, as "mist" is slang for manure in German.[12]

As mentioned earlier, in international business, language can be a problem even if the language in question is the same language spoken in different countries. Use of words and contexts differ from country to country. For example, the Spanish word for "wastebasket" in Colombia is *caneca;* in Puerto Rico it is *zafacón;* and in Venezuela it is *basurero.* In an interesting case, Electrolux, a Swedish appliance maker, introduced its vacuum cleaners in the United Kingdom with the tagline "nothing sucks like an Electrolux." In introducing the vacuum cleaner in the United States, the company used the same previously successful tagline from the United Kingdom with disastrous results. In the United States, "sucks" has an entirely different meaning (in fact several meanings, none of them very complimentary). This example demonstrates the complexities of selling products in countries where the same language may be spoken, but the local slang and use of words may be different.

Social Structure

Social structure is a society's fundamental organization; it determines the roles of individuals within different groups. A social group is a collection of two or more people who identify and interact with one another and have common interests. The different groups that members of a society belong to include family, households, social class/caste, and other similar institutions, such as friendship groups and reference groups. Social structure also determines individuals' social positions and their relationships to others within the group.

International companies strive to understand social structures in their management of foreign operations. In many societies, traditional social structures are strong and have great impact on how workers relate to one another. It has been observed that a key distinguishing characteristic of work behavior in societies is the way in which members relate to one another as a group.[13] Companies may use social classes to segment markets. Social groups are also used in international advertising as a way to disseminate information.

Family. Family units differ in size and structure from country to country. The basic family unit is the nuclear family, which is made up of a father, a mother, and their children. The nuclear family structure is often found in industrialized countries, including Australia, Canada, most of Europe, and the United States. Even in these countries, however, the traditional nuclear family structure is changing. With the high divorce rate in these countries, it is common to find families where only one of the parents resides with the child (or children).

In many societies, an extended-family structure exists. An extended family is made up of the basic nuclear family plus grandparents, uncles, aunts, and other relatives. Countries in Africa, Asia, the Middle East, and Latin America have extended-family structures. The relationships and influences of family members differ in an extended-family structure as compared to a nuclear-family structure. In an extended-family system, grandparents and uncles may have influence over children and their behavior. Therefore, while marketing products to children in these societies, companies may have to consider the role of other extended-family members in influencing the purchase decision.

Household. A household includes single people or unrelated individuals living in a single dwelling. Mostly found in industrialized countries (the United States, for example), households are targeted by companies as potential purchasers of goods and services. In households that have more than one individual, the group dynamics and social relationships can be strong, as in the case of friends or classmates living together; a household can also be simply an arrangement among people to save on living expenses, in which case the social structure is loose and does not influence behavior. In either case, the structure forces consumption of common household items such as appliances and furniture. Each type of household has a distinctive set of buying habits.

Social Class. Social class refers to relatively homogeneous divisions in a society, divisions that are hierarchically ordered and whose members share similar values, interests, and behaviors. Social classes exist in every society and are quite often determined by social status, including income level, education, occupation, area of residence, and other such variables. Typically, people in a particular class have similar buying habits and seek similar products. In fact, they also exhibit similar brand preferences. They tend to behave more alike than people from other social classes. Hence, social classes tend to be used by companies for segmenting markets and determining market trends. In extreme cases, the social class structure may be very rigid and formalized into a caste system, as in India. Whereas social mobility is easy under a social class system, it is virtually impossible to change under the caste system.

Religion

In many industrialized countries, especially in Europe, religion has lost its position as a cultural institution that influences society's value systems. Sweden, for example, is a secular country with no national role for religion, and, to some extent, this is true in China, too, though for different reasons. In Sweden, religion has lost its impact on society due to the country's economic success and the liberal attitudes adopted by its people; in China, the years of communist rule have made religion less of a factor in people's daily lives. But in many countries, religion plays a critical role in people's lives. To some extent, religion's impact touches people's secular lives, as well. It is important for international companies to understand and adopt practices that will satisfy religious decrees or beliefs. The religious taboo on eating meat among the Hindus in India led to the introduction of veggie burgers by McDonald's. Similarly, in Muslim countries where Islamic law prohibits charging interest on loans, banks have devised other alternatives such as offering shares to depositors and charging a nominal fee. The success of these alternate means to charge customers has led many Islamic banks in the Persian Gulf area to enter many of the predominantly Muslim countries of North Africa.[14]

The four major religions of the world are:

- Christianity (including Roman Catholic, Protestant, and Orthodox), with more than 1.7 billion followers
- Islam, with more than 1.2 billion followers

- Hinduism, with more than 750 million followers
- Buddhism, with more than 350 million followers

Christianity and Islam are termed "global religions" because their followers are found in many countries of the world, whereas religions that are dominant in one culture or country—Hinduism, for instance—are called cultural religions. Hinduism is found largely only in India. Islam is the fastest-growing of the world's religions and its followers are passionate about their beliefs. The other important religions of the world are Sikhism, Judaism, and Shinto. Confucianism holds a similar place in the lives of its followers, though it is technically a philosophy of life rather than a religion.

Many human values and attitudes are derived from religious tenets. The direct consequences of religion can sometimes be seen and felt in how managers and businesses behave in international negotiations and competition. For example, the Protestant work ethic states that there is more economic growth when work is viewed as a means of salvation and when people prefer to transform productivity gains into additional output rather than additional leisure. In other words, you need to give glory to God and at the same time work hard. This has led to the hard-charging work ethic of many Western societies. Buddhists believe in spiritual life, self-control, and the attainment of nirvana (salvation) rather than amassing wealth. There is very little conflict and aggression among the followers of Buddha, resulting in calm interpersonal relationships. Buddhism and other similar religions are also the roots of the collectivistic societies in Far East Asia. Similarly, followers of Hinduism tend to view the world and its purpose in terms of spiritual redemption and, to a lesser degree, accumulation of wealth. Islam asks of its followers their total dedication to Allah (the prophet); anything and everything they do, including how businesses are conducted, is viewed through this belief.

Values

Values are the belief systems that underlie a society's behaviors, the things that people believe to be important. People are emotionally attached to these belief systems, so to some extent they influence people's behavior. The work ethics that are practiced by different societies are value based. For example, the Japanese believe that work is very important, and their philosophy is "live to work." In contrast, the Europeans' philosophy is "work to live." Both philosophies are culture based and deeply rooted in their respective value systems. Therefore, values are important to international companies because they affect human behavior in organizations. In addition, some universal value elements are observed among international managers from different countries. In a study of managers from five different countries, researchers observed that managers from Australia and the United States were similar in social processes used to devise strategies for industrial development. The researchers also found similarities between American managers and Japanese managers in their pursuit of international expansion.[15] Despite these similarities, international companies must manage their employees in a way that recognizes prevailing cultural value systems. Treating all employees the same, irrespective of their cultural backgrounds, can often lead to disastrous results. Take, for example, the experience of an American company that introduced the merit system to its operations in Japan. To help coordinate the various individual tasks, the American manager delegated one individual to be the leader of one of the groups. In no time, the group was functioning poorly, with performance levels lower than those before the change was made. In investigating the cause of the decline in productivity, the American manager realized that he had essentially destroyed the harmony of the workgroup. Japan is a collectivist society, where individuals in a group are all equal; no single individual is ranked above the rest. By appointing a leader, the manager had created disharmony in the system. The employee who was appointed leader did not want to be the leader, and the group did not feel appreciated.

Attitudes

Attitude is a person's enduring favorable or unfavorable evaluations, emotions, and tendencies toward some object or idea. Attitudes put people into a frame of mind of liking or disliking, and in general, attitudes lead people to behave in a fairly consistent way in similar situations. For example, attitudes toward time vary among cultures. For Swedes, being on time is very important, and they will adhere to this attitude at all costs. In Mexico and other South American countries, however, the attitude toward time is casual; therefore, being prompt may not be given the high priority there that it receives in other cultures, particularly if a family member or other relationship simultaneously vied for the individual's attention. Business executives from Japan, Sweden, and the United States, where being prompt and on time for meetings is very important, find it difficult to function in societies where time is viewed casually.

People's attitudes affect the international companies' operations in two ways. First, a manager's attitude affects how he or she runs a foreign subsidiary; attitudes about work, time, and age need to be considered in managing employees. People's attitudes regarding family-career trade-off, workplace relations, and salary scales differ from country to country. In Asian countries, women often choose family over career, whereas in many Western countries, women balance family and career. Important cultural differences exist in attitude toward age. In Asian and Arab cultures, age is respected and elders are revered. Important positions in companies are often held by experienced older people. In the United States, however, age does not matter. Companies often appoint capable young people to very senior positions. In international operations, this can sometimes lead to problems. Sending a young fast-track executive to negotiate with senior government officials in Japan is probably unwise.

Second, in selling products and services in a given market, international companies must consider people's attitudes toward them. For example, Levi Strauss has sold jeans in the United States using functional and reliable positioning, whereas in many overseas markets, it stresses its American/Western toughness as a strong reason to buy its products.

Customs

Customs are ways of behaving under specific circumstances. Like culture, customs are handed down from generation to generation. Customs dictate how people react to situations. For example, a custom that varies from country to country is the role of alcohol in business dealings. In Asian countries, alcoholic drinks such as beer, liquor, and sake are usually shared at business events and are part of the business custom, whereas in the United States, alcohol consumption has no place in business.[16]

Aesthetics

Aesthetics play an important role in culture. Cultural preferences in color, beauty, arts, and architecture are unique to each society. International companies need to recognize these cultural differences in packaging and advertising their products and services. For example, the use of the color green in any commercial transactions is unacceptable for Islamic countries (it is the color of their flag), and red in China is a royal color and therefore not used for commercial purposes. The color of mourning differs from country to country: in the West it is black, in Japan it is white, and in many Latin American countries it is purple, and therefore avoided in some product categories, especially clothing. International companies need be aware of host countries' preferences, which may differ from those of the home country, in order to avoid business blunders.

Artifacts

Artifacts are buildings, monuments, architectural objects, and other works of art built by people to reflect some of the values and beliefs of their respective societies. These buildings are designed and built to last for a long time. Some ancient structures such as the Great Wall of China, the Parthenon in Athens, the pyramids of Egypt, and the Coliseum in Rome have withstood the passage of time and speak volumes about the people of that time. Similarly, seventeenth- and eighteenth-century monuments such as the London Bridge, the Taj Mahal in India, and the Eiffel Tower in Paris also tell us about the people of that era. More recently, buildings such as the Empire State Building in New York, the Tokyo Tower, and the Petronas Twin Towers (at present the tallest building in the world) in Kuala Lumpur, Malaysia, all reflect something of the people and society in their respective countries.

FRAMEWORK OF CULTURAL CLASSIFICATION

Cross-cultural management is defined as the study of the behavior of people from different cultures working in organizations. To understand the cultural variations across countries, researchers have created useful frameworks that make it easier to compare them. A variety of cultural classification models have been developed to assess cultural similarities and differences, four of which are presented here. By no means do these four provide all the answers to cultural issues faced by international managers, but collectively they present a useful framework for understanding cultural differences. These models may also assist international companies in managing employees successfully across cultures.

The four cultural frameworks discussed here are:

- Hofstede's cultural dimensions
- Kluckhohn and Strodtbeck's value orientation
- Hall's low-context high-context approach
- Ronen and Shenkar's cluster approach

HOFSTEDE'S CULTURAL DIMENSIONS

By far the most discussed work on cultural classifications was written by Gert Hofstede, who as human resources manager at IBM surveyed about 100,000 IBM employees in many countries in the 1980s.[17] Based on his study, Hofstede proposed five dimensions of culture (he first proposed four; later, in 1989, he added the fifth).

- Individualism-collectivism
- Power distance
- Uncertainty avoidance
- Masculinity-femininity
- Long-term/short-term orientation

A few of these dimensions were originally proposed in 1961 by the anthropologists Florence Kluckhohn and Fred Strodtbeck, but Hofstede is the one who studied them extensively in a corporate setting.

Individualism-Collectivism

Individualism-collectivism refers to the degree to which a society accepts individual actions or the degree to which individuals perceive themselves to be separate from others. In a collectivist society, group actions are emphasized. In some ways, the individualism-collectivism dimension is the most observed and practiced of the five dimensions studied by Hofstede.

In individualistic societies, such as Australia, Canada, the United Kingdom, and the United States, people exhibit more individualistic behavior, often pursuing their own goals, and more likely making decisions that affect their own situations. In collectivistic societies, people tend to consider the group's interest first and put the good of the group ahead of their own personal welfare. Countries that have been found to have collectivist societies include China, Colombia, Greece, and Mexico.

For international companies the individualism-collectivism dimension is a very important consideration in the management of foreign operations. In individualistic societies, individual performance is rewarded, individual initiatives are encouraged, and individual decision making is the norm; the corporate cultures in these countries tend to be more impersonal. Research has shown that employees from individualistic countries prefer individual rather than group-based compensation practices.[18] Corporate policies in individualistic-oriented cultures tend to allow individuals to take initiatives, work on their own, and make individual decisions. In collectivistic societies, groups make decisions, work is performed in groups, and compensation packages are based on the groups' results. In addition, in collectivist societies, group performance is more important, and the organizational structures tend to reflect a "family" orientation.[19] Corporate policies in collectivistic cultures are set up to encourage group results, group actions, and harmony within the group's structure.

Power Distance

Power distance refers to the degree to which a society accepts hierarchical (power) differences; societies will accept either equal or unequal distribution of power. In countries where power is distributed evenly, that is, where power distances are low, there is greater acceptance of ideas among people. In these societies senior executives consult with their subordinates in the workplace. This behavior is also exhibited within families and in other social settings. In countries with low power distance, children are encouraged to participate in family decisions and students are encouraged to discuss and present their points of view in the classrooms. Low power distance is also called "power tolerance." Low power distance countries include Austria, Denmark, Norway, and Sweden.

In high power distance countries, the society believes that there should be a well-defined order in which everyone knows their individual positions. In these societies children are supposed to respect their parents and obey them, the teacher is the center of the educational process, and subordinates are told what to do by their superiors. Higher power distance countries include India, Mexico, and the Philippines.

For international companies, the implications of power distance dimensions affect organizational structure, decision making, and overall management of foreign operations. Studies have shown that power distance and uncertainty avoidance hinder the acceptance of new products in some countries.[20] Generally, in high power distance countries, international companies need to set up centralized decision making, a well-defined hierarchy, and close control. The opposite may be adopted in low power distance countries.

Uncertainty Avoidance

Uncertainty avoidance refers to the degree to which a society is willing to accept and deal with uncertainty; in other words, it ranks how a society deals with risk. In countries with high uncertainty avoidance, people seek security and certainty. They are comfortable knowing the parameters of their lives and are eager to avoid risk. People in these societies do not want to deal with ambiguous situations. Countries with high uncertainty avoidance include Japan, France, Greece, and Portugal. In countries with low uncertainty avoidance (uncertainty acceptance), people like change and constantly seek new opportunities. In these countries routine activities and certainty in future actions lead to boredom, and people tend to be less productive. Countries with low uncertainty avoidance include Denmark, Sweden, the United Kingdom, and the United States.

In a study that assessed cross-cultural differences in the perception of financial risk, researchers found that the risk judgment differed with nationality and culture. The attitudes toward risk of respondents from Western societies such as the Nether- lands and the United States differed from those respondents in Eastern societies such as China.[21] This finding was consistent with cross-country variations in uncertainty avoidance, suggesting that multinationals operating in countries with high uncertainty avoidance countries have to provide clearly defined work rules and job security (such as lifetime employment, which until recently was offered by Japanese firms). In contrast, when operating in countries with low uncertainty avoidance, international companies should provide opportunities for quick decision making and should also encourage risk taking.

Masculinity-Femininity

Masculinity-femininity refers to the degree to which traditional male values are ac- cepted and followed in a society. In a highly masculine society, behaviors such as aggressiveness and materialism are viewed favorably. Cultures with a strong mascu- linity dimension have clearly differentiated sex roles, and men in these societies tend to be dominant. Men in masculine societies are expected to work and provide for the whole family. Highly masculine countries include Austria, Italy, Japan, and Mexico. In highly feministic societies both men and women tend to work and provide for the family. The sexes have less defined roles and share the responsibilities of parenting, doing chores, and shopping equally. Countries with a stronger femininity dimension include Denmark, Finland, and Sweden.

The masculinity-femininity dimension impacts the operations of international companies in several ways. For example, companies that operate in feministic cul- tures find that it is more important to maintain easy work schedules and offer better fringe benefits (maternity/paternity leaves), and they find their employees to be less interested in promotions. In these countries workers also tend to be more concerned with community and environmental issues. In countries with a greater masculinity dimension, workers are interested in pay raises and promotions and tend to be much more goal oriented.

Long-Term/Short-Term Orientation

Long-term/short-term view refers to time orientation and view of life and work in terms of a time horizon, either long-term or short-term. People living in cultures that are long-term oriented, such as Brazil, China, India, and South Korea, tend to be thrifty; they worry about the future, and they are more dedicated to tasks and causes. Some experts refer to long-term orientation as a Confucian philosophy. Short-term oriented cultures, such as Canada, New Zealand, the United Kingdom, and the United States, worry about the present, seek instant gratification, and are less likely to save. International companies operating in long-term oriented cultures may find it necessary to treat their workers differently than do those that operate in short-term oriented cultures.

Researchers have observed the collective effects of Hofstede's five cultural dimensions in marketing situations. Studies have found that consumers from collectivist, high power distance, uncertainty-avoidance, and Confucian (long-term oriented) cultures such as China and Taiwan definitely have different preferences in their consumption of goods and services when compared with masculine, individualistic cultures such as the United States.[22]

Criticism of Hofstede's Cultural Dimensions

Hofstede's cultural dimensions are probably the most studied and discussed of all cultural dimension models. Hofstede's is also one of the few cultural models to receive worldwide publicity. Since it is based on a large sample covering many countries, it is generally viewed as a reliable model. In addition, some of the dimensions identified by Hofstede have been identified by other anthropologists and social scientists. In empirical studies by Sondergraad (1994);[23] Hoppe (1998);[24] and Neelankavil, Mathur, and Zhang (2000),[25] some of Hofstede's results on a few of the dimensions have been validated.

The criticisms leveled against Hofstede's cultural dimensions relate to:

- appropriateness of the sample
- labeling of the terms
- other biases

Appropriateness of the Sample. Hofstede's survey was conducted at one company, IBM. Because IBM is a large multinational company with a strong corporate culture, its employees may not be a representative sample of the general population. Doubts exist about results based on a sample from a single company; therefore, researchers are not sure whether Hofstede's original four dimensions would have been identified if the study had been done across many companies. Despite Hofstede's large sample size, researchers question the validity of the results based on the fact that the responses may have actually represented the values of just a few.

Labeling of Terms. Hofstede studied business cultures. The information he gathered and the conclusions he reached may not shed light on the core societal culture and the values that are prevalent in a given society. Additionally, Hofstede studied managers' attitudes, which may not necessarily reflect a society's behavior patterns. In fact, a few studies have demonstrated that cultural categorization is based on dominant cultural value orientations; it does not provide a complete explanation of cultural similarities and differences among cultures (a general criticism of all cultural dimension models).[26]

Other Biases. Hofstede's survey was based on an instrument (questionnaire) and scales that were developed for people in Western societies. Therefore, the terms used in the questionnaire may not be exactly translated across cultures and in some cases may have entirely different meanings in different cultures. Some research studies have shown that questionnaires in organizational psychology are skewed by Western assumptions

Table 2.1

Summary of Hofstede's Cultural Dimensions

Dimension	Definition	Characteristics	Countries
Individualism-collectivism	Extent to which the self or the group constitutes the center point	Interest of the individual versus the group	*Individualistic:* Australia, Canada, United Kingdom, United States *Collectivistic:* China, Colombia, Greece, Mexico
Power distance	Extent to which hierarchical differences are accepted, ranging from power respectability to power tolerance	Centralization versus decentralization	*Power respect:* Brazil, India, Mexico, Philippines *Power tolerance:* Austria, Denmark, Norway, Sweden
Uncertainty avoidance	Extent to which uncertainty or ambiguity is tolerated, ranging from uncertainty avoidance to uncertainty acceptance	Structure versus less structure (more rules or fewer rules)	*Structured:* Japan, France, Greece, Portugal *Less structured:* Denmark, Sweden, United Kingdom, United States
Masculinity-Femininity	Extent to which traditional masculine (aggressiveness and assertiveness) values are emphasized	How sex roles are defined and practiced	*Masculine:* Austria, Italy, Japan, Mexico *Feminine:* Denmark, Finland, Sweden
Long-term–Short-term	Extent to which a society values thrift and respect of social obligations	Short-term view vs. long-term view	*Long-term view:* Brazil, China, India, South Korea *Short-term view:* Canada, New Zealand, United Kingdom, United States

and values that might not be appropriate for use in more traditional societies.[27] In fact, Hofstede originally had only four dimensions. The fifth, long-term orientation, based on Chinese philosophies, was added much later. Other problems associated with Hofstede's study include the difficulties of measuring cultural variables that are highly subject to contextual interpretation and judgment.

Despite these criticisms, Hofstede's work has been recognized as a centerpiece of corporate cultural studies and is widely referred to by scholars and practitioners of international business research. Table 2.1 summarizes Hofstede's five cultural dimensions.

KLUCKHOHN AND STRODTBECK'S VALUE ORIENTATIONS

Anthropologists Florence Kluckhohn and Fred Strodtbeck were the first (1961) to describe a cultural framework that was based on dimensions or factors.[28] They proposed a framework for identifying cultural differences using six dimensions based on past versus future and beliefs in individual versus group. To arrive at their cultural dimensions, Kluckhohn and Strodtbeck looked at the following set of relationships in a society:

- Are people viewed as good, bad, or a combination?
- Do people live in harmony with or subjugate (conquer) nature?
- Should people in a society act in an individual manner, or should they consider the group?
- Should people accept and enjoy the current situation or change and make it better?
- What is the concept of space in a society; that is, do people think that most things are private or public?
- What is the temporal orientation of a society—past, present, or future?

Based on their research, Kluckhohn and Strodtbeck concluded that most societies have a dominant cultural orientation that could be explained through six cultural dimensions:

- Human nature
- Relationship to nature
- Human relationship
- Activity orientation
- Concept of space
- Time orientation

Human Nature

Human nature refers to society's belief in people. Some societies, such as the Japanese, believe that people are essentially good. In these societies, people trust one another and are more likely to rely on verbal agreements. There are also societies in which people are viewed as essentially evil; hence, these societies enact codes and set up rules of behavior. The result of the mistrust in such societies is that they draw up detailed contracts in business dealings and specify up front the penalty for not fulfilling the contract. Contracts with penalty clauses are common in many European countries. A third type of society views people as both good and evil. In these societies, of which the United States is an example, people are viewed as changeable, and the members of these societies try to develop systems to modify behavior.

The human-nature dimension may provide international companies with the clues that dictate how they run their operations. Therefore, international companies may have a very participative form of management, with unwritten rules and verbal agreements, in a country where people are viewed as essentially good. In countries where people are viewed as evil, a more directive form of management should be adopted, with written rules and formal contracts. For the third group of countries, where people are viewed as both good and evil, employees may be rewarded for good behavior and punished for bad (evil) behavior. In a study conducted in China, researchers found that trust played a significant role in resolving conflicts between expatriate managers and their Chinese workers.[29]

Relationship to Nature

The relationship to nature refers to a society's relationship between people and nature—in other words, whether people live in harmony with or subjugate nature. Societies that believe in living in harmony with nature, such as people in Middle Eastern countries, tend to alter their behavior to accommodate nature. Countries where the people view themselves as able to master nature, such as Australia, tend to harness the forces of nature.

International companies can make use of the relationship-with-nature dimension by encouraging innovation, changing existing beliefs, and implementing planning in those countries where people believe that they can conquer (master) nature. In societies where people tend to view nature as part of their lives, international companies should be more environmentally conscious, for example, by using biodegradable packing and by selling goods and services that foster ecological concerns.

Human Relationship

The human relationship (the same as Hofstede's individualism-collectivism dimension) refers to a society's understanding of relationships among people. In some societies, people focus on themselves in their actions, decisions, and interactions. These societies are said to be individualistic; and examples include Denmark, Sweden, and the United States. The opposite of individualism is groupism, or collectivism. In collectivist societies people tend to place the interests and welfare of the group ahead of themselves. In these societies group accomplishments, group decisions, and group interactions are encouraged. Groupism is practiced in countries such as China, Japan, and South Korea.

For international companies operating in collectivistic countries, group decisions must be emphasized and individual recognitions and rewards should be avoided.

Activity Orientation

Activity orientation refers to the primary mode of activity in a given society, that is, whether people in the society accept or attempt to change their current situations. Societies that accept the status quo, such as Brazil, Italy, and Mexico, go along with the flow of events and tend to enjoy the current situation. In those societies where change is desired, people seek ways to improve the current situation by setting specific goals, planning for the future, and working toward results. People in Finland, Sweden, and Switzerland normally tend to be change oriented.

International companies can use the activity dimension in decision making and the development of long-term plans. If they are operating in a society that looks for change, employees should be encouraged to innovate and suggest ideas for improvements, and they should be rewarded for successful innovations.

Concept of Space

The concept of space describes the extent to which a society views meetings between people as private or public. In countries that view space as private, such as the United Kingdom, people do not get too close to one another. Open discussions are not common, and ideas are restricted to just a few at one time. The opposite is true for those countries in which space is considered public, such as Italy. In these countries, participation is encouraged, decision making is more democratic, and feelings are expressed publicly.

International companies must consider the space concept in running their foreign operations. In a very private society, for example, management-employee meetings and discussions must be managed differently than those that take place in a public society.

Time Orientation

The time orientation (somewhat similar to Hofstede's long-term/short-term view) is the extent to which people view their value systems based on time frames. Are their value systems governed by the past, present, or future? In some societies, the past is very important. People in these societies use historical experiences and traditions to guide them in their day-to-day activities. These societies also make use of the past in their business dealings. For example, the Chinese are traditionalists and use the past as their reference point in conducting business.

In some societies the past is not that important; the present and the immediate are what counts. Instant gratification is the norm among people that value the present. Businesses in these societies tend to develop short-term plans. Companies publish quarterly financial reports and managers are rewarded on short-term goals. The United States is often cited as a society focused on the present.

Societies that are future oriented are interested in long-term results. Japan is an example of a society that is long-term oriented. The Japanese people have one of the highest savings rates in the world, and they value lifetime employment. Japanese companies emphasize long-term planning; for example, Matsushita Company (now Panasonic) set up a 100-year business plan, but more commonly Japanese companies have 25-year plans.

The time orientation has significance for international companies not only in terms of corporate planning, but also in terms of how their employees view their day-to-day activities. In past-oriented societies, traditional practices never go away; hence, management has to be careful when introducing new systems. International companies that operate in future-oriented societies have difficulty operating in a present-oriented society. Japanese companies operating in the United States encounter difficulties in instituting long-term business plans for American managers. Table 2.2 summarizes the six Kluckhohn-Strodtbeck cultural dimensions.

Table 2.2

Summary of Kluckhohn-Strodtbeck Cultural Dimensions

Dimension	Definition	Characteristics	Countries
Human nature	Extent to which people view one as good or evil	Focus on good, evil, or a combination	*Focus on good:* Asian countries (Japan)
			Focus on evil: European countries
			Focus on good and evil: United States
Relationship with nature	Extent to which people live in harmony or try to subjugate (harness) nature	Belief in accepting, altering, or managing their destinies	*Accepting:* Middle Eastern countries
			Harnessing: Australia, United Kingdom, United States
Human relationship	Extent to which people believe in independence or dependence	Individualistic versus group oriented	*Individualistic:* Denmark, United Kingdom, United States
			Group oriented: China, Japan, South Korea
Activity orientation	Extent to which people accept the current situation	Expression of feelings vs. seeking change	*Accept:* Brazil, Italy, Mexico *Change:* Finland, Sweden, Switzerland
Concept of space	Extent to which a society views meetings as private or public	In private society people are distant; in public society people encourage participation	*Private:* United Kingdom *Public:* Italy
Time orientation	Extent to which people view the past, present, or future as important	Past provides the solutions; effects of present are important; effects in the long run	*Past:* China *Present:* United States *Future:* Japan

HALL'S LOW-CONTEXT–HIGH-CONTEXT FRAMEWORK

In explaining the use of language and how information is obtained, Edward T. Hall characterized the differences in cultures as low-context and high-context cultures.[30] In low-context cultures, the words used by the speaker convey precisely what the speaker has in mind. Hence, in obtaining information in a low-context culture, only firsthand information is considered relevant. Communication in low-context societies is direct and people avoid small talk. Many European countries and the United States are considered low-context cultures.

In high-context cultures, it is not the words alone that convey the message, but also the context. Cultural clues are important in understanding what is being communicated, making the context as important as the spoken words. When interpreting information in these cultures, one has to be sensitive to the peripheral information. In countries with high-context cultures, the person's status and the importance of the situation are just as important as the communication itself. High-context cultures are found in Asia, Latin America, and the Middle East.

From a practical standpoint, the context dimension of culture affects communication, information gathering, and decision making. For managers from low-context cultures supervising subordinates from high-context cultures, information provided by subordinates may sound as if it is an excuse as they explain the current status of the task in a roundabout way. The opposite may happen if managers are from high-context cultures are supervising subordinates from low-context cultures. Managers from high-context cultures may feel that their subordinates are too aggressive and do not like to follow orders. The low-context–high-context dimension is equally problematic in business negotiations, as either side may feel offended due to differences in approaches. Many negotiations between Japanese executives and Western European executives have been strained due to communication problems.

It is important for business executives from low-context cultures to understand that in high-context cultures, building a good relationship is the first order of business and must occur before actual long-term arrangements are made. The initial meetings between the parties are simply to earn one another's trust. Therefore, bringing lawyers to early meetings sends the wrong signal (implies a lack of trust). In this environment, negotiations and agreements take a long time; managers from low-context cultures must be prepared for delays in completing business arrangements.

The low-context–high-context cultural dimension also affects international companies' advertising strategies. In Austria, Germany, and the United Kingdom, advertising is fact based and contains few words. Therefore, companies from high-context cultures need to adapt to the direct approach used by low-context cultures in presenting their messages. For example, Japanese automakers' ads in Europe are very direct and to the point in comparison to the lengthy ads used in Japan. In high-context cultures, advertisements take on emotional overtones and the ad copy is long. International companies from low-context cultures need to adjust their ad copy to fit into the cultural context in which they are operating. For example, in high-context countries Procter & Gamble's ads for its Joy brand of dishwashing soap are especially descriptive and explain in detail the merits of the soap.

RONEN AND SHENKAR'S CLUSTER APPROACH

By grouping countries that share cultural dimensions such as language, Simcha Ronen and Oded Shenkar were able to classify countries into nine clusters:[31]

- Anglo
- Arab
- Far Eastern
- Germanic

Table 2.3

Ronen and Shenkar Culture Clustering

#	Culture cluster	Characteristics
1	Anglo (7 countries): Australia, Canada, Ireland, New Zealand, South Africa, United Kingdom, United States	Common language, British influence in business and law
2	Arab (6 countries): Abu Dhabi, Bahrain, Kuwait, Oman, Saudi Arabia, United Arab Emirates	Common language, common religion, common customs and practices, proximity to one another
3	Far Eastern (8 countries): Hong Kong (not a country anymore), Indonesia, Malaysia, Philippines, Singapore, Taiwan, Thailand, Vietnam	Common Asian traditions and customs
4	Germanic (3 counties): Austria, Germany, Switzerland	Common language, historic links, and proximity to one another
5	Independent (4 countries): Brazil, India, Israel, Japan	No common characteristics
6	Latin American (6 countries): Argentina, Chile, Colombia, Mexico, Peru, Venezuela	Common language, former colonies of Spain, proximity to one another
7	Latin European (5 countries): Belgium, France, Italy, Portugal, Spain	Some common cultural values and proximity to one another
8	Near Eastern (3 countries): Greece, Iran, Turkey	Historic links and proximity to one another
9	Nordic (4 countries): Denmark, Finland, Norway, and Sweden	Many common cultural dimensions, historic links, proximity to one another

Source: Simcha Ronen and Oded Shenkar, "Clustering Countries on Attitudinal Dimensions: A Review and Synthesis," *Academy of Management Review,* 10, no. 3 (1985): 435–454.

- Independent—nothing in common
- Latin American
- Latin European
- Near Eastern
- Nordic

The basic premise of Ronen and Shenkar's cultural clustering is that similarities among cultures do exist. It follows, then, that it is possible for international companies to implement standardized strategies across countries. In addition, Ronen and Shenkar's culture clustering can be used to select countries for market entry. By using a similar analysis for countries in the same clusters, international companies can more quickly evaluate potential locations. If there are cultural differences between the home country and the host country, an international firm may want to avoid the uncertainty these countries present. Cultural differences may foreshadow difficulties in adapting to local conditions. For example, recognizing the similarities in cultures, many U.S. companies often choose Canada and the United Kingdom as their first overseas markets. Similarly, China is the first entry point for some Taiwanese companies.

International companies have also used cultural clustering to design organizational structures that take into consideration the similarities and differences among cultures. In designing organizational structures, international firms try to create balance between international/global integration (coordination of activities) and local responsiveness (response to specific needs by the subsidiary). This balancing act is often dependent on how culturally similar or dissimilar the home and host cultures are. For example, Unilever's organizational setups in Germany and Switzerland are similar, whereas the organizational structure in India is totally different from that found in Europe. Table 2.3 presents the Ronen and Shenkar culture clustering.

OTHER CULTURAL CLASSIFICATIONS

Besides the four frameworks of cultural dimensions that have already been examined, there are two other cultural classification models that are often discussed in the international business context. The first is the cultural classification by S.H. Schwartz and the second is the Charles Hampden-Turner and Fons Trompenaars cultural model.

Schwartz's classification focuses on the social relationships and social environment in which people interact. Schwartz's model identifies three key dimensions: (1) embeddedness versus autonomy; (2) hierarchy versus egalitarianism; and (3) mastery versus harmony.[32] The first dimension, embeddedness versus autonomy, explains people's cultural orientation toward social relationships. In some societies, people are very independent and express their feelings with no regard for others (autonomy). Countries in which individuals seek autonomy include Denmark, France, and Germany. In contrast, societies that exhibit embeddedness (also called conservatism) are more traditionalists. Countries in which embeddedness is observed include Singapore, Taiwan, and Turkey.

The hierarchy versus egalitarianism dimension deals with the roles of people in social situations—those who seek important roles versus those who are more concerned with their relationships with others. Countries such as China and Thailand are very hierarchical; countries such as Estonia and Mexico are more egalitarian. Schwartz's third dimension deals with mastery of nature versus harmony. In some societies, people value success, and in others they pursue harmony with nature and tend be less ambitious. People in Brazil and Spain are found to be driven by ambition, whereas people from Italy and Finland are more concerned with the broader social system.

Hampden-Turner and Trompenaars developed a classification that is based on the premise that foreign cultures are basically not very different, but rather mirror images of one another. According to their theory, a society's values and rewards are based on order and sequence of looking and learning. In a very basic sense, we need to understand why in some societies people write their given name first and family name last, as in many Western cultures, whereas in many Asian cultures the family name comes first. At the same time, most Western societies are individualistic and

Asian societies are collectivist (community oriented). Is there a link between these two patterns? Is the reason that members of Western society write their given name first because they are very individualistic in their behavior, and vice versa? Similarly, in some societies people write left to right and in others they write right to left (Arabic language). How much of this is value driven? Based on their research, Hampden-Turner and Trompenaars developed three value dimensions: (1) universalism (applies to many) versus particularism (emphasizes exceptions); (2) individualism versus communitarianism (collectivism); and (3) specificity (precision or getting to the point) versus diffuseness (larger context).[33] There are similarities between Hampden-Turner and Trompenaars's classifications and other cultural classifications, most obviously Hofstede's individualism-collectivism and Hampden-Turner and Trompenaars's individualism/communitarianism.

Some overlap exists among all the cultural dimension models. For example, the individualism-versus-collectivism dimension is mentioned in three of the models. Similarly, Hofstede's power distance dimension is the same as the hierarchy dimension in Schwartz's framework.

Clearly, culture can have a powerful effect on international business operations. Because people belong to different societies that have their own cultural norms, beliefs, and values, their behavior and expectations at the workplace are affected. If international companies make a concerted effort to understand foreign cultures, some of the problems associated with differences in culture may be reduced.

One suggestion for global managers to be successful in overseas markets is to develop five cultural competencies; *cultural self-awareness, cultural consciousness, ability to lead cultural teams, ability to negotiate across cultures,* and *a global mindset.*[34] Though these skills are extremely useful, in practice they are hard to teach. In understanding different cultures, it becomes apparent that it is quite difficult to master and be proficient in all their variations.

All the cultural models that are presented here have some common themes, but they do not address each and every unique aspect of the hundreds of cultures that exist around the world.

CULTURAL GENERALIZATION

The cultural models presented here, along with others, may give the impression that one can easily capture, compartmentalize, and learn about other cultures. The truth of the matter is, cultures cannot be classified, it is not easy to understand them, and learning individual cultures is a long and tedious process. Some cultural differences are easy to observe and learn, such as a society's acceptable attire or how to greet people. However, it is difficult to learn the culturally ingrained responses to situations that are second nature to the locals but completely unfamiliar to foreign executives. The best way to learn a culture fully is to immerse oneself in that culture, that is, to live and practice the culture for a long period of time and learn the language. Time, however, is one item that international businesses and their executives do not have. Therefore, many international managers end up receiving only a macro treatment of culture and never become well-versed in the deep-rooted cultural values, norms, and customs of their host nations. It is no wonder that many international blunders can be traced to cultural misunderstandings.

Cultural generalizations based on different models, though useful, are often the problem in learning about foreign cultures. Armed with a few cultural dimensions, executives feel confident that they are ready to conduct business in foreign countries. But these dimensions may not provide the complete picture. Some of the information gathered about foreign cultures may be stereotypes that can pose even more problems. A few examples of stereotypical generalizations include: "Americans are brash and make quick decisions," "Japanese are slow to come to an agreement," and "Italians love to talk." There are so many cultural variations and nuances that it is not possible to understand or memorize all of them for every country.

CULTURAL CONVERGENCE

Advances in technology that have enabled people to travel and communicate in ways that were difficult if not impossible just a decade ago have made the world smaller and brought people closer. This phenomenon has led to a better understanding of foreign cultures and an acceptance of values and norms that until recently had been foreign to many. In addition, some uniform consumption patterns have emerged that seem to transcend cultures. In a study conducted among Web users, it was found that the satisfaction levels across cultures provided equivalent measurement.[35] Take, for example, the success of Starbucks coffee in China, a tea-drinking society; the proliferation of American-style fast food in Japan, India, and Latin American countries; the widespread wearing of denim jeans among young people in many parts of the world; and the success of Japanese cuisine in America (especially raw fish, which differs from the traditional preferences.) Add to this the spread of globalization; it is not surprising to see more similarities in cultural practices.

CULTURE SHOCK

Even after managers complete their cross-cultural training in preparation for an international assignment, many are likely to feel disoriented upon arrival at the new location. For instance, someone accustomed to calling colleagues by their first names must adjust to the widespread use of titles and last names in the workplace. In some countries, the degree of respect given to people and use of proper names in addressing people is very important.[36] How does one adjust to people coming late for meetings? How does a manager from a cold weather country adjust to hot and humid climates? This disorientation faced by foreign workers is generally referred to as "culture shock."

Culture shock is defined as "a generalized distress one experiences in a new and different culture because of a lack of understanding of the local culture." If often occurs because the foreign worker is facing an unfamiliar set of behavioral cues that are different from the ones he or she is used to or knows about.

Most experts agree that culture shock is accentuated by the difficulty in interacting in the local environment, leading to a focus on the negative aspects of the local culture and its people. The more successful foreign workers are those who are willing to learn the culture, accept the differences in cultures, and adapt to the new environment. There are no shortcuts in preparing international managers to be ready for cultural shock, but training, role-playing, and exposure to people from different cultures and environments can often make the transition a little easier.

CULTURAL ORIENTATION

Understanding foreign national cultures and adapting to these cultures in the business world depend on two factors: (1) the cultural similarities found between the home country's culture and the host country's culture, and (2) the managers' attitudes toward other cultures. The attitudes of managers and their companies toward outside cultures can be classified as *ethnocentric, polycentric,* or *geocentric.*

ETHNOCENTRISM

Ethnocentrism—the belief that one's own culture is better than or superior to other cultures—is one of the most common attitudes found among international managers. Managers with an ethnocentric attitude often ignore important host-country cultural values. For example, a study of Chinese workers employed by multinational companies found that the expatriate managers were persistent in maintaining their own cultural values in relationship building.[37] Of course, this resulted in poor working relationships between the locals and the expatriates. It was also noticed that the expatriate managers tried to change the cultural orientation of the host-country personnel, which did not help the situation. International companies that tend to have an ethnocentric attitude more often use a centralized organizational structure. These companies often dictate policies and procedures from headquarters, with very little input from subsidiary personnel. Interestingly, the managers themselves may not be aware of their ethnocentric attitudes, and herein lies the challenge for international firms in handling their executives' ethnocentric behavior. Ethnocentrism has been identified as a major cause of many international business difficulties.

POLYCENTRISM

Polycentrism is the recognition that it is important to understand the differences in cultures and act accordingly in interacting with people from other cultures. International companies and their polycentric managers try to accommodate cultural differences, and to facilitate its local responsiveness, the company is often organized in a decentralized structure. Some experts feel that while polycentric firms adapt readily to various countries, this adaptation can lead to serious inefficiencies for the firm (as it is often unable to capitalize on economies of scale). This situation may ultimately have a negative impact on the firm's competitiveness. Trade-offs between local adaptation and cost efficiency usually depend on the nature of the product or service being marketed. For example, consumer packaged-goods companies may need to be more sensitive to national differences than, say, firms selling industrial goods. International companies that have a polycentric attitude may also be reluctant to adopt certain practices and procedures simply because they were successful in the home country or other host countries; in this way, polycentric companies are being sensitive to a given host-country personnel's attitudes and behaviors.

GEOCENTRISM

Geocentrism is the belief that in certain cultures change can be made and in others one has to adapt to the host culture. In these cases, international companies and their managers base their decisions and manage their operations after thoroughly understanding the host culture and its unique features. The geocentric attitude avoids the main problems associated with ethnocentric and polycentric attitudes, and the international company is able to introduce proven systems and be innovative at the same time.

CHAPTER SUMMARY

Culture is a critical environmental variable that international companies need to consider in entering and managing their foreign operations. Mistakes rooted in cultural misunderstandings are some of the most common blunders committed by international executives. Hence, there have been many attempts made to identify similarities and differences between cultures through cultural dimensions.

A good working definition of culture is *the knowledge, beliefs, art, law, morals, customs, and other capabilities of one group distinguishing it from other groups.* Culture is a learned behavior that is passed down from generation to generation and evolves over a long period of time. The key institutions that instill culture are family, schools, and religion.

Language, religion, and social structures are important correlates of culture that influence international business operations. Researchers have attempted to study and understand the reasons for cultural similarities and differences. Based on these studies, researchers have developed various classifications of country cultures. The most cited and discussed cultural classification is the one proposed by Gert Hofstede. Hofstede identified five cultural dimensions that may be used to find similarities between cultures. The other classifications of culture include those of Kluckhohn and Strodtbeck; Hall; and Ronen and Shenkar. Though each of these systems explains some of the similarities between cultures, they do not provide all the answers to cultural behavior and the differences found between cultures.

International companies need to recognize the importance of culture and use it to avoid major mistakes. The influence of culture should be considered in developing entry strategies, designing organizational structures, managing subsidiary operations, and developing marketing strategies.

In understanding cultural influences, international businesses have to recognize concepts such as cultural generalization, cultural convergence, cultural shock, and various types of management orientation such as ethnocentrism, polycentrism, and geocentrism.

KEY CONCEPTS

Cultural Components
Cultural Dimensions
Culture Shock
Cultural Convergence
Cultural Orientation

DISCUSSION QUESTIONS

1. What is culture?
2. Identify the key elements of culture.
3. How is culture learned?
4. What are the key institutions that influence cultural behavior?
5. How do societies communicate, and what role does language play in international operations?
6. Explain the role of religion in culture and how it affects international business operations.
7. What are social structures? How do international companies use social structures in designing their organizational structures?
8. What are cultural dimensions?
9. Identify and discuss some of the important cultural dimensions.
10. What is cultural convergence?
11. What is culture shock?
12. Explain and discuss ethnocentrism, polycentrism, and geocentrism.

ADDITIONAL READINGS

Ajiferuke, Musbau, and Jean J. Boddewyn. "Culture, and Other Exploratory Variables in Comparative Management Studies." *Academy of Management Journal* (June 1970): 153–63.

Ashkansay, Neal M., and Celeste P.M. Wilderom. *Handbook of Organizational Culture and Climate.* Beverly Hills, CA: Sage Publications, 2000.

Dunlop, J.T., F.H. Harbison, C. Kerr, and C.A. Myers. *Industrialism and Industrial Man Reconsidered.* Princeton, NJ: Princeton University Press, 1990.

Gannon, Martin J., and Associates. *Understanding Global Cultures: Metaphorical Journeys through 17 Countries.* Beverly Hills, CA: Sage Publications, 1994.

Griffin, Ricky W., and Michael W. Pustay. *International Business.* 4th ed. Upper Saddle River, NJ: Pearson-Prentice Hall Publishers, 2005, chap. 4.

Krech, David, Richard S. Crutchfield, and Egerton L. Ballachey. *Individual in Society.* New York: McGraw-Hill, 1962.

Punnet, Betty Jane, and David A. Ricks. *International Business.* Boston, MA: PWS-Kent, 1992, chap. 6.

Shenkar, Oded, and Yadong Luo. *International Business.* Hoboken, NJ: John Wiley & Sons, 2004, chap. 6.

APPLICATION CASE: BUSINESS NEGOTIATIONS AND CULTURAL PITFALLS—MEXICO

Two companies had been shortlisted for a major infrastructural contract in Mexico: one was an American and the other Swedish. Both companies were invited to Mexico to present their proposals to the relevant ministry and to start negotiating the terms of the deal.

The Americans put a lot of effort into producing a high-tech, hard-hitting presentation. Their message was clear: "We can give you the most technically advanced equipment and quality of service at a price our competitors can't match." The team, which consisted of senior technical experts, lawyers, and interpreters, flew down from the company's New York head office to Mexico City, where they had reserved rooms in one of the top hotels for a week.

In order to put on the best possible performance for the minister and his officials, the Americans arranged to give the presentation in a conference room at the hotel. They brought all the necessary equipment with them from the United States. All the arrangements had been written down in great detail and sent to the Mexican officials two weeks earlier.

At the agreed-upon time, the American team was ready to present, but they had no one to present to. The people from the ministry arrived at various times over the next hour. The ministry staff did not apologize for being late, but just began to chat amicably with the Americans about a wide range of nonbusiness matters. The leader of the American team kept glancing anxiously at his watch. Finally, he suggested that the presentation should start. Though the Mexicans seemed surprised, they politely agreed and took their seats. Twenty minutes later, the minister, accompanied by some senior officials, walked in. He looked extremely angry and asked the Americans to start the presentation again from the beginning. Ten minutes later, the minister started talking to an aide who had just arrived with a message for him. When the American presenter stopped talking, the minister signaled that he should continue. By this time, most of the Mexican representatives were talking amongst themselves. When invited to ask questions at the end, the only thing the minister wanted to know was why the Americans had told them so little about their company's history.

Later, during lunch, the Americans were very surprised to be asked questions about their individual backgrounds and qualifications, rather than technical details about their products. The minister had a brief word with the American team leader and left without eating or drinking anything.

Over the next few days, the American team contacted their Mexican counterparts several times in an attempt to fix a meeting time and start the negotiations again. The Americans reminded the Mexican team that they had to fly back to the United States at the end of the week. But the Mexican response was always the same: "We need time to examine your proposal amongst ourselves first." At the end of the week, the Americans left Mexico angry and frustrated.

QUESTIONS

1. Who do you think received the contract?
2. Explain in specific detail the American team's steps (right or wrong) that produced this outcome.

ADDITIONAL READINGS

Shirley Taylor, "Communicating across Cultures," *British Journal of Administrative Management* (June-July 2006): 12–21.

SOURCE

Chris Fox, "Cross-Border Negotiation," *British Journal of Administrative Management* (June-July 2006): 20–23.

3 Economic and Other Related Environmental Variables

Economic variables such as the gross domestic product, balance of payments, inflation, and other such factors have a great impact on the operations of a global company.

LEARNING OBJECTIVES

- To understand the environmental variables that affect international business
- To understand the influence of macroeconomic factors on international operations
- To understand the variables used to measure the strengths and weaknesses of individual economies
- To understand the differences among industrialized, emerging, and developing economies
- To understand the differences among market-based, centrally planned, and mixed economies
- To learn about the underground, or parallel, economies and their effects on international companies
- To understand techniques to conduct country risk analysis
- To understand the importance of competitive analysis in international business operations

Aside from the cultural factor, discussed in Chapter 2, the environmental factors that affect an international business include a country's economy, competition, infrastructure, technology, political stability, and government regulations. In this chapter, the effects of economy, competition, infrastructure, and technological factors are discussed.

THE ECONOMY

The last 20 years have brought the world more trade, more globalization, and more economic growth than in any such period in history.[1] The economy of a country affects businesses in many ways. Economic downturns might result in a reduction in consumer expenditures, affecting sales revenues. A drop in a country's gross domestic product (GDP; the total value of all goods and services produced in a country in a given period of time) or gross national income (GNI; includes the total value of goods and services produced within the country together with external net income received in the form interests and dividends; the World Bank uses the GNI measures to report on a country's economic activity) may imply a contraction in a country's total output. A decline in a country's currency value may suggest an underlining weakness in the economic structure of country and, hence, may mean difficulties for businesses.

Recognizing the possible impact of this key external variable, international managers continuously monitor economic factors to be prepared for the dynamic shifts that occur in each country's economic activities. The unexpected Asian crisis in July 1997 sent shockwaves throughout the region. As a result, many investors were unwilling to provide loans and subsidies to developing countries. The ensuing credit crunch led to an economic slowdown in many developing countries, which resulted in a decrease in demand for foreign goods, affecting many international companies. Similarly, the continuing decline in the value of the U.S. dollar against the European euro and the British pound is affecting businesses on both continents.

More recently, the credit crisis of 2008 that started in the United States has had global financial repercussions; the crisis is engulfing developing countries from Latin America to Central Europe, raising the specter of market panic and even social unrest. The list of countries under threat is growing by the day and now includes such emerging market stalwarts as Brazil, South Africa, and Turkey. The fast-growing economies of the world depend on money from Western banks to build factories, buy machinery, and export goods to the United States and Europe. When those banks stop lending and the money dries up, as it did in 2008, investor confidence vanishes and the countries suddenly find themselves in crisis.

International managers consider the changes in the economic environment when selecting countries for market entry, and when developing specific market-related strategies. Among the various external factors, the economic environment is more consistently structured and the information on economic activities for most countries is readily available; hence, this external factor can be accessed easily.

In international markets, the level of a country's economic activity as measured by its GDP, GNI, inflation rate, and/or exchange rates is critical to a company's operations. These economic variables attempt to describe a set of conditions that influence the company's strategic operations. A growing and robust economy implies higher consumption expenditures by consumers and better revenues for companies. A higher inflation rate creates economic instability and leads to increases in commodities prices, and a depreciating local currency makes imports cheaper and domestic exports more expensive, resulting in trade deficits.

Evaluating countries for market entry or for developing operational strategies depends to a large extent on the soundness of the selected country's macroeconomic conditions. Economic strength is dependent on the structural foundation of the economy for sustained economic growth and economic stability. Specific components of a country's economic strengths include investments, both internal and foreign, domestic consumption, the population's real income levels, performance of the individual sectors within the economy, and infrastructure development.

Local and foreign investments add to the factors of production, including the creation of jobs. They also stimulate the economy through the introduction of advanced technologies, higher productivity levels, and overall improvements in key sectors of the economy. A case in point is the phenomenal economic growth in the United States during the 1990s that was brought on by investments in technologies during the previous decade. Equally important are changes in the consumption expenditures, specifically per capita consumption. Increases in consumption expenditures imply that the people have steady jobs, their real incomes (income minus rate of inflation) are rising, and many of them are very confident about the robustness of the economy. When consumption expenditures in a country decline, its economy suffers. A case in point is the situation that the Japanese economy experienced in the late 1990s. Due to general weaknesses in the economy and a lack of confidence in the government leaders to pull the economy out of its downturn, many consumers in Japan reduced their consumption expenditures, which further destabilized the economy.

Economic strength and stability are also affected by the performance of a country's economic sectors—agriculture, manufacturing, and service. Quality of output, efficiencies in each sector, use of technology in each sector, and overall productivity levels greatly influence the economy. A strong and stable economy normally relies on the development of its economic sectors. Countries with a strong manufacturing base, such as China, or those that rely heavily on the service sector, as the United States does, normally have strong economies. Countries that rely heavily on the agricultural sector and have relatively fewer workforces in the manufacturing and service sectors typically have underdeveloped economies. Countries in Africa, parts of Asia, and Latin America are good examples of countries that are underdeveloped. These countries are not competitive and receive very little foreign investment, which further hinders their economic development.

As mentioned earlier, an economy's strength is normally deduced through key economic variables such as GDP/GNI growth rates, per capita GDP/GNI, inflation, current account balance (part of the balance of payments), and external debt.[2]

GROSS DOMESTIC PRODUCT AND GROSS NATIONAL INCOME

Gross domestic product (GDP) can be calculated by totaling up the amount of a country spent on final goods and services; this is called the *expenditure* method. It can also be calculated by totaling up all the wages, rents, interest incomes, and profits earned by all factors in producing the final goods and services; this is called the *income* method, or gross national income (GNI). The GDP/GNI is used as a measure of a nation's total output. The GDP/GNI growth rate measures the annual increase in a nation's total output from the previous year to the next. For example, the German economy grew by 2.7 percent in 2006, a moderate increase; in contrast, the Chinese economy grew by 9 percent during the same year, a substantial growth rate. The growth rate is a good indicator of a nation's economic vitality. The stronger the growth rate, the more robust the economy. For international companies, countries with a strong growth rate are attractive locations for investment.

Per capita GDP/GNI is a nation's total GDP/GNI divided by its population. The

Table 3.1

Inflation Rates for Few Select Countries, 2007

	Country	Inflation Rate (%)
1	Zimbabwe	1,035.5
2	Iraq	53.2
3	Guinea	30.0
4	Sao Tome and Principe	23.1
5	Yemen	20.8
6	Myanmar	20.0
7	Uzbekistan	19.8
8	Congo	18.2
9	Afghanistan	16.3
10	Serbia	15.5

Source: "World Statistics," http://www.infoplease.com/January 2008.

GDP/GNI per capita is a better reflection than overall GDP/GNI of the well being of the country's people. Based on GNI per capita figures for 2006, the people of Switzerland at $58,050 seem to be leading a very good life. On the other hand, with a GNI per capita for 2006 of only $230, the people of Malawi seem to have a difficult life.[3] For international companies, the higher the GNI per capita, the better the market potential, as the people in the country with higher GNI per capita can afford to spend more on a vast variety of goods and services.

INFLATION

Inflation is another factor that international companies use to measure a country's economic strength. Inflation is defined as an increase in the overall price level of goods and services in a country. The rate of inflation is calculated by averaging the percentage growth rate of the prices of a selected sample of commodities. Inflation affects many aspects of an economy, including prices of goods and services and prices of raw materials and components used by companies in the manufacture of goods. The inflation rate also determines the real cost of borrowing and affects a country's exchange rate. Real interest rates are calculated by subtracting inflation from the nominal interest rate. Most countries control inflation through monetary and fiscal policies. Japan and the United States, for example, have a good record in keeping inflation under control through monetary and fiscal policies.

Inflation rates vary from country to country. Most industrialized countries try to maintain low inflation—in the single digits. For example, for the year 2007 the inflation in Japan was 0.8 percent; during the same time period Serbia registered a 15.5 percent rate of inflation. Developing economies have difficulty maintaining single-digit inflation, however. For example, Zimbabwe experienced an inflation rate of 1,035.5 percent for 2007, and Iraq's inflation rate for 2007 was 53.2 percent. Table 3.1 presents the inflation rates for selected countries for the year 2007.

Due to fundamental structural problems, it is difficult for developing countries to keep inflation under control. For most developing countries, an unending cycle of high unemployment and low incomes combined with scarcity of goods and services leads to a general rise in price levels. Long-term inflation is caused by excessive demand, called *demand-pull inflation,* or a rise in costs, called *cost-push inflation* or *supply-side inflation.* Demand-pull inflation occurs when there are general increases in the aggregate demand and the supply of goods and services lags behind—that is, consumers are purchasing too many goods, and the producers are not able to meet the needs, resulting in higher prices. In cost-push inflation, input costs keep rising; the producers pass this increase on to the consumers.

Setting prices is never an easy task for international companies. Prices are affected by many factors, including competition, price elasticity of demand, government regulations, and other internal factors. However, when a firm must set a price within a high-inflation market, these factors become compounded.[4]

BALANCE OF PAYMENTS

Balance of payments refers to all of a nation's transactions in goods, services, assets, and donations with all of its trading partners. It is a double-entry bookkeeping system that is balanced at the end of a specific time frame, usually a year. Balance of payments consists of two separate accounts: (1) the *current account,* which is made up of all of a country's exports and imports, any income earned or remitted because of assets, and employee compensation received or paid, and (2) the *capital account,* a financial transaction between countries in which assets are purchased or sold. The current account is the one most watched by policy makers and international companies.

The difference between a country's exports and its imports in goods and services is referred to as its balance of trade. A trade surplus is said to occur when a country's exports are greater than its imports; a trade deficit occurs when a country's imports are greater than its exports. Countries such as Japan and China have huge trade surpluses each year. China had a trade surplus of $262.2 billion for the year 2007, a nearly 50 percent increase from the previous year.[5] In contrast, the United States runs deficits every year. The U.S. trade deficit for just one month (March 2008) was close to $60 billion.

EXTERNAL DEBT

A country's external debt is its total borrowing through foreign government sources or private banks. Many developing countries borrow from foreign sources to finance their developmental programs, as they themselves lack the required capital. In many instances, the poorer countries are not able to pay back the amount outstanding, and banks have to reschedule their debts. An agreement is reached whereby the debtors are given extensions on their payment schedules, and in some cases a portion of the debt may be written off. During the 1970s and 1980s some American banks, primarily Citigroup and JPMorgan Chase, lent considerable funds (close to $700 billion) to foreign countries, including Brazil, Mexico, and Venezuela. Table 3.2 presents the current external debt of selected countries. Countries with large external debts

Table 3.2

External Debt for Selected Countries, 2007 (estimate)

#	Country	External Debt (in $ billions)	External Debt as a % of GDP
1	Brazil	557.1	43.9
2	China	614.1	18.9
3	Mexico	204.8	23.1
4	Russia	90.0	7.0

Source: Central Intelligence Agency, "Country Statistics," *The World Factbook.* Available at https://www.cia.gov/library/publications/the-world-factbook/ (accessed June 10, 2008).

have fundamental problems in their economies. Any economic downturn among the industrialized countries hurts poorer countries' exports, reducing their capacity to pay back the loans. The profits and other remittances of international companies that plan to operate in these countries may be compromised.

ECONOMIC DEVELOPMENT AND INTERNATIONAL BUSINESS

Traditionally, international companies have sought countries that have substantial market potential—specifically, the industrialized countries of the world, such as Japan, most of the Western European countries, and the United States. These countries provide economic stability but also a larger than average consumer base that can buy goods and services beyond basic necessities. For example, the European Union had an estimated population in 2006 of 457 million. Of this population, nearly 70 percent or 320 million were in the middle-income category, providing a substantial consumer base to which foreign companies could sell their goods and services. Because of the economic stability and high purchasing power of the fully developed countries' population, international companies find the business environment in these countries safer. For example, companies such as Boeing and Coca-Cola in the United States, Switzerland's Nestlé, and Unilever of the Netherlands derive a substantial portion of their revenues from a select few countries. Coca-Cola obtains about 15 percent of its revenues from Japan alone, and Nestle receives about 20 percent of its revenues from the United States, the world's two largest economies. Hence, a country's economic development has considerable influence on whether an international company will invest in it.

Less industrialized countries offer smaller markets for international companies and also have marginal growth rates. The total market potential of all the less developed countries put together is relatively small. Hence, the business environment in these countries is riskier for international companies. But some radical changes are taking place in the flow of globally based companies' investments and operations. In recent years, because of the saturation of industrialized countries' domestic markets and the dynamic changes that have occurred in some of the developing economies, international companies are investing in these economies to tap into the newfound opportunities. For example, countries such as Brazil, China, the Czech Republic, Hungary, Malaysia, Peru, and Thailand are attracting attention in the corporate sphere. In fact,

China has become the world's "manufacturing base," with many foreign companies investing heavily there. Currently China is the world's single largest cellular phone user, with more than 432 million subscribers. By the year 2020, China will be the second-largest market for automobiles, with expected sales of 9 million cars per year. It is no wonder that the world's major automobile manufacturers, including Mercedes-Benz of Germany, are setting up manufacturing operations in China.

A country's economic development is measured by the following variables: per capita GDP/GNI, wealth distribution, quality of life, literacy rates, and life expectancy. Using a country's level of economic activity, various international agencies such as the United Nations (UN), the World Bank, and the International Monetary Fund (IMF) have grouped countries of the world into different classes. The traditional (and old) economic development classifications included industrialized/fully developed countries; newly industrialized countries; less developed countries; and underdeveloped, or third world, countries. These classifications are often based on a multitude of factors including the level of industrialization, the country's wealth, availability of capital for investments, and the general well-being of the country's citizens. Under this system, Canada, France, Germany, Japan, Singapore, Sweden, the United Kingdom, and the United States would be classified as "industrialized," or "fully developed," nations. "Newly industrialized" countries include Brazil, South Korea, and Taiwan. Examples of countries that are considered "less developed" or "developing" are Chile, India, Malaysia, Mexico, Peru, and Thailand. And Angola, Burundi, and Myanmar are countries that could be classified as "underdeveloped."

The current classification of a country's stage of economic development no longer contains categories such "third world" or "underdeveloped," but rather more acceptable terms such as "developing" or "less developed." Each international agency uses not only different terminology to classify countries but also different variables to group them. For example, the IMF uses terms such as "advanced economies" that include both "developed countries" and "newly industrialized economies." Similarly, the United Nations generally uses just two categories to classify countries—"developed" and "developing" economies.

Perhaps the simplest and most useful classification of countries based on their stage of economic development was developed by the World Bank, which uses GNI as the sole variable to classify countries. A country's gross national income is defined as "income generated by a country's residents from domestic and international activity." Using GNI per capita, the World Bank classifies countries as "high income" (54 countries), "upper-middle income" (37 countries), "lower-middle income" (56 countries), and "lower income" (61 countries). The exact statistics used by the World Bank to group the countries are as follows:

High income	$10,726 or more
Upper-middle income	$9,075–2,936
Lower-middle income	$2,935–736
Low income	$735 or less

Table 3.3 presents selected countries classified according to GNI.

Table 3.3

Selected Countries as Classified by the World Bank, 2006

#	Country	GNI per Capita (Current US$)
High-Income Countries		
1	Australia	33,940
2	Canada	36,280
3	Denmark	36,190
4	Germany	32,680
5	Italy	28,970
6	Japan	32,840
7	Netherlands	37,940
8	Singapore	43,300
9	United Kingdom	33,650
10	United States	44,070
Upper-Middle Income Countries		
1	Argentina	11,670
2	Chile	11,300
3	Gabon	11,180
4	Hungary	16,970
5	Malaysia	12,160
6	Mexico	11,990
7	Slovak Republic	17,060
8	South Africa	8,900
9	Uruguay	9,940
10	Venezuela	10,970
Lower-Middle Income Countries		
1	Albania	6,000
2	Belarus	9,700
3	Brazil	8,700
4	Ecuador	6,810
5	Egypt	4,940
6	Honduras	3,420
7	Jordan	4,820
8	Morocco	3,860
9	Philippines	3,430
10	Thailand	7,440
Low-Income Countries		
1	Bangladesh	1,230
2	Chad	1,170
3	Eritrea	680
4	Haiti	1,070
5	Kenya	1,470
6	Liberia	260
7	Nigeria	1,410
8	Senegal	1,560
9	Tajikistan	1,560
10	Vietnam	2,310

Source: The World Bank, "World Development Data." Available at http://devdata.worldbank.org/data-query (accessed June 10, 2008).

A problem faced in GNI and other economic statistics is the question of comparability between various data. Is 100 euros in Berlin equivalent to 600 Chinese yuan at an exchange rate of €1.00 = 6.00 yuan? The answer is no. With €100, a German family would probably be able to buy one week's worth of food and beverages. In contrast, a Chinese family might need only 100 yuan to buy food for a week. Since 1 yuan is not equal to €1, the Chinese person is spending only €16.60 (100/6.00) per week, compared to the German's €100. Therefore, a simple conversion of a country's GNI per capita or GDP per capita into another currency in which country statistics are maintained (U.S. dollars or euros) might not be an accurate measurement of that country's economic state.

To overcome the conversion problem, international organizations such as the United Nations have developed a technique to compare economic statistics across countries. The technique, known as "purchasing power parity" (PPP), is defined as the number of units of a currency required to buy the same amount of goods and services in the domestic market that could be bought with the U.S. dollar in the United States. For example, suppose a basket of essential goods (food, rent, clothing, and the like) for a family in the United States costs $1,000.00. That same basket of goods costs a family in the Philippines P1,000. When the cost of goods is converted from pesos into U.S. dollars, a family in the Philippines spends only $200, at an exchange rate of US$1 = P50. Therefore, it appears that a Filipino family needs only a fifth (200/1000) of the expenditure of an American family to buy the same quantity of essential goods. Hence, according to purchasing power parity, if the GDP per capita of the Philippines was $1,000, using the PPP method it will be recorded as US$5,000 (multiplied by a factor of 1,000/200 = 5).

The World Bank does not use straightforward official exchange rates or the purchasing power parity approach to a country's economic data; instead, it uses the "Atlas" methodology. Conversions using the Atlas method are normally more stable and take into account historic exchange rates by utilizing three factors: (1) the average of the current exchange rate, (2) the exchange rates for the two previous years, and (3) the ratio of domestic inflation to the combined inflation rates of the European Union, Japan, the United Kingdom, and the United States. In calculating the conversion of economic data using the Atlas approach, the World Bank adjusts the two-year historic domestic exchange rate by the ratio of domestic inflation to the combined inflation of the four aforementioned groups/countries. Table 3.4 presents GNI per capita for selected countries using the Atlas method and the PPP method.

Because of the lower cost of living in countries such as Argentina, Bangladesh, and Colombia, the GNI per capita using the PPP method is higher than the GNI per capita using the Atlas method for these countries. In contrast, for Norway, the GNI per capita using the PPP method is much lower than the Atlas method.

In addition to the GNI classification of countries, the World Bank uses a measure of indebtedness to group countries when compiling global economic data. Using indebtedness as an economic factor, countries are classified into four groups: "severely indebted" (53 countries, including Argentina, Indonesia, and Turkey); "moderately indebted" (39 countries, including Bolivia, Malaysia, and Slovak Republic); "less indebted" (44 countries, including Algeria, Guatemala, and Thailand); and "not classified" (77 countries, including the wealthiest in the world such as the Nordic countries).

The GNI classification of economic development is useful for a broad-based macroanal-

Table 3.4

GNI per Capita for Selected Countries Using the Atlas and PPP Methods, 2006

Country	GNI per Capita (Atlas Method)	GNI per Capita (PPP Method)
Argentina	5,150	11,670
Australia	35,860	33,940
Bangladesh	450	1,230
Canada	36,650	36,280
Colombia	3,120	6,130
Germany	36,810	32,680
Ireland	49,960	33,740
Malaysia	5,620	12,160
Norway	68,440	50,070
Philippines	1,390	3,430
Sweden	43,530	34,310
United States	44,710	44,070

Source: The World Bank, http://devdata.worldbank.org/data-query (accessed June 10, 2008).

ysis of countries. However, in evaluating countries or formulating operational strategies, international managers make use of the more traditional economic indicators such as GDP growth rate, GDP per capita, rate of inflation, current account balance, and so on. These statistics have more direct influences on the consumption patterns of a population.

Countries can also be classified by their overall economic systems. An economic system explains how a country allocates its resources. A country's resources may be owned by private citizens, by private companies, collectively by the country's people, or by the government. When private citizens and private companies own and control resources, the economy is referred to as a "market-based system." When the government owns and controls resources, the system is referred to as a "centrally planned economy" or a "command economy." Ownership of resources translates into control of the resources and the right to allocate them, as in the case of the Netherlands and the United States. In a market economy, most of the resources are owned and controlled by the private sector. In a centrally planned economy, such as those found in Cuba or North Korea, the resources are owned and controlled by the public sector. There are some economies where the resources are owned and controlled by the private sector and the public sector, as seen in France and India. Table 3.5 presents countries organized by their economic systems.

MARKET-BASED ECONOMY

If given a choice, international managers prefer to operate in a market-based economy because, by definition, it is consumer driven; that is, consumers have unlimited choices, and their decisions are not controlled by outside forces. The freedom the consumers enjoy also extends to firms operating within the country. In a pure market-based system, companies decide what to produce, what to sell, at what prices to sell their goods and services, and how to market them. Supply and demand dictates prices; they are not preset by any entity—government or private. That is, when the demand for

Table 3.5

Types of Economic Systems in the World

Type of economy	Selected countries	No. of countries
Market-based	Hong Kong, Singapore, United States	10
Mixed	Brazil, Canada, India, Japan, Mexico	125
Centrally planned	Cuba, North Korea	27

a particular product increases, companies may raise prices to take advantage of this opportunity, and when demand falls, they may lower price to stimulate demand.

For international companies, operating in a market-based economy implies that the country's economic framework is open to accepting foreign companies and foreign investments. In an open economy, the country's economic structure is invariably sound, and private companies can thrive under these conditions. A company's success or failure is totally dependent on its own strategic actions and the actions of its competitors. This is similar to the environment that most international companies are used to in their home countries, and therefore the level of uncertainty for these companies is minimized.

CENTRALLY PLANNED ECONOMY

In a centrally planned economy, the consumers have no freedom of choice regarding what they can buy, and most of the country's goods and services are produced by government enterprises. Consumers buy what is available, and within a product category only one brand is available. If a family wishes to buy sneakers, the only brand that is available is the one made by the government factory producing them, unlike in market-based economies such as the United States, where there are plenty of choices. In a centrally planned economy, resources are allocated to various production facilities based on the plans of the country's government, which considers itself a much better judge than the private sector of what is good for its people. It can divert resources to various segments of the economy as it sees fit. Economic principles of demand and supply do not function in a centrally planned economy. Hence, the quality, prices, and marketing of goods and services are determined by the government. One advantage for the people in a centrally planned economy is that the prices of commodities remain the same during high demand as well as low demand. The downside of the system is that when supply of a product runs out, no efforts are made to add to the supply, no matter what price a consumer is willing to pay.

The general principle behind centrally planned economies is that everyone in a society should be able to buy and consume goods and services equally. The concept of rich versus poor does not exist in these economies. Since the breakup of the Soviet Union, few countries follow a centrally planned system. In fact, China, which used to have a centrally based economy, is slowly shifting toward a mixed economy.

Operating in centrally planned economies is often a struggle for international companies. Their success is dependent on factors that are outside their control. International companies have to fit their plans into an overall country-based economic plan developed by the country's government. Depending on the industry, this quite often puts an international company at odds with local governments. For example, if the Cuban government in its current five-year (2005–2010) economic plan has identified food production, health services, and infrastructure as the key sectors toward which to direct its efforts, and if Unilever plans to enter the Cuban market by introducing a brand of detergent, the Cuban government may not necessarily deny Unilever's request to invest in Cuba, as it seeks foreign investments; at the same time it may not be too helpful to the company, either.

MIXED ECONOMY

In a mixed economy, the resources are owned and controlled not by individuals or the government alone, but by both groups. In fact, there are more mixed economies in the world than there are either market-based or centrally planned economies. The principle behind mixed economies is that there are some segments of production that for various reasons should be controlled by the government and some that should be left to the private sector. Transportation, energy production, telecommunications, and distribution of food are segments typically controlled by the government. The reasoning is that these are the lifelines to the existence of a society, and leaving their control to the private sector may threaten the supply of these essential goods and services, especially during a national crisis. Mixed economies range widely regarding how much of the private sector controls the resources versus how much the public sector controls the resources. France, India, and the Scandinavian countries are good examples of mixed economies.

In mixed economies, the opportunities in some sectors of the economy are very attractive for international companies, as they may not have to compete with public-sector companies. The market environment for nonpublic-sector undertakings in many of these mixed economies is similar to that of market-based economies. They are driven by market forces, although at times the government may decide to take over a particular sector if it determines that this action will serve the public's best interest. For example, the French government has slowly reestablished its presence in the energy industry, especially in the production of electric power, to safeguard against foreign control of this sector.

ECONOMIC FACTORS AND INTERNATIONAL BUSINESS STRATEGY

Analysis of the economic and other environmental factors that affect foreign countries and their markets can help international managers understand the behavior of these markets and assist them in developing effective strategies. By predicting market trends and analyzing the size, potential, and characteristics of countries' markets, international managers can develop unique strategies to tap into the potential of these countries. However, the many differences among countries make this process difficult. Countries vary in size, economic development, economic policies, and view of investments from abroad. Countries from the former Soviet Union bloc, for example, do not necessarily look favorably on foreign companies. The governments of these countries make it difficult for foreign companies to invest in them, even if it would mean improvements in their economic conditions. Sometimes these countries fear a change in their political systems due to the influence of international companies. It is difficult for governments that have been immersed in socialistic ideals to suddenly forgo these ideals and embrace democratic rules and privatization.

Frequently, international companies find foreign countries' economic systems totally alien in comparison to their own domestic economic environment. The learning process for these companies can be time-consuming and difficult. For example, the Japanese economy was a puzzle to many American and European companies: the close relationship between Japanese companies and the various Japanese government agencies, whose role was to help private companies and act on their behalf in negotiations, was new to the American and European managers. Since many international companies operate in multiple countries, they are required to learn different economic systems. For example, Siemens of Germany operates in 137 countries, and the economic patterns that they encounter in Europe are vastly different from those they find in the Latin American region. The economic compositions of countries vary widely; no two systems are exactly alike. What is learned in one system may not be transferable to another. A company that operates in Brazil may find the economic system in Argentina quite different, even though both countries are situated in the same region. Therefore, international managers have to learn a new system every time they enter a new country.

Economic systems in some countries are very volatile. Without warning, the local economy may enter into a downward spiral; overnight the rate of inflation may hit double digits; and the local currency may be devalued by 20 to 40 percent in no time, as happened in Argentina in the fall of 2004. Each of these events places great stress on the operations of international companies. International managers must always be prepared to deal with such sudden changes.

As economic conditions shift, international companies have to adjust their corporate strategies. Compared to domestic economic forces, international economic factors are quite dynamic and difficult to predict. Unfamiliarity with local economic conditions also makes it difficult for international managers to plan for sudden swings in a country's economy. For example, a rise in inflation might affect the costs of inputs such as labor and material. A sudden appreciation in the local currency might make exports of goods and services more expensive and cause a country to lose its competitive advantage. An increase in the local country's external debt may affect government expenditures and soften consumption expenditures. In fact, changes in economic variables affect the overall business environment. These changes mean that international companies that operate in many countries must react to shifts in economic conditions in a timely, effective, and well-programmed manner.

To address the difficulties of planning in an uncertain world economy, international managers follow a systematic strategy-formulation process. The individual steps in the process are: *scenario analysis, business analysis, strategic action plans, execution, and monitoring/control.* Most of these steps are standard management prescriptions used in developing strategies. Due to uncertainties in the international context, however, these tasks become increasingly important. (Some steps are presented in later chapters in the discussion of functional strategies.) Because of its impact on the overall business environment, scenario analysis is the first step undertaken by most international companies. It helps international managers to develop alternative business strategies.

Scenario analysis is built on the assumption that the future of an economy or event can be realistically and systematically predicted and that it is possible to identify the chain of events that might take place in certain situations. Scenario analysis is defined as *quantitative and qualitative descriptions of the possible future state of an organization developed within the framework of relevant interdependent factors or events in the external environment.* That is, scenario analysis (1) focuses on the external environment, (2) considers the future of this environment, (3) identifies the interdependence of the various factors that affect this environment, and (4) uses research to predict future events.

Scenario analysis is an exercise in identifying the events in the environment that are most likely to affect a company's performance. These future events are developed under logical assumptions about what might impact the market and include existing uncertainties. International managers developing scenario analyses may use them to forecast possible actions that would minimize or overcome existing uncertainties, asking themselves what the best possible course of action would be in a given scenario. To be useful, the scenario analysis should focus on the one or two most likely possibilities and use indicators that confirm or refute the laid-out scenario.[6] A good example of the application of scenario analysis comes from Southwest Airlines. It was one of the few American companies that entered into a futures contract to buy oil at $34 per barrel during the gradual price increases of crude oil in the summer of 2005. When the price reached $77 in the summer of 2006, Southwest was competitively well placed in controlling its costs, as it was paying only half the amount for oil that other U.S. domestic airlines were paying. Similarly, Deutsch Bahn (DB), the German railway system, wanted to predict the ridership under different scenarios for its express trains, which take people to different parts of the country and connect them to the other rail systems in Europe. DB considered the effects of gasoline prices on automobile and air travel, and it also considered weather patterns that may influence people's travel plans when calculating the number of trains that it should put into service each year. This action resulted in substantial cost savings for the railways.

As we have said, the economic scenario is made difficult due to its unpredictability. Despite their sophistication, the existing econometric models that use complex simultaneous regression equations are unreliable. Two years ago, no one could have predicted that a barrel of crude oil would hit $135; nor could anyone have predicted that the downturn in the Japanese economy would last for more than 10 years. Recession, the spiraling cost of energy, interest rate hikes, and trade deficits are all variables that do not behave logically.

In developing a scenario analysis, the following steps may be helpful.[7]

- Enumerate the strategic intent of the analysis—the analysis may help international companies to forecast the environment in preparation for subsequent decisions or for evaluating strategies against chosen scenarios.

- Conduct a trend-impact analysis—using information, media scanning, forecasts, judgments, and past experiences to identify possible trends.
- Create scenarios—predict which events will occur, at what time, and in what order.
- Outline actions—for each possible scenario, develop an action plan to take (what should be done).

ECONOMIC FACTORS AND COUNTRY RISK ANALYSIS

In selecting a country for entry, international companies conduct a risk analysis to consider those factors that expose them to various types of risks. Aside from financial losses, international companies face (1) loss of intellectual property rights (for example, many pharmaceutical companies have lost their patent rights in India; local Indian companies have produced generic drugs that are sold at reduced prices, outselling international companies); (2) loss of brand image; (3) liability lawsuits (for example, in 1999 Coca-Cola products were banned in six European countries after children in school cafeterias became ill after drinking Coke; this was a public relations nightmare for Coca-Cola, and the company lost close to $300 million in sales after the recall of its products); and (4) human loss (in some Latin American countries expatriate executives have been kidnapped, and a few have lost their lives). Factors used in country risk analyses include political stability, economic conditions, banking and finance risk systems, laws and regulations, and cultural dynamics. In addition to these factors, international companies may analyze the quality of infrastructure, level of technology, quality of life, and a country's external debt.

Depending on the industry, some factors may be more important than others. For example, for a fast food company, the cultural and infrastructure variables might be more critical than the technology factor. For a telecommunications company, however, the technology factor will most likely be more critical than many others. In most instances, however, researchers believe that the economic and political factors are most important in an assessment of a country's risk. In analyzing countries, researchers assign weights to each factor and then rank the risk element for each country. For example, in its semiannual country risk rankings, *Euromoney,* a U.K. publication, assigns a weight of 25 percent each to the economic and political factors.

Euromoney uses a multiple approach in arriving at its rankings, taking into account both qualitative information and quantitative data in assessing a country's risks. To obtain some of the qualitative data, *Euromoney* polls economists, political analysts, and insurance brokers. The quantitative data is collected from the World Bank, the International Monetary Fund, and credit agencies such as Moody's and Standard & Poor's to arrive at a score for each country. Table 3.6 lists the nine variables considered by *Euromoney* in its ranking of countries and the respective weights assigned to each variable.

Using these variables, *Euromoney* ranks 185 countries of the world every six months. Table 3.7 lists the 10 *least* risky countries to invest in based on *Euromoney's* March 2008 rankings. Table 3.8 lists the 10 *most* risky countries to invest in based on *Euromoney's* March 2008 rankings.

Table 3.6

Variables Used in *Euromoney's* Country Rankings

	Variable	Weight %
1	Political risk	25
2	Economic performance	25
3	Debt indicators	10
4	Debt in default	10
5	Credit ratings	10
6	Access to bank financing	5
7	Access to short-term finance	5
8	Access to capital markets	5
9	Forfaiting (discount rate on letter of credit)	5

Table 3.7

The Ten Least Risky Countries of the World, March 2008 *Euromoney* Rankings

	Country	V1	V2	V3	V4	V5	V6	V7	V8	V9	Totals
1	Luxembourg	25.00	25.00	10.00	10.00	10.00	5.00	5.00	5.00	4.88	99.88
2	Norway	24.67	22.93	10.00	10.00	10.00	5.00	5.00	5.00	4.65	97.47
3	Switzerland	24.71	21.63	10.00	10.00	10.00	5.00	5.00	5.00	4.88	96.21
4	Denmark	24.54	19.58	10.00	10.00	10.00	5.00	5.00	5.00	4.27	93.39
5	Sweden	24.68	18.40	10.00	10.00	10.00	5.00	5.00	5.00	4.88	92.96
6	Ireland	24.39	18.09	10.00	10.00	10.00	5.00	5.00	5.00	4.88	92.36
7	Austria	24.36	18.01	10.00	10.00	10.00	5.00	5.00	5.00	4.88	92.25
8	Finland	24.76	17.32	10.00	10.00	10.00	5.00	5.00	5.00	4.88	91.95
9	Netherlands	24.50	17.58	10.00	10.00	10.00	5.00	5.00	5.00	4.88	91.95
10	Austria	23.74	17.53	10.00	10.00	10.00	5.00	5.00	5.00	5.00	91.27

Source: Euromoney magazine, "Country Risk Analysis," March 2008. Available at http://www.euromoney.com/Article/1886310/country-risk-March-2008-overall-results.html.

Some large international companies do not rely on rankings published by the business press, but conduct their own country risk analyses. Most of the factors considered by these companies are similar to the ones published by the business journals. For example, the U.S.-based American Can Company assigns the most weight to economic and political risk factors in developing its own country risk ranking lists. Table 3.9 lists a few of the key factors used by American Can in its country risk analysis and the respective weights assigned to each factor.

The World Economic Forum (WEF) conducts a global competitiveness ranking of countries using both publicly available data and an executive opinion survey. For the 2007–2008 report, WEF polled more than 11,000 business leaders. Table 3.10 lists the top 10 competitive countries among the 131 WEF polled. United States was ranked as the top country by WEF, followed by Switzerland and three other Nordic countries—Denmark, Sweden, and Norway—ranking third, fourth, and sixth. Similarly, in the "Doing Business" report released by the World Bank,

Table 3.8

The Ten Most Risky Countries of the World, March 2008 Euromoney Rankings

	Country	V1	V2	V3	V4	V5	V6	V7	V8	V9	Total
						Variables					
176	Micronesia	13.84	3.98	0.00	0.00	0.00	0.00	0.77	0.44	0.00	19.03
177	Zimbabwe	0.56	0.07	6.97	10.00	0.00	0.00	0.19	1.13	0.00	18.92
178	Zaire	4.48	2.98	0.00	10.00	0.00	0.00	0.58	0.86	0.00	18.89
179	Liberia	4.58	1.78	0.00	10.00	0.00	0.00	0.19	0.38	0.00	16.93
180	Cuba	3.85	5.75	0.00	0.00	3.44	0.00	0.58	0.60	0.61	14.82
181	Marshall Islands	9.83	3.41	0.00	0.00	0.00	0.00	0.00	0.38	0.00	13.61
182	Somalia	0.00	2.37	0.00	10.00	0.00	0.00	0.58	0.38	0.00	13.32
183	Iraq	1.74	3.22	0.00	0.00	0.00	0.00	0.19	0.95	0.00	6.11
184	North Korea	0.29	4.50	0.00	0.00	0.00	0.00	0.58	0.64	0.00	6.01
185	Afghanistan	1.71	3.46	0.00	0.00	0.00	0.00	0.19	0.08	0.00	5.45

Source: Euromoney magazine, "Country Risk Analysis," March 2008. Available at http://www.euromoney.com/ Article/1886310/country-risk-March-2008-overall-results.html.

Table 3.9

Relative Factor Weights Used by American Can for Analyzing Country Risk

Factor	Weight (%)
Political stability	26.0
Political freedom	7.0
Quality of infrastructure	6.7
Inflation	3.6
Currency stability	3.3
Balance of payments	3.3

Table 3.10

The Global Competitiveness Rankings, 2007–2008

Rank	Country	Score (out of 7)
1	United States	5.67
2	Switzerland	5.65
3	Denmark	5.55
4	Sweden	5.54
5	Germany	5.51
6	Finland	5.49
7	Singapore	5.45
8	Japan	5.43
9	United Kingdom	5.41
10	Netherlands	5.40

Source: The World Economic Forum, "World Competitive Ranking." Available at http://www.weforum. org/en/initative/gcp/Global%/20competitivness/20report/index.htm.

Denmark, Finland, Norway, and Sweden were ranked near the top as well. The United States was ranked second.

These rankings by the various agencies show that there is some uniformity in all rankings, and their lists are quite reliable.[8]

UNDERGROUND ECONOMY

Most of the economic data compiled by individual national governments and various international organizations is the result of reported economic activity by corporations, small businesses, and individuals. The official economic statistics, called the "observed economy," are measured by totaling all expenditures for newly produced goods and services that are not resold in any form. These expenditures include consumer spending, investment by businesses, government expenditures, and net exports. It is believed that in many countries reported economic activity is understated, as some corporations, small businesses, and private citizens do not fully disclose their financial records. There may be many reasons for underreporting income and related financials, including internal tax codes and other government regulations. It is generally alleged that the higher the income tax rate and the more bureaucratic the process of reporting financial statements and filing taxes, the greater the nondisclosure of incomes.[9]

The economic activities that go unreported are commonly referred to as "underground economic activities." The underground economies are sometimes called "parallel economies," "shadow economies," or "submerged economies." Underground economies were originally thought to be a problem of developing economies or centrally planned economies (economic systems found in predominantly socialist countries including China and the bloc of countries that made up the former Soviet Union). Recent statistics compiled by business journals such as the *Economist* paint a different picture. In fact, many of the culprit nations of huge underground economies are some of the most developed countries of Western Europe, particularly Italy and Spain. In addition, three Scandinavian countries with some of the highest tax rates due to their social welfare systems are among the top six countries in terms of highest underground economies. The size of the underground economies among developing countries remains high due to structural deficiencies and corruption. Some estimates place the figure between 35 and 44 percent. Table 3.11 presents countries with the highest percentage of underground economies among the industrialized countries in relation to their total GDP.[10]

For international companies, operating in an economy that is to a large extent based on the parallel economy poses problems. As foreign companies, they need to adhere to the country's laws, and their actions are scrutinized much more carefully than are those of domestic companies. At the same time, local competitors have an advantage, as they are used to these conditions and can operate under the radar.

In addition to economic factors, the other four environmental factors that need to be discussed are *competitive environment, infrastructure, technology,* and *quality of life.*

COMPETITIVE ENVIRONMENT

Competitive environment can be divided into two parts: macro and micro. In the macro competitive environment, the country's competitive advantage or disadvan-

Table 3.11

Estimate of Underground Economy as Percentage of Total GDP, 2006

	Country	Total GDP[a] Current ($ hundred million)	% of Underground Economy of GDP[b]	Corporate tax (%)[c]
1	Australia	768.20	13.00	30.00
2	Belgium	392.00	21.00	33.99
3	Canada	1,251.50	16.00	36.60
4	Denmark	275.20	19.00	24.00
5	France	2,230.70	16.00	34.33
6	Germany	2,906.70	16.00	25.00
7	Ireland	222.60	10.00	20.00–42.00
8	Italy	1,844.70	26.00	33.00
9	Japan	4,340.10	9.00	30.00
10	Netherlands	657.60	14.00	29.00–34.50
12	Norway	311.00	20.00	28–51.3
13	Spain	1,224.00	24.00	15.00–45.00
14	United Kingdom	2,345.00	12.00	30.00
15	United States	13,201.80	9.00	35.00

Sources:
[a] The World Bank, http://www.worldbank.org/data/countryclass/countryclass.html (accessed October 15, 2007).
[b] "Black Hole," *The Economist,* August 28, 1999, p. 59.
[c] Worldwide-Tax.com, available at http://www.worldwide-tax.com (accessed January 2007).

tage as a whole is considered. In the microenvironment, the competitive advantage or disadvantage at the firm level is evaluated. The macro competitive environment deals with attractiveness of countries to investors. As Michael Porter put it, "Why do some nations become the home base for successful international competitors in an industry?"[11] A few countries are more attractive than others for some specific industries. For example, Switzerland is home to many of the leading pharmaceutical companies; similarly, China is home to many of the garment manufacturers of the world, and India has many of the leading software development companies of the world. Countries attain competitive advantage through various means, including factor-input costs (India and China), economic stability and regulatory environment (Switzerland), size of domestic market (Europe and the United States), and technological developments (Germany and Japan). None of these reasons by themselves may provide the competitive advantage a country seeks, but a combination of these factors may explain some of it.

At the micro level, international companies face an array of competitors with varied and unique advantages. Some of the competition comes from local companies, which are already entrenched in the host country—*local competitors.* Others are international firms operating in the global marketplace—*global competitors.* A third category of competitors are companies from the same country as the international firm—*home competitors.* For example, for General Motors operating in Germany, BMW, Mercedes-Benz, and Volkswagen are local competitors; Fiat, Renault, Saab, and Toyota are global competitors; and Ford Motors is the home competitor. By understanding the competitive and strategic advantages of each of these groups, an international company might be able develop its own unique strategies.

International companies conduct competitive analyses to identify current and potential competitors, to predict the possible strategic actions of these competitors, and to account for unforeseen events that may give competitors an advantage. In identifying current competitors, companies consider the following key variables:

- How similar are the company's product or service offerings to those of other firms in the same country? For example, Coca-Cola and Pepsi-Cola both offer cola products that could easily be substituted for each other. Therefore, these two companies are competing directly with each other for the same target customers. In contrast, Coca-Cola and Cadbury Schweppes offer carbonated beverages, but their products are not similar; Cadbury Schweppes offers more noncola products.
- How similar are the benefits that customers derive from the company's products to those they derive from the products or services that the other firms offer? Once again, the more similar the benefits derived from the products or services, the higher the substitutability. Weight Watchers and Jenny Craig, two American companies, offer diet programs, but their methods of losing weight are different, even though customers signing up for the two programs seek the same benefit.
- Lastly, a company should consider how other firms define the scope of their market. Again, the more similar the companies' definitions of the target customers or markets, the more likely the companies will view each other as competitors. For example, BMW, Lexus, and Mercedes-Benz focus on the high end of the automobile market, where as Hyundai focuses on the low end of the market. Therefore, BMW, Lexus, and Mercedes-Benz compete with one another, but they are not in direct competition with Hyundai.

International companies have learned to deal with many of the competitive challenges that they face on a daily basis. Some successful companies use systematic approaches to survive the intense competitive pressure they face. One such approach is to compare competing firms on key variables that may provide a competitive edge. For example, in the automobile industry critical competitive factors may include fuel efficiency, level of safety, engine performance, roominess, and acceleration. Some of these factors are easily measurable: fuel efficiency (EPA ratings), safety (crash tests), acceleration (industry standards), and roominess (cubic feet of space or distance between the front seats and the backseats). Using these factors, a company could do a brand-by-brand comparison across competitors. Table 3.12 presents competitive analysis for competing brands of cars.

By reviewing the matrix shown in Table 3.12, Ford, for example, could evaluate its competitive position vis-à-vis of other brands. It is clear that if these factor rankings hold true, in order to be competitive and attract more buyers, Ford will have to improve its offerings in many areas. The systematic approach to competitive analysis helps international companies weigh their positions in each country and develop strategic steps to be successful.

Table 3.12

Systematic Competitive Analysis—Automobiles (Sedans)

Brand	MPG (city/highway)	Safety (good, acceptable, marginal, poor)	Engine Performance (high, medium, low)	Roominess	Acceleration (0 to 60 in seconds)
Accord	24/33	Good	High	Moderate	8.6
Century	19/30	Good	Medium	Moderate	8.5
Camry	23/32	Acceptable	High	Moderate	8.6
Maxima	20/28	Good	Medium	Moderate	8.2
Taurus	19/28	Good	Medium	Moderate	9.0

Source: National Automobile Dealers Association, McLean, Virginia, and Insurance Institute for Highway Safety, http://www.iihs.org/vehicle_ratings/ratings.html (accessed January 2008).

INFRASTRUCTURE

Infrastructure is the collection of systems, activities, and structures that facilitate logistics and communications. The efficiency of an infrastructure affects production and business operations. These systems and structures are able to move the raw materials and finished goods of a country from suppliers to the marketplace, that is, facilitate both upstream and downstream distribution. For international companies, the networks of roads, railroads, communication systems, and warehouse facilities are critical variables in their choice of target countries. Infrastructure undertakings require substantial government investment, and countries that are in the developmental stages find it harder to allocate funds for this area than established economies do. At the same time, to attract foreign investors, developing countries need to provide the basic means of transporting supplies to manufacturing plants and finished goods to markets.

Industrialized countries continuously improve their infrastructure facilities to lower costs and improve delivery time. New airports are built to accommodate travel and shipment of goods. Take, for example, Hong Kong International Airport (HKIA), built at a cost of $300 billion, which can be used for passenger travel, cargo, shipping, and air delivery. As a gateway to China and other Asian countries, HKIA has become one of the most important hubs for international passenger and cargo flow. This facility has attracted many foreign businesses, which find it cheaper and faster to redistribute goods through Hong Kong. Similarly, Japan has built the longest combined rail and road bridge in the world, at a cost of $7.6 billion; it connects the island of Shikoku with Honshu, the main industrial and commercial center of Japan. The route hops from island to island and is made up of six separate bridges. Seto Ohashi bridge reduces travel time between these two islands from two hours to ten minutes, facilitating the transportation of goods and improving the economy of Shikoku.[12]

TECHNOLOGY

Technology has become a key driving force in the development of industrialized countries. It enables these countries to increase productivity, lower costs, and improve the general welfare of their citizens. Use of technology in the agricultural sector has helped the United States to attain a level output with only 3 percent of its labor force devoted to farming. Use of computers and software such as CAD (computer-aided design) has helped automobile manufacturers to design and introduce new models of automobiles in less than three years (compared to the seven or eight years that it took previously). Use of broadband communication technology helps companies to transmit data and information in an instant to any part of the world. Technology allows international companies to gain competitive advantages through the introduction of innovative and better-quality products, to lower costs, and to achieve internal efficiencies.

Technology is broadly defined as *the science of systematic knowledge used by industries to help in the production and marketing of goods and services.* Technology in business has three components—technology of production, technology of processes, and technology of management.[13] Technology used in the development and manufacturing of goods is called "product technology." This type of technology is responsible for the invention of new ideas and the innovation of products. Toyota is known for its production and product technology. Technology used to organize and coordinate activities of operations is called "process technology." Procter & Gamble has been very successful through its emphasis on process technology. This technology helps companies to take the innovations to the marketplace more efficiently. Technology that enables management to improve efficiencies, manage its people better, and improve communication and decision making is called "management technology." This technology helps companies apply their new knowledge across all parts of their organizations. GE is a good example of a company that has attained significant competitive advantage through its management technology.

For companies in high-technology industries such as aircraft manufacturing, chemicals, computers, pharmaceuticals, and telecommunications, the level of technology available in a country quite often dictates whether the firm will invest in that country. Therefore, in assessing countries for entry, technology—along with the economy, political stability, and business regulations—becomes a critical environmental factor that these companies consider. In some instances, international companies may consider *transfer of technology* into some of the less sophisticated countries if the long-term market potential is attractive. Transfer of technology implies that international firms are willing to disseminate their scientific knowledge where it is not currently available. By doing so, they are able to achieve a competitive advantage in these countries, at the same time helping the local country attain a level of technological advancement that it had not yet achieved on its own. In fact, many governments of developing countries may insist on transfer of technology as a requirement before permitting foreign firms to enter their countries. A major concern for international companies in transferring technology into other countries is the protection of their technology against pirating and misuse. Consequently, international companies seek intellectual property rights protection when transferring technology.

QUALITY OF LIFE

Quality of life issues deal with people's comfort and fulfillment in all aspects of life in a particular town, city, or locality. Factors that contribute to quality of life include

Table 3.13

World's Top Ten Cities in Terms of Quality of Life, 2006

Rank	City	Country	Index
1	Zurich	Switzerland	108.1
2	Geneva	Switzerland	108.0
3	Vancouver	Canada	107.7
4	Vienna	Austria	107.7
5	Auckland	New Zealand	107.3
6	Dusseldorf	Germany	107.3
7	Frankfurt	Germany	107.1
8	Munich	Germany	106.9
9	Bern	Switzerland	106.5
9	Sydney	Australia	106.5

Source: City Mayors, "Quality of Life Rankings." Available at http://www.citymayors.com/features/quality_survey.html (accessed March 7, 2009).

standard of living; quality of education; availability of public transportation; health services, including life expectancy and availability and quality of hospitals and medical facilities; crime rate; availability of cultural attractions; freedoms of speech, religion, and politics; job opportunities; and weather conditions.

Various research groups rank cities by their quality of life. Two such groups are Mercer Consulting and the Economist Intelligence Unit. The Mercer Consulting annual Worldwide Quality of Living Survey covers 350 cities and is based on 39 different criteria, including political, social, economic, environmental, personal safety, health, education, and transport factors, as well as the availability of other public services. Cities are ranked against New York as the base city, which has an index score of 100. The Economist Intelligence Unit, a global business intelligence research firm, uses nine factors in its quality of life index, including such items as material well-being, health, and family life. Table 3.13 presents the world's top 10 cities in quality of life based on the Mercer Consulting survey.

Based on the survey, Zurich and Geneva, Switzerland, are the top two cities in terms of quality of life. Both Switzerland and Germany have three cities each among the top 10 in the Mercer Consulting survey, as reported by city mayors. Honolulu (ranked twenty-seventh) and San Francisco (ranked twenty-eighth) are the only two U.S. cities that are ranked among the top thirty.

Besides quality of life, an equally useful ranking for international companies in selecting locations for setting up operations is a list of the most expensive cities of the world. A survey for the City Mayors group conducted by UBS, the Swiss financial company, ranks the most expensive cities based on living costs in 71 metropolises. The City Mayors is an international network of professionals working to promote strong cities. The cost of living is based on a shopping basket containing 122 goods and services geared toward Western European consumers. Cities are ranked against New York as the base city, which has an index score of 100. Moscow is the most expensive city in the world. Three of the other 10 most expensive cities are in Asia: Tokyo, Seoul, and Hong Kong. Table 3.14 lists the 10 most expensive cities to live in.

Table 3.14

The Ten Most Expensive Cities in the World, 2008

Rank	City	Country	Index
1	Moscow	Russia	105.5
2	Tokyo	Japan	100.0
3	London	UK	94.6
4	Oslo	Norway	93.4
5	Seoul	South Korea	87.3
6	Hong Kong	China	86.3
7	Copenhagen	Denmark	85.8
8	Geneva	Switzerland	84.3
9	Zurich	Switzerland	82.2
10	Milan	Italy	80.6

Source: City Mayors, "Most Expensive Cities." Available at http://www.citymayors.com/economics/expensive_cities2.html (accessed January 14, 2007).

International executives use the quality of life and cost of living index in assessing countries for entry. Both indexes are critical in attracting qualified employees from within the country and from overseas. In addition, since international companies pay for the cost of living of its overseas staff, a more expensive city may drive up the cost of operations.

Chapter Summary

The economy of a country is an important variable that international companies consider in selecting countries for entry as well as for developing strategies. A country's economic strength is measured through its gross domestic product, rate of inflation, balance of payments, and external debt.

A country's economic development is classified by a variety of factors, including GDP per capita and income levels. Different international organizations, such as the International Monetary Fund, the United Nations, and the World Bank, classify countries using different variables. The World Bank classifies countries using the gross national income (GNI) factor, with the categories high income, upper-middle income, lower-middle income, and lower income. High income countries have a GNI per capita of more than $10,726; upper-middle income countries have a GNI per capita between $3,466 and $10,725; lower-middle income countries have a GNI per capita between $876 and $3,465; and lower income countries have a GNI of $875 or less. When countries are compared across economic data, due to variations in purchasing power, income levels across countries may not be comparable. To rectify this problem, most international organizations use a factoring approach called "purchasing power parity" (PPP). Purchasing power parity is defined as the number of units of a currency required to buy the same amount of goods and services in the domestic market that the American dollar would buy in the U.S. market.

Countries are also classified by the economic systems that they follow or use to allocate their resources. The three basic economic systems are market based, centrally planned, and mixed. In a market-based economy, the allocation of resources is driven by demand and supply; in a centrally planned economy, the government decides on the allocation of resources based on its developmental plans; and in a mixed economy, some resources are allocated by the government and some are allocated by the private sector.

Many international companies use scenario analyses to plan their activities in foreign countries. A scenario analysis helps international managers to operate under uncertainties and in volatile conditions by asking "what if" questions. Knowing the answers to these questions, companies can develop alternate strategies.

Strategically, international companies analyze economic factors to decide on a country for entry and also to develop strategies. In choosing a country for entry, international companies conduct a country risk analysis, which evaluates the critical economic variables that may impact the companies' entry. Factors such as GDP per capita, prevailing inflation rate, interest rate, and balance of payments are some of the economic factors that international companies consider. Larger global companies conduct their own country risk analyses, but smaller companies rely on freely available analyses that are conducted by governments or a business press. One such country risk analysis is published every six months by *Euromoney*.

A major concern for international companies in entering a country is the level of economic activity that goes unreported. Called the "underground," or "parallel" economy, these individual and corporate activities are not part of the country's economic data. International companies have to be careful in their activities in a foreign country; the underground economy may sometimes pose problems, especially if an international company directly competes with smaller companies that are part of the underground economic system. These local companies may have cost advantages that are not feasible for international companies.

Competitive environment is also a critical factor in the operations of international companies. Local competitors have unique advantages because of their knowledge of the local conditions, relationships with local distributors, and influence with the local government. In conducting a competitive analysis, companies should consider how similar their products are to the products and services offered by their competitors, how similar the target customers are, and how similar the benefits derived from the products or services are.

Infrastructure is another external variable that international companies consider in their decision-making framework. Infrastructures are systems that facilitate logistics and distribution. It is essential that countries selected for entry by international companies have some sort of infrastructure in place. These systems facilitate the supply of goods from the raw-material stage to the production centers, and then on to the markets where they are sold.

Technology is another environmental variable that has been the driving force behind the growth of many economies. Use of technology helps international companies improve productivity, reduce cost, and remain competitive. For those firms that are in a high-tech industry, the level of a country's technological capability may be a critical factor in considering that country for market entry.

International companies use quality of life and cost of living indexes in selecting countries for entry. Cities with higher quality of life and lower cost of living are attractive, as they may be used to induce qualified personnel to relocate.

KEY CONCEPTS

Economic Factors
Types of Economies
Economic Stages
Country Risk Analysis
Underground Economy
Competitive Environment

DISCUSSION QUESTIONS

1. Why is the economy of a country a critical environmental variable?
2. How is the level of economic activity in a country measured?
3. What is current account balance?
4. How are the countries of the world classified in terms of their economic development?
5. What is purchasing power parity?
6. What are the three types of economic systems?
7. Differentiate between market economies and centrally planned economies.
8. What is scenario analysis? How do international companies make use of scenario analysis?
9. What is country risk analysis and how is it conducted?
10. Identify the critical variables considered by *Euromoney* in its country rankings.
11. What is an underground economy?
12. How important is the competitive environment?
13. How do international companies conduct competitive analysis?
14. Why is the infrastructure of a country important for international companies?
15. Why is the level of technology in a country important for international companies?
16. What are some of the factors used in ranking quality of life indexes?

APPLICATION CASE: CHINA'S ECONOMY AND FOREIGN DIRECT INVESTMENT FLOWS

The People's Republic of China (China) is one of the fastest-growing economies in the world. Since the late 1990s it has consistently attained double-digit economic growth rates. Between 1997 and 2007, China's average economic growth was more than 10 percent. For the period 1980 to 2006, China's GDP per capita rose from $300 to $2,000. This economic growth is fueled by considerable inflows of foreign direct investments (FDI flows), which have poured millions of dollars into the manufacturing sector, making China the manufacturing center of the world.

Over a five-year period, net FDI flows into China doubled from $38.4 billion in 2000 to $79.1 billion in 2005. In just the past 10 years, China has been the beneficiary of FDI flows of more than $200 billion. Inward FDI flows account for nearly 10 percent of the gross fixed capital formation of China compared to 4 percent for the United States. China receives FDI flows from many countries, including Hong Kong, Japan, South Korea, and the United States.

In addition to the FDI flows, China has also benefited from an increase in its exports, which has resulted in a current account balance of nearly $180 billion. These surpluses have helped China accumulate foreign reserves in excess of $1.2 trillion. China is the second-largest holder of U.S. long-term debt securities, at $677 billion, surpassed only by Japan, which holds about $827 billion. China, with a GDP of more than $10 trillion (PPP), ranks second only to the United States in terms of size of the economy. The two key economic policies that have stimulated the Chinese economy are trade liberalization and the opening of the country for foreign trade and investments. China's trade policy changed from import-substitution and self-reliance before economic reforms to export promotion and openness.

China has become an attractive market for international and global companies, first as a low-cost manufacturing center, and second as a vast consumer market. With a population of more than 1.3 billion, China alone can be a major market for foreign companies. Currently there are more than 14 million U.S. businesses operating in China; among them Boeing, Ford, GE, GM, Motorola, and TRW have large operations in China.

China is expected to become one of the largest markets for many products, including automobiles, commercial aircraft, and computers. By late 2009 the Chinese automobile market is expected to reach 7 million cars per year, the second-largest market after the United States. Similarly, China will have the second-largest airline industry in the world and will need about 1,790 commercial aircraft, worth more than $83 billion over the next 10 years. Moreover, China will be the second-largest market for personal computers after the United States, and it already has the largest mobile network in the world, with over 432 million cellular phone users.

QUESTIONS

1. What has led to China's phenomenal economic growth?
2. How do you think China's expected economic dominance will affect the Asian region?

4 The Political and Legal Environment

International business decisions are affected by developments in the political and legal environment. Political instability that results in sudden changes in the government and its policies are risks that international businesses face on a regular basis.

LEARNING OBJECTIVES

- To identify and understand different political systems
- To understand the working relationships between governments and international companies
- To understand political risks
- To understand the factors affecting a host government's political system
- To learn how to analyze political risks
- To understand the world's major legal systems
- To understand the various aspects of business affected by the legal system

THE POLITICAL ENVIRONMENT

A country's political and legal environments are interrelated. The political system integrates society into a viable, functioning unit, and the legal environment helps the society maintain its peace and order. Governments that are designed to rule a country are set up through a political system. Governments create laws and regulations that affect every aspect of life in a country, including how businesses are operated. Stable political systems generally have stable governments that enact laws to benefit the population and at the same time encourage a receptive environment for businesses. For many years, the political landscape of Africa has been strewn with governments that have been dictatorial and have ruled with an iron hand. As these rulers suppressed democratic movements, their relationships with the rest of the world seemed to have been frayed. Recent studies conducted on African nations seem to indicate that the Northern African groups of countries that have followed more open political systems have fared better in their relationships with Europe and North America than the rest of Africa.[1] International businesses face increased political risk when there is uncertainty about the stability of the host country's political system. For example, if President Hugo Chávez of Venezuela goes ahead with his threat to nationalize the country's telecommunication and electric utilities, Verizon Communications of the United States could lose up to several hundred million dollars.[2] Political risk is not a new threat facing international companies; it has existed for centuries—for as long as there has been business activity across national borders. Due to advanced telecommunication technologies, many of the decisions and actions by various governments in many parts of the world are instantly flashed by the media for everyone to know. In a knowledge-based environment, information seems to help improve the democratic control of policy makers.[3]

Political risk has taken on a new meaning and significance because of the proliferation of international business activities over past 30 years and also due to the changes in governments of many countries of the world. Since 1950 many countries in Africa, Asia, Eastern Europe, and Latin America have gained independence from their former colonizers and taken steps to rule themselves. In the process many of these countries have had unsettled governments that were either autocratic or weak, resulting in unpredictable shifts in laws and business regulations. Many multinational companies anticipate changes in government and make their decision to invest accordingly. That is, if an international company expects a left-wing government to take over in a country, then they will decide against investing in that country, but if they expect a right-wing government to be elected then they will definitely decide to invest in that country.[4] In the past, political risk analysis was more of an art than a science and was designated to staff analysts with very little input from upper management. In an environment such as this, political risk assessment was hit or miss, resulting in some costly investments. For example, during the Vietnam War, a U.S. oil company that in 1968 was contemplating an aggressive program of oil exploration in South Vietnamese waters based its rosy forecasts on the expectations of a win by the South Vietnamese government with the help of U.S.-led forces. The international managers were expecting to reap great rewards from these exploration efforts. But the company's analysts working in the United States predicted a downfall of the South Vietnamese government within a few years and recommended abandoning the project. In spite of these warnings, senior management went ahead with the project based on the line manager's recommendations. Needless to say, the oil company had to abandon the project in the early 1970s, costing the company millions of dollars.[5] Without a focused environmental scanning, many international companies have been caught off guard by large-scale environmental shifts.[6] For the oil company, not having a systematic political risk analysis with considerable support from top management was the reason that it failed in recognizing the seriousness of the political situation in South Vietnam.

Most senior executives of international companies recognize the importance of conducting political risk analyses. They also understand that it is easy to distinguish between very stable political countries and very unstable political countries. The difficulty is in recognizing the gray area between the two extremes. Therefore, conducting an integrated and scientific political risk analysis is critical to the success of international companies. Effective strategic planning requires that international companies conduct a thorough environmental assessment, especially a political risk assessment, or PRA.[7,8]

POLITICAL SYSTEMS

Political systems are institutions that set standards, rules, and policies to govern a society. These institutions include political parties, political organizations, interest groups, and members of the leading industry groups. There are many types of political systems, including autocracy, democracy, monarchy, one-party states, plutocracy, socialism, and theocracy. The three basic and most common political systems are:

- Democracy
- One-party states
- Theocracy

Democracy

Democracy is a political system in which elections by a country's citizens form the basis for the formation of a government. A truly democratic system must have free and fair elections. Over the years, multiparty democracies have proved to be the most stable, and the experiences of international companies in such a system have been risk free. When elections are not controlled or manipulated by any single party or entity (notably the existing government) and are free of outside influences, the result is a free and fair election. In some countries of Africa, Asia, and Latin America, the ruling party controls the election process, leading to fraudulent results.

There are two types of democracies—direct and republic. In direct democracy, the government is formed by elected officials voted on by the citizens, and most laws are directly enacted by the citizens. The earliest form of direct democracy was practiced by the Greeks in Athens in the fifth century B.C.E. In modern times, direct democracy exists to some extent in Switzerland, where citizens vote on issues that affect their communities and districts. In a republic form of government, citizens elect representatives, who, in turn, vote on laws. The leader of the government most responsible for running the republic is called president (as in the Philippines and the United States), prime minister (as in India and the United Kingdom), or chancellor (as in Germany). The Roman Empire was the earliest known republic.

One-Party States

In the one-party system, only one political party is allowed to form the government. Countries such as Cuba, China, and North Korea that have communist rules are prime examples of countries with one-party states. Communism implies a classless society and a means of equalizing living conditions for all. Therefore, in communist countries, wealth is distributed equally and no single individual owns any property. In these societies, collectivism is practiced. There are no elected officials in one-party systems; rather, a group of party leaders rule the country. Under such a system, the will and preferences of the population are secondary to the overall well being of the country, as determined by the leaders of the party in power.

Theocracy

Theocracy is a form of government in which a particular religion plays a critical role in the formation of the government and influences the enactment of laws and regulations. In some instances, religious leaders may hold key government posts. The government in Iran is an example of a theocratic system. Once again, in this system, the will of the people may not be the basis for the laws of the country; instead, laws are based on religious edicts. For example, in Iran, serving alcohol in restaurants is not permitted, as it is against the country's religious codes.

For an international company to succeed in a foreign country, its management must first determine if its corporate philosophy and practices fit with the host country's political and legal environments. The political process faced by international companies, though not unique compared to that faced by domestic firms, is more complex and problematic.[9] The political process in a domestic market is at least a known entity, and companies have experience with the political system. Furthermore, they might even have some influence in the home country's political process. In addition, they can anticipate changes and plan accordingly. In the international arena, the political process is an unknown quantity for international companies, and they have very little influence in the host country's political process. Internationally, political problems range from catastrophic events such as revolution to a broad range of destabilizing issues, including endemic corruption, labor unrest, crooked elections, religious violence, and incompetent economic management.[10]

MODELS TO ANALYZE INTERNATIONAL COMPANIES' RELATIONSHIPS WITH HOST GOVERNMENTS

Three models have been suggested to analyze the relationship between international companies and the host country's government.[11] All three models make the assumption that the relationship and interactions between the international company and the host government are conflictual-adversarial, especially in the case of developing countries. This assumption may not always be true. When an adversarial relationship exists, the models suggest that the relationship could be labeled as:

- *Sovereignty at bay.* Most countries consider themselves to be sovereign states that are free from external control. The host country views the international company as a threat. First proposed by Jack Behrman,[12] the sovereignty at bay model posits that the multinationals enterprise (MNE) is in a more powerful position than the national government in their relationship to each other. This leads to conflicts, as the host country views the MNE as a threat. When the host country is less developed, the MNE, with its financial strength, seems to have control over most negotiations, especially if the MNE's operations are in a vital industry such as mining, transportation, food, or the like.

- *Neomercantilism.* The host country sees benefits in its relationship with the international company. Therefore, the relations between the MNE and the host government are more cordial. This leads to favorable treatment of the foreign company and both parties benefit from such a relationship.
- *Dependency.* In the dependency relationship, there is more cooperation between the international company and its host government. The extent of the relationship may vary depending on the economic level of development of the host country. If the host country is a fully industrialized country, the relationship between the country and the MNE might be that of two equals. However, if the host country is a developing or less developed country, the government in this case might be more dependent on the MNE, and the balance of power may shift in favor of the MNE.

Though all the three models have some merit, international companies must use their judgment in assessing the kind of relationship they can develop with the host country's government and not be constrained by theories or labels.

FACTORS IN POLITICAL ENVIRONMENTS

Political risks faced by international companies are due to sudden changes in the existing political conditions that affect government policies and rules toward foreign and domestic companies. International business executives agree that a stable government that is hospitable to foreign companies attracts foreign direct investment (FDI) and encourages international businesses to establish operations in that country. FDI is the acquisition abroad of physical assets, such as plant and equipment, with operating control residing with the parent company. Research has shown that a country's political system influences an international company's decision to invest in a foreign country. Studies have identified that a democratic form of government is important for FDI flows in the service sector.[13] While FDI is beneficial to the investing company, it also provides valuable foreign currency reserves to the host country. These investments, therefore, help the host country to improve its own economic conditions. More on FDI and its workings is discussed in the international finance chapter of this text (Chapter 5).

The purpose of a sound political system is to integrate various parts of a society into a single functioning unit.[14] A country's political policies are established through a continuous interaction of people, philosophies, and institutions. The aggregated viewpoints of politicians, businesspeople, interest groups, and the general masses form the core principles of a country's political system.[15] The needs and proposals of this wide group of interested parties are then considered by the government and proposed as policy alternatives. Policy initiatives may be further influenced by lobbying groups, who have their own vested interests. In many countries the U.S. Chamber of Commerce acts on the behalf of American international companies on policy initiatives that may be detrimental to them. These policy initiatives then become a country's laws, which are implemented by the government's bureaucrats.

Many factors influence a country's political environment, including ideology, nationalism, unstable governments, traditional hostilities, public-sector enterprises (the proportion of businesses that are government owned), terrorism, corruption, and international companies.

Political Ideology

Political ideology is a set of ideas, theories, and goals that constitute a sociopolitical program. Ideology is the thought process that guides individuals in the formation of institutions or social movements. Since no single ideology is acceptable to all the people in a given country, diverse political views coexist side-by-side, forming a pluralistic society. In India, for example, more than 36 ideological views coexist, forming the greatest number of political parties in a democratic country. The major ideological systems that form governments to manage a country's economic policies include:

- Capitalism
- Socialism
- Conservativism and liberalism
- Communism
- Authoritarianism

Capitalism is an economic system in which the means of production and distribution of goods and services are for the most part privately owned; the businesses in a capitalistic system operate for profit, and market forces determine demand and supply. In capitalism, or the free-enterprise system, the government's role is limited. Capitalism is practiced in most Western European countries, Japan, and the United States.

Capitalism goes hand in hand with democratic forms of government. Democracy implies rule of the people, by the people, for the people. In a democratic system, people make the decisions. Democracy affords its people unique rights that are the envy of people living under other forms of government. Democracy guarantees people the following basic rights:

- Freedom—freedom of expression, freedom of opinion, freedom of association, freedom of the press, and freedom to organize. These freedoms allow the citizens to participate in the government and express their views without the fear of repercussions. Freedom of the press ensures the dissemination of views, opinions, and other relevant information whether it is favorable to or critical of the ruling party.
- Elections—democratic governments are elected by the people. Elections are held periodically to ensure representation by the people's choices and a smooth transition of the government.
- Limits on terms—a major benefit of democracies, the term limit placed on elected officials guarantees that they do not become complacent and that they continue to work for the people. For example, the president of the United States is allowed to serve only two four-year terms.
- Independent judiciary—The independence of the judicial systems guarantees the

people a place for bringing up disputes, an assurance of fair trials, and protection of individual rights.

Socialism is the opposite of capitalism. Under this system, the government owns or controls the production and distribution of goods and services. The goal of the state-run enterprises in a socialist system is not profits but rather the availability of basic commodities for all of its citizens at reasonable prices.

Conservativism and liberalism are not political systems; they represent people's views of the role of the government. Conservatives feel that the government's role should be minimal and encourage private ownership. Liberals feel that there is a role for the government in the free-enterprise system that includes social spending by the government to benefit its people.

Communism proposes a classless society. In communist countries, the government owns and controls production and distribution of all goods and services. Communism promotes the seizure of power by suppression of internal opposition. It is a single-party rule, with communists being in power. Examples of countries with communism as the core political ideology are China, Cuba, and Russia.

Authoritarianism describes a government in which authority is centered in one person within a small group, and that person is not accountable to the nation's people. In most instances of authoritarianism, a single person rules the country, as in the case of dictatorships, and tries to control the people through intimidation. Zaire under the rule of President Mobutu Sese Seko is a good example of an authoritarian regime. During his rule as president for life, Mobutu controlled all aspects of civilian life and plundered the nation of all its resources. In some instances, a junta made up of three or four military leaders may rule the country and try to control the people, as in the case of Myanmar.

Nationalism

Nationalism is the attachment and dedication of people to their own country. Some experts suggest that in earlier times, when people of a country shared the same race, language, and religion, it made sense to be nationalistic. In the twenty-first century, however, many countries are based on borders that were politically drawn, and the homogeneity that was there before does not exist anymore; hence, the true spirit of nationalism no longer exists. For example, immigration has made the United States into a country of diverse nationalities, languages, and religions.

Unstable Governments

A government is considered stable if it is able to maintain power and sustain uniform rules and regulations; that is, its political, fiscal, and monetary policies are predictable. In an unstable government, political, fiscal, and monetary policies change suddenly and drastically. As mentioned earlier, a stable government encourages foreign direct investments.

Control of power by the government does not imply that it holds on to the power by force, but by democratic means. In fact, when a group of people maintain power by force, that government is not very attractive for foreign investors.

Traditional Hostilities

Traditional hostilities are those that constitute a deeply rooted hatred between people of the warring countries, and the conflict is long-standing. Affinity or animosity between nations reflects how closely aligned or estranged they are based on historical, religious, cultural, and political realities.[16] These affinities or animosities affect international companies. Businesses from friendlier countries are welcomed by the host countries, and those viewed as unfriendly are not so welcome. For example, most French international firms are welcome in many of the western African countries, as these countries were former colonies of France, and they therefore have a friendly relationship with each other. Conflicts in central Europe and the Middle East are historic in nature—they are deeply rooted and will not end soon—and the resulting instability has discouraged foreign investments. The lack of FDI flows might have deprived these countries of potential economic growth.

Public Sector Enterprises

When a government gets involved in the business sector, its objective is to provide goods and services at a reasonable price to its citizens. In most instances, though, the entry of governments into the business sector results in poor-quality products, fewer choices, and inefficient utilization of resources. International companies find it difficult to operate in countries where the large businesses are in the hands of the government. Government-owned companies have distinct competitive advantages over foreign-based companies: they are not driven by profits and consequently can control prices to the detriment of international companies. Moreover, the governments that already own businesses may be tempted to expropriate foreign-owned companies if they view them as threats.

Terrorism

Part of the problem of unstable political environments is terrorism. Terrorism consists of unlawful acts of violence committed by individuals or groups against people and their institutions. Terrorism violates the basic principles of human rights, and unfortunately it has become a worldwide phenomenon. To spread their cause, terrorists groups have kidnapped people for ransom, murdered kidnapped individuals, hijacked planes, and bombed buildings. In the past 30 years, 80 percent of terrorist attacks against the United States have been aimed at American businesses.[17] Therefore, American international companies are very sensitive to the issue of terrorism and spend considerable sums of money to protect their operations from terrorist attacks. Terrorism creates political instability, and international companies are reluctant to invest in countries and regions that are hotbeds of terrorism, such as Latin America and the Middle East.

Corruption

Corruption is defined by the United Nations as the commission or omission of an act in the performance of or in connection with one's duties, in response to gifts, promises or incentives demanded or accepted, or the wrongful receipt of these once the act has been committed or omitted. In simple terms, corruption implies some form of illicit and criminal behavior for personal enrichment.

Corruption is part of the political process, as it is tied to the lack of political will to root it out. Corruption is a means for shady politicians to enrich themselves and perpetuate their rule. For international companies, corruption increases the cost of operations and creates an uneven playing field—that is, those companies that bribe officials are granted favors, while those that follow the rules are at a competitive disadvantage. Chapter 1 contains a more detailed discussion on corruption.

International Companies

International companies also play a role in influencing political systems with their financial strength (some companies such as ExxonMobil and Wal-Mart have revenues greater than the GNP of many of the countries in which they operate). International companies are sometimes drawn into local politics because of the friendly or adversarial relationship that may exist between the company's home country and the host country in which they operate. For example, the Cold War defined much of what U.S. international companies could do in some overseas markets. The U.S. government basically influenced the actions of U.S. corporations, including which countries they could invest in and which goods and services they could sell abroad. If the U.S. government's policy changed toward a traditionally hostile nation, then that country became an immediate opportunity for American companies, as in the case of China.[18] On the other hand, the United States views Cuba as an unfriendly country, so American companies are prohibited from operating there. At other times, international companies may be drawn into host countries' politics through pressures from the international community at large. For example, some multinational companies left South Africa and its apartheid policies in the 1970s as a result of the diplomatic stance taken by European countries. U.S. international companies are not always passive victims of political forces; at times they are the force.[19] Through their links to the U.S. government and strong financial and economic might, some U.S. firms become indirect yet active participants in local politics and influence the actions of the local governments.

COUNTRY RISK ASSESSMENT

One of the critical decisions that an international company has to make is the choice of which country to enter. As discussed in Chapter 3, in selecting a country for entry, international companies assess the country's risk by analyzing various factors, including political dynamics. Political risk is one of the major factors that most companies consider in evaluating country risk.[20] Political risk is defined as the fear of losses incurred by international companies through sudden and unexpected changes in the host country's political environment. These losses can vary in nature from financial to human to corporate image to intellectual property rights to expropriation. Because of the vulnerability to political risks, many international companies have started conducting nonmarket-related scientific research, including studies that shed light on political risks and issues.[21]

In most country risk analyses, the factors that carry the most weight are economic and political variables. Political risk is one of the key factors that all international companies consider in assessing countries.[22] Political instability is caused by the sudden changes that occur in a given environment. These changes might be in the form of revolutions, social unrest, labor strikes, wars, or terrorism. Such conditions pose problems for international companies. Political unrest often results in economic upheaval and may pose a risk to humans, especially expatriates. Some international companies conduct their own political risk analysis by actually visiting the country they are interested in and exploring its political environment firsthand. A few others rely on the opinions of trusted and knowledgeable people, including academic scholars, consultants, journalists, and diplomats. These approaches generally take time; consequently, many international companies use their own internally developed models to assess political risk or employ outside research suppliers to conduct these assessments. For example, Embraer of Brazil was able to set up a joint venture partnership with a Chinese aerospace company after conducting a thorough political and business analysis, even though the Chinese authorities wanted to build their own aerospace industry.[23]

Many research studies have reviewed the practices of international companies in assessing political risk as they conduct country risk analysis. It is generally agreed that the political environment has become more complex in recent years. The unification of Europe, the breakup of the Soviet Union, the emergence of China as a superpower, the continuing conflicts in the Middle East, and the collapse of governments in Africa have changed the economic landscape and heightened the political risk for international companies.[24] In a study of American-based international companies, researchers observed that these companies conduct mostly an organizational-based analysis of political risk.

Many of the political risk analyses conducted by external agencies use a combination of factors in assessing a country's political risk. The PRS Group, an East Syracuse, New York-based research company, ranks countries on political risk using two methodologies: Political Risk Services and International Country Risk Guide (ICRG). ICRG uses 12 factors, including government stability, socioeconomic conditions, internal conflicts, external conflicts, and corruption (see Table 4.1 for all 12 factors used by ICRG and the corresponding weights for each factor). The scores are based on a rating scale that uses various internal and external sources to assess the risk for each factor. The list of factors used by ICRG provides a glimpse into the underlying causes that may lead to a destabilized political environment. The PRS Group also publishes the *Political Risk Yearbook,* which is available online and contains detailed information on the political, economic, and general business environment in most countries of the world.

Table 4.1

ICRG Factors and Corresponding Weights

	Factor	Explanation of Factors	Weight (%)
1	Government stability	Consistency of policy and continuity	12
2	Socioeconomic conditions	Unemployment, consumer confidence, poverty	12
3	Investment profile	Profit repatriation, payment delays, expropriation	12
4	Internal conflict	Civil war, terrorism, coup threats	12
5	External conflict	Cross-border conflicts, wars, foreign pressures	12
6	Corruption	Bribery, fairness in awarding contracts	6
7	Military politics	Military's influence in politics and the government	6
8	Religious tensions	Single dominant religion that exerts influence in framing government policies	6
9	Law and order	Crime rate, independence of the judicial system	6
10	Ethnic tensions	Periodic ethnic conflicts, acts of genocide	6
11	Government accountability	Responsiveness of government to people's concerns	6
12	Bureaucracy	Qualifications and abilities of government officials	4
	Total		100

Source: Political Risk Services, *International Country Risk Guide.* Available at http://www.prsgroup. com/ (accessed June 2008). International Country Risk Guide, http://www.countryrisk.com/reviews/ar-chives/000029.html, June 2008.

The scores obtained for each country provide the level of political risk associated with that country. The higher the score, the less risky that country's political environment. The ICRG scores are grouped into five categories, as follows:

Score	Risk
00.00–49.90	Very high risk
50.00–59.90	High risk
60.00–69.90	Moderate risk
70.00–79.90	Low risk
80.00–100.0	Very low risk

Using these ratings, ICRG lists the level of political risk faced by international companies in many parts of the world. Table 4.2 lists the 10 least politically risky countries of the world.

Strategic Actions

International companies must develop specific strategic action plans to overcome political instability before they enter a foreign country. These plans can help the companies to be better prepared for anticipated or unanticipated political shifts. To protect themselves from adverse political events by reducing some of the risk factors, international companies rely on forecasting models to predict the risk-reward matrices. In addition, many companies operating in overseas markets might also insure themselves as a protection against political upheavals in the country in which they are

Table 4.2

Ten Least Politically Risky Countries

Country	Factor 1	Factor 2	Factor 3	Factor 4	Factor 5	Factor 6	Factor 7	Factor 8	Factor 9	Factor 10	Factor 11	Factor 12	Total
Luxembourg	11.0	11.0	12.0	12.0	11.5	5.0	6.0	6.0	6.0	5.0	5.0	4.0	94.5
Finland	9.5	9.5	12.0	11.0	11.5	6.0	6.0	6.0	6.0	6.0	6.0	4.0	93.5
Ireland	10.5	11.0	12.0	11.5	11.0	3.5	6.0	5.0	6.0	5.5	6.0	4.0	92.0
Sweden	8.5	10.0	12.0	11.0	11.5	5.5	5.5	6.0	6.0	5.0	6.0	4.0	91.0
Netherlands	8.5	10.5	12.0	11.0	12.0	5.0	6.0	5.0	6.0	4.5	6.0	4.0	90.5
New Zealand	9.0	10.0	11.5	11.5	<11.0	5.5	6.0	6.0	6.0	4.0	6.0	4.0	90.5
Austria	9.0	10.0	12.0	11.5	11.5	5.0	6.0	6.0	6.0	4.0	5.0	4.0	90.0
Canada	9.5	8.5	12.0	12.0	11.0	5.0	6.0	6.0	6.0	3.5	6.0	4.0	89.5
Norway	7.5	10.0	11.5	11.5	11.5	5.0	6.0	5.0	6.0	4.5	6.0	4.0	88.5
Switzerland	<8.5	10.5	11.5	12.0	11.5	4.5	6.0	5.0	<5.0	4.0	6.0	4.0	88.5

Source: Political Risk Services, *International Country Risk Guide*. Available at http://www.prsgroup.com/ (accessed June 2008). International Country Risk Guide, http://www.countryrisk.com/reviews/archives/000029.html, June 2008.

operating. For example, global financial companies that face political risks such as nationalization of the banking industry have developed sophisticated computer models that test insurance policies against worst-case political scenarios.[25] Similarly, a few international companies have developed models that assesses the effects of political risk on direct investment projects by considering all the elements that generate losses and relating them to the risk's evolution process.[26] As more and more international companies enter the transitional economies of Central and Eastern Europe—economies that can experience significant political turbulence—they have adopted some unique strategies to overcome the uncertainties. A few of these international companies have developed a diverse network that includes the host government, local businesses, and public partners to help them navigate through the political minefield.[27] Of course, this opportunity for networking might not always be available, which means international companies must devise other approaches to combat political uncertainties. Before the advent of computer-generated models, many international companies dealt with political risk by investing in a wide group of countries, thereby spreading out the risk that they would encounter through political instability; this strategy is known as the portfolio approach[28] and to some extent is still very useful.

Generally, international companies are well prepared to deal with most political uncertainties, and if the risks are very high, they pass up the opportunity to invest in such countries. The key concern for international business executives is the loss of their assets. Research has shown that after the initial difficulties and insecurity, international businesses find that political risk might actually decrease once they are able to understand the intricacies of the system.[29] One of the reasons for such a shift might be the familiarity of the situation and the subsequent confidence international business managers develop in dealing with the existing uncertainty. The keys to developing political strategies are understanding how political decisions are made, how the government operates, what some key current political agendas of the ruling government are, and the general political climate. If the governments are democratically elected, it is much easier to formulate strategies for avoiding political risks because drastic shifts in the political environment can be predicted. In contrast, the more authoritarian the government, the more difficult it is to predict the political shifts. One approach to deal with political risk is to understand the key issues and follow the steps outlined below.[30]

- Identify the specific political actions facing the company.
- Analyze the issues upon which these political actions are based.
- Determine which interest groups are behind the political actions.
- Identify the parties affected by the political actions (other international companies).
- Identify the key players that may have a role in the political actions (legislators, government agencies, and so on).
- Formulate strategies based on company goals, resources, core competencies, and management know-how.
- Identify the potential outcome of implementing the outlined strategies in the host country and home country (determine, for example, whether the strategies or its effect are unpopular).
- Select the most suitable strategy from a list of options.

Although the aforementioned steps seem simple, in practice they can be challenging. Often it can be difficult to identify the key players and interest groups in the system, specific political actions might not be clear, the effects of some political actions are not apparent, and the possible strategic options might be limited.

THE LEGAL ENVIRONMENT

The following quotes from Newton Minow, the former chairman of the U.S. Federal Communications Commission, seem appropriate in understanding the international legal landscape.[31]

> "In Germany, under the law, everything is prohibited, except that which is permitted."

> "In France, under the law, everything is permitted, except that which is prohibited."

> "In the Soviet Union, under the law, everything is prohibited, including that which is permitted."

> "In Italy, under the law, everything is permitted, especially that which is prohibited."

Like other environmental variables, legal systems vary from country to country. The two key differences observed in the legal systems around the world are *the nature of the system* and *the degree of independence of the judiciary*. Most of the world's legal systems are derived from three major legal structures. These are

- *Civil law.* Legal codes are the basis of civil law. Rules are developed for every aspect of life, including how to conduct business. Most countries of the world, including Germany and Japan, follow the civil law system.
- *Common law.* The common law system is based on traditions, precedent, customs, usage, and interpretation. Common law is practiced in about 30 countries of the world, especially former British colonies. The United States follows the common law system.
- *Theocratic law.* Theocratic law is based on religious doctrines and teachings. Most Islamic countries follow the theocratic legal system.

The key differences in the three legal systems center on how the legal system is developed and how the courts decide on issues. Civil law is based on *how the law is applied to the given facts and on the application of preset codes.* Common law is based on *the courts' interpretation of events;* and theocratic law is based on *what is acceptable within the religious precepts.*

Besides these three legal systems, many other tribal legal systems are practiced in Africa, some parts of Asia, and Latin America. Such systems are based on traditions and cultural influences. Until recently, these legal systems were not studied and analyzed because very few international companies ever ventured into the more remote parts of the world where they prevail. An increase in exploration and heightened interest in the search for natural ingredients and minerals has forced some international companies to deal with tribal legal systems that have no written records.

For international companies that operate in more than one foreign country, variations in laws from country to country pose problems. Additionally, there is no single body of codes or laws that applies across country borders. Hence, disputes between international companies and host governments are harder to resolve than domestic disputes. To facilitate resolution of disputes between international companies and host governments, a few international agreements have been reached, resulting in the establishment of institutions that can be used for mediation. These institutions include the World Trade Organization (WTO), the International Court of Justice (ICJ), and the International Labor Organization (ILO).

The WTO was set up to negotiate trading agreements and resolve trade disputes between countries. The ICJ, also called the World Court, renders legal decisions involving disputes between countries and helps resolve broader issues that may affect international companies. The ILO is a multilateral organization that promotes the adoption of humane labor conditions.

At the macro level, a country's legal system affects international companies in many different ways, including how they conduct business in the host country, how they deal with cross-border legal issues, and how they deal with international treaties (tax treaties between countries, trade agreements, intellectual property rights agreements, and the like). At the micro level, a country's legal system affects many aspects of business, including

- Ownership
- Mode of entry
- Taxation
- Labor laws
- Currency controls
- Expatriates issues
- Price controls
- Antitrust laws
- Product liability
- Repatriation of profits
- Tariffs and other nontariff barriers

Every country has its own set of laws governing the aforementioned aspects of business. International companies must review these laws carefully to ensure compliance.

OWNERSHIP

Ownership laws are those that govern the extent to which foreigners can own businesses and the types of businesses that they can own. These laws are meant to ensure that sensitive industries—industries that may have national security implications, such as media, food distribution, and defense—are not owned by foreigners, as they could become a national safety issue.

Individual countries' ownership laws are intended to help the growth of domestic businesses, increase competitiveness, and encourage transfer of technology and management skills. Typically, international companies have superior products, efficient production technology, and sound management and marketing skills that often overpower those of domestic companies. The protection afforded by their governments through ownership rules provides the local companies with some relief and gives them an opportunity to compete.

In many industrialized countries, foreign companies are allowed to have 100 percent ownership (these are referred to as wholly owned or fully owned subsidiaries). In most cases, international companies prefer 100 percent ownership of their subsidiaries, as it gives them complete control of their operations. It also allows them to apply their own management and marketing skills, and protect their technology and intellectual property rights (IPR) without interference. But in many countries of the world, foreign ownership is restricted to joint ventures only. Even in joint ventures, foreign companies are restricted to minority ownership. For example, in China, joint ventures are restricted and in some cases entirely prohibited in such industries as banking, insurance, and distribution. Similarly, in India, foreign ownership in the telecommunications industry is limited to 49 percent, and in Brazil, foreign ownership is limited to 20 percent in aviation and mass media.

MODE OF ENTRY

Laws governing mode of entry deal with how foreign-owned companies can enter a given country. These laws specify whether a foreign company can enter through exports, licensing agreements, franchise operations, strategic alliances, joint ventures, or Greenfield investments. For example, in China, the government permits foreign-owned service companies to enter Chinese markets only through joint ventures (Chapter 6 discusses the various entry modes and the advantages and disadvantages of each).

TAXATION

Most countries levy some form of tax on their citizens as well as businesses in the form of personal tax, business tax, value-added tax, or some other tax. Through taxation, governments collect revenues from their people and businesses. Revenues are used for providing services that benefit its citizens, such as police protection, social programs, national defense, and infrastructure. In addition, tax revenues are used by governments to redistribute income, discourage consumption of some products (such as alcohol and tobacco), and encourage consumption of domestic products (through tariffs). Tax laws vary from country to country and govern various issues including tax levels, tax type, tax treaties, and tax incentives.

Tax levels determine the amount owed by individuals (as income tax) and busi-

Table 4.3

Tax Rates for Select Countries

Country	Income tax rate (%)	Corporate tax rate (%)	Tax treaty with other countries
Belgium	25–50	33.99	Yes
Brazil	15–27.5	34	Yes
Canada	15–29	36.1	Yes
China	5–45	33	Yes
Egypt	20–40	40	Yes
France	48.09	34.33	Yes
Germany	15–42	25	Yes
India	10–30	30–40	Yes
Italy	23–43	33	Yes
Japan	10–37	30	Yes
Mexico	3–29	29	Yes
Netherlands	0–52	29.6	Yes
Spain	15–45	35	Yes
Taiwan	6–40	25	Yes
United Kingdom	0–40	30	Yes
United States	0–35	35	Yes

Source: Worldwide-tax.com, The Complete Worldwide Tax & Finance Site, www.worldwide-tax.com, January 2007.

nesses (as corporate profit taxes) to the government. These levels can range from zero tax policy to 70 percent tax policies. Table 4.3 presents tax rates for a selected group of countries.

Tax types are the various categories of taxes a government levies against its citizens and businesses. The most common types of taxes are the following:

- Personal income tax—levied on the income of individuals
- Corporate income tax—levied on corporations on incomes earned
- Capital gains tax—levied on sales of assets when the asset is sold for an amount greater than its cost
- Value-added tax—levied at each step of the production-to-distribution process.

Tax treaties are arrangements between governments that agree (1) to share information about taxpayers, (2) to cooperate in tax law enforcement, and (3) to avoid double taxation (that is, an individual from one country working in another is not subject to income taxes in both countries). Tax treaties define and explain "tax terms" and "taxable activities." Some of the tax terms defined includes *income, source of income,* and *residency.*

Tax incentives are exemptions and allowances offered by governments to encourage foreign direct investment and other forms of participation by international companies. These incentives may include reduced corporate tax rates for a period of time, additional depreciation allowance, and foreign tax credit (credits offered to individuals or companies for taxes paid in another country).

LABOR LAWS

Labor laws are enacted to protect workers' rights. Most countries have laws that deal with working conditions, workplace safety, minimum wages, hiring practices, termination guidelines, health benefits, working hours, sick leaves, vacation leaves, and general working conditions. Most of these laws apply to international companies, too.

The governments of some countries have passed laws mandating minimum wage rates for workers. This ensures that workers are compensated sufficiently to earn a decent living. For example, in the Philippines, by law, the minimum wage rate has been set at 250 pesos per day (equivalent to $5.00 a day or 63 cents an hour) and in the United States as of 2008, minimum wage was $7.50 an hour (in some states such as Washington, the rates are higher, at $8.75 per hour).

CURRENCY CONTROLS

Most developing countries have currency exchange controls that deal with the purchase and sale of foreign currencies. These countries tend to have weak economies, and they impose regulations on foreign exchange transactions to stem the outflow of foreign currencies and help shore up their own currencies. Some of the currencies held as reserves by many of the world's countries are the euro, Japanese yen, Swiss franc, and the U.S. dollar. Developing countries hold foreign currencies as reserves to undertake economic development projects such as infrastructure improvements, including investing in electricity generation and water works. In order to make these advances, foreign governments have to buy industrial goods such as farm equipment (tractors), road-building equipment (earth movers), construction equipment (bulldozers), and transportation equipment (railroads, ships, airplanes). If controls were not imposed on foreign exchange transactions, individuals and companies in these developing countries could easily use up their limited amount of foreign reserves and cause economic disaster.

In countries that impose exchange controls, the government allocates and controls the trading of foreign currencies. Individuals entering and leaving these countries must declare the value of funds that they have in foreign currencies. Anyone wishing to buy foreign currency must have a permit to do so, and, normally, the amounts are limited.

EXPATRIATE ISSUES

Expatriates are foreign workers brought into a country by international companies. These workers include technical staff, specialists, and executives. International companies bring in expatriates for a variety of reasons, including (1) to ensure control over their operations, (2) to establish policies and procedures that are in line with those of the parent company, and (3) to provide training to executives that might be tapped for future senior assignments. For host countries, the presence of expatriates results in lower opportunities for local personnel. In addition, expatriates also inhibit the development of local managers. In some countries, the government restricts the number of expatriates an international company can bring in.

In addition to restrictions on the number of expatriates that can be brought into a country, host governments in some cases might restrict expatriates born in certain countries. For example, European and American international companies are not permitted to bring Israeli expatriates into some Middle Eastern countries.

PRICE CONTROLS

Some countries have laws that govern commodities prices. These countries prohibit upward price spirals, especially on food items. The intent of these laws is to protect the citizens from sudden changes in commodities prices that cause unnecessary strain on the poor. In addition, these laws are intended to control inflation.

ANTITRUST LAWS

Antitrust or restrictive trade practices laws are intended to free up competition and enable the free market system to operate efficiently. Antitrust laws are generally directed at price fixing, the sharing of competitive information, and the formation of monopolies. Most of the industrialized countries of the world have some form of antitrust laws on their books. The recently formed European Union monitors business operations within its member countries, including operations of international companies. The European Union's antitrust laws govern issues such as cartels and price fixing (Article 81 EC) and price discrimination and exclusive dealings (Article 82 EC). In 2002, the European Union's Competition Commission played a critical role in blocking the proposed merger of General Electric and Honeywell, both U.S. firms. The rationale for the commission's action was that the merger would create a virtual monopoly that might hinder overall competition in the field of electricity generation in Europe.

In the United States, the major antirust laws are the Sherman Act, the Clayton Act, and the Robinson-Patman Act. The Sherman Act, passed in 1890, was the first of many U.S. government actions addressing such competitive issues as cartels and antitrust activities. The U.S. government did not actively enforce the Sherman Act, and its effectiveness was questioned by many. The Clayton Act was passed in 1914 to address some of the weaknesses of the Sherman Act. Specifically, the Clayton Act addressed price discrimination and business merger issues. The Robinson-Patman Act, passed in 1936, was a further refinement of the earlier acts; it governed such issues as price discrimination and exclusivity that reduces competition. Under the act, the same goods could not be sold to different purchasers at different prices if the effect of such sales reduced competition or made it difficult for small, independent retail firms to stay in business.

PRODUCT LIABILITY

Product liability laws are intended to hold manufacturers, their executives, and their outside directors responsible for causing injury, harm, death, or any other damage to consumers.

The challenge for international companies is how to deal with the different legal systems that provide various consumer safeguards. In some countries, the scarcity of lawyers and the long delays in the legal process discourage consumers from seeking legal help to collect compensatory or punitive damages from companies whose products may have failed or caused them harm. A good example of a country that has few cases of product liability is Japan: lawyers in Japan are scarce, the Japanese Bar Association sets all legal fees, and foreign lawyers are not allowed to file cases against companies. In contrast, in the United States, consumers use the court systems to extract damages for various reasons, including for injuries and deaths caused by using a particular product. In fact, one U.S. automobile company was hit with 250 product liability suits in just one year.[32]

REPATRIATION OF PROFITS

International companies operate in foreign countries to earn profits. Once they earn these profits, foreign-owned companies normally repatriate their profits to the parent office. The profits generated from various operations are then pooled as a source of funds for investments. In many countries, international companies have the freedom to transfer funds and profits as they wish; in others, however, the host government restricts these outflows through local laws. These laws basically ensure the channeling of profits by the international companies to local investments, as well as the protection of the foreign currency reserves held by the country. International companies' continuous outflow of profits may weaken the local currency and raise concerns of inflation.

TARIFFS AND OTHER NONTARIFF BARRIERS

Tariffs are taxes on imported goods that raise the prices of imported goods and services, thereby discouraging their local consumption. The purpose of tariffs is to restrict the flow of imports that may jeopardize the host country's industries and put pressure on foreign currency reserves. Through the passage of various laws, these countries are able to control the flow of imports. Tariffs aid and protect local producers and reduce competition. Though the intent of the tariff is to develop local industries, in most cases it fails to attain the stated objective. Because local businesses lack some of the basic ingredients for efficient use of resources, they are not able to compete with the larger and more efficient foreign firms. The price and quality of locally produced goods and services never attain international standards, and local consumers suffer. For example, after gaining independence from the British, the Indian government levied high duties on imported cars (as much as 150 percent) and also restricted foreign investments in the automobile sector. The intent was to develop its own automobile industry. But the automobile industry was not able to produce efficient cars at reasonable enough prices for the industry to prosper. Car models that were introduced in the 1950s continued to be manufactured and marketed year after year without change or improvement. Once the government opened the industry to foreign manufacturers, the competitive dynamics were altered. Foreign manufacturers introduced more fuel-efficient and better-performing cars at much lower prices, resulting in a considerable drop in the local producer's market share, from more than 85 percent of the market in the 1950s to only 7 percent of the market in 2000.

CHAPTER SUMMARY

Political and legal environments play a critical role in international business. Some political and legal factors create problems for international companies in managing their operations in the host country.

The purpose of a sound political system is to integrate various parts of a society into a single functioning unit. The aggregated viewpoints of politicians, businesspeople, interest groups, and the general masses form the core principles of a country's political system. Political systems are influenced by ideology, nationalism, unstable governments, traditional hostilities, proportion of government ownership of businesses, terrorism, corruption, and the activities of international companies.

There are five basic ideological systems that form governments to manage a country's economic policies: (1) capitalism, (2) socialism, (3) conservative versus liberal views, (4) communism, and (5) authoritarianism. Democratic forms of government and capitalism go hand in hand.

International companies conduct political risk analyses before entering foreign markets. Political strategic actions assist international companies in better managing their operations.

Like the political environment, a country's legal system plays a critical role in a company's operations. Legal systems vary from country to country, but differences can be categorized as differences in the nature of the legal system and the degree of judicial independence. The three major judicial systems are civil law, based on legal codes and rules; common law, based on precedents; and theocratic law, based on religious precepts.

At the macro level, a country's legal system affects how international businesses operate in the host country, how the system affects cross-border issues, and how laws affect international treaties. At the micro level, the legal system affects specific aspects of business operations, including ownership, taxation, antitrust issues, and trade regulations. The best laid plans by an international company may be sabotaged by political upheaval or legal obstacles, the apparent signs of which the company may have totally missed or misunderstood.

KEY CONCEPTS

Political Systems
Political Ideology
Political Risk Assessment
Legal Systems

DISCUSSION QUESTIONS

1. What is the purpose of a political system?
2. Define a political system.
3. What are the components of a political environment?
4. What are the key influencers of a country's political environment?

5. What is a political ideology?
6. How many different political ideologies exist?
7. What are the basic differences between capitalism and socialism?
8. What specific strategies does an international company develop to handle diverse political systems?
9. What are the two key differences in legal systems among countries?
10. Identify and explain the three major judicial systems.
11. Enumerate the various business activities that come under the legal system.
12. How can international companies prepare to deal with the legal environment when entering a new market?

APPLICATION CASE: ADAPTING FINANCE TO ISLAM

Deutsche Bank entered the Malaysian market in 1967 with one branch. Focusing mainly on affiliates of foreign companies, the bank did well, but it was not a force in the retail business of banking. Competitors such as HSBC (Hong Kong Shanghai Bank Corporation), which had a presence in Malaysia since 1884, and Citigroup were much bigger and had multiple branches. To further extend their reach in the banking sector, HSBC bought out the Mercantile Bank of Malaysia and became one of the largest foreign banks in the country. Meanwhile, by 2006, Deutsche Bank had two offices in Malaysia and employed 130 professionals.

A major problem for most overseas banks, including Deutsche Bank, was understanding banking rules in a predominantly Muslim country that must adhere to the laws of the Koran. Islamic laws prohibit charging interest on loans; for bankers, this means sharing borrowers' risks. Therefore, Islamic banking rules resulted in financial institutions treating their customers as shareholders, sharing a portion of the profits. Hence, when a bank wants to lend funds to one of its customers to buy a house or other property, it enters into a partnership by forming a joint venture to raise the capital to acquire the property. The customer and the bank become the joint owners of the property, and each has its respective shares based on a ratio equivalent to the capital raised. The bank then leases its share to the customer. The customer makes monthly payments over an agreed-upon period of time. Over time, the bank's share diminishes and the customer becomes the 100 percent owner of the property.

Similarly, to avoid the problems created by interest earned on deposits by customers, local banks in Muslim countries enter into an agreement with their customers through which the bank is allowed to invest a customer's deposits for profits. The ensuing profits are then shared between the customer and the bank according to a predetermined profit-sharing ratio. The local Islamic banking institutions, which were controlled by nationals, thrived under this law, but foreign banks had difficulty understanding the law's nuances and adapting to them. However, HSBC—through its merger with Mercantile Bank of Malaysia—and Citigroup—by hiring locals as senior executives—were able to succeed under the Islamic banking laws. Deutsche Bank, with its entrenched European-style banking, had problems adjusting to the local religious laws.

QUESTIONS

1. As Malaysia's country manager for Deutsche Bank, would you train your foreign staff to adapt to the Islamic laws, hire a few Malaysians as senior executives, or remain as an institutional banker? Give reasons for your choice.

SOURCE

This case was developed from information gathered from the Deutsche Bank, Citigroup, and HSBC Web sites, and also from an article on Islamic banking in Malaysia by Arnold Wayne titled "Adapting Finance to Islam," *New York Times,* November 22, 2007, pp. C1, C4.

5 International Trade and Foreign Direct Investments

Since NAFTA went into effect, U.S. trade with NAFTA partners has more than doubled. Today, nearly half of total U.S. exports to the world go to Canada and Mexico. The only "giant sucking sound" we have heard over the last 10 years is the sound of U.S. goods and services headed to Mexico and Canada.[1]

LEARNING OBJECTIVES

- To understand the economic reasons for international trade
- To recognize the impact of international trade on domestic welfare
- To appreciate the role of the World Trade Organization (WTO) in regulating trade
- To understand the economic reasons for foreign direct investment
- To learn the impact of foreign direct investment on domestic welfare
- To offer insights into the future of global trade and investments in the twenty-first century

INTERNATIONAL TRADE

International trade refers to the exchange of goods and services between countries. In prehistoric times, when there were no formal countries or boundaries, international trade was simply a barter of goods between two individuals or groups separated by a "long" distance, which over time spanned continents. Evidence exists of trading routes connecting Egypt, Mesopotamia (the area around modern-day Iraq), and the Indus Valley civilizations (near modern-day Pakistan and western India) as early as 3000 B.C.[2] Trade did not take place only via land routes, however. The Phoenicians (modern-day Lebanese) were sea traders who established trading posts throughout the Mediterranean coasts in 1000 B.C.E.

International trade continued to flourish right through the periods of the Greek and Roman empires, increasing in volume as technological advances progressed in shipbuilding and navigation. Famous personalities in the history of international trade include Venetian Marco Polo, who traveled to China in the thirteenth century, and Vasco de Gama, from modern Portugal, who opened the spice trade when he sailed around Africa to India in 1498. In the 1600s, Holland became a center of trade in several commodities, including financial futures contracts. In 1688 Edward Lloyd

117

opened a coffee house in London where marine insurance was openly traded. Today Lloyd's continues to be a leading market for insurance in the world.

The term "international trade," as understood today, is more applicable to the practice that took place after the formation of nation-states in the eighteenth century, when feudal states coalesced and formed specific boundaries and a formal currency was created to establish clear legal and political boundaries. However, boundaries continued to change as a result of wars or popular uprisings, making it difficult to measure the exact volume of trade between nation-states prior to the twentieth century. Recent examples include Italy, whose boundaries were only defined in 1870, and Ireland, which separated from the United Kingdom in 1922 and became a separate country formally after World War II.

Irrespective of boundaries, when does trade benefit a nation-state or country? From an economic perspective, it is clear that individual traders engage in the export and import of goods and services to enjoy monetary benefits. However, it is not clear whether international trade benefits a country as a whole. Initial works on the topic, written as early as the 1500s, all considered international trade as beneficial only if a country managed to export, rather than import, in exchange for gold or silver. This doctrine, termed mercantilism, was widely popular until the nineteenth century.

MERCANTILISM

The theory of mercantilism evolved gradually as trade increased in importance after the fifteenth century. Exporting allowed a country to obtain gold and silver, the two most widely accepted forms of payment prior to the introduction of paper money. Gold enabled a country to become rich and powerful and increased its ability to finance wars. However, excess gold without a corresponding increase in output can lead to inflation in the economy. If inflation continues, it is difficult for a country to maintain its exports, as prices become less favorable. Under the *price-specie flow mechanism* proposed by the British economist David Hume in the middle of the eighteenth century, such increases in prices ultimately reduce exports, and the balance of trade is restored back to equilibrium. (*Specie* refers to gold and silver.)

Unfortunately, mercantilism continued to be popular and accepted by rulers and thinkers alike until the 1800s. Monarchs and feudal lords encouraged the expansion of exports, mostly to finance wars. It was easy to justify and enact laws—and to intervene militarily—to protect local industry and employment. It was not until the dissemination of works by Adam Smith (1732–1790) and later economists, which showed how countries could be better off when engaged in mutually beneficial two-way trade, that mercantilism philosophy fell from favor. Two-way trade required countries to specialize in products where they possessed distinct advantages in productive efficiency, as explained in the next section.

THEORY OF ABSOLUTE ADVANTAGE

With his book *The Wealth of Nations,* Smith became the first economist to openly oppose the doctrine of mercantilism. He was a proponent of laissez-faire economics and is considered the first free market economist. Instead of focusing only on exports, Smith argued that it was beneficial for countries to specialize in the production of goods in which they enjoyed productive efficiency. Goods can be exported in exchange for other goods produced more efficiently elsewhere. The net result is an overall increase in output for all countries, as shown in the following example.

Assume that Country A and Country B, for a given amount of capital and labor, can produce 100 bushels and 50 bushels of wheat and 200 yards and 300 yards of textiles, respectively.

	Wheat	Textiles	If Resources Are Divided Equally
Country A	100 bushels	200 yards	50 bushels of wheat and 100 yards of textiles
Country B	50 bushels	300 yards	25 bushels of wheat and 150 yards of textiles

If the resources in each country are divided equally between farming and textiles, the combined output is 75 bushels of wheat and 250 yards of textiles.

Adam Smith's theory of absolute advantage requires each country to specialize in goods in which it enjoys a production advantage. In the above example, Country A has an absolute advantage in producing wheat, while Country B has an absolute advantage in producing textiles. If Country A specializes in and devotes all its resources to wheat, the total output is 100 bushels. Similarly, if Country B devotes all its resources to textiles, its output will be 300 yards. Through specialization, total output increases by 25 bushels of wheat and 50 yards of textiles.

This additional output can be shared by both countries through trade. For example, Country A could export 40 bushels of wheat to Country B in exchange for 125 yards of textiles. This leaves Country A with 10 more bushels of wheat and 25 more yards of textiles than it would have if it had produced both the wheat and the textiles on its own. Country B will end up with 15 more bushels of wheat and 25 more yards of textiles than it would have if it had produced both products on its own. This simple example highlights the benefits of specialization under Adam Smith's theory of absolute advantage. The actual gains to each country will depend on the exchange rates and the countries' bargaining power.

THEORY OF COMPARATIVE ADVANTAGE

The theory of absolute advantage requires each country to have an absolute advantage in the production of at least one good. For some countries, the advantages come about because of weather or geography. For example, coconuts and pineapples can grow only in temperate climates, while production of oil and gas requires the natural elements to be located physically in the country. For other countries, the advantages may be realized through efficient production processes, superior managerial skills, or technological superiority.

What happens when one country does not have the capacity to produce goods more efficiently than another? Smith's model will not work, because without specialization and increased output, trade may not take place to benefit both countries. However, David Ricardo (1772–1823) showed that it was still possible for countries to engage in trade, even without possessing an absolute advantage. According to Ricardo, as long as a country possessed a comparative advantage in producing one of the goods to be traded, mutually beneficial trade could still take place. The following example demonstrates how this is achieved.

Assume for given amounts of land, labor, and capital, Country A and Country B can produce the following:

	Wheat	Textiles	If Resources Are Divided Equally
Country A	100 bushels	200 yards	50 bushels of wheat and 100 yards of textiles
Country B	50 bushels	150 yards	25 bushels of wheat and 75 yards of textiles

In the above example, Country B does not have an absolute advantage in producing either wheat or textiles. However, Country B has a *relative* advantage in producing textiles over wheat. To understand this, recognize that Country A has to give up 2 yards of textiles for every 1 bushel of wheat produced (2 : 1 ratio). Country B has to give up 3 yards of textiles for every 1 bushel of wheat (3 : 1 ratio). This difference in ratios means that Country B has a relative advantage in producing textiles over wheat compared to Country A. Ricardo showed that trade can still take place if Country B specializes in producing textiles.

How much should Country A and Country B produce in order to maximize total output? There are several possibilities, but one scenario is for Country A to specialize and produce 80 bushels of wheat. This would use up 80 percent of its resources, and the remaining 20 percent could be used to produce 40 yards of textiles. Country A can keep 50 bushels of wheat for itself and export the remaining 30 bushels to Country B. Country B could specialize in producing 150 yards of textiles and export 75 yards of textiles to Country A. Country A will now have a total of 115 yards of textiles, 15 yards more than if it were to spread its resources equally, without trade. Country B will have a total of 30 bushels of wheat, 5 bushels more than if it were to equally split its resources, without trade.

Ricardo's theory of comparative advantage was instrumental in showing countries that international trade benefits all participants through specialization. It provided a new paradigm to international trade theory by rejecting the principles of mercantilism and offering a new approach that relied on specialization, two-way trade, and mutual benefits. Unfortunately, it required cooperation and coordination between countries that was often difficult to achieve, especially when domestic politics conflicted with the consequences of free trade, specialization, and reliance on other countries for imports of necessities or sensitive goods.

Indeed, it took a long time for specialization and free trade to be associated with increased output and mutual benefits. The mercantilist philosophy continued to shape public policy right up to World War II. Countries were often in dire need of gold and money to finance their wars, and exports provided the quickest means to earn bullion. Nationalist and labor groups often managed to blame free trade for loss of industries and increased unemployment. Industrial and agricultural groups lobbied governments to impose tariffs and laws that discouraged imports of goods, especially those that threatened domestic production. It was not until the end of World War II that the principles of free trade were formally incorporated into global treaties under the auspices of the General Agreement on Trade and Tariffs (GATT; now the World Trade Organization [WTO]).

The free trade theories of Adam Smith and David Ricardo continue to be relevant today. One area of trade they do not delve into is why some countries produce goods more efficiently than others. It is assumed that natural resources and technology play a role in the way countries are able to gain relative advantage in production. Two theories that purport to explain the patterns of trade are discussed in the next section.

HECKSCHER-OHLIN FACTOR PROPORTIONS EXPLANATION FOR INTERNATIONAL TRADE

Eli Heckscher (1879–1952) and Bertil Ohlin (1899–1979), two Swedish economists, were among the first to offer explanations for the differences in trade specializations. They proposed that the abundance of productive resources determines the ability of a country to produce goods efficiently. If a country has an abundant source of labor, it should be effective in producing labor-intensive goods. In contrast, if a country has an abundance of capital, it should specialize in producing capital-intensive goods. Although capital in economics usually refers to the nonlabor equipment and machinery required to produce goods, it also can include money for investments in the purchase of capital goods.

The Heckscher-Ohlin (H-O) model is intuitively very consistent and appealing, but it was not able to predict actual behavior in international trade. In 1954, Wassily Leontief (1906–1999), found that that the Heckscher-Ohlin proposition did not hold up empirically for U.S. trade patterns. His analysis showed that the United States continued to export labor-intensive goods and import capital-intensive goods in spite of having significant advantages in producing capital goods. The abundance of endowments themselves appears not to be sufficient to guarantee the production of goods efficiently. The use of technology and the effective management of the production process also play a role in exploiting factors of production to increase output.

China and India are other examples that violate the H-O theory. Both countries continue to lag in the production of agricultural output compared to countries with lesser amounts of labor resources. For example, Europe and the United States have continued to maintain their superiority in the production of agricultural commodities. The explanation lies in their efficient implementation of farming methods, which includes the use of harvesters, fertilizers, and pesticides, better drainage systems, crop rotation, and cross-fertilization of seeds. Farms in the midwestern United States continue to yield higher quantities of wheat and corn per acre than anywhere else in the world. Thus, an abundance of natural resources alone does not appear to be able to predict trade patterns. The efficient use of technology and capital also factor into a country's ability to specialize in production.

THE PRODUCT LIFE CYCLE THEORY

The product life cycle (PLC) theory provides another explanation for patterns in international trade.[3] Under this hypothesis, the flow of trade depends on the stage in the life cycle of a product. It does not discount the comparative theories or the H-O hypothesis.

Rather, it complements them by adding another dimension to the explanation, the nature of the product itself. Trade depends on the demand for a product by overseas customers. As demand increases, not only is the product exported, but it eventually gets produced overseas, a phenomenon unheard of in the times of Smith and Ricardo.

The PLC hypothesis begins with the premise that new products are usually developed in countries where purchasing power is high—in other words, rich countries. This period is defined as the *introductory stage.* The product is manufactured locally using available capital and labor. Demand for the product that spurred its innovation is less sensitive to the price or cost of the product. This is followed by the second stage, the *growth stage,* in which the product gets accepted more widely and usage increases. Prices fall as market share increases and additional features are added to the product to satisfy the demands of a larger clientele. During this period, the product may change from being a luxury or exclusive item to being one of necessity. An example is a copier machine or an automobile. Initially the product is considered an item of luxury to a consumer, but over time it becomes a necessity.

During the latter part of the introductory stage and the beginning of the growth stage, the product is likely to be exported to other countries as foreign consumers become aware of its availability. Demand is most likely to come from other rich countries that can afford the initial high prices. During the growth stage, some production may take place overseas, as the higher demand for the product cannot be satisfied by domestic production alone. Although patent protection may prevent duplication of the product, near substitutes are likely to enter the market.

The next stage, defined as the *mature stage,* sees a flattening of the demand curve as the product gets well established both locally and overseas. Production takes place around the globe. Trade continues to increase as products are shipped from overseas facilities to new markets. Products may even be imported back to the country that first manufactured them as a result of cheaper manufacturing costs overseas. Innovations and new features are likely to be standardized across competitor products, and prices are likely to stabilize into a long-run equilibrium.

The final stage of the life cycle process is the *declining period,* when the product is replaced by new innovations. During this declining phase, production is likely to take place in countries that are able to produce the product at the lowest cost. Industrialized and rich countries are likely to be the largest importers of these products.

To a large extent, the PLC theory provides a coherent explanation for the patterns of trade of popular consumer durables. It can also predict the trade flows of raw materials that are used in the production process and the sale of after-market supplies. Unfortunately, the theory is better at explaining ex post trade patterns rather than providing a formal framework for future trade flows. This is because at the product level, it is difficult to predict the demand, cost of production, exchange rates, innovations, and other factors affecting supply and demand for the product during the life cycle.

GLOBAL PATTERNS OF TRADE: STATISTICS

As international trade increases, the standard of living increases for all countries involved, as more output is available to their citizens. Although international trade

Table 5.1

Merchandise Exports by Region

Region	1948	1963	1983	2003	2005
World[1]	$58	$157	$1,838	$7,369	$10,159
United States[2]	21.7%	14.9%	11.2%	9.8%	8.9%
Canada[2]	5.5%	4.3%	4.2%	3.7%	3.5%
Mexico[2]	0.9%	0.6%	1.4%	2.2%	2.1%
European Union[2]	n.a	27.5%	30.4%	42.4%	39.4%
Africa[2]	7.3%	5.7%	4.5%	2.4%	2.9%
Middle East[2]	2.0%	3.2%	6.8%	4.1%	5.3%
Asia[2]	14.0%	12.4%	19.15%	26.1%	27.4%
Japan[2]	0.4%	3.5%	8.0%	6.4%	5.9%
China[2]	0.9%	1.3%	1.2%	5.9%	7.5%
India[2]	2.2%	1.0%	0.5%	0.8%	0.9%

Source: World Trade Organization, World Merchandise Exports by Region and Selected Economy, Table II–2. Available at http://www.wto.org/english/res_e/statis_e/its2006_e/its06_overview_e.pdf (accessed August 27, 2008).
[1]In billions of U.S. dollars.
[2]In percentages (of world total).

has been increasing since the 1500s, its dramatic growth during the second half of the twentieth century provides clear evidence that cooperative efforts benefit all countries. During the interwar period between 1918 and 1939, countries around the world, including the United States, were still engaging in antitrade policies. After World War II, a concerted effort was made to increase international trade. As a result, it grew at an unprecedented pace, not only among rich countries, but also between rich and poor countries. Table 5.1 illustrates the increase in trade in the last six decades. Trade increased from $58 billion in 1948 to more than $10 trillion in 2005, for an annualized growth rate of more than 10 percent. The largest increases took place between 1963 and 1983, when trade increased at an average rate of 13.1 percent annually. Between 1983 and 2003, it increased by 7.2 percent annually.

Table 5.1 also shows some variations in trade patterns by region. The proportion of international trade as a percentage of total trade in the United States dropped gradually from a high of 27.1 percent in 1948 to 8.9 percent in 2005. Within North America, Canada's share of world trade also declined to 3.5 percent from a high of 5.5 percent in 1948, while Mexico's gradually increased to a high of 2.1 percent in 2005.

The increase in trade in the European Union (EU) is difficult to measure because countries are continuously being added to the bloc. Table 5.2 shows the members that have been gradually admitted to the union. The European Union, with 27 member countries as of January 1, 2007, had a combined share of 39.4 percent of world trade in 2005, with Germany and France registering the highest share at 9.5 percent and 4.5 percent, respectively. The proportion of trade in Asia has also been showing a steady growth since 1963, registering 27.4 percent in 2005. As expected, China experienced rapid growth, reaching 7 percent in 2005, while Japan's share declined to 5.9 percent in 2005 from a high of 9.9 percent in 1993. India's share has been

Table 5.2

European Union Members

Year	Countries	Total	Comments
January 1, 1958	Belgium France Germany Italy Luxembourg Netherlands	6	Establishment of the European Economic Community (EEC)
January 1, 1973	Denmark Ireland United Kingdom	9	No referendum keeps Norway out
January 1, 1981	Greece	10	
January 1, 1986	Spain Portugal	12	Euro becomes official currency in 2002 except in the UK
January 1, 1995	Austria Finland Sweden	15	Euro is the currency of Austria since 2002
May 1, 2004	Cyprus Czech Republic Estonia Hungary Latvia Lithuania Malta Poland Slovakia Slovenia	25	
January 1, 2007	Bulgaria Romania	27	Slovenia adopts the Euro
January 1, 2008			Malta and Cyprus adopt the Euro

Source: Adapted from European Union, "Key dates in the history of European integration." Available at http://europa.eu/abc/12lessons/key_dates/index_en.htm (accessed July 7, 2008).

showing a gradual increase, reaching approximately 0.9 percent in 2005. In contrast, the proportion of trade in Africa has decreased from a high of 7.3 percent in 1948 to 2.4 percent in 2003.

WORLD TRADE ORGANIZATION

The World Trade Organization (WTO) is the successor to the General Agreement on Tariffs and Trade (GATT). GATT was created as part of the Bretton Woods agreement at the end of World War II.

The economic events that occurred between World War I and World War II convinced several economists that the best approach to achieving postwar recovery was for all countries to grow together toward full employment and output. GATT's mission was to ensure that the trading rules were fair to all countries, and a coordinated approach was required to encourage countries to produce goods efficiently and export freely.

The initial work of GATT was to reduce the tariffs imposed by countries on imports of commodities. Tariff reductions were later extended to other consumer and capital goods. Between 1986 and 1994, under the aegis of the Uruguay Round of conferences, countries began to work on reducing barriers to the free flow of services, agriculture, capital, and intellectual property. The WTO is the result of this round of negotiations. It should be noted that GATT, although much maligned and criticized by various groups at times, deserves much of the credit for the successful growth in trade in the postwar period.

The main objectives of the WTO, which was formally created in 1995, are to formulate and implement trade rules through multilateral trading agreements rather than bilateral agreements. The WTO's members come from 150 countries, with another 30 countries in various stages of negotiations to join the organization. An important task of the WTO is to handle disputes between countries in areas of trade violations, including allegations of dumping, hidden taxation, and subsidies. The WTO, like its predecessor, prefers to reach agreement by consensus, but unlike GATT, majority voting is allowed in cases when a consensus is not achieved. A majority-approved law is applicable only to those countries that accept the vote.

INTERNATIONAL TRADE IN THE FUTURE

International trade will continue to increase in the near future as more countries improve their production capabilities and innovations continue to spur new products. Earlier models that helped explain the growth and pattern of international trade are less applicable today because of changes in the production environment. The major change in international trade—one that began as early as the middle of the nineteenth century—has been the movement of labor and capital across national boundaries. A phenomenon such as this affects the dynamics of trade because goods can now be produced using labor and capital imported from overseas. The United States, where waves of immigrants contributed to a rapid increase in the speed of industrialization, is the best example of this dramatic change in the international trade environment. The United States also imported capital goods and machinery from Europe, which, combined with new labor, made the country into a major manufacturer and consumer. As its production processes became more efficient, it became a major exporter of capital and consumer goods. Similarly, Japan, in spite of being an island with scarce arable land and natural resources, became an industrial power by importing oil, steel, and other natural resources to skillfully produce consumer durables for export around the world. The old theories of comparative advantage would never have predicted that Japan, with few natural resources, would become a leading exporter of industrial goods in the second half of the twentieth century.

The second major change in the international trade environment was the formation of multinational corporations in the twentieth century. Multinationals changed the dynamics of international trade because their wealth and power allow them to establish production centers around the globe. Today they have the flexibility to relocate globally, enabling them to maximize output at the lowest cost. Multinationals have the ability to transform a country with few resources into a fledgling modern industrialized state. Hypothetically, even in a country with few natural resources, unfavorable climate, and a lack of skilled workers, multinationals can set up factories to produce a range of goods from basic agricultural produce to advanced microchips. In such cases, multinationals must construct the required infrastructure, including roads and electricity, import the necessary raw materials, and recruit skilled labor to produce and export the output. It should be noted that such an investment does not guarantee a country will prosper, since development can be impaired by a corrupt government or exploitation by multinationals themselves. Singapore and Taiwan are examples that are close to such a model where multinationals were major contributors to their development.

Multinationals foster the movement of labor and capital through foreign direct investment. Foreign direct investment in recent years has been a major factor to increase in global trade, accounting for nearly one-third of international trade flows. Hence, international trade today cannot be studied in isolation. This new paradigm recognizes that international trade and foreign direct investment go hand in hand, unlike in the past. This topic is explored in the next section.

FOREIGN DIRECT INVESTMENT

Foreign direct investment (FDI) represents capital investments made by firms in another country. When IBM invests in the construction of a plant in Belgium to manufacture semiconductors, it represents U.S. FDI in Belgium. The United States is considered the sending country and Belgium the receiving country of FDI. Similarly, when Lenovo acquired IBM's personal computing division in 2004, it represented FDI by a Chinese company in the United States. The United States is the receiving country of the FDI. The companies that engage in FDI are usually multinational corporations (MNCs) or transnational companies (TNCs).

It is not necessary for a multinational to own 100 percent of an overseas firm for its investment to be classified as FDI. An investment is considered FDI as long as the multinational has a controlling interest in the overseas firm. The amount of shares a multinational must own to possess a controlling interest can vary and in some cases can be as low as 10 percent.

It should be noted that there is a difference between foreign direct investment and overseas portfolio investment. The latter refers to the purchase of stocks in an overseas company for passive investment. A mutual fund, for example, may purchase up to 10 percent of an overseas company's shares and seek no controlling interest. The fund is interested only in receiving dividends with the prospect of selling the shares in the future at a higher price. It is difficult to separate overseas portfolio investment and foreign direct investment, as there are no clear guidelines or accepted practice for distinguishing them.

The U.S. State Department considers 15 percent ownership in a company sufficient for classification as FDI. The European Union classifies FDI as follows: "Foreign direct investment (FDI) is the category of international investment made by an entity resident in one economy (direct investor) to acquire a lasting interest in an enterprise operating in another economy (direct investment enterprise). The lasting interest is deemed to exist if the direct investor acquires at least 10 percent of the equity capital of the direct investment enterprise."[4] This is consistent with the definition used by the Organisation for Economic Co-operation and Development (OECD), an influential group of 30 countries that generates research for policy making.

For measurement purposes, countries prefer to categorize FDI by outward (OFDI) or inward investment (IFDI). OFDI refers to outward foreign direct investment made by residents of one country to another country. It represents an outflow of money and investment from domestic investors to foreign countries. OFDI is usually perceived negatively by domestic residents because it reduces investment and employment in the domestic market. The positive aspect of OFDI is that at some future date earnings from the overseas operations will be repatriated back to the originating country in the form of dividends and interest, bringing income and foreign currency to the domestic country.

IFDI refers to foreign direct investment by foreign residents in the domestic economy. Although it represents investment and employment in the domestic market, it is also sometimes viewed negatively by domestic residents. The reasons are usually nationalistic, as ownership of assets by foreigners rouses jingoistic sentiments among certain segments of the population. A recent example in the United States includes that of Japanese investments during the 1980s. Japanese firms, flush with dollar reserves after a period of rapid growth of exports, found investments attractive in the United States because of the weakened dollar compared to the yen. It also represented a strategic move because the weak dollar made it difficult for Japanese firms to maintain their exports from Japan to the United States. As a result, several car companies, such as Honda, Nissan, and Toyota, and other manufacturers decided to build plants in the United States.

Politicians and nationalists initially portrayed the investments as an economic invasion, and the press often hyped the so-called Japanese domination of corporate America. Over the years, this antagonism has disappeared, and time has shown that the owners' origin is irrelevant. What matters most is whether the capital is being invested wisely to employ workers and produce goods competitively.

FORMS OF FOREIGN DIRECT INVESTMENT

There are three ways for companies to engage in foreign direct investment: construct new plants or facilities (greenfield investments), acquire existing plants or facilities (brownfield investments), or establish licensing arrangements.

Greenfield investments refer to the establishment of new plants and offices overseas by multinational corporations as a means of FDI. The process usually involves setting up a separate corporation in the host country, either as a 100 percent–owned subsidiary or as a joint venture with a local partner. The capital for the investment is usually sent by the parent company in the form of equity or a combination of equity and debt. The parent company maintains full control over the operations of the plant, including control of the board of directors and the senior management.

Brownfield investments refer to the acquisition of existing firms or plants as a means of FDI. Such investments save a multinational from building new plants and incurring the associated costs of obtaining regulatory approvals, zoning, and dealing with local contractors. Recent data suggest that 70–80 percent of new FDI takes place in the form of mergers and acquisitions. Another benefit of brownfield investments is the savings in time and money because a multinational does not have to recruit new staff or establish vendor, supplier, and bank relationships. A disadvantage of acquiring a firm or existing business is that it may be difficult to introduce change, especially in countries with pro-labor laws and weak corporate governance. If a multinational acquires a foreign firm with the intent to restructure the business and change the existing work flow process, it may find it difficult to reassign workers or close down divisions. Such institutional rigidities may turn out to be costly in terms of both capital and employee morale.

Licensing agreements refer to contractual agreements between a parent company (the multinational) and a local company, allowing the local company, with or without partnership, to produce goods or services in exchange for fees and royalties. This arrangement eliminates the risks associated with operating in an unfamiliar local environment. Instead, the responsibility for the production and marketing of goods is fully passed on to the local investor. A disadvantage of this approach is that the local vendor is provided access to private business information, including technology that may be misused in the future, resulting in new competition to the parent company.

TYPES OF FOREIGN DIRECT INVESTMENT

FDI can also be classified by the types of investments a company makes, based on whether they are horizontal or vertical to the existing line of business.

Horizontal FDI

Horizontal FDI refers to overseas investment in plants and services in the investing company's existing line of business. This is the most popular form of FDI. For example, in June 2007, Hilton announced plans to build more than 55 hotels in Russia, Britain, and Central America, to be completed in 2012, with total construction costs exceeding $1.7 billion. In May 2007 Dell announced that it would open a second plant in Hortolandia, close to São Paulo, Brazil, where 70 percent of Dell's Brazilian customer base is located. The new plant manufactures Dell's traditional line of notebooks and desktops. Both these initiatives are classified as horizontal FDIs because both companies are expanding their original line of business overseas.

Vertical FDI

Vertical FDI refers to overseas investments in plants or services that contribute either to the upstream or downstream segment of a business. For example, in 1998, Total SA of France announced plans to acquire Petrofina SA of Belgium. Total SA was primarily in the business of oil exploration and extraction. Petrofina, in contrast, specialized in the post-production marketing and refining of oil, considered downstream operations. Hence, Total was acquiring a line of business downstream. Other examples include automotive companies purchasing steel manufacturers, or McDonald's purchasing farms to raise chickens and grow potatoes so they can supply their franchisees with consistent ingredients.

Motives for Foreign Direct Investment

In a perfectly competitive market, there is no reason for FDI because a company should be able to distribute its products to all markets at some equilibrium price. A company that produces a good in New York should be able to sell it throughout the United States at one equilibrium price, plus transportation costs. Similarly, if the world market is perfectly competitive, the company should sell its output globally at one equilbrum price and geographic boundaries should be of no consequence. The only reason for FDI to take place is the existence of market imperfections. A majority of studies have focused on the macroeconomic imperfections in the marketplace to explain the motivations for FDI. Another branch of study has looked at FDI from a microeconomic perspective; the skills and know-how of a firm require that it be located overseas to exploit its full productivity.

Among the various theories offered in the literature, John Dunning's eclectic OLI paradigm provides an overview of both the imperfections in the market and the uniqueness of the firm to explain FDI.[5] The O stands for ownership, L for location, and I for internalization.

- Ownership advantages refer to the special know-how belonging to a firm. It can be in the form of a patent, technological skill, managerial skill, or process skill that gives the firm an advantage in the production of a good or service.
- Location advantage refers to the exploitation of local resources that would otherwise be unavailable to provide added value to the product. An example would be the extractive industry, where the special know-how to dig very deeply for ores still requires the company to be located near the mines.
- Internalization refers to the process by which it is more efficient for the multinational to execute the project through intracompany transfer than to transfer its know-how to a third party. There can be many reasons for this scenario, including special expertise as well as the potential loss of the know-how.

Dunning's OLI paradigm is able to integrate the multiple motivations for FDI into three broad and simple categories. It recognizes the impact of both macro and micro factors involved in the decision to go overseas and substitute FDI for trade.

Other authors have classified the motives strictly from the perspective of the multinational as it operates in a global environment without national boundaries. Multinationals engage in FDI to seek resources and markets and to achieve global efficiency and strategic fit. Strategic fit may encompass several different criteria such as securing markets, cutting costs, and accommodating other factors, including import barriers, shortage of foreign exchange, and uniqueness of product.

Resource-Seeking Motives

Multinationals are very adept at seeking locations globally to produce output at the lowest cost. The lower costs may be the results of cheaper labor, lower transportation costs, and lower costs of raw materials. Overseas expansion can also be viewed within the context of the product life cycle (PLC) theory. As discussed earlier, during the second stage of the PLC, when demand rises overseas, a firm may be better served by plants established near customers. Overseas expansion also allows companies to devote more attention to the tastes and needs of their overseas customers and build separate R&D facilities for the overseas markets. Competition or the threat of competition can also force companies to seek cheaper resources. If a competitor sets up plants overseas to produce goods more cheaply than it can at home, it becomes difficult for a domestic company to maintain its competitive edge.

Market-Seeking Motives

Another reason for multinationals to engage in FDI is to create or increase new market share, usually near their existing markets. The production of cars in the United States by foreign automobile manufacturers is one example of market-seeking FDI. Volkswagen was the first foreign car company to open a plant in the United States, in Westmoreland, Pennsylvania, in 1978. Within a few years, many foreign car companies entered the market, beginning with Honda in Marysville, Ohio, in 1982. Similar competitive positioning behavior is now being practiced by U.S. car manufacturers overseas. In anticipation of a booming market, GM started to assemble Buick cars in China in 1999. GM has now been joined by other U.S. car companies. Ford opened its first factory in China in February 2003 and has already announced plans to build a few additional plants. Such expansion also provides diversification benefits. For example, while GM has announced plans in late 2008 to close plants in North America as a result of an impending economic recession, it continued to open plants in China where demand for cars is expected to grow for the foreseeable future.

In vertical FDI, the strategic motive focuses on gaining a competitive advantage on a company's upstream or downstream operations. Mergers and acquisitions that seek to control upstream and downstream operations are subject to antitrust laws in order to prevent the likelihood of a monopoly. In 2008, ALCOA, the world's largest producer of aluminum, announced a joint venture with Vietnam's premier minerals development company, Vietnam National Coal-Mineral Industries Group (Vinacomin), to develop its aluminum industry. This will enable ALCOA to consolidate its upstream operations by having access to Vietnam's high quality bauxite reserves.[6]

Import Barriers

Another strategic reason for a company to use FDI to enter new markets or expand its operations in existing markets is to overcome trade barriers, usually import restrictions. Countries often discourage imports by imposing high import duties, labeling requirements, health certifications, and quality tests. Some countries may have legitimate reasons for imposing restrictions on imports, most often as a result of scarce foreign exchange. A developing country with limited foreign reserves may want to discourage the import of luxury items such as perfumes, jewelry, and expensive cars and instead encourage the import of capital equipment into vital or fledgling industries. A country may also attempt to encourage selected industries to develop without fear of foreign competition. The effectiveness of these measures depends on their implementation;

they can have negative consequences if they are exploited by domestic companies for their own benefit.

For example, India banned the imports on luxury cars and charged very high duties on other cars in the 1950s to promote its domestic car production. This led to the development of three local car manufacturers who dominated the domestic market for many years. Unfortunately, the lack of competition provided no incentive for these companies to improve the quality of their cars, and over time they began to lag behind cars produced overseas. When import restrictions were removed in the 1990s and foreign cars began to penetrate the Indian market, domestic manufacturers were forced to focus on quality and service. By 2006, fierce competition among several car companies led not only to increased quality but also to reduction in the prices of all cars. In 2007, Tata Motors (an Indian car manufacturer) and Nissan-Renault announced plans to start manufacturing cars that would cost less than $3,000, a clear signal that competition, and not import barriers, helps local manufacturers in the long run.

Trade barriers have been coming down in recent years as a result of the work of GATT and the WTO. Several studies have confirmed the impact of trade barriers on FDI, including research by Theo Eicher and Jong Woo Kang (2004), who demonstrate empirically that when trade barriers are low, overseas companies prefer to export but will opt for FDI when trade barriers are high.[7]

Shortage of Foreign Exchange

As mentioned earlier, developing countries often face a shortage of foreign exchange earnings, forcing governments to restrict their use for the import of essential items such as capital goods, oil, and food. Luxury items such as cars get a lower priority. Strategically, it makes sense for a foreign car manufacturer to produce locally rather than exporting to a country that lacks foreign exchange. If the initial investment can be obtained locally, the company needs only to secure foreign exchange sufficient to remit profits as dividends back to the parent country, a much smaller amount than if they imported the cars to the country.

Nature of Product

In some cases, the nature of the product or service requires that the company invest locally in a plant or an office (Dunning's location-specific advantage). Two prominent examples are power plants and extractive industries. These industries require huge capital investments in the local area and a long-term commitment. Such projects are also very risky and require contractual agreements with the local government that will guarantee the safety of their investments for many years. In some cases, it is possible for firms to license their technology and collect only royalties and special fees for its use.

Other examples of foreign direct investment that require local presence include several service industries such as the legal, financial, banking, and food services. In the food industry, for instance, it is common for firms to franchise their services with a local owner. The franchisee pays the parent company a percentage of the revenue in exchange for use of the brand name and the process for food preparation and compliance with the franchisor's standards. The franchisee is also expected or required to import the ingredients from the franchisor for preparation of their food products.

NEW TRENDS IN FOREIGN DIRECT INVESTMENT

As the WTO continues to reduce tariffs across the globe, firms are finding it strategically necessary to reduce their costs of production at all stages of the product life cycle. The trend is no longer to move overseas in the third stage of the product life cycle; rather, the process may begin as early as the first stage. An entrepreneur or company today has the luxury of patenting a product first before deciding on the location to manufacture the output. With information from the Internet, and assisted by the various branch offices of the U.S. Chamber of Commerce, companies can obtain quotations and proposals worldwide to develop prototypes of their products.

Technological advances have also made it possible for a firm to develop a product initially in electronic format, using advanced 3-D modeling and manufacturing software. The software enables the computer to test the product for durability, strength, wear and tear, and safety. Additional software also enables the prototype to be generated with different types of materials unique to each country. Based on the results, a firm can decide to produce products in multiple locations using different materials and processes.

COSTS AND BENEFITS OF FOREIGN DIRECT INVESTMENT

The impact of FDI on both the sending and receiving countries depends on a number of factors. There is a general consensus that FDI provides significant benefits to the receiving or host countries in terms of employment, income, trade, investments in human capital, infrastructure development, and technology transfers. Noneconomic benefits include better corporate governance, awareness of the environment, social equality, and political freedom. There are also costs associated with FDI, particularly if host countries' economic policies are not geared to spread the benefits of FDI in a positive manner. Inappropriate policies can lead to income inequality, social unrest, pollution, degradation of the environment, depletion of resources, and political instability. We first examine the impact on employment and income to both the sending and receiving country, followed by the impact on trade, investment, and technology transfer.

The impact of FDI on employment and income to the sending country is still open to debate. When U.S. companies open subsidiaries overseas to take advantage of cheaper labor costs, the initial impact on employment and income is usually negative. Labor unions and economists complain that sending jobs overseas also generates negative externalities to the domestic economy. When a company closes a plant down, it also affects ancillary industries and local businesses. The net effect on society may be larger than the savings generated for the company shareholders. Others have argued that it is not labor costs that drive firms overseas but rather the tax breaks and other financial incentives host countries provide to multinational corporations. However, many economists cite the low unemployment rate in the United States over the last two decades prior to 2008 as an indicator that FDI does not lead to lower employment and income. Rather, the income from export services has been growing steadily over the years, indicating that overseas investments are beginning to pay off.

From the perspective of the receiving country, the influx of FDI often means more jobs and income and a boost to the economy. Unfortunately, there can also be negative externalities. Labor exploitation is among the most common criticisms leveled against multinationals, especially when they operate in developing countries. They are often accused of using child labor, compromising on worker safety measures, paying substandard wages, and contributing to environmental degradation. It is difficult to take sides on this issue as it can be viewed from several standpoints.

For example, on the issue of substandard wages, one needs to use the proper benchmark to evaluate the wage level. The most appropriate index to use is the median wage within the country or industry sector. By and large, most multinationals pay higher than the local wages, but without proper controls, it is still easy for labor to be exploited, most notably by firms that use contracted labor. In August 2007, China Labor Watch, a watchdog group in New York, reported that it investigated eight factories supplying toys to well-known companies in the United States such as Disney, Hasbro, and Sega and found widespread violations, including mandatory overtime, verbal and sexual abuse by managers, and hiring of underage workers.[8]

Another consideration is the impact on employment and income when FDI is achieved through mergers and acquisitions (M&A). In the case of FDI through M&A, employment may either drop or not increase in the initial phase. This can happen if the multinational introduces new technology or work flow processes that improve efficiency in the firm. However, if the firm succeeds in its reorganization, employment should increase in the long run.

TRADE, INVESTMENTS, AND TECHNOLOGY TRANSFERS

One of the benefits of FDI for a receiving country is increased investments that may not otherwise be available. When FDI flows into a country, the immediate benefits that result from the influx of investment are increased employment and income to local industries. The sending country generates a positive payoff only after a period of time when it is able to repatriate profits and dividends. FDI can also lead to technology transfers and eventually help a receiving country upgrade its human capital and productive capacity. This transfer may hurt the sending country in the long run if the technology is duplicated or it results in an erosion of its technological lead. If FDI leads to increased exports to a country, then it offers additional benefits in that the country also earns foreign exchange through trade.

FDI's impact on trade, investments, and technology transfers is considered next for three industries: manufacturing, services, and extractive.

Manufacturing Industry

FDI for manufacturing is undertaken by companies that plan to produce goods for local consumption or for export to other countries, including their home countries. Such investments require machinery and other equipment to be imported from overseas for installation in the receiving country. Examples include IBM building a semiconductor plant in France or Siemens building a power plant in India.

Trade. Whether FDI increases or decreases a receiving country's exports depends on the reasons for the establishment of the plant. If the multinational opens the plant because it is unable to meet local demand through exports, it is very likely that all the output will be sold in the local market. If the plant was constructed for cost-savings reasons, then the output is likely to be exported back to the sending country and exports will increase for the receiving country.

Investments. Plant production, especially new investments (greenfield investments), usually require substantial investment in building infrastructure, equipment, and manpower. Plant construction also leads to investment in ancillary industries that are in close proximity to the new plant.

Technology Transfer. There is some transfer of technology whenever plants are constructed overseas. The extent of the transfer depends to the kind of technology chosen and the ease of adoption. If the technology is simple and requires low levels of investment, it will be easier for local countries to imitate it or create near imitations. If the technology is sophisticated or requires a large investment, it is unlikely for technology to be transferred for many years.

Services Industry

FDI for establishing services overseas is made in the hotel and food businesses, theme parks, retail chains, and transaction services including banking. Examples include Hilton opening a chain of hotels in Mexico, American Express opening offices in Colombia, and Disney opening a theme park in France. The core business model remains the same globally, although local culture and tastes may require adaptations and changes to the mix of services and delivery.

Trade. Most service industries usually cater to domestic consumption. However, some services such as those in the leisure business may cater to foreign tourists that can help earn foreign exchange indirectly for the country (export of services). Examples include tourist resorts run by global brands such as Hilton, Starwood Group, and Novotel, which are usually frequented by tourists and foreign businesspeople.

Investments. The investments required to establish services overseas are usually lower than those for plant construction. In the service industry, the main investments are in buildings and manpower. The returns on service investments are typically high, especially for brand-name companies. Examples include Citibank and HSBC for banking services and McDonald's and Burger King for food services. However, service industries face higher risk than others, for they are subject to expropriation or excessive regulation and are also often easy targets for nationalistic politicians.

Technology Transfer. Technology transfer is limited to the training of individuals and the delivery of services. Such expertise may in the long run be transferable to local companies. It is not yet clear whether technology transfers by service industries hurt overseas companies. Well-known brand-name companies are difficult to replace, and any negative effects may only be marginal.

Extractive Industry

FDI for the mining and excavation of minerals and fossil fuels requires large investments, usually in the form of capital goods and equipment. Extractive FDI has received much criticism in the recent past because of the environmental degradation associated with this industry.

Trade. The output of extractive industries is usually exported and can earn large amounts of foreign exchange for the receiving country. However, the earnings can be very volatile because demand for commodities is influenced by the global economy and sometimes by the economies of a few countries. If these select countries experience a recession, then the exports of the receiving country are also affected. The impact of a recession is felt more strongly in countries that have only one or two commodities as their main foreign exchange earners. A decline in export earnings has significant effects on a country's overall economy. According to a 2004 report by the Food and Agriculture Organization of the United Nations (UN), approximately 43 developing countries relied on a single commodity to generate 20 percent of their export earnings. Most of them were in sub-Saharan Africa, Latin America, or the Caribbean and exported products such as sugar, coffee, cotton, and bananas.[9]

Investments. Investments in the extractive industries are usually large and tend to continue for many years. In 2007, the UN Conference on Trade and Development (UNCTAD), a body of the UN that monitors global foreign direct investment, reported that Africa remains the largest recipient of mining FDI where total inflows reached $56 billion.[10] In oil extractions, as well as in the mining of bauxite (used to make aluminum) and gold, investments can run into billions of dollars. The offshore drilling, open-pit quarrying, and dredging industries are now coming under scrutiny, especially in relation to labor exploitation and environmental concerns. Consequently, further investments have been demanded by UNCTAD for improvements in mining technology during and after the projects are completed.

Technology Transfer. Although the capital investments for extractive industries are high, the technology can range from simple, as in open-pit quarrying, to highly complex, as in offshore drilling. Multinationals possess significant advantages in high technology extraction. As in the case of manufacturing, it takes many years for complex technology to be transferred to the receiving countries.

Table 5.3

Global Foreign Direct Investment (FDI) Inflows and Outflows (in billions of U.S. dollars)

Region	1994–1999 Annual Average	2003	2005
FDI Inflows			
Europe	220.4	274.1	433.6
Japan	3.4	6.3	2.8
USA	124.9	53.1	99.4
Africa	8.4	18.5	30.7
Asia	92.4	110.1	199.6
World	548.1	557.9	916.3
FDI Outflows			
Europe	326.5	317	618.8
Japan	22.8	28.8	45.8
USA	114.3	129.4	−12.7
Africa	2.5	1.2	1.1
Asia	43.5	19	836
World	553.1	561.1	778.7

Source: Adapted from United Nations, "World Investment Report 2006: FDI from Developing and Transition Economies: Implications for Development," Table 1, p. 2. Available at http://www.unctad.org.

FDI STATISTICS

In a 2006 survey by UNCTAD, total global FDI outflows were estimated at $778.8 billion while inflows totaled $916.3 billion, as shown in Table 5.3. This represents nearly 10 percent of global trade flows. FDI and trade go hand in hand, with FDI serving as a major catalyst for trade. For example, a majority of U.S. and European firms that have invested in China send the output back to the home countries—another way of contributing to international trade.

Table 5.3, which is based on information from the UN's "World Investment Report 2006," also shows that the bulk of FDI inflows and outflows are concentrated in Europe. The inflows and outflows do not equal each other because of reconciliation errors. In Japan, FDI outflows ($45.8 billion) are much higher than inflows ($2.8 billion). In contrast, the United States has continued to be a magnet for FDI, with $99.4 billion in inflows. The outflows show a negative $12.7 billion. Developed countries are also a target for investment, accounting for 36.5 percent of total inflows and just 15.1 percent of total outflows. Africa has received an increasing share of FDI as well, from $8.4 billion in the late 1990s to $30.7 billion in 2005, with South Africa receiving 21 percent of the total inflows.

A new pattern in international trade is for developing countries to invest more in developed countries. This phenomenon reflects a maturity of industries in the developing countries and a readiness to compete with the rest of the world. In December 2007, Tata Motors from India successfully bid $2 billion for the Rover and Jaguar divisions of Ford, which represents the first major acquisition of a car company in a developed country.

Table 5.4

Role of Foreign Affiliates in Global Foreign Direct Investment (in billions of dollars and percent)

Variable	Value at current prices		Annual growth rate
	1982	2005	1996–2000
Sales of Foreign Affiliates	2,620	22,171	10.1
Total Assets of foreign Affiliates	2,108	45,564	21.0
Export of Foreign Affiliates	647	4,214	4.8
Employment of Foreign Affiliates	19,537	62,095	11.0
Royalties and License Fees Receipts	2,247	12,641	3.6

Source: Adapted from United Nations, "World Investment Report 2006: FDI from Developing and Transition Economies: Implications for Development," Table 3, p. 7. Available at http://www.unctad.org.

Table 5.5

The World's Top 10 Multinational Corporations, Ranked by Foreign Assets, 2004 (in billions of dollars and percentage)

Corporation	Country	Foreign Assets	Percentage of Foreign Asset	Foreign Sales	Percentage of Foreign Sales
General Electric	USA	44,890	59.8	5,689	37.2
Vodaphone Group	UK	24,875	95.8	5,330	8.5
Ford Motor	USA	17,985	58.9	7,144	4.2
General Motors	USA	17,369	36.2	5,913	3.1
British Petroleum	UK	15,451	80.0	23,238	8.2
ExxonMobil	USA	13,492	69.1	20,287	7.0
Royal Dutch/Shell	UK/NL	12,993	67.4	17,028	6.4
Toyota Motor	Japan	12,296	52.6	10,299	6.0
Total	France	9,871	86.1	12,326	8.1
France Telekom	France	8,566	65.3	2,425	4.1

Source: Adapted from United Nations, "World Investment Report 2006: FDI from Developing and Transition Economies: Implications for Development," Table 4, p. 8. Available at http://www.unctad.org.

Table 5.4 shows the growth in assets of foreign affiliates, representing nearly $46 trillion in 2005. In addition, cross-border mergers and acquisitions totaled $716 billion. Finally, the exports of affiliates accounted for $4,214 trillion, providing evidence of the importance of FDI in increasing trade globally.

Table 5.5 shows the top 10 multinationals, or transnational corporations, in the world. In 2005, there were 77,000 parent companies with 770,000 foreign affiliates (not reported). They generated employment and produced $45 trillion in output. Japan, Europe, and the United States continue to dominate the list of the top companies in the world. France, Germany, the United Kingdom, Japan, and the United States account for 73 of the top 100 companies in the world. This is slowly changing, however, as more firms from developing countries, especially India and China, enter the market.

Figure 5.1 **The Extractive Industry Transparency Initiative**

The Extractive Industry Transparency Initiative (EITI) was formed under the auspices of UNCTAD in 2002 to improve the governance in resource-rich countries. The goal of the initiative is to ensure that the wealth generated from the earnings is distributed properly for economic growth and poverty reduction. The EITI has members throughout the globe, including twenty African countries. The basic principle of EITI is that there should be sufficient transparency in the business of extraction that governments are forced to spend the earnings carefully and for the benefit of the citizenry as a whole. Open information on the amount of extraction, payments, and costs ensure that the people of the country have a voice in the distribution of the wealth.

Source: David Mayer-Foulkes and Peter Nunnenkamp, "Do Multinational Enterprises Contribute to Convergence or Divergence? A Disaggregated Analysis of US FDI," Working Paper 1242, University of Kiel, Germany, May 2005. Available at www.ssrn.com (accessed July 11, 2008).

FOREIGN DIRECT INVESTMENT AND POLITICS

The amount of foreign direct investment that flows from one country to another is affected by the government policies in both the sending and receiving countries. A country can use tax incentives and disincentives or impose burdensome rules and regulations to influence FDI outflow or inflow. Which approach is used depends on the political system in each country and their philosophy toward FDI. At one extreme is the negative view, based on the early Marxist interpretation, that multinationals seek access to foreign markets to only exploit the local resources. At the other extreme is the positive or free market view that claims FDI is always beneficial for the recipient country. In reality, whether or not FDI is beneficial depends on a range of factors, including policies set by the local government, goals of multinationals, and the skills of local labor.

Negative View

Taken primarily from Marxist literature, the negative view of FDI tends to consider all FDI as exploitative; multinationals are seen as being interested only in taking advantage of cheap labor. This may true in some cases, especially in the extractive industries, and it usually happens when the local government is corrupt and exploits the benefits from the FDI to enrich a few. The situation is made worse if the land and environment are left in a polluted condition after the ores have been extracted completely. David Mayer-Foulkes and Peter Nunnenkamp found that U.S. FDI in developed countries tends to increase the benefits for the recipient country, but its effect has been the opposite for developing or poorer countries. See Figure 5.1 on the Extractive Industry Transparency Initiative (EITI).

Positive View

Proponents of free markets and free trade usually point to the positive aspects of FDI. The negative impact is less severe in nonextractive industries, where the production of output or services requires the use of the local land, capital, and labor. This is especially true if FDI is managed carefully by the host countries through multilateral agreements that ensure a level playing field for both domestic and foreign investors. The benefits come not just from employment, taxes, and net income, but also from the positive externalities. Employment through FDI leads to the development of improved employee skills and higher income, which eventually lead to additional development of local industry. Technology transfers, direct and indirect, ultimately benefit the local residents of the receiving country.

FDI has always been a sensitive issue because, unlike international trade, the investment includes ownership of assets and repatriation of profits. When Japan exported cars in the 1970s to the United States, there was not as much ill will as when the Japanese began to make investments in the United States. For example, the purchase of Rockefeller Center by Mitsubishi in 1989 raised a chorus of criticism by politicians and industry leaders. Some authors suggested that it amounted to discrimination because Britain and the Netherlands were also very large investors during this period, yet their investment in the United States never became a hot issue.[11] Similarly, during the 1960s and 1970s, nationalistic politicians in Europe and Asia found it easy to associate FDI by U.S. companies with exploitation of the country's economic wealth.

FOREIGN DIRECT INVESTMENT AND GOVERNMENT POLICIES

Many countries use tax policy as a means to lure or repel foreign direct investment. Tax breaks are a common means to attract FDI into a country. They can come in the form of zero taxes on the parent company for the first five years, followed by gradual increases over the remaining years. Withholding taxes, in addition to normal corporate taxes, are used to discourage FDI. Withholding taxes are levied on companies when they have to repatriate their profits or dividends back to the parent company. By increasing withholding taxes, countries can make the cost of FDI higher to potential investors.

Example of Withholding Taxes

Assume that a U.S. multinational in Singapore generates revenues of S$10 million and incurs costs of S$6 million in variable and fixed costs. If the tax rate is 40 percent, then its after-tax earnings available to shareholders are as follows:

Revenues	S$10,000,000
Costs	S$6,000,000
Gross profit	S$4,000,000
Taxes (40 percent)	S$1,600,000
Net income	S$2,400,000

This amount can be sent back to the parent company in the form of dividends. However, most governments will impose a withholding tax. Assuming that this tax is 15 percent, this means the multinational is allowed to send only S$2,400,000–S$360,000 = S$2,040,000 back to the parent company. Withholding taxes provide incentives to companies to reinvest their money back in the foreign country.

Subsidized Loans

Another way for countries to attract FDI is to provide subsidized loans to foreign companies and lower their cost of investments. Although it imposes a cost on the local country or city to attract the industries, the subsidized loan is justified if its costs can be recouped. Typically, the higher employment and income generated by the investments will result in greater tax revenues to the lending country or city.

Regulation

Many companies use outright regulation to prevent or encourage FDI. To prevent FDI, countries can usually invoke reasons such as national security or protection of specific industries. For example, the United States has stringent rules on trading with countries designated as those that promote terrorism. Such rules make it difficult for U.S. firms to engage in any kind of investment in those countries. In August 2007, Iran, North Korea, Syria, Cuba, and Sudan were on the list.

In 2006, Dubai Ports World acquired the British P&O shipping company to become the world's third-largest shipping operator. P&O also had contracts to operate port facilities in six cities in the United States, including Philadelphia and Miami. The issue became political when Miami-based Continental Stevedoring & Terminals, a rival port operator, went to court to block the acquisition on national security grounds. Although it was approved by the Committee of Foreign Investment of the U.S. Treasury, politicians found it easy to exploit the issue based on the backlash of the September 11 hijackings. The result was that Dubai Ports decided to sell those contracts as part of the agreement to acquire P&O.

Ownership Restrictions

Restricting the percentage of foreign ownership in a company is an effective way for countries to regulate the flow of inward FDI. Nearly all countries have some laws restricting foreign ownership. A popular restriction in many countries is to limit the percentage of foreign ownership to 49 percent, allowing domestic shareholders to have a majority control. The reasons usually cited for ownership restrictions are the protection of strategic industries and providing breathing room for infant industries.

Strategic Industries. Countries like to ensure that firms in sectors deemed to be of strategic importance are owned by domestic investors. The sectors usually include telecommunications, utilities, airlines, financial services, and media. In the United States, for example, when the semiconductor industry was threatened with closure due to cheap imports from Japan and Asia, there were calls to protect this industry by providing subsidies. It was deemed a critical sector because shortages of chips could affect a majority of industries. Indeed, in 1985, a glut of chips forced many U.S. companies to abandon production. Japanese companies continued to produce them at a loss estimated at US$4 billion; however, Japan's investment paid off as demand soared back and increased sixfold by 1990.[12] Companies in the United States were forced to buy chips at highly inflated prices until production was ramped up by domestic companies.

Similarly, shortages in critical components such as oil and steel can lead to severe repercussions in the domestic market if supply is restricted. Governments have to decide which industries are strategically critical and pass appropriate laws to encourage those companies to stay at home. Unfortunately, categorization of strategic industries can be tainted by domestic politics and corporate lobbying, which can instead lead to unnecessary protectionism.

Infant Industries. Many countries provide protection to domestic infant industries in order to give them time to develop and to protect them from foreign competition. Examples include India, which for many years protected its car industry, and Brazil, for its aerospace industry. However, protection can be misused and companies may stagnate rather than innovate and achieve higher standards. The result is a likely deterioration in the quality of the output, and protection may have to be continued to maintain employment and output locally.

FOREIGN DIRECT INVESTMENT IN THE TWENTY-FIRST CENTURY: THE ROLE OF PRIVATE EQUITY

The growth of free market policies around the globe in the last quarter of the twentieth century has resulted in dramatic changes in the flow of foreign direct investment. A new element has been injected into the dynamics—the role of private equity. Private equity firms purchase companies and manage them with the intent of either listing them in the public markets at some future date or selling them to other private investors. In 2007, private equity firms engaged in a record $700 billion in takeovers and also raised more than $500 billion in 2006 as new capital. The power of private equity is beginning to be recognized by governments and the financial markets. This is because acquisitions by private equity can impact domestic companies based on the portfolio of firms in the current inventory.

Example

Assume that two private equity firms raise $100 million each to engage in purchases of companies. Assume that the existing inventory of the firms is as follows:

Private Equity A		Private Equity B	
Auto parts firm in Belgium	$25 million	Software firm in Thailand	$50 million
Electrical retail firm in Poland	$50 million	Bicycle company in India	$25 million
Yet to be invested	$25 million	Yet to be invested	$25 million

Assume that both firms plan to bid for an engineering firm in the United States. In order to optimize their global efficiency, the firms may develop different business plans after the acquisition. Private Equity A may choose to reduce the engineering staff in Belgium and Poland and consolidate all the operations in the United States.

Employment in the U.S. engineering firm will increase at the expense of the Belgian and Polish firms. Private Equity B may choose to reduce the engineering staff in the United States and funnel more of the work through its engineering base in Thailand and India.

Depending on which firms succeed, the impact of private equity can affect employment and flow of capital in several countries because the firms operate on a global portfolio basis. As private equity becomes a dominant factor in FDI, the flow of capital will be influenced by its growth.

FOREIGN DIRECT INVESTMENT AND TRADE

The flow of international trade is affected significantly by the flow of foreign direct investment. FDI can either complement trade or act as a substitute for trade. Earlier studies had pointed to a negative correlation between FDI and trade, especially bilateral trade. Recent studies overwhelmingly show a positive relationship between FDI and trade.[13]

This interaction requires new policies and coordination by and between countries. If FDI results in increased trade for both countries, it makes sense to lower trade barriers to the fullest extent possible. However, the benefits of trade through FDI may not be immediate, and the short-term effects of FDI can be destabilizing for a country. The World Trade Organization has to balance the social and economic consequences of FDI and trade to achieve the right balance of free trade policies.

CHAPTER SUMMARY

The beginnings of international trade can be traced back to 3000 B.C.E. with the discovery of several trading routes in Asia Minor. In the sixteenth century, the economic policies of mercantilism, which emphasized the dominance of exports over imports, prevailed in Europe. By the nineteenth century, Adam Smith and David Ricardo showed the flaws in the philosophy of mercantilism and replaced it with the benefits of specialization and mutual trade. Trade has been increasing ever since, achieving very high rates after World War II. Global trade policies, encouraged by the World Trade Organization, are lowering trade barriers for all forms of business activity.

Foreign direct investment, or FDI, is another phenomenon that grew significantly in the second half of the twentieth century. FDI represents capital investment—such as building a factory or purchasing a company—in another country. When foreign capital is invested in the domestic market, it is labeled as inward FDI. When domestic residents invest capital abroad, it is defined as outward FDI. The motivations for FDI include (1) seeking new markets and cheaper resources, (2) avoiding trade barriers, and (3) strategically increasing efficiency of a firm's foreign operations.

When a company establishes a plant overseas, it usually imports capital goods to the foreign country. It may or may not export goods out of the country. FDI also contributes to the transfer of technology, which can benefit both countries. From a political perspective, FDI can be a sensitive issue. Foreign investment in domestic markets may be viewed negatively—as loss of ownership—to domestic outsiders.

Similarly, when domestic companies go overseas, critics will point to the loss in employment and income as negatives for the home country.

FDI and international trade will grow as long as trade barriers continue to fall under the stewardship of the World Trade Organization. Although there are occasional calls for protectionism, the growth of FDI and international trade continues unabated as we head toward a truly global market.

KEY CONCEPTS

International Trade Theory
Global Trade Patterns
Trade and the Economy
Foreign Direct Investment (FDI)
Global FDI Pattern
FDI and Trade

DISCUSSION QUESTIONS

1. Why is it difficult to measure international trade prior to the eighteenth century?
2. What is mercantilism and why is it not possible to maintain a mercantilist policy for long?
3. Assume that Country A can produce 100 units of wheat and 400 units of steel for a given amount of land, labor, and capital. Country B can produce 200 units of wheat and 350 units of steel with the same volume of land, labor, and capital. Show how specialization can increase total output. How much additional wheat and steel would each country get if they were to share the gains equally?
4. What is the difference between absolute advantage and comparative advantage in international trade?
5. Assume that Country A can produce 100 units of wheat and 200 units of steel for a given amount of land, labor, and capital. Country B can produce 50 units of wheat and 150 units of steel with the same volume of land, labor, and capital. Show how specialization can increase total output.
6. What is the basic premise of the Heckscher-Ohlin theory on international trade? Has empirical evidence supported this theory? Explain.
7. Explain how the product life cycle (PLC) theory can provide an explanation for trade flows between countries.
8. What is the WTO, and what role does it play in international trade?
9. Distinguish between foreign direct investment and foreign portfolio investment.
10. What are the forms and types of FDI? Explain the differences.
11. What are the major motivations for FDI? Explain them within the context of Dunning's OLI paradigm.
12. How can governments affect the flow of FDI into or out of a country? Explain how withholding taxes can affect the flow of FDI.
13. Discuss the relationship between FDI and international trade.

APPLICATION CASE: SIEMENS IN ARGENTINA

In recent years, as foreign direct investments have increased globally, the number of disputes over cross-border agreements has also increased. In 2008, an estimated 200 cases were pending with several tribunals.[14] The absence of a true global multilateral set of standards and rules to govern global investments has led companies and countries to use a variety of international tribunals to settle their cases. This, in turn, has led to a patchwork of rulings that are inconsistent and often contradictory across cases. One popular tribunal chosen by investors is the International Center for the Settlement of Investment Disputes (ICSID), an autonomous institution set up in 1995 under the auspices of the World Bank with 155 signatory countries. The ICSID finds itself struggling to adopt uniform rulings as the cases between sovereign nations and private companies are often complex and by no means clear-cut. One recent case involved Siemens AG in Argentina.

In 1998, Siemens IT Services of Argentina, a subsidiary of Siemens AG of Germany, was awarded a $1.26 billion contract by the government of Argentina to develop a national identification and immigration control system. The government was then headed by President Carlos Menem of the Justicialist Party. In 1999, Fernando de la Rúa of the Radical Civic Union Party became president of the country and annulled the agreement, citing irregularities in the procurement process. In 2001, Siemens took the case to international arbitration on the grounds that its contract was unjustly terminated. Six years later, after extensive hearings, the ICSID ruled in favor of Siemens and ordered the government of Argentina to pay $217 million in restitution and release $20 million posted by the company as performance bond.

In a separate incident in 2003, the auditors of a bank in Liechtenstein discovered a number of suspicious transactions originating from a company named Martha Overseas in Greece. The country of Liechtenstein had recently agreed to make its banking services more transparent in order to combat money laundering. Upon further investigation, the bank discovered that the disputed account belonged to an executive of a subsidiary of Siemens AG in Greece. The investigators gradually realized that they were uncovering one of the largest bribery scandals in corporate history. Siemens executives routinely used slush funds in overseas accounts to bribe officials in various countries throughout the world. A slush fund is not set aside for a specific purpose; slush fund money is sometimes used for questionable, or illegal, expenses. The scandal became public only when German authorities raided the offices of Siemens in November 2006. Nearly a decade earlier, Siemens was fined 200 million euros for its alleged role in bribing officials in several countries. As the investigation continued, U.S. and Swiss investigators found additional evidence of slush finds exceeding over $2 billion.

On August 15, 2008, Argentinean officials raided the offices of Siemens in Buenos Aires, the capital of Argentina. The new raids were prompted by evidence supplied by the German authorities indicating that Siemens may have continued to pay bribes to Argentinean politicians and government officers until 2004, even while the ICSID was holding hearings to determine the contract termination case. Argentina thereafter officially asked the ICSID to reconsider its earlier findings and rescind the $217 million in fines imposed in 2007. The request was based on the following grounds—if a company engages in bribery to obtain contracts, investment disputes do not fall within the purview of bilateral treaties, and that includes the current treaty between Argentina and Germany. It is very likely that ICSID may be forced to rescind its earlier decision and step out of the case altogether as evidence of the illegal payments are verified.

Siemens, a 160-year-old company, is bracing for further losses as a result of investigations worldwide. The company employs over 400,000 people in 160 countries and has a reputation for engineering excellence. This episode makes it clear that it is difficult for international arbitration panels to settle disputes when companies are confronted with local political environments that demand bribery in order to win contracts. In the United States, the Foreign Corrupt Trade Practices Act of 1977 strictly prohibits the bribing of foreign government officials to win contracts. In Europe, similar provisions were enacted on November 21, 1997, when the 30 OECD member countries and five nonmember countries—Argentina, Brazil, Bulgaria, Chile, and the Slovak Republic—adopted a Convention on Combating Bribery of Foreign Public Officials in International Business Transactions. After a period of lax intervention, European authorities are finally beginning to crack down on such behavior. In August 2008, German authorities initiated multimillion euro lawsuits against several of Siemens's previous executives for having knowledge of such clandestine activities and not taking actions to stop them.

QUESTIONS

1. Do you agree with the Argentinean authorities' decision to request the ICSID to rescind its earlier ruling and fine of $217 million? Why or why not?
2. Do you think laws preventing bribery will create a level playing field for business worldwide? Why or why not?

6 Entry Strategies

Companies can enter foreign markets using a variety of methods and various strategies. Each entry strategy provides unique benefits, but international companies also face many difficulties. Therefore, companies planning international expansion need to consider various factors in selecting an appropriate entry strategy.

LEARNING OBJECTIVES

- To learn about the various international market entry methods
- To understand the decision-making process in selecting a particular entry strategy
- To understand the export/import process
- To understand elements of export/import strategy
- To understand the differences between direct and indirect selling
- To understand the differences between licensing and franchising arrangements
- To understand the various strategic alliances that international companies undertake
- To understand the use and importance of joint ventures
- To understand why companies enter into joint venture agreements
- To understand why companies invest in a wholly owned subsidiary
- To understand the benefits and major issues faced by companies that invest in a wholly owned subsidiary

In deciding to go international, a company must choose an entry strategy to achieve its international expansion goals. Entry strategies set the stage for an international company's success in its expansion into overseas markets. Choosing the right entry strategy saves money and time, provides strategic advantages, and lessens the risks associated with international operations. The choice of a particular entry strategy is most often a result of a thorough analysis of the company's strengths and weaknesses and a comprehensive external environment analysis that includes the market potential. Some key internal factors that are considered include a company's core competencies and its risk threshold, or how much financial risk the company is willing to take. In entering a foreign market, a company can choose from a minimal investment option to one that requires a large investment. International companies can choose from four distinct entry strategies: exporting/importing, licensing/franchising, joint ventures, and wholly/fully owned subsidiaries. Licensing/franchising, joint ventures, and wholly owned subsidiaries require direct investments in the foreign country. Each strategy is designed for gaining entry into foreign markets under varying conditions. These entries are not necessarily unique to large international companies; small and medium-sized companies also use them.

As mentioned earlier, the selection of an entry strategy is often dictated by both internal and external factors the company faces. The firm's size, the number of products/services it offers, its financial position, its marketing expertise, and the number of countries the company operates in are some of the internal factors that may dictate its entry strategy. In the external environment, factors such as market size, potential growth of the market, regulatory environment, intensity of competition, knowledge of the market, and the host country's economic and political conditions might all play a role in the choice of entry strategy.

It is also possible that once a company selects a particular entry option, it might decide to shift into another mode based on internal and external changes. For example, a company that started out as an exporter might sometime in the future decide to enter into a joint venture agreement or even invest in a wholly owned subsidiary. Toyota Motors entered the U.S. market with exports of its vehicles from Japan; eventually it built manufacturing plants in the United States to serve the growing market it had captured. International companies have sometimes taken the reverse approach; that is, after starting out as a wholly owned subsidiary, a few have downsized their operations and used exports to cater to the needs of the market. For instance, after many years of operations in India, IBM left the country and returned as an exporter of its hardware and software.

A brief description of each entry strategy follows.

EXPORT/IMPORT STRATEGY

Exports are goods and services produced by a company in one country that are sold to customers in a different country. Importing is the purchase of goods and services by a company in one country from sellers located in another country. Importing is the reverse of exporting. Since importing is not necessarily a market expansion, but a means to efficiently distribute goods and services that reach a country, the discussion that follows will center on exporting.

Exporting is an easy entry strategy that is used by small, medium-sized, and large companies. Large global companies such as Boeing, Embraer (Empresa Brasileira Aeronáutica S.A.), GE, Panasonic, Philips, Siemens, and Toyota export their products all over the world. Similarly, large service companies such as AIG, Deutsche Bank, Goldman Sachs, and SAP export their services to many parts of the world. At the same time, these large companies also have wholly owned subsidiaries in many countries. Large global companies, therefore, may have export entry strategies *and* wholly owned subsidiaries to exploit the opportunities offered by larger markets in different ways.

Exporting is also used by smaller companies that do not have the resources or management expertise for engaging in a wholly owned subsidiary, but see the potential to sell in a given market through exports. In fact, there are more exporting companies in each country than those that have full-fledged invested operations. For every Boeing, there are literally thousands of small companies that are involved in exporting. For large and small companies, exports provide an opportunity to sell goods and services in other countries, increase their revenues, gain additional profits, test the market for further expansion, gain experience, and achieve economies of scale in their domestic operations. Exports are also known to improve productivity levels within companies and raise national productivity levels. In a study of 500 export managers in the United Kingdom, researchers found that exporting firms experienced faster productivity growth than nonexporting firms and, therefore, contributed more to national productivity growth.[1]

For some companies, an export strategy might be part of a well-laid international plan that evaluates markets, identifies potential, assesses competition, develops a marketing program, and identifies potential distributors. However, involvement in export might occur by chance; that is, a foreign distributor may request that a company's goods and services be sold in the distributor's country. The Internet and other worldwide media have exposed consumers to goods and services more rapidly than ever before. This has led to an increased demand for goods and services from many corners of the world. Through Web marketing, consumers in many countries are able to purchase goods and services that they find unique, that serve a particular need, and that are priced reasonably. Therefore, it is not uncommon for customers surfing the Web or reading a catalog in China to order cosmetics, computers, clothing, and other goods from a company based in another part of the world.

Small, independent entrepreneurs in particular find exporting attractive, as it requires no additional investment, very little additional personnel, minimal marketing effort, and an opportunity to increase revenues and profits at reasonably low risk. Exporting allows both small and large companies to tap into a new market without investing much time and effort and at the same time provides valuable lessons in entering foreign markets. Research has shown that the current performance of a company involved in exporting is influenced by the firm's past experiences.[2] Research has also shown that small and medium-sized companies can improve their export performance by better understanding the export process and also by increasing the level of commitment to exporting.[3] Exporting is also a good way to diversify risks; that is, economic downturn and loss of revenues in the domestic market could be compensated by the additional revenues and profits from exports. Exporting has proved useful in smoothing seasonal fluctuations in sales providing tax advantages; many governments, including that of the United States, encourage exports by offering tax incentives to international companies.

The disadvantages of exporting include higher transportation costs, which in some instances price a firm out of a market. Exporters also face trade barriers in the form of tariffs and nontariff barriers such as additional documentation, tedious inspections of goods, additional certification, and port-of-entry restrictions. In addition, many exporters face problems with inefficient and ineffective local agents. Finally, exports result in relatively lower rates of return compared to other modes of entry. Exporting

Figure 6.1 **The Export Process**

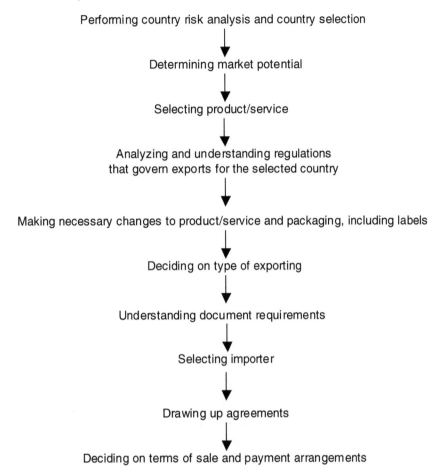

Performing country risk analysis and country selection

Determining market potential

Selecting product/service

Analyzing and understanding regulations
that govern exports for the selected country

Making necessary changes to product/service and packaging, including labels

Deciding on type of exporting

Understanding document requirements

Selecting importer

Drawing up agreements

Deciding on terms of sale and payment arrangements

allows companies to have control of the operations side of the business, but they must forfeit strategic marketing controls: most of the marketing functions are undertaken by the importer and the local distributors.

THE EXPORT PROCESS

The decision to export begins with the expectation that a company is committed to expanding its operations into overseas markets. Once it is established that a company wants to grow through international expansion, some critical steps must be taken in order for the firm to succeed in the foreign market. Although export strategy is relatively less complex than other entry modes, it does require careful planning and execution. The specific steps in the process are presented in Figure 6.1

Some of these steps are uniform to all the four modes of entry. For example, performing country risk analysis and determining market potential must be completed for exporting, licensing/franchising, joint venture, and wholly/fully owned subsidiaries. However, deciding on a type of exporting and selecting an importer are tasks performed only in exporting. Each of these steps must be carefully executed, especially by first-time exporters. After a firm has exported to a few countries, the lessons learned could make this process a little more easier.

PERFORMING COUNTRY RISK ANALYSIS AND COUNTRY SELECTION

The country risk analysis conducted for exporting is similar to the one conducted for most international expansion strategies. As outlined in Chapter 3, a country risk analysis evaluates a country's various external variables that might cause a company to lose assets, its intellectual property rights (IPR), its image, its competitiveness, or human life.

Country selection is often based on two key factors: market potential and country risk assessment. Country risk is evaluated by understanding the factors or variables that have an effect on the product (or industry) that is considered for export. The many variables that determine a country's risks include its economy, politics, culture, regulatory environment, social factors, technology, infrastructure, sophistication of the banking and financial systems, and geography. All of these variables are not necessarily critical for all types of goods and services. For example, in exporting chemicals to industrial users, factors such as the economy, political stability, and level of technology might be more critical than, say, cultural and social factors. Once identified, the critical factors may hold varying degrees of importance on the export plan, with some having a greater effect than others. Consider the case of the chemical exporter: the importing country's economy (because chemicals are an industrial product) and level of technology will probably have a greater impact on that company than the level of banking and the financial system. However, for an investment bank exporting its services to a foreign country, the level of the banking system would typically be of greater importance than technology.

Country risk assessment is undertaken by identifying the critical factors that affect a company's international operations, measuring each variable, and assigning weights to these factors to reflect the importance of each identified variable. In some of the large multinational companies, country risk assessment is conducted by internal staff who are specialized in this area, as these companies constantly need to identify potential countries (i.e., these companies expand their markets on a regular basis). Medium-sized international companies that do not have internal staff can hire professionals to conduct risk assessment studies. Some of the leading consulting service companies that provide risk assessment services include Control Risks Information Services, the Economist Intelligence Unit, and Standard and Poor's Rating Group. For smaller companies that do not have the internal staff or the funds to hire consultants, there are a few publicly available sources that are useful in assessing country risks. These include *Euromoney,* Japan External Trade Organization (JETRO), the *Financial Times,* and the U.S. Department of Commerce.

DETERMINING MARKET POTENTIAL

Market potential is the maximum available sales for a specific product/service in a given country for all companies operating in that industry. The potential is the upper limit of the size of the market. In most instances, this potential is never achieved because of less-than-optimal marketing efforts, environmental factors, consumer uncertainties, and substitutes that are close enough to the one marketed by the companies. For example, India's full market potential for automobiles is more than 3 million cars per year. At the present time, only 2.2 million cars are sold in India because of factors such as the high cost of the automobile, the poor road conditions, the cost of gasoline, and the high tariffs levied on imported automobiles. For these reasons, the Indian automobile market has never reached its full potential.

International companies are reluctant to enter foreign markets (even through exporting) unless the market potential is sufficiently large. Considering the cost of entry and the risks associated with international operations, companies avoid countries that offer a small potential with very few growth possibilities. Total market potential and demand for a company's goods and services are not one and the same. As explained, market potential is the upper limit in a given market, whereas a demand for a company's particular product is the estimated share of the total potential for that product that a company can achieve under ideal conditions. Most exporting companies try to establish a "sales forecast," which is the realistic goal within an expected demand under the total market potential.

SELECTING PRODUCT/SERVICE

Companies sell many products and services. In fact, larger companies may have hundreds of different products. For example, Unilever markets more than 660 different products in various countries of the world. Similarly, Citigroup offers nearly 100 different services to its retail and corporate clients. For the purposes of exporting, companies with multiple products/services must decide on one or a few on which to concentrate. When a company first begins exporting to a particular country, there might not be a demand for all the company's products/services. For example, when Deutsche Bank entered Malaysia for the first time, it offered only transactional services to its corporate clients and did not enter the retail banking sector until nearly a decade later. Similarly, when Natura Cosmetics of Brazil entered the Mexican market, it exported only skin care products for women, not its whole range of beauty care products. The limited offerings of smaller companies with a single product or service make the choice of the product/service to export easier.

In selecting the product or service to export, it is important to conduct market research in the chosen country to identify opportunities as well as constraints. Specifically, market research helps companies (1) to ascertain the demand for the product and the specific needs of the market, (2) to identify a target market, (3) to understand the unique characteristics of the market, and (4) to identify regulations that affect imports to the country. Selection of the product or service is sometimes made easier if a company receives unsolicited orders from abroad. In such instances, there is no need to conduct market research.

Analyzing and Understanding Regulations

Companies that export goods and services need to understand the specific regulations that apply to exporting to a particular country. These regulations include types of products that can be exported, regulations that cover the size or volume of the product, packaging and labeling restrictions, restrictions on the choice of distributors, rules regarding transfer of funds, and tariffs and quotas.

Foreign countries restrict the flow of goods and services to their countries for many reasons, among them

- To protect domestic industries; if a local industry is in its infancy, imported goods and services might affect its growth
- To force importers to comply with environmental controls; for example, many of the Nordic countries restrict importing goods that are packaged in nonbiodegradable material
- To protect the health of the people; for instance, the United States restricts toys containing lead-based paints (the 2007 recall of toys made in China is a good example of this)
- To comply with the local standards; requiring the metric versus English system of measurement is an example
- To prohibit goods and services that influence culture, especially clothing, movies, videos, and music
- To restrict goods and services from countries that are considered unfriendly, as in the case of many Middle Eastern countries restricting importation of goods and services from Israel
- To generate revenues; in other words, tariffs and other import duties not only help countries restrict flow of goods and services, they also generate revenues

Making Necessary Changes to Product/Service and Packaging, Including Labels

Companies that export goods and services quite often have to make adjustments to items that they sell to comply with local laws, cultural taboos, buyer preferences, local standards of living, local market conditions, and geographic and climatic conditions. For example, in introducing its retail banking services in Malaysia, Deutsche Bank had to revise how it calculated interest owed by clients in order to comply with the edicts of the Koran, which prohibits charging interest. Similarly, a German floor-tile manufacturer had to apply stronger glue to all the tiles exported to many Asian countries to address the hot and humid conditions there (if it had not done so, many of the tiles would have buckled and separated from the floors). Likewise, Unilever modified its shampoo packaging to introduce single-use sizes in many developing countries to reflect the standards of living (the price of full-size shampoos was prohibitive for local consumers).

Product and service changes to suit local conditions may take the form of minor modifications or major alterations. Simply changing the language on a package's label or changing the size of the package might be considered a minor modification. However, shifting the steering wheel from the left to the right in automobiles sold in Japan or making changes to appliances to fit the size constraints of small apartment units in some foreign countries are considered major modifications.

Finally, exporting companies have to consider the issue of warranties and after-sales service. Most products come with a warranty, especially high-priced items such as computers, appliances, automobiles, and telecommunications equipment. The question arises of who will perform the after-sales service, and how. On the one hand, the exporter's reputation is at stake; on the other, it might not be practical to provide overseas service from the exporting country. Normally, if the country is well developed, the warranty service can be provided locally. Exporters have also used local distributors to provide after-sales service by training the distributors and giving them incentives. If a country does not have the technology or skills to provide service locally, exporters have asked their customers to ship the products back for servicing or in some cases provided after-sales service at a third location. For example, Singapore and Australia are often used as warranty fulfillment centers by American and European exporters.

UNDERSTANDING THE DOCUMENT REQUIREMENTS

Exporting requires extensive documentation that describes the product, its origin, package size, value, and so on, and contains all pertinent information from both the exporter's and importer's point of view. Fortunately, beginning and even experienced exporters can make use of freight forwarders, specialists who act as travel agents for shipping cargo instead of people. These agents specialize in maritime as well as air freight. The various services provided by freight forwarders include quoting freight rates for all modes of transportation, preparing the necessary documents, making arrangements for the transportation and shipment of the product, and clearing customs and other regulatory requirements.

Some of the required export documents include the following:

- The *commercial invoice* is similar to invoices that are found in most domestic sales. The commercial invoice contains: the exporter's address; the importer's address; the invoice date; the number of units being shipped; the terms of sale, that is, whether it will be free on board (FOB) or cost insurance and freight (CIF); and the country of origin. A sample commercial invoice is presented as Figure 6.2.
- The *packing slip* contains the same information as the invoice except that it does not contain the price.
- The *bill of lading* is a receipt given by a carrier of goods, which could be a trucking company, a shipping company, or an air carrier, that agrees to carry the shipment to its final destination. The bill of lading is made to the order of the buyer and is a document of title. It can be used by the holder of the bill of lading as collateral for a loan.

Figure 6.2 **Sample Commercial Invoice**

COMMERCIAL PRO FORMA INVOICE

Date: _____ _____   Reference Number: _____ _____

Shipper:	Consignee/Importer:

VIA AIRFREIGHT

Country of Origin:	Country of (Temporary) Destination:

MARKS & NUMBERS	NO. OF PKGS	DESCRIPTION OF GOODS	WGT	QTY YDS	UNIT VALUE*	TOTAL

Value for Custom Purposes only.

Source: U.S. Department of Commerce, Economics and Statistics Administration, and U.S. Census Bureau, Bureau of Export Administration, Form 7525-V, "Shipper's Export Declaration." Available at http://www.census.gov/foreign-trade/regulations/forms/new-7525v.pdf.

- The *shipper's export declaration* contains information found in the commercial invoice and lists the relationship between the exporter and the importer (for example, if the importer is a subsidiary or under the control of the exporter), the names of the ultimate and intermediate consignee, transportation details (type of carrier, port of embarkation, port of disembarkation), and other pertinent information. Figure 6.3 is a sample shipper's export declaration.
- *Certificate of origin* is similar to a bill of lading and is requested by an importer to ensure that the origin of the goods is as stated in the commercial invoice and the bill of lading. Figure 6.4 is a sample certificate of origin.
- *Legalization and consularization* is required by some countries; a few of the documents must be approved by their consulate offices before shipping the items.
- *An insurance policy* is necessary in most cases of exports to cover any damages and losses that might occur in the shipment of goods.

DECIDING ON THE TYPE OF EXPORTING

Exporting channels can be direct or indirect. In direct exporting, an exporter deals directly with an overseas buyer, is actively involved with the operations, has control of the many aspects of the export process, and takes some risks. Because of the significance of the various activities associated with direct exporting, management has to commit substantial time and attention to achieve success. The direct exporter must be involved in the selection of the markets and distributors, must make most of the payment arrangements, and must do the follow-up work with the distributors. Direct exports have the potential to reap optimal results.

In indirect exporting, an intermediary is used to locate buyers, ship the goods, and collect payments. Several kinds of intermediaries are available, including export trading companies and export management companies. These are specialized agents who have knowledge of the various markets, well-established contacts with distributors in each country, and a wealth of experience. These intermediaries can be located through foreign government consulate offices or, in the case of many industrialized countries, through their own government agencies. For U.S. exporters, the Department of Commerce is a useful agency to identify intermediaries. The principal advantage of indirect exporting, especially for inexperienced small companies, is that it provides an easy means to penetrate foreign markets. Indirect exporting is easier to implement, requires fewer resources, and demands far less management time and commitment. Typically, indirect exporting results in less-than-optimal profits and market expansion. In service industries such as banking and insurance, direct selling is used with a branch or sales office to service the local customers. Figure 6.5 presents various export channels in direct versus indirect exporting.

The decision to use direct or indirect exporting depends on many factors, including the company's human resources capabilities, its financial resources, its size, the type of goods and services being exported, its prior knowledge of the importing country, prior exporting experience, and the country's general economic and business conditions.

Figure 6.3 **Sample Shipper's Export Declaration**

SHIPPER'S EXPORT DECLARATION

1a. U.S. PRINCIPAL PARTY IN INTEREST (USPPI) (Complete name and address)		
ZIP CODE	**2.** DATE OF EXPORTATION	**3.** TRANSPORTATION REFERENCE NO.
b. USPPI'S EIN (IRS) OR ID NO.	**c.** PARTIES TO TRANSACTION ☐ Related ☐ Non-related	
4a. ULTIMATE CONSIGNEE (Complete name and address)		
b. INTERMEDIATE CONSIGNEE (Complete name and address)		
5a. FORWARDING AGENT (Complete name and address)		
5b. FORWARDING AGENT'S EIN (IRS) NO.	**6.** POINT (STATE) OF ORIGIN OR FTZ NO.	**7.** COUNTRY OF ULTIMATE DESTINATION
8. LOADING PIER (Vessel only)	**9.** METHOD OF TRANSPORTATION (Specify)	**14.** CARRIER IDENTIFICATION CODE	**15.** SHIPMENT REFERENCE NO.
10. EXPORTING CARRIER	**11.** PORT OF EXPORT	**16.** ENTRY NUMBER	**17.** HAZARDOUS MATERIALS ☐ Yes ☐ No
12. PORT OF UNLOADING (Vessel and air only)	**13.** CONTAINERIZED (Vessel only) ☐ Yes ☐ No	**18.** IN BOND CODE	**19.** ROUTED EXPORT TRANSACTION ☐ Yes ☐ No

20. SCHEDULE B DESCRIPTION OF COMMODITIES (Use columns 22–24)

D/F or M (21)	SCHEDULE B NUMBER (22)	QUANTITY – SCHEDULE B UNIT(S) (23)	SHIPPING WEIGHT (Kilograms) (24)	VIN/PRODUCT NUMBER/ VEHICLE TITLE NUMBER (25)	VALUE (U.S. dollars, omit cents) (Selling price or cost if not sold) (26)

27. LICENSE NO./LICENSE EXCEPTION SYMBOL/AUTHORIZATION	**28.** ECCN (When required)
29. Duly authorized officer or employee	The USPPI authorizes the forwarder named above to act as forwarding agent for export control and customs purposes.

30. I certify that all statements made and all information contained herein are true and correct and that I have read and understand the instructions for preparation of this document, set forth in the **"Correct Way to Fill Out the Shipper's Export Declaration."** I understand that civil and criminal penalties, including forfeiture and sale, may be imposed for making false or fraudulent statements herein, failing to provide the requested information or for violation of U.S. laws on exportation (13 U.S.C. Sec. 305; 22 U.S.C. Sec. 401; 18 U.S.C. Sec. 1001; 50 U.S.C. App. 2410).

Signature	Confidential – Shipper's Export Declarations (or any successor document) wherever located, shall be exempt from public disclosure unless the Secretary determines that such exemption would be contrary to the national interest (Title 13, Chapter 9, Section 301 (g)).
Title	Export shipments are subject to inspection by U.S. Customs Service and/or Office of Export Enforcement.
Date	**31.** AUTHENTICATION (When required)
Telephone No. (Include Area Code)	E-mail address

This form may be printed by private parties provided it conforms to the official form. For sale by the Superintendent of Documents, Government Printing Office, Washington, DC 20402, and local Customs District Directors. The **"Correct Way to Fill Out the Shipper's Export Declaration"** is available from the U.S. Census Bureau, Washington, DC 20233.

Figure 6.4 **Sample Certificate of Origin**

CERTIFICATE OF ORIGIN

The undersigned _
(Owner or Agent, or Co.)

for _
(Name and address of shipper)

that the following mentioned goods shipped on S/S _
(Name of ship)

on the date of _ _ _ _ _ _ _ _ _ _ _ _ _ consigned to _

_ are the product of the United States of America.

MARKS AND NUMBERS	NO. OF PKGS., BOXES, OR CASES	WEIGHT IN KILOS		DESCRIPTION
		GROSS	NET	

Sworn to before me

Dated at _ _ _ _ _ _ _ _ _ on the _ _ _ _ _ day of _ _ _ _ _ 19 _ _ _ _

this _ _ _ _ _ day of _ _ _ _ _ 19 _ _ _ _

_ _ _ _ _ _ _ _ _ _ _ _ _ _ _ _ _ _   _
                                                 (Signature of Owner or Agent)

The _ , a recognized Chamber of Commerce under the laws of the State of

_ , has examined the manufacturer's invoice or shipper's affidavit concerning the origin of the merchandise and, according to the best of its knowledge and belief, finds that the products named originated in the United States of North America.

Secretary _

Source: UNZ & CO., Form No. 10-906. Copyright © 1990 UNZ & CO. Available at http://www.haasindustries.com/files/certificateOfOrigin.pdf.

Figure 6.5 **Export Channels**

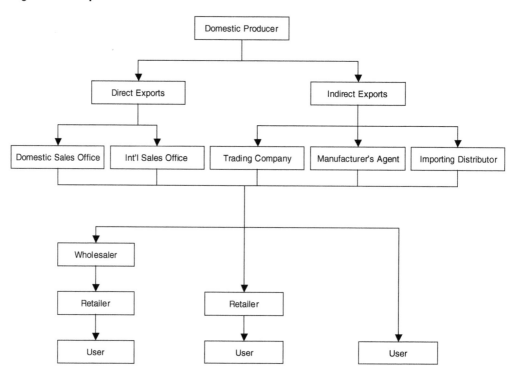

SELECTING AN IMPORTER

For companies that use indirect exports, the selection of the right importer is critical. Since the key marketing functions in the selected country are handled by the importer, an importer that has experience, knows the market, and can handle the local problems could be the difference between success and failure.

Importers can be small or large. The smaller companies, whose only business is to import, deal with fewer product categories and handle imports to just one country. At the same time, there are large multinationals involved in imports (besides conducting other businesses) that are active in many countries, handle a variety of products, and have a large number employees who specialize in certain functions such as dealing with the documentation, making payments, and arranging logistics.

One of the key factors to consider in selecting a qualified importer includes the firm's financial strength. Through research, credit checks, and other available secondary information, an exporter must determine whether the importer has the capital resources to make payments for the goods imported. Financial capability is a precondition to selecting a viable importer. The next factor to consider is the importer's experience. Exporters do not want an importer to learn the business with their products, as this will make it difficult to penetrate the market, and the importer's learning curve will make it hard to generate profits. The third factor to be considered is the importer's local market knowledge: it should be extensive, since the importer handles local marketing efforts, and the importer should demonstrate knowledge of the distribution system, the targeted customer, and the competition. It is also useful to determine the number of employees working with the importer, the size of its facilities, and its location.

DRAWING UP AGREEMENTS

International transactions require carefully drawn contracts and agreements. These are meant to protect both the exporter and the importer. The terms of the contract should include length of the specified arrangement, payment options, payment defaults, antipiracy clauses, geographical limitations, liability and safety issues with the exported product, who will fulfill warranty and guarantee services and how they will be fulfilled, and termination clauses. The contracts and agreements are drawn by legal specialists, and many are similar in content.

DECIDING ON TERMS OF SALE AND PAYMENT ARRANGEMENTS

The final steps in the exporting process (in some cases these may be agreed upon very early in the process) are the terms of sale and payment arrangements. Many conditions need to be agreed upon regarding terms of sale, but the critical ones are accounts payable and payment arrangements. Normally, exporters will not ship goods unless they have been guaranteed payment for the goods by a third party, usually a bank. The guarantee of payment is normally handled through a letter of credit (LC). An LC is a document with which the importer's bank extends credit to the importer and the bank agrees to pay the due amount to the exporter. In some cases, especially if the exporter has had a long-standing business arrangement with the importer, the exporter may extend terms that allow payment to be due after the goods have landed in the entry port. These terms may be for 30 to 60 days after the goods have arrived to help the importer manage its cash flow. Even in extending the credit terms, an exporter will still insist on drawing up a letter of credit to assure timely payments.

In some instances, an exporter might settle for a barter arrangement instead of a letter of credit for two reasons: (1) to gain entry into a market where economic conditions prevent the importer or the importing country from paying in foreign currencies, or (2) if some of the local commodities can easily be traded in the world market and, in some cases, the barter commodity is a raw material for the exporter. For example, in the 1980s Pepsi exported its products to the Soviet Union, which paid the company in either sugar or vodka. Sugar was a raw material in many of Pepsi's soft drinks, and vodka was easily traded for cash. Barter is also used in trade between countries. In an agreement between Indonesia and Thailand, Indonesia agreed to supply Thailand with small aircraft, train carriages, and fertilizer in exchange for rice from Thailand. The critical issue in barter is establishing equivalency between the bartered goods. Is one ton of Thai rice equal to one aircraft? In practice, the value is determined by the market value of the goods exchanged. In case of barter, it is necessary to negotiate the value of each barter for each transaction.

DIRECT INVESTMENTS

Entry strategies such as licensing/franchising, joint ventures, and wholly owned subsidiaries involve direct investments. Licensing/franchising and joint ventures are also referred to as "collaborative arrangements"—formal, long-term contractual agreement between companies.

Investments in foreign countries involve capital movement as well as noncapital movement. Most FDI flows does involve some capital movement, but licensing/ franchising involve other types of assets, including management expertise, technical systems, and so on. International companies may undertake investments in foreign countries for specific benefits, as detailed below.

RATIONALES FOR FOREIGN DIRECT INVESTMENT

Benefits

Spread the Investments and Reduce Risk. By operating in many countries, international companies can spread their overall risk, especially in managing operations in politically unstable countries. For example, British Petroleum (BP) has drilling and refining operations in the United States, the Middle East, Latin America, and Africa. It considers its operations in the United States and most of Middle East to be in politically safe regions, but its operations in Africa are vulnerable to political unrest. Because of its safer operations in other parts of the world, BP can limit its losses while operating in riskier regions such as Africa.

Avoid Local Competition. International companies enter into collaborative arrangements to improve their competitive position. By joining with local companies, a foreign company might gain a stronger position in the market than if it had acted alone. For example, in the early 1990s, Pepsi-Cola Corporation entered into a joint venture agreement with Punjab Agro Industrial Corporation, a state-owned entity in India, and Voltas Ltd. to distribute agricultural-based products as well as market its soft drink brands. The move helped Pepsi gain a stronger competitive position vis-à-vis its U.S. rival Coca-Cola, as well as in relation to its competitors.

Gain Market Knowledge. For most international companies entering foreign markets, the most vexing problem is a lack of knowledge of the local market. Collaborative strategies help these companies gain instant knowledge of the local market conditions through their partners.

Benefit from Specialization. By operating in countries that have distinct competencies that differ from the strengths of the collaborating firm, the collaboration will be mutually beneficial.[4] For example, Coca-Cola is strong in the bottling and distribution of soft drinks but lacks expertise in manufacturing the promotional items they sell such as clothing, caps and so on. To tap into the expertise that Coca-Cola lacks, it might enter into a collaborative arrangement with a foreign promotional items manufacturer.

Benefit from Geographic Diversification. By operating in multiple countries, international companies can smooth out revenues and earnings by generating income in countries whose economies are doing well even while underperforming in those that face an economic downturn. For example, Coca-Cola's operations in Asia had double-digit growth in 2006, a stark contrast to its flat revenues and earnings in the United States that same year.

Gain from Country of Origin Effects. Many consumers associate quality of goods and services on the basis of where they are made. For example, Switzerland is well known for its outstanding watches, France and Italy are known for their designs, Japan is known for producing quality automobiles, and the United States is recognized for its investment banking capabilities. Therefore, companies set up operations in foreign countries to gain from the country-of-origin effects. For example, GM's Opel automobiles, manufactured in Germany, are more highly regarded than its comparable U.S.-made vehicles.

Reasons

Avoid Legal Constraints. Many countries impose restrictions on imports and wholly owned subsidiaries to encourage local businesses to undertake operations that otherwise would be controlled or owned by foreigners. For example, China restricts full ownership of companies in many industries. One way for international companies to avoid these restrictions is to form partnerships with local businesses.

Reduce Costs. Many of the developing countries of Asia and Latin America have much lower labor costs, which attract foreign investors. The lower labor costs and reduction in other operational costs such as transportation and some utilities help companies to price their goods and services lower than in their home markets. The lower price tag in turn attracts segments of the local market that now can afford these products. For example, Whirlpool entered into a joint venture agreement with an Indian company to produce washing machines. Washing machine usage in India until then was very low due to the high cost of the machines and the fact that many Indian households had servants who did the wash. Once Whirlpool machines were available in the Indian market, sales of washing machines skyrocketed, as consumers were attracted by the lower prices as well as the status symbol associated with owning a washing machine.

Reduce Transportation Costs. A major problem with exporting is the added cost of transportation that is incurred by the buyer, especially for those products that have to travel long distances. For example, the distance between the United States and Japan is nearly 10,000 miles. For some products, such as clothing and toys shipped from China to the United States, the transportation cost is double the actual cost of the product itself.

Avoid Duties and Tariffs That Some Countries Impose on Imports. Even with growth in the number of countries joining the WTO, trade barriers in some form still exist. The most common trade barriers are in the form of tariffs that increase the landed price of a given product. For example, India levies tariffs of more than 100 percent on imported automobiles. Because of the high tariffs, many foreign manufacturers, such as Ford, GM, Hyundai, and Volkswagen, have set up joint venture operations in India.

Gain Control of Operations. Direct investments allow international companies to have a measure of control over their operations that would not exist in an exporting venture. One of the problems in exporting is a company's lack of control over its own marketing and related activities. Without this control, a company may fail to reach its full sales potential, may experience poor customer relations, and may encounter weak after-sales service. Through direct investments, an international company has much more control over its operations in a foreign country.

LICENSING AND FRANCHISING

Under a licensing arrangement, a firm grants "rights" to some process or other intangible property—such as patents, formulas, designs and the like—to another company for a specified period of time in exchange for a fee. For example, many clothing brands such as Vanderbilt jeans and Ralph Lauren Polo shirts license their designs for manufacture by companies in countries where they do not have distribution arrangements. The company providing the license is called the "licensor," and the recipient is called the "licensee."

Franchising is a specialized form of licensing in which the original company not only sells the use of a trademark—an essential asset for conducting business—but also assists the recipient on a long-term basis in the actual operations of the business. Some companies set up multiple franchise operations through a single business partner, who then might decide to open others in the country (subfranchisees). This helps the franchisor establish many outlets in one country without having to deal with a large number of individual operators. For example, Holiday Inn has many franchise hotels all over the world that are owned and managed by local entrepreneurs, but Holiday Inn provides assistance in terms of personnel, marketing, accounting, and food and beverage operations. A good number of franchise operations are from the United States. Most of these operations are in the service sector, especially hotels and fast foods. The franchise-granting company is called "franchisor," and the company receiving the franchise is called the "franchisee." Licensing and franchising are entry modes that have low developmental costs and relatively low risks. Countries that have been the beneficiaries of franchising arrangements seem to have high income levels, a well-educated population, and entrepreneurs willing to take risks.[5] In the United States, the franchising industry employs 11 million people, generating about 4.4 percent of the U.S. economic output.[6] For the remainder of this chapter, licensing and franchising will be discussed as if they are one and the same.

Advantages of Licensing/Franchising

Licensing/franchising offers a faster way than other modes of entry into foreign markets. Because the investment needs are small and the local operations are handled by the licensee/franchisee, the licensor is required to do very little analysis of the market. Licensing and franchising help companies extend their markets very quickly, and some of the risks of the expansion are borne by the licensee/franchisee. In some instances, licensing agreements also provide valuable technological benefits for the licensor. For example, Merck & Co. of the United States was able to obtain valuable ultraviolet-absorbing technology used in skin care products from Sol-Gel Technologies, its Israeli licensee.[7] Although licensing and franchising arrangements are easy to establish, it is important that the licensee/franchisee be carefully selected.

Selection of Licensing/Franchising Partners

The three principal considerations in most collaborative arrangements are decisions about operational factors, the importance of negotiations, and payment arrangements.

Factors that come to play in setting up licensing/franchising arrangements include the partners' financial capabilities, business knowledge, understanding of the local markets, experience, and enthusiasm for the business, all of which must be carefully evaluated. For example, Outback Steakhouse was very successful in South Korea when the local franchisee was given the freedom to use its local market knowledge and cultural patterns in developing local marketing strategies.[8] Similarly, in a study of franchising operations in Ireland, researchers found that franchises succeeded when the local company approached the agreement with higher commitment and used its knowledge of the local market in developing strategies.[9]

A second consideration in all collaborative entry strategies is the importance of negotiations between the two parties. This is a critical consideration in joint ventures, where the involvement is much more than an arrangement between partners involving investments, operational factors, and sharing of profits. Unless the partners in collaborative strategies feel that each party is being treated fairly, the collaboration will fail. Internationally, the process of negotiations is complex and takes considerable time, especially in the case of joint ventures.

A third factor in licensing/franchising agreement that requires special attention is the payment arrangements. In licensing/franchising, unlike in joint ventures, the parties in the agreement must reach an understanding on the terms of the fees and royalties to be paid to the licensor/franchisor. For the foreign company, this represents payments for its brand name and other intellectual property rights. There are no set standards for these payments, and, hence, the parties have to negotiate to arrive at fair fees or royalties. Some of the factors that play a role in the final settlement of the payments include volume of sales, future potential for growth, the life (perishability) of the technology, the extent of the contract, the relationship between the parties, and the licensor/franchisor's level of experience. The payment negotiations should also include how often (quarterly, semiannually, or annually) and in what currency payments will be made.

Disadvantages of Licensing/Franchising

Licensing/franchising is not without its share of problems. One of the disadvantages of licensing/franchising is the foreign company's lack of control over technology and intellectual property rights, especially in cases of high-tech companies operating in countries that lack piracy laws. A few companies, including Vanderbilt (jeans) and Apple (iPods), have seen their products copied and sold back into the market at a much cheaper price. In licensing/franchising, since the local entrepreneur is the one who handles the marketing of goods and services, the franchisor/licensor does not get a chance to learn about the local market. This also removes the learning curve experience for the foreign company's future international market expansions. Another disadvantage in licensing/franchising arrangements is that the foreign company does not fully benefit from market growth. For example, when Disney decided to enter Japan with its theme park in 1981, it was not sure how the Japanese would react to Disney characters such as Mickey Mouse, Pluto, and the like and decided to license the local partner instead of investing in a joint venture operation. Against all odds, Disney Tokyo became a huge success and the only revenues Disney gained from the success were the fees, not the profits, which would have been 10 to 20 times greater.

JOINT VENTURES

Joint ventures are direct investments in which two or more companies share ownership. Joint venture agreements can be established between companies and, in some cases, between a foreign company and the host government, with the foreign company's ownership at anywhere from 1 percent to 99 percent. The company that holds a majority in a partnership arrangement has controlling interest in the joint venture. Most joint venture agreements are long-term arrangements. Many developing countries encourage and provide incentives to foreign companies setting up joint venture operations. For these countries, joint ventures provide the maximum benefit.

Joint ventures allow developing countries to receive badly needed capital, valuable technology, and aid in the development of local entrepreneurial skills. Such business ventures also provide employment, help build local managerial talent, and make quality goods and services available to the people. Among the entry strategies, joint venture partnerships are probably the most popular and the most preferred by developing countries. Entering into a joint venture with a local partner provides the foreign company with an opportunity to learn about the partner's technology and operating methods, which might result in enhancing the competencies of the foreign company.[10] Joint ventures definitely have many advantages; but research has shown that nearly half of them dissolve after a few years.

Critical Factors in Forming Joint Venture

The critical factors in forming a joint venture are finding the right partner, developing mutual trust, sharing common business goals, resolving control issues, establishing an active partnership, and viewing shared benefits as greater than if each partner went on its own.

The Right Partner. As it is true in most collaborative strategies, one of the most important steps in joint ventures is finding the right partner. Joint venture partnerships are established when a foreign company actively seeks local partners in foreign countries or responds to proposals it receives from host-country businesses to form joint ventures. Before making a final decision, international companies seeking joint venture partners typically do exhaustive research on their most viable options, including contacting their embassies, reviewing business newspapers for leads, or hiring international research companies to select a joint venture partner. Failures in joint venture arrangements have been traced to problems between partners.[11] The selection of a suitable partner or partners is based on the value that the local partner brings to the table. Usually, the foreign firm is able to bring financial capital, technology, machinery, and personnel. The local partner's share might include capital, raw material and parts, knowledge of the market, government contact, and a supplier network. In selecting a partner, a foreign company is interested in whether the partners' assets and skills complement their own, and whether the foundations for a successful working relationship exist.

Mutual Trust. Joint venture partnerships are built on trust. One partner should not take advantage of another, and both should strive to make the joint venture a success. Some companies have successfully built trust through their actions as partners, that is, by investing time and effort in the joint venture to make its operations a success.[12] The day-to-day operations of a joint venture involve individuals working together, and, human behavior being what it is, problems can arise that undermine the joint venture. Since international joint venture arrangements are between companies from different countries, cultural and language differences can cause misunderstandings that lead to mistrust. Therefore, it is imperative that the managers involved in the joint venture maintain their focus on the goals of the partnership, openly discus issues before they become too complex to manage, and seek common ground when problems occur.

Common Business Goals. Right from the start, joint venture partners should establish mutually beneficial goals. These goals must be easily measurable, must be beneficial to all the partners, and must be equitable and fair. Most problems in joint venture arrangement arise from the sense that one of the partners is benefiting more from the venture than another. It is also critical that achievable goals be negotiated early in the relationship.

Control Issues. In a joint venture arrangement, because of the differences in ownership percentages, one partner (the majority owner) might have more control over the joint venture's operations. This may lead to differences in goals and strategies that could be viewed by one partner as not in its best interests. It is difficult for the minority partner to impose its ideas even if they are better for the joint venture operation.

Active Partnership. To be successful, joint venture partners must be active in the venture's operations. If one partner gives more management attention to the joint venture and the results are less than optimal, the other partner might blame the more active partner for the losses. There should not be a silent partner in a joint venture, as it creates mistrust and friction between the partners.

Shared Benefits. Finally, each partner should be convinced that it would not be able to achieve more if it had conducted the business on its own. That is, each partner should believe that the partnership results in much greater rewards than a lone venture would.

Advantages of Joint Ventures

A discussion of the many advantages of joint ventures follows.

Lower Investments. Because more than one partner is involved in a joint venture, the investment required of each partner is much lower than if a business began the venture on its own.

Shared Risks. As in the case of investments, risks are also shared, and each partner's exposure to those risks is lowered.

Taking Full Advantage of Market Potential. Since the foreign company is involved in some aspects of the operations and marketing, it has the opportunity to explore the local market fully.

Taking Advantage of Local Regulations. Many developing countries restrict entry of foreign companies but are willing to allow them to form joint venture partnerships. In some instances, to attract foreign companies to form joint ventures, countries may offer incentives in the form of tax breaks, discounts on utilities, and easier terms for repatriation of profits.

Partners' Complementary Skills and Resources. Quite often, the joint venture partners have complementary skills that give them a strong competitive position. For example, Motorola of the United States formed a joint venture with WiPro Technologies of India. Together, they deliver managed services and computing mobility that taps into the cellular phone technology of Motorola with the software expertise of WiPro Technologies.[13]

Making Full Use of the Profit Potential. As in the case of making full use of sales potential through joint venture partnerships, these arrangements also result in fully utilizing the profit potential of the market.

Gaining Relationships with Government, Suppliers, and Customers. Host countries' governments view joint ventures as the preferred mode of entry, so the foreign investor who forms joint ventures is perceived more favorably and gains politically. Besides, the local partners in joint ventures are usually business owners who have long-standing relationships with government agencies, suppliers, and customers, which then become part of the joint venture network. This relationship helps the foreign company succeed where going on its own would have posed problems, as it would have to establish its own network and build relationships from the bottom up.

Acquiring Knowledge of the Market. One of the reasons foreign owned companies fail in overseas markets has been attributed to their lack of knowledge of local market conditions and difficulties posed by the cultural differences. By taking on a local partner, the foreign company is able to instantly acquire knowledge of the local market and existing cultural nuances, and it becomes easier for the foreign company to develop strategies that succeed.

Gaining Experience. International companies that look for growth in foreign countries learn from each experience they have with a new market. By joining a local joint venture partner, the international company gains experience with minimal risk as its local partner can help it to navigate through difficult situations. Each joint venture experience makes the next one that much easier. For example, GE was always reluctant to undertake joint venture agreements; it was driven by having control of its operations, and in joint ventures companies need to cede at least some of the control. But once GE entered into a joint venture arrangement with a French company, it found it to be a very easy form of entry, and since then it has entered into many joint venture partnerships.

Disadvantages of Joint Ventures

One of the disadvantages of joint ventures is the lack of control over the overall business operation. For successful international companies, this is a major issue: at times they cannot implement their proven and successful strategies because of interference by the local partner. Equally troublesome for international companies is the loss of control over their technology. There have been incidents in which local partners have pirated foreign technology and then competed against their previous joint venture partners not only in local markets but also in other overseas markets. Even with a local partner, joint ventures are high-cost, high-risk investments, because the expectations of the foreign company are very high and the results of the joint venture might not meet those expectations. Joint ventures are not easy to manage due to differences in philosophies, cultures, business practices, and prevailing goals.

WHOLLY OWNED SUBSIDIARIES

The most complex and high-risk form of direct investment occurs when a foreign company owns a local subsidiary outright. It can accomplish this by acquiring a local company, or it can build from the bottom up by buying or leasing land, building a plant, and embarking on business operations in the host country; this is referred to as a "greenfield investment." There are definite advantages to acquiring a local company, including the shorter time required to set up such an operation compared to starting from scratch. Additionally, there are difficulties in transferring resources to a foreign operation, especially when the local conditions are drastically different from those in the home country.[14]

Wholly owned subsidiaries assume that the international company is ready to fully explore the foreign market and reach the full potential the market offers. Through wholly owned subsidiaries, an international company takes full control of all its operations, including marketing. Control is very important for some companies, particularly those that have managerial or technical expertise. Sharing this expertise—as a firm would in a joint venture, for instance—might lead to piracy and reverse competition. Having a wholly owned subsidiary is a high-investment venture, but if successful it can be an added benefit in a global expansion strategy. When companies invest in a wholly owned subsidiary, they also lessen the probability of developing local competitors. In essence, this approach, which is referred to as *appropriability theory,* denies competitors access to resources.[15] Wholly owned subsidiaries are not the normal mode of expansion for small companies, since the investments and risks are so high. Besides tapping into the full potential of the new market, wholly owned subsidiaries offer larger companies the protection of their technologies, an important factor for high-tech companies specializing in electronics, chemicals, pharmaceuticals, and telecommunications.[16]

Wholly owned subsidiaries are a gamble because of the high investments involved and the risk of entering into an unknown market. Lack of knowledge about local conditions, difficulties in building supplier networks, cultural differences, and host-country regulations that mostly favor local companies make full ownership of a foreign subsidiary challenging. The type of subsidiary ownership a foreign company chooses is also to some extent the outcome of the host-country market and regulatory environment. For example, most foreign companies that invest in the United States do so in the form of greenfield investments. Hence, companies such as Canon, Nestlé, Olympus, Siemens, Toyota, and Unilever operate as wholly owned subsidiaries of their parent companies. However, investments in developing countries and some of the emerging markets take the form of joint ventures or other type of ownership, including licensing/franchising and exporting. As mentioned earlier, developing countries prefer joint ventures because they assist local companies in gaining managerial expertise and technical knowledge while providing employment. For example, most foreign operations in China are in the form of joint ventures. Wholly owned subsidiaries also take time to implement, whereas a joint venture can be up and running fairly quickly.

COMPARISON OF THE VARIOUS MODES OF ENTRY STRATEGIES

When ranking various entry strategies by ease or difficulty, it appears that an export entry is the easiest to implement, but the exporter does not have control of the operations and is not able to develop the full potential of the local market offers. On the other hand, a wholly owned subsidiary offers full control and the foreign company is able to exploit the market's full potential, but this mode of entry is risky and takes time to implement. The other two modes of entry, joint ventures and licensing/franchising,

Table 6.1

Comparison of Various Entry Strategies

Factors		Exporting	Licensing/ Franchising	Joint Ventures	Wholly Owned Subsidiaries
1	Ease of entry	High	Medium	Medium/high	High
2	Speed to market	High	Medium	Medium/high	Low
3	Regulatory constraints	Medium	Low	Medium	High
4	Market penetration	Low	Medium	Medium/high	High
5	Access to customer feedback	Low	Low	Medium	High
6	Control of operations	Low	Low	Medium	High
7	Management commitment	Low	Low	Medium	High
8	Cost, tariffs, fees	Med.	Medium	Low	Low
9	Capital needs	Low	None	Medium	High
10	Profit potential	Medium	Low	Medium	High
11	Financial risks	Low	Low	Medium	High
12	Technology risks	Medium	High	Medium	Low
13	Economies of scale	High	Low	Medium	Medium
14	Nationalization risk	Low	Low	Medium	High

do not offer control of the operations but are easy to implement. Table 6.1 presents a comparison of the ease and difficulties involved in the various entry strategies.

CHAPTER SUMMARY

In entering foreign markets, international companies have four distinct entry modes available: exporting, licensing/franchising, joint ventures, and wholly owned subsidiaries. Of the four modes of entry, exporting is the easiest to implement. It also has the advantage of low investment and allows international companies to gain knowledge and experience in international markets. However, exporting does not allow the company to exploit the full potential of the market, and the loss of control of operations and marketing could pose problems in the future.

Licensing/franchising is another low-investment entry mode that some companies pursue. Like other foreign market strategies, licensing/franchising has its share of problems, including the fact that it does not allow the international company to exploit the full potential of the market, and it can result in loss of control—especially in the area of intellectual property rights, which might lead to piracy and related problems.

The joint venture is the entry mode most commonly used by international companies, as it provides sufficient control and allows the international company to fully exploit the market. It is also the entry mode preferred by developing countries. In addition, the local partner complements the expertise of the foreign company with its superior knowledge of local market conditions and also can help the joint venture partnership through its relationship with the local supplier network.

Wholly owned subsidiaries provide the maximum control of foreign operations with the potential to fully exploit the local market. At the same time, this entry mode requires the highest investment and carries with it high risks.

KEY CONCEPTS

Export Process
Export Strategy
Licensing/Franchising
Joint Ventures
Wholly Owned Subsidiary

DISCUSSION QUESTIONS

1. Identify the four entry modes used by international companies in entering new markets.
2. When and why would you use export as an entry mode?
3. What are some of the disadvantages of exporting?
4. Identify the various collaborative strategies used by international companies in entering foreign markets.
5. Discuss the advantages and disadvantages of licensing/franchising agreements.
6. Why and when do international companies use joint ventures?
7. What is the biggest advantage of using greenfield investments in international business?
8. Compare the four entry modes. Does any single one appear to have an advantage over the others?

APPLICATION CASE: GENERAL ELECTRIC

General Electric (GE) is a diversified global company with its headquarters in Fairfield, Connecticut. In 2006, GE's worldwide net earnings were $21 billion on revenues of $163 billion. GE has been at the forefront of both industrial and consumer goods and services. Under its legendary CEO Jack Welch, the company was known for its commitment to excellence and its market dominance in all the various business areas in which it was involved. With Welch at the helm, GE would withdraw from a market if it did not hold either the number one or number two position in terms of market share. Yet another of GE's strict philosophies was: "If you don't have full control, don't do the deal." This meant that GE's mode of entry into a new country was either as an exporter or as full owner of a subsidiary.

For years, GE would enter a new market by buying up a small company and taking it to the top through its proven strategic initiatives and management approach. Internally, the process of taking small operations into market leaders was referred to as "GE-izing." Lately, GE's approach to entering foreign markets has become difficult because of shifting market conditions, including the growth of large local competitors. During the 1980s and 1990s, GE would enter a new country with a bag full of money and buy up whatever it wanted. But these days, if there are opportunities to gobble up small companies, it is being done by private equity funds with even greater money power. According to GE's current CEO, Jeffrey Immelt, the days when it could buy whatever it wanted are pretty much over. It seems that it is better for GE to partner with a number three company that wants to be number one. In the past, GE had a few joint ventures—for example, its 50/50 partnership with Snecma, the French manufacturer of aircraft engines—but these ventures came about after GE had explored other ways to gain access to a particular market technology. In the case of the Snecma joint venture, GE could not have bid for Airbus engine contracts without the help of the French government.

In a shifting marketplace and with globalization forcing companies to be nimble and have shorter reaction time, GE is slowly rethinking its philosophy of "control" over its operations. For GE, the global market is an increasingly important factor in driving its growth strategy. Much of its growth in the past few years has come from its overseas operations. More important, the growth markets are the emerging countries of Asia, including China. GE has very little market presence in China or in other Asian countries. In many of these countries, the legal and cultural landscape is a difficult to understand, making it better for an international company to have a local partner who is familiar with the local market conditions. Therefore, when an opportunity arose for GE to set up a retail lending arm in South Korea with Hyundai Capital, it explored the feasibility of being a minority joint venture partner, with a 43 percent stake in the new venture. Hyundai Capital offers credit cards, auto loans, and mortgages. Each of these services requires a thorough understanding of local consumer behavior, cultural nuances of lending, and the financial legal systems. GE could not have embarked into this environment alone and been successful.

QUESTIONS

1. Analyze GE's entry strategy philosophies of the 1980s and 1990s in comparison with their philosophies of today.

SOURCE

This case was developed from articles in *International Herald Tribune* and *Wall Street Journal.*

7 Functional Integration

Businesses are organized around functions, but their activities need to be coordinated in order to efficiently employ the resources of an international company.

LEARNING OBJECTIVES

- To understand the importance of functional integration
- To identify the critical factors in the integration of the various functions of an international company
- To understand the procedures used in integrating functional areas
- To understand the complexities of integrating functions in an international organization

Businesses are organized around functions as a way to benefit from specialization of activities. Most medium-sized and large international companies are organized into eight functional areas: accounting, administration and legal, finance, human resources management (HRM), management information systems/information technology (MIS/IT), marketing, production and operations management (POM), and research and development (R&D). The strategic decisions a company develops center on these functions. Hence, we have human resources strategy, marketing strategy, and so on. The critical question for managers is, how will an international company manage these diverse functions in developing the most effective strategies and maximizing the available resources? International companies view development of their strategies as a collective effort, even though the company develops strategies specific to each function. In other words, strategies for a function such as marketing are developed in conjunction with and through the coordination of activities in the areas of production, finance, R&D, and so on. Coordination is the critical process in linking and integrating an international company's various functions and activities. Figure 7.1 presents how the functions are linked to one another.

Due to the growing emphasis on customer satisfaction and customer relations, companies have been forced to rethink their organizational emphasis away from individual functions and toward more interdependent customer groupings. Research has shown that interdisciplinary thinking and a cross-functional approach to streamline process and delivery strategies improve overall coordination of functions.[1] Some researchers suggest that companies need to organize to make full use of the synergies between individual

Figure 7.1 **Functional Linkages**

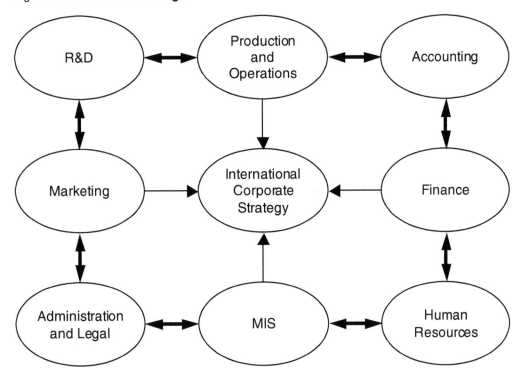

functions to provide the necessary focus on customers.[2] For example, Intel Corp., under CEO Paul Otellini since 2005, reorganized to bring together its engineering, software-writing, and marketing functions to offer a much more coordinated group that can service its customers more effectively.[3] The interdependent and well-coordinated functional linkages that many companies are introducing are turning out to be an effective way to gain an advantage in a highly competitive global environment by creating capabilities that are strengthened through synergies.[4] It seems synergy through integration is the catchphrase for attaining organizational effectiveness.[5]

In fact, academic research has shown that there are some functions that are naturally linked to one another. Functions such as R&D, manufacturing, and marketing seem to flow logically from one to the other. Studies have shown that superior business performance can be achieved through integrative approaches.[6] That is, the innovations created by R&D are implemented in the manufacturing process and in the development of new products, and these are then sold by the marketing department to potential customers. Hence, the integration of these functions is necessary for the production and successful marketing of goods and services.[7] Similarly, marketing and information systems go hand in hand, and their activities should be integrated. Marketing strategies across countries and functions can be made more effective by sharing these strategies through information systems and avoiding duplication.[8]

Global integration of functions within an organization is essential in managing the multifaceted activities of international companies that are spread over many regions. Through coordination and control of business operations, international companies can integrate corporate functions more smoothly.[9] International functional coordination results in linkages among geographically dispersed units and their varied functions. Because international business is an interdisciplinary area, a thorough understanding of the independence of each function is required, along with the ability to recognize the interdependence of the various functions; that is, each function is only effective when combined with other functions. For example, international operations deal with the generation of goods and services for consumption by users. But to produce goods and services, the operations side of the business has to have the right personnel (HRM), and depends on the finance group for the necessary funds, the accounting department for control of the operations, the R&D department for technologically superior materials and innovative products, and the marketing department to use its resources for selling the goods and services.

Individually, each function undertakes specific and unique activities that benefit from specialization. For example, assembly workers in a manufacturing plant that produces automobiles are more efficient in that function than at evaluating an investment opportunity. Evaluating investment opportunities is best left to the people in the finance department. Specialization results in more efficient use of resources within a functional jurisdiction. In-depth knowledge of a function and repeated use of the knowledge allows personnel within a function to be more productive; this is known as *the learning-curve effect.*

Following is a summary of activities that fall under each of the eight functions. (A detailed treatment of six of the critical functions is presented in Chapters 8 through 13).

PRODUCTION AND OPERATIONS MANAGEMENT

The following activities are associated with production and operations management. (See Chapter 8 for a more complete discussion of this topic.)

SOURCING

Sourcing is part of supply-chain management. International and domestic companies search globally for sources of raw materials and components to take advantage of lower prices and better designs: in some instances, a few countries serve as the exclusive sources for some raw materials. For example, Brazil is the largest producer of coffee beans and South Africa is the largest producer of diamonds. Hence, these countries offer the best opportunities to obtain coffee beans and diamonds, respectively.

SETTING UP MANUFACTURING FACILITIES

International companies set up manufacturing facilities in many parts of the world to be closer to their markets. For example, Siemens of Germany has many manufacturing facilities in Europe (Denmark, Germany, and the Netherlands), Asia (Singapore), and the Americas (the United States). These different facilities produce different products, depending on the particular demand for a product, the available level of technology, the labor force's skills, and investment requirements. Therefore, an international company operating in multiple countries might have a highly sophisticated and technologically advanced manufacturing plant in one country and a labor-intensive and low-technology manufacturing facility in another country. Michelin, the French tire maker, has quite a few manufacturing plants in Europe, including those in France, Germany, and Italy, that are fully automated and employ very few assembly workers, but its plants in Asia, including one in India, are labor intensive and tend to have low-technology assembly lines.

LAYOUT

Modern manufacturing facilities and service centers to handle customer transactions are built around efficiency and maximization of available space. This involves bringing people, machines, and space together. The layout helps companies manage the flow of material, people, and machines in the most efficient way in producing goods and services.

DESIGN AND TECHNOLOGY ISSUES

Design of goods to some extent influences the amount and types of materials and other inputs that are required to produce a product. For example, in the 1980s many automobile manufacturers began using plastic components instead of metal in the assembly of cars to reduce the weight of the car and achieve higher gas mileage. This shift from metal to plastics was made possible through design changes and the development of stronger plastics and epoxies for attaching the plastics. Also, when international companies implement standardization strategies across countries, they rely on universally accepted designs to accomplish this cost-saving strategy. In designing the overhead luggage bins in its latest versions of planes, for instance, Boeing placed the door openings at the bottoms of the luggage bins instead of the top to accommodate height differences between passengers from different countries (many of the European passengers being taller than some of their Asian counterparts).

QUALITY CONTROL

Good quality is essential for the success of a company's products and services. Quality control is the management of the quality of finished goods and services. Quality is relative, though, and standards vary from country to country. In an industrialized country, where multiple brands of goods and services are available and where the competition is intense, companies might have to offer very high-quality products. In countries with limited offerings, where consumers do not have many choices, the quality of the products offered might not meet the standards of industrialized countries. For example, the cars in Germany are of much higher quality than the ones available in Bolivia.

INVENTORY MANAGEMENT

Inventory management encompasses the activities involved in developing and managing the inventory levels of all materials, components, and finished goods to maintain an adequate supply of these items to ensure availability. With an efficiently designed inventory control system, international companies can save on costs and ensure timely supply of materials and finished goods in the marketplace.

FINANCE

The following activities are associated with the finance function. (See Chapter 13 for a more complete discussion of this topic.)

FINANCING

Financing is the acquisition or sourcing of funds for use by an international company for operations and investment. Most international companies have a variety of sources for raising capital, both internal (within the company) and external (from outside sources). Internally, companies raise funds from retained earnings and through dividend policy, intracompany borrowings (especially from subsidiaries), and the management of accounts receivables and payables (lead/lag effect). External sources consist of equity, loans, bonds (including Eurobonds), and government grants, including incentives and subsidies.

INVESTMENTS

Investments are decisions a company makes on how its available funds should be allocated. Investment decisions are influenced by many factors, including the company's investment policies, the types of projects selected for investment (for example, should the company invest in a manufacturing plant in China or a joint venture arrangement in Vietnam?), and the returns on each investment. Investment decisions are governed by the fact that each company has limited resources and, hence, needs to utilize the funds judiciously. Most investment decisions are made by evaluating the projects using one of the more accepted assessment techniques, such as net present value (NPV), internal rate of return (IRR), or adjusted present value.

WORKING CAPITAL MANAGEMENT

Working capital management is the selection of the best possible mix of cash, marketable securities, accounts receivables, and inventory (current assets) that can be used to maximize the value of the firm. For international companies, there are the additional considerations of exchange controls, currency fluctuations, and countries' differential tax rates. The objectives in working capital management are to manage the company's cash resources efficiently and to achieve maximum conservation and utilization of the available funds.

DESIRED CAPITAL STRUCTURE

A company's desired capital structure is important in deciding how the firm's total sources of funds should be divided between equity and debt. Furthermore, for loans, management must determine how much of the debt should be divided between long-term and short-term financing. A company's responses to these issues determine the amount of financial leverage the company is employing. The capital structure of firms varies from industry to industry and from firm to firm.

MANAGING FOREIGN EXCHANGE RISKS

By definition, international companies operate in more than one country. Hence, they transact business in multiple currencies and are frequently exposed to the risks associated with fluctuations in currency exchange rates, that is, the amount of gains or losses attributed to currency fluctuations. International companies are exposed to a variety of risks, including transaction risk (the effect of exchange rate change on foreign-currency-denominated transactions) and translation exposure (change in the value of a firm's foreign-currency-denominated accounts due to changes in exchange rates).

DEBT POLICIES

Each international company has its own set of guidelines on how much debt it is willing to service during the life of a project. Some are willing to finance their operations from debt, and others consider this too risky. Some companies' tolerance for debt capacity, that is, the amount of debt-type securities a firm can service, is relatively higher than that of other companies.

MARKETING

The following activities are associated with the marketing function. (See Chapter 11 for a more complete discussion of this topic.)

SELECTING TARGET MARKETS

A target market consists of potential buyers of a company's goods and services. In selecting a target market, international companies distinguish the market by important consumer variables such as demographics, buyer behavior, and the like, and then decide to sell to one or more of these groups, called the target markets. In marketing a particular product, an international company may target the same group (also called segment) in every country in which it operates, or it may target a different market from country to country. For example, in selling its shampoo products, Unilever may target a segment made up of middle-class consumers in Europe and the United States, but may target just the upper-middle-class group in Indonesia.

UNDERSTANDING CONSUMERS' NEEDS

People need basic items such as food, clothing, and shelter to survive. In addition, people need products and services to look good, to be entertained, to participate in leisure activities, and so on. Different groups of consumers satisfy these needs through different products. For example, to satisfy hunger, some consumers may go to a grocery store and buy ingredients to cook a meal at home, some may buy a pizza from a pizza parlor, and still others may eat at a fancy restaurant and spend a considerable amount of money to satisfy their basic need. Each of these situations provides opportunities for marketers to sell goods and services to various target markets by country.

INTERNATIONAL MARKET RESEARCH

International market research is a systematic technique to collect and analyze information from different countries. This information is used by international marketing managers to make strategic decisions. The necessary information may be gathered from internal sources or external sources, or it may be obtained through research vendors who provide specific information on particular problems or issues a company faces.

DEVELOPING PRODUCTS AND SERVICES

After selecting the target market and identifying the needs of its customer base, international companies have to place their products and services in the chosen market. For global companies, it is often a question of determining which of their product items are best suited for the various international markets. If possible, companies would like to sell the same product or service that is sold in their domestic market without any modifications (otherwise known as standardization). For example, Gillette's Mach 3 Turbo shaver has the same features and packaging in United Kingdom that it has in the United States. In some instances, due to differences in taste, purchasing power, or regulations, international companies are forced to modify their products when they enter new markets. McDonald's sells veggie burgers in India instead of beef burgers, as eating beef is taboo according to Hindu religion.

SETTING PRICES

Setting prices is a critical activity for international marketers. On the one hand, price produces revenue for the company, and as such, it puts pressure on the marketers to produce as much revenue as possible. On the other hand, for customers, cost is a major factor in the decision to purchase goods—they like to pay as little as possible for a given product. Marketers have to find a fine balance between these two aspects of pricing. Most companies set their prices based on cost, demand for the product, and the unique competitive advantage that a particular brand might have in the marketplace. Price is a flexible marketing element that can be changed very quickly, is often copied equally quickly, and is used for comparison purposes by customers.

SELECTING CHANNELS OF DISTRIBUTION

Marketers use channels, or marketing intermediaries, to get their products from the manufacturing facilities to the customers. This is the downstream part of the supply chain. Even though some international companies such as Dell Computers and Avon Cosmetics use direct channels rather than intermediaries, most companies do not sell directly to the consumer. Channels allow marketers to focus their attention on their core competencies and not be diverted into activities that may be handled more efficiently by another source. The main purpose of channels is to facilitate the movement of goods and services from their source to the place where there are customers who want them. Channel membership (the number of intermediaries) varies from country to country, and international marketers select channels that best suit their requirements

PLANNING COMMUNICATION STRATEGIES

To succeed, marketers must not only produce quality products but also must let the target customers know about them. Passing on the necessary information to customers to generate sales is achieved through a comprehensive communication program. In communicating with their customers, international companies need to decide on a specific target group, have a clear message, and make sure that the target group understands that message. International companies make use of different media to reach their customers, including television, print media, the Internet, and so on. One of the most important issues for international marketers to consider is the cultural and legal barriers that restrict their message content or selection of a medium.

RECOGNIZING THE IMPORTANCE OF CUSTOMER RELATIONS

Most companies realize that acquisition of new customers is a costly activity, so companies make every attempt to retain as many of their existing customers as possible. Customer relations management (CRM) attempts to streamline the process of customer acquisition and retention through a systematic approach. The focus of CRM is to manage the relationship between a company and its customers through proactive initiatives such as understanding individual customer needs, understanding customers' likes and dislikes, gathering as much information on each customer as possible, responding to customers' concerns in a timely manner, and generally being a concerned partner rather than viewing customers as adversaries. The emergence of computerized databases and sophisticated communication systems has helped international companies manage this activity much more easily.

EVALUATING MARKETS AND OBTAINING FEEDBACK

Customer feedback enables companies to identify weaknesses in their marketing strategies and provides the necessary information to modify these strategies. Customer feedback should be continuously collected to improve the product/service and a company's marketing program. Through scanner data, information from syndicated service companies such as Nielsen, and customer surveys, international companies are able to obtain extremely valuable feedback.

HUMAN RESOURCES

The following activities are associated with the human resources function. (See Chapter 12 for a more complete discussion of this topic.)

RECOGNIZING THAT HUMAN RESOURCE MANAGEMENT IS PEOPLE DRIVEN

Human resources management (HRM) recognizes people as an organization's key resources.[10] Managers, staff, and technicians run the operations of a company. Hence, utilizing this resource efficiently is critical to an international company's success. Japanese companies, with their people-driven philosophy and lifelong employment policy, have achieved phenomenal success in international markets. For many American companies, the ethnocentric and parochial human resource systems and policies that they inherited, which focused on the parent company and were projected onto the rest of the world, are found to be a barrier to the implementation of effective global organizational processes.[11]

KNOWING THE EXISTING SKILLS AND TRAINING OF COMPANY PERSONNEL

To develop an effective human resources management program, a company has to identify the existing skills, qualifications, experience, and potential of its employees by conducting a sort of audit or inventory. This is especially true for international companies because of their widespread operations and the cultural diversity of their employees. By recognizing its internal capabilities, a company can develop a more realistic HRM plan for its operations.

HUMAN RESOURCES PLANNING

Human resource planning is a systematic way to project the HRM needs of an international company throughout its operations. It outlines the specific jobs to be filled by location; the necessary qualifications and experience of each employee; where various employees should come from (that is, the home country, the host country, or a third country); and the optimal mix of these employees. By planning ahead, international companies are able to fill present vacancies and hire for future needs.

RECRUITING AND SELECTION

Recruiting and selection encompass the process of finding the most suitable person for a specific job. Companies have to identify, screen, and select candidates from a pool of possible recruits. For international companies, sources of recruits include internal candidates, candidates from competitors in the home country, internal candidates from the company's regional or subsidiary offices, candidates from host-country competitors, and other host-country nationals. Through various screening devices, interviews, and tests, companies try to select the best possible candidate for each job opening.

COMPENSATION

Compensation packages are set to attract the most qualified personnel. Most international companies compensate their employees based on the prevailing compensation packages in their industries. International companies operating in developing countries tend to pay higher salaries and benefits than most local companies do. For international companies, this premium package leads to hiring the most qualified individuals in a given country. Furthermore, most locals prefer to work for international companies rather than local companies due to the higher compensation package and the prestige associated with working for an international company.

TRAINING AND DEVELOPMENT

International companies provide their employees with training in an effort to help the employees complete their assigned tasks effectively. These programs may be directed at enhancing specific job-related skills, such as training in a particular software package, or may be more general in nature, such as providing cultural orientation to an employee assigned to a foreign country. The purpose of all training programs is twofold: (1) to improve the productivity of an employee, and (2) to prepare an employee for new assignments.

PERFORMANCE REVIEW

Performance reviews are meant to provide feedback to employees about how they are performing their assigned tasks. These performance reviews can be used for awarding bonuses, identifying employees who may be ready for greater responsibilities, or identifying areas where an employee needs additional training. Performance reviews need to be objective and fair. Many sophisticated instruments have been developed to conduct performance reviews.

EXPATRIATE ISSUES

A unique HRM issue faced by international businesses is the hiring of personnel who are not citizens of the host country. These staff could be from the home country or from a country other than the host country (a third country). Personnel who are not citizens of the host country are referred to as expatriates ("expats," for short). Expatriates normally hold senior-level positions or are part of the technical staff. Though expensive to maintain, expatriates offer some distinctive benefits to the international company: they provide a link to the home office, they serve as managers who may be considered for future promotions, and they may act as a protection against pirating of intellectual property rights.

LABOR RELATIONS

Labor relations are the various activities that encompass labor-management interactions. Labor relations are governed by laws, economic conditions, the level of unionization in the country, accepted business practices, cultural values, and societal norms. For international companies, maintaining normal working relations with the labor force is critical. Compared to local companies, international companies are more vulnerable to poor labor relations and may become the target of negative publicity. Unionization of labor varies from country to country. In some countries such as the United States, only a small portion of the workforce is unionized, whereas in other countries such as Germany, most factory workers are unionized. International companies must learn to operate under different unionization systems.

ACCOUNTING

The following activities are associated with the accounting function. (See Chapter 14 for a more complete discussion of this topic.)

ACTING AS A STRATEGIC CONTROL MECHANISM

Accounting systems are used to identify a company's economic status and to provide reasonable judgments of a company's financial health to investors, government agencies, and the public. Through its role as an internal watchdog, the accounting department provides the necessary checks and balances to company executives as they develop strategic initiatives. Through accounting reports, managers are constantly reminded of the available funds, cost overruns, and inefficiencies in project management.

DEVELOPING REPORTS

One of the more visible tasks of accounting is generating reports, such as the balance sheet, income statements, budgets, cash-flow statements, and so on to assist international managers in managing their day-to-day operations. These reports also provide information to the public on the performance and health of the company.

TAX MANAGEMENT

Taxes affect a company's cash flow and profitability. Each country's tax laws and corporate tax rates are different. It is critical that the international tax specialist in an international company understands the home country's tax policy on foreign operations as well as the tax policies of all the countries in which the company is operating. Tax management impacts an international company's decisions on where to invest, as well as the mode of entry it should employ (exports, licensing/franchising, joint ventures, or a wholly owned subsidiary).

Accounting for Transactions That Are Denominated in Foreign Currencies

Financial reports such as income statements and balance sheets for international companies are consolidated reports that combine all the activities of the company across all countries. As a result, one of the tasks of the accounting department in an international company is to translate financial reports from foreign currency to home-country currency. Depending on the home country, international companies have to follow the rules of their home countries while consolidating all the reports into one currency. For example, for U.S-based international companies, Financial Accounting Standards Board (FASB) statement 52 describes how international companies must translate their foreign-currency financial statements into U.S. dollars.

Assimilating and Working through Different Accounting Standards and Governing Bodies Found in Various Parts of the World

Accounting standards differ from country to country, and so do the governing bodies that maintain these standards. For example, in the United States, the standards are influenced by business practices and the monitoring agencies are industry based. In contrast, in France, Germany, and Japan, the standards are based on laws and the governing agencies tend to be government sponsored.

Management Information Systems

Management information systems (MIS) are a critical component in coordinating the activities of the various functions in an international company. In a knowledge-based, information-driven global economy, it is vital that international companies develop a comprehensive system to manage the flow of information that is continuously being assembled. A well-organized information system is an assembly of components that is designed to collect, retrieve, process, store, and disseminate information to the various functional departments of an organization. Such an organized system provides the necessary information to decision makers and also assists the international company in coordinating its various activities. Recognizing the importance of information flows to the modern global economies, many international companies are utilizing the advances in information technology to create more interdependent functional organizations.[12] The various components of an MIS include computers that are able to process/analyze and disseminate information; telecommunications systems that are used for collecting, distributing, and retrieving information; statistical packages that are used to analyze data; databases that are used to store the vast information that is generated by these systems; and software packages that are used for processing information and connecting the system to the various functional areas of an international company.

Because the operations of an international company are spread out in different countries and through different time zones, MIS acts as the linchpin through direct communication links with the various subsidiaries and their operations on a 24/7 basis. These links often provide real-time information and are usually interactive so that everyone can respond easily to the dynamic changes in the environment and directives from upper management. The various activities of an MIS department focus on information, processing, and dissemination/distribution.

INFORMATION

The starting point of MIS is information. Various data and information that are generated during a company's normal business activities need to be collected, organized, and stored for future use. These data or information may include cost data, sales data, employee salaries, the various transactions a company might engage in, and so on. In addition, an international company might gather external information from its suppliers, information about its competitors, and information about the external environment.

PROCESSING

The raw data or information that is collected in the previous step needs to be converted into useful information. MIS achieves this by sorting the data/information into categories, subjecting it to statistical or other forms of analysis, reconfiguring the data/information, and then storing it in subsystems that can be retrieved for decision making or other useful purposes. For example, the raw cost data that is collected by the accounting department may be sorted into subcategories that can then be analyzed to form a line item in the income statement, such as cost of goods sold or marketing expenditures.

DISSEMINATION/DISTRIBUTION

Once the information has been collected, analyzed, and processed, it must be distributed to persons and or departments that can use the reconfigured data for some action. Through computer technology and modern telecommunications systems, MIS is able to provide managers with interactive access to real-time information. This is a tremendous help in a fast-paced, dynamic global environment. For example, companies have found that they are able to satisfy their customers' needs and achieve a higher rate of customer retention through the development of customer-centric information systems.[13] Similarly, manufacturing companies have found that they can reduce their costs and improve quality through greater application of information technology in their outsourcing strategy.[14]

RESEARCH AND DEVELOPMENT (R&D)

For many international companies, the road to success is through innovation. Whether this innovation is in product development, process engineering, or operational innovation, they all tend to provide companies with significant competitive advantages. Most innovations are a result of R&D efforts by individual companies or the collective efforts of government, industry, and academia. Understanding the importance of R&D for the economic development of a country and its resulting effects on worker productivity, many governments initiate and also encourage R&D efforts by industries. By far, the United States allocates the largest amount of funds for R&D. For the year 2007, U.S. spending (both public and private sector spending) on R&D reached $350 billion, and it is projected to rise to $365 billion.[15] Historically, Japan was the second leading country in terms of overall R&D spending, but in recent years, China has overtaken Japan in R&D spending, reflecting its resurgent dominance in the global economy. For the year 2007, China's spending on R&D was in the range of $217 billion, while Japan spent $151 billion.

Based on industry statistics, it appears that U.S. pharmaceutical industries spend about 15 percent of their revenues on R&D, followed by technology industries (computers, telecommunications, and the like), which spend about 7 percent of their revenues on R&D, and industrial companies (appliances, automobiles, and so on), which spend about 3.5 percent of their revenues on R&D.[16] In the United States, the semiconductor industry alone spent more than $30 billion on R&D for the year 2005.[17]

Among the global companies, GE and Toyota are recognized as leaders in innovation, especially in the areas of product and process innovation. The GE global research division has been the cornerstone of GE technology for more than 100 years. With more than 2,500 of the world's brightest researchers spread out in multidisciplinary facilities around the world, GE has maintained its competitive edge in aircraft engine technology, turbine technology, and medical devices. Similarly, Toyota has outpaced most of its competitors through its focus on manufacturing engineering and new product development. Through its R&D efforts, Toyota has achieved significant efficiencies in manufacturing and quality control.[18] In 2005, Toyota's R&D spending was in excess of $7 billion, or 4 percent of its total revenues. Corolla and Camry are the best-selling automobiles in their class, and by the end of 2008 Toyota is slated to be the number one automobile manufacturer in the world in terms of total vehicle production.

The research and development efforts of a country are to some extent influenced by the types of industries that are dominant in the country, the size of the domestic market, the government's philosophy on R&D, and a country's tax policies. Those countries that have industries concentrated in chemicals, computers, high-technology firms, and pharmaceuticals have a distinct advantage in overall R&D spending compared to countries that are agricultural and have only light-manufacturing industries. Therefore, China, Japan, the United States, and countries in Europe that have more of the technology-driven industries and also have a large domestic market to sustain R&D expenditures tend to lead the way in R&D spending. The governments of these countries spend on R&D to stimulate the economy and improve labor productivity. They also stimulate R&D expenditures within the private sector through their liberal tax policies on R&D spending.

CHAPTER SUMMARY

As explained in this chapter, an international company is comprised of many functional areas. Each division is a standalone unit but it cannot be effective unless it is paired with other functional areas to produce and sell goods and services. In order for an international company to be efficient and successful, all the various functions and their activities need to be organized, coordinated, and integrated.

International companies must ask the question, What is the critical factor of each function that makes that function efficient? For example, it could be shown that for R&D to be effective, the two most critical factors are people and information. Likewise, manufacturing is dependent on people and information. Therefore, companies can benefit from the integration of manufacturing and R&D. By integrating the modes of each function, management can achieve the synergistic effects of functional integration.[19]

Functional integration is not necessarily implemented in all areas of a business at the same time. In some cases, it may be necessary to integrate just a few of the functions to achieve efficiency. For example, research has shown that functional integration has been very useful in logistics management. By integrating the activities of logistics with supply-chain management, it is possible to improve efficiency and reduce long-term distribution costs.[20] In the financial services area, the challenge is to find the optimal balance that will maximize cost reductions, boost sales, and increase customer retention. Therefore, in financial services firms, it is essential that the operations and marketing departments integrate their strategies to reduce costs and retain loyal customers.

As more and more international companies try to improve functional integration to cut costs, improve strategic effectiveness, and ensure success, they are reevaluating their existing organizational structures with an eye toward smoothing coordination among the functional areas of their organization. Some major international companies such as IBM and Fidelity Investments have dismantled their product/service-driven organizations to create customer-centered organizations in an attempt to be more responsive to customer needs; all of their functions are linked to this single goal. These companies have achieved functional integration by making a key account manager responsible for all the functional activities that lead to the development, sales, and after-sales activities within the organization.[21]

Research has shown that international companies can achieve their corporate goals by integrating administrative mechanisms within many of the company's functional divisions.[22]

KEY CONCEPTS

Functional Linkages
Functional Integration
Strategic Decisions

DISCUSSION QUESTIONS

1. Why are international companies organized into functions?
2. List the key functions in an international company.
3. How are the various functions linked?

4. Why is functional integration and coordination important for companies to be successful?

5. Which of the eight functions would be most essential for a small exporting company?

APPLICATION CASE: BMW IN INDIA

BMW is one of the leading luxury automobile manufacturers in the world. Headquartered in Munich, Germany, the company was established in 1916. Its brands of automobiles are recognized for their high quality and high performance. BMW's models include the MINI Cooper and the Rolls-Royce. Classified as luxury automobiles, they have extremely high brand recognition, and the firm as a whole has a loyal customer base.

BMW automobiles are exported to many parts of the world. Starting in the 1970s, the company embarked on a major expansion program in an effort to increase its international market share of luxury automobiles by setting up manufacturing facilities in selected countries. Its first plant outside of Germany opened in 1972 at Rosslyn (near Pretoria), South Africa. Since then, BMW has set up 17 manufacturing plants in six countries, including Austria, the United Kingdom, and the United States. The U.S. manufacturing facility was established in 1994 and is located in Spartanburg, South Carolina. In addition, as China's economy grew and the Chinese government encouraged foreign investment, BMW saw an untapped potential market there for luxury cars. In 2003, BMW established a manufacturing plant in Shenyang, China, to cater to the growing Chinese market.

The success of BMW in China led the company to explore other opportunities in Asia, and India was selected as a new market. Like China, India was considered a less-developed country for years, having never attained a large measure of economic success. In 1991, however, the country reversed its previous policies of restrictive foreign investment rules and opened up to foreign investors. Since then, India has achieved high economic growth rates, averaging over 8 percent for the five-year period from 2002 to 2006. The automobile market in India is growing at an annual rate of 16 percent.

Typically, BMW conducts extensive research before it chooses a country for investment. The selection is based on country risk factors, market potential, and a feasibility study that projects costs, revenues, and potential profits. In proposing a new operation in a foreign country, BMW involves most of its functional divisions in coordinating the various activities so that it has a reasonable chance to succeed. It is critical for BMW that the functional entities communicate with one another in developing an overall strategy. After conducting a thorough analysis of the data, BMW decided to set up an assembly plant in India to target the affluent group of consumers who could afford a high-end luxury car. By 2004, India had 20 automobile manufacturers, primarily foreign manufacturers with Indian joint venture partners. Although some luxury automobiles were imported into India, Mercedes-Benz was the only luxury manufacturer in India at that time. Mercedes sold approximately 2,000 cars annually.

Based on the feasibility study, BMW decided to construct an assembly plant in Chennai, South India, with an initial capacity of 1,700 cars on a single shift (BMW's target was to sell 2,000 cars by 2008). With an initial investment of €20 million that included the factory, machinery, and a subsidiary office in Delhi, BMW was ready to sell luxury cars in India. In selecting Chennai, BMW considered the availability of a skilled labor pool, the cost of operations, and the availability of suppliers. All components to assemble the cars—except for seats and door panels—would be imported from Germany. In 2007 in the Indian subsidiary, BMW sold 743 of the 3 Series models, 320 of the 5 Series models, and 251 of the 7 Series models, for a total of 1,387 cars, far exceeding its first-year target of 1,000. Reflecting the demand for its cars, BMW plans to streamline its production facilities at an additional cost of 500,000 euros and increase annual production in India to 3,000 cars.

QUESTIONS

1. Is BMW's time-consuming integrative approach justified under the current global competitive environment? Explain.

SOURCE

Most of the information for this case was obtained from press releases in newspapers, including the *Economic Times,* the *Telegraph,* and the BMW Web site (http://www.BMW.com, accessed January 14, 2007).

International Production & Operations Management and Supply-Chain Management

One of the most critical business functions in organization is operations management. It is responsible for transforming inputs into finished goods and services. Supply-chain management is the coordinating of materials, funds, and information to facilitate the transfer of materials and components from their source to the marketplace in the form of finished goods and services.

LEARNING OBJECTIVES

- To understand the scope and strategic importance of international production and operations management
- To understand the application of production and operations management to business operations
- To understand the various decisions and their importance to the process of international production and operations management
- To recognize the significance of quality management and understand the techniques used to manage quality
- To understand the importance of inventory control in the production and operations process
- To understand the role and importance of supply-chain management

Businesses produce goods and services that are marketed to potential consumers. All other functions of an organization, such as marketing, finance, human resources, accounting, research and development, and information technology, interface with operations management to produce goods and services. With the availability of fast-paced computers and advanced models of enterprise resource planning, international companies can achieve high-level efficiencies in their production and operations management (POM) systems.[1] Operations management is not restricted to the manufacture of goods but also deals with the production of services. POM concepts are equally applicable in the service sector and in manufacturing. Service industries such as banking, insurance, health care, retail sales, and not-for-profit organizations also make use of POM techniques. Take for example, a large hospital. In order to operate efficiently, the hospital has to coordinate all the activities that need to be completed to provide the best possible patient care. Most of the activities performed by the medical director, doctors, nurses, hospital administrators, technicians, and other staff fall within the field of operations management. These activities include scheduling surgeries, assigning doctors and nurses, preparing the surgical wards, buying medicine, equipment, and other supplies, managing the food service, supervising the staff, taking care of the repairs and maintenance, and keeping the hospital clean. In order for the hospital to run efficiently, its functions have to be coordinated and managed as if they were an assembly line operation. Whether the hospital is in New York or Lagos, Nigeria, similar operational systems must be applied.

Operations management helps with the creation of goods and services. That is, it transforms inputs into finished goods or services through tooling, assembly, coordination, transportation, and storage. The transformation in the case of a desktop computer may be in assembling circuit boards, memory chips, and other components to produce a finished product. Similarly, a bank also has to assemble various services in order to provide a bank loan or other banking products. In the manufacture of computers, it is easy to see the transformation from parts into finished goods. On the other hand, the transformation of a bank product such as a mortgage loan is not so obvious. It is easier to understand the transformation of goods and services from the input stage to the finished stage through the concept of *value added*. Value added is the difference between the input costs and the price of outputs. Hence, in the case of a PC, one could easily discern the difference between the input and the output. A customer is willing to pay $600 for a personal computer (PC), knowing that the console by itself may be worth only $50. In the case of the banking service, the difference between the input and the output cost is not as clear, but value is added through a service such as a home loan that the bank packages for a borrower. If the borrower feels that the fee charged (price of the service) by the bank is more than is warranted, he or she may go to another bank or may decide against taking the loan. Production and operations management provides significant strategic advantages to international companies. Of all the factors that contribute to strategic/competitive advantages, it is believed that more than 25 percent is derived from operations management.[2]

OPERATIONS MANAGEMENT IN MANUFACTURING VS. SERVICES

The applications of operations management in the manufacturing and service sectors are identical, but these sectors differ in many other ways. As mentioned earlier, manufacturing involves transformation of material and components into tangible output. For example, steel, rubber, plastic, and machine parts are assembled to obtain a finished automobile—a tangible good. In contrast, service involves transformation without a tangible output. Take the case of educational services: the output cannot be seen or touched, but transformation of knowledge occurs in the form of an intangible output. Manufacturing and services are similar in *what* is done, and, therefore, the major difference between them is in *how* it is done. The similarities between the two are easy to understand. Both require inputs (for an automobile it may be steel and other necessary materials, and for education it is the students, instructors, and instructional materials). Both are based on design and managerial decisions such as how much to invest, whom to hire, and where to locate. But services have four major characteristics that make them different from goods/products and that greatly affect their design, processing, and marketing. These are:

- *Intangibility.* Services are intangible because they cannot be seen, felt, tasted, smelled, or heard before they are bought. Because a service is intangible, its quality is not known by the buyers before they purchase it. Buyers will draw inferences about quality and results of the use of a service from other evidence, including references from people who have used a particular service. Therefore, service providers must be able to manage the available evidence from the intangibles to their advantage.[3]
- *Inseparability.* Services are produced and consumed simultaneously. The buyer and the provider of a service are both integral parts of that service. Since the customer is present as the service is produced, provider-client interaction is a unique feature of services.
- *Variability.* Service quality and the extent of the service received can vary from transaction to transaction. Service outcomes are dependent on who provides them and when and where they are provided. Hence, the service quality provided by one bank teller may not be the same as the next.
- *Perishability.* Services cannot be stored as physical goods. Physical goods can be manufactured, placed in inventory, distributed through multiple channels, and consumed later, whereas services, because of their inseparability, are consumed as they are being provided. Storing services for future demand is not possible.

In addition, a product can be mass-produced, and through automation almost all units can be uniform. In service, each transaction can be different from the previous experience, as it is provided by humans and not machines.

INTERNATIONALIZATION OF PRODUCTION & OPERATIONS MANAGEMENT

The globalization process, with its borderless network of operations, has created a complex system of manufacturing and operations management that is indifferent to where goods are manufactured, where services are offered, and where these goods and services are distributed. The dynamic shift in the world over the last decade has resulted in China becoming the manufacturing center of the world and India becoming the information-technology hub of the world. As international companies seek cost advantages to compete successfully in the international marketplace, they constantly look for countries that have lower input costs. In addition, the technological advances achieved during the late twentieth century have helped companies adopt more advanced manufacturing systems, including lean manufacturing. Lean manufacturing improves productivity through cost and time management.[4] The growth in globalization has opened opportunities for small entrepreneurs in many countries. Many of these small entrepreneurs use modern management and operations concepts and extended value chain management practices to be competitive.[5] As businesses from industrialized countries scan the globe for lower input costs, they modify their strategies to take advantage of opportunities available in developing countries that may offer a reasonably skilled labor force at a fraction of the cost in their own countries. Many companies seek competitive advantages through production and operations management.[6]

DECISIONS IN PRODUCTION & OPERATIONS MANAGEMENT

An international firm setting up a POM system has to make some strategic decisions. These decisions assist companies in utilizing their resources in the most effective and efficient way in transforming inputs into outputs. The nine most critical strategic POM decisions are:

1. Location—where to set up operations
2. Product—which product design to adopt and which products to introduce in which market
3. Process—how to utilize people, material, machines, and technology to produce high-quality products at the lowest possible cost
4. Quality—how to meet and exceed customers' quality expectations
5. Layout—how to set up machines and manage the interaction among people, materials, and machines
6. Scheduling—setting up time, date, and volume of output
7. Purchasing—cost, quality, and delivery are critical decisions in purchasing
8. Inventory—managing the inventory levels to meet unexpected demand at the lowest possible costs
9. Human resources—assigning tasks based on skills and requirements of the operation

Each of the above strategic decisions has to be made individually to result in synergy and cost effectiveness.

LOCATION DECISIONS

Strategy

One of the critical long-term strategic decisions companies make is where to locate their operations. As discussed in Chapters 2 and 3, companies carry out detailed assessments of risks in selecting countries. After selecting the country in which to set up operations, international companies have to decide where to locate their manufacturing plants or service centers based on many factors, including the upstream and downstream efficiencies in the supply-chain process. Upstream distribution deals with the supply of materials and other components used by manufacturing plants and service centers. Downstream distribution handles the supply of finished goods and services to the marketplace. In the era of globalization, locational decisions are not necessarily confined to where the market for the finished good or service is, but may depend on other factors, including input costs. Therefore, international companies may sometimes locate their plants and service centers far away from the actual marketplace to take advantage of labor costs and/or the availability of a skilled workforce. For example, Canon Inc. and Olympus Optical Co. Ltd. of Japan have major manufacturing operations in China, but the markets for these companies' products are elsewhere. Similarly, Siemens of Germany has a major research facility in India, but most of the work assigned at this center targets Siemens's markets in Europe and North America. American companies, too, have established manufacturing facilities outside the United States. For example, Motorola and General Motors have major operations in China. In 1992, Motorola announced plans for a $120 million plant in China, which has since been completed. It has also set up a software-engineering laboratory in India. In addition, Motorola has 18 R&D laboratories in Europe with 14 manufacturing plants, accounting for about 23 percent of the company's total revenues. Clearly, location decisions transcend national boundaries.

In selecting a location, international companies consider some key variables that influence their decisions, including the items below.

1. *Availability of skilled workers, staff, and technical people.* It is important that the company selects a location where it has easy access to qualified employees. For example, many garment manufacturers have moved their production facilities to China to tap into the skilled and inexpensive labor force available there. In fact, in China there are cities that produce just one type of clothing, and all key manufacturers have plants in these cities. Some of the factory towns have even been renamed for the garments that they produce—for example, "Socks City," "Underwear City," and so on.

2. *Wages and salaries that affect input costs.* The cost of goods sold is affected by wages and salaries. For example, as the hourly rates of factory workers in Germany and other European countries rise, companies such as Volkswagen are relocating their manufacturing operations to lower-wage locations such as Poland and the Czech Republic.

3. *Worker productivity rates.* Hourly rates alone should not be the criteria for selecting a location; productivity should also be part of the equation. Productivity is the rate of output per unit of input. If hourly rates are high but the productivity is high, too, it may be worth remaining in the present location, as there may be no significant difference in the input costs in a different location. For example, if the hourly wage rate in the United States is $20 and a worker in the United States can produce 10 units of output per hour, the cost per unit is $2. In contrast, if the hourly wage rate for similar work is $5 in Mexico and the Mexican worker is able produce two units of output per hour, the cost per unit is $2.50. In this instance, there is no significant benefit for an American company to relocate its operations to Mexico. In studies done across manufacturing plants in various countries, researchers have found that productivity levels are influenced by management competency and workers' skill levels.[7]

4. *Local tax rate.* Depending on the corporate tax rate, international companies may select those countries that have lower rates to increase the profitability of their operations. For instance, the corporate tax rate in Egypt is roughly 40 percent, whereas in Brazil it is 33 percent. If all other factors of production are the same, an international company would set up its operations in Brazil to take advantage of the favorable tax rates.

5. *Distance to suppliers (upstream).* The cost of transporting required raw materials and other supplies affects the cost of goods sold. Hence, international companies may select locations that are close to suppliers to reduce the upstream supply cost. This is especially true for the mining and oil exploration industries, as transportation costs for these industries are very high. Therefore, oil refineries are usually located near where the oil wells are drilled.

6. *Distance to markets (downstream).* Companies locate their operations close to markets to reduce distribution costs. In industries where the consumer purchase rate is high (consumers go to stores often to buy such goods), it is critical that companies locate their operations close to markets. Soft drink companies such as Coca-Cola and Pepsi-Cola have many independent bottlers in a given country to make sure that the supply of their beverages reaches the markets quickly.

7. *Logistics.* Logistics helps with the movement of goods and services from one point to another. It involves transportation, loading and unloading, communication, storage, tracking, and rerouting if necessary. One aspect of logistics issues concerns the downstream and upstream distribution of materials and finished goods. In the modern era, with the new technologies available, logistics has become a key activity for businesses to improve efficiency and reduce costs.

8. *Availability of utilities.* The supply of utilities such as water, electricity, and gas is essential for operations, especially in the manufacturing sector. In selecting locations, international companies that require these utilities may try to select countries that have a reasonable supply of water, electricity, and gas. For example, automobile and appliance manufacturers who operate heavy machinery in their production processes require a continuous supply of electricity and would be constrained if it were not available. In many developing countries, power supplies are not reliable, and in some instances there are frequent power outages. Companies that operate in these countries most often invest in their own power generation to augment the local supply. This additional investment adds to the cost of operations.

9. *Local government regulations.* Regulations are often enacted to assist the overall well being of a country's people. Some of these regulations may also be unfavorable for foreign investors. Regulations that are meant to protect local industries from competition can be an impediment to foreign companies. For example, ownership regulations that require foreign companies to own only a minority position in a company are intended to help local entrepreneurs. Similarly, regulations that levy higher duties on imported goods are intended to help local companies compete against foreign goods that may be more attractive to local customers because of their superior quality.

10. *Local government incentives.* In some instances, countries encourage the flow of foreign investments to improve their economic condition. In order to attract foreign investors, some countries offer incentives including tax relief, lower utility rates, or low-cost land. In a highly competitive environment, countries offer substantial incentives to attract foreign investors. Even within individual countries, states/provinces may offer incentives to attract foreign investors. For example, the state of Alabama in the United States offered Mercedes-Benz of Germany various incentives that totaled $253 million, including tax breaks. In addition, the state government promised to buy

25,000 new Mercedes-Benzes. The reward: an investment estimated to be worth $300 million, 1,500 high-paying jobs, and the satisfaction of outbidding 30 other states.[8]

11. *Quality of life considerations.* Quality of life issues help companies attract skilled workers to the location and are used as incentives to attract qualified expatriates to manage overseas operations. Quality of life issues include environmental factors, cost of living, educational facilities, transportation, personal safety and health, cultural facilities, and other public services. For example, in the annual rankings by the mayors of major cities of the world for 2007, the best cities for relocation were Zurich, Switzerland, with a score of 108.1 points, followed closely by Vienna, Austria, and Geneva, Switzerland, tied at 108.0 points (where New York is the base city, with a score of 100 points). These cities were followed by Vancouver, British Columbia (107.6), Auckland, New Zealand (107.3), and Düsseldorf, Germany (107.3).[9] The mayors also ranked Moscow, Russia, as the most expensive city to live in, followed by Tokyo, Japan; London, England; and Oslo, Norway for 2008.

12. *Economic factors.* (Already considered in the selection of the country.) Companies may weigh each of these variables differently depending on the industry they are in, their market position, and their competitors' actions. For example, when General Electric decided to set up its research center in Bangalore, India, it chose a location where other high-tech firms were located—Bangalore is referred to as the Silicon Valley of India—and that had a large pool of skilled workers, with an excellent quality of life that was attractive for relocation. Similarly, when BankBoston was planning its expansion strategy into Latin America, where it generates about 20 percent of its profits, it chose São Paulo, Brazil, as the gateway to service the region. BankBoston made the decision on the basis of the size of the country (Brazil is the largest country in Latin America), proximity to other countries such as Argentina, Chile, and Peru, and the importance of São Paulo as a banking center, where offices of many foreign banks are located.[10]

Locational Decision Analysis

In selecting locations, international companies conduct elaborate feasibility studies to make sure that their choice is in the best long-term interest of the firm. Studies have shown that international companies decide on facility locations based on economic, infrastructural, and legal factors.[11] If a wrong location is selected, the firm faces insurmountable difficulties, including loss of competitive advantage (a competitor may have already selected a better location), financial loss (forgone profits, costs of selling off assets, and uprooting cost), and loss of market position. International companies do not follow a single approach to decide on a location. Many of them use different models that are found to be beneficial in certain environments and under certain situations. But market size appears to be a key variable that many international companies consider seriously. Studies of American, European, and Japanese companies have shown that market size as defined by the number of manufacturing establishments in a country is strongly associated with foreign manufacturers' locational decisions.[12] Probably the fact that there are so many manufacturers at one site implies that the market is large, a supplier network is in place, and the collective wisdom of so many manufacturers could not be wrong. To evaluate locations, some companies use analyti-

Table 8.1

Break-Even Analysis to Select Locations (€)

Item	Hanover	Rotterdam
Overhead	80,000	100,000
Total variable	200,000	150,000
Total cost for producing 100,000 units	280,000	250,000
Cost per unit	28.00	25.00

cal techniques to make the selection as objective as possible. Two such approaches are locational break-even analysis and the factor rating method.[13]

In the break-even analysis approach, both fixed costs and variable costs are esti-mated by location, and the selection is made on the basis of the lowest unit cost. For example, an international firm has to choose between two locations, say, Hanover, Germany, and Rotterdam, the Netherlands. The cost associated with manufacturing 100,000 units of its product is shown in Table 8.1. If all the factors remain the same, the company should select Rotterdam on the basis of lower unit cost.

In the factor rating method, an international company first identifies the critical factors in its operations, then assigns weights based on the importance of each of the critical factors, and finally arrives at a score that reflects the importance of each factor. For example, a company might identify hourly wage rate, worker productivity, taxes, and quality of life as the most important factors in selecting a location. The company has two choices, Manila, Philippines, or Saigon, Vietnam. Based on past experience, it assigns the following weights to each of the four selected factors: wages = 30 percent; productivity = 30 percent; taxes = 25 percent; and quality of life = 15 percent.

Using available information from government and other sources, it rates (on a 10-point scale, where 10 is best) each city on the four factors, as shown below.

Factor	Manila	Saigon
Wages	7.0	8.0
Productivity	6.0	5.0
Taxes	7.0	5.0
Quality of life	5.0	4.0

Using the factor weights and factor ratings, the international company can select between Manila and Saigon on the basis of the factor weights, as shown in Table 8.2. If all other fac-tors remain the same, the company should select Manila as its location for operations.

PRODUCT DECISIONS

Most international companies produce and sell hundreds of different goods and ser-vices. For example, Unilever, the British- and Dutch-owned conglomerate, offers more than 660 different items, from food products to detergents, in many of its markets. After selecting a new location, Unilever has to make a choice of which product(s)

Table 8.2

Factor Weights to Select Locations

		Ratings		Weighted scores	
	Weight	Manila	Saigon	Manila	Saigon
Factor	(%)	(/10)	(/10)	(col. 2 × col. 3)	(col. 2 × col. 3)
Wages	30	7.0	8.0	21.0	24.0
Productivity	30	6.0	5.0	18.0	15.0
Taxes	25	7.0	5.0	17.5	11.5
Quality of life	15	5.0	4.0	7.5	6.0
Total				64.0	56.5

to sell there. Usually, international companies do not introduce all their products to the market when they start out in a new country. They normally try to introduce the most marketable product and slowly build up the line. This approach reduces the risk of failure and allows management to be focused and to direct all its attention to that single product. In some instances, an international company introduces two or three products if they are viewed as linked and if they complete a single package. For example, when Citicorp, the large global full-service bank, enters a country for the first time, it may initially introduce checking and savings accounts and, after some time, introduce other services such as credit cards, car loans, and so on.

Cost is the compelling reason why international companies in a new country prefer to introduce an existing product that has been successful in other countries. The experience gained in marketing one product in other markets is a valuable competitive advantage. In some instances, due to market forces, an international company may introduce a totally new product in the new country. Take, for example, the experience of McDonald's Corporation. When the company was planning to enter the Indian market, it realized that it would not be successful in India with its standard beef hamburgers, as many Indians do not eat meat, especially beef, for religious reasons. Hence, the company experimented with a vegetable burger, called a "veggie burger," which was successfully introduced into the Indian market.

PROCESS DECISIONS

The manufacturing and operations process transfers inputs into finished goods and services. Process function brings together people, material, machines, and technology in the transformation of products and services for use by customers. Hence, process management is equally applicable to all organizations—goods and services, for profit and not-for-profit. It addresses such issues as:

- Which aspects of the process should be done in-house, and which should be outsourced? In the internal business context, this is becoming a critical issue as companies seek lower wage areas to manufacture and process services using modern technology. For example, many of the world's computer companies are using China and Taiwan as their manufacturing bases to make use of the relatively inexpensive, yet technically skilled, labor force. Similarly, many financial institutions are outsourcing their customer service departments to call centers in India and the Philippines. Chapter 9 discusses the outsourcing area in detail.

- What is the best proportion of human skills to the level of technology (labor-intensive processing versus technology-driven processing)? For international companies that have manufacturing plants in nonindustrialized countries, the choice of how much technology should be applied in manufacturing is a complex issue. On the one hand, technology-driven manufacturing is cost efficient and can produce high-quality finished goods; for example, most of the automobile manufacturing in Europe is totally automated. On the other hand, the workers in many nonindustrialized countries lack the skills to operate highly sophisticated machinery; these countries have an abundant labor force and high unemployment, both of which favor low-technology processing. The automobile-manufacturing process in China, India, and Mexico has higher labor content. In addition, the higher the technology, the more capital intensive the operation, which raises the financial risk. Even in commercial banking, the question is: How much of the automated banking system that is the norm in the United States and many other industrialized countries is feasible or practical in countries with low literacy rates?

- How can the selected process help the company attain quality, reduce cost, and increase flexibility? As discussed earlier, with higher technology components in the manufacturing process, the human element is reduced, which in turn cuts down on the number of errors, resulting in better quality. A robot that welds parts on an assembly line can produce welds of the same strength 24 hours a day, with consistency, and with little waste. In contrast, if this task is given to a human, fatigue, boredom, and other factors would produce inconsistent results and a greater amount of waste. Flexibility in process management is equally important. Firms improve their ability to compete by examining each step of their processes and responding quicker than their competitors to market and consumer changes.[14]

- How can process management be improved? Competitive pressures and shifts in the environment dictate that companies constantly seek improvements in their manufacturing processes.[15] For example, Toyota's move to lean manufacturing has enabled the company to cut production costs by 10 percent or more. This has led other automobile manufacturers to play catch-up.

Process management is important to many aspects of a business organization, from accounting to manufacturing. From an accounting point of view, process management seeks better ways to perform accounting functions such as cost analysis. In manufacturing, process management helps determine product designs that maximize customer value.

The two major process decisions that companies have to make involve (1) the type of process to be used, and (2) the extent to which the company wants to achieve integration.

Type of Process to Be Used

Companies have a choice in organizing their operations around the products that they plan to sell or around the process that they plan to use in producing a particular product. Depending on the choice, the company's resources—especially an international company's resources—have to be organized for optimal operations. For international companies, the choice of a process may vary from country to country, depending on factors such as capital investment, labor costs, level of labor skills, local regulations, size of the market (volume), and whether the process is for the short term or the long term (life of the existing technology).

The five types of processes most often used by companies are: *project based* (single item), *job based* (consulting assignments), *batch* (garment manufacturing), *line process* (assembly line operations), and *continuous process*. When an international company such as Bechtel is involved in a major construction project, the process selection is project based and highly customized. No two bridges or buildings are alike; hence, each project needs to be customized to suit the needs of the customer. In contrast, the processing of many consumer goods is volume driven, and the same process is applied continuously, as in ExxonMobil's oil-refining process or Pinnacle Foods Group, Inc.'s Duncan Hines cake mix production process. The different types of processes are influenced by level of customization, volume of output, and variations within a product category. In many developing countries, the number of variations in a given product is limited compared to that in industrialized countries. For example, the number of models of automobiles available in Argentina, Bangladesh, Egypt, and Vietnam is far fewer than the number available in many European countries. Similarly, in packaged goods such as soap and shampoo, the varieties available in Bolivia, China, and Thailand are fewer compared to the choices that American consumers might have.

Integration

Most companies purchase some materials or parts from outside vendors. For example, automobile manufacturers such as GM, Toyota, and others buy sheet metal, plastic, batteries, and tires from suppliers that specialize in these items. Similarly, Coca-Cola buys sugar and packaging materials from outside companies. The extent to which a company processes all its required materials, parts, and components is referred to as integration. Integrating activities that precede or follow the manufacture or assembly of goods and services is called *vertical integration*. Vertical integration flows in two directions: backward and forward.[16] For example, when a jeans manufacturer also manufactures cloth, thread, and buttons that it uses to make the garment, the process is called backward vertical integration. Now, if the same garment manufacturer also retailed the jeans that it manufactured, this would be referred to as forward vertical integration (see Figure 8.1).

The more processes in the supply chain that an organization performs itself, the more vertically integrated it is. For example, Purdue grows its own chickens, manufacturers its own feed for the chickens, and does its own packaging. On the other side of the spectrum, Dell Computers outsources most of its parts, components, and technical services.

Figure 8.1 **Vertical Integration**

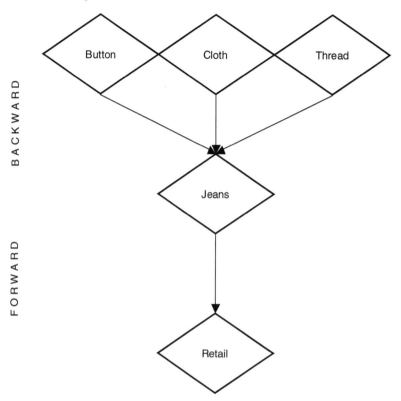

The decision by a company to integrate fully is referred to as a *make* decision. In contrast, when a company outsources many of the required items/functions for its product, it is referred to as a *buy* decision. The advantages of integration, or the make decisions, are (1) total control over the process, including product quality, (2) economies of scale, (3) timely deliveries, (4) protection of intellectual property, and (5) cost efficiencies through centralization of product design and R&D. For example, Mercedes-Benz designs all its cars and has a vast R&D facility in Germany to direct its state-of-the-art developments in automobile engineering. The advantages of outsourcing, or the buy decisions, are (1) the organization can focus on its core competencies, (2) management can concentrate on key strategies that affect its products/services rather than get involved with noncore businesses, (3) the company can obtain parts and components from suppliers who have specialized expertise in single items (Intel is much better suited to developing chips than HP or Dell), (4) the costs are lowered by buying from suppliers who have economies of scale, and (5) because of globalization, more supplier options are available. Modern technology allows companies to coordinate the activities of these suppliers, who are located in different countries. For example, many financial institutions and large hospitals have technicians, such as radiologists, in India who read X-rays, CAT scans, and MRIs and have the reports ready for next day by taking advantage of the time differences between the United

States and India. In a global economy that transcends distances and time with opportunities for cost savings, very few companies are fully integrated.

QUALITY DECISIONS

Quality is one of the most critical factors in the success of a product or service. Quality is the ability of the product or service to satisfy customers' expectations. Quality translates into value for the customer: it does not imply that a customer is getting the very best product or service, but within a given price range, it implies that it is the best available product. A customer looking for an automobile that runs well, is fuel efficient, is the safest in the market, has a lot of room, is equipped with the best sound system, has a quiet ride, and will not break down might have to pay more than $50,000. There are automobiles under $15,000 that are reasonably good, and there are automobiles that are priced at $50,000 that are excellent in comparison. For a customer who can only afford an automobile in the $15,000 range, the higher quality found in the automobile that costs $50,000 is meaningless; that customer is not going to be able to buy such an automobile. Hence, quality is a range of satisfaction for different segments of consumers at different price levels. However, quality does imply that the product or service has some minimum standards of performance and that those consumers who buy the product benefit from it.

From a firm's point of view, quality is a strategic tool it can use to attract customers, create brand loyalty, and gain a competitive advantage. Many Dell customers believe the company makes excellent computers and place special value on the ability to customize their purchases. Buyers of Dell computers have implicit faith in the quality of the company's products. Similarly, business travelers select a particular hotel chain such as the Marriott or the Hyatt Regency expecting a certain quality of service and presumably willing to pay the price for it. Quality cannot be measured in a single dimension; therefore, comparisons across products or services are not possible. Quality can mean different things for different people. For some, it may be the *performance,* or the main characteristics of the product or service. For example, in a five-star restaurant, it may be the status of the chef and the impeccable service of the waitstaff that make the difference for the customer. For some, quality implies *reliability,* or consistency of performance. A photocopier purchased for home use, for instance, should not break down during the first six months of use. For some, quality may simply mean *reputation* of a given brand. For example, owners of BMW automobiles buy them because the brand is well known and has an excellent reputation.

Although quality has many dimensions, the fact is that if consumers perceive a product/brand to be of poor quality, they will not buy that brand. Therefore, for companies, quality has implications that may determine their financial success. Whereas high quality results in customer loyalty, repeat purchase, brand recognition, and increased profits, poor quality results in loss of customers, higher costs, and, in some cases, liability (court settlements due to injuries).

In manufacturing high-quality products, firms try to control certain aspects of their operations. The first and the most critical aspect of the quality process is controlling product failures that result from defective parts or workmanship. This is an internal failure, and most quality-control procedures are developed to minimize internal failures. Businesses' quality-control systems have evolved over the years from very simple approaches to the more sophisticated methods that are employed by many international companies.

In the early part of the twentieth century, most companies checked product quality after production runs. However, this approach to quality control posed problems for companies that produced thousands of units in a single run. It was not possible to check all the units produced, so companies designed quality-control checks called *statistical quality control* (SQC) to monitor the final quality of a particular product. This procedure was widely used by many of the international companies of that era. SQC is based on statistical techniques of sampling. That is, by using small samples, companies determined the quality level (defective rates) of the whole production run. In SQC, a random sample of finished products is measured against predetermined standards. Hence, the defective rate of a production run of 100,000 units might be decided by testing a sample of a few hundred units. In SQC, the margin of error in testing the sample can be established at the 90, 95, or 99 percent level. Therefore, based on the results of the sample, a technician testing a batch would conclude that the defective rate was not too high and that it fell within the boundary of tolerance at the 95 percent significance level (or other pre-established level). Based on the sample test, the quality-control technician would either accept the whole batch or reject it. If the technician were to reject the sample, a check of the whole production batch would have to be done to remove the defective units from the batch.

As the international environment became more competitive and the importance of product quality became an issue for consumers, the SQC process seemed to lack the precision that was required in this evolving environment. Companies started relying on process quality control, also called *statistical process control* (SPC), to improve quality. Unlike SQC, which checks batches of output, SPC checks quality at every step of the production process, including the supplier level. Though this was an improvement over the SQC methodology, it did not fully solve quality-control problems. Companies realized that SQC and SPC were focused on the production part of the process without taking into account the design stage of the product. They soon realized that in the quality game it was critical to *prevent* mistakes rather than finding mistakes and correcting them. Therefore, companies such as Toyota Motors of Japan started focusing on the design stage of their products. For Toyota, the design stage not only included designing a better product but also designing better machinery and better processes to reduce mistakes at the source. To implement this new emphasis on design at all levels of production, Toyota works very closely with all its suppliers to assure a continuous supply of high-quality parts and components.

The next phase in the evolution of quality control was the introduction of quality theories and philosophies that addressed management issues. These theories were pioneered by individuals who viewed the quality problem in a holistic way and postulated that most product defects are preventable. Some of the prominent theorists who introduced these philosophies were W. Edwards Deming, Joseph M. Juran, Philip B. Crosby, and Kaoru Ishikawa. The major contributions of these four quality philosophers are summarized in Table 8.3.

The next phase in the quality-control evolution was the introduction of the *total*

Table 8.3

Quality Philosophers and Their Philosophies

Name	Philosophy
W. Edwards Deming	Cause of poor quality is the system 14-point prescription to achieve quality (consistency, constancy, finding problems, etc.)
Joseph M. Juran	80 percent of defects are controllable "Fitness-for-use"–quality planning, quality control, and quality improvement
Philip B. Crosby	Concept of zero defect Management commitment, persistence, articulation, and doing right
Kaoru Ishikawa	Cause-and-effect diagrams for improving quality Use of quality circles to involve workers in quality improvement

Sources: W. Edwards Deming, *Quality, Productivity, and Competitive Position* (Cambridge, MA: MIT Center for Advanced Engineering Study, 1982); Joseph M. Juran, "The Quality Trilogy," *Quality Progress* 19, no. 8 (1986): 19–24; Philip B. Crosby, *Quality without Tears: The Art of Hassle-Free Management* (New York: McGraw-Hill, 1984); and William J. Stevenson, *Production/Operations Management,* 5th ed. (Chicago: Irwin Publishers, 1996), p. 101.

quality management (TQM) concept, a comprehensive strategy that combines the process element with human resources involvement in controlling defects and reducing costs. Introduced first in Japan, it has its roots in the quality-control principles that were proposed earlier by Deming, Juran, and Ishikawa. In general terms, TQM can be defined as *an organization-wide approach to continuously improving the quality of an organization's product and processes that are important to the customers.*[17] Total quality management focuses on three primary areas:

1. Its goal is total satisfaction of both the internal and external customers.
2. It is management driven.
3. It seeks continuous improvement of all systems and processes.

This approach was a drastic shift from the previous quality-control systems. First, there was recognition that product and service quality was important for customer satisfaction. Second, top management involvement was necessary to achieve quality. Third, quality is not a onetime effort, but implies continuous improvement. Finally, quality has to be applied to all systems. The critical elements of the TQM approach are:

- *It is customer driven.* The final arbiter of all goods and services is the customer. If the customer does not perceive value in a product, no amount of promotional campaigns will translate into sales.
- *It is championed by a firm's leadership.* Quality should be understood as an important component within an organization, and this needs to be embraced by all, including senior management.

- *It is employee driven.* For quality programs to be successful, they should be adhered to by everyone in the organization. The easiest way to achieve this goal is to make every individual employee responsible for quality.
- *It focuses on continuous improvements.* Quality is not static. It is a dynamic process and should be reviewed and improved upon on a regular basis.
- *It uses benchmarks to recognize deficiencies.* As goods and services compete in the marketplace, comparisons of brands are inevitable. The TQM procedures recommend that firms evaluate performance on the basis of external standards, especially among key competitors. The goal is to find the best possible practice of quality management and to introduce the technique into the organization.
- *It emphasizes design quality.* Producing superior-quality products depends on both the actual transformation of inputs into outputs and also on design of the product.

TQM techniques have been successfully utilized by many companies worldwide, including Toyota and Sony of Japan, Philips Electronics and Siemens of Europe, and General Electric and Ford Motor Company of the United States. In the United States, 14.1 percent of manufacturing firms use TQM.[18]

The next phase in the evolution of the quality-control process was the development of Six Sigma principles. Six Sigma is a disciplined methodology that uses data and statistical analysis to measure and improve a company's operational performance by identifying and eliminating defects. Sigma is the standard deviation of a normal distribution. In Six Sigma, the parameter values fall under 99.99966 percent of the normal curve. Adopted in 1987 by Motorola, an American cellular and other advanced technology manufacturer, Six Sigma attempts to reduce defects to a maximum of 3.4 items per one million. Compared to the traditional SQC systems that operated at two sigma (43,600 defects per million) or at three sigma levels (2,600 defects per million), the Six Sigma approach virtually eliminates all defects. In the United States, companies that use two sigma quality standards end up redoing close to 33 percent of their work, adding to overall cost. Based on the success of Motorola's Six Sigma approach, GE quickly adopted the technique to improve its own quality-control program.

The Six Sigma technique has resulted in higher quality output at Motorola and GE, improving customer satisfaction and reducing costs for both companies. At Motorola, the reported cost savings over the years is estimated to be nearly $16 billion.[19] General Electric saved close to $750 million through its Six Sigma program in 2003 and $1.5 billion in 2004.[20] About 4.9 percent of American manufacturers use Six Sigma to improve quality.[21] International companies using Six Sigma initiatives transcend both manufacturing and service companies, and the technique is used in many parts of the world. Table 8.4 presents a partial list of the international companies that make use of Six Sigma quality procedures. Implementing Six Sigma quality-control procedures involves setting up and monitoring procedures. Table 8.5 presents the key steps in Six Sigma and its differentiating features.

Manufacturing companies have used Six Sigma to improve quality and precision of process outputs. Six Sigma has been found to be equally beneficial to service companies, which use it to design, measure, analyze process losses, and guide process improvements.[22] For example, because of Six Sigma, Bank of America was able to

Table 8.4

Partial List of International Companies Using Six Sigma

Company	Country	Company	Country
Amazon.com	United States	Johnson & Johnson	United States
American Express	United States	Mayo Clinic	United States
Bank of America	United States	Motorola	United States
Bharat Heavy Electrical	India	Nokia	Finland
Boeing Corp.	United States	Samsung Corp.	South Korea
Daimler-Chrysler Corp.	Germany	Singapore Technologies	Singapore
Dell Computer Corp.	United States	Sony Corp.	Japan
Deloitte & Touche Ltd.	United States	Sumitomo Chemicals	Japan
DuPont Corp.	United States	Tata Group of Companies	India
Eastman-Kodak	United States	Toshiba Corp.	Japan
Ford Motor Company	United States	3M	United States
Glaxo-Smith Kline	United Kingdom	Toyota Motors	Japan
Hondo Motors	United States	Volvo	Sweden
IBM	United States	Xerox	United States
JPMorgan Chase	United States		

Source: 209 Six Sigma & Quality Article Archive. Available at http://www.isixsigma.com/library (accessed June 2008).

Table 8.5

Steps in Six Sigma and Its Differentiating Features

Steps in Six Sigma	Differences from other techniques
1 Identify the product/service	Six Sigma is more of a business strategy
2 Identify the customer	It is a disciplined statistical problem-solving technique
3 Identify what specific benefits customers seek	Resources are dedicated to continuous performance improvement
4 Determine attributes that should be offered to satisfy the customers' needs	Six Sigma is customer driven
5 Define the work process	Emphasis is on training
6 Modify the process to eliminate waste	Results are measured by quantifiable costs/revenues
7 Ensure continuous improvement through measurement, analysis, control, and refinement	Six Sigma uses a fact-based approach; there is no room for guesstimates

reduce payment errors by 22 percent and deposit errors by 83 percent in 2007.[23] Also, Bank of America completed thousands of Six Sigma projects in 2003 alone, improving its profits and gaining considerable competitive advantage in the process.[24] From an organizational standpoint, Six Sigma is implemented by trained personnel who have achieved a degree of competence in its technique. Individuals trained in Six Sigma can attain different levels of expertise, which are identified by different colors of belts, similar to the martial arts belt. (At the first level is the Green Belt, followed by the Black Belt, and finally the Master Black Belt.)

In a competitive global environment, international companies have to deliver goods and services to meet customer needs. However, it is not possible to introduce a uniform quality-control technique in every country. Due to cost considerations and difficulties in adopting some of the more sophisticated techniques, international companies may use two or three different techniques across different countries. In any event, it is critical that international companies produce goods and services that meet the expectations of their customers, wherever they are.

LAYOUT DECISIONS

Layouts are arrangements of machines and work centers and the flow of materials designed to transform inputs into finished goods/services most efficiently. Well-designed layouts increase productivity and reduce costs. Consider a manufacturing plant that assembles automobiles. The number of parts that go into assembling an automobile run into the thousands. Therefore, if the plant floor is laid out poorly, parts may not arrive in time at the point of assembly, or workers may have to travel unnecessarily long distances to obtain the necessary tools to complete the assembly process. Even in service industries, the layout is important. Take for example, the branch office of a bank. The flow of people that are being serviced by the tellers, customers waiting to see the bank officers, customers waiting for the safety deposit area, and the customers waiting for an ATM machine all have to be taken care of without confusion or delay. Consequently, a bank branch should be organized to help the flow of customers and provide quick and efficient service. Traditional straight-line assembly lines are now being modified to take advantage of robotics, computer networks, and just-in-time inventory systems. One such innovation is the U-shaped assembly line, which reduces the worker and machine downtime by organizing the parts and equipment around the workers. A few studies have shown that the U-shaped layouts used by companies that have adopted lean manufacturing are very effective in optimizing assembly line operations.[25] Also, companies that use U-shaped assembly lines claim improvements in their worker productivity.[26]

There are different types of layouts—product based, process based, and fixed position. Product-based layouts are used to process a large volume of products or customers. The process is standardized and repetitive. For example, serving a large number of customers in an office cafeteria is a good example of product-based layout. In the case of a cafeteria, the focus is on serving the food. Product-based layouts may be arranged in a straight line or may be U-shaped. U-shaped layouts are more compact, and distances between workstations are reduced. When the processing is not standardized and instead presents a variety of requirements, product-based layouts are inefficient. In these situations, it is best to use a process-based layout, which divides processes into groups that complete similar tasks. In a tire plant, for instance, the rubber-mixing section of the plant is a separate department from the tire-curing department; once the process in one department is completed, a batch of semifinished products is taken into the next department to be processed. In a fixed-position layout, workers, materials, and equipment are brought to the workstation for completion of the process. For example, in the construction of an electric power generator, a fixed-position layout might be used. The generator position is fixed, but technicians, various materials, and equipment are brought to the site to complete the generator. Fixed-position layouts are most often used with construction projects where the project is bulky and cannot be moved around for processing. Besides the three layouts mentioned here, others have been developed due to improvements in technology. One such layout is called the cellular layout, in which machines are grouped to perform similar tasks. As cellular layouts require a continuous flow of information, they are used in countries where communication technology is well advanced and computer networks are easily available.

International companies adopt different types of layouts in different countries to adapt to local conditions. In countries where the use of technology is low, companies may adopt more labor-intensive techniques, which may require different layouts than the ones used in more advanced countries. Consider Michelin Tires of France: it has a completely automated system of tire assembly that requires very few workers, with the plant layout geared for fewer worker movements to complete the assembly because it is completely dependent on computers and neural networks. In contrast, Michelin's factory in Thailand has more workers, and the layout is designed to facilitate the movement of people and materials.

SCHEDULING

Organizing the timing and flow of materials to complete the production process while meeting market demands is the function of scheduling. The demands on people and the specific tasks each worker needs to complete must be planned ahead of time to provide a smooth sequence of task completions. Scheduling therefore involves assigning due dates to specific jobs to utilize all available resources efficiently. In some industries, products have to arrive at specific time periods. For example, 60 percent of all retail sales in the United States take place in a five-week window between the last weekend in November and the twenty-fourth of December. In industries where the market due dates are known beforehand, companies do a backward scheduling; that is, they schedule the final step first, and other steps in the process are then scheduled in reverse order. In industries where the product is mass-produced and consumers purchase the product frequently, it is critical that the product be available at all times. Household products such as food, soap, and cosmetics are produced continuously to keep stock levels steady; in such instances, companies follow a forward-scheduling method, beginning with the purchase of raw material, the delivery of components, and so on. Forward scheduling is also used in industries where the products are made to order and companies plan the schedule after receiving orders. In the construction industry, scheduling is done once the construction project is commissioned.

The basic objectives of scheduling, whether for a domestic company or an international company, are to ensure that the production process is completed in a timely and efficient manner. There are some key differences between scheduling for goods (manufacturing) and scheduling for services. In the manufacturing operations, the emphasis is on material delivery, assembly, and delivery of finished goods, whereas in services the most critical resources are the people, and maximizing their efficiency is an overriding scheduling concern. Keep in mind that services cannot be stored, so scheduling plays an even bigger role in the service industry. In other words, manufacturing scheduling can rely on inventory to smooth out the scheduling process; this opportunity is not available in the service industry. In industrialized countries, order quantities are large and scheduling is critical to the delivery of goods to the marketplace. In developing markets with smaller sales volumes, scheduling is simpler. Scheduling to a great extent depends on the following factors:

- *Market size.* The larger the market, the greater the volume of materials that need to be ordered, and scheduling such a vast quantity of inputs complicates the scheduling process.
- *Product type.* Products that are complex (assembling a robot is more difficult than assembling a ballpoint pen), bulky (assembly of an automobile versus assembly of a plastic toy), have high input costs (assembly of a Rolex watch versus assembly of rubber slippers), or are purchased infrequently (a personal computer that is purchased once in three years versus a bar of soap that may be purchased once a month) tend to require careful planning. A misstep in the scheduling process could tie up resources and cost the company its market position.
- *Resource utilization.* In the final analysis, the goal of organizations is to utilize scarce resources efficiently and to make goods and services that satisfy their customers. Poor scheduling may hold up the production process and reduce the efficient utilization of people and machines.
- *Inventory cost.* Inventory helps companies to manage the uneven demand for goods in the marketplace. If the cost of inventory is low, companies can take chances with the accuracy of their scheduling, as inventory provides the needed buffer and satisfies the customer demand in the marketplace.
- *Willingness of customers to wait for the product.* Customers are willing to wait for unique products and products for which there are no substitutes. A patient may wait for the highest quality reading glasses but may not wait for a particular brand of ballpoint pen. Similarly, a customer may wait three months for a luxury automobile but may not wait more than a week for an automobile that has mass appeal.

PURCHASING

Most international companies have to purchase many items from outside suppliers to complete the production process. For example, Toyota Motors buys tires for its automobiles from Bridgestone, Deutsche Bank buys software programs for its financial analysis from SAP of Germany, and Coca-Cola buys aluminum cans from Alcoa Corporation. The main reason why international companies purchase materials and other components from outside suppliers is to be able to focus on their core competencies. Toyota is much better at assembling cars than producing tires; Deutsche Bank is knowledgeable in banking and finance, but not necessarily in developing sophisticated software; and Coca-Cola is a master formulating popular soft drinks but has little expertise in making aluminum cans. Therefore, most companies end up purchasing materials rather than making them internally. The decision to make or buy is one that companies have grappled with for ages.

Table 8.6

Pros and Cons of Make-or-Buy Decisions

	Pros of Make Decision	Pros of Buy Decision
1	Lower production cost	Lower acquisition cost
2	Ensure adequate supply	Preserve supplier commitment
3	Avoid unreliable suppliers	Obtain superior capabilities
4	Utilize surplus resources	Avoid investment in additional capacity
5	Obtain desired quality	Reduce inventory costs
6	Avoid supplier collusion	Ensure constant supply of items
7	Make unique items that may be difficult to buy	Limited internal resources
8	Avoid layoffs	Reciprocity
9	Protection of intellectual property	Items that are protected by patents
10	Increase the size of the company	Focus on core competency

Source: Jay Heizer and Barry Render, *Production and Operations Management: Strategic and Tactical Decisions* (Upper Saddle River, NJ: Prentice Hall, 1995), p. 531.

The make-or-buy decision has its pros and cons. Companies weigh these advantages and disadvantages in making their final decision as to make items internally or buy them from an outside supplier. Table 8.6 presents the advantages of make-versus-buy decisions.

The advantages of the "make" decision are the disadvantages of the "buy" decisions, and vice versa. In the twenty-first century, it is difficult to find a company that produces all its input factors internally. Some companies make less and buy more from outside suppliers. The use of outside suppliers is called outsourcing. For example, Toyota Motors of Japan makes only 28 percent of its car materials and components internally; the rest it buys from outside sources. International companies take advantage of their global reach by purchasing components from suppliers located all over the world. Using efficient suppliers, international companies can drive down the cost of goods sold. In a study of 50 U.S. firms that used outsourcing, a majority (69 percent) mentioned cost savings as the overriding reason for buying parts and components from outside suppliers.[27] Boeing, an American aircraft manufacturer, buys about 20 percent of the parts for its Boeing 777 airplane from Japan. Besides the cost benefits, outsourcing helps companies sell their products and services to customers in the countries that provide the materials and components they buy, as the local buyers take pride in their own country's involvement in the processing of a particular product or service.

In some industries, however, it is customary to make most of the parts and components internally. For example, companies that are in the extraction industry, such as mining and oil drilling, make their core products internally. ExxonMobil Corporation of the United States drills for crude oil, refines the crude to make petroleum and petroleum-based products, and distributes them through their outlets. Recall from earlier in this chapter that when a company has control over the different stages of the production process from raw materials to distribution, the process is referred to as vertical integration. International companies may be vertically integrated in their home countries or in countries where they have a sizable market, but rarely do they have integrated operations in smaller markets.

NEWER DEVELOPMENTS IN MANUFACTURING PROCESSES

Competitive pressures and recent developments in communication technologies and network computing have enabled international companies to develop advanced manufacturing strategies.[28] Two such developments are *lean manufacturing* and *flexible manufacturing*. Lean manufacturing was first introduced in Japan and is now utilized by many companies in Europe and the United States. In lean manufacturing, the resources needed to complete a process are reduced considerably; that is, the objective of lean manufacturing is to use fewer workers, less inventory, and as little space as possible. To achieve lean manufacturing, companies have to hire more skilled workers to perform specific tasks, use flexible equipment, produce items in smaller lot sizes (batches), use inventory efficiently, and set up machines to optimize space. Skilled workers not only learn tasks quicker but also are able to solve problems when they occur. Flexible equipment helps companies to organize multitask functions and save valuable production time. By using smaller lot sizes, companies make it less likely that a large number of defective items will be made before they are discovered. Lower levels of inventory are achieved through better scheduling and just-in-time (JIT) systems, which reduce waste and inventory costs. Finally, in lean manufacturing systems, the setup of various assembly line machines and conveyor belts that bring parts and components is organized to be closer to workstations and occupy the least amount of space. Lean manufacturing operations stress the importance of eliminating waste at all levels, especially at the process stage.[29]

Research has shown that for lean manufacturing to work, companies need to build the necessary social systems as well. Simply copying techniques from successful Japanese companies without integrating social systems capable of supporting the new technical changes will not work. Social systems include the interactions of the people working on the process, the organizational structure in which they operate, and the existing corporate culture. Therefore, for American companies to implement lean manufacturing, they first have to transform their companies from autonomous and individualized structures to a teamwork-oriented and collaborative problem-solving culture.[30] Companies that have implemented lean manufacturing systems have vastly improved the efficiency of their operations. In the United States, approximately 35.7 percent of manufacturing firms make use of lean manufacturing systems.[31]

Flexible manufacturing is a system that allows production facilities to respond more quickly to varying demand patterns. This system integrates the core competencies of supply-chain members to respond to market shifts and helps the introduction of customization at a mass level (Dell Computer Corp. is an example of a firm that employs this system successfully). Mass customization uses a flexible manufacturing process to produce and deliver customized products and services for individual customers around the world through computer-aided manufacturing systems. Developed by Toyota to customize production, flexible manufacturing attempts to save unnecessary downtime and improve efficiency in the assembly line. The core principle of the flexible manufacturing system is its ability to switch from making one product type or model to making another that is in greater demand at a faster rate using the same assembly platform. This system can reduce months of the factory downtime formerly necessary to switch the assembly line to accommodate building a different model. The key to flexible manufacturing is standardized equipment for every step in the process. For example, Ford Motor Company uses flexible manufacturing at its new factories in Norfolk, Virginia, and Kansas City, Missouri. Ford estimates that the new factories could save $2 billion over six years. In addition, Ford is able to switch assembly lines in as little as 15 percent of the time it used to take, and the cost of building these new plants is 22 percent lower than the cost of building the old ones.[32]

INVENTORY

Maintaining inventory helps companies to meet the fluctuating and unexpected demand patterns observed in the marketplace. Specifically, inventory helps international companies to accomplish the following:

- Meet the normal (forecasted) demand and the unexpected demand for goods.
- Uncouple the production process from distribution; that is, inventory can be used to balance the production process, so that, regardless of the demand (seasonal, cyclical), the production run can be maintained at the same level throughout the year, reducing costs through underutilized resources during slow seasons.
- Hedge against inflation. In international operations, firms are often confronted with double-digit inflations in developing countries, which increase the costs of manufactured goods. By maintaining inventory, these companies can reduce costs during high inflationary periods.
- Take advantage of quantity discounts.
- Protect against stock outs. Stock-out problems occur both at the upstream and downstream distribution ends of a supply chain. When there are stock outs at the upstream end, companies may not have materials and parts to maintain production runs. In contrast, when there are stock outs at the downstream point, the company not only loses potential sale but also may have dissatisfied customers.

Inventories can be maintained at different levels of the production stage. Hence, companies may have raw-material inventory, work-in-progress inventory, and finished-goods inventory. For example, automobile companies may stock up on steel (materials), inventories of partially assembled cars (work-in-progress), and fully assembled cars (finished goods). Finished-goods inventory may be held at any point in the distribution process—at the factory warehouse, at the transportation company's facilities, and at the distributor warehouses. For international companies that operate far from their home bases, maintaining inventory is a critical strategic activity. For companies that export, transportation of goods may take weeks and in some cases months to reach their destinations. In such instances, having a reliable stock of goods for sale is crucial to their operations. For companies that have to import raw materials and other parts for assembly, holding these items as inventory ensures continuous and trouble-free production runs.

Holding material and goods in the inventory system can be expensive and, if not managed properly, can increase the cost of operations and reduce profits. There are many costs associated with managing inventories, including:

- *Holding costs* (also called carrying costs). These are the costs of keeping items in a storage facility. They include costs such as rent for the facility, security, and staffing (staff used in maintaining records of the incoming and outgoing materials and goods).
- *Ordering costs.* Any costs associated with placing an order are part of the ordering costs. These costs include salaries, order processing, and supplies.
- *Setup costs.* Setup costs are costs incurred in starting an inventory system. These costs include purchase of machinery (forklifts, computers, etc.), conveyor systems, and investment in materials handling.
- *Transportation costs.* Transportation costs are the costs incurred in shipping inventory items to the storage facility.
- *Opportunity costs.* Opportunity costs are defined as the required return that is forgone by choosing one investment over an alternative investment of similar risk. By investing capital in the inventory of materials and goods, a firm may be losing an opportunity to obtain greater returns by investing that capital in an alternate investment opportunity.
- *Spoilage/breakage/obsolescence costs.* By placing a large quantity of materials and goods in storage, a firm may face changes in style or upgrades in technology that render the items in the inventory obsolete (use of a newer generation of chips in computers makes the older models less desirable), or items may spoil over time (products that have a limited shelf life, such as food items and some pharmaceutical products).
- *Insurance costs.* To lower the risk of spoilage/breakage/obsolescence, companies may buy insurance to protect the value of their items in inventory.
- *Stock-out costs.* Stock-out costs are costs associated with the loss of sales due to lack of inventory. Stock-out costs have a short-term effect and a long-term effect. In the short term, a firm may lose a sale because the item/brand is not available, but the consumer may return to buy the brand during the next purchasing cycle. However, if the stock out of the brand occurs frequently, consumers may abandon the brand and buy a competing brand.

To control inventory costs, international companies develop models that help them rein in some of the costs associated with inventory management. This is especially true in those countries where transportation and storage systems are inadequate, making inventory costs much higher than in those countries that have excellent infrastructures. In managing inventory, companies try to minimize the costs incurred in ordering, transporting, and placing items in storage. However, inventory costs are not linear. While *some* of the costs associated with holding inventory are directly proportional to the quantity held, other costs are inversely proportional to the quantity held. Holding costs, for example, are directly proportional to the quantity held. Therefore, as the quantity of items held increases, the holding costs rise. In contrast, setup costs decrease with larger quantities. The same amount of start-up costs may be required to hold 100 units or 10,000 units. Similarly, ordering costs normally decrease with larger orders. Due to the conflicting nature of costs, attaining cost effectiveness implies finding a balance between rising costs and decreasing costs. Holding costs, opportu-

Figure 8.2 **Total Inventory Costs and Economic Order Quantity**

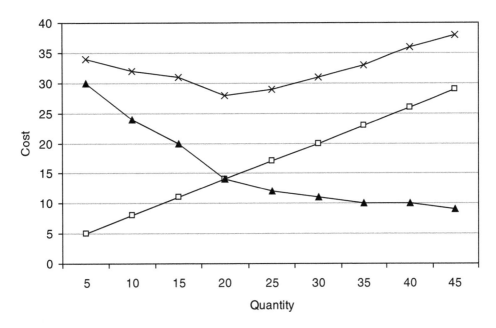

nity costs, and other such costs will increase if larger inventories are maintained, but annual setup costs, ordering costs, and other such costs decrease with larger orders. If the objective of inventory control is to minimize total cost, an order quantity has to minimize both types of cost. This concept is illustrated in Figure 8.2.

The three cost lines shown on the figure are: total cost, costs that are inversely proportional to quantity, and costs that are directly proportional to quantity. The total inventory cost is lowest at the point of intersection of the two types of cost. The size of order that minimizes the total cost of maintaining inventory is called *economic order quantity,* or EOQ. Economic order quantity depends on many factors, including volume of annual sales, cost of the item, holding cost, ordering cost, and so on. Therefore, if the unit cost of an item to be held in inventory is very high, only a small amount of the item should be placed in inventory; otherwise, the opportunity cost with the tied-up capital may be very high. On the other hand, if the demand for an item is very high, it is important for it to be easily available; therefore, a company may stock up on this item. There are many models available that assist managers to determine the EOQ. A simple model to compute EOQ is presented below (the derivation of the EOQ formula is not presented here).

$$EOQ = \sqrt{\frac{2DO}{UH}}$$

where D = annual demand in units, O = ordering and setup costs, U = unit cost, and H = holding cost/year.

Example:

ABC, a German manufacturer of high-end toys, purchases console boxes from South Korea. These console boxes are used in game boards sold by the company. The company sells about 1,000,000 game boards per year. The holding cost per unit for one year is €4.00, the unit cost is €10.00, and the ordering/setup cost per order is €16.00. Calculate the optimal order quantity that ABC should place with its South Korean vendor.

For this problem, D = 1,000,000, O = €16.00, U = €10.00 and H = €4.00.

$$\text{Therefore, EOQ} = \sqrt{\frac{(2)(1,000,000)(16.00)}{(10.00)(4.00)}} = \sqrt{\frac{32,000,000}{40}}$$

$$= \sqrt{800,000} = 894.427$$

Maintaining inventory is expensive and can increase the cost of goods sold. Recognizing this problem, some Japanese manufacturers, especially Toyota Motors in the 1950s, experimented with a novel idea in which production runs would be maintained not by securing large inventories of required parts, but by asking suppliers to deliver the parts on demand. Called the *just-in-time (JIT) system,* it was a phenomenal success, and most Japanese companies and some European and American companies adopted the JIT system. By eliminating inventory, Japanese companies were able to reduce their inventory cost by 40 percent.[33] The just-in-time system is a balanced system in which no inventory is maintained but materials and parts are brought in as required. In the JIT system, the exact numbers of required parts/components arrives at the factory as they are needed.

The just-in-time system has been extremely successful in Japan and is part of the lean production manufacturing and TQM processes adopted by many Japanese companies. The focus in lean manufacturing and JIT is on avoiding waste and reducing unnecessary downtime. In the United States and parts of Europe, JIT is not yet universally accepted. It appears that there are some fundamental differences in how businesses are organized in Japan and in the West. Japanese firms have very close relationships with their suppliers, and they have an ownership stake in many of them. The term *keiretsu* is used to describe a group of companies with interlocking businesses and shareholdings. Japanese companies also rely on a single supplier for a specific part. Furthermore, most of the suppliers that deliver parts and components are located close to the manufacturing plants. In this type of arrangement, it is easier to practice JIT than when multiple suppliers are used and they are located far from each other. JIT systems rely on transportation to serve as their temporary warehouse. In the United States, most suppliers are geographically far away from their customers;

U.S. companies spread their orders across many suppliers, reducing their control over the suppliers (ownership or otherwise). In addition, for many U.S. manufacturers, strained global supply lines have further complicated their use of the JIT system. If conditions fit, however, JIT is an excellent form of inventory control.

To make JIT work, there has to be a philosophical shift in the thinking about the manufacturing process. "Just in time" implies more than timely deliveries. It assumes that the design is optimal, the machines are in good condition, the workers are well trained, scheduling is based on excellent forecasts, and there are no delays along the entire production line. The goals of JIT are very simple: avoid all disruptions along the production process, design the process to be flexible so it can accommodate quick changeovers, reduce setup times, minimize inventory, and eliminate waste.

HUMAN RESOURCES

Human resources are the key to the success of any production and operation system. A well-trained workforce that understands the entire operations system can be highly productive, improve quality, reduce downtime, and reduce waste. All functions in an organization are either handled or managed by people. Therefore, the various tasks in the operations management area—the decision about where to locate, the processing of materials, maintaining quality, scheduling the flow of materials, designing layouts, and managing inventory—are all completed by people.

Human resources planning for POM is similar to planning for human resources in other functional areas. This area is examined in greater detail in the international human resources chapter (Chapter 12). That is, in managing human resources, firms have to draw detailed job specifications, recruit the right people, provide continuous training, motivate the workforce to optimize their capabilities, empower workers, provide incentives, evaluate their performance, set up an appropriate salary structure, and provide a work environment that is interesting and challenging.

OPERATIONS MANAGEMENT STRATEGIES AND SUPPLY-CHAIN MANAGEMENT

For operations management to function efficiently, it needs to be supported by an equally efficient supply chain. A supply chain is defined as the activities that facilitate the movement of materials, parts, and other needed supplies for the processing of goods and services for delivery to the final customer. Supply-chain management improves the efficiency and effectiveness of a firm's total operations. Efficient supply-chain management requires the coordination of all resources that are applied to the supply-chain activities. As material and transportation costs rise, international companies seek efficient supply-chain systems to control these costs, which are estimated to be nearly 80 percent of revenues.[34] As more and more companies make use of worldwide suppliers, supply-chain bottlenecks can increase operating costs and eat into a company's profits.[35] In the international context, the supply-chain system assists managers in acquiring materials and parts from low-cost suppliers that may be located thousands of miles and several time zones away. For example, Dell Computer Corporation buys its supplies from more than 200 suppliers, over half of which are located outside the United States. More than 50 percent of its major suppliers are in countries in Asia, 12 hours ahead of Eastern Standard Time (EST) in the United States.[36]

Source management, or *sourcing,* is the selection and retention of reliable suppliers. Companies seek suppliers that can offer them the highest quality materials and parts at the lowest possible cost. For example, since the late 1990s, China has become a major auto parts manufacturer, supplying auto parts to many major automobile manufacturers. East China's Zhejiang province exported $192 million worth of auto parts during the first four months of 2004.[37] Once a good supplier is located, it is important that a company build a close relationship with the supplier and make it part of its extended team.

For international companies that operate across countries, sourcing strategies vary from country to country. European companies that supply manufactured parts to American companies quite often try to locate their facilities closer to the users of their products. In contrast, Japanese companies prefer to export parts and components made outside the United States.[38] Sourcing strategies are constantly evolving due to technological changes, spread of globalization, and open market conditions. International companies have many more options when it comes to selecting suppliers, and companies try to take advantage of the abundant supplier sources that are currently available, especially for commonly used materials, parts, and other supplies. Outsourcing—that is, buying goods and services from outside suppliers, is also a major part of the supply-chain management system.

Supply-chain management can be divided into sourcing, logistics, management of suppliers, customer relations management, and continuous improvement of the system.

SOURCING

Sourcing relates to finding outside suppliers to obtain materials, parts, and supplies that a firm needs to process its goods and services. It is not economical and in some instances it is impossible for a firm to make all the materials, parts, supplies, and services that it needs. For example, it is typically more cost effective and cost efficient to have the offices cleaned by outside janitorial service companies than to hire workers and manage them internally. Firms focus on their core competencies in managing organizations, and for IBM, managing a janitorial service to clean its offices does not fall under its expertise in developing software and computer systems. In sourcing decisions, international companies focus on cost effectiveness and, at the same time, maintaining high quality standards. In a global environment, outsourcing has been extended to include any suppliers in any part of the world that can supply materials, parts, or services that are either not available locally or can be obtained at lower prices (a detailed discussion on outsourcing is included in Chapter 9.)

LOGISTICS

Logistics refer to activities that facilitate the movement of materials, parts, and supplies to processing facilities, as well as activities that deliver the finished goods to the marketplace. This includes the shipping of materials, parts, supplies, and finished goods from various locations to storage facilities, processing centers, and end markets. Logistics also include coordinating the various activities, tracking shipments, and ensuring safe deliveries of shipments to all the points in the chain. In the international context, logistics can be troublesome. Materials, parts, and supplies have to travel greater distances, a single tracking system may not be sufficient, and government bureaucracy may further complicate the logistical process.

MANAGEMENT OF SUPPLIERS

Suppliers are crucial to the success of a supply-management system. The more involved the suppliers are, the more likely the supply-chain system will function smoothly. Suppliers can be of great help in designing parts and materials, adjusting production to fit into the processing system, improving the quality of finished items, reducing costs, and improving reliability. Suppliers should be considered partners and companies should develop long-term relationships with them. For international companies, managing their suppliers is challenging, as they may not have the same level of relationships with the suppliers as the local companies do. In addition, international companies' supply-chain systems are more geographically widespread, thereby adding to the difficulties.

CUSTOMER RELATIONS MANAGEMENT

Customer relations management (CRM) is made up of systems developed to learn and understand consumers by integrating all information about each individual customer into a database. CRM systems are able to add value to customer transactions by customizing some of the activities. Development of CRM systems offers companies fast access to records of actual customer buying behaviors. The supply-chain management system through CRM is able to link the manufacturing process to the customer transaction system. Supply-chain management systems can be improved to serve customers better through CRM systems. Studies have shown that a good CRM system can assist companies in acquiring and retaining customers. Companies such as IBM, Procter & Gamble, and Unilever have successfully adopted CRM systems that have provided them with valuable information about the characteristics and behavior of their customers. With the help of CRM, the supply-chain management system is able to coordinate a company's internal resources and capabilities for more effective and efficient utilization of its resources.[39] For international companies that operate in large markets and where the local communications and transportation systems are fully developed, use of CRM has become necessary in a highly competitive environment. In developing countries with smaller markets and a smaller customer base, international companies do not make full use of supply-chain management systems, and hence the use of CRM is rare.

CONTINUOUS IMPROVEMENT SYSTEMS

As supply-chain management coordinates the activities of various internal functional units and external suppliers, it provides opportunities for improving every aspect of the system from source to delivery of goods to the marketplace. By analyzing individual components of the system, managers can focus on those activities that reduce costs and improve efficiencies. For example, suppose through its tracking system that a company finds it has a bottleneck at a distribution center. It can immediately study the problem and try to rectify it instead of waiting for complaints from distributors. Continuous improvement implies preempting problem situations. International companies do not apply continuous improvement systems across all countries due to cost considerations or the marginal benefits derived from such systems in smaller markets. The investments are not worth the benefits in countries where the markets are not fully developed.

CHAPTER SUMMARY

The production and operations management (POM) function transforms inputs into finished goods and services. Production and operations management concepts and principles are equally applicable in the service sector and in manufacturing. Because of the inherent differences between manufacturing and service, some POM applications may vary in practice. The key difference between the manufacturing sector and the service sector is in the tangibility of goods in manufacturing versus the intangibility of the service sector. Therefore, POM concepts are applied differently in manufacturing and services.

The nine key decisions in POM are: location, product offering, process, quality, layout, scheduling, purchasing, inventory, and staffing. Each element of the decision process has to be carefully evaluated in setting up the POM operations.

Location decisions are affected by many factors, including labor costs, productivity, taxes, and quality of life. International companies typically weigh the most critical factors that affect their firms and/or their industries in arriving at a location decision. Many international companies use quantitative techniques to arrive at a location decision that avoids subjective and otherwise biased choices. Similarly, the quality issue is influenced by many factors, including customer expectations, competitive environment, and costs. Recently, international companies have adopted more well-known quality-control techniques, such as total quality management (TQM) and Six Sigma. These techniques provide management with tools that improve the overall quality of their goods/services offerings. Many of these techniques assign much of the responsibility for quality at the lowest level of the assembly by empowering assembly line workers to take the initiative in producing quality products and services. Quality is achieved by monitoring and evaluating a product or service through each and every step of the assembly line process.

Every decision in the POM process is important. Therefore, international managers have to direct each of the steps in POM to offer quality goods and services to customers.

KEY CONCEPTS

Operations Management in Manufacturing and Service Industry
POM Decisions

Location Decision
Quality Control
Inventory Management
Supply-Chain Management

DISCUSSION QUESTIONS

1. Identify the key differences between the manufacturing sector and the service sector.
2. Why is manufacturing of goods and services shifting to less industrialized countries?
3. Identify the nine major decisions to be made in POM.
4. What are the critical factors used by international companies in deciding on a location?
5. What is upstream distribution?
6. What is downstream distribution?
7. How is the break-even analysis approach used for location decisions?
8. Discuss the factor weights method of selecting locations for setting up foreign operations.
9. What is process management?
10. Discuss vertical integration.
11. What is TQM, and how is it applied?
12. Why is the Six Sigma approach to quality useful to companies?
13. How do layout choices affect operations management?
14. Discuss make-or-buy decisions.
15. What are some of the newer developments in manufacturing processes?
16. How and why do companies use inventory?
17. Explain the just-in-time (JIT) system of inventory management.
18. What is supply-chain management?

ADDITIONAL READINGS

Chase, Richard B., F. Robert Jacobs, and Nicholas J. Aquilano. *Operations Management for Competitive Advantage.* New York: McGraw-Hill/Irwin, 2004.

Fagan, Mark L. "A Guide to Global Sourcing." *Journal of Business Strategy* (March–April 1991): 21–25.

Heizer, Jay, and Barry Render. *Production and Operations Management.* Upper Saddle River, NJ: Prentice Hall, 1996.

Krajewski, Lee J., and Larry P. Ritzman. *Operations Management: Strategy and Analysis.* Upper Saddle River, NJ: Prentice Hall, 2006.

Stevenson, William J. *Production/Operations Management.* Chicago: Irwin, 1996.

APPLICATION CASE: TOYOTA AND LEAN MANUFACTURING

Lean manufacturing helps companies achieve efficiencies far beyond the normal rates by combining techniques and philosophies in optimizing operations. Lean manufacturing was introduced by Toyota as the Toyota Production System (TPS) to better compete with its more entrenched and larger competitors from the United States and Europe. Toyota's TPS and lean manufacturing systems borrowed heavily from Henry Ford's principles of the 1930s.

In the last 10 years, Toyota has been the most successful automobile manufacturer in the world. In 2007, it surpassed General Motors as the world's leader in automobile sales. Toyota's automobiles are known for their quality, design superiority, and high profit margins. Because of the efficiency obtained through lean manufacturing, the company has one of the lowest costs per automobile in the industry—an advantage that translates into high profit margins. For Toyota, lean manufacturing has meant lower operating and overhead costs, higher revenues per employee, lead time cut by over 50 percent, and higher employee satisfaction.

By designing vehicles on common platforms, Toyota is able to change production runs to suit market and customer needs, as well as to adjust to the supplier logjams that delay production runs. In its various assembly plants spread throughout the world, the lean manufacturing systems are practiced without fail.

The principles of lean manufacturing focus on:

- Understanding customers' needs
- Adhering to continuous improvements in manufacturing and process engineering
- Recognizing and eliminating waste by cutting down on overproduction, reducing inventory through just-in-time delivery systems, achieving zero defects, and reducing unnecessary processes
- Motivating the workforce

Lean manufacturing is achieved by:

- Analyzing customers and markets
- Assessing current process and improving on it
- Training the workforce
- Integrating lean manufacturing into every function, including engineering, design, marketing, R&D, and supply-chain management
- Educating suppliers
- Accepting lean manufacturing as a corporate culture that is driven down from the top management to the lowest paid employee

SOURCE

Adapted from Process Quality Associates Inc., "Lean Manufacturing." Available at http://www.pqa.net/ProdServices/leanmfg/lean.html (accessed March 2008).

9 Global Outsourcing or Offshoring

> Europe has only lost eight percent of its jobs due to outsourcing and that's also a very
> important message because the problem is not all about outsourcing. . . .
> Europe's share of global exports has gone up in the last five years and
> I think that is a very important message as well.
> —*Mark Spelman, Chairman, American Chamber of Commerce, Belgium, 2008*[1]

LEARNING OBJECTIVES

- To introduce the phenomenon of overseas outsourcing as a global trading activity
- To distinguish between offshoring, inshoring and near-shoring
- To examine the growth of the new phenomenon of offshoring services
- To distinguish between Internet technology (IT) and business process offshoring (BPO)
- To understand the advantages and disadvantages of offshoring
- To assess the factors for an effective global offshore strategy

As explained earlier in Chapter 5 on international trade and investments, global trade has been increasing at an unprecedented pace since the 1950s. More countries than ever before are engaged today in exports and imports leading to increased income and consumption globally. The creation of the General Agreement on Tariffs and Trade (GATT) in 1945, and its successor, the World Trade Organization (WTO), helped spur the growth by successfully lowering trade barriers among countries. Foreign direct investment (FDI), the process by which companies set up plants and factories in other countries, also increased in volume. In the early years after World War II, FDI flowed from the United States to Europe. As European countries recovered from the war and demand for both capital and consumer products increased, U.S. firms found it more convenient to serve the markets by establishing plants overseas rather than exporting products from the United States. Not only was it economical, but products could be tailored to local markets and distributed through local channels.

In the 1970s, U.S. multinationals continued to increase their FDI, but this time to take advantage of the lower cost of production available in developing countries. The preferred countries were the then newly industrialized countries (NICs) of Hong Kong, South Korea, Taiwan, and Singapore. The combination of cheap labor and favorable business climate allowed multinationals to expand production and ship the output back to the United States. Over time this led to the closure of many plants and factories in the United States.

When companies opt to locate plants overseas to save costs, it can have a major impact on the domestic economy. The direct effect is a loss of jobs, especially if a factory is closed or downsized. A secondary effect is the loss of ancillary industries that support the main plant or factory, impacting a wider swath of the local economy.

The loss of manufacturing jobs in the United States accelerated in the 1980s, when China opened its borders to FDI. U.S. and European companies flocked to China not only because of the cheap labor but also because of the availability of natural resources and a strong infrastructure, built by the Chinese government to attract as much foreign investment as possible. In the United States, the loss of manufacturing jobs became a politically sensitive issue. Although Congress made several attempts to dissuade U.S. companies to move overseas, they were not successful.

In the 1990s, another form of job outsourcing to companies overseas began in the United States. Service-related, or "white-collar," jobs began to migrate to developing countries. The first wave began in the early 1980s, when data-entry jobs were exported to the Caribbean countries. Airline companies such as American Airlines and Delta and telephone companies such as AT&T found it cost-effective to ship paper copies of data to offshore companies located in the Caribbean for input into large IBM machines. When Internet technology boomed in the 1990s, low-level computer programming jobs began to be outsourced to such countries as Poland, Romania, India, and China. In due course, U.S. companies found that they could transfer clerical, back-office, and call-center work to these countries and take advantage of the lower wages. With a huge pool of English-speaking engineers, India managed to establish a lead among all the countries by providing a variety of Internet-technology-related services to companies globally.

The outsourcing of service jobs to companies overseas has created controversy again in the United States and Europe. Politicians and labor organizations continue to condemn multinationals for putting profits first, before labor and local development. Research on the effects of overseas outsourcing on the domestic economy is still in its infancy. Most economists would agree that free trade and open FDI lead to long-term benefits to all countries, including increased employment and income. This has proved to be true for the United States, where in spite of the outsourcing of both manufacturing and service jobs beginning in the late 1970s, the overall rate of unemployment in the United States has remained low. The highest unemployment peaked in November 1982 at 10.8 percent and thereafter registered a steady decline, averaging 5 percent through the 1990s and until 2007. In 2008, unemployment increased dramatically as a result of a financial crisis caused by the collapse of the housing bubble in the United States. How this crisis, that has spread to countries globally, affects traditional relationships between FDI, international trade, and outsourcing remains to be seen.[2]

Some economists contend that the loss of manufacturing jobs from developed to developing countries is inevitable as technical know-how is passed on to these countries and their labor force improves its skills. The low unemployment rate up to 2007 reflected significant flexibility on the part of U.S. labor, which is essential for adaptation in today's global market. When manufacturing jobs were lost, U.S. labor moved to the service sector to compensate for the losses. In contrast, European unemployment rates have remained high, between 9 and 11 percent, with the exception of the Netherlands and Ireland. The reasons for the high rates have been attributed to the labor forces' lack of flexibility and innovation.[3]

Before we discuss different aspects of the new form of outsourcing, we define new terms that have crept into the English lexicon over the past few decades: *offshoring, inshoring,* and *near-shoring.* We begin with the generic term *outsourcing.*

OUTSOURCING, OFFSHORING, INSHORING, AND NEAR-SHORING

OUTSOURCING

The term "outsourcing" denotes the contracting by a company of selected work, previously performed in-house, to a third-party vendor. The location of the third-party vendor is immaterial; it may be domestic or overseas. The work may be relatively minor and peripheral to the company's main activity, for example, janitorial services, facility maintenance, landscaping, or worker training. Alternatively, it can involve work that is more integral to the core business of the company, such as manufacturing, accounting, payroll, or marketing.

A company may choose to manufacture and assemble all the components of its product in-house, or it may choose to manufacture only selected components that are considered noncore elements. Another option, or business model, for a company is to outsource the manufacturing of all the components and perform only the assembly work in-house. A third possible model is to outsource the design, marketing, and accounts receivable (collection of payments) services while performing the manufacturing and operations in-house. Outsourcing can include a combination of core and noncore activities, and the actual model chosen will depend on the strategic mission of the company and potential cost savings.

Thus, outsourcing has the following characteristics:

1. The work may be peripheral or integral to the business of the company.
2. The third-party vendor may be located in a domestic or a foreign country.
3. The work may or may not be defined by a long-term contract.
4. The outsourced work may be performed in-house or at the location of the third-party vendor.

As a result of negative publicity surrounding the practice, the term "outsourcing" has taken on a narrower definition, referring only to jobs sent overseas. In the business and academic world, however, to clearly distinguish between kinds of outsourcing activities and locations, three new words have supplemented the term "outsourcing": "offshoring," "inshoring," and "near-shoring."

OFFSHORING

Since outsourcing can be domestic or foreign, a more appropriate and common term used today for jobs that are sent overseas is "offshoring." Offshoring has the following characteristics:

1. It includes both manufacturing and service jobs outsourced overseas, although the term is more commonly used for service jobs.
2. It includes transfer of jobs by companies to their own overseas affiliates managed by their own staff. Such offshore affiliates are called captive firms.
3. It includes offshore work offered to joint ventures, where the company owns an affiliate in partnership with a local vendor.

INSHORING

"Inshoring," the opposite of offshoring, is a practice in which companies bring the job back to the country of domicile. This can happen when companies terminate their offshoring contracts or close down their captive affiliates.

It also includes jobs sent by overseas vendors back to the United States, the country that originally provided the outsourcing orders. For example, many large Indian service vendors that were the beneficiaries of offshoring from U.S. firms have now opened offices in the United States and employ U.S. workers. There are three reasons for the growth of inshoring:

1. As overseas vendors perform more complex jobs, they require skilled labor that is available only in the United States.
2. As overseas wages increase, the cost differential between U.S. and overseas workers narrows and the offshoring is reversed.
3. Some business models require managers to be posted at client sites in order to ensure effective communication between the company and the overseas vendor.

Inshoring is relatively a new term. The volume of inshoring is expected to increase as the dollar continues to depreciate and the wage differentials between the United States and offshoring countries narrow over time.

NEAR-SHORING

"Near-shoring" is a practice in which companies send work offshore to countries that are geographically close. This practice has come about because companies in the United States are finding that the logistics of managing projects in faraway countries such as China, India, and the Philippines can be problematic. This is of particular concern to U.S. manufacturing firms that have sent work offshore to countries in Asia.

The reasons cited for the preference of near-shoring are as follows:

1. *Logistics Costs:* Companies that send work offshore to Asia have to pay extra for transportation costs. The fourfold increase in oil prices in 2008 makes transportation costs a significant factor, especially for the delivery of heavy items such as cars, cranes, and the like.

2. *Inventory Costs:* The amount of inventory a company maintains when working with an overseas production facility is usually higher the farther away the location of the vendor. In addition, companies with a single offshore transit point are vulnerable to disruptions and must also carry more inventory. A strike by the International Longshore and Warehouse Union on April 7, 2003, to protest the Iraq war led to delayed shipments that hurt many companies in the United States practicing lean inventory management.

3. *Time Zone:* Near-shore countries usually have the same time zone as the contracting company, which allows for easier management of the offshore unit. The disadvantage of using a firm in the same time zone is the inability to get jobs done during off-hours for delivery the subsequent morning.

4. *Free-Trade Zone:* The signing of the Dominican Republic–Central America–United States Free Trade Agreement (CAFTA-DR) in 2005 has made it financially more attractive for U.S. companies to set up offshoring centers in the near-shore countries of the Dominican Republic, El Salvador, Guatemala, Nicaragua, Honduras, and Costa Rica.

5. *Exchange Rates:* As the dollar continues to depreciate, the cost of offshoring increases, thereby reducing the benefits of sending work overseas. In contrast, the currencies of nearby countries tend to move together.

The advantages of near-shoring, based on the aforementioned factors, are especially relevant for the manufacturing industry. The major beneficiaries of near-shoring by U.S. companies are those countries located in Latin America and South America. There is talk that Latin America and South America could improve their infrastructures and labor skills to become the new India and also excel in offering services, aided in part by their geographical proximity to the United States.[4] Similarly, the beneficiaries of near-shoring by European companies are countries in North Africa and Eastern Europe.

OFFSHORING OF SERVICES: INTERNET TECHNOLOGY VS. BUSINESS PROCESS OFFSHORING

Offshoring of services has become an important element of global trading activity. As a new phenomenon, it is not clear whether the impact of offshoring service jobs has the same impact as that of manufacturing jobs.

One difference between manufacturing and services offshoring is that the latter has been spurred by rapid advances in Internet technology. Internet technology makes it possible to send a wide variety of service jobs overseas, some of which were once thought immovable and believed to require physical presence at the performance site. For example, surgeons can now perform delicate operations on patients in another country using robotics and Internet technology, termed "telesurgery." A new paradigm for global trade and economics may have to be defined as Internet technology changes the work process to accommodate labor that can be sourced globally.

The new technology offers much more flexibility when a company is developing a global business model. Companies can now outsource or send offshore any or all components of the business process. In addition, a company can plan such that a lack of inventory caused by a disruption in production or service in one country can be compensated for immediately by a contracted company in another country. Managing an offshoring project requires a completely new business approach, as it involves incorporating additional variables such as culture, attitude, work ethic, and leadership style. Before we discuss the offshoring of services in detail, we define the two most popular forms of jobs that are offshored: IT and business process.

"Internet technology offshoring," or "IT offshoring," is the term used for offshoring all services related to a company's use of computers and Internet technology. Most of these projects involve the development of programs and software for companies, including customized and automated processes, business applications, web portals, and scientific equipment. In addition, IT managers of offshore companies work on in-house program development and maintenance. IT offshoring may be outsourced to third-party vendors or to a captive subsidiary of the company itself.

IT offshoring services mushroomed in the 1990s as Internet technology became established in the commercial sector. Shortages of trained programmers in the United States forced companies to search the overseas market, and India became a popular destination. Not only was there a large labor pool specialized in engineering, but the language of instruction in most colleges was English.

In the late 1990s, there was worldwide concern about what was termed as the year 2000 crisis, commonly referred to as the Y2K crisis. The problem stemmed from the two-digit programming code used in a majority of software for the "year" variable. For example, the year 1990 was written as "90" and 1980 as "80." As the year 2000 approached, it was not clear how the programs would interpret the "00"—as "1900" or as "2000." This potential problem would affect not only software applications but many of the algorithms embedded in microchips. Unless the year was specified clearly, there was a danger that applications would fail to operate on January 1, 2000, shutting down systems around the globe. Doomsday scenarios were predicted by the popular press, including the possibility of airplanes failing in mid-flight and nuclear power plants shutting down.

Private companies and government organizations undertook a major effort to rewrite critical programs. This rework required a massive amount of labor skilled in programming, and India was the only country that could supply it at short notice. The year 2000 proceeded without any major disaster, and it is still unclear whether it was a real problem and whether the reprogramming averted potential disasters.

An interesting offshoot of this programming effort was that India was ready with a large pool of skilled labor to provide IT services. Coincidentally, companies throughout the world had just begun to incorporate IT programs at a rapid pace into their workflow processes. India benefited the most from this upsurge, as companies began to send their IT services offshore. In 2007, six major companies in India—Satyam, Wipro, Infosys, TCS, Cognizant, and HCL (known as SWITCH)—accounted for 2.4 percent of the global

IT services and 3.6 percent of IT services in the United States. They also accounted for 1.9 percent of European IT services, an increase from 1.5 percent in 2006.[5]

"Business process offshoring," or BPO, is the term used to denote a variety of work processes that are outsourced to foreign countries. They include a whole spectrum of company work ranging from data entry, payroll, human resources, and budgeting to pension fund management. Broadly speaking, any work process apart from IT services that can be outsourced to a third-party vendor can be defined as a BPO. BPO services can be sent offshore to captive companies or to third-party vendors.

BPOs are subdivided into back-office or front-office services.

BACK-OFFICE SERVICES

Back-office activities relate to the business functions of a company that are processed at the back of the office and usually do not require interaction with customers. The following are some examples of back-office services that are sent offshore, listed by type of institution.

Financial Institutions

Commercial banks, investment banks, credit card companies, and other financial companies perform a range of back-office work at the end of the day. This labor-intensive work includes recording, verifying, and settling all trades and transactions incurred during the day. For investment banks, the work involves documenting the day's trades made by hundreds of brokers engaged in buying and selling commodities, foreign currencies, and securities. The back office of American Express, for example, processes all credit card purchases recorded during the day and updates the statements of clients worldwide. With Internet technology, these updates now take place in China and India during the middle of the night in the United States.

Insurance Companies

Every day, insurance companies process thousands of claims by customers, requiring continuous updates of client records, verification of claims, and payments. In the case of medical insurance, claims processing requires checking and recording all patient bills, Medicare payments, and the posting of balances and notices.

Hospitals

Doctors usually use a handheld voice recorder to document the diagnoses of their patients; these recordings are later transcribed into an electronic or paper format. This labor-intensive process is now outsourced offshore by a majority of U.S. hospitals to third-party vendors in countries such as India and the Philippines. Medical transcription, as it is termed, involves a pool of typists located overseas who transcribe the recordings into electronic documents that are then sent back the United States by the following business day.

Other forms of back-office processes include payroll services, human resource services, legal services, and bookkeeping services.

FRONT-OFFICE SERVICES

The front office usually handles sales-related jobs, including marketing, advertising, account maintenance, and customer support. The majority of front-office BPO services are performed through call centers that provide support services such as technical support, customer service, and telemarketing. Call centers require the establishment of a full infrastructure of trained personnel who are able to make and receive overseas telephone calls. Computer companies were among the first group of companies to outsource these services offshore.

Support centers for software- and hardware-related products require a highly skilled labor force that understands the products thoroughly and are able to answer all customer queries. The most frequently chosen offshoring destinations are Ireland, Canada, India, Mexico, Jamaica, and the Philippines. Not only do companies need to invest heavily in setting up the offices and training the local workers, they also have to monitor the offshore employees' progress continuously. An advantage of call centers located offshore is that they are able to offer customer support services around the clock. The most popular support services are discussed next.

Customer Service Support Center

Many companies provide customer support services through offshore affiliates or vendors that are able to respond to basic service requests and answer low-level queries. If a customer's request requires personal attention or the query is complex, the call is transferred back to a U.S. call center. The types of companies that have set up offshore customer support service centers include telephone, insurance, mortgage, and software companies.

Help Desk

Companies have also established help desks at their offshore locations to provide a variety of troubleshooting services and assist companies in effectively selling their products. The initial help desks were set up for computer- and software-related companies. Today, offshore help desks are being created for both consumer and industrial companies. For example, Siemens, a large German multinational, outsourced their help desk services offshore to Ireland to take advantage of that country's lower wages. All queries on a range of consumer products are routed to the company's Irish offshore center.

Many companies separate their technical and customer service centers, providing one resource for corporate accounts and another for individual and home accounts. Since corporate accounts usually provide larger profit margins, companies may choose to route business service calls to local centers while serving individual or home accounts with offshore services.

Telemarketing and Sales Calls

Another front-office activity being sent overseas is telemarketing services. Teams of salespersons in various call centers around the globe call customers in the United States to sell a company's services or products. Cost savings has been the primary reason cited for offshoring telemarketing services. The most frequently chosen destinations for telemarketing call centers are India, the Philippines, Mexico, Jamaica, and Canada.

Several types of telemarketing services can be provided by offshoring companies. The most popular services include:

1. *Sales:* Call centers are given a list of targeted people to call, and the company's product or service is sold directly to the customer. Insurance and mortgage products, long-distance telephone services, and banking services are often sold through call centers. Bonuses are typically provided for successful sales.
2. *Appointment Setting:* Call centers are given lists of targeted people to set up appointments for the marketing team. This is usually done for products or services that cannot be sold directly to customers but require negotiations, pilot projects, or detailed discussions.
3. *Lead Generation:* Lead generation is perhaps the most difficult of all services since target customers are not clearly identified and therefore may not expect the call. Call centers are provided with a general list of companies or phone numbers, and telemarketers are tasked with generating sales, mostly through a hit-or-miss approach.
4. *Market Research:* Call centers perform a variety of analyses required for market studies. Data is collected through direct phone calls, e-mails, surveys, or other research. Market research services conducted in this manner include market profiling, customer satisfaction surveys, competitor evaluations, and analysis of lost sales and customer retention.
5. *Database Update:* Companies' databases, including client lists, office locations, new employees, or other information pertinent to a business, must be kept up-to-date. Call centers contact companies, persons, or other entities to perform the updates to the databases.

The performance of offshore call centers has recently come under criticism due to an increase in complaints about the quality of service, including callers' difficulties in understanding foreign operators' accents. This has led many companies to reevaluate the benefits and effectiveness of offshoring front-office services. A well-publicized case is that of the computer company Dell Inc., whose technical support services came under intense criticism for providing a mediocre level of service. Dell was forced to reroute most of its corporate client services back to the United States. Similarly, Conseco, an insurance and financial services firm based in Carmel, Indiana, purchased an offshoring firm in 2002 with plans to move 14 percent of its workforce to India. At the end of the first year, it decided to sell the company, citing difficulties in managing the offshore location.[6]

However, these failures were short-lived. In due course, both companies reopened or expanded their offshoring activities. On April 8, 2008, Conseco awarded a five-year outsourcing contract to one of India's largest offshoring companies. In July 2007, Dell opened a manufacturing plant in Chennai, India, to meet the growing demand for computers in India. This will be their third plant in the Asia-Pacific region (plants have already been established in Penang, Malaysia, and Xiamen, China).[7]

The return can be explained partly by the higher learning curve and migration pains required when services are outsourced to foreign vendors. With improvements in the quality of foreign labor, extensive training, and improved delivery by call centers, both companies have recognized that offshoring in the end pays off with proper project management. Another reason cited for their return to India has been the growth in the internal market of India for a range of consumer products and services as a result of its growing middle class. Companies planning to tap into this market will have an advantage if they already have established a subsidiary or office there.

The offshoring of services is expected to grow for the foreseeable future. As discussed earlier, there is a learning curve when companies send services offshore to countries with different cultures. Companies have to be patient and should plan on spending sufficient time to fine-tune the offshoring process if it is to be implemented successfully.

FUTURE OF OFFSHORING SERVICES

A study by McKinsey and NASSCOM (a trade group representing Indian offshoring services) concluded in 2005 that India accounted for 46 percent of global BPO services and 65 percent of IT offshoring services. The total value of these services was expected to reach $60 billion by 2010. The biggest impediment to the increase in offshoring was the lack of resources in India to keep up with the expected demand. The study projected an increase in demand of more than 25 percent per year for the foreseeable future.[8] In the meantime, other countries have recognized the benefits of accepting offshoring service jobs and are investing heavily in the appropriate infrastructure to attract them. A 2008 survey by Gartner reported a list of 30 countries that were acceptable to U.S. companies for offshoring services, listed in Table 9.1. Among the 10 criteria used were language proficiency and availability, including written proficiency and competency; government support; and potential labor pool.[9]

The last few years have also seen an increase in companies from Europe, Japan, Australia, and New Zealand offshoring service jobs. As offshoring becomes an integral component of multinational planning by non-U.S. firms, the choice of countries will depend on the language skills (other than English) that can be offered. The following is a list of locations with advantages in offering offshoring services in languages other than English.

1. *Northern Ireland:* Northern Ireland's labor force is able to deliver services in 18 languages throughout Europe and South America. The country's long civil war pushed its younger population to study overseas, and over the years these individuals have returned to their home country equipped with various IT and BPO skills for offshoring services.

Table 9.1

Thirty Acceptable Countries for U.S. Offshoring Services

Americas	Asia-Pacific	Europe, Middle East, and Africa
Argentina	Australia	Czech Republic
Brazil	China	Hungary
Canada	India	Ireland
Chile	Malaysia	Israel
Costa Rica	New Zealand	Northern Ireland
Mexico	Pakistan	Poland
Uruguay	Philippines	Romania
	Singapore	Russia
	Sri Lanka	Slovakia
	Vietnam	South Africa
		Spain
		Turkey
		Ukraine

Source: Denise Dubie, "Gartner: Top 30 Offshore Locations for 2008," Network World, May 20, 2008. Available at http://www.networkworld.com/news/2008/052008-gartner-top-offshore-locations.html?page=1.

2. *South Africa:* South Africa's long history with the Netherlands allows the country to provide services in Dutch.
3. *Brazil:* Brazil has the largest Japanese population outside of Japan and has been effective in servicing Japanese projects.
4. *Dalian, China:* Dalian, a city in northeast China, has a large Japanese-speaking population; Japan occupied it in 1895 and later leased it from China until 1945.
5. *Guatemala:* Guatemala has a bilingual population that can provide services in both Spanish and English.
6. *Algeria, Tunisia, and Morocco:* Their long history with France has provided all three countries with a large educated population that is capable of providing a variety of services in French.

China is touted as the next country to dominate the offshoring market for services as it possesses the requisite infrastructure and labor. Although offshoring of manufacturing services to China is expected to continue and grow in the near future, it is facing strong competition from other countries. Wage inflation and strains on China's infrastructure are also expected to exert a downward pressure on its growth. A recent scandal involving lead found in children toys and the discovery of diethylene glycol in toothpastes from China created a massive recall by many toy makers and dental product manufacturers. The Chinese government has acted swiftly to curb the abuses, but they have exposed the vulnerability of the country's dependence on the manufacturing sector. The Ethical Corporation reported that FDI to China from the European Union fell 29.4 percent in 2007; from the United States during the same period it fell 12.8 percent.[10] As a result, China is focusing on efforts to increase its capabilities in offering offshoring services. A recent report in *McKinsey Quarterly* predicted that if China pursues an aggressive strategy, the value of the offshore services sector could reach $56 billion by 2015.[11]

TOWARD A GLOBAL OFFSHORING STRATEGY

Although U.S. companies have been outsourcing work offshore for more than three decades, with Europe and Japan following shortly thereafter, offshoring is still a new phenomenon for a majority of companies. This is because the process of offshoring is more complicated than that of domestic outsourcing. First, the company has to ensure that the offshoring is consistent with its strategic objectives. Second, it has to ensure that the organizational structure is in place to handle the flow of communication between the United States and overseas offices. Third, the company has to ensure that the workflow from offshore units is fully integrated into the domestic business units.

Once the decision has been made to send work offshore, the following steps must be followed to ensure successful implementation.

1. Determine those sectors that should be outsourced domestically and those that should be sent offshore. The following factors have to be considered for the offshoring of any manufacturing or services jobs:

- *Critical Functions*: Identify noncore and core services. Core services are those that can cripple a company if the offshoring fails or if there is an interruption in delivery; for example, the failure to deliver components can halt work in an assembly line.
- *Domain Expertise*: Estimate the level of difficulty for the foreign vendor to acquire the company's domain expertise. If it can be copied and duplicated easily, it may be too risky to offshore.
- *Scalability*: Identify offshored services that can be scaled up in the event they are successfully implemented. A what-if scenario analysis can help determine the best time to expand or opt out of offshoring.

2. Perform a cost-benefit analysis for offshoring the services. This can be a tricky task, as a complete and thorough analysis requires reliable and detailed information on offshoring costs. A number of factors have to be taken into account when undertaking the analysis:

- *Single or Multiple Vendors:* A company must choose between employing single or multiple vendors. The advantages of using a single vendor are lower costs as a result of economies of scale and easier communications management. A disadvantage is the potential bottleneck that may occur if there is a failure in the delivery of services by the single vendor.
- *Captive or Third-Party Vendor:* Costs will be affected by whether the company sets up its own office or plant (captive unit) or outsources the work offshore to

a third-party vendor. In general, it is more expensive to set up a captive center, but a captive center provides more control over the management and execution of projects.

• *Large or Small Vendor:* It is important to evaluate potential vendors thoroughly. Large vendors usually have the expertise to provide the required services and additional skills that can benefit a company. However, they are typically more expensive and may be bureaucratic. Not only may small vendors be cheaper, but they usually provide more attention to a company's requirements. In all cases, it is essential that the vendors have the capacity to perform the requested services.

3. Implement the process slowly and ramp it up in tandem with the success of each leg of the project. The following issues need to be considered for successful implementation.

• Establish a set of criteria to measure the progress or success of each leg of project. This will include a timetable for completion of projects with a reasonable time allotted for the learning curve.
• Create and assign the appropriate personnel responsible for managing each of the projects outsourced or sent offshore. For large and multiple projects, the person in charge should be the chief technology officer (CTO) or the chief information officer (CIO).
• Perform periodic evaluations based on the established criteria to recommend continuation or abandonment of the projects.

ADVANTAGES AND DISADVANTAGES OF OFFSHORING SERVICES

It is difficult to measure the gains or losses from offshoring services to both the sending and receiving countries. Research has only recently begun on the impact of offshoring of services, and the issue continues to be influenced by the politically sensitive nature of the topic. Labor groups and politicians of sending countries see offshoring as a net loss to society; critics find it easy to bolster their case by highlighting the losses to the local economy without looking at the overall picture. Similarly, most economists and business professionals see offshoring in a positive light but tend to underestimate the impact of job relocations, labor anxiety, and lack of worker commitment that can negatively impact the economy in the long term. The following points highlight some of the observable gains and losses to both the receiving and sending countries.

Receiving Country

At first glance, it would seem evident that the country receiving the offshoring services is always a net beneficiary. While this may not always be true, some of the possible positive impacts are:

1. Offshoring increases employment and generates income to the economy.
2. Offshoring leads to the development of ancillary industries, contributing further to the growth and income of the economy.

3. Over time, the skills and talents acquired while providing the offshoring services are turned inward to serve the growing internal market and help propel the country to the next level.

Negative impacts include the following points:

1. Offshoring may increase the wage rates in the economy, usually as a result of a shortage of skilled labor to meet the growing demands of the offshoring market. Both China and India are examples of countries that are experiencing double-digit wage increases as a result of the growth in offshoring activities. As companies compete to attract a limited number of skilled workers, upward pressure on wages can affect other sectors of the economy.
2. Offshoring may lead to increases in inflation rates as a result of the growth in purchasing power of a growing middle class. The increased offshoring to India and China has resulted in the development of sizable middle classes in those countries. India experienced 8 percent inflation in 2007, while China experienced 4.8 percent inflation in 2007, well above the targeted 3 percent.
3. Offshoring can lead to a growing disparity in income and living standards between the urban and rural sectors of the country. Both China and India are witnessing this phenomenon, which has resulted in an accelerated migration of people from rural to urban areas. If the income inequality is not contained, it could lead to social unrest.
4. The high wages and inflation rates eventually force companies to search for other countries to meet their needs for offshoring services.

In sum, receiving countries have to be careful to manage the growth of their economies, as offshoring generates income and employment. Policies have to be put in place to prevent high wages, price inflation, uneven development, and currency appreciation. This requires that resources be allocated in a well-balanced manner. The government has to balance its infrastructure spending between supporting the offshoring industry and supporting other population groups in the country.

SENDING COUNTRY

A report in 2005 by the General Accountability Office (GAO), an independent U.S. government agency that provides objective research and information for Congress, reported the following benefits and costs to the United States as a result of the sending services offshore in recent years.[12] Costs include:

1. Offshoring leads to downward pressure on wages and reduces the standard of living in the sending country.
2. Offshoring leads to job losses and increases the unemployment rate in the sending country.
3. As wages decline and profits increase for shareholders, offshoring may widen income inequality in the sending country. Shareholders stand to benefit the

most when jobs are sent offshore. The flexibility provided to companies with offshoring opportunities can only result in continual downward pressure on local wages.

4. Offshoring may impact national security, as transfer of technology enables other countries to specialize in products that are important for a country to maintain its lead in critical sectors. An often-used example is the loss of the semiconductor industry to foreign companies in 1985, when there was overproduction around the world. A sudden shortage of processor chips can have a devastating effect on a range of industries.

Offshoring may lead to loss of privacy as personal data is passed on to vendors in countries that have lower standards of corporate governance. This is of particular importance because of the increase in the offshoring of financial institutions' back-office functions from the United States to foreign countries. The Gramm-Leach-Bliley Act of 1999 mandated that banks take adequate precautions to maintain the privacy of their clients' personal data. The Federal Banking Agencies (FBA), consisting of the Office of the Comptroller of the Currency, the Board of Governors of the Federal Reserve System, the Federal Deposit Insurance Corporation, the National Credit Union Administration, and the Office of Thrift Supervision, recently issued tougher guidelines to cover the work performed by service providers located offshore.

However, offshoring has its benefits, as well:

1. Offshoring increases productivity and, in the long run, increases real wages. If companies increase productivity by offshoring, the benefits should also accrue to the company's remaining workforce.

The GAO report states that total labor compensation as a percentage of net income in the United States declined from 66 percent in 2001 to 64 percent in 2004. In addition, wages and salaries declined from 55 percent of net income in 2001 to 52 percent in 2004. It is not yet possible to conclude whether offshoring depresses wages in the receiving country. More data is required to infer the impact of offshoring on wages and salaries.

2. Offshoring does not reduce employment; rather, it increases it in the long run. Long-term unemployment has remained steady in the United States despite the migration of manufacturing jobs to foreign countries. The U.S. unemployment rate has fallen from 5.8 percent in 2002 to 4.6 percent in 2007. Critics have argued, however, that the unemployment rate by itself may not be a good indicator, as the standard of living may be lower due to lower real wages and purchasing power.

3. Offshoring leads to lower prices and inflation, enabling U.S. consumers to have more opportunities to increase consumption.

Most economists would agree that offshoring reduces prices and benefits consumers in the long run. Wal-Mart is a classic example of how imports from China have managed to keep inflation rates in the United States low for decades. It is estimated that Wal-Mart is China's eighth-largest customer, ahead of Russia and Germany.[13] It is somewhat of a paradox that Wal-Mart is the favorite shopping center for a majority of America's middle- and low-income population while being equally responsible for the loss of millions of jobs in the United States.

Table 9.2

U.S. Inflation Rate, 2000–2007

Year	Inflation Rate	Year	Inflation Rate
2000	3.38%	2004	2.68%
2001	2.83%	2005	3.39%
2002	1.59%	2006	3.24%
2003	2.27%	2007	2.85%

Source: U.S. Bureau of Labor.

Inflation rates, according to the U.S. Bureau of Labor Statistics, for the years 2000 to 2007 are listed in Table 9.2. Although inflation rates increased in 2008, this increase cannot be blamed on offshoring; rather, steep increases in energy prices and global food shortages are mostly responsible for the upward trend.

There is sufficient evidence to indicate that offshoring leads to higher wages, lower prices, and higher productivity for the sending country in the long run. As in the case of the receiving country, it is necessary for policies to be put in place to ensure that the short-term effects of offshoring on income and employment are not disruptive. Appropriate policies have to be established to ensure that the country remains competitive in the long run.

ORGANIZATIONAL STRUCTURE IN OFFSHORING

There are several ways for companies to structure their offshoring projects when they go overseas. They can set up captive units or joint ventures, or contract out to direct or indirect third-party vendors.

Captive Units

A firm may decide to pursue offshoring services on its own and set up a captive unit; in other words, the firm will own and manage the overseas company. Companies can start from scratch or purchase a local company to form the captive unit. Setting up a captive unit is the equivalent of FDI. Just as IBM may choose to open a factory in Belgium, a bank may choose to set up a unit or purchase a vendor in another country to perform its business processes. The unit will hire local labor to perform the services, while senior management may be sent to the site from the parent company.

Joint Ventures

In a joint venture, a firm teams up with a local company to form an offshore affiliate and provide offshoring services. The agreement may restrict the type of offshoring activities that can be performed by the joint venture; for example, it may not be permitted to offer services similar to those performed by the firm's competitors. Control is usually shared equally. Over time, if the joint venture is successful, the firm may acquire the remaining ownership of the local company. The model, termed "BOT" (build, operate, and transfer), has been used successfully by many companies.

For example, in May 2008, Barclays Bank decided to set up a 5,000-seat captive unit in India to perform BPO services. Barclays had originally invested 50 percent in a local company called Intelenet Global Services. It had asked the company to build a 1,000-seat unit and operate it on Barclays' behalf until it purchased the unit. However, in this particular case, Barclays decided not to take the transfer (purchase the company) but instead decided to build its own.[14] One reason cited was data security, and this concern has led many other banks—including Citibank, American Express, Standard Chartered, Deutsche Bank, and HSBC—to set up their own captive units in India.

Direct Third-Party Vendors

The other approach for offshoring is to contract the jobs to third-party vendors. There are many benefits to using third-party vendors.

1. It requires no investment in infrastructure.
2. With lower overhead, the risk is lowered. If the offshoring is a failure, the investment losses will be borne by the vendor.
3. It allows a company to choose among the best vendors.
4. If the vendors implement the projects successfully, they can be acquired later and integrated into a captive unit.

The disadvantages are the following:

1. The company must transfer technology and other know-how to a third-party vendor, who may use it for their other clients.
2. Costs may be higher when compared to a company setting up its own captive unit.
3. Without complete control of management of the offshoring unit, the company faces the risk of delays and nonimplementation.
4. Personal data and privacy may be compromised.

In the initial years of offshoring, most companies preferred setting up captive units in India. However, as wages and attrition rates increased in response to the fierce competition for talented workers, the average cost has continued to rise. In May 2007, a study by Forrester Research showed that even though 300 firms had opened captive firms in the previous two years in India, 60 percent of them were struggling with managing them.[15] It predicted that by 2010, 40 to 60 percent of them would select one of four possible exit strategies:

1. Exit from the offshoring business completely. The prediction is that 10 percent of the exiting firms will choose this option.

2. Engage in a hybrid strategy where firms outsource some of the work and reduce the overhead of the captive unit. About 25 percent of the exiting firms are expected to choose this option.
3. Adopt a termite approach, where captives partner with vendors and hollow out the center, leaving only project management functions for the parent company. About 40 to 50 percent of exiting firms are expected to choose this approach.
4. Outsource all the jobs to offshore units and close the captive unit. About 10 percent of the exiting firms are expected to follow this approach.

In a subsequent study by Everest Research Group in September 2007, a poll of 102 executives from 56 firms yielded different results. Although some major firms are expected to exit the Indian market, most plan to stay and expand their captive offices. In 2002, among the Forbes 200 companies, 44 firms had established captive centers in India; that number increased to 71 in 2003 and to 110 in 2006.[16]

Indirect Third-Party Vendors

Some companies outsource jobs to domestic companies that, in turn, have offshoring offices. Indirect third-party vendors provide advantages and disadvantages similar to those provided by direct offshoring, with the exception that the job is made easier because the contracting company has to communicate only with the domestic outsourcer. Care has to be taken to ensure that the relationship between the domestic outsourcer and its affiliate overseas is sound, reliable, and effective. It may be risky if the domestic outsourcer is using multiple vendors overseas instead of owning its own affiliate.

WHICH COMPANIES DO THE MAJORITY OF OFFSHORING?

Although a large number of firms have begun to send service-related jobs offshore to India, China, the Philippines, and Mexico, the number of firms sending work offshore is still a very small percentage of the total. A survey by Robert Half in January 2008 of 1,400 chief information officers shows that only 5 percent of them have sent technology jobs offshore. Companies with more than 500 employees were more likely to send work offshore, accounting for 11 percent of this group. About 43 percent of the companies that are presently outsourcing plan to increase their offshoring, while 13 percent plan to decrease it.[17]

The National Academy of Public Administration published a report in 2006, commissioned by U.S. Congress and the Bureau of Labor Statistics of the Department of Commerce, on the activity of offshoring services between 1998 and 2004. The panel concluded that:

1. The outsourcing of services to domestic companies between 1998 and 2004 far outstripped the offshoring of services to overseas companies.
2. Offshoring levels in all industry groups were very small during this period.
3. No consistent pattern of growth of offshoring services could be found among the industries. In fact, there was substantial variation among industries and across time.[18]

One therefore has to keep the total picture in perspective when evaluating the offshoring phenomenon. Even though offshoring is increasing in volume, it still is and probably will remain a small component of total service activity in the United States.

Europe is expected to catch up with the United States in terms of offshoring services. Strong unions and a business culture that focuses on maximizing stakeholder rather than shareholder wealth had European companies less enthusiastic about offshoring jobs. However, with the enlargement of the European Union to 27 countries and the growth of European markets in developing countries, companies are now beginning to send services offshore. A 2007 Gartner study predicted that offshoring from Europe will increase by 60 percent in 2008, with the preferred destinations being India, China, Russia, and Brazil.[19]

In the United States, government agencies have also been offshoring some of their IT services in spite of complaints from several protectionist lawmakers. This issue became a politically sensitive topic during the presidential election year of 2004. Two states, New Jersey and Arizona, prohibited the offshoring of government-related work. It is not clear whether laws banning offshoring are in the best interest of the states' citizens.

To highlight the issue, assume that a state awards a two-year contract worth $3.75 million to an offshore company for processing work. Assume the lowest domestic bid is $5 million, meaning the offshore company saves the state 25 percent. The $1.25 million saved allows the state to hire or retain approximately 25 individuals for a year at $50,000 per year. Thus, the decision not to offshore should be based on real long-term costs and benefits.

A 2006 report by the GAO stated that 43 of the 50 states and the District of Columbia sent some work offshore. The types of work sent to offshore locations included software development and assistance in managing the food stamps program, unemployment insurance, and other temporary assistance programs.[20]

REASONS TO GO OFFSHORE

There are several reasons for a company to go offshore, with cost being the dominant factor. Other factors include access to talent, flexibility, and market penetration.

Lower Costs

Lower costs are the primary reason for offshoring projects. However, cost alone is not sufficient to justify offshoring, as other factors have to be considered, including an ability to maintain the business model for an extended period of time. This is especially true for projects that require multiyear implementation and maintenance.

Access to Talent

Many companies are finding a large pool of well-trained engineers and technicians in offshoring countries that are otherwise unavailable in the home country. The new term for this kind of offshoring is "BKO," or business knowledge offshoring. Those firms that have made offshoring a success with noncore activities are most likely to move to the next step of knowledge offshoring, which includes R&D and product design work.

Flexibility

An outsourcing or offshoring model provides flexibility to companies because it requires lower investments and overhead. It allows companies to ride through peak and trough cycles with fewer disruptions. It also allows firms to ramp down during changes in market conditions without incurring much severance pay. Finally, it enables companies to spread their risks and focus on their core missions.

Market Penetration

A number of firms are now strategically looking to integrate their offshoring activities with long-range marketing plans to penetrate developing countries. As China and India become major consumers, companies are finding it strategically important to set up subsidiaries and offices in these countries in order to establish their presence. The process is similar to the FDI strategies adopted by the United States in Europe and by the Japanese in the United States. These investments eventually led to large markets for the firms as consumer spending increased in their favor.

A 2007 study by PricewaterhouseCoopers of 226 senior executives of private companies and service providers revealed seven reasons to outsource and send some of their services offshore. About 51 percent of the companies had revenues in excess of $1 billion. The service providers were located in China, India, the United States, and the United Kingdom.

Reasons to Offshore	
Lower costs (important or very important)	76 percent
Gain access to talent	70 percent
Farm out activities that others can do better	63 percent
Increase business-model flexibility	56 percent
Improve customer relationships	42 percent
Develop new products or markets	37 percent each
Geographic expansion	33 percent

The executives also highlighted the obstacles to outsourcing and offshoring.[21]

Reasons Not to Offshore	
Proving cost benefit	48 percent
Lack of experience	48 percent
Company values favor using in-house employees	45 percent
Lack of skills in managing outsourcing	37 percent
Need to clean up operations before outsourcing	37 percent
Ethics of moving jobs offshore	22 percent
Concerns about public reaction	21 percent

In sum, larger companies are the major users of offshoring of both manufacturing and services to overseas countries. Cost is the major factor in this decision, but other factors such as access to talent, expertise, and increased business flexibility are a close second.

CHAPTER SUMMARY

The growth of offshoring manufacturing to developing countries began with the opening of plants and factories in Europe by U.S. multinationals. Later, U.S. companies moved to developing countries to take advantage of cheap labor and a favorable business climate. Offshoring of manufacturing increased in pace when China opened its borders to FDI in the late 1970s. In the 1980s, a new form of offshoring began to take place—that of service, or white-collar, jobs. This service offshoring was made possible by the rapid advances in Internet technology.

The two major types of offshoring services are IT offshoring and business process offshoring. The offshoring of IT services began in the aftermath of the Y2K problem, as U.S. companies found a ready pool of programmers overseas, primarily in India. In due course, companies started sending offshore services related to the various workflow processes; this practice was termed business process outsourcing, or BPO. BPO services were classified into back-office and front-office services, both of which are popular today. Among front-office services, call centers that make and receive calls are the most popular and continue to flourish in spite of some negative publicity generated through to customer complaints.

The decision to use offshoring must be planned carefully by the company. A number of issues must be considered prior to beginning any offshore project. They include identifying which jobs should be outsourced, evaluating the likelihood that the company's domain expertise may not be duplicated, choosing to go with a single or multiple vendors, and estimating the costs and benefits of each leg of the offshoring process. The company also has to ensure that the organization is staffed appropriately to handle the communication and flow of work between the parent and offshore affiliates. Finally, a set of criteria has to be established to monitor the progress and success of the offshore projects.

There are several advantages and disadvantages in offshoring services to overseas affiliates or vendors. For the receiving country, the benefits are increased employment and income to the economy. The negative impacts include high wages and inflation. For the sending country, the negative impacts include the short-run loss of jobs and downward pressure on wages. The long-run benefits, however, may be higher income and employment. For both countries, it is necessary that government policies not oppose offshoring, but it is important that the governments manage the offshoring process intelligently, and avoid disruption of their respective domestic economies.

There are four major ways to structure offshoring projects: through captive units, joint ventures, direct third-party vendors, and indirect third-party vendors. Each structure offers different costs and benefits, with captive units providing the most control and the use of indirect third-party vendors providing the least. The most expensive choice is for a company to set up its own captive unit, while the most cost-effective choice is to go directly to third-party vendors.

The reason to go offshore is usually motivated by cost reductions. However, other factors include access to talent, flexibility to manage the business, and integration with the company's long-range strategic market penetration.

In sum, the global outsourcing or offshoring of both manufacturing and services will continue to increase in the near future. This phenomenon can be compared to the growth of FDI after 1945, when U.S. companies set up plants and factories overseas initially to serve local markets and later to take advantage of lower costs. In the 1990s, the next wave of offshoring service, or white-collar jobs, began to grow in volume and breadth. As Internet technology continues to innovate, the kinds and forms of offshoring services will continue to grow and evolve to incorporate all forms of business activity. In spite of this growth, offshoring of services will remain only a small part of a country's total service activity.

KEY CONCEPTS

Global Offshoring
Business Process Offshoring
Internet Technology Offshoring
Global Offshore Strategy

DISCUSSION QUESTIONS

1. What factors led to growth in the outsourcing of manufacturing from the United States to developing countries? What is the difference between FDI made by the United States to Europe and that made to developing countries?
2. Distinguish between manufacturing and service offshoring. Provide some examples.
3. Why did India become a favorite destination for U.S. companies to outsource IT services offshore?
4. Distinguish between the offshoring of IT services and business processing offshoring (BPO).
5. What is the impact of services offshoring to the domestic economy?
6. Compare offshoring, inshoring, and near-shoring. What are some of the characteristics of offshoring and inshoring?
7. What reasons are offered for the growth in near-shoring?
8. What was the Y2K problem and how did it spur the offshoring of IT services overseas?
9. Define business process outsourcing, or BPO. Provide some examples of back-office services that are sent offshore by U.S. companies.
10. Explain the front-office services provided by BPO firms. How are they different from back-office services? Have the front-office BPO services to India been successful?
11. What factors need to be considered in deciding whether to send any business processes offshore to an overseas affiliate or vendor?

12. What changes need to be made to the internal organizational structure if a firm decides to send work offshore?

13. What are the different structures that can be set up for offshoring projects overseas? What are the pros and cons for each method?

14. What are some of the reasons for companies to send services offshore? What are some of the reasons for not offshoring services?

APPLICATION CASE: EVALUESERVE AND KNOWLEDGE PROCESS OUTSOURCING

The outsourcing of services to India and other developing countries began with Internet technology (IT)–related projects in the 1980s. Most of the jobs focused on providing direct and indirect support to the IT departments of large companies in the United States and Europe. The work entailed writing software programs to run hardware effectively, creating and maintaining Internet sites, and developing application software. Business process outsourcing (BPO) evolved as the next growth industry as companies outsourced the development of complex systems to streamline, automate, and standardize their workflow processes. Beginning in 2000, BPO services gave way to knowledge process outsourcing services (KPO), defined as the delivery of customized and complex processes requiring advanced analytical and specialized knowledge unique to each project.

The number of companies that outsource KPO services to India come from a variety of industries. In the pharmaceutical industry, specialized services outsourced by U.S. and European companies include clinical trials, research and development, genetic engineering, treatment of new diseases, and biotechnology design. In the financial services industry, outsourced projects include market research, stock analyses, risk management and economic analysis. In the area of legal services, outsourced work to India includes reviewing litigation reports, performing due diligence on a variety of contracts, researching past cases, and drafting preliminary analyses and contracts. A common denominator for the success of KPO projects is the recruitment of skilled personnel holding advanced degrees in science, medicine, the humanities, and management. India possesses a natural advantage by having large pool of English-speaking people with a variety of advanced degrees from hundreds of universities.

One leading KPO firm is Evalueserve, founded in 2000 by Alok Aggarwal and Marc Vollenweider. Aggarwal earned his Ph.D. in computer science from Johns Hopkins University and joined IBM in 1984. He went to New Delhi, India, in 1998 to head the IBM India Research Laboratory, which he started while working in the United States. Vollenweider received his M.B.A. from INSEAD (a graduate business school in France) and joined the management consulting firm McKinsey & Company in Switzerland, where he became a partner in 1998. The next year he moved to India to become the head of the McKinsey Knowledge Centre in Delhi.

Vollenweider was recruiting a number of experts for McKinsey to perform market analytics and business research to service their clients around the world. His department grew from 12 to 125 MBAs in the span of a year. Aggarwal was recruiting students with doctorates and master's degrees to perform a variety of tasks for IBM. His department grew from nothing to 70 employees in a similar period. Both recognized that the demand for individuals with advanced degrees from India would grow substantially to satisfy the growing need for advanced analytical work for industries in the West. A chance meeting in early 2000 resulted in both quitting their jobs in November 2000 to start Evalueserve with the mission of serving clients worldwide on specialized and complex projects. After a few difficult years, the company grew to over 2,500 professionals in 2008.

The KPO sector in India is currently worth about $4 billion but is expected to reach $10 billion by 2012.[22] The industry currently employs 40,000 individuals, but demand is expected to grow to 100,000 by the year 2012. However, there are several problems facing KPO industries in India, including Evalueserve.

One such problem is a shortage of talent. As the number of KPO firms has increased, the available pool of professionals in India has not been able to keep up with demand. The country is also facing stiff competition from Russia, the Philippines, Pakistan, Malaysia, Egypt, and Indonesia—nations that are also producing advanced graduates in record numbers. Evalueserve has opened offices in Russia, Romania, and Chile to diversify their talent base as one strategy to ensure a steady supply of qualified employees.

Another problem in India is the high attrition rate that has become endemic in this industry. As companies compete for the limited amount of talent, labor costs have increased exponentially, making it difficult for companies like Evalueserve to maintain their cost advantage. In a recent interview, Aggarwal cited "job hopping" as a serious concern for Evalueserve as employees continue to jump jobs, sometimes four to five times in a few years.[23]

Data security and the release of proprietary information is another problem. KPO services usually require clients to divulge confidential information on their core activities and their domain expertise. This is different than outsourcing BPO services, where the outsourced work is usually peripheral to the company's core activities. A leakage of KPO information to a client's competitors can be potentially damaging—if not catastrophic—requiring firms like Evalueserve to design and implement the highest level of security and risk management practices.

The 2008 economic slowdown in the United States and Europe provides some interesting challenges to the KPO industry in India. If the slowdown reduces demand for their services, Evalueserve may use this opportunity to consolidate its operations and focus on strategies to combat labor shortage and improve security systems. On the other hand, it is possible that the slowdown may increase business as Western companies seek to further reduce their costs. Evalueserve may have to scale up their operations more than anticipated while simultaneously solving the aforementioned problems.

QUESTIONS

1. How is knowledge process outsourcing (KPO) different from the other forms of services provided by outsourcings firms in India and other emerging countries.
2. What suggestions can you provide to Evalueserve to resolve their labor shortage and security concerns?

10 The Foreign Exchange Market

The currency depreciation that we have experienced of late should eventually help to contain our current account deficit as foreign producers export less to the United States. On the other side of the ledger, the current account should improve as U.S. firms find the export market more receptive.
—*Alan Greenspan*[1]

LEARNING OBJECTIVES

- To understand the role of foreign currencies in international trade
- To comprehend the historical use of money and foreign exchange as a medium of exchange
- To appreciate the growth of the foreign exchange market into the largest financial market in the world
- To examine the factors that affect foreign exchange rates
- To understand the importance of foreign exchange markets to multinational corporations

If goods are purchased by a citizen of one country, with one currency, from a citizen of another country, with a different currency, the buyer in most cases prefers to make the payment in his or her own currency. This requires an exchange of currencies from that of the buyer to that of the seller. The purchase or sale of any goods from a citizen of one country to a citizen of another will always result in two simultaneous transactions:

1. Physical exchange of the commodity
2. Purchase or sale of a foreign currency

The purchase or sale of the foreign currency affects only one of the parties in the exchange. If an American importer purchases US$100,000 worth of goods from a Japanese manufacturer and the invoice is billed in Japanese yen, the burden falls on the American importer to purchase Japanese yen to complete the transaction. If the contract is invoiced in U.S. dollars, the Japanese seller is responsible for converting the American dollars that were received into Japanese yen to complete the transaction. The party that has to convert the currency takes the risk that the exchange rate on that date of conversion is favorable to that party.

The venue for the purchase and sale of foreign currency is the foreign exchange market. The dynamics of international business cannot be appreciated without a thorough knowledge of the structure and workings of the foreign exchange market. This is all the more important today, as foreign currencies can be delivered in multiple formats: wire transfer, credit card, letters of credit, and other special instruments. Corporate managers engaged in exports and imports must be aware of all the available alternatives and evaluate their costs and benefits if they are to select the most appropriate methods of payment.

DEFINITION OF FOREIGN EXCHANGE

A *foreign exchange rate* refers to the price an individual pays in one currency to purchase another currency. A currency is similar to any other commodity, such as gold or food; its price is determined by the demand and supply for the commodity. Just as a fisherman quotes US$2 for a pound of fish, a foreign exchange dealer quotes a price for the purchase or sale of another currency. If a dealer quotes US$1.25 / €, he or she is quoting US$1.25 for the purchase or sale of €1.

The foreign exchange can also be quoted with the dollar as the unit of commodity; in other words, instead of dollars per euro, the cost can be quoted in euros per dollar. The rate per dollar is the inverse of the rate per euro, in our example, €0.80 per US$1.

$$1 / 1.25 = €0.80 / US\$1$$

This is similar to changing the fisherman's quote from $2 per pound of fish to half a pound of fish per dollar, that is, from US$2 / pound to ½ pound / US$1.

In the foreign exchange markets, the two forms of quotes are defined as direct or indirect:

Direct quote = HC / FC
Indirect quote = FC / HC

where HC = home country and FC = foreign currency.

For example—If the direct quote for an American investor is US$2.00 / €1, then the direct quote for a German investor is €0.50 / US$1.

If the indirect quote for an American investor is €0.50 / US$1, then the indirect quote for a German investor is US$2 / €1.

Note that a direct quote for an American investor is an indirect quote for a German investor.

Question: What is the direct quote for a Japanese investor who wishes to purchase the euro if the indirect quote is €0.006 / ¥1?

Answer: The direct quote for a Japanese investor is ¥ / € or 1/0.006 =
¥166.67 / €1.

Hints: To type the symbol € using your keyboard in Windows OS, with the
number lock on, press ALT and 0128.

To type the symbol ¥ using your keyboard in Windows OS, with the
number lock on, press ALT and 0165.

Exchange rates are available for either immediate delivery or for future delivery.
A spot rate is the price of a foreign currency for immediate delivery. Until recently,
immediate delivery in the United States meant two days for most currencies and one
day for Canadian dollars. Assume you purchased €100,000 in exchange for dollars at
a spot rate of US$1.21 for a total of US$121,000. The actual deposit of the $121,000
and €100,000 into the respective bank accounts takes two days because of the time
required for confirmation and initiating the transfer, a process defined as clearing
and settlement.

Advances in online technology have now made it possible for a spot transaction to
be settled on the same day it is made. The CLS Group (Continuously Linked Settlement; www.cls-group.com) is a consortium of the world's largest banks that is able
to settle all spot transactions on the same day for more than 50 currencies. The goal
of the group is to offer same-day settlement and clearing services for all currencies
in the world.

A forward rate is the rate for the purchase or sale of a foreign currency for delivery
at a future date. For example, a trader agrees to purchase €100,000 from another dealer
for a price agreed upon today, for delivery to take place in three months. No money
is exchanged today. At the end of three months, both traders are obligated to deliver
as promised. In every other feature, the forward rate is similar to the spot rate. The
most common periods for forward currencies are 30-, 60-, and 90-day deliveries.

APPRECIATION AND DEPRECIATION OF CURRENCIES

In all competitive markets, prices play an important role in equating supply and demand
for any product. If prices increase, demand for the commodity declines and supply of
the commodity increases, resulting in a new equilibrium price. In the short run, price
changes can cause disruptions in the production of output and services, while in the
long run, demand and production will adjust to the new price levels.

To understand the effects of price increases and price decreases of foreign currencies, it is first necessary to formally define currency appreciation and depreciation.
If the price of the euro increases, that is, moves from US$1.20 / € to US$1.25 / € to
US$1.30 / €, the dollar is said to be depreciating, or, conversely, the euro is said to
be appreciating. If the price of the euro decreases, that is, moves from US$1.20 / €

to US$1.15 / € to US$1.10 / €, the dollar is said to be appreciating, or, conversely, the euro is said to be depreciating. One way to remember the difference is based on whether the buyer has to pay more or less for a currency. Paying more implies hardship and therefore can be associated with a depreciation of the currency. If an American pays less for a foreign currency, one can consider that as good news and recognize that the dollar has appreciated.

A depreciating dollar is a boon to an American exporter, because it reduces the effective price to the foreign buyer of American commodities. To illustrate:

Assume the current or spot price of the euro is US$1.20 / €.
Assume the price of a candy bar in the United States is US$1.20.
Assume the price of a candy bar in Germany is €1.
Assume now the dollar depreciates drastically (for illustration purposes) to US$2.40 / €.
A German can now purchase two candy bars from the United States for €1.

Thus, whenever the dollar depreciates, U.S. goods become cheaper for German importers and exports will increase from the United States.

The opposite is true for an American importer; that is, a depreciating dollar will have a negative impact. Using the same numbers as above, assume the importer has been purchasing candy bars from Germany at a price of €1.00, or US$1.20, each. If the dollar depreciates to US$2.40 / €, then the U.S. importer has to pay two times more to purchase the euro in order to import one candy bar from Germany.

As shown above, changes in the price of currency have opposite effects on exporters and importers. When the dollar depreciates against the euro, it has a positive effect on U.S. exports but a negative effect on German exports. A depreciating dollar is equivalent to an appreciating euro to a German exporter. When the price of the euro goes from US$1.20 / € to US$2.40 / €, it becomes twice as expensive for an American importer to purchase commodities from Germany. Hence, German exports will fall. However, the depreciating dollar will be a boon to a German importer because he or she can purchase twice the amount from the United States per dollar.

Question: Assume the exchange rate between the Norwegian krone (KR) and the Brazilian real is NK2.5/real. Assume the export price of a particular brand of Adidas shoes from Norway is NK700. If the exchange rate changes to NK3.5/real, has the Norwegian krone depreciated or appreciated? Will the exports of shoes from Norway increase or decrease?

Answer: Since more Norwegians krones are required to purchase one Brazilian real, the Norwegian krone has depreciated (and the Brazilian real has appreciated). This will make Norwegian shoes cheaper for Brazilians, and exports of shoes from Norway should increase. A pair of these Adidas shoes will now cost the Brazilian buyers 200 reals instead of 280.

Table 10.1

Partial List of Major Currencies and Rate against the U.S. Dollar

Country	Currency	Alphabetic Code	Numeric Code	Rate on March 21, 2008
Afghanistan	Afghani	AFN	971	48.599/$
Australia	Australian dollar	AUD	036	1.1150/$
Austria	Euro	EUR	978	0.6371/$
China	Yuan renminbi	CNY	156	7.0525/$
France	Euro	EUR	978	0.6371/$
Kuwait	Dinar	KWD	414	0.4190/$
India	Indian rupee	INR	356	38.96/$
Norway	Norwegian krone	NOK	578	5.2614/$
Russian Federation	Russian ruble	RUB	643	

Source: Exchange rates from XE—The World's Favorite Currency and Foreign Exchange Site, available at http://www.xe.com. (accessed March 21, 2008). The alphabetic and numeric codes shown in Table 10.1 have been compiled by the International Standards Organization (ISO, www.iso.org). The ISO is comprised of the national standards institutes of 157 countries, and its mission is to develop a set of standards for various business activities, to make it easier for firms to operate in a global environment. Based in Geneva, Switzerland, it is a nongovernmental body that began by establishing standards for the electrical and engineering fields and later expanded to include all kinds of industrial services.

Note: The exchange rates shown are direct rates for each country

MAJOR CURRENCIES OF THE WORLD

Most countries issue their own currencies, which come in all sorts of shapes and colors. A partial list of the major currencies and their rates against the dollar is shown in Table 10.1.

Most of the currency names originated with the "weights" used to measure silver or gold. For example, the dollar came from the word *thaler,* from the city of Joachimsthal in modern-day Bohemia, where the coins, minted by the Count of Schlick, were trusted by traders for their consistency and uniformity. As a result, the "thaler" circulated extensively in Europe. The pound is another unit of weight, as are the lira (from the Latin *libra,* a unit of weight) and peso (from Latin *pensum,* meaning weight). The Indian rupee came from the Sanskrit word *rup,* meaning silver, and the Israeli shekel referred to the weight for a given quantity of silver.

THE EURO

The euro is an exception in that it was created recently by design and with the consent of participating countries in the European Union (EU). For the first time in history, countries volunteered to give up an existing currency to create a common currency. The euro began in 1999 as the currency of 11 EU countries (Belgium, Germany, Spain, France, Ireland, Italy, Luxembourg, the Netherlands, Austria, Portugal, and Finland), and was joined by Greece in 2001.

The history of the euro dates back to 1957, when the Treaty of Rome established plans for the creation of the European Economic Community. Further integration continued in small steps until the Maastricht Treaty agreement in 1992 paved the way for the creation of a common currency. A set of criteria was agreed upon for member countries to fulfill prior to adopting the euro, including having stable inflation and interest rates, deficit spending of less than 3 percent, and total public debt at below 60 percent of GDP. By 1999, with the exception of Greece, all countries managed to stay within the prescribed targets. On January 1, 1999, the exchange rates of 11 countries were locked in at the predetermined rates. Greece managed to fulfill the minimum criteria to join the group in 2001. On January 1, 2002, the currency of all 12 countries was officially changed with the issuance and distribution of the new currency. In January 2007, Slovenia adopted the euro, followed by Malta and Cyprus in January 2008. On January 1, 2009, Slovakia adopted the Euro and became the 16th country to join the Euro club.

Most economists agree that the euro has been a great success, which bodes well for the ultimate creation of a single global currency.

HISTORY OF FOREIGN EXCHANGE

Prior to 800 B.C.E., bartering was the principal means of exchange of goods, with cattle and grain serving as the mediums of exchange between neighboring communities. The rate of exchange depended on the demand and supply of the goods at the time of the transaction. If harvest in a given year was weak, less grain could be exchanged for cattle or any other product. If fishing in a given season resulted in a large harvest, more fish would be exchanged for other goods, especially since fish is a perishable product.

Bartering has the disadvantage that the goods have to be physically transported for the exchange to take place. As trade within and between city-states increased and the distances between them widened, it was a natural evolution for traders to settle on a common currency to serve as a medium of exchange. Precious metal was an obvious choice since it was available universally and was transportable.

The first coins were minted in electrum (a combination of silver and gold) in Asia Minor around 650 B.C.E. Later Greece and other city-states began minting their own coins as well, and the process of exchange within a city-state was consequently made simpler.[2] However, a problem with the use of metal coins was the difficulty in verifying the purity of the coins, usually gold or silver. Coins coming from kingdoms that minted them in pure gold or silver were sought after, such as those made by Croesus of Lydia in 550 B.C.E. Unfortunately, this was not the norm for most periods. City-states could mint pure coins only if they had sufficient gold or silver to produce the needed amount of coins. When a city-state did not have sufficient pure metals, often in times of wars, the coins were *debased,* as in the regimes of Nero in C.E. 60 and Henry VIII in the mid-1500s.

Debasement has two effects:

1. It leads to the hoarding of pure coins, which leaves only debased coins in circulation. Such a phenomenon, termed Gresham's law, essentially states that bad money drives out good money.

2. It leads to inflation because more coins are printed relative to the amount of reserves.

In a monetary system where coins of precious metal are used as a currency of exchange, foreign exchange rates are influenced more by debasement than by the real demand and supply for the coins. If pure gold or silver coins are used as a medium of transaction, the coins' country of origin does not matter; they can always be melted down and sold again. The value of the exchange depends on the amount of expected debasement, determined at the venue of exchange.

The two commodities that ultimately became the common denomination of exchange were gold and silver, for several reasons:

1. Scarcity: unavailable in abundance, requiring huge investments to extract
2. Divisibility: can easily be melted and shaped to any required quantity
3. Homogeneity: homogeneous and malleable
4. Durability: does not lose luster over time
5. Transportability: easily transported
6. Consistency: no variation in composition

The scarcity of gold eventually led to it being preferred over silver as a reserve currency.

PAPER MONEY

The determination of foreign exchange became more complicated with the advent of paper money, introduced first in China as early as C.E. 800. Marco Polo brought the concept to the West in the late 1200s, but its use as a currency did not become popular until the 1600s. The acceptance of paper money requires a much stronger trust in the issuer, since paper money could become worthless overnight.

In a world of paper money, the exchange of foreign currency requires two things:

1. Confidence that the paper currency can be exchanged for something valuable, such as gold or silver, on demand
2. Confidence by both the buyer and seller that the paper currency will maintain its value over time without a loss in purchasing power

The risk of paper currency becoming worthless overnight was a major reason why its acceptance was often limited to the local geographic area in which it was issued. Rarely was paper money accepted outside a country. In the United States, this concern continued right up to the twentieth century because the issuers of notes were usually private banks, which could fail and close down overnight. An additional problem was the counterfeiting of money, which was rampant at times in many countries.

As an example, the Massachusetts Bay Colony, one of the 13 original colonies, issued the first paper money in the New World in 1690 to finance military expeditions.

When the colonies were banned from printing currencies by the British government in 1764, the Continental Congress reissued new currency in 1775 to finance the Revolutionary War. It lost value soon after, however, because of counterfeiting and the lack of assurance that it would be repaid in gold or silver.

Congress tried twice to set up central banks, once in 1791 and again in 1816, but both ventures were short-lived. In 1861, when the government ordered the U.S. Treasury to issue noninterest-bearing demand notes, termed "greenbacks," the currency finally stabilized. To this day, all notes issued after 1861 can be redeemed at full face value. In 1913, the Federal Reserve Act created the Federal Reserve Board (the Fed) to oversee the U.S. monetary system and authorized it to issue all notes. Once credibility was established, the exchange rate for the dollar depended less on speculation and became a function of demand and supply.

The history of the central bank in Britain is somewhat different. The Bank of England was established in 1694 as a private bank to manage the accounts of the monarchy. It also did commercial business by accepting deposits and issuing its own handwritten notes. As a result of its close relationship with the monarchy, the Bank of England was regarded by many as an (un)official central bank. Indeed, during major crises, it served as the banker of last resort and issued credit by handwritten paper that was redeemable with gold or coinage. The bank was nationalized in 1946.[3]

GOLD STANDARD

One way for a government to instill confidence in its currency is to state its value in terms of gold or silver. The gold standard, sometimes supplemented by silver, has been the mainstay for foreign exchange pricing for more than 200 years. The gold standard was adopted informally as early as 1717, when Sir Isaac Newton was the master of the mint in England. But the gold standard in conjunction with bank notes became popular only in the early 1800s, with England formally adopting it in 1821, followed by Germany in 1875, France in 1878, the United States in 1879, and Russia and Japan in 1897.

Here is a simple way to understand how the foreign exchange rate is determined under the gold standard:

- Assume the U.S. government announces that it will always be prepared to exchange one ounce of gold for $35.
- Assume the UK government announces that it will always be prepared to exchange one ounce of gold for £17.50.
- If traders trusted both governments to stick to their pledges, the exchange rate would be set at:

£1.00 = US$2.00   *(US$35 / £17.50)*

Trust is a key ingredient in the effective working of a gold standard system. To achieve this trust, it is necessary for governments to print only as much currency as can be supported by the gold it holds in reserve.

What happens when traders lose faith in a government to back its currency with gold? For example, assume the UK government is unable to stick to its pledge of converting its pounds to gold on demand. Investors holding pounds will start selling their notes in exchange for gold. As investors rush to the Bank of England to demand gold, the country will be left with fewer gold reserves, which will force it to print less money. Investors will also be unwilling to trade at the old price of US$2.00 / £1, and the value of the dollar will increase in relative terms. In other words, the exchange rate will move from US$2.00 / £1 → US$1.90 / £1 → US$1.80 / £1 as traders are willing to accept fewer dollars to get rid of their pounds.

When will the dollar stop appreciating or, equivalently, when will the pound stop depreciating? According to the classical theory of the *price-specie-flow mechanism,* the flow of gold determines the final equilibrium price. As gold flows from one country to another, the receiving country will be able to print more banknotes, which in turn will lead to high inflation. Over time, the receiving country will see an increase in imports and a decrease in exports, allowing gold to flow back to the original country.

If equilibrium is not restored automatically, the country could officially change the price of gold. In the earlier example, England could increase the price of gold to £20 per ounce. This action effectively devalues the pound, and the new exchange rate will be US$35 / £20 = US$1.75 / £. However, until the beginning of the twentieth century, most countries were reluctant to use this method as a means to devalue their currency, mainly for reasons of national pride and a belief that a strong currency is a sign of national strength.

The gold standard served as the basic framework for foreign exchange transactions throughout the 1800s. When gold and silver were convertible to currency, it was termed the *bimetallic* standard. By 1870, nearly all countries in the West had converted to the gold standard, and it flourished well until 1914. The advent of World War I forced all countries to abandon their pledge to convert gold to currency. After the war, many countries returned to the gold standard, but the turmoil and chaos that followed this period resulted in many countries abandoning it soon after.

THE BRETTON WOODS SYSTEM (MODIFIED GOLD STANDARD)

During the interwar period leading up to World War II, there were major breakdowns in exchange rate management. Several countries, hoping to stimulate exports and improve their balance-of-trade, devalued their currencies, with the result that exchange rates fluctuated abruptly, trade further slowed, confidence in all currencies declined, and global depression deepened and spread.

As World War II was drawing to an end, economists were concerned that the mistakes made during the interwar period should not be repeated. Under the new system agreed upon in Bretton Woods, New Hampshire, the United States proposed to guarantee the convertibility of the U.S. dollar at $35 per ounce of gold (at the end of the war, the United States held approximately 60 percent of the world's gold). Other countries were to peg the price of their currency to gold, although they were not required to offer convertibility. No country could devalue its currency without the collective permission of all countries. The International Monetary Fund and the World Bank (officially the International

Figure 10.1 **Foreign Exchange Rates: United States vs. Foreign Countries**

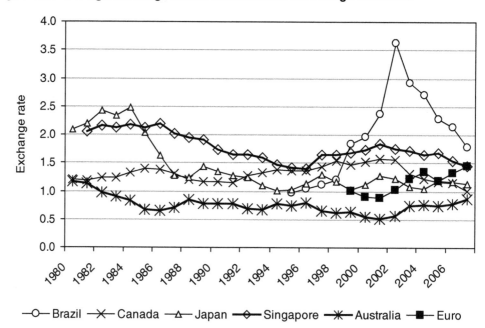

—○— Brazil —✕— Canada —△— Japan —◇— Singapore —✳— Australia —■— Euro

Source: Author complied data from the Federal Reserve Board of St. Louis Foreign Exchange database, available at http://research.stlouisfed.org/fred2/ (accessed October 22, 2008).

Bank for Reconstruction and Development, or IBRD) would provide short- and long-term financing to ensure that countries were able to maintain currency stability while promoting growth.

The modified gold standard system of Bretton Woods worked very well in the aftermath of the war. European countries were able to restore faith in their currencies and allow convertibility in 1959. Unfortunately, the system was ultimately abandoned because of a lack of trust in the United States to guarantee full convertibility. Continued deficits and the inability to control spending in the 1960s meant that not enough gold was available to the U.S. government to support the dollars circulating outside of the United States. On August 15, 1971, President Richard M. Nixon closed the so-called gold window.

FREE-FLOATING EXCHANGE RATE SYSTEMS

The breakdown of the modified gold standard was in some ways a boon to the development of the modern international financial system. The aftermath led many countries to float their currencies, that is, to allow their value to be determined by supply and demand. Unfortunately, this meant that exchange rates were more volatile than when the rates were fixed. The increased volatility can be troublesome to businesses whose sales or purchases are denominated in other currencies, especially if the movements are temporary.

The United States was one of the few countries that strictly adhered to the doctrine of free float and rarely intervened to stabilize the exchange rates. As a result, U.S. exchange rates have been extremely volatile since the 1980s, as shown in Figure 10.1. In contrast, the European countries continued on a path of managed floating, which meant that although the currencies were allowed to float, the governments ensured that they stayed within a fixed band of 2.5 percent against the dollar. If they fell outside this band, the government would intervene to bring the exchange rate back to within the specified band. This has led to a more stable environment for European companies operating in international markets.

SIZE OF THE FOREIGN EXCHANGE MARKET

The foreign exchange market is one of the largest markets in the world, with approximately $3 trillion traded every day. The Bank for International Settlements (BIS), based in Basel, Switzerland, and considered the central bank of central banks, tracks the daily trades of the exchange market among the global banks. A country's central bank is usually the monetary authority that implements the country's monetary policy, including printing and issuing money. Table 10.2 summarizes the total volume of foreign exchange transactions traded in U.S. dollars in 1995, 2001, and 2007.

The average daily turnover in 2007 was approximately $3.2 trillion per day, nearly 68 percent more than the 2001 volume of $1.90 trillion. The most common form of transaction was the foreign exchange swap, where the spot is sold against the forward, assuring the dealer a fixed spread. The most common forward rates are 30-, 60- and 90-day contracts. The next most common currency transaction was the spot transaction. In the recent past, spot transactions took two days for final settlement, except for those in Canada, which took one day. However, with the advent of electronic trading and competition, most spot currencies are now delivered on the same day.

The dramatic increase in trading per day makes the foreign exchange market one of the largest in the world. It reflects the growing importance of overseas trading for all countries and the interdependency of the world community. Such high volumes of transactions require an efficient mechanism and institutional structure to be in place globally if the markets are to function smoothly. The foreign exchange infrastructure today is extremely well developed, making it one of the most efficient markets in the world.

The major players in the foreign exchange market are the large international banks. There is no centralized location for trading. Instead, banks throughout the world purchase and sell foreign exchange via telephone, fax, and the Internet. The purchase or sale of foreign exchange can be classified into two categories: wholesale and retail. A majority of the trading is in the wholesale market, where banks purchase or sell deposits in minimum amounts of $5 million. The rest of the trades are made by corporations and individuals.

Table 10.3 shows the daily foreign exchange turnover by country. The largest market by volume is London, followed by New York and Tokyo. Other cities where active foreign exchange activity takes place include Sydney, Hong Kong, Singapore, Paris, and Frankfurt.

Table 10.2

Global Foreign Exchange Market Turnover

Amounts are daily averages in April, in billions of U.S. dollars.

	1995	2001	2007
Spot Transactions	494	387	1,005
Outright Forwards	97	131	362
Foreign Exchange Swaps	546	656	1,714
Total	1,190	1,900	3,210

Source: Bank for International Settlements; Triennial Central Bank Survey, "Foreign exchange and derivatives market activity in 2007," December 2007, p. 4. Available at www.bis.org (accessed June 16, 2008).

Table 10.3

Foreign Exchange Market Turnover by Country

Amounts are daily averages in April, in billions of U.S. dollars.

	2001		2007	
	Amount	Percent of total	Amount	Percent of total
United Kingdom	504	31.2	1,359	34.1
United States	254	15.7	664	16.6
Japan	147	9.1	238	6.0

Source: Bank for International Settlements; Triennial Central Bank Survey, "Foreign exchange and derivatives market activity in 2007," December 2007, p. 6. Available at www.bis.org (accessed June 16, 2008).

Commercial Banks account for a major portion of the foreign exchange activity. In 2007, 12 banks in the United Kingdom and 10 banks in the United States accounted for over 75 percent of the total turnover in the country. These ratios have declined in recent years due to consolidations in the banking industry. In 1998, the numbers were 24 percent and 20 percent, respectively.[4] However, with Internet technology, more alternative platforms of trading are emerging, and the dominance of banks may be reduced, as smaller, more focused, and specialized companies encroach on their markets.

DETERMINATION OF FOREIGN EXCHANGE RATES

This section examines the factors that affect the prices of foreign currencies. The primary reasons for prices of foreign currencies to increase and decrease are similar to those of every other product—changes in demand and supply. Some variables that affect demand and supply are common to most currencies, while others are unique to the country of origin.

In a perfectly competitive market, prices move in anticipation of changes in demand or supply. As a result, information plays a major role in the pricing of currencies, in both content and timing. A small country that does not trade much may have few traders specializing in that currency. With fewer traders, price changes may be slow and infrequent. In contrast, if hundreds of traders participate actively in the market, the price of a currency can move up and down in near unison as no single trader wants to be left behind. The most liquid currencies in the world are the U.S. dollar and the euro.

For a truly free floating exchange rate regime, where prices are determined solely by demand and supply, it is necessary for foreign exchange markets to operate without government intervention or institutional restrictions. Such markets do not exist today, because most countries impose some form of restriction on the transfer of foreign currencies. In the United States, it is not possible for individuals to open foreign currency accounts overseas or write checks in foreign currencies.

Countries that earn a limited amount of foreign currency through exports are usually the ones that impose the most restrictions. This allows them to allocate the scarce foreign exchange to industries of economic importance. For example, a small country earning scarce foreign exchange through the sale of one commodity may allow the imports of capital goods but ban the imports of luxury goods.

Such barriers to the free movement of foreign currencies distort currencies' true market prices. As a result, forecasting exchange rates is complicated and requires a broad understanding of the market environment in which foreign exchange is traded.

The following factors play a major role in the determination of foreign exchange rates for all countries.

INFLATION RATES

The difference in inflation rates between two countries affects the foreign exchange rates between two countries. The country with the higher inflation rate will experience a depreciation of its currency relative to the other country, a phenomenon termed "purchasing power parity."

INTEREST RATES

Since interest rates and inflation rates go hand in hand, the relationship is similar to that of inflation rates. Ceteris paribus, the country with the higher interest rate should see its currency depreciate relative to the other country.

EXPORTS AND IMPORTS

If a country is successful at exporting, it has the ability to earn more foreign exchange. If all other things remain unaltered, higher exports increase the demand for that country's currency, causing it to appreciate against the dollar. Assume China's exports to the United States continue to increase. The increased demand for Chinese yuan (renminbi) to pay for Chinese goods will lead to an appreciation in the Chinese currency unless the government intervenes to prevent it.

Conversely, when a country imports more goods than it exports, its demand for foreign currencies will increase and its currency will depreciate relative to those of other countries. Take the example of Brazil and Mexico. Mexico is a major exporter of oil, while Brazil is a major importer of oil. Oil is priced in dollars. When oil prices increase, Brazil has to purchase more dollars to pay for the oil. Mexico will receive dollars for its sale of oil. As a result, ceteris paribus, the Brazilian real will depreciate against the dollar when oil prices increase, while the Mexican peso will appreciate.

PARTICIPANTS IN THE FOREIGN EXCHANGE MARKET

The major participants in any trading market are the actual users and suppliers of the commodity. Also included are middlemen, or traders, who link the suppliers to the users. Together, these participants determine the demand and supply of the commodity.

Take, for example, a fish market. The suppliers of fish range from individual fishermen to companies with vessels that catch large quantities of fish. The buyers of fish range from restaurants and supermarket chains to large food companies. The major transactions take place at wholesale markets, and the large number of buyers and sellers ensures liquidity and depth in the market. In addition, there are speculators who purchase and sell fish for the purpose of making quick profits. The presence of speculators also adds depth to the market in that trading activity increases, with traders able to request prices from more sources. When trading is active, the likelihood of price distortion is minimized.

The foreign exchange market is very similar to the commodities markets. The only difference is that foreign exchange is not directly consumable but rather allows for the purchase of a consumable product or service. As discussed earlier, all transactions are conducted via phone, faxes, or the Internet. Once a deal is agreed upon, the exchange actually takes place by way of a transfer from one bank account to another.

The major participants in the foreign exchange markets are commercial and noncommercial banks, nonbank brokers, central banks, and corporations and individuals.

COMMERCIAL AND NONCOMMERCIAL BANKS

Commercial and noncommercial banks are some of the largest players in the foreign currency markets. Commercial banks are depository institutions that accept deposits from individuals and corporations and convert them to loans. Well-known commercial banks include JPMorgan Chase, Bank of America, ABN AMRO, and Barclays. Noncommercial banks are investment banks that underwrite securities, trade shares, and provide corporate advisory services, as well as insurance companies that have large foreign exchange desks. Examples include Oppenheimer Holdings, Lazard Capital Markets, and Brown Brothers Harriman.

These institutions usually have large trading floors where they buy and sell foreign exchange both for their clients as well as for their proprietary trading. Most of the larger banks in major cities are market makers for different currencies, while smaller banks serve as brokers between their clients and the larger banks. The difference between market makers and brokers (for any commodity) is described below.

Market makers are always willing to buy or sell a currency. For example, if a bank is a market maker for the Japanese yen, it must be prepared to buy and sell yen at all times. Market makers do not charge commission; rather, they make their profits on the spread between the buy and sell (ask) prices. They are expected to quote irrespective of market conditions. As a result, they are expected to hold some inventory of the currency.

Brokers are intermediaries that connect buyers and sellers. They earn their income purely through commissions and, as a result, are not required to hold inventory.

NONBANK BROKERS

Several large specialized brokers in the foreign exchange markets play an important role in the smooth trading of currencies. Some of the better known brokers include HIFX Plc, Tokyo Forex & Ueda Harlow Ltd, and Tullet Prebon. The advantage of using a broker in selling or purchasing foreign currency is that brokers are able to provide a range of quotes from different market makers. This also enables companies to keep their trades anonymous, which can be useful especially when large trades are to be executed. Usually, when the market realizes that a party is selling a large block of a currency, the price tends to get depressed.

CENTRAL BANKS

Central banks of all countries are also major players in the foreign exchange markets. Central banks have an obligation to keep their currencies stable, especially from speculators who may inject wide swings to currencies prices—a phenomenon known as volatility. To avoid excessive volatility, central banks may intervene by buying or selling foreign currencies. For example, if the Federal Reserve Board decides that the current price of dollar against the euro, say US$1.35 / €1, is weak, it can offset this imbalance by purchasing dollars from the market. If a significant amount of dollars is removed from the market, the scarce dollar will induce traders to offer fewer dollars per euro. This should result in a dollar appreciation, for example, from US$1.35 / €1 to US$1.25 / €1 to US$1.20 / €1, and so on.

CORPORATIONS AND INDIVIDUALS

Another group of purchasers and sellers of foreign exchange are individuals and corporations. Corporations that export and import are active participants in the foreign exchange market. Individuals, on the other hand, are usually small-time purchasers, most often for their travels overseas as tourists.

EXCHANGE RATE REGIMES

As described earlier, the breakdown of the Bretton Woods system induced several countries to adopt a freely floating exchange rate regime. The European countries formed an alliance and adopted the European exchange rate mechanism, which required countries to manage exchange rates to reduce volatility. The world today is divided into countries that have either fixed exchange rate or floating exchange systems. Most central banks continue to monitor their exchange rates, even if they prefer that rates be determined by market forces.

FIXED-RATE REGIMES

In today's fixed-rate regimes, countries do not peg their rates to a commodity such as gold or silver; rather, they peg them to another more stable and stronger currency. A majority of countries, including many of the Arab states, have pegged their rates to the dollar, while others have pegged to the euro or yen, or to a basket of currencies. China, which has pegged its currency to the U.S. dollar for a long time, has recently committed to freeing its exchange rates, albeit slowly. There are pros and cons to pegging the exchange rates to one currency.

Assume a country such as Kuwait fixes the rate at 3 dinars to a dollar (KD3 / US$1). In a fixed-rate system, it is the responsibility of the government to ensure that the rate does not deviate from KD3 / US$1 plus or minus a few basis points. Assume that the country increases its imports, thereby increasing the demand for dollars against the dinar. Ceteris paribus, that would mean the dinar will have pressure to depreciate, that is, to KD3.10 / US$1 to KD3.20 / US$1 to KD3.30 / US$1. The Central Bank of Kuwait will have to sell dollars from its reserves if it chooses to stop this decline and return the price to KD3 / US$1. If the bank runs out of dollars to continue this intervention, it will be forced to devalue its currency to a higher rate, perhaps KD3.30 / US$1. In a fixed exchange rate regime, the responsibility to maintain the exchange rate at a predetermined level can impose a burden on the country.

FLOATING-RATE REGIMES

In a fully floating and free regime, exchange rates are determined purely by supply and demand for the currency. Few countries allow absolute freely floating rates. The United States, considered one of the few countries to rarely interfere in the exchange rate, has intervened occasionally to stabilize exchange rates. The intervention is undertaken by the Federal Open Market Committee of the Reserve Bank of New York and the Department of the Treasury. They do not attempt to affect the price of the currency but to avoid excess volatility in the markets. This is different from intervening to maintain the currency within a stated rate.

Many countries, including those of the European Union, prefer to float their foreign exchange rates but intervene to keep the rates within desired ranges so as not to cause major volatility. This system is referred to as a "managed float."

MULTINATIONALS AND FOREIGN EXCHANGE

Understanding the foreign exchange market is extremely important for all firms that engage in international trade, whether they are large multinationals or small firms. Exposure to foreign currency risks can significantly affect a company's cash flows. Foreign exchange also affects a company's pricing decisions, which in turn can affect the demand for the company's products. A financial manager has to monitor the market continuously and forecast the direction of the exchange rates. However, forecasting of exchange rates is both a science and an art that requires a much broader understanding of the forces affecting exchange rates in a dynamic global environment.

The following is a list of areas where foreign exchange plays a role in affecting business decisions.

PRICING OF PRODUCTS

When a company plans to sell or purchase goods from another country, it is very important to predict the expected foreign currency prices several years ahead. A wrong prediction can lead a company to price its product low and sell at a loss. For example, assume a company sells a product for US$100 in the United States and plans to export the goods to the United Kingdom. If the exchange rate is currently US$2 / £1, it may seem appropriate to export the product at a price of £50. However, if the dollar appreciates in the future and the exchange rate changes from US$2 / £1 to US$1.75 / £1 to US$1.50 / £1, then the amount received by the company for the products sold in the United Kingdom will be lower: £50 × US$1.50 = US$75, which will result in a loss for the company.

Managers have to make assumptions on expected future exchange rates and price their products accordingly. One way for managers to obtain expected spot rates is from forward rates. If traders in the market expect rates to be US$1.50 / £1 one year from today, the one-year forward rate is likely to be in the vicinity of US$1.50 / £1. Several studies have looked at whether forward rates are unbiased predictors of the expected spot rates in the future. The results have been mixed. Nearly all studies have found forward rates to be unreliable predictors in the short run, but some studies have found them to be reliable in the long run. Several reasons have been offered to explain this anomaly. In the short run, new information can change the spot prices from the expected prices. In the long run, the models should include a risk premium that is demanded when investing over a longer time horizon.

PRICING OF RAW MATERIAL

The purchase or import of raw materials or other inputs from overseas presents exchange rate risks similar to those posed by the export of products overseas. In this case of imports, a depreciation of the dollar will increase the cost of purchased goods. For example, assume a U.S. company imports raw materials from Malaysia at a rate of US$0.25 per ringgit (RM). If the dollar depreciates to US$0.30 / RM1, and then to US$0.35 / RM1, the cost of the imports will increase, and the company may be better off seeking alternative sources.

In today's global markets, even a company that does not import or export is vulnerable to exchange rate fluctuations, because its competitors may be engaged in imports and exports. If a competitor is able to obtain products cheaper as a result of favorable exchange rates, this may affect the domestic company's ability to compete effectively. Exchange rate fluctuations also provide opportunities to earn extra profits.

For example, assume a competitor imports 50 percent of its inputs from overseas. If the dollar depreciates, the cost of imported items increases and the competitor may be forced to raise its prices. Alternatively, if the dollar appreciates, the cost declines and the competitor may be able to lower prices.

PAYMENTS AND RECEIVABLES

Managers of multinationals have to consistently monitor changes in exchange rates to ensure that their incoming receivables and outgoing payments are not affected significantly. If exchange rates are expected to change, managers must take appropriate action to offset potential losses. One example of a counteraction is termed "leads and lags in payments."

Take the case of a company that expects to receive £100,000 every three months for exports of goods to a regular client. If the manager forecasts that the pound will appreciate in the near future, that is, from the existing spot rate of US$1.50 / £1 to US$1.75 / £1 to US$2 / £1, he or she may prefer to delay receiving the money. This is termed "lagging the receivables." The manager should collect the payments in pounds and invest it in the United Kingdom in anticipation of the pound appreciation. Alternatively, assume the company has to make a payment of £100,000 every three months. If the pound is expected to appreciate, it would be better for the company to "lead the payments," that is, make them sooner rather than later.

If the dollar instead of the pound is expected to appreciate—say, from US$2.00 / £ to US$1.75 / £ to US$1.50 / £—the reverse strategies should be adopted for the above example. The company is better off leading the incoming receivables and lagging the outgoing payments.

INVOICING CENTERS

Perhaps the most vexing issue for multinationals is managing the multitude of transactions among their own subsidiaries; multinationals are continuously making and receiving payments between parent companies and subsidiaries. If the transactions are in different currencies, not only are transaction costs high, but they are also exposed to exchange rate risks. One of the ways to reduce these costs is to create an invoicing center that can consolidate and net the payments and receivables from the various subsidiaries, as shown in the example below.

Suppose a U.S. parent company has three subsidiaries, located in Belgium, Brazil, and Japan. The companies purchase and sell among themselves raw materials, intermediate goods, and finished products. Figure 10.2A shows the flows in all four currencies. Payments and receivables are made between Japan and Belgium and between the United States and Brazil (diagonally in the figure). In total, there can be six inflows and six outflows in various currencies among the participants.

Assume that an invoicing center is set up in Luxembourg, as shown in Figure 10.2B. All overseas payments are now channeled through the invoicing center, resulting in savings not only in the number of transactions performed but also in the exposure to foreign exchange.

263

Figure 10.2 **Payments among Parent and Subsidiaries**

A. Without an Invoicing Center

B. With an Invoicing Center

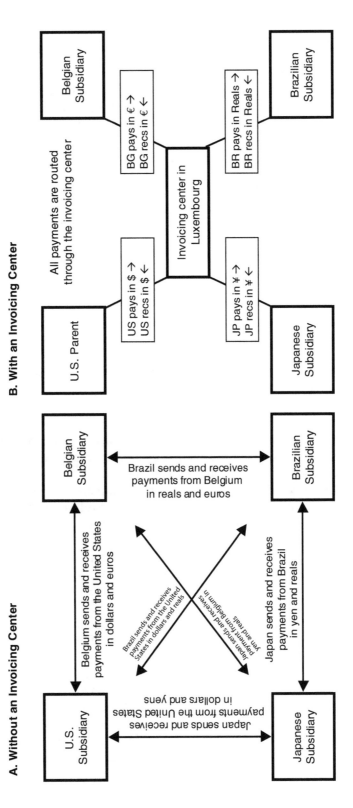

CHAPTER SUMMARY

This chapter provides an overview of the foreign exchange markets, defined as the venue for purchasing and selling foreign currencies. Foreign exchange is required whenever a transaction takes place between residents of different countries that do not share a common currency. The increased pace of industrialization and trade in the twentieth century contributed to the foreign exchange market's development into one of the largest and most efficient in the world, approaching $3 trillion per day.

A foreign exchange rate is defined as the price of a foreign currency. When paper money replaced the gold and silver coins as a medium of exchange, the value of a foreign currency was initially determined by the official rate set by each government or nation-state. If the rates deviated from the fixed rate, then countries had to intervene in the markets by purchasing or selling their currencies to maintain that rate. Since the 1970s, more countries have opted for their exchange rates to float freely and be determined by the demand and supply for the currency.

Foreign exchange is quoted in direct or indirect terms. If a foreign currency is quoted as home currency per unit of foreign currency, it is defined as a direct quote. When a currency is quoted in foreign currency per unit of home currency, it is termed an indirect quote. Foreign currency is available for spot (immediate) exchange or forward deliveries. Forward rates for many currencies are available for 30-, 60-, and 90-day deliveries.

If a country has to pay more for a foreign currency, we consider the home currency to have depreciated or the foreign currency to have appreciated. When a home currency depreciates, goods in the home currency become cheaper because the foreign purchaser pays less to acquire the home currency. As a result, a depreciating currency will increase exports and reduce imports for the country. As exports continue to increase, ceteris paribus, there will be an increase in demand for the home currency, and eventually this will cause the rates to return to equilibrium.

The main determinants for the demand and supply for a foreign currency are exports, imports, and the inflation and interest rate differentials between the countries. The higher the relative inflation rates or interest in a country, the more likely its currency will depreciate against the other currency.

The major players in the foreign exchange markets are the major international banks, followed by nonbank brokers, central banks, and corporations and individuals. The bulk of the trading takes place between the major banks, defined as wholesale trades. Wholesale trades account for 85 percent of all foreign currency transactions.

Finally, understanding foreign exchange markets is important for managers of multinational corporations. Managers need to be aware of the future direction of foreign exchange rates in order to price goods for overseas markets and source raw materials for production. Foreign exchange rates also affect pricing in domestic markets because procuring raw materials at cheaper rates enables companies to sell their output at competitive domestic rates. If foreign exchange rates are volatile, it makes it much more difficult for the manager to make long-term decisions required for successful business planning.

KEY CONCEPTS

Gold Standard
Fixed Exchange Rates
Floating Exchange Rates
Foreign Exchange Market

DISCUSSION QUESTIONS

1. Define foreign exchange. What are the two ways that foreign exchange can be quoted?
2. If the direct quote for the Norwegian krone in New York is US$0.1550 / NK1, what is the indirect quote?
3. If the exchange rate of the dollar to the euro changes from US$1.55 / €1 to US$1.65 / €1, did the dollar appreciate or depreciate? Is that good or bad for U.S. exports?
4. What are some of the reasons that gold and silver became the accepted choice of coins to serve as a medium of exchange?
5. Who are the major users of foreign exchange? Distinguish between market makers and brokers in the foreign exchange markets.
6. What are some of the major factors affecting the price of a currency? If the inflation rate in a country increases relative to that of another country, will its exchange rate depreciate or appreciate?
7. What is the difference between fixed and floating exchange rate regimes? What is managed float?
8. Why is it important to have an understanding of foreign exchange rates for pricing a company's products? Is it only relevant for the pricing of exported goods?
9. Explain how an invoicing center can help reduce costs to a multinational.

APPLICATION CASE: DOLLARIZATION AND THE CASE OF ECUADOR AND EL SALVADOR

The euro and the dollar are the two most dominant currencies in the world. As of 2006, the value of euro notes in circulation exceeded that of the dollar. This can be explained partly by a fall in the value of the dollar and partly by the preference for Europeans to pay in cash for most transactions, in contrast to Americans who prefer to use credit cards. In addition, more countries are qualifying to join the European Union, requiring the European Central Bank to print more euro notes and coins.

The success of the euro indicates that it is possible for the world to eventually adopt a single currency. The euro is successful because all countries using the euro agree to a common monetary system. A country has to be accepted into the eurozone in order to be a member of the monetary system. Another way for a country to attach on to another currency, preferably a stronger one, is to officially "adopt" the currency without being a member of the monetary system. The term for such official adoption is "dollarization," and the term arose because the dollar was the most likely currency to be adopted in the past. Today, it could easily be called "euroization" or "rublization" or "yuanization," depending on the currency adopted.

Two countries that recently "dollarized" their currencies were Ecuador in 2000 and El Salvador in 2001. Only five other independent nations in the past have adopted the dollar as their official currency, East Timor, the Marshall Islands, Micronesia, Palau, and Panama. This list excludes all U.S. territories and those countries that use the dollar "unofficially" (as a result of a failure of their local currency).

It is not clear whether countries benefit when they adopt a stronger currency like the dollar. In the case of Ecuador, the dollarization appears to have worked well; however, the experience for El Salvador has been mixed. The success or failure may depend more on the economic conditions that existed in the country both prior to and after the currency's adoption.

In Ecuador, inflation had reached over 100 percent in 1999, the year before dollarization, leading to a dramatic depreciation of their local currency, the sucre. In 1997, the sucre was selling at 3,500 per dollar; by 2000, its value had fallen to over 25,000 per dollar. A room at a top-rated hotel that normally cost US$50 in 1997 dropped to US$7 per room for an American tourist. The country's financial markets had collapsed, and adoption of the dollar was one of the few options available to the government. The aftermath was very encouraging, as inflation fell to 10.7 percent in 2002 and continued its downward drift thereafter to 3.9 percent in 2007. The reason for the drastic drop in inflation was obvious: local politicians could no longer print money as needed, and instead dollars had to be earned by exports or obtained through official borrowing.

The long-term results for Ecuador have also been encouraging. The U.S. State Department estimates the average GDP in Ecuador increased to 4.6 percent since 2000, supported by the exports of oil and nontraditional items and by remittances from abroad. Per capita income increased from US$1,296 in 2000 to approximately US$3,270 in 2007, and the poverty rate fell from 51 percent in 2000 to 38 percent in 2006. These statistics might have improved even more if not for the high level of corruption and political tension that still exists in the country. The growth rate finally slowed down in 2007. It is unclear how the global slowdown in 2008 will affect the country's economic progress in the coming years.

Conditions in El Salvador were different from Ecuador when they dollarized their currency. There was no immediate financial crisis and inflation rates were low prior to dollarization. A number of structural reforms had been initiated between 1998 and 2000, that including the privatization of banks, the strengthening of the tax code, and the breaking up of the state monopolies in telecommunications and electricity. Dollarization was chosen deliberately as a means to prevent deterioration in the value of their local currency.

The U.S. State Department reports that El Salvador's economy grew at 4.7 percent in 2007, and poverty has been reduced from 66 percent in 1991 to 30.7 percent in 2006. However inflation increased from 2.3 percent in 2001 to nearly 3.6 percent since the dollarization. Although the interest rate declined during this period, it did not manage to attract foreign investments into the country, primarily because of low productivity and overdependence on agriculture. When the dollar became strong in early 2000, exports from El Salvador also suffered as Chinese imports into the country increased. The recent decline in the dollar should help both countries increase their exports.

Most economists would agree that it does not make economic sense for every country, and in particular small countries, to have their own currency. Currencies of small economies are more susceptible to outside shocks that can have major impacts on their income and employment. Yet the experiences of Ecuador and San Salvador do not provide clear evidence of whether dollarization is a solution for small countries, especially those with weak currencies. During the financial crisis of 2008, investors throughout the world showed a preference to buy dollars, a term referred to as a "flight to safety." Whether the dollar will continue to be considered a safe haven will depend on how the United States handles the crisis and its aftermath.

If the United States is unable to rein in its deficit spending, it will not only lose value but also its reputation as the currency of choice for the world. In that event, the world may end up with several dominant currencies—the euro, the dollar, the Russian ruble, and the Chinese yuan are the more likely dominant currencies. This is probably better than having the current system of over 200 currencies.

QUESTIONS

1. How does dollarization differ from the adoption of the euro as the national currency?
2. What was the impact of dollarization in Ecuador and El Salvador?

11 | International Marketing

> The success of most companies depends on their ability to market goods and services to potential customers in a competitive global environment.

LEARNING OBJECTIVES

- To understand the role of marketing in international operations
- To understand the marketing environment
- To understand the strategic variables in marketing
- To be familiar with critical international marketing activities

Goods and services are produced for eventual sale to consumers in a given market. The marketing function generates revenues and is the source of company profits. Until and unless consumers buy goods and services, there is no business to run. Therefore, marketing plays an important role in a company's day-to-day operations. Marketing's functions include selecting the target market, choosing the goods and services to offer to the customers, packaging and labeling the product, setting the price, distributing goods and services, promoting the product, applying customer relations management, and establishing feedback mechanisms to obtain relevant information from the users of the goods and services. In fact, among the various costs associated with producing and selling goods and services, quite often marketing and selling expenses account for a major portion of the total cost.

The American Marketing Association (AMA) defines marketing as "an organizational function and a set of processes for creating, communicating, and delivering value to customers and for managing customer relationships in ways that benefit the organization and its stakeholders." The key concepts in the definition of marketing are that *marketing is a process;* it *delivers value to the customers;* it *manages customer relationships;* it attempts to meet a *firm's organizational objectives,* while at the same time providing *benefits to its stakeholders.* Companies deal with two types of customers: they sell goods and services to the final consumers, who purchase items for their own use or to be used by others in a household setting; and they sell goods and services to business customers (also called industrial or institutional customers), who further a product/service or in some way add value to the product/service for resale to the final consumers.

FINAL AND INDUSTRIAL CONSUMERS

Final consumers buy essential and nonessential items on a regular basis as part of their daily purchases. For example, when a member of the family buys food items, appliances, or automobiles, he or she is buying these items to be used by the individual and family and household members. The purchases by this group are referred to as final consumption. If, however, individuals or companies buy goods and services that are then used to make other products or services, this type of consumption is referred to as industrial consumption. The purchase of raw materials such as crude oil, steel, and plastic, and component parts such as tires, motors, and copper wires is normally associated with industrial consumption. The individual or the company that buys these goods and services does not consume them but makes something else out of them and then sells that product or service to the final consumers. For example, Volkswagen's purchase of tires from Michelin to be mounted on the VW Jetta, a car model it assembles in the thousands, is an industrial consumption. In contrast, an individual's purchase of the same tires as replacements for worn-out tires is final consumption. Similarly, Unilever's purchase of food for its employee cafeteria, or a fleet of cars for its senior executives, is referred to as industrial consumption. Unilever's purchases are part of its operations, and they help the firm to produce soap, detergents, toiletries, and so on. Hence, it is not the types of goods and services that determine if the purchase qualifies as final or industrial consumption, but how the goods and services are used after they are purchased.

Purchases by businesses tend to be larger in volume than purchases by final consumers. Also, in industrial purchases, prices tend to be negotiated. Some companies, such as the British retailer Marks & Spencer, sell goods and services only to final consumers. At the same time, there are others that sell only to industrial consumers; for example, the Indian-based Tata Iron & Steel Company sells steel and other fabricated metals only to industrial consumers such as appliance manufacturers and automobile manufacturers. There are also companies that sell goods and services to both the final and industrial consumers; GE, IBM, Philips, Samsung, and Sony are all international companies that deal with both final and industrial consumers. In the case of GE, it sells household appliances to final consumers, but it also sells electric turbines and aircraft engines to industrial customers. Similarly, Philips sells electric bulbs to final consumers as well as to industrial consumers.

GOODS VS. SERVICES

In our discussion, we have stated that international companies sell goods and services. These terms are most often used interchangeably, but there some key differences between goods (also called products) and services. Products are *tangible* items that are purchased by consumers for consumption either immediately or for later use. For instance, a consumer may buy a box of cereal that he or she may consume in one sitting or over a period of time. Among tangible products, there are other differences, too. Products are classified as nondurables or durables. Durable products have a long life and nondurables have a shorter life. Items such as milk and eggs are nondurable items. Consumers buy these types of products often. Durable products are also tangible, but they last longer. Products such as appliances, clothing, and automobiles are considered durable products.

Services are *intangible* items that consumers purchase. Besides intangibility, services have three key characteristics: *inseparability, perishability, and heterogeneity.* Inseparability implies that services are consumed as they are transacted; perishability implies that services cannot be stored, so they are consumed as the service is transacted; and heterogeneity implies that the same service varies from vendor to vendor in form, quality, and the time it takes to transact that particular service. Restaurants, banks, and consulting are examples of services. Marketing principles apply equally to goods and services.

MARKETING ACTIVITIES

An international marketer undertakes two broad-based activities. The first is managing the environment, and the second is managing the marketing variables (programs). Marketing activities for domestic and international markets are similar in the sense that all the individual activities associated with domestic marketing are also undertaken in international markets. The critical difference between the two lies in the environment within which the marketing programs are developed.

MARKETING ENVIRONMENT

The marketing environment is made up of all the forces that exert influence on and shape consumer purchases and a company's marketing programs. The environmental variables include competition, a country's economic activities, political stability, government laws and regulations, culture and its influences, societal influences, technology and its impacts on consumers, geography as it influences marketing and consumption of goods and services, and existing distribution structure (for international companies, changing an existing distribution structure is difficult; hence, it is an uncontrollable variable). Geographic considerations, especially climatic differences, may have to be recognized in introducing products.[1] Culture has been found to exert great influence on the customer's choice process, especially for products with significant cultural content such as magazines and films. When a product is marketed internationally, the cultural similarity between the country of origin and the country where the product is marketed influences the rate of adoption in the new country.[2] International marketers do not control the environment in which the basic marketing activities are conducted (environmental variables were discussed in detail in Chapters 2 through 4).

The environmental variables faced by domestic and international marketers are the same; that is, both face economic, political, cultural, and other external variables, but the differences lie in the level of complexity between the domestic and international variables. The external environment exerts influences over a company's operations as well as on the consuming public. The domestic environment is easy to understand, familiar to the managers, and easy to predict. Companies always have an advantage when they are selling in a domestic marketing environment because both the company and its consumers share the same environmental variables. In contrast, the international environment is difficult to understand, unfamiliar to international managers, and difficult to predict. In addition, the countries in which international companies operate are not all alike. Significant differences among the countries further complicate the task of the international manager. That is, an international company has to evaluate, understand, and influence individually each of the markets it is in. If there are similarities among the different countries, the international company has an opportunity to standardize some of its marketing strategies. For example, when Pepsi-Cola sells its beverages in China as well as in Germany, it needs to understand that these two countries have totally different environments, and strategies used in each have to be planned carefully. In contrast, in marketing the same products in Canada and the United States, Pepsi can easily standardize such strategies as packaging and advertising.

To be successful in overseas markets, international companies must thoroughly analyze and understand the marketing environment. The external factors will also shape how each firm develops its strategies. For example, in predominantly Muslim countries such as Indonesia, Kuwait, and Saudi Arabia, products with pork as the main ingredient, such as sausage, are not sold or marketed in any form. Similarly, countries that are less developed and that are classified as low income do not provide many sales opportunities for baby diapers, detergents, and household appliances. Therefore, it is important that international companies evaluate the external environment thoroughly before marketing goods and services to a particular country.

INTEGRATED MARKETING PROGRAM

An international company manages the following marketing variables:

- Products and services
- Branding and packaging
- After-sales services (warranties, returns, repairs, and complaints)
- Price
- Distribution (retail selection, channel management, logistics, and inventory management)
- Communication (message content and medium—sales force, advertising, sales promotion, and public relations)

An international marketing environment is mostly an uncontrollable variable, whereas marketing variables are mostly under the international company's control. It is through these variables that an international company gains competitive advantage and succeeds in the different countries in which it operates. In developing strategies using marketing variables (also known as a marketing mix or marketing program), both domestic and international companies have to coordinate the various marketing activities to achieve synergy among the variables. Called the integrated marketing approach, this strategy has helped companies achieve competitive advantages that boost their success in a globally competitive environment.[3] That is, in developing a marketing program, the company must ensure that the philosophy and attributes of the product or service are in harmony with consumer needs. In addition, the packaging strategy, price, distribution, and communication must all be aligned with the attributes of the product or service.

Collectively, all the marketing variables should send the same signal to consumers; for example, moderately priced products that are typically distributed through discount stores would not appeal to the affluent market just because they were advertised in a prestigious business magazine such as *Fortune.* In this case, consumers would be confused, because they would not be sure if the product was meant for the mass market or for the premium market. To achieve synergy, a moderately priced product must be targeted to the general public (mass marketed) at a reasonable price in retail stores that are frequented by the targeted group; furthermore, its availability should be communicated through advertisements in general appeal magazines and during television programs that are popular among mainstream shoppers. For example, Timex watches targets middle-income consumers in many countries; priced reasonably, Timex watches are marketed in department stores, superstores, discount outlets, and specialty stores (in this case, stores that sell only watches and jewelry) and are advertised through popular magazines, television, and billboards. In contrast, luxury products such as Rolex watches are targeted to a few affluent consumers; are priced high (more than $10,000); and are distributed through high-end retailers and advertised through prestigious magazines (*Vogue, Fortune,* and similar publications), premium television programs (golf tournaments), and select newspapers (*Financial Times, Wall Street Journal,* and the like). The key component of success in developing marketing programs is to make sure that all the variables are well orchestrated and they all communicate the same philosophy.

Because international markets vary from country to country, developing synergies across markets is not always possible. Due to differences in consumers' purchasing power and cultural variations, quite often what has worked in one market may not work in another. Major appliances from manufacturers such as GE and LG Electronics, automobiles from manufacturers such as Hyundai and Toyota, and cosmetic products from Estée Lauder and Revlon are typically marketed to wealthy households in developing countries. These consumers are not price sensitive and view these products as prestigious. These same brands are often targeted to the mass market in industrialized countries. So, in marketing these products in overseas markets, international companies may completely shift their strategy from mass-produced and mass-marketed products to top-of-the-line brands, depending on the target market.

In some situations, international companies may be backed into different market segments, even though that was not their primary intention. For example, when Pepsi-Cola was first introduced in the former Soviet Union in the early 1970s, only politburo officials could afford the soft drink, and it was also served at major banquets more as a novelty drink than as a simple soda. The result was that Pepsi was never accepted as a drink by the masses in the USSR. Hence, its distribution and pricing remained as an exclusive product. But when Coca-Cola introduced its soft drinks into Russia after the fall of communism in 1991, the public was ready for soft drinks. Similarly, when McDonald's opened its first restaurant in the United Kingdom in 1974, the Duchess of Kent and her children were among the first to line up at the restaurant,

Figure 11.1 **Integrated Marketing Program and Its External Environment**

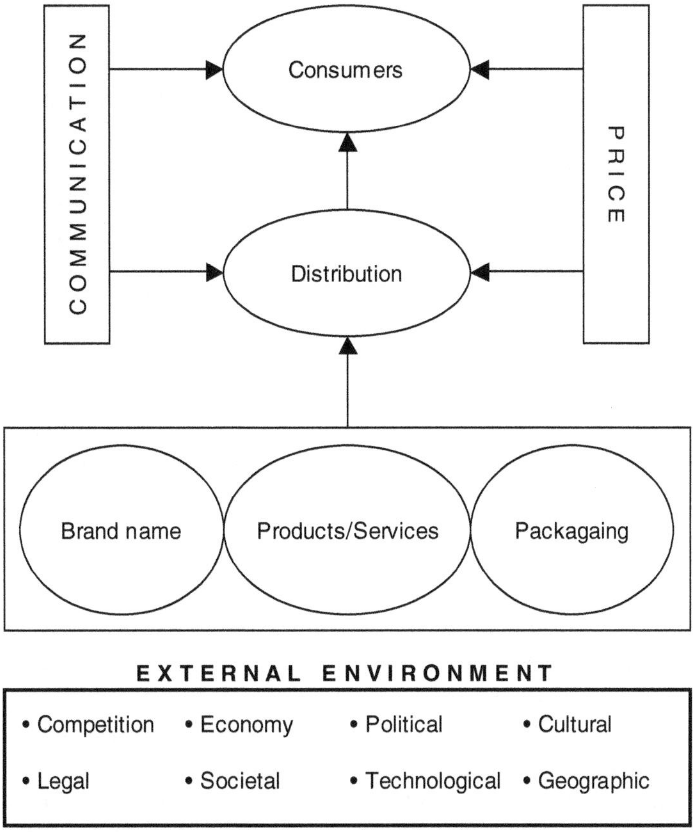

which became a liability for McDonald's; it took the company years to correct the notion that McDonald's was an exclusive restaurant.

Figure 11.1 presents the interrelationships among marketing activities.

BASIC STEPS IN INTERNATIONAL MARKETING

As with domestic marketers, companies operating in international markets also have to follow some specific steps, including identifying target consumers and developing a comprehensive marketing program. The program developed should include selecting products and services with attributes that benefit the consumers, setting the appropriate price, making the product or service available to consumers at their convenience using existing distribution channels, providing the necessary information to educate the consumers about the benefits of using a particular product, and, finally, setting up a formal feedback system to evaluate the performance of the product or service in the marketplace.

Recent developments in technology and communications have, in effect, made the world smaller. Globalization—that is, the interweaving of national economies—and the effect of it in the formation of a wider market that transcends national boundaries is shifting companies' strategic emphasis from a single-market approach to multiple-market considerations. For example, online retailing has created a global market that transcends national boundaries.[4] The multiple-market approach makes it possible for companies to standardize product offerings, creating a universal segment. Therefore, international companies find consumers with similar needs that will buy the same product regardless of their locations. Coca-Cola, for example, is very popular in many countries and is sold in nearly 200 of them. Similarly, BMW automobiles, Colgate toothpaste, Head & Shoulders shampoo, Philips light bulbs, and Sony television sets are popular with customers all over the world. This approach, called universal segmentation, is becoming a targeted strategy by many international companies. The challenge facing international marketers today is to develop products and strategic plans that are competitive in the intensifying global market.

Global competition and the large number of firms that operate in these markets have forced international companies to develop sophisticated marketing strategies that exploit the opportunities provided by the globalization of markets.

DEVELOPING AN INTERNATIONAL MARKETING STRATEGY

As in the development of domestic marketing strategies, international marketing strategies also start with the consumer. In a consumer-driven marketplace, identifying the right target group and determining its needs is essential for companies to succeed. Basically, target market selection focuses on certain clearly defined groups of consumers that are likely buyers/users of a specific product or service. In international markets, target groups may vary from country to country. For example, in most European countries, buyers of major appliances such as refrigerators, dishwashers, and washing machines tend to be middle-class and lower-middle-class families. In comparison, in some Asian countries, appliances are often purchased by families from the upper and upper-middle classes.

Following are the basic steps in developing an international marketing strategy:

- Choose consumers and market—Which consumer groups should the company target?
- Conduct marketing opportunity analysis and forecast sales—Does a substantial market exist, and what are the potential sales in units?
- Decide on mode of entry—How should a company enter the overseas market? Through exports, by way of joint venture, or by establishing a wholly owned subsidiary?
- Determine product and service offerings—What specific product/service benefits are desired by the target group? Do the existing product attributes meet consumers' needs?
- Establish price points—What should be the final price of the product?
- Select channels for distribution—Which channel of distribution should the company use?

- Develop a comprehensive communication program—What message should the company deliver to its consumers?
- Select media for reaching consumers—Which media should the company use in delivering its message?
- Implement a customer relations program—What programs should the company introduce to establish customer contact?
- Set up a feedback mechanism to evaluate the marketing program—What mechanism should the company use to obtain market-related feedback?

The above steps may seem familiar to students who have taken an introductory marketing course. As mentioned earlier, the basic steps in domestic marketing and international marketing are the same. The difference is in the implementation of these strategies in the marketplace: some differences stem from whether the target group is domestic or international; others stem from variations in the external environment.

In developing a comprehensive international marketing strategy, companies often use their experiences in other countries or markets as a starting point to avoid costly mistakes. Companies that are entering an overseas market for the first time need to be careful in making sure that they have studied the consumers and markets carefully and have considered all possible scenarios. Following is a discussion of the various steps that companies take in marketing goods/services in foreign markets.

CHOOSE CONSUMERS AND SELECT MARKET

Consumers as a Variable

Consumers are the focus of all marketing programs. Hence, it is critical that international marketers analyze customers to identify, learn about, and understand the factors that affect their purchases. Consumers can be identified using many variables, including demographic variables such as age, income, gender, education, occupation, marital status, and family (household) size; benefits sought from a particular product; quality preferences; purchase behavior, that is, their rate of consumption of a product (usage rate); and how often they purchase the product. Some marketers also make use of psychographic variables, especially consumers' lifestyles. Values and lifestyles are used wherever data on them is available to identify target markets. In the United States, SRI International measures values and lifestyles (VALS) of individuals on an ongoing basis, and the data is available to subscribers, who use them to target specific consumer segments.[5] In international marketing, psychographics are not used for segmenting markets as often as it is done in the United States and other industrialized countries. Availability of information and measurement issues are the main reasons why psychographics are not used as often internationally to identify and understand consumer groups.

To improve the effectiveness of marketing strategies, marketers have used consumer segmentation as a possible approach to improve their earnings performance.

Segmentation offers companies with a group of consumers who may have similar needs and wants and could be reached through similar marketing communications and distribution channels. In segmenting markets, international marketers make use of the consumer characteristics to group customers with similar characteristics. Some of the characteristics used to segment markets are the same as the ones used to analyze customers—demographic variables, buyer preferences, purchase behavior, and psychographics. For example, a consumer segment for Chanel perfume could be made up of females, age 25 to 45, single, living in metropolitan areas, with a college degree, and earning between €25,000 and €50,000.

Segmentation assumes that international marketers are able to identify specific groups that are different in their consumption behavior and that the groups are measurable through certain characteristics. For example, in India, income has been used as a segmentation factor based on clear response differences between groups in the consumer market. Income was a variable that was easily measured, and the segment was identified as the "premium segment."[6] If marketers are able to distinguish two groups through certain characteristics but are not able to identify which group corresponds to the different purchase or consumption patterns, then segmentation is not an appropriate marketing strategy.

International marketers use marketing mix strategies to influence consumers to purchase specific brands of a product category. The factors that influence consumers most are price, quality, availability, attribute-need (fit), recommendation of others, and information.

Identifying Countries/Markets

In an ever-growing global market with a vast untapped potential, there are many opportunities for international companies to market goods and services. Companies such as Coca-Cola, IBM, Philips, Siemens, Sony, Thomson, and Unilever constantly look for potential markets to reach new growth targets. Although some of these companies operate or sell in more than 100 countries, their quest for newer markets is a mainstay of their strategic direction. The task of selecting an appropriate new country or market is made difficult by the divergent goals or the trade-offs between two goals that companies face. On the one hand, the company has to identify a country with the greatest potential; on the other hand, it has to consider a country with the least amount of risk. Often, these two goals are not complementary. For example, Luxembourg is often rated as one of the safest or least risky countries for foreign firms to invest in, but Luxembourg has a small population, just over 450,000. Though the country is safe for investment purposes, the size of the population does not provide an attractive opportunity for most goods and services. In selecting a new country for entry, international companies analyze such factors as the number of potential consumers for a given product or service, the consumers' ability to purchase these products or services, the competitive environment, various external risks (economic, political, regulatory, and the like), and the companies' ability to generate profits in these new markets. Chapters 2 through 4 discuss some of the environmental factors and how companies select countries for entry.

CONDUCT MARKETING OPPORTUNITY ANALYSIS

Entry into a new market does not assume that all potential consumers in that market are ready to buy a new product or service. Factors such as the specific needs of the consumers in the new market, the level of competition, and the price of the product or service offered are all factors that affect consumption rate in a given market. For example, introducing SUVs in a country where the roads are narrow and the price of gasoline is high may not fit the needs of the local consumers. Similarly, the introduction of compact cars by General Motors in Japan will definitely not succeed, as the Japanese have some of the best made compact cars in the world.

To develop a viable international marketing strategy, companies need to conduct a market opportunity analysis and forecast the potential sales in a new market. A critical part of market opportunity analysis is estimating the size of the total market, that is, the number of units that the market can absorb by all firms selling the product. Market forecast is the number of units a company is able to sell in a given market for a specific period of time. Market opportunity analysis involves (1) determining market potential, (2) conducting a sales forecast, and (3) evaluating the overall opportunity.

Market potential is the maximum number of units of a particular product that can be sold to a specific target group. This includes the opportunity *by all firms* serving the market. The market potential is the upper limit of possible sales for a product in a given market and may not always be achieved by a single company. Actual industry sales (by all companies) are lower than the potential due to many reasons, including a lack of interest among the consumers for the product, ineffective marketing strategies, and the availability of substitutes that equally satisfy a similar consumer need. For example, in introducing its Prell shampoo in India, Procter & Gamble as well as other shampoo manufacturers were not able to reach the projected market potential, as traditional homemade herbal concoctions served the needs of the consumers at a much lower cost. Hence, in estimating market potential as well as in defining the target market, it is important to incorporate criteria such as affordability.

A target market may be defined as *a specific segment or segments within a potential market (country) that is defined through a set of variables that can be identified and reached and contains the most likely adopters of a given product or service that a firm wants to pursue.* The target market is the focus of most marketing programs. For example, among the 6 million new car buyers in China, Ford may define its target market for its Ford Explorer as predominantly male consumers ranging in age from 25 to 50 years, in the top 10 percent of the socioeconomic income level, who consider themselves the trendsetters in their society. This particular segment might encompass fewer than 50,000 consumers among the potential 6 million automobile buyers. But for Ford, this is the target that they will concentrate on in developing their marketing strategy.

FORECAST SALES FOR THE SELECTED TARGET GROUP

The sales forecast is the expected unit sales for a given product in a given market within the market potential. It can be calculated for the whole industry or for a single firm. A sales forecast is the result of a detailed marketing program within a given marketing environment. Therefore, it is important for companies to establish their potential sales for a given time frame (typically one, two, or five years). There are many techniques available to international companies for forecasting their sales. These include using historic sales analysis of similar market introductions (comparative analysis), using estimates made by the sales force, expert opinion, retailer/distributor estimates, time-series analysis, and market research studies.

If the company is already in a country and would like to forecast future sales, it would definitely make use of historic sales data in arriving at the target number. In this situation, estimates by the sales force or the existing dealer network estimates may be acceptable as well; however, quite often these figures are inaccurate and biased, as each group may not state the true potential lest they be held responsible for the estimates. In instances when the company has many years of data, it is appropriate to use time-series analysis or regression analysis, as the forecast may be more objective.

When a company enters a new country/market for the first time, it is often difficult to forecast sales accurately. The lack of information coupled with inexperience in the country is often mentioned as the reason for not being able to forecast sales precisely. For international companies that are attempting to enter foreign markets for the first time, the problem of predicting sales accurately is even more difficult because such companies do not have any prior experience in international marketing.

If the company is attempting to enter a new country and does not have any histori-cal data to analyze, it can use a comparative-analysis approach, expert opinion, or market research. In a comparative-analysis approach, the international company will forecast the sales based on actual sales in a country where it had previously marketed its product or service. For example, Adidas, the German-based sneaker manufacturer, can use its sales figures for tennis shoes from a few years earlier in Japan to estimate the sales for the same type of shoes in South Korea, making some adjustments for the size of the target group (the population of Japan is more than 128 million, whereas South Korea's is just short of 49 million).

In using experts to predict sales, international companies rely on individuals who are knowledgeable about the country in question. These may include individuals who have had selling experience in the country, consultants, home country consular of-ficials, and trade associations such as the National Automobile Dealers Association, the International Chemical & Plastic Manufacturers Association, American Chambers of Commerce Abroad, and other similar associations.

DECIDE ON MODE OF ENTRY

As discussed in Chapter 6, companies enter international markets through exports, licensing arrangements, strategic alliances, joint ventures, or wholly owned subsid-iaries. Each of these approaches varies in the level of involvement and the level of control exerted over the foreign operation. In exports, a firm has minimal control over its marketing efforts in overseas markets. With a wholly owned subsidiary, a firm can manage its foreign operations with total control. Whether a company enters a market through exports or through a wholly owned subsidiary, its objectives are the same, that is, to penetrate a new segment and expand its global markets.

The entry strategies of international companies are not static. Many companies that start out as exporters eventually move into higher-order operations such as joint ventures or fully owned subsidiaries. For example, when Japanese automobile manufacturers entered the U.S. market in the early 1960s, they first opted for exports (as they did not have brand recognition in the United States), and only when they had gained substantial market share did they decide to put up fully owned factories in the United States. International companies may also use different entry strategies for different countries. For countries that have significant market potential, a company may elect to enter through a fully owned subsidiary, as Nestlé did during the early stages of its forays into overseas markets. For countries that are not fully developed but may provide future opportunities for expansion, an international company may decide to use exports to enter the market. For example, Nestlé entered many of the markets in Africa through exports when it was exploring the market potential in the region.

DETERMINE PRODUCT AND SERVICE OFFERINGS

In the final analysis, consumers purchase goods and services to satisfy specific needs. The basic transaction between companies and consumers is in the exchange of goods for payment. Therefore, the starting point of all marketing activities and the focus of marketing strategy have to be about a product. In developing product strategies, an international company considers two factors. The first is the stage of the product life cycle (PLC), and the second is the product position in relation to competing brands.

Every product goes through a life cycle of various stages from introduction to decline. Even though every product has its own life cycle, each may vary in length of time. That is, the life cycles of some products such as designer clothes and toys may be less than a year; some others such Bayer Aspirin and Coca-Cola have been in the market for more than 100 years. Depending on the stage of a product's life cycle, different marketing strategies may be applied. For instance, in the introductory stages, heavy communications strategies might be employed, whereas in the saturation stage, the focus of marketing strategy may be to attain distribution in every possible outlet. International marketers have the opportunity to extend the life of a product by exploiting the differences in economic and market conditions among countries. A product that is developed in an industrial country may be introduced in emerging countries at a later time, making it possible for the product's life to be extended. For example, as Gillette, the maker of shaving items, introduces its Fusion Power razor in the United States and a few other countries, it will introduce its previous model, the Mach 3 Turbo, into Argentina, Brazil, and South Africa, thereby extending the overall life of the Mach 3 and other razor products. In fact, it has been noted that there are still some earlier models of razors that were introduced in the 1960s that remain in the markets in some countries of the world.

Developing unique and/or distinctive product positions is part of the overall marketing strategy. Product position refers to the perception of consumers of a particular brand within a product category that distinguishes the brand on some attributes from other competing brands. These attributes could be superior quality, higher price value, ease of use, image, or any other feature that consumers may use in selecting a

particular product. International marketers make every attempt to attain a preferred
product position. For example, among credit card customers, American Express has
a position of prestige in comparison to MasterCard or Visa.

In international marketing, a factor that is often of some concern for companies
is the *country-of-origin effect* on consumers' perception of the product. Country-of-
origin effects can be positive or negative: products made in some countries are well
known for their quality and value. It is possible that when the customer becomes
aware of the country of origin, it might affect the product's image and, therefore,
its sales.[7] For example, automobiles from Germany, electronics from Japan, and
watches from Switzerland all have positive images in most consumers' minds. In
contrast, automobiles from Russia, designer clothing from Laos, and wines from the
Philippines have negative product images, as these countries are not known for the
manufacture of these products. Country-of-origin effects are product specific, not
brand specific. It also appears that there may be degrees of country-of-origin effects
among consumers from different countries. In a recent study, it was observed that
Japanese consumers were found to be more sensitive than American consumers to
the country-of-origin effect.[8] International marketers that have positive country-
of-origin effects should leverage this benefit to their advantage in their marketing
strategies, while those that do not should design strategies that emphasize other
features to counter the negative product image. For example, in introducing Chilean
wines to the United States, the distributors who handled these wines emphasized
the value of the wines rather than the fact that they came from Chile, which is not
a traditionally strong wine-producing country.

Identify Specific Product/Service Benefits Desired by the Target Group

Consumers buy goods and services to derive predetermined benefits. Hence, a customer buying a Volvo is attracted by the car's reputation as one of the safest cars in the
market. In international markets, the benefits sought by consumers differ from country
to country. A consumer in one country may desire a particular brand of product for its
quality, whereas a consumer in another country may be interested in its convenience
factor. For instance, bicycles in China are used as a major mode of transportation
and are used by people who are mostly in the lower socioeconomic segment of the
population. For buyers in China, bicycles should be simple in design and relatively
inexpensive (under $25). In contrast, in the United States, bicycles are used mostly
as recreational vehicles, and buyers are willing to spend hundreds of dollars (if not
thousands) on each. Hence, these bicycles are equipped with all available gadgetry
and are technological marvels. For American bicycle manufacturers to be successful
in the Chinese market, they have to totally revamp their machines to suit the benefits
sought by the Chinese bicycle buyers.

While entering a new country/market, international companies need to conduct
market research to identify specific benefits that consumers seek in a given product
category. Information on consumers and markets may be gathered through international market research. For international companies, their first attempt in gathering
consumer or market-related information may be through internal records. Reports such

as cost data, accounting reports, sales reports, inventory reports, annual advertising expenditures, and consumer data (especially for service companies such as banks, insurance companies, and other financial institutions) are all useful information in understanding purchase patterns, media preferences, and so on that can be useful in developing marketing programs. For international companies that operate in multiple countries, comparing data across markets may shed some insights that may also be applied in developing marketing strategy. Besides the internal sources of information, international companies sometimes seek out other secondary data that may be useful. Information from government agencies, international organizations such as the International Monetary Fund, the United Nations, and the World Bank, and trade publications and other published information can be useful in understanding markets (Appendix 2 provides a summary of activities of the international agencies). Many of these sources are relatively inexpensive (some of them may even be free), and with modern technology such as Internet access they are easy to locate.

Many of the larger international companies monitor markets on a regular basis and employ qualified staffs who from time to time conduct market-related research. These companies also sometimes hire outside research suppliers to carry out specific research studies. Companies such as VNU of the Netherlands, the Kantor Group of the United Kingdom, and Information Resources of the United States are all research suppliers that conduct a variety of studies and have operations in many countries of the world. In fact, VNU has operations in 81 countries.

Determine If the Existing Product Attributes Meet International Consumers' Needs

In the previous step, the international marketer was able to identify the specific benefit(s) that a segment of consumers sought from a product category. At this stage, the international marketer should evaluate its product or service offering to make sure that the attributes of the offering match the benefits sought by its target group. *Product or service attributes are defined as features and characteristics that provide specific benefits to consumers.* For example, attributes of a personal computer may be its overall quality, memory, speed, integrated audio capability, and so on. In international marketing, due to influences of culture, consumers may seek more than just physical attributes. Based on an individual consumer's culture, preferences may be influenced by taste, color, and form—attributes that are more psychological than physical. Research has shown that consumer perceptions of quality vary from country to country, and market-perceived quality is difficult to compare across cultures.[9]

Successful international marketers recognize that consumers seek total satisfaction from a purchase. Total satisfaction implies that the marketers consider both the physical and psychological satisfaction that consumers desire. For example, when Heineken, a Dutch beer company, having experienced the surge in low-caloric light beers in the United States, introduced its Amstel Light in some European countries, many consumers rejected it. For these consumers, who enjoy their full-bodied beer, the taste of light beer did not appeal to them. Although Amstel Light was successful in the United States, it never caught on in Europe. Similarly, refrigerators in many developing countries are viewed as a symbol of one's wealth and success, and, hence, are often exhibited in the living room, a practice not seen in European and American homes.

In introducing products into foreign markets or developing new offerings, international companies have to make sure that their products meet the physical and psychological aspects of consumers' needs. That is, if a group of consumers buys a particular brand of shampoo for its medicinal qualities (such as removal of dandruff) and at the same time the preferred color of the shampoo is blue, an international company has to determine if its product has such medicinal benefit as well as the color sought by the consumers in that country. Similarly, Volvo automobiles are renowned for their safety features, but traditionally their cars have been boxy and, according to some observers, ungainly in shape and design. If, in a given market, a large segment of the population considers safety the single-most-critical physical attribute in an automobile but also values attractiveness of design, then Volvo would appeal to only a small segment of that market. (Recognizing this problem, Volvo did introduce sleeker designs in the late 1990s.)

Product or service attributes, both physical and psychological, can offer an international company unique competitive advantages. A company has a competitive advantage in a brand of a particular product category (e.g., Arial is a brand within the product category detergents) when it has greater value in benefits than competitors' products. Through exceptional quality, convenience, user friendliness, added value, and cultural symbolism, international companies are able to gain competitive advantage. Companies must first identify and understand the needs of consumers and develop unique attributes that can retain customers and gain their confidence and patronage. For example, Toyota, which is renowned for its quality, has a competitive advantage over other automobile manufacturers that helps it outsell most competitors in its class of vehicles (Corolla in the subcompact category and Camry in the four-door sedan category). Similarly, Apple's iPod, with its unique features and attractive design, is the preferred brand of MP3 player among teenagers and adults alike all around the world.

International Product Standardization

If the conditions are right, international companies prefer to market the exact same product in all countries. This strategy, called standardization, offers unique advantages to companies that can implement it. Some of the key advantages of standardization are economies of scale in production, R&D efficiency, distribution effectiveness, and strategic synergy, resulting in cost savings. Standardization also avoids duplication of efforts and streamlines operations. Using a standardization strategy, international companies are able to compete strongly with other global brands.

Standardization is the ultimate goal of most international companies. In fact, the globalization process, as outlined by Theodore Levitt,[10] assumes that companies are able to standardize products and services as consumers seek the best products at the lowest prices from anywhere in world. To achieve standardization, international companies must find common ground in consumer segments that have similar purchasing power, seek similar benefits, and are in countries that have similar external environments. It is virtually impossible to find two exactly similar countries that can adopt similar products. Country variations do exist, and, therefore, it is not easy to standardize products. However, marketers have found ways to circumvent these difficulties. One strategy is to offer products and services that marketers feel have particularly strong consumer appeal and sell them as "what everyone wants" rather than worry about the details of "what everyone thinks they might like."[11] When Starbucks introduced its brand of coffee houses in China, it ignored the fact that the Chinese are predominantly tea drinkers and instead believed that its brand of coffee, which was appealing to the younger middle class all over the world, would succeed in China, too. Similarly, when Kellogg's and General Mills, two American-based cereal companies, introduced Corn Flakes and Cheerios in India, they did not worry about the fact that most Indians have a hot home-cooked breakfast each morning. Instead, they felt that the convenience of just pouring milk into ready-made cereal would appeal to busy executives, working women, and children, and they did succeed in changing the breakfast habits of Indians in the metropolitan areas.

In Europe, where it is assumed that there are some similarities among the countries, including their state of industrialization, efforts to standardize products have not always been successful. To succeed in these countries, the practical approach has been not to standardize products and marketing programs across the region, but to find groups of countries that have similar marketing characteristics. For example, the authors of a recent research study found that companies can succeed through standardization by pairing countries such as Germany and France, the United Kingdom and France, and others.[12]

Product Strategy When the Product Attributes Do Not Match Consumer Needs

If the product or service attributes do not match the specific benefits sought by a target group, the international company has a few strategic options available. First, it can consider whether consumers may be convinced through demonstrations, experts' testimonials, or other communication techniques that the attribute its product possesses is important and desirable. For example, Philips, a Dutch conglomerate that sells fluorescent light bulbs to the industrial market, wanted buyers to change the product emphasis from how much light bulbs cost and how long they last to the total cost of buying the bulb, including the high disposal cost caused by toxic materials in the bulbs. Philips had a new version of a light bulb that was environmentally friendly and easy to dispose of but cost more than conventional bulbs. Instead of using the traditional channel of convincing purchasing managers to buy the bulbs, Philips pitched the new bulbs (Alto) directly to the CFOs, who understood the significance of the overall cost. Through this strategy, Philips was able to capture 25 percent of the industrial fluorescent lamp business in the United States.[13] Similarly, Starbucks was successful in China without adapting to the local tastes. The company did not change any of its product offerings but relied on its marketing program to sell coffee to a heavily tea-drinking population. Toyota has succeeded globally by emphasizing the fuel efficiency of its cars and changing the mindset of consumers worldwide about the most important attribute in a car even before the present oil crisis (especially in the United States, where car buyers were less concerned about fuel efficiency).

International companies that feel they cannot convince foreign consumers of their products' merits have tried other approaches, including changing their products' attributes for the new market. For example, McDonald's has been successful in many countries by adapting to local tastes: in the Middle East, all the food is halal approved; in Mexico, McDonald's offers a chorizo (spicy sausage) platter of eggs, rice, and beans; and in India, its menu includes a veggie burger.

Packaging and Branding

Packaging and branding go hand in hand. Brand names are typically placed on every package. Consumers quite often recognize their favorite brands simply by looking at the package. For example, Heineken beer is recognized worldwide by its distinctive green bottle. Similarly, Citigroup is recognized by its logo (an umbrella over its brand name). A strong global brand image is a definite competitive advantage for companies that can achieve it. Studies have shown that consumers do not process brand experience at a rational and conscious level, but rather through a complex system of psychology and motivation.[14] Developing global brands is probably the most important strategic initiative that international companies can undertake.[15] To be recognized globally while standing for excellence, companies must (1) start with a very good product or service, (2) develop unique competitive advantages, (3) be in the public's view, (4) sell to a large market, (5) have a distinctive name, and (6) be marketed in many countries. In addition, global brand recognition is achieved through heavy promotional activities that require financial resources. International companies have also been successful through co-branding, or linking brands through relationships with other brands.[16] For example, many desktop computer companies such as Dell and HP have successfully co-branded their products by linking with Intel. The world's 10 most recognizable brand names in 2007 were Coca-Cola, Microsoft, IBM, GE, Intel, Nokia, Toyota, Disney, McDonald's, and Mercedes-Benz.[17]

Most consumer products are packaged so as to protect the product as well as to provide useful information. Consumers see the package before they see the product inside, so packaging has significant marketing implications. If all other factors remain the same, a consumer may select a brand simply because of the attractive features of the packaging. Hence, cosmetic companies and packaged goods companies spend a considerable amount of resources in developing package designs that are unique, appealing, and create awareness.

In international markets, due to language differences, cultural tastes, and government regulations, companies have to make changes to the packaging to adapt to the host country's needs. For example, the governments of many countries require all weights and measurement to be in metric. Numerous other packaging problems have been caused by a company's failure to adapt to local conditions. Take the case of Brugel, a German children's cereal brand, which featured birds, dogs, and other animals on the packaging to attract children's attention. This product was placed in the pet foods section of supermarkets in China based on its package features. If the company had used some Chinese labeling, it could have avoided this problem. Since Japanese companies spend a considerable amount of time and money on packaging, foreign products that are marketed with poor packaging convey poor-quality products to the Japanese. In Brazil, Coca-Cola's Diet Coke ran into problems, as "diet" in that culture implied medicinal use, and the product therefore required daily recommended consumption on the label.

ESTABLISH PRICE POINTS

Wherever consumers buy goods and services, the price of the item is a major consideration in their choice of a brand because it is the most easily comparable measure. Therefore, setting the price of goods and services is an important strategic step for international companies. Price can be used to attract consumers, add value to a company's offering, gain competitive advantage, maximize profits, and acquire and retain distributors. The factors that affect prices are costs (direct and indirect), distribution costs, break-even level, market size, demand estimates, price elasticity of demand, competitors' prices, local taxes, and the host country's regulations.

In international marketing, setting a final price is complicated by the differences in input costs, rates of inflation in the host country, exchange-rate fluctuations, differences in price elasticity of demand, different break-even levels, and the purchasing power of the consumers in a given country. Hence, it is not unusual to find that the price for the same product differs from country to country. For example, a package of 100 Tylenol 500 mg tablets has a retail price of US$9 in the United States, P325 in the Philippines (the equivalent of US$6.50 at an exchange rate of P50 per dollar), and Rs150 in India (the equivalent of US$3.00 at the exchange rate of Rs50 per dollar). Similarly, the Canon PowerShot S3 IS digital camera sold for US$556.95 at retail stores in the United States, for €546 in Germany (the equivalent of US$873), and £238.00 in the United Kingdom (the equivalent of US$454).

From a strategic point of view, price is viewed as *value* gained by the consumer. Value is defined as the ratio of the benefits derived from a product to its price. That is Value = benefits/price. Therefore, the more benefits a customer derives from a given product, the greater the value associated with it. International companies can charge high prices if they can show that their products have high value. Many consumers are willing to pay high prices for luxury goods such as Rolex watches and BMW cars, as they perceive these as high-value brands. The value quotient can be increased by increasing the benefits derived from a product, by decreasing its price, or by doing both (combining an increase in benefits with a decrease in price).

International companies that enter a new country for the first time may have a difficult time deciding on the exact price to charge for their products because they lack prior experience with that particular market. In such cases, companies have several options: They may set the price based on their cost structure by computing all the costs first and then adding a predetermined profit to arrive at the final price. For example, if the direct and indirect cost associated with producing and marketing a product is US$10, and if the company typically aims for a 10 percent profit over cost, the final price would be US$11. Another common approach in pricing a product in a new market is to set the price on the basis of a competitor's price, assuming the competitor's products have similar attributes and are marketed to the same target group. In some instances, when the company is not sure of a direct competitor, an average price for the industry may be used as a benchmark.

If the international company has prior experience in other markets, it can use these experiences as a guide in setting a final price. For example, Sony has little difficulty in setting a price for its television sets in a new market: it uses its vast experience and knowledge in determining the exact cost of producing and marketing television sets all over the world.

In establishing the price points for a product or service, international companies have to continuously monitor the environment. The actions of competitors, changes in raw material costs, changes in rate of inflation, exchange-rate fluctuations, and government regulations are just some of the factors that must be monitored. Any change in a competitor's price has to be considered seriously. An upward shift in price may be a deliberate action by a competitor to change its image and the prestige associated with its brand. If the target consumer group accepts this price change, it may be willing to pay more for the competitor's brand, resulting in a loss of sales for the company. For example, if BMW raises its price by 5 percent on its 500 series of cars, then Mercedes-Benz and Lexus may opt to raise their prices, too. Sometimes companies may lower their prices to take market away from their competitors. Most often these price reductions are quickly matched by all competitors in an attempt to protect market share. If British Airways reduces its price on its London-to-New York route, this move will be quickly replicated by Air India, American Airlines, and others flying the same route. Unless a company has some unique cost benefits such as lower production costs or advantages in distribution efficiencies, the window of opportunity for a price advantage is small. Price is the easiest of all marketing strategies to copy.

SELECT CHANNELS FOR DISTRIBUTION

Distribution is the marketing activity that makes it possible for companies to reach their consumers and complete a sale. Distribution activities include channel management, logistics, transportation, and inventory management. Logistics is an integral part of distribution and is a critical activity within the marketing function.[18] Distribution is divided into two categories: upstream and downstream. Upstream distribution manages the flow of goods and services from various suppliers to the manufacturers or service companies, basically for industrial consumption. For example, the distribution of raw materials such as steel, tires, and batteries that are purchased by an automobile manufacturer is considered upstream distribution. In contrast, distribution of goods and services that reach retailers for consumption by final consumers is called downstream distribution. What follows is a discussion of downstream distribution in international markets.

Channels help companies move goods and services from manufacturer to consumers. The major function of channels is to have products available where and when the customers want them. Hence, channels fulfill the utilities of place and time. Through retailers, companies reach consumers at various locations within the country. In many countries, foreigners are barred from investing in retail activities so as to protect national interests (distribution of staple items is considered vital to a country's security).[19] Some of the other functions performed by channels are buying and selling (transferring ownership from a company to a buyer), breaking the volume down, transporting goods and services, maintaining inventory levels, providing information, and promoting goods and services to final consumers. In international markets, the channel functions vary from country to country. For example, in Japan, it is typical to use six to seven intermediaries in transferring a product from the source (producer) to the final consumer. Therefore, some of the first-level channel members in Japan may be just selling agents who do not actually buy the product but sell it for a fee. In the United States, a typical channel for distributing consumer goods uses three or four intermediaries, a much shorter channel compared to Japan's distribution system. Typically, the first level of channel members in the United States is made up of wholesalers, who buy and sell goods and services. In industrial marketing, the number of channel members is even fewer—at most one or two intermediaries— because the volume of a purchase by each industrial consumer, shorter channels are justified. For example, when Henkel, a German-based multinational company that sells household items, buys toner cartridges for its photocopying machines, it buys them in the hundreds; an individual consumer probably buys two or three toner cartridges per purchase. Shorter channels are efficient when the products are bulky. Costs of handling, loading, and unloading bulky products can add to overall costs, and, hence, shorter channels are more practical in such cases. Also, shorter channels are economical when order lots are larger.

Within the channels, each member or intermediary performs different functions. A company may decide to carry out all the channel functions internally (direct channels), or have independent, outside businesses carry out the channel functions (indirect channels). With indirect channels, companies use intermediaries to complete the distribution function. Some companies use just one intermediary, and others may use many. The number of intermediaries depends on the product, consumption rate, and specific country in which the distribution is set up. In automobile distribution, for instance, only one intermediary is used, as the product is bulky and consumers do not buy this product that frequently; in contrast, toiletries are distributed through three or four intermediaries, as they are purchased frequently by consumers. The number of intermediaries used determines the length of the channel; when only one or two are used they are referred to as short channels, and when three or more are used they are referred to as long channels.

Companies that opt for direct channels sell their goods and services directly to the final consumers. These companies undertake all the essential functions that are necessary to have the product or service available to the user. There are definite advantages in opting for direct channels. Companies that perform their own channel functions have direct access to their customers and hence come to know their needs better. This helps them to improve their customer retention rate. This direct contact also helps them to gather information that may be used to streamline strategies and to help generate new product ideas. In addition, these companies have better control of their distribution costs. On the downside, a direct channel is very expensive. A company that decides to undertake all the channel functions by itself incurs the related costs associated with them without the benefit of spreading these costs over many product categories of many companies, which an independent distributor is able to do. Doing one's own distribution also implies assuming many unrelated activities that may not be within a company's core competencies.

In spite of the difficulties, a few international companies are involved with direct channels, and they are more popular in industrial marketing, where order size justifies shorter channels. Many manufacturers have started the use of virtual stores as a direct distribution channel in addition to their existing indirect retail channels. When manufacturers start their own direct channels, however, conflicts can arise with the existing retail channel system. To avoid these conflicts, some manufacturers distribute excess stock at retail stores through their direct online system.[20] Companies that sell door-to-door, mail-order companies, telephone-order companies, and Internet-based sellers all use direct channels. For example, the Avon cosmetic company sells its products through representatives in door-to-door sales; Amazon.com sells many varieties of products through the Internet; and Dell Computers uses the telephone to take customer orders. Some of the large industrial companies such as Boeing, Hyundai, Mitsubishi Heavy Machinery, Philips, and SAP have their own sales offices in foreign countries that call on customers directly. Most service companies—commercial banks, insurance companies, and investment banks—always use direct channels to reach their customers. Hence, HSBC of the United Kingdom has branch offices in different countries of the world. Similarly, the Swiss-based UBS AG, an investment bank, has offices in many countries to serve the needs of its retail customers and business clients.

Some service companies do use indirect channels to reach a wider geographic area quickly. Through licensing and franchising arrangements, these companies are able to provide their services to customers in many parts of the world with much lower risks to the franchisor. Licensing is an arrangement whereby one company gives rights to another for the use of a brand name or trademark for a predetermined fee. Franchising is a similar arrangement, in which, for a fee (royalty), one company (the *franchisor*) sells to another party (the *franchisee*) the use of a trademark that is the essential asset for the franchisee's business. As the franchisors themselves do not invest directly in these operations and can assign the actual operational details to the franchisee, the financial exposure to these companies is reduced. Some of the benefits for international companies that use licensing or franchising systems are that they are able to cover a territory with little investment and receive highly motivated businesspeople to work for them without having to keep them on their payroll. Furthermore, franchisees have local knowledge and expertise that can be leveraged to a competitive advantage. Lack of knowledge of host country market conditions is a common problem faced by most international companies. The franchisors are also guaranteed income through licensing fees or royalties. On the downside, franchisors lose some control over their brand names and management expertise to host country nationals who may end up being future competitors. Also, the available market potential may not be fully exploited by the franchisee.

International companies that sell their goods and services to final consumers usually use indirect channels to distribute their products. These companies use a combination of importers, agents, wholesalers, and retailers to sell their products to final consumers. The type of channel members available and the level of services they provide in each market may vary from country to country. For example, until China entered the World Trade Organization (WTO) in 2001, distributors in China provided only basic transportation and warehousing services. Since many of these distributors were state designated, they operated under a monopoly. Therefore, many international companies had to use fragmented, tiered, and rigid top-down distribution networks that were expensive and inefficient. Because of the WTO-mandated guidelines, however, China had to revamp its distribution system and open the business for private as well as foreign-owned companies. These changes have led to improved services and a much more efficient distribution system. Before China joined the WTO, the distribution system was made up of three to four intermediaries, and now it is made up of just one or two.[21] Therefore, it is very important for international companies to study a host country's distribution channels and systems to develop a competitive strategy.

Distribution costs, if not controlled, may lead to unprofitable operations. Many international companies continuously search for ways to streamline their distribution systems to lower their costs. Some of these changes may include a total revamping of not only the distribution system but other operational activities as well. A small Ohio-based industrial parts company with distribution in more than six countries established new channels by shifting its manufacturing to five locations around the world with six major distribution centers. Before this shift in the manufacturing-distribution matrix, all manufactured parts flowed through the company's U.S.-based manufacturing plant. After the revamped system, each manufacturing plant, through its distribution centers, delivered parts to its customers at a faster rate, knocking 3 percent off the company's distribution costs.[22] Similarly, Dell Computers and Nokia in China have improved their distribution systems through the removal of unnecessary layers of bureaucracy.[23]

Distribution systems in each country are often already established; hence, an international company may be forced to adapt to the host country's system. In some countries, like Japan, the distribution system is complicated, and foreign companies, even successful retail chains like Carrefour SA, have difficulty succeeding there.[24] Most of the difficulties in Japan are attributed to the tradition-bound structure, which is difficult for foreign companies to understand. Companies like Toys "R" Us have taken on local partners in Japan to maneuver through an archaic system that is deeply entrenched and functions effectively. Similarly, in the Philippines, food distribution is handled first by large trading agents, followed by wholesalers, and then by food brokers, finally reaching the end consumers through retailers. Nestlé's entry into the Philippine market has been greatly affected by the nation's distribution chain. The chocolate maker has very little choice but to use the existing distribution system. If it wants to set up its own system, it may run into government regulations (in the Philippines, food distribution cannot be handled by foreign-owned companies), as well as increased investments in an activity in which the company has very little expertise, and, more important, lacks geographic coverage. Nestlé may not be able to reach all potential international consumers due to a lack of the wide network of retailers that the independent businesses handling distribution are able to provide. International

Table 11.1

Types of Channel Members Used in Selected Countries

Country	Product	No. of Channel Members	Type of Channel Members
Australia	Food items	1 to 2	Large food retailers buy direct. Small retailers use a food distributor.
Brazil	Food items; toiletries	2 to 4	
China	Nonfood items and prescription drugs	2 to 3	Dealer/distributor and retailer or Dealer/distributor, wholesaler, and retailer
Denmark	Food items; toiletries	1 to 3	For large chain retailers, just one; For small retailers, broker and retailer
India	Food items; toiletries	2 to 5	
Japan	Food items	5 to 6	Agent 1, Agent 2, distributors, wholesalers, and retailers
New Zealand	Food items; toiletries	2 to 4	
Philippines	Food items; toiletries	3 to 4	Brokers, distributors, and retailers
South Korea	Food items; toiletries	1 to 2	For packaged items, direct to the retailer; For fresh produce, wholesalers to retailers
Thailand	Drugs	2	Wholesaler and retailer
United States	Food items (meats); toiletries	3	Wholesalers, jobbers, and retailers

marketers must get their goods into the hands of consumers, either by distributing them themselves or by handing them to specialists who can do it more efficiently.[25] Table 11.1 presents types of channel members used by selected countries in the distribution of various items.

Inventory management and warehousing are part of the distribution system. Through inventory, companies are able to manage the uneven demand patterns that occur in the marketplace. Because of distances and operating in different time zones, inventory management in international marketing becomes even more critical than it is domestically. Inventory helps companies to regulate the flow of goods through distribution channels. The advantage of maintaining an adequate inventory level is that consumers will always be able to find the products they need (fulfilling the time utility function of distribution), and retailers will not be out of stock of a particular brand of product. Consumers may be willing to wait for items such as automobiles and even some appliances, but for products such as milk, soap, detergent, and other household items, they will not wait. If a particular brand is not available, consumers will switch brands.

The key decisions in inventory management are when to order and how much to order. There are many costs associated with inventory management. Some of these costs are storage (also called carrying) costs, ordering costs, handling costs, transportation costs, opportunity costs, insurance costs, allowances for breakage or spoilage, and stock-out costs. Maintaining a large inventory is expensive, and marketers try to control these costs. In industrial marketing, some manufacturers use the just-in-time (JIT) manufacturing process. This inventory system is designed to minimize inventories and their associated costs, and also to control waste. (Inventory management and JIT are discussed in Chapter 8.)

DEVELOP A COMPREHENSIVE COMMUNICATION PROGRAM

Communication programs are meant to inform current and potential consumers of the benefits of using a company's products and services. Well-organized and well-managed communications should be able to (1) tell potential consumers why they should use a particular brand of product, (2) persuade those customers that the company's brand is best by showing its advantages over competing brands, (3) build loyalty, (4) serve as a champion for the company's brands, and (4) inform consumers about the company. In some industries such as cosmetics, household items, and toiletries, communication costs are a major portion of the overall marketing costs. International companies such as Nestlé, Procter & Gamble, and Unilever spend more than US$4 billion annually in communication-related activities. To achieve the various goals of communication and at the same time be cost efficient, many companies develop models to simulate scenarios and map outcomes. Some of the basic steps in most communications strategies are:

- Identifying the target audience
- Setting communication goals
- Designing the message
- Selecting media
- Developing a promotional budget
- Evaluating communication programs

To be effective, a communications strategy should first identify the target audience, which ranges from current users of a company's products, to potential purchasers of a company's products, to those who may influence the purchase of the company's products, or any other group that may directly or indirectly help the company sell its goods and services. As mentioned earlier, in international markets, the target audience may differ from country to country, and, therefore, companies may have to adjust their message to the audience targeted.

Once the target audience is identified, the next step is to develop a message that conveys the reasons why a given target audience should consider using or buying a company's products. Message design should achieve the following: gain the audience's attention, hold their interest, help them make a decision, and help them to recall a specific brand when considering a purchase in a product category. In international markets, it is important that message content be effective and be consistent with the country's cultural values. As explained in Chapter 2, "International Business Environment: Culture," numerous marketing campaigns have failed because of improper usage of language or unintentional breaches of cultural norms.

To be successful, marketing communications have to be received by the selected audience; therefore, selection of the right media vehicles helps companies reach their target audience. The three basic vehicles to communicate with target audiences are personal selling, advertising, and sales promotions. Despite their differences, all three can be used together to attain improved synergy in communicating with the target audience. Many domestic and international companies are developing integrated marketing communication programs to attain maximum communication impact.[26] An integrated marketing communication program is defined as a comprehensive plan that evaluates the strategic roles of a variety of communication initiatives including advertising, sales promotions, direct response, and public relations.

Personal Selling

Personal selling is a direct two-way communication that is possibly the most effective means of communicating with target consumers. As salespeople represent the company, they are the final, but critical, link to consumers. Because of the direct two-way communication, salespeople are able to answer questions, remove doubts, customize the message to suit the consumer, and gather pertinent information that may be useful in refining marketing strategies and introducing new products. Moreover, personal selling is one of the few marketing activities that can be measured for its effectiveness. Marketers are able to measure the effect of incremental spending on the sales force in sales revenues or profits.

Even though personal selling has many benefits, one of its main drawbacks is its cost. Because of salaries and fringe benefits, the cost for reaching 1,000 customers through personal selling in comparison to reaching the same number of customers through advertising is relatively very high. Assuming an average compensation package of $75,000 per salesperson, and assuming that each salesperson is able to reach 10 customers per day, it will cost a company $30,000 to reach 1,000 customers (10 customers × 250 days/year = 2,500 customers @ $75,000 = 75,000/2.5 = $30,000.00). An advertisement during the Super Bowl cost only $5 to reach the same number of customers, and in the case of most magazines, the cost to reach 1,000 customers ranges from $3 to $35. In addition to its cost, developing a sales team is administratively time-consuming, especially in the international marketing context. In some cases, international companies cannot bring expatriates to the host country to be part of the sales force. This may pose problems for international companies in industries such as pharmaceuticals that deal with intellectual property items. Because of the above reasons, personal selling is most often utilized in industrial marketing situations, where it is important to customize communications and obtain feedback, and where order size justifies the higher costs associated with this approach.

Advertising

Advertising is a nonpersonal communication approach that utilizes media vehicles to reach a target audience. The objectives of advertising are the same as those of the overall marketing communication program. Ads inform a given audience about products, give reasons why customers should buy the products, tell where the products are available, and provide information about the company that markets the products. Many international companies use advertising as a communication vehicle because of its cost efficiency and the variety of media that are available. On the downside, advertising is a one-way communication vehicle; in addition, most media are cluttered with hundreds of advertisements vying for viewers' at-

Table 11.2

The World's Ten Largest Advertisers, 2007 (US$ million)

Rank	Company	Country	Advertising Expenditure
1	Procter & Gamble	United States	8,190
2	Unilever	Netherlands	4,272
3	General Motors	United States	4,173
4	Toyota	Japan	2,800
5	L'Oréal	France	2,773
6	Ford Motors	United States	2,645
7	Time Warner	United States	2,479
8	Daimler Chrysler	Germany	2,104
9	Nestlé	Switzerland	2,033
10	Johnson & Johnson	United States	1,968

Source: "Top 100 Global Marketers," *Advertising Age,* November 19, 2007, p. 4.

tention, and the effectiveness of this type of communication is difficult to measure. To improve advertising effectiveness, many companies use coordinated advertising campaigns to make their products popular.[27] Creatively, it is very challenging to develop messages to reach a culturally diverse audience.[28] Some international companies have tried to standardize their message content and/or media choice in multiple countries if target audiences are found to be similar. But most often, even with the same target audience within the same region, there are obstacles to standardization due to minor variations among customers.[29]

International companies spend a considerable amount of money, time, and effort in developing and placing advertisements. Total media spending for all companies worldwide reached US$98 billion during 2007.[30] That year, the leading advertiser in the world was Procter & Gamble, with an annual expenditure of US$8.2 billion, followed by Unilever with US$4.3 billion. Five of the top advertisers are American companies. Four of the top advertisers are automobile companies. Table 11.2 presents the world's 10 largest advertisers. The total U.S. advertising expenditure at $47 billion alone is nearly half of all the advertising expenditures of the world. As a region, Europe is the second largest advertiser in the world at US$31 billion. Table 11.3 presents advertising expenditures by region, and Table 11.4 presents the 10 leading advertisers in the United States.

The actual development of an advertising campaign and the message design are most often managed by advertising agencies. Advertising agencies offer an international company many services that are best handled by an outside supplier who specializes in message design, creative input, artwork, media placement, market research, publicity campaigns, and consulting. Not all advertising agencies offer every service mentioned here; some offer just creative input, and a few others specialize in media. Globalization of markets and the growth in international marketing have been matched by the internationalization of advertising agencies. Most of the large ad agencies, including Omnicom Group, WPP Group, Interpublic, Publicis, Dentsu, and Havas, have offices in nearly 100 countries to match their clients' operations. In some

Table 11.3

Advertising Expenditures by Region, 2007 (US$ million)

Rank	Region	Advertising Expenditure	% of Total
1	United States	46,015	47.1
2	Europe	31,121	31.8
3	Asia	14,915	15.3
4	Africa, Latin America, and Middle East	3,616	3.7
5	Canada	2,093	2.1
6	Total	97,760	100.00

Source: "Top 100 AD Spending by Region," *Advertising Age*, November 19, 2007, p. 7.

countries, international companies may hire local ad agencies for their knowledge of the particular market, and in some instances, the host countries' laws may require a local partner, as in the case of Vietnam.

For advertising to reach its audience, it needs to use media vehicles. The major advertising media are print (newspapers and magazines), broadcast (radio and television), outdoor, direct mail, and electronic media.

Because of specific considerations, cultural influences, and regulations, all media are not available for advertising in all countries. Television and radio in some countries are controlled by the government and, hence, not available for the placement of advertisements. In Brazil, broadcast advertisements must appear just before or after the start of a program or during station breaks; in Vietnam, space for advertisement in print media is limited to only 10 percent. These restrictions and cultural influences pose problems for international marketers in their attempts to reach their customers. Therefore, it is essential that international companies plan ahead and develop alternatives in case the preferred media are not available to them.

For international marketers, the decision to place advertising in one or more of the seven available media vehicles is governed by two factors: which ones offer the best chance of reaching the target audience and which are the most cost effective. Most companies use a collection of media (called a media mix) to reach the various segments of the market. Each medium has advantages and disadvantages.

Newspapers are relatively inexpensive, reach a wide audience, have high believability in most countries, and can be reviewed again and again. Since most newspapers are printed in black and white, they are not useful in communication campaigns that need to show vibrant colors such as cosmetics, clothing, food, and automobiles (in some countries this problem has been overcome with special full-color advertising inserts). Newspapers in some countries focus on just the news and have limited space for advertising, as in Japan. For some advertisers, newspapers' target audience may be too broad.

Magazines reach a specific target segment, as there are many specialized magazines that attract certain groups (*Business Week,* the *Economist,* and *Vogue,* are three good examples). Magazines can also be geographically segmented through regional editions (*Time* magazine has an Asian edition and a European edition). Magazines have high-quality reproduction, including color and a long life (people keep magazines

Table 11.4

The Ten Largest Advertisers in the United States, 2007 (US$ million)

Rank	Company	Advertising Expenditure
1	Procter & Gamble	5,230.1
2	AT&T	3,207.3
3	Verizon Communications	3,016.1
4	General Motors	3,010.1
5	Time Warner	2,962.1
6	Ford Motors	2,525.2
7	Glaxo Smith Kline	2,456.9
8	Johnson & Johnson	2,408.8
9	Walt Disney Co.	2,293.3
10	Unilever	2,245.8

Source: "Leading National Advertisers," *Advertising Age*, June 5, 2008, p. 8.

for a long time), and have pass-along readership. On the negative side, magazines are relatively expensive and have a long lead time (some magazines require at least six months' lead time to buy advertising space).

Radio is a good backup medium that is inexpensive and useful in reminding a target audience about a company's products. Radio has a wide reach in many countries, as most people have radios. On the negative side, radio suffers from a lack of visual presentation, and ads are usually very short. In addition, some of the more popular stations that have a significant listener base may have too many advertisements and hence more clutter (clutter is defined as greater number of advertisements in a given time period). Studies have shown that respondents are twice as likely to recall a particular advertisement among those that they were exposed to low clutter compared to those who heard the same advertisements in a high-clutter situation.[31]

Combining both audio and visual presentations, television is a popular medium that the masses watch for news and entertainment. The audiovisual presentation improves the attention rate of the audience, is appealing to their senses, and helps the target audience recall the ad's message. Placing advertisements on television is very expensive (the cost of single minute of advertising during the 2006 Super Bowl was $4 million). The television medium also suffers from clutter, as there are too many ads, and each ad may be shown for only 15 to 30 seconds. In many countries, such as China, advertising on television is strictly controlled. In Sweden, advertisements focusing on children are restricted. Hence, this medium is not always available to international companies.[32]

Outdoor advertising is a flexible medium that has high exposure and is inexpensive. However, some countries have many regulations governing outdoor advertising, and this type of advertising does not have audience selectivity; therefore, it is limited to certain product categories.

Direct mail may be customized both in message content and in customer targets. Hence, it is useful for certain product categories, such as financial services. Direct mail assumes that the mail system in a country is efficient and that the target audience's addresses can be located easily. But in many developing countries and also in some industrialized countries, the postal system is not efficient, and finding addresses is next to impossible.

The Internet has become a worldwide medium that is gaining popularity, especially among the young. The Web is a low-cost medium (the cost is less than US$1 to reach 1,000 potential customers), and it is an interactive system that can help international companies answer questions and gather relevant information from potential customers.

Sales Promotion

Sales promotions are a collection of communication initiatives that do not fall under the personal selling or advertising categories. Any communication device that can be creatively developed to inform a target audience about a product, a service, an idea, or an organization is a sales promotion. In the United States, commonly used sales promotion tools are sampling (giving out free samples), coupons, rebates, low-interest financing, premiums, contests, and tie-ins. As the list of tools suggests, it is difficult to categorize them under a single label. Internationally, common sales promotion tools are price discounts, in-store demonstrations, coupons, sweepstakes, games, and buy one, get one free (BOGO) specials. For example, during the 2006 World Cup, Bimbo, Mexico's leading bakery, teamed up with Jorge Campos, Mexico's star soccer player, for a promotion campaign tied in to the World Cup championship.

Sales promotions are useful for gaining attention because they are incentive laden. Expected responses from successful sales promotion tools are brand switching, purchase acceleration, stockpiling, product trials, and increased spending. Supermarkets are heavy users of sales promotion devices.[33]

Because of regulations, a few sales promotion tools that are permissible in the parent country may not be used in the host country. For example, in Belgium there is a maximum limit on discounts (33 percent), and in many European Union countries, games and sweepstakes tied to product purchases are banned.[34] Similarly, in many Asian countries, cash gifts are restricted by local laws.

IMPLEMENT A CUSTOMER RELATIONS PROGRAM

Customer relations management (CRM) is a powerful tool in the hands of marketers that can be used to segment markets, preempt customers' concerns, customize marketing strategies, and evaluate current marketing programs. CRM systems integrate pertinent customer information into a single location and help businesses use technology and human resources to gain insight into customers' behavior. CRM offers fast access to records of actual customer purchasing behavior. Through advances in computer technology and database management, it has become easier and less expensive for companies to set up CRM systems that provide unprecedented opportunities to customize products and meet customers' needs.[35] Some international companies hire consulting companies that specialize in CRM to develop their relationship programs. International CRM Solutions provides multilingual sales and service support for clients throughout the world, including the Asia-Pacific region, Europe, Latin America, and North America. Some financial service companies have successfully implemented CRM in a few countries using their existing information technology (IT) departments.[36]

Set Up a Feedback Mechanism to Evaluate the Marketing Program

Strategic marketing programs are dynamic and require adjustments during their implementation stage. Feedback systems should track the results and monitor changes taking place in the marketing environment, especially competitive efforts. To fine-tune the program, international marketers need information about the program's success. The type of information sought can be performance measures such as revenues, market share, regional penetration, and dealer acceptance rate, and more specific consumer information such as who purchased the product, where they purchased the product, and the reasons why they purchased the product.

There are many techniques to track programs. Some are simple; others rely on specialized data. Some are internally generated information, and others are obtained from outside suppliers. Tracking sales data by customer and/or by region is useful for understanding the direct effects of a marketing program. This adaptation can be compared to using historical data for comparative analysis. International companies also compare sales data across countries to identify patterns. In addition, companies can compare sales and other related data to preestablished benchmarks such as industry averages or the dominant competitor's performance. Information can also be obtained from consumers through market research that may help companies in evaluating their marketing programs. Distributors, as well, are a good source of information that may help international companies identify problems with their marketing programs.

Syndicated companies such as Nielsen and Ipsos Group S.A. conduct studies and monitor sales of goods on a regular basis. The studies are available to subscribers for a fee. These and other companies provide single-source data (data that allows researchers to link purchase behavior, household characteristics, and advertising exposure at the household level) that is customer and market specific.

Chapter Summary

Marketing activities generate sales and in turn revenues and profits. Hence, studying marketing activities is one of the most critical business functions for an international company. The basic marketing activities for a domestic market and an international market are the same, but the external environment in which an international company operates is more challenging and difficult to predict. In developing marketing programs for international markets, it is useful to know the various regulations that govern some of these activities. The regulations vary across countries, and international marketers may have to adapt their strategies to comply with the regulations.

The primary focus of all marketing programs is the consumer. Strategic actions such as product/service development and others are intended to influence purchases. To understand the consumers' needs and the benefits they seek from a product, international marketers obtain consumer- and market-related information. International marketers deal with both final and industrial consumers. Final consumers purchase goods and services for their personal consumption, whereas industrial consumers purchase goods and services to make other goods and services and then sell them to the final consumers.

Standardization of products and marketing programs is the ultimate goal of international companies. Standardization reduces costs and improves efficiency. But due to variations in the external environment, standardization is not always possible. Therefore, international companies may end up adapting their products and marketing programs to suit the host countries' market conditions.

Strategic marketing variables include product, brand, packaging, price, distribution, and communication. To be successful, an international marketer should coordinate all the various marketing activities to benefit from the synergy that can be derived from the interplay of the activities.

It is important for international marketers to assess their marketing programs to identify and make any changes that may be necessary. Using internally available data, companies can fine-tune their programs to improve their results.

KEY CONCEPTS

International Marketing Environment
Target Market
Marketing Variables
Standardization
Integrated Marketing Approach
Customer Relations

DISCUSSION QUESTIONS

1. What are the differences between the domestic and international marketing environments?
2. What are the differences between final and industrial consumers?
3. What are the differences between products and services?
4. What is standardization?
5. What are the benefits of standardization?
6. What are the key marketing activities?
7. Discuss international product life cycle (PLC).
8. What is product positioning?
9. Why is it difficult to standardize prices across markets?
10. Identify the critical issues in international distribution.
11. What is an integrated communication program?
12. What are the major challenges for international marketers in communicating with a target audience?

13. What is customer relations management?
14. What are country-of-origin effects, and how can they be utilized to an international company's advantage?
15. Why do international companies set up feedback systems?

APPLICATION CASE: NATURA—A BRAZILIAN SUCCESS STORY

Natura was established in 1969 as a laboratory and retail store in São Paulo, Brazil. Its first line of products consisted of men's grooming items; in 1972, the company added a women's line of cosmetics. From its inception, Natura's business philosophy was to build relationships: the company fostered relationships with its customers, suppliers, and employees while building its customer base by providing innovative, high-quality products. In a shift from industry norms at that time, Natura made a decision to sell through a well-organized sales force—called consultants—directly to its customers, bypassing the established distribution channels; this is the same practice used by Avon, a large, U.S.-based multinational cosmetic company.

With its customer-focused business philosophy, its quality products, and its system of direct distribution, Natura grew by leaps and bounds. In 1974, the company's annual revenues were just over $5 million; it had revenues of $180 million in 1990 and $350 million four years later. By 2006, the company had grown to be a major player in the cosmetics and beauty care industry, with sales of more than $2.7 billion, 5,125 employees, and about 568,000 consultants. Having captured 20 percent of the Brazilian cosmetics market, Natura was competing head-on with such industry giants such as Max Factor (a division of Procter & Gamble), L'Oreal, and Unilever.

Back in the 1990s, as the Brazilian economy grew, the government decided to open its markets to foreign competition in many industrial sectors, including cosmetics. At the same time, Natura decided to expand its operations into other Latin American countries, including Argentina, Bolivia, Chile, Mexico, and Peru. Through its well-trained sales consultants, Natura was able to do well in many of these countries.

Besides its business philosophy and direct sales approach, Natura succeeded through innovative product introductions that took advantage of its consultant network's extensive customer knowledge. Through R&D efforts and market research, Natura identified attractive target segments in each of the countries it entered and then developed products that solved unique customer-related beauty problems. For example, by offering a three-in-one skin care product, the company was able to outsell its competitors, who had three different products for the same purpose. The savings were substantial, and the use of just one product instead of three made the Natura cream a convenient, time-saving choice for customers. In addition, Natura used many indigenous ingredients found in the Amazon jungles of Brazil that were less harsh on the skin, especially in humid tropical climates.

Natura offers a full range of cosmetic, facial care, skin care, and hair care products for men and women of all ages. In 2006 alone, Natura launched 213 new products.

The company has several lines that cater to specific target segments by addressing their unique needs. For example, one of its successful product lines, called "Mamae e Bebe" (translated as "Mom and Baby") is aimed at mothers and infants and addresses the needs of both. By concentrating on introducing new products and targeting different needs, Natura always seems to leave its rivals behind.

QUESTION

1. Enumerate and discuss the strategic actions that helped Natura, a small company, compete successfully with some of the large, foreign-owned cosmetic companies.

12 International Human Resources Management and Organizational Structures

Of all the resources managed by an organization, the human resources are the most critical of all. Organizational structures dictate the divisions of workforce and distribution of roles to facilitate the orderly functioning of a firm.

LEARNING OBJECTIVES

- To explain the role of human resources in an international company
- To understand the various functions of human resources management
- To understand the differences between centralized and decentralized organizations
- To understand the differences between using local managers and using expatriate managers
- To understand the importance of labor-management relations
- To distinguish and describe different types of organizational structures
- To discuss factors that affect organizational decision making in an international firm
- To understand the role of divisional and departmental setups in organizing for international business

Managing a modern-day international company with its dynamic competitive environment requires a strong internal governance process that starts with the people that administer it.[1] As more and more companies embrace the resource-based view (RBV) of strategy, the employees offer the core competencies for sustainable competitive advantage.[2] Moreover, research studies have shown that the companies most effective in conducting business globally must excel in people management, among other factors.[3] Human resources, also referred to as human capital, are probably the most important resource that international companies possess.[4] The success of international companies in their human resources development process has led government agencies of foreign countries to use those same techniques in training their staff, especially in handling crisis situations.[5]

The people who manage an international company are part of human resources management (HRM). The human resources management function in an international company involves many activities, among them identifying staffing needs, writing detailed job descriptions, and recruiting and hiring the right people. Each of these

301

activities is undertaken in a complex and challenging international environment. The spread of globalization has forced international companies to staff multicountry operations with qualified people from all parts of the world rather than looking internally for expatriates to manage operations.[6] In an international company, human resources managers become even more critical than in a domestic environment, as these people play a key role in the overall international strategic planning process.[7]

International companies' personnel include people from different countries; therefore, a major challenge for an international company is to manage this diverse group of staff with different cultural backgrounds and to encourage them to work as a team, interacting with one another to achieve corporate goals. Running a modern globally oriented company requires a highly specialized yet closely linked group of global managers, regional and local managers, and worldwide functional managers.[8] The task sounds challenging, and it is; hence, the difficulties of managing a dispersed and disparate workforce in a globally oriented organization. Some large international companies have thousands of people working for them in many different countries. For example, Unilever, the Anglo-Dutch company based in the Netherlands, operates in 150 countries and employs 247,000 people worldwide. Managing such a vast number of staff in different parts of the world requires a well-organized human resources department that can react to varied requests from subsidiaries. To make each subsidiary thrive, international companies have to successfully transfer business practices from the parent company to local subsidiaries. A key to this diffusion, or transfer, is the parent company's human resources practices.[9] By deploying staff from corporate headquarters, international companies are able to transfer management skills to a wide group of personnel across countries, thereby developing the capabilities of the staff with the foreign assignment and becoming a training ground for career development.[10]

One of the primary questions international companies have to address is the issue of how much control host-country managers should be given. This issue, the two sides of which are broadly labeled "centralized" operations and "decentralized" operations, reflects where the power and control of operations are vested. In a centralized organization, most of the power and control are held at the company's headquarters; the managers at the company's central location make decisions for the subsidiaries. In a decentralized organizational structure, many decisions are made by managers at the subsidiary levels. Large international companies fear the loss of control in a totally decentralized organizational setup. To ensure control in a decentralized organizational system, companies develop formal strategic control processes that allow them to exert some form of control to achieve broader corporate goals.[11] Some international companies have developed a middle-of-the-road approach, wherein the control and power do not reside at either extreme.

It is difficult to balance these two divergent systems. In industries where transfer of technology or knowledge is critical, the more centralized form of organizational structure is recommended.[12] For example, setting retail prices, selecting media for advertising, and making sales force management decisions in the local market may be done by subsidiary managers. However, major investment decisions, budget allocations for R&D, and selecting countries as targets for marketing goods and services would be made at the headquarters level. Philips, the Netherlands-based electronics company, has a centralized system for currency hedging but allows individual countries to allocate the gains or losses resulting from these hedging actions.[13] The relationship between headquarters personnel and subsidiary personnel is critical in the success of international companies. Headquarters personnel must be able to effectively coordinate and control worldwide operations to improve efficiency and reduce duplication and waste. Subsidiary managers and staff should be able to understand local conditions and make smart decisions that have a positive impact on their local operations.

Human resources management is made up of many individual functions. These functions collectively help an international company manage and coordinate the activities of its staff in different countries.

MANAGING THE HUMAN RESOURCES FUNCTION

The human resources functions in an international company are:

- Identifying the staffing needs of an international company
- Writing out detailed job descriptions
- Recruiting the right people
- Developing an adequate and fair compensation plan
- Instituting an evaluation process
- Setting up training programs to develop international managers
- Managing the placement of expatriate and host-country personnel

As companies grow, the need to staff this growth requires that an international company recruit and train new employees. Many of the larger international companies plan their staffing needs well in advance to coincide with their expansion plans into overseas markets. In some companies, human resources needs are planned two to three years in advance, as many American companies do. In contrast, Japanese companies normally plan their future staffing needs nine to ten years in advance.

In identifying staffing needs, international companies have to complete the following steps:

- Determine the number of new employees to be hired for a specific time period
- Ascertain the functional department(s) to which the new employees will be assigned
- Determine the time frame in which these new employees should be hired (for instance, immediately, in the next 12 months, or in the next two years)
- Determine if the new positions could be staffed by current employees
- Determine if new staff should be hired for assignments at headquarters or at the subsidiary level
- If the staff is required at the subsidiary level, determine the countries in which these new staff will be employed
- Describe the job specification for each new position
- Identify the essential qualifications, including technical and language skills, of the persons to be hired
- Identify financial considerations, including budget allocations (which budget the staff will be assigned to)

- Determine whether the new position can be filled by a local staff member or must be filled by an expatriate staff member

DETERMINE THE NUMBER OF NEW EMPLOYEES TO BE HIRED FOR A SPECIFIC TIME PERIOD

The request for new employees may come from many areas, including functional departments within the organization, subsidiary operations, or HRM itself. In larger international companies, procedures are set up so that each functional manager or country manager requesting new staff has to submit paperwork for review by upper management. The official procedure includes justifying the need for additional personnel, deciding on the applicants' required qualifications and experience, estimating the salary level for each open position, figuring out which budget will be charged for paying the new staff, and establishing the date for the new staff to begin work. In smaller organizations, procedures may be much more informal, but all staff additions must be justified. Whether the procedures are formal or informal, at the end of the process, management must be able to determine the number of new employees needed by the company for a given period of time.

In identifying staffing needs, some larger international companies periodically conduct an inventory of their current personnel and their various skills. The items included in the personnel database include educational background (degree[s] earned), special skills, work experience, yearly performance evaluations, training programs attended, and so on. Table 12.1 presents the skeletal framework of the matrix used in an HRM personnel/skill inventory.

This information is stored in an HRM database and can be accessed whenever there is a need to identify internally qualified staff. The personnel/skills inventory provides the company with information about where it can locate a specific skilled person within the company, if such a skill level is required. Most companies go to great lengths to find internally qualified people to fill an open position; only if they cannot find a qualified internal candidate do they actively recruit from outside. There are many benefits for a company in seeking internal candidates first, including that management knows the strengths and weaknesses of its employees, these employees are familiar with the company's products and services, and, finally, internal hiring provides opportunities for staff to grow within the organization. Additionally, internal hirings are excellent for motivating staff.

ASCERTAIN THE FUNCTIONAL DEPARTMENT(S) TO WHICH THE NEW EMPLOYEES WILL BE ASSIGNED

In most instances, the request for new staff comes from a particular functional department at the headquarters or subsidiary level. Typical functions in most organizations are accounting, administration and legal, finance, HRM, information technology (IT), marketing, production and operations management (POM), and research and development (R&D). It is also possible that in some instances, based on future expansion plans, HRM and senior management may decide to add new staff to a new functional area or add staff to fulfill the needs of a newly created department or even

Table 12.1

Skeletal Framework of the Matrix Used in HRM Personnel/Skill Inventory

Employee ID	Current Position	No. of Years in This Position	No. of Years in the Company	Educational Background	Additional Certification	Internal Training	Language Skills	Other Factors
001								
002								
003								
004								
005								
006								
007								
008								
00n								

a new division. For example, as customer relations management (CRM) became part of business operations, many international companies added this function and were compelled to add new staff independent of the existing departmental needs. Similarly, many foreign-based companies in the United States, such as HSBC, Siemens, and Nestlé, were forced to add compliance officers for improving internal controls and audit trails in their subsidiaries, as required by the Sarbanes-Oxley Act of 2002.

DETERMINE THE TIME FRAME IN WHICH THESE NEW EMPLOYEES SHOULD BE HIRED

Recruiting the right staff for a specific position is time-consuming and expensive. A new employee who does not fit within the corporate culture or is not able to fulfill the tasks assigned causes unnecessary delays, additional expenses, and an increased workload for the existing staff—situations that may bring down the morale of the employees. Therefore, many international companies plan ahead so that they can take their time in identifying the right person and avoiding costly mistakes. International companies usually start their hiring process six months to a year in advance. The length of time needed depends on the availability of a pool of candidates, the level of the position that is going to be filled (from a simple clerk to a technical manager), the number of vacancies to be filled, host-country regulations, and the amount of training needed to prepare the employee for taking the post.

In some instances, an international company will fill in a position with minimal planning due to an urgent need for a replacement or to fulfill a need brought on by shifts in the marketplace in one of its subsidiary operations. For example, when Apple's iPod became an instant success, it had to hire additional marketing and sales staff in the United States and many of its overseas operations to handle the unusually high demand.

DETERMINE IF THE NEW POSITIONS COULD BE STAFFED BY CURRENT EMPLOYEES

Once the number of new staff and the time within which they have to be hired are determined, an international company normally looks for people within its organization. As mentioned earlier, internal hiring provides opportunities for present employees to advance and improves morale. This is especially true if the position to be filled is of a sensitive nature, such as dealing with intellectual property rights or handling confidential financial, technical, or R&D information. These positions are better filled by people who have experience and who have been with the company for some time; they provide an opportunity for a well-deserving employee to move up within the organization. If the position to be filled is not critical—a clerical position, for instance—and is not at a level to which an existing employee can be promoted, international companies may not spend too much time reviewing internal candidates.

DETERMINE IF NEW STAFF SHOULD BE HIRED FOR ASSIGNMENTS AT HEADQUARTERS OR AT THE SUBSIDIARY LEVEL

Where new staff will be assigned depends on where the request for new employees originated. If the request for a position comes from headquarters, then the new staff will be placed at headquarters. If the request for a position comes from one of the subsidiaries, then the new staff will be placed at that subsidiary. Requests for new employees may also come from regional offices for assignments at either the regional office or in one of the local operations. When operating in many countries, international companies often set up regional offices to manage the disparate operations. Countries are often grouped by geographic proximity. For example, Coca-Cola is divided into six geographic divisions: (1) North America, (2) Africa, (3) East Asia, South Asia, and Pacific Rim, (4) European Union, (5) Latin America, and (6) North Asia, Eurasia, and Middle East.

One of the decisions a company faces when placing new staff, whether at headquarters or at the subsidiary level, is whether to use expatriates to fill the positions or to hire host-country nationals. That is, the company must determine whether it is better to send staff from its existing operations (headquarters, regional offices, or one of its subsidiaries) to an operation in another country or to rely on local staff. In considering this issue, we need to define the term *expatriate*. Expatriates are noncitizens of the country in which they are working. For instance, if Canon, a Japanese company, sends one of its staff from Japan to work in China, that employee is considered an expatriate (also called an "expat"). A more detailed discussion of expatriates versus host-country citizens is presented later in this chapter.

If the Staff Is Required at the Subsidiary Level, Determine the Countries in Which These New Staff Will Be Employed

If the request for additional staff is from one of the subsidiaries, the question of where to assign the new staff is quite simple. The subsidiary requesting the new staff either will recruit locally or will be assigned a staff member from the regional office or headquarters. In some instances, the decision to add a new staff member at the subsidiary level may come from headquarters to improve the operation, in which case the new staff may be recruited at the parent country and then assigned to the subsidiary in the host country.

Describe the Job Specification for Each New Position

It is essential that the department, unit, or division requesting the new staff be able to spell out exactly what the job entails. Called "job specification," this explains in detail the various tasks that the person hired should accomplish, to whom the new staff member reports, with whom they have to interface, what qualifications they need, and how their performance will be measured.

Identify the Essential Qualifications, Including Technical and Language Skills, of the Persons to Be Hired

To recruit the right person for a particular job, the department, unit, or division requesting the new staff member must have a clear idea of the qualifications required to undertake the assignment. Normally, the qualifications are an output of the job specification. That is, if the accounting department is requesting an additional auditor to monitor the various subsidiary operations, the basic qualification required may include an undergraduate degree in accounting and a certification that qualifies the individual to sign off on accounting reports, such as balance sheets. In the United States, an auditor must have a certification of public accountancy (CPA) to be able to sign off on accounting reports.

IDENTIFY FINANCIAL CONSIDERATIONS, INCLUDING BUDGET ALLOCATIONS

Before requesting approval for hiring a new employee, the requesting department or unit should have the necessary funds. Budget allocations are necessary to keep control of costs and to make sure that all expenditures are preapproved. Budgets are a detailed forecast of all expected cash inflows and outflows by the international company for all its activities and are prepared well in advance. Budgets have a specific time frame, usually a year, but in some international companies they can be set for a longer time period. If the control measures are not in place, there may be cost overruns that affect the net earnings of the company.

DETERMINE WHETHER THE NEW POSITION CAN BE FILLED BY A LOCAL STAFF MEMBER OR MUST BE FILLED BY AN EXPATRIATE STAFF MEMBER

Expatriates

In hiring staff for international operations, management has a choice of hiring local staff or sending in personnel from other countries. Personnel from other countries may include employees from headquarters, regional offices, or another subsidiary. These outside staff members are referred to as expatriates. As explained earlier, expatriates are noncitizens of the country in which they are working: they may be home-country nationals, that is, citizens of the country in which the international company is headquartered, or third-country nationals, that is, citizens of neither the country in which they are working nor the headquarters country. For example, a manager sent by Mercedes-Benz from Germany to its operations in the United States is a home-country national; however, a Chinese manager from Mercedes-Benz's operations in China who is sent to the United States is a third-country national. In both cases, the managers deployed are considered expatriates.

Most often, if the new assignment is not critical (clerk, assembly line worker, or technician, for example), it is not necessary for international companies to send in personnel from other countries. These positions, if filled by expatriates, might unnecessarily increase the cost of operations at the subsidiary level. In contrast, if the position is a managerial or highly skilled position (chemist, IT specialist, and the like), the decision to hire locally versus sending in an expatriate becomes quite involved.

Compared to 20 or 30 years ago, when there were many expatriates working in subsidiary operations, in recent years the numbers of these employees have been declining. International companies have found competent local personnel with sufficient skills; the cost of sending an expatriate has risen; some host-country governments have regulations that prohibit excessive hiring of expatriates; the expatriate burnout rate is high; and expatriates, especially those from the headquarters country, are often not willing to relocate to operations in foreign countries.

Job burnout among expatriates is a major concern for international companies. In some cases, expatriates have not been able to handle the strains of working overseas and have either failed as managers or have left their jobs earlier than planned. Research conducted on expatriate burnout has identified several reasons for this. In one study, researchers found that the expatriates had difficulty adjusting to local cultures and business practices.[14] Other frequently mentioned reasons for expatriate burnout are lack of job satisfaction,[15] role conflicts,[16] and the inability of most Western-based expatriates who come from rule-based individualistic countries to adjust to the relationship-based collectivistic countries that are mostly in their economic development stages.[17]

There are many compelling reasons why international companies rely on expatriates to fill some positions in their subsidiary operations:

- International companies are not able to find qualified personnel in host countries.
- The nature of the position involves sensitive areas such as proprietary technology, confidential operational procedures, complex mathematical models, and so on.
- Transfer of technology is involved. That is, when a company is starting up a new operation, introducing a new product, making a major modification to a product, or introducing a totally new production process, international companies use expatriates to accomplish these tasks.
- A subsidiary operation needs to be controlled. A subsidiary is just a part of the larger entity, and, hence, its activities need to be synchronized and coordinated with the activities of all other subsidiaries. Having a person from headquarters is of great help in this process.
- Host-country personnel need to be introduced to and educated about the company's policies and procedures (so the subsidiary operates as headquarters operates). This uniform application of policies and procedures is very useful in managing vastly diverse operations.
- Managers must be provided with a training ground for understanding the complexities of managing across diverse environments in preparation for senior postings.[18]

There are disadvantages to sending expatriates to foreign countries:

- There are additional costs. Expatriate personnel are normally paid a premium to accept positions in overseas subsidiaries. In addition, there are other costs, such as moving expenses, housing allowances, educational allowances for children, annual home leave, adjustments for host-country taxes, and household help allowances.
- It takes time for the expatriate manager to get acclimated and to begin handling the daily tasks.
- The expatriate's family members may not adjust to local conditions, creating tension at home and making the expatriate less productive.
- There may be resentment from local staff, as each incoming expatriate takes away an opportunity for local personnel to move up within the organization.

- The reentry of expatriate managers back into their home country is not smooth. During their absence, there may have been shifts in assignments and the previously established network with other managers and staff may not exist anymore.
- There may be legal restrictions in bringing foreign-born managers into the host country.

A few countries (India, among others) have enacted laws that restrict the number of foreign personnel that can work in a subsidiary. Host governments enact these laws to force foreign companies to train local personnel in advanced technical and managerial skills to improve the skills of local staff. In addition, host governments view expatriates as an unnecessary financial drain (outflow of funds) on the economy.

Therefore, when determining whether to fill a position with an expatriate, international companies have to carefully weigh the pros and cons and decide whether it is in the best interest of the company to send a foreign national as a manager to a subsidiary operation.

A related issue concerning expatriates is whether to send a worker from the home country or from a third country. If the international company's desire is to have control of subsidiary operations, protect intellectual property (or another sensitive area), and/or introduce new products, procedures, and methods, it is always better to use home-country nationals. Home-country nationals are more apt to have the required experience and related qualifications for this type of work than third-country nationals.

If the position at the subsidiary is not in a sensitive area and does not involve introduction of products, procedures, or methods, it is best to send third-country nationals. Third-country nationals may have compatible qualifications in the nonbusiness area, such as cultural or language similarities. For example, it is easier for Indian expatriate managers to function in Bangladesh or Sri Lanka than it is for European expatriate personnel because of the cultural similarities among India, Bangladesh, and Sri Lanka.

The process of selecting expatriate personnel for overseas assignments has to be handled carefully. Many of the problems attributed to expatriate failures can be traced back to the selection of the wrong people for the job—people who did not want to leave their home country, were not prepared for the complexities of working in a different culture, did not know how to adjust to staff that had different skill levels, and in some instances did not have the necessary technical competence to function effectively.

As this discussion shows, international companies should consider the following factors critical when selecting an expatriate to fill a position with a foreign subsidiary.

Technical Competence. The person selected for overseas operations must have advanced technical knowledge of the position through education, training, and/or work experience; remember that technical knowledge is frequently lacking at the subsidiary level, so technical competence is the key reason why expatriates are needed in host countries.[19] For example, a person selected to head the finance department in a subsidiary must have the necessary financial background to be effective. Research studies have shown that technical competence, usually indicated by past domestic or foreign job performance, is the greatest determinant of success in foreign assignments.

Cultural and Linguistic Adaptability. Individuals who come from cultural backgrounds similar to that of the host country or know the host-country language seem to perform well as expatriates. Studies have shown that it is possible to select expatriate staff using cross-cultural social intelligence tests that have proven to be effective.[20] For example, an expatriate from Argentina who is sent to Chile would have a better chance of succeeding because these two countries have similar cultures and Spanish is the official language of both nations.

Willingness to Accept Foreign Assignment. Any expatriate must not only be competent and adaptable but also be willing and eager to take the foreign assignment. Those who view the foreign assignment as a challenge and adventure are more likely to succeed than those who view it as just a job. Research studies have shown that expatriates from Australia, the Netherlands, and the United Kingdom are more willing to be placed overseas than the French, Germans, Italians, Spanish, and Swiss.[21]

Family Cooperation. It is equally important for the international company to ascertain the willingness of the spouse (if the expatriate is married) and children to be in a foreign country. Many expatriates have failed due to the inability of family members to adjust to the local environment.[22]

Local Staff

If the international company's business is affected by local environmental conditions such as culture, language, business practices, laws, and established relationships, then it is better for the company to hire local staff. The greater need for local adaptation, the better it is for the international company to use local managers because they understand local conditions better than foreign nationals do. For example, if local distributors are more likely to trust and work with locals, hiring a marketing manager from a foreign country would create problems. Similarly, if government officials speak only the local language, sending an expatriate with no knowledge of this language to negotiate with the host government is bound to fail. In this circumstance, it is better to hire a local to participate in the negotiations.

To a great extent, the importance of the decisions to be made, the experience of the host-country managers, and the confidence of the upper management in the local managers will influence the amount of control and decision making that will be transferred to the subsidiary level. Following are several other reasons to hire locals:

- Hiring local managers is less expensive than sending an expatriate to the subsidiary. For starters, local managers are paid comparable local salaries that are lower than the salaries paid to expatriates. The company does not have to pay the various allowances (moving, educational, housing, and others) to the locals that are commonly paid to expatriates.

- There may be political or diplomatic reasons why locals may be better suited for the position than expatriates. For example, BP, a UK-based international company, would be better served by appointing Argentinean managers to key posts rather than having British managers attempt to deal with the local government and other business entities in Argentina; territorial disputes and conflicts between the United Kingdom and Argentina still exist over the Falkland Islands, which are located in the southern Atlantic Ocean about 300 miles off the coast of Argentina.
- Hiring local managers may help establish better relationships with the subsidiary's workforce, which may enhance overall morale. Moreover, it is easier to recruit experienced new local employees if the managerial positions are held by locals.
- International companies that have hired local managers have found that these employees have some good ideas and initiatives that could help the international company. In fact, research has shown that adequately trained local managers reach high productivity levels and gain a critical knowledge base.[23]

Nonmanagerial Staff

Generally, a firm's nonmanagerial staff, including accountants, clerks, factory workers, technicians, and others, is hired locally. International companies have to address some major issues in hiring nonmanagerial local staff:

Managing the Staff. The process of recruiting, training, motivating, and compensating local employees differs from country to country. As the international company moves to different countries, it normally faces different hiring and training methods. It is difficult to adapt one model of human resources guidelines across countries and cultures. For example, in Japan it is customary to form teams to work on tasks. Because Japan is a collectivistic society, teamwork is part of the culture and is accepted freely. When the same team orientation is introduced in individualistic countries, such as Germany, it may not work.

Wages and Benefits. Compensation and associated benefits vary from country to country, so international companies have to set wages according to the prevailing rate in the country in which they are operating. This can be beneficial for the international company, as it often saves on costs. For example, an American automobile assembly worker earns on average $28 per hour, whereas a similar Mexican worker earns the equivalent of $5 an hour. Also, benefits, which in some cases are high, differ from country to country. In the major industrialized countries of Canada, France, Germany, Japan, and the United States, not only do workers receive wages, but they also receive other benefits such as medical insurance, holidays, and pension plans. These costs can become a competitive disadvantage for the company. In many developing countries, including China, Indonesia, and the Philippines, international companies do not have to pay into a health insurance system, saving the company worker-related expenses. The wage and related compensation factors may be one of the critical reasons why China is one of the largest low-cost manufacturing centers in the world. Table 12.2 presents average wage rates for selected countries.

Table 12.2

Average Hourly, Weekly, and Monthly Wage Rates in the Manufacturing Sector for Selected Countries (US$), 2006

	Country	Hourly Wage Rate	Weekly Wage Rate	Monthly Wage Rate
1	Austria	19.38	—	—
2	Australia	—	870.00	—
3	Canada	17.76	—	—
4	Czech Republic	—	—	884.32
5	China	—	—	102.00[a]
6	Ireland	19.04	758.10	—
7	Japan	—	—	3569.10
8	Netherlands	—	1,082.72	—
9	Philippines	5.32	—	—
10	Romania	—	—	383.83
11	Singapore	—	—	2,364.70
12	South Korea	—	—	2,799.35
13	Spain	16.97	—	2,382.50
14	Taiwan	—	—	1,298.40
15	United Kingdom	19.25[b]	—	—
16	United States	16.50–25.00[c]	—	—

Source: ILO Statistics and Database, June 19, 2007. Available at http://www.ilo.org/.

Notes: The International Labor Organization (ILO) reports labor rates in hourly, weekly, and monthly rates depending on how each country reports the data. The ILO reports rates in local currency. Rates have been translated in U.S. dollars using the average exchange rate for the year.

[a]As reported by China Labor Watch, July 2006, pp. 1–4.

[b]UK Statistics Authority, available at http://www.statistics.gov.uk/.

[c]U.S. Bureau of Labor Statistics, June 19, 2007. Available at http://www.bls.gove/oes.

In hiring local personnel, international companies need to understand local labor laws. Each country has laws, rules, and guidelines that stipulate hiring requirements. These may include minimum age requirements, minimum wage policies, hiring quotas (among them, requirements to hire certain minorities), and minimum and maximum hours that employees must work. For example, in Finland, workers are represented through unions, and wages, benefits, and such are governed by law.

Labor unions are another factor that many international companies face in dealing with workers in different countries. The labor movement and the unionization of the workforce have lost some of their earlier strength, especially compared to the influence they had at the turn of the twentieth century. In many countries, union membership has declined considerably. For example, in the United States, only about 18 percent of the total present-day workforce is unionized, and in France less than 10 percent is. There are many reasons given for this decline, including improvements in working conditions and labor laws that provide some level of protection for workers. Even with the decline in worldwide union activity, though, unions are active in many countries, including Sweden and Japan. Unions in different parts of the world are organized differently. Some countries have national unions; others have industry-based unions; and a few others, such as Japan, have unions that are organized at the company level. For international companies, dealing with these various types of union structure is difficult; therefore, they must approach each situation differently. Wherever the union is a force, international companies should exercise care in dealing with them. Unions have been known to target large multinational companies for wage and benefit increases, knowing that these companies have the financial resources to support such raises and are averse to creating labor discord in a foreign country.

ORGANIZATIONAL STRUCTURES

Organizational structures and human resource functions are key elements in organizing for effective management of an international company. Most international business failures can be traced to two key factors: *people* (managers making poor decisions) and *organizational structures* (inadequate structures creating problems in coordination, communication, and management control).

Organizational structures (also called organizational designs) are used by international companies (or any organization) to arrange their business activities in an orderly fashion among their various working units. Such structures show (1) where the formal power in a company is vested, (2) what the lines of decision making look like, and (3) who is responsible for certain activities. They also outline formal reporting arrangements. Organizational structures are even more critical for international companies, as they need to coordinate, communicate with, and control many operations that are geographically diverse. Having control of its operations helps an international company ensure that each of its many subsidiaries is working toward a common goal. Control is the ability of the parent company to guarantee the quality of its offerings and coordinate the activities of all its units to meet corporate objectives. On the one hand, excessive control by the home office might endanger the subsidiary decision-making process, resulting in slower reactions to local competitive initiatives. On the other hand, a lack of control might lead to duplication of effort, especially in areas such as research and development, raw-material sourcing, financing, and promotional campaigns. Duplication leads not only to inefficiencies in decision making but also to cost increases. Organizational structures are greatly influenced by the external environment in which they have to operate.

Organizational structures normally reflect where the level of authority and control in a company is vested. When decision making is concentrated at headquarters and the structure exerts tight control, the system is called *centralization*. If subsidiaries are granted a high degree of autonomy and are subject to relatively loose controls, the structure is referred to as *decentralization*. In the present business climate, with dynamic shifts in the external environment, companies are usually neither totally centralized nor totally decentralized. Some functions, such as research and development, will be centralized, but the media planning for the local market and the final price that a customer pays might be left to local managers.

The organizational structures of most companies are dynamic and evolving, reflecting current trends and environmental conditions. For example, in a 10-year span between the 1980s and 1990s, Coca-Cola transformed its organization from a divisional structure to a geographic structure. In contrast, in early 2000, Procter &

Gamble transitioned from a geographic structure to a product structure in managing its worldwide operations.

The driving forces in changing organizational structures are:

- To adapt to changes in the competitive environment
- To improve efficiency so as to reduce cost
- To improve decision making so that line managers can react faster to changing market conditions
- To improve coordination among the various units (headquarters, regional offices, and subsidiaries)
- To improve customer relations
- To facilitate innovation and introduce new products at a faster rate

Many companies entered foreign markets through exports. The management of exports was normally assigned to a department within the organization. As their sales and revenues grew, some international companies established joint ventures and/or wholly owned subsidiaries in these markets. With increasing revenues from overseas markets, many companies set up international divisions that managed the various overseas operations. Many of the large international companies of the twenty-first century derive more than half of their revenues and profits from international operations. In addition, the trend toward globalization has created a new set of challenges for international companies, requiring them to view their organizational designs differently than in the past.

The global design adopted by a firm must deal with the need to integrate three types of knowledge to compete effectively: *area knowledge, product knowledge,* and *functional* knowledge.[24] Even with the trend toward globalization, international companies have not adopted one single design that they feel is the most effective. Depending on the industry, the size of the firm, and other factors, each company develops its own design. In addition, an international firm may be an exporter, a licensee, a joint-venture operator, or a wholly owned subsidiary. Each of these operations has unique aspects that make the organizational setup different for different types of operations. To compound the problem even further, some large international companies may be involved in all the aforementioned activities. The organizational structures of international companies are a continuous experiment in arriving at an optimum level of efficiency and improvements in decision making. Organizational research has identified six distinct organizational structures that international companies use:

1. Divisional structures
2. Product structures
3. Geographic structures
4. Functional structures
5. Matrix structures
6. Hybrid structures

A concise description of each of the six structures follows.

DIVISIONAL STRUCTURES

Divisional structures are one of the earliest forms of organizational designs found among international companies. As mentioned earlier, they are an outgrowth of the first forays of companies into foreign markets. In this structure, the international operations and functions of a company are clearly separated from its domestic operations. The international division centralizes in one entity all of the responsibility for international activities. Divisional structures are simple and easy to set up. Headed by a senior executive, the international division is responsible for all international activities from identifying markets to recruiting personnel for international assignments. These divisions exert full control over the company's international operations. Over the years, in some companies, sales by the international division eventually equaled or surpassed those of the domestic operation in terms of size, revenues, and profits.

The focus of the divisional structure is the international operation's separation from domestic operations, which allows it to tap into various overseas markets and grow without implications for the domestic operations. In divisional structures, the management of international operations might be left in the hands of specialists. Because the problems encountered by foreign managers are unique to the international arena, this setup has some merit. Foreign exchange transactions, for example, are uniquely international, and therefore the person dealing with this function needs to be a specialist in that area. These specialists then allocate and coordinate resources for international activities under a single unit, the international division, providing a better overall direction and enhancing the firm's ability to respond quickly to market opportunities. Moreover, the divisional design allows the firm to independently serve international customers.

In those firms that had international divisional structures—for example, Ford Motors and IBM, both of which operated for many years under the divisional structure—staff members were able to focus the firm's undivided attention on exploring the international market.[25] This autonomy allowed the division to be recognized as a profit center and eliminated possible bias against international activities that may have existed with international sales when they were handled under a domestic department. Figure 12.1 presents a divisional organizational structure.

As shown in Figure 12.1, the international division is totally independent of the domestic division. In this example, the international division is organized around regions and further segmented by countries. In some instances, a division may be organized into functional units (finance, marketing, and production, for instance) or even product divisions (cosmetics, detergents, paper products, and so on for a firm like Procter & Gamble).

The primary emphasis in divisional structures is the independence of the international area from its domestic counterpart and the recognition that the overseas environment is complex and different from the domestic environment. This allows the division to be treated as a profit center with decision-making authority on how to operate the business in foreign countries and foreign markets. Besides the independent nature of the divisional structure, the other main advantage of the divisional design is the locus of power at the divisional headquarters, which is useful in negotiations with

Figure 12.1 **International Divisional Structure**

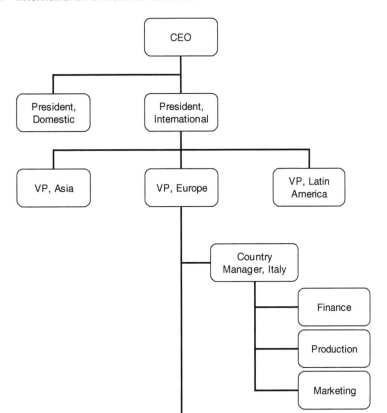

governments and other businesses, especially with potential joint-venture partners. Additionally, the divisional structure is useful in exploring worldwide markets.

One of the disadvantages of divisional structures is that they are not very effective if the international company is involved in many countries and sells a large number of products. Too many products or markets overwhelm the capacities of the international division; for example, it is difficult for employees to know the whole product line. Similarly, it is difficult for employees in the international division to know or understand the local needs of a large number of countries.

PRODUCT STRUCTURES

Many international organizations operate through product-based structures. These companies focus on their product offerings as the basis for organizing into various units. Take the case of Procter & Gamble and Kimberly-Clark, two diversified American consumer packaged goods companies that formerly used a geographic

organizational design: both companies have recently adopted product-oriented organizational structures. Procter & Gamble was reorganized from four geographical units
into seven global business units responsible for each of its product areas worldwide.
In this setup, the various domestic product divisions are responsible for international
line and staff functions. Because the global product design forces managers to think
globally, it facilitates geocentric corporate philosophies. This is a useful mind-set
as firms work to develop greater international skills internally.[26] Similarly, in 2004,
Kimberly-Clark, with sales in more than 150 countries, reorganized to form three
divisions to manage its three main product categories—personal care, consumer tis-
sues, and business-to-business items.[27] In addition, it divided its business operations
into developed- and developing-market divisions to increase effectiveness and reflect
fundamental differences between these two types of countries.

Companies that operate with a product structure may have regional experts to assist
the product group. This type of structure is best suited for coordination of domestic
and international activities related to a product category. The goal with this structure
is to reduce duplication in such areas as product research, systems development, and
package design. When an organization has a product-based arrangement, the head
of the domestic product division is the most important post in the company. All the
international activities are coordinated from a product point of view. The international
activities are secondary to the product.

Product-based structures are set for greater control of international operations,
and the feedback from various countries is used to develop a strong overall product
strategy. For example, in 1991, IBM restructured its organization from a geographic
structure to an industry/product-based structure to better serve its global customers'
needs. The new structure is based around specific industries such as banking, insurance,
government, retail, and utilities. Since adopting the industry-based structure, IBM has
improved its bottom-line performance, and its customers are equally pleased with the
improved service that they have been receiving. Similarly, GE is organized around
its various businesses, including aircraft engines, consumer products, financials, and
industrial products. Each product group identifies investment opportunities and is
responsible for the marketing of any goods or services that are developed from the
investment. Figure 12.2 presents a product-based organizational structure.

In the product structure shown in Figure 12.2, specialists with some country or
regional expertise are assigned to assist the CEO. These specialists may be recruited
from each of the regions or may come from the parent organization. The divisional
head of each product exercises a greater role than the country managers in the function and management of the unit. Country managers are mostly administrators who
coordinate the activities of the various functional departments.

Business research in product-based organizations may be centralized at headquarters, with each region or country assigned the task of conducting the research with
assistance from the central office. In some companies, the research function is totally
decentralized, with each country undertaking its own research and some coordination
at the regional or central level.

The advantages of the product-based structure are strong coordination across
functional areas to support the product group, improved customer service, and the

Figure 12.2 **Product Structure**

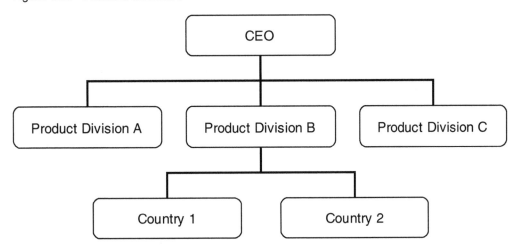

ability to manage products that are unique. For example, IBM has found that servicing government orders across countries requires uniquely developed solutions to IT problems that are different from solutions created for business customers.

A critical disadvantage of divisional structure is that, although this structure avoids duplication in product development, it creates some confusion for the regional or country managers, as they have to report to as many product heads as there are product divisions. In addition, this type of design requires more personnel to manage the international operations than other designs, thereby increasing the overall cost of operations.

GEOGRAPHIC STRUCTURES

In a geographic structure, responsibility for all international activities is in the hands of a regional or country manager reporting directly to the chief executive officer or an international divisional head. This type of organization simplifies the task of directing worldwide operations, as the person in charge is directly in contact with a senior officer at the firm's headquarters. In this case, the country operations become just another division of the company for allocation of resources. Geographic structures ensure that sufficient funds are made available to the country operations.

Besides the advantage of the allocation of resources, this structure helps local managers to contribute considerably more to the decision-making process. With their knowledge of the local market conditions, they are able to direct the company's efforts more effectively than if they were managed directly from headquarters. The geographic structure leads to improved service to the firm's customers and enables international companies to develop a pool of local managers, adding diversity to the management ranks.

Geographic structures are most often found in companies with diverse product categories requiring a strong marketing approach. These structures also tend to be

Figure 12.3 **Geographic Structure**

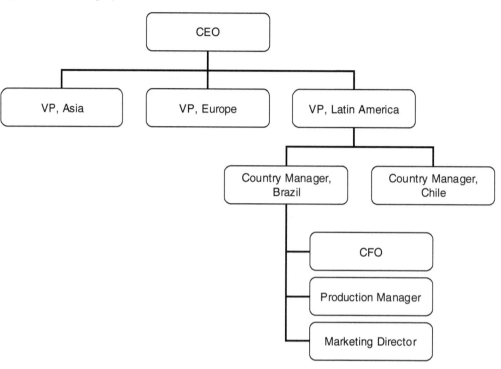

used more by packaged goods companies such as Coca-Cola, Campbell's, and RJR Nabisco. The companies in these categories face intense competition, require constant modifications to their strategies, and come under foreign government scrutiny. For local governments, especially those in developing countries, some of these products are not high-priority items (soft drinks, packaged food, and tobacco) and therefore do not help in the country's economic development programs. Geographic structures are also favored by international companies that depend on their marketing capabilities more than their manufacturing efficiency or technology. Companies such as Apple computers and Heineken are market driven and have adopted a geographic organizational design. Many financial institutions such as AIG and other global banks and insurance companies have organized their operations around regions and countries.

On the negative side, geographic structures require each foreign operation to have both product and functional specialists. Therefore, a geography-based international organization requires more staff than other structures in the international division to provide support to the geographic units. Studies have shown that in a few cases the geographic structures have generated dissonance between the organization and local staff.[28] This type of structure also creates problems in terms of coordination of the activities of the various product offerings. Figure 12.3 presents a geographic organizational structure.

In the setup shown in Figure 12.3, the functional managers report to country heads. These country managers are directly under regional managers. The regional manag-

Figure 12.4 **Functional Structure**

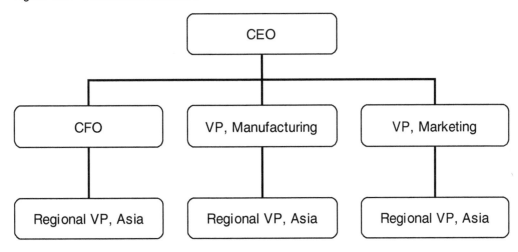

ers report either to the company CEO or to a high-ranking executive at corporate headquarters.

FUNCTIONAL STRUCTURES

The philosophy behind the functional structure is that it is more efficient to have functional expertise than product or country/regional expertise. In this type of structure, the senior executive responsible for each functional area—production, finance, or marketing—is responsible for the same functions at the regional and country levels. Function-based organizations are most often found among companies with a limited product line, such as companies in the petroleum industry and industrial product companies (office equipment) or those whose products are highly technical (robotics). After its merger with Mobil, Exxon changed its organizational structure from a geographically based design to a function-based structure. The company felt that it could make better use of its expertise in refining (operations), marketing, and financial capabilities through this structure. Function-based organizations are able to manage individual departments very well. This leads to efficiency through economies of scale. In those companies that have limited product lines, this type of design is useful in developing successful strategies through effective coordination among the various functions.

One of the disadvantages of the functional structure is the difficulty in coordinating activities among functional units both at headquarters and at the country level. The coordination between various functional units is either left to the CEO at the country level or handled by a senior executive at headquarters. Figure 12.4 presents a function-based organizational structure.

As can be seen in Figure 12.4, the marketing executive coordinates the same activities in every country in which the company has operations. This is true for the other company functions as well, such as manufacturing, finance, and so on.

MATRIX STRUCTURES

The previously identified organizational structures, though useful in specific situations, have deficiencies in coordinating and implementing the various activities of an international firm. To reduce these problems, some international companies have tried to combine the structures. Called matrix organizations, this type of structure blends the product, geographic, and functional elements, while maintaining clear lines of authority. Some large global companies have adopted a matrix organizational design, including Boeing, the U.S.-based aerospace company; Nokia, the Finnish cellular phone manufacturer; the New Zealand Dairy Board, New Zealand's government-sponsored dairy farmers cooperative; and the large Anglo-Dutch consumer goods company Unilever.

In a matrix organizational structure, a subsidiary reports to more than one group (functional, product, or geographic). This design is based on the theory that because each group shares responsibility over foreign operations, the groups will become more interdependent and exchange information and resources with one another.[29] In matrix organizations, the area and product managers have overlapping responsibilities. A manufacturing manager in Japan will report not only to the vice president of manufacturing but also to the regional manager for Asia at the world headquarters. In this case, the lines of responsibility and resultant flow of communication occur both horizontally and vertically across the main dimensions. Generally, in a matrix organizational structure, it is customary to have staff personnel coordinate the various lines of authority and communications, including the research function. However, final responsibility for all activities and the decision-making authority rests with the senior management.

The New Zealand Dairy Board, with sales in more than 120 countries, has found the matrix structure to be effective in managing its global operations. The cooperative is organized around geographic areas (Asia, Europe, and so on) that revolve around specific products (such as powdered milk) with overlaid functional strategic business groups (finance, marketing, and the like). The change from the board's previous geographic organizational design involved developing pilot category teams, specialized training for employees, and shifts in employee responsibilities. The matrix structure is very flexible and allows management to pursue both global and local strategies at the same time without difficulty. Matrix structures also encourage team decision making, which is useful in building consensus and consequently improves programs implementation.

Many international managers agree that the matrix structure is the most complex form of international organizational design.[30] Although matrix structures were meant to take advantage of the merits of product, geographic, and functional forms, in practice they create new problems of their own. Since matrix structures form managerial teams with no single person in charge, the focus is on building team consensus. This slows the decision-making process. Also, in instances of a lack of consensus, top management has to step in to resolve conflicts, taking valuable time from these senior executives. ING group, a large Dutch financial institution, recently reorganized itself from a matrix structure to a product-based structure

Figure 12.5 **Matrix Organization Structure**

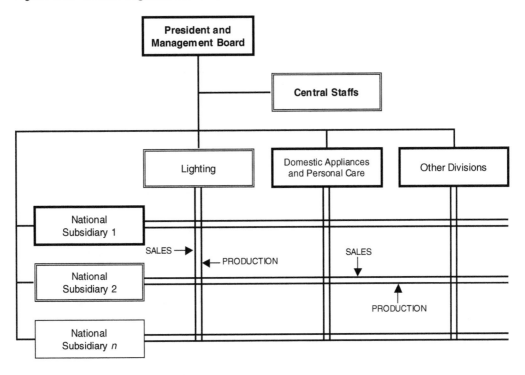

because of difficulties in attaining coordination under the matrix structure. Figure 12.5 presents a matrix organizational structure.

As can be seen in Figure 12.5, the lines of communication tend to be quite complex. The vertical and horizontal reporting systems can often cause delays in decision making and sometimes lead to confusion. Overall, however, these designs do help in opening multiple channels of communication.

HYBRID STRUCTURES

Hybrid structures are variant forms of matrix structures. In the hybrid structure, a matrix form of structure exists at the senior level of management, and one of the other forms of organization design (functional, geographic, or product) is adopted at the other levels. Hybrid structures are designed to improve the organization's effectiveness when it faces new challenges. These challenges may be the result of the acquisition of a new company, the introduction of a new product line that is different from its existing portfolio of products, or the process of becoming a major supplier to a large single customer.

Hybrid structures are not seen as permanent organizational designs, but rather temporary arrangements to address changes brought on by unexpected or unplanned events. Figure 12.6 presents a hybrid organizational structure.

Figure 12.6 **Hybrid Organization Structure**

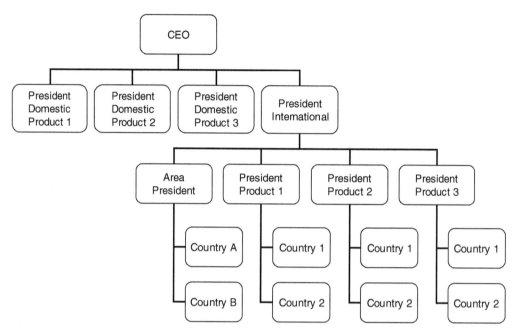

The advantages of the hybrid structure stem from the division of the activities of managing an international company between senior managers and line managers. Senior management is able to make decisions on broad-based corporate strategies and be responsible for the upstream activities in the value chain. Meanwhile, line managers are able to concentrate on functional and local issues and are left to handle the downstream activities in the value chain, which is their main concern. One drawback to the hybrid structure is that, like the matrix structure, they are complex and difficult to operate. In addition, this design offers no clear-cut responsibilities for controlling costs and profits, and, hence, profitability of the company may suffer.

NEW DEVELOPMENTS IN ORGANIZATIONAL STRUCTURES

Besides the six organizational designs discussed above, from time to time, international companies experiment with structures that improve their decision making and give them a competitive advantage. International companies that build infrastructures such as airports, oil-drilling platforms, highways, and bridges have successfully used project-management systems that are organized around specific parts of the project.[31] The customer-based organizational structure and the transnational network structure are two systems that some international companies use. In the customer-based organizational design, the focus of senior management and the whole organization is the customer. Resources and strategies are designed to acquire and retain customers. Solectron Corporation, an electronic manufacturing service company, has set up its organization around customers by merging various regional areas such as the account

Figure 12.7 **Transnational Network Organization Structure**

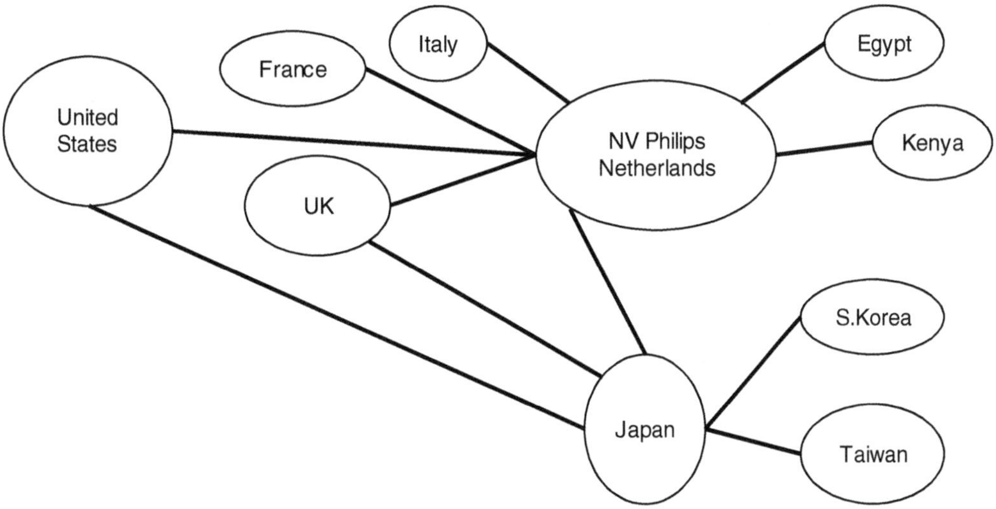

Source: Sumantra Ghosal and Christopher A. Bartlett, "The Multinational as an Interorganizational Network," *Academy of Management Review* 15, no. 4 (1990): 603–625.

management teams to provide customers with a more globalized support structure.

In some companies, customer-based structures are set up to improve the organization's effectiveness in servicing one large customer such as the government, or, in the case of advertising agencies, in servicing a single client that has substantial billings and for whose global advertising the agency is responsible.

The transnational network structure is designed to take advantage of the global economies of scale that are available for an international company and at the same time be responsive to the demands of the individual host countries in which the company operates. As the name suggests, this design connects the various country operations to the regional offices and headquarters. In transnational network structures, all the subsidiaries are linked through a network arrangement that facilitates communications among all the subsidiaries and at the same time maximizes the utilization of resources.[32] The transnational structure is a complex organizational design that requires multilevel communication networks that overlap functional, geographic, and product levels within the organization. This structure is often used by companies that have a vast number of products in many regions of the world. Figure 12.7 presents a partial transnational network structure that is used by Philips of the Netherlands.

Philips's three main regional offices—in Japan, the United Kingdom, and the United States—are linked to headquarters in the Netherlands. Each regional office is linked to subsidiaries in countries close to it. The headquarters in the Netherlands administers the subsidiaries in the Middle East and Africa.

As observed from the previous discussion, there is no single organizational design that fits all the requirements of an international company. Developing an effective organizational structure is an evolving process due to the internal and external changes that take place in an international company. It is one of the critical tasks of senior management to adopt a design that helps the company to manage a vast variety of products and services over a number countries spread across the world. It is important that all the managers and key personnel perform their duties within the context of the prevailing organizational structure. Table 12.3 presents the advantages and disadvantages of using some of the organizational structures discussed here.

Chapter Summary

Human Resources

Human resources are among the most critical resources that an international company manages. As a crucial function, human resources are central to an organization's success. The human resources management (HRM) functions are the activities that help an international company to attract, develop, and maintain an efficient and productive workforce.

Some of the specific tasks within attracting, developing, and maintaining a competent staff include developing job specifications, recruiting qualified candidates, developing training programs, administrating a compensation plan, instituting motivational programs, setting up an evaluation system, and placing the staff in various international operations.

The actual operations of HRM are a function of the degree of centralization versus decentralization of control an international company wants to exert. In centralized organizations, most of the power and control of the company is vested at its headquarters. In a decentralized organization, much of the decision making is left to country-level managers. The actual choice between centralized versus decentralized operations depends to a large extent on the international company's corporate philosophy, the type of products and services it sells, the size of the company, and the host government's regulations. Technology-oriented international companies that have proprietary products such as pharmaceuticals and whose managerial decisions have long-term effects tend to prefer centralized forms of governance. In fast-paced industries such as soft drinks that require immediate actions on the part of country managers, a more decentralized approach may be adopted.

Another important consideration in international HRM is the hiring of local managers versus sending in expatriates. Expatriate managers are faced with complex and challenging external environments. As a result, they need the ability to adapt to host-country cultures and business customs that are often unfamiliar to them. In addition, they may be called upon to deal with government officials, a task that is not normally assigned to line managers at headquarters. Expatriates are useful in maintaining corporate polices and procedures, transferring technology, and controlling operations. On the downside, expatriates are expensive, their local knowledge is often minimal, and their presence hinders the development of talented local managers.

Labor-management relations and union issues are another set of concerns that the HRM department has to deal with. Unions in different parts of the world are organized differently. In some countries, there are national unions; in others, there are

Table 12.3

Advantages and Disadvantages of Different Organizational Structures

Organizational Structure	Advantages	Disadvantages	Representative Organization
Divisional structure	Useful in negotiations with joint-venture partners and governments (experience) Able to explore more effectively world-wide markets	Not effective to operate in many countries Not effective when selling a large variety of products	IBM
Product structure	Strong coordination across functional areas to support the group Useful when products are unique	Not efficient due to duplication of product strategies across countries Needs more personnel to manage, increasing the cost of operations	Procter & Gamble
Geographic structure	Serves customers' unique needs Better control over regional markets	Duplication of functional tasks Needs more personnel to manage, increasing the cost of operations	Coca-Cola
Functional structure	Efficient (economies of scale in each function) Useful with few products or locations	Difficult to coordinate the various functions, as they are separated from one another Not practical for companies with a large number of product lines or operations in many countries	ExxonMobil
Matrix structure	Is flexible enough to pursue global and local strategies Promotes team decision making	Difficult to make decisions because of multiple layers and multiple reporting Problematic because staff must deal with multiple bosses	New Zealand Dairy Board
Hybrid structure	By dividing the activities between senior management that handles most of the upstream activities in a value chain and the local managers that handle the downstream activities, this design helps companies develop focused strategies It is able to improve coordination and be responsive to market factors.	Complex structure that is difficult to operate Also, it is not clear who controls the costs and profits.	Xerox
Transnational network	Responsive to local situations at the same time taking advantage of global economies of scale Combines functional, product, and geographic areas, which may result in high-quality strategic decisions	Complex structure that is difficult to operate Duplication of efforts, as subsidiaries are independent of headquarters and can pursue any area, including R&D	Philips

industry based unions; and in a few others, the unions are organized around individual companies. Dealing with these different types of unions is difficult; international companies have to approach each situation as unique and not attempt a broad strategy that applies to all situations.

ORGANIZATIONAL STRUCTURES

Organizational structures are used by international companies to arrange their business activities in an orderly fashion among their diverse working units. Organizational structures show where the formal power is vested and who is responsible for certain activities. They assist an international company in improving coordination of activities, decision making, controlling operations, and enhancing the communication process.

International companies use different types of organizational designs in managing their global operations. There are six to eight different types of organizational designs in use today. Use of a particular structure by an international company is an evolving process. Factors such as the company's focus, its product offerings, the number of countries it has operations in, and changes in the external environment may dictate a change in the company's organizational structure.

The most commonly used organizational structures by international companies are divisional structures, product structures, geographic structures, and functional structures. It is critical that an organizational structure reflects a company's strengths. With the dynamic transformations that are constantly occurring in the business environment, some large international companies are experimenting with newer organizational designs such as matrix, hybrid, and transnational networks to react to the rapid changes.

KEY CONCEPTS

Human Resource Functions
Human Resource Planning
Expatriates
Organizational Structures

DISCUSSION QUESTIONS

1. What is the human resource function in an international company?
2. Why is the human resource function important for an international company?
3. Enumerate and discuss the various human resource functions.
4. Discuss the differences between centralized and decentralized organizations.
5. Identify the conditions or factors that influence the choice of centralized versus decentralized organizations.
6. What is an expatriate?

7. Discuss the merits of sending expatriates to manage overseas operations.
8. When is it appropriate to hire local managers?
9. How does unionization affect international companies' operations?
10. In general, are unions beneficial for employees? If so, why?
11. What is an organizational structure?
12. What is the purpose of an organizational structure?
13. Discuss the various organizational designs.
14. Discuss the contributing factors in a company's choice of an organizational design.
15. In your opinion, are there one or two organizational designs that are superior to others?

APPLICATION CASE: CHIBA INTERNATIONAL

Chiba International of Japan, maker of high-precision electronic parts, has its U.S. operations in San Jose, California. The company's electronics parts are used in the final assembly of integrated circuits, particularly the expensive memory chips used in computers and military hardware. Chiba International is a subsidiary of Chiba Electronics Company and is rated as one of the most profitable companies in Japan on the basis of "management earnings stability" and "overall performance" by the *Nihon Keizai Shimbun,* Japan's preeminent business paper.

Chiba started its U.S. operations in 1994 with a small sales office and later established a manufacturing facility through the acquisition of an American competitor. The company has been quite successful in the United States and currently employs an American workforce in its manufacturing plant. Moreover, 14 out of the 24 top executives and 65 of the 70 salespeople in the California plant are also Americans.

Chiba, like other Japanese companies, has an underlying philosophy that it preaches and practices. In Japan, all employees have to memorize this philosophy and are required to recite it at the morning assembly held each workday. The Japanese have found that the recital and expression of the philosophy is fundamental to the success of making each employee part of a work-based family and, therefore, is responsible for the high morale exhibited by the company's workforce.

To be successful in the United States, Ken Morikawa, the general manager of the Chiba operations in San Jose, would like to have his American workforce feel a part of the overall company family. He is convinced that the only way to achieve this is by educating his American workforce in the Japanese system of human resources management principles, including the practice of reciting the company's philosophy each day. The problem for Morikawa is how to go about implementing this practice. First of all, he is not sure that American workers unfamiliar with the practice would be willing to learn and recite the philosophy at an assembly each morning, so he wonders whether he could introduce this concept piecemeal—slowly and carefully. Second, in order to be useful, the philosophy needs to be translated into English. How accurately would the translation reflect the company's original philosophy? Morikawa's plan is first to give each employee a leaflet explaining the company philosophy; then the employees will be given a few training sessions to explain the philosophy, and finally

Morikawa will have them recite it. The English translation of Chiba's philosophy is presented below:

> As the sun rises brilliantly in the sky,
> Revealing the size of the mountain, the market,
> Oh, this is our goal.
> With the highest degree of mission in
> Our heart we serve our industry,
> Meeting the strictest degree of customer
> Requirement.
> We are the leader in this industry and
> Our future path
> Is ever so bright and satisfying.

QUESTIONS

1. In your opinion, would the American workers adopt the philosophy?
2. If you were Mr. Morikawa, how would you go about implementing the company philosophy to the American workforce?

SOURCE

Part of this application case was developed from the work of Nina Hatvany and Vladimir Pucik, published in John B. Cullen and K. Praveen Parboteeah, *Multinational Management: A Strategic Approach,* 4th ed. (Mason, OH: Thomson/South-Western Publishers, 2008), pp. 725–73.

13 International Financial Management

LEARNING OBJECTIVES

- To understand the various financial transactions undertaken by a multinational manager
- To recognize the various financial institutions that will be faced by an international financial manager
- To be aware of the various methods of payment available to an international financial manager
- To understand the role of stock markets and the Eurodollar currency markets in international finance
- To recognize how regulatory agencies in the United States and overseas countries can affect international financial decision making

INTERNATIONAL EXPANSION

When a company expands its business beyond its national borders by exporting or importing goods or services, the company's financial manager has to deal with additional variables such as exchange rates, tariffs, and regulatory, legal, and cultural issues. The financial manager's responsibilities increase further when the company establishes subsidiaries abroad, as he or she must deal with additional issues such as borrowing and lending in local markets and interacting with foreign governments, agencies, and institutions.

The goal of this chapter is to provide an overview of the major decisions as well as the elements of the financial environment that will be faced by international financial managers. These include the various institutions in the marketplace, including banks and insurance companies, stock and debt markets, and regulatory agencies. Understanding the roles and structures of these institutions, which are integral to overseas business transactions, will help international financial managers appreciate the decision-making challenges facing them.

We first identify the business variables that are important to financial managers when they expand into international business activities. We then discuss the institutions that are associated with the variables and the choices available to the multinational manager.

Stage 1: Exports and Imports

A company's exposure to the overseas markets usually begins with the sale or purchase of goods or services from other countries. The financial manager's role in handling the overseas activities of exports and imports requires dealing with the following.

Foreign Currency

A financial manager is responsible for the timely payment of bills and collection of receivables. If invoices to overseas customers are stated in dollars, there are no exchange-rate issues, and the manager faces the same problems as domestic clients. If the invoices are stated in foreign currencies, the manager needs to possess a good working knowledge of the foreign exchange markets and the various international payment options available for handling the monetary transactions. In many countries, a significant amount of paperwork is also required prior to sending or receiving payments.

Tariffs

The financial manager needs to deal with the various tariffs imposed by different countries, some of which are convoluted and complicated. Tariffs can affect the pricing of goods and services directly or indirectly. If the tariffs are high, the company may be forced to lower prices in order to make their products affordable to customers. Similarly, if a company is purchasing goods, it will have to be aware of the duties and fees imposed by U.S. customs authorities in order to determine the final cost of the product and the price to charge locally.

Shipping

The financial manager has to evaluate the costs associated with the various shipping options available for the export and import of goods. In most cases, the mode of transportation is determined by the characteristics of the product, including size, weight, durability, and other factors. The packaging of the goods is an additional factor for consideration. Innovations in packaging can affect the mode of shipment and, in turn, the pricing of the product.

Insurance

In international business, it is important to insure products shipped abroad for non-delivery or delay. Unlike domestic shipments, the time lag for replacement is much longer for overseas shipments. In addition, insurance for liability protection may also be required in the event of a failure of the product or service. In the past, this was less of a concern, as it was too cost prohibitive for an importer to pursue legal action for noncompliance, especially for small companies. The process was also very cumbersome, especially in Europe and Asia, where it could take years to settle a case. However, in recent years, lawsuits against foreign companies have become routine, and the threat of overseas litigation has forced companies around the world to reconsider their insurance options. For instance, three employees of the software company SAP, based in China, sued the company on grounds of unlawful termination, something that would have been unheard of a few years ago.[1] In addition, various national governments are playing a role in litigation. Microsoft, for example, continues to face legal challenges from the European Union on its monopoly status of its operating software, in spite of having reached an agreement with the U.S. Justice Department.

STAGE 2: ESTABLISHING A SUBSIDIARY

The second stage in a company's overseas plan usually entails establishing an office or a subsidiary in a foreign country, which poses considerable challenges to a financial manager. The following variables impact financial decision making in the establishment of an overseas office.

Taxes

The financial manager has to be aware of the different types of taxes in a country and their impact on payment flows between the parent company and the subsidiary. Reconciling taxes can be challenging when the parent's and the subsidiary's statements of accounts have to be consolidated in accordance with the local accounting standards.

Banking Relationships

Since a subsidiary is a separate freestanding incorporated company in a foreign country, it will usually establish its own financial relationship with a local bank. Although the subsidiary can obtain loans from the parent company at lower interest rates, it encounters exchange-rate risk when it is has to repay the money. In addition, there is often substantial paperwork involved in overseas borrowing. A subsidiary usually prefers to work with the local offices of major international banks, especially with the branch office of the parent company's bank.

Capital Markets

Larger subsidiaries usually have to access the local stock and debt markets to issue stocks and bonds for their financing needs. If a subsidiary funds its long-range requirements by borrowing in local currency, it can be paid from its earnings in the local market and avoid exchange-rate risks. Although the parent is able to issue shares and bonds overseas on behalf of its subsidiary, exchange-rate volatility and paperwork may make it more convenient to let the subsidiary raise the capital in the local markets.

STAGE 3: ESTABLISHMENT OF MULTIPLE SUBSIDIARIES

The final stage in the overseas expansion of multinationals is the creation of multiple subsidiaries in several countries. Cash will flow not only between a subsidiary and the parent but also among subsidiaries. The management and control of cash flows among subsidiaries can become quite complex, requiring financial managers with considerable expertise to manage the payments. For example, a subsidiary may choose to provide credit to another subsidiary for purchase of its goods with the stipulation that the payment be made directly to the parent, saving time and transaction costs. Such payments have to be done carefully to ensure they do not violate the laws of each country.

The next sections discuss the various institutions faced by financial managers when completing international transactions.

INTERNATIONAL BANKS

The bank is a focal point for most international financial managers, as payments have to be made to vendors and funds collected from customers throughout the year. In the case of overseas operations, financial managers must deal with banks that have expertise in foreign exchange and the facilities to offer foreign currency services. There are several types of international banks that can assist multinational managers in transferring payments from one country to another.

COMMERCIAL BANKS

Commercial banks are depository institutions that accept deposits from customers and make loans to corporations and individuals. Smaller commercial banks usually do not have a foreign exchange desk; instead, they use a larger commercial bank to perform the international transactions on behalf of their clients. Large commercial banks have their own foreign exchange traders, who buy and sell currencies and hold inventories. A commercial bank still requires a correspondent associate in the other country to make a payment on behalf of its client to an overseas customer. The correspondent associate role can take the form of a commercial relationship with a local bank in the country, or the commercial bank can choose to set up its own affiliate or branch.

SUBSIDIARIES

Large commercial banks find it advantageous to set up their subsidiaries in major financial markets. A subsidiary is usually an incorporated company in a foreign country. When located in a foreign country, the subsidiary is a freestanding legal entity separate from the parent company. It is treated as a domestic company by the local authorities. The parent company's ownership of the overseas subsidiary may be less than 100 percent, but the parent still maintains control of management. If management is shared, the arrangement is usually defined as a joint venture. A subsidiary has to file taxes locally, prepare financial statements based on local standards, and report to the monetary and taxing authorities of the country where it is established. A banking subsidiary usually offers a full range of services in the local country. Its presence overseas makes it very convenient for the parent bank to offer a range of payment services to its multinational clients located in that country.

BRANCH OFFICES

A commercial bank also has the choice of setting up a branch office in a foreign country to handle its overseas transfers and payments. A branch office is just a legal extension of the parent company and is not treated as a separate corporate entity. The branch office may or may not accept deposits from local customers. If it does not take local deposits, it will lend to local customers using equity capital or loans from the parent bank. A commercial bank will find it useful to set up a branch office in a foreign country if its clients conduct regular business in that country. It will be able to perform the transfers and payments of its clients more efficiently and with less paperwork.

Foreign banks similarly set up branches in the United States to facilitate business with their clients that have moved here to set up subsidiaries. In the United States, all branches of foreign banks are regulated by the International Banking Act of 1978. Branches are allowed to accept deposits from domestic residents only if they exceed US$100,000 and therefore are not eligible for deposit insurance provided by the Federal Deposit Insurance Corporation (FDIC).[2] There is no minimum amount for deposits accepted from foreigners.

CORRESPONDENT BANKS

It is not possible for a commercial bank to have subsidiaries or branches in every country. Most commercial banks instead establish correspondent banking relationships with banks in countries where they do not have a branch or subsidiary. A correspondent bank will facilitate the transfer of payments for an overseas bank, and the relationship is usually two-way. For example, if Citibank agrees to handle all payments and transfers in the United States for Shanghai Pudong Development Bank, the latter will perform similar services for Citibank in China.

A commercial bank usually maintains a deposit in the correspondent bank, which serves as a means of payment for services received from the correspondent bank. Maintaining a corresponding banking relationship is very important for banks that have multinationals as their customers. A multinational makes and receives multiple payments from around the world and usually prefers to have one bank handle its global transactions. That bank must have the ability to provide services in every country.

REPRESENTATIVE OFFICES

Many commercial banks also establish representative offices in foreign countries to service the overseas subsidiaries of their domestic clients. A representative office does not accept deposits, engage in lending, or offer other banking activities. Its sole role is to act as a liaison between its client and the foreign banks located in the overseas country. In the United States, the Foreign Bank Supervision Enhancement Act of

1991 requires that foreign banks wishing to set up representative offices in the United States first obtain approval from the Federal Reserve Board, even though technically a representative office does not perform any banking function.

OFFSHORE BANKS

Large multinationals and major banks also establish offshore banks, which are usually located in what are termed "tax-haven countries." The offices are usually shell entities with a minimal staff. These shell companies typically hold cash on behalf of the parent bank and disburse the money when needed to different parts of the world. The countries with the greatest number of offshore banks are the Bahamas, the Cayman Islands, Bahrain, Singapore, Luxembourg, Panama, and the Netherlands Antilles. Offshore banks serve a useful function for banks that are engaged in international transactions because they allow banks to park their cash for temporary periods as they shift their resources globally. Multinationals also find it convenient to deposit money in offshore banks for short-term periods.

Assume that a U.S. multinational has US$20 million from its UK operations that it wishes to hold for six months before spending it on a planned investment in Spain. If the multinational brings this money back to the United States, it will be subject to corporate taxes. The multinational may choose to deposit the funds in a UK bank. However, assume it also has the option of depositing the funds in an offshore bank that pays a higher interest rate. Offshore banks are able to offer higher deposit rates because they face fewer regulatory requirements. In this case, it is obvious that the better choice is to deposit the funds with the offshore bank.

Offshore banks also enable multinationals to plan their cash inflows and outflows on a global scale. For example, assume the amount of funds in the earlier case was not sufficient for the multinational's Spanish investment. The UK subsidiary may request the parent bank to collect additional funds from its various subsidiaries. This is best accomplished by the parent company pooling all the money in a central account at the offshore bank.

The growth of offshore banks led the Federal Reserve Board in 1981 to allow the establishment of an international banking facility (IBF) in the United States. This allows a commercial bank to create its own offshore unit within the United States. The offshore unit can be lodged within the bank premises and for all purposes is legally assumed to be an office located offshore. Deposits in the IBF are not subject to U.S. banking regulations. An IBF is allowed to accept deposits only from foreigners. It can perform all the functions of an offshore bank. The 1981 rule resulted in the establishment of several IBFs by major banks in the United States and slowed the growth of offshore banks overseas.

Table 13.1 lists the results of a survey undertaken by *Global Finance,* an online magazine, which ranks the most popular banks by region for delivery of foreign exchange services. The researchers interviewed corporate executives and industry analysts covering 70 leading foreign exchange banks around the world. The questions were both objective and subjective in nature. Citigroup ranked among the best for companies located in North and South America.

Table 13.1

World's Best Foreign Exchange Banks in 2005

North America	Citigroup
Latin America	Citigroup
Western Europe	Deutsche Bank (Honorable mention: BNP Paribas and UBS)
Central and Eastern Europe	Bank Austria Creditanstalt
Scandinavia	Nordea
Middle East	National Bank of Kuwait
Africa	Standard Bank
Asia-Pacific	HSBC
Southeast Asia	DBS (Singapore)

Source: Gordon Platt, "World's Best Foreign Exchange Banks 2005, Global Finance Selects the Leaders in the World's Biggest Financial Market," *Global Finance*, January 2005. Available at http://globalf.vwh. net/content/?article_id=694 (accessed July 12, 2008).

INTERNATIONAL TRANSACTIONS

RECENT DEVELOPMENTS IN TRANSFERS AND PAYMENTS

Internet technology has revolutionized the way companies send and receive payments in foreign currencies.

Most banks today offer Web-based programs for companies to send and receive overseas payments from their corporate checking accounts. The most common method of payment for corporate international transactions is through wire transfers, which take between one and three days. Most programs also allow for scheduling of payments so that if a company has to make a periodic or recurring payment, the financial manager can state the payment dates and amounts in advance and the program will automatically make the payments.

Another improvement in international payments is in the clearing and settlement of stocks and bonds purchased in overseas markets. The actual confirmation and delivery for the purchase or sale of a stock or bond used to vary between three to seven days, with the exception of transactions between the United States and Canada, which usually was completed in a day. The terms used in the market are T + 3 for three days and T + 7 for seven days for actual receipt of payments. Today, the purchase or sale of securities and receipt of payment for a majority of countries can be concluded in T + 1 days.

TERMS OF PAYMENT IN INTERNATIONAL TRANSACTIONS

There are four terms of payment for export and import of goods, and they offer different benefits and risks to the seller (exporter) and buyer (importer).

Advance Payment

A seller may demand an advance payment prior to shipping any goods.

- This provides full security to the exporter, who will not have to worry about nonpayment.
- In advance payment, the risk is borne completely by the buyer or importer who is now exposed to nondelivery of goods, delay, or unacceptable quality.
- The importer also incurs an additional interest expense because the payment is made prior to receiving the goods. Most advance payment transactions are done when the two parties are unfamiliar with each other or the importing country is politically unstable.
- Advance payments in international business are not common. On the contrary, the terms of payment for most international transactions are on credit with payments made only after the delivery of the goods.

Letters of Credit

A letter of credit (LC) is a document issued by a bank that guarantees a bank will pay the specified amount on a specified date when an exporter completes his or her contractual agreement of shipping the goods and presenting all documents specified in an export agreement. It allows an exporter to safely ship goods on credit as long as he or she receives a letter of credit from the importer's bank. The usual terms of payments are 30, 60, or 90 days after the shipment of goods.

- The importing bank is obligated to make the payment as long as the documents, usually a bill of lading from the shipping company and insurance papers, are in order.
- The importing bank does not require verification of the goods unless specified in the agreement. In that case, a customs document may also have to be included to ensure that the goods are in accordance with the terms of the contract.
- The LC is the most common form of payment in international transfers of goods. This is partly because the exporter's agreement is with the importer's bank and not with the importer. The payment should be guaranteed as long as the importer's bank is in good standing.
- An LC is usually irrevocable, which means that if any changes have to made, they require the agreement of the exporter, the importer, and the importer's bank.
- An LC can be confirmed by the exporter's bank for a small fee. This will provide a double guarantee in that if the importing bank is unable to make the payments for any reason, the exporting bank is obligated to make the payments. It is recommended that the exporter get an LC confirmed if the importing bank is located in a country that is politically unstable or has foreign exchange problems.

Documentary Collections

A documentary collection, or DC, is a transaction in which the title of goods is exchanged when the importer's bank accepts the documents sent by the exporter's bank. The importer's bank will make a payment immediately if the document sent by the exporter's bank is a document against payment (D/P), or will agree to make the payment on the specified due date if the document is a document against acceptance (D/A). A DC is similar to an LC except that neither of the banks provides any guarantee of payment.

- A DC is commonly used when the parties have a well-established relationship or the transactions are between parties in countries where the legal system is reliable for enforcement of nonpayment.
- Using a DC is less expensive than using an LC.
- A DC is often used with shipments by sea because it is easier to maintain ownership of goods until the documents are accepted. It is more difficult to maintain ownership of goods with air or road shipments because of the potential delay that may occur for the document to reach the foreign bank on time.

Open Revolving Account

In an open revolving account, an exporter sends the documents after shipping directly to the importer, who will make the payments based on the terms and conditions of the agreement. Usually an open purchase order (P.O.) is requested from the importer, against which the exporter will invoice after each shipment. For example, a German company will issue a €1 million P.O. valid for two years, against which the exporter is asked to ship goods worth €20,000 per month. Each month, the exporter will ship goods and send an invoice for €20,000 for payment. When the amount left in the P.O. is low, the companies may choose to add an additional amount to the old P.O. or issue a new P.O.

- In an open revolving account, the risk of payment is borne completely by the exporter.
- Open revolving accounts are usually undertaken by companies with longstanding relationships and in transactions where the importer is considered to have a strong financial standing.
- An open revolving account is a very strong selling tool for the exporter because it shows confidence that the exporter will meet the quality required by the importer and does not expect any rejection of delivery.

METHODS OF PAYMENT

Wire Transfer

Wire transfer is the most common form of payment in international transactions. Most banks today offer Web-based programs to directly transfer money from a company's checking account to a client's bank, with fees ranging from US$12 to US$20 per wire transfer for high-volume customers.

The following information is usually required for wire transfers.

SWIFT Number. All banks use a messaging system to notify the recipient bank of the arrival of funds. The most popular service is provided by the Belgium-based Society for Worldwide Interbank Financial Telecommunication (SWIFT), with bank customers in

208 countries. To identify a bank, SWIFT uses an eight- and eleven-letter bank identifier code (BIC), based on ISO (International Standards Organization) standard 9362.[3] For example the code BNPAFRPP stands for BNP-Paribas, located in Paris, France. The first four characters, BNPA, stand for BNP-Paribas. The next two letters, FR, stand for France, and the last two, PP, stand for Paris, the location of their headquarters. The eleven-digit code adds a three-letter identifier for the branch. For example BNPAFRPPMAR would route the message to the Marseilles branch (MAR) of BNP-Paribas. The last five digits of the code are alphanumeric, meaning they can be numbers or letters.[4]

Routing Number. In addition to the messaging number sent by SWIFT, all banks require routing numbers for the actual delivery of the payment. The routing numbers vary for different countries, although efforts are being made to consolidate them to a single format.

ABA Number. In the United States, the routing number is known as the ABA number, so termed because it was created by the American Banking Association in 1910. The components of the nine-digit code are as follows: the first four digits represent one of the 12 Federal Reserve districts, with the first two identifying the city. For example, 01 is Boston and 02 is New York. The next four digits are a unique bank identifier code, and the last digit is a check digit that is used to verify the accuracy of the routing number.

IBAN Number. In Europe, the international bank account number (IBAN) is used as the routing number. It is an alphanumeric code that can be as long as 34 characters. It is based on ISO standard 13616–1:2007 and consists of the following components: the first two characters identify the country, the next two are check digits to ensure that all the numbers are in order, the next four are letters that identify the bank, and the last component is a six-digit number for the branch. The rest of the numbers represent the customer's account number.

Other Countries. Most countries have their own unique identifier code for routing numbers. Canada has an eight-digit number for checks and a nine-digit routing number for electronic delivery, assigned by the Canadian Payments Association. India recently introduced the Indian Financial System Code (IFSC), which will be applied to all branches in the near future. The Reserve Bank of India (the equivalent of the Federal Reserve Board) issues the IFSC. It is made up of four letters to identify the bank and a digit for future use, followed by six digits to identify the branch.

Credit Cards

The use of credit cards as a method of payment for international transactions is increasing as transactions over the Internet increase in volume. The three major card companies that dominate the market are American Express, Visa, and MasterCard. The seller usually has to pay a discount of between 2 and 4 percent based on the card and the agreement terms. American Express issues its own cards, while Visa and MasterCard issue cards through banks and other financial institutions. Payments through credit cards in international business are usually made by customers for small transactions and do not apply to large corporate transactions.

Paper Checks

The use of paper checks as a means of payment has declined considerably over the years, as the cost of this method of payment has increased relative to wire transfers. Not only is check payment expensive, but it also takes a long time for the payment to clear. The importer has to first send the check via mail to the exporter who then deposits in his or her bank. The exporting bank has to mail the check to the foreign bank on which it has been drawn. The money is then transferred via correspondent banks before being credited to the exporter's account. Even with the use of Internet technology that allows checks to be scanned and sent electronically to another bank, the time delay is still significant, somewhere between two and four weeks.

INTERNATIONAL SHIPPING

The financial manager must often evaluate the various delivery options available to a company and the financial impact of each option. The major forms of transportation to overseas markets are by sea and air, with sea shipments accounting for more than 80 percent of the total. Some goods are limited in the type of transportation that can be used to ship them.

1. If the product is bulky or heavy, it cannot be shipped by air. For example, cars and trucks have to be shipped by sea transport. Although in theory a car can be shipped by air, it is prohibitively expensive.
2. If the goods are perishable, they must be transported by air. For example, fresh flowers from countries in South America have to be shipped by air in order to reach customers in Europe or the United States by the following morning.
3. Hydrocarbons, such as oil and gas, must be transported via ships because they need to be enclosed in special tanks or bulk containers.

SHIPMENT BY SEA

There are three types of global shipping:

1. *Dry Bulk:* These carriers transport mostly dry raw materials or food, such as stones, steel, iron, wheat, rice, and maize, which must be transported in bulk and require a significant amount of space.
2. *Wet Bulk:* These carriers transport mostly raw materials such as hydrocarbons (oil and liquefied gas), as well as several kinds of wet chemicals.
3. *Tanker:* These carriers transport mostly finished products that are shipped in containers. The container sizes are standardized—usually 20 or 40 feet in length—so they can be loaded from ships directly to trains and trucks.

Table 13.2

The Top Five Airports for Transport of Air Cargo

	City	Country	Tonnage	Comments
1	Memphis	United States	3,840,574	Hub for Federal Express
2	Hong Kong	China	3,772,673	Asian hub for many companies
3	Anchorage	United States	2,826,499	Major transit for transpacific routes
4	Seoul	South Korea	2,555,582	Major hub for Air Korea
5	Shanghai	China	2,494,808	UPS China base

Source: "The World's Top 50 Cargo Airports," *Air Cargo World,* July 2008. Available at http://www .aircargoworld.com (accessed July 12, 2008).

SHIPMENT BY AIR

The use of air cargo has been increasing consistently over the past three decades as larger and more fuel efficient planes have been developed to carry products over long distances. Air cargo volume fell in 2008 because of a spike in oil prices, but most analysts are forecasting that the growth of air cargo will continue for the foreseeable future. The Official Airline Guide (OAG) has estimated that air cargo growth between 2008 and 2011 will average 5.6 percent. In addition, the 2008 report estimates that air freight will increase from 152.1 billion FTKs (freight tonne kilometers) to 274.1 billion FTKs by 2017.[5] The top five airports for transport of air cargo are listed in Table 13.2. The next five busiest air cargo airports are in Paris, Tokyo, Frankfurt, Louisville, and Miami.

For goods that can be sent either by sea or by air freight, a financial manager must perform a cost-benefit analysis after considering all factors that can affect pricing. Air shipment is preferable if costs of holding inventory are very high. When goods are sent by ship, a company is usually required to hold a significant amount of inventory because of the delay incurred when goods are transported from the seaport to the final destination. However, sea shipment is preferred if the product is combustible or not suitable to extreme temperatures.

RECENT DEVELOPMENTS IN OVERSEAS SHIPPING

Sea shipments will continue to increase in volume as countries develop and engage in more exporting and importing of goods. Current technology does not foresee breakthroughs in air technology that will make it cheaper to send all goods by air. However, in some industries such as publishing and engineering services, advances in Internet technology have made it unnecessary to ship goods at all.

Publishing

In the publishing industry, the ability to send complete books overseas electronically for either download or professional publication eliminates the need to send books physically across borders. In the documents-processing industry, the availability of software to authenticate signatures allows formal documents, including contracts, invoices, architectural drawings, and the like, to be sent electronically. Banks are now able to send scanned checks electronically to their overseas counterparts for verification prior to making payments to their clients.

Engineering

The development of 3D technology has enabled engineers to create products first on the computer and to test them completely before producing a prototype for physical testing. Three-dimensional models of mechanical parts can be sent overseas electronically to be reproduced using special prototyping machines. This process not only eliminates the need to send prototype models but also allows for multiple configurations to be tested based on the availability of local materials and processes. Innovations in robotic technology are expected to develop additional new ways of producing goods and services remotely and reduce the demand for transportation.

INTERNATIONAL INSURANCE

Multinational managers have to be familiar with the insurance coverage required for manufacture and delivery of goods and services to their overseas customers. In the case of overseas customers, additional coverage is required for political risk. Political risk refers to the risk of loss due to changes in political structure or government policies that affect, directly or indirectly, the conduct of business transactions in the foreign country.

SHIPMENT INSURANCE

All shipments, domestic or international, require insurance coverage in the event of nondelivery of goods or services. The reasons can vary from damage to shipments to lost shipments to bureaucratic delays or theft. Most of the major insurance companies around the world and some shipping companies provide a range of insurance services for international shipments. Shipments by sea are covered by marine cargo insurance, while shipments by air may be covered by both marine and air cargo insurance, which is also offered by air carriers. The usual coverage for export insurance is 110 percent of CIF, defined as the total of cost (of product), insurance, and freight.

In the United States, the government also offers insurance to encourage exports of goods and services and assists companies in short-term financing and protection against nonpayment. The services are provided by the Export-Import Bank of the United States, usually called the Ex-Im Bank. The Ex-Im Bank does not compete with the private sector. It provides insurance services only if companies are unable to obtain financing or insurance from private financial institutions.[6]

POLITICAL RISK INSURANCE

Perhaps the most difficult insurance to obtain is political risk insurance, especially for countries that have unstable governments or weak corporate governance. The major political risk is the nationalization or appropriation of a company's assets that leads to a complete blockage of its funds. In the United States, political risk insurance is obtained from the Overseas Private Investment Corporation (OPIC), a government agency, and from the Multilateral Investment Government Agency (MIGA), an affiliate of the World Bank.

OPIC

The Overseas Private Investment Corporation, an independent U.S. government agency, was established in 1951 to encourage private companies to export by providing financing and political risk insurance. It also makes funds available for investment in countries that are currently not attractive to the private sector. Political risk insurance protects firms against expropriation, currency inconvertibility, political violence, and stand-alone terrorism.[7]

MIGA

The Multilateral Investment Government Agency is an affiliate of the World Bank, and its goal is to encourage foreign direct investment (FDI) to developing countries to stimulate growth and reduce poverty. MIGA protects investors and lenders against expropriation, currency inconvertibility, war, civil disturbances, and breach of contract. It covers only new investments and does not exceed US$420 million to any one country. It also provides insurance for financial institutions that provide financial support for equity or debt instruments.[8]

STOCK EXCHANGES AND MARKETS

Financial managers of large multinationals often have to go to the public markets to obtain financing in the form of stocks and bonds. Until the 1980s, there were few well-developed financial markets in the world. The major markets were located in New York, London, Tokyo, Frankfurt, and Paris. In the 1980s, countries around the word began to liberalize their financial markets and develop their stock and debt markets. Today, most of the large companies overseas issue stocks and bonds in the local markets to meet their long-term financing needs. This practice replaced their main form of financing, loans through local commercial banks.

New York and London continue to dominate the stock markets. Large foreign companies prefer to list their stocks in these two markets because of their established reputation, experience in handling large trades, deep pool of investors, and strict rules that protect minority shareholders. These factors, termed corporate governance, were weak in many of the newly emerging stock exchanges in the early years of development. Insider trading, which can be disadvantageous to small and overseas investors, was the biggest problem in most of these countries.

This landscape has changed in the past decade as more countries have clamped down on stock market abuses and tightened corporate governance rules. As a result, there has been significant growth in the listing of overseas shares in stock markets around the world. These developments have led to a wave of consolidations among stock exchanges. The largest stock exchanges continue to be in New York and London; a discussion of three of the world's major exchanges follows.

NYSE-EURONEXT

The merger of the New York Stock Exchange, one of the largest in the world, and Euronext, an Amsterdam-based Pan-European exchange, led to the creation of NYSE-Euronext, the largest exchange in the world in terms of listed firms.

The NYSE opened in 1792, with 24 members, and the first stock listed was the Bank of New York. In 1972, the NYSE incorporated itself as a not-for-profit organization, and in 2006, it became a for-profit company. It is only one of the exchanges listed in the S&P 500 index. For most of its existence it traded through open pits, where traders bought from and sold to each other through hand signals and shouting at the pits. Although it offered electronic trading through its SuperDot system in 1984, it did not expand its services until recently. The NYSE ARCA electronic trading platform now handles most of the daily trades. In 2007, the NYSE was trading more than 5 billion shares per day.

Euronext was formed on November 22, 2000, when the stock exchanges of Amsterdam, Paris, and Brussels merged to create a Pan-European exchange. In 2002, Euronext merged with the Portuguese stock exchange and the London International Financial Futures Exchange. In 2008, NYSE-Euronext merged with the American Stock Exchange (AMEX) to consolidate its leading position in the world. It now boasts a total of 5,600 listed companies.[9]

NASDAQ OMX

NASDAQ OMX also considers itself one of the largest exchanges in the world. Although the listed companies total only 4,400 firms in 2008, the exchange provides trading support for more than 60 exchanges located in 40 countries. NASDAQ was one of the first companies to offer electronic trading when it introduced the small-order execution system in 1984. It continued to grow by listing stocks that were unable to meet the requirements of the NYSE and AMEX, then the two leading exchanges. As electronic exchange became better established, NASDAQ was in the enviable position of having a strong lead in the delivery of automated trades. In 2007, it merged with OMX—a derivatives exchange that began in 1985 and grew by merging with several Nordic exchanges, including the Stockholm, Copenhagen, and Iceland exchanges. OMX was well known in the market for its use of advanced technology in the creation of trading platforms.

LONDON STOCK EXCHANGE

The London Stock Exchange, or LSE, is considered one of the oldest exchanges in the world, beginning its activities around 1698. Most of the trading was informal and took place at Jonathan's Coffee House in Change Alley. In 1751, 150 brokers officially formed a club to buy and sell shares at the coffee house.[10] In 2007, the LSE merged with Italian

Borsa to form the largest stock exchange in Europe. In June 2008, the exchange had more than 3,200 stocks listings, including the Alternate International Market (AIM), which caters to smaller companies and demands lower requirements to list their stocks.

AMERICAN AND GLOBAL DEPOSITORY RECEIPTS

When companies list their stocks in overseas markets, the shares are usually traded by investors in the local economy. It is difficult for a U.S. investor, for example, to trade stocks of a company traded on the Australian stock exchange. The U.S. investor also faces exchange-rate risk because the stock will be priced in Australian currency. To encourage U.S. investors to purchase foreign stocks, a bank can purchase foreign shares and place them in a trust. It then issues new shares that are valued in American dollars. The prices are based on the prices traded in the home market. The new shares are called American depository receipts (ADRs) and have become a popular instrument for U.S. investors wishing to hold foreign shares.

Assume that a German company, called AKR GmbH, has 1 million shares trading in the German stock market at €10 each. The current exchange rate is US$2/€1. An American bank could purchase 100,000 shares of AKR in Germany and put them in a trust. The bank then creates AKR ADRs and sells shares in the United States for US$20 each. These shares can be traded on either the NYSE or the NASDAQ by American investors. For example, assume that the price of the AKR share in Germany increases to €20. The price for AKR ADRs will increase to US$40, assuming the exchange rate stays the same at US$2/€1. The American investor can now sell the ADR to another buyer at a purchase price of US$40. Any dividends paid by the company in Germany will also be paid to the American investor in U.S. dollars.

ADRs have been growing in popularity for the past 20 years. Foreign companies have found it beneficial to list their stocks this way for two reasons: to increase their investor base and to raise capital in the United States. The deep market in the United States allows foreign companies to raise capital less expensively than in their home country.

The recent development of stock exchanges around the world has led companies to seek and list ADRs in other countries, too. If a depository receipt is trading on more than one stock exchange, it is called a global depository receipt (GDR). Between 2002 and 2004, among all new depository receipts in the world, ADRs accounted for 64 percent and GDRs for 36 percent of the total issued. In the period between 2004 and 2006, the ratio stood at 55 percent for GDRs as opposed to 45 percent for ADRs.[11] J.P. Morgan introduced the American depository receipt in 1927 for a British retailer, Selfridges & Co. Today, more than 2,000 companies from 80 countries have issued depository receipts. What was once an American phenomenon has become a global one.

EURODOLLAR MARKETS

A financial manager of a multinational must be knowledgeable not only about international stock markets but also about debt markets. Most subsidiaries abroad borrow from local commercial banks to satisfy their financing needs. However, because of the financial market liberalization around the world, multinational managers are finding that they can go directly to the local public markets, with or without the help of investment banks, to obtain debt financing. In addition, parent companies can satisfy their financing needs by tapping the Eurocurrency market, where currency instruments are traded outside the borders of the respective countries

The Eurocurrency market can be best explained by the development of the Eurodollar market in the 1950s. The original Eurodollar can be traced to Russia and the Eastern European countries that formed the Soviet bloc after World War II. Fearing that their dollar deposits in U.S. banks would be confiscated by the U.S. authorities, they moved their dollar deposits to European banks, where they opened dollar accounts. The banks found a ready market for dollars in U.S. multinationals and European companies. The banks lent the money in dollars for repayment in dollars, though they were located in Europe. The person or corporation that borrowed the money would, in turn, deposit the dollars in another bank. As a result of the multiplier effect, the dollar deposits grew in volume. They were not subject to local banking laws because they were not in the currency of the country. Over time, companies began to issue bonds and other instruments in dollars, and eventually this led to the rapid development of the dollar market outside of the United States. All dollars that are traded outside the United States became known as Eurodollars. It does not matter if the dollars are deposited in a bank account in Singapore or Japan; they are still termed Eurodollars.

The success of the Eurodollar market also led other currencies, such as the German deutsche mark, French franc, and Japanese yen, to be deposited outside their countries. They were called Euromarks, Eurofrancs, and Euroyen, respectively. Multinationals such as IBM could borrow Euroyen to finance their Japanese operations and Euromarks for investment in Germany. Approximately two-thirds of the Eurocurrency market is still dominated by the Eurodollar. London is the largest center for dollar deposits, estimated at US$1.86 trillion, approximately 25 percent of the total. The next largest repository of U.S. dollar deposits is in the Cayman Islands.[12]

REGULATORY AGENCIES

A major concern for managers of multinationals is the myriad of regulatory agencies that must be dealt with in the course of conducting overseas business. Companies that engage in exporting, invest in overseas ventures, and set up joint ventures or subsidiaries are all likely to face the following kinds of regulators, both in the United States and around the world.

U.S. Customs and Border Protection, formerly the U.S. Customs and now part of the Department of Homeland Security, monitors both exports and imports of goods. A company that imports goods to the United States faces different schedules of duties. If the country is classified as developing, it may be subject to lower rates than the general rates. Countries that do not have normal trade relations with the United States, such as Cuba and North Korea, may have rates higher than the general rates. In addition, user fees are applied based on mode of entry. The harbor processing fee is charged for goods entering by ship, while a merchandise processing fee is applied for most other imports.[13]

The Office of Foreign Assets Control, a part of the U.S. Department of the Treasury, monitors international financial transactions. The office ensures that investments are not undertaken in countries where investment is prohibited by law. Today, all overseas investments, including manufacturing of goods and delivery of services, have to abide by the controls put in place by Congress, mostly to combat terrorism-related activities.

The International Trade Administration, a division of the U.S. Department of Commerce, promotes U.S. trade and investment, ensures that fair trade is implemented among countries, and monitors companies to ensure that they are complying with trade laws and agreements. The Bureau of Industry and Security (BIS), another division of the Commerce Department, monitors the export and licensing of goods that are restricted by law, requiring multinationals to seek its assistance in verifying that they are compliant with the laws.

The U.S. Internal Revenue Service (IRS), part of the Department of the Treasury, monitors the reporting of foreign-exchange earnings and the associated tax implications. Multinationals have to pay taxes on income repatriated from their foreign subsidiaries to the parent company. In addition, they have to consolidate the income statements and balance sheets of all their subsidiaries and compute the net taxes owed. This often entails getting interpretations and clarifications as to whether certain transactions meet the definitions of the local accounting standards, requiring frequent consultations with the IRS.

The customs authority of the foreign country, with the exception of countries located in economic unions or free trade areas, subjects all exports to that foreign country to customs duties. There are no customs duties within countries in the European Union. The North American Free Trade Agreement has also eliminated a majority of tariffs among Mexico, Canada, and the United States. There are many other free trade areas around the world where duties are not assessed for the member countries. Free trade areas can make a big difference to financial strategies. Assume, for example, that a multinational plans to open a subsidiary in or near Europe to service the European Union market. Assume that the multinational must choose between opening the subsidiary in Spain or in Morocco, where the labor rates are much lower. A cost-benefit analysis must be done to determine if the benefits of having zero tariffs within the EU offsets the gains of cheaper production in Morocco.

The taxing authority of the foreign country charges taxes for income earned by a multinational in that foreign country. All multinationals have to deal with a number of taxing authorities under different tax laws. Tax treaties between countries also determine the amount of taxes to be paid by subsidiaries of foreign corporations. If the foreign taxing authority charges a tax rate higher than the U.S. corporate tax rate, the IRS will issue a credit for the extra taxes paid. There are attempts to harmonize taxes within economic unions and free trade zones, but the goal for a unified global taxation is still quite far from fruition.

The monetary authorities of the foreign country, the equivalent of similar agencies in the United States, are also entities faced by U.S. multinationals when they do business overseas. Handling some government agencies can be challenging because of the prevalence of bribes and other unofficial payments expected by government officials in some countries. The United States has a strict policy of not making any illegal payments overseas under the Foreign Corrupt Trade Practices Act of 1977, explained in the next section. In addition, financial managers have to keep abreast of new laws passed by host governments that are implemented by the various branches of their monetary authorities.

Other agencies that can impact trade include the consumer protection offices of both the exporting and importing countries, local taxing authorities, social agencies, and sometimes even political lobby groups. From a financial perspective, they either add to the direct costs of doing business overseas or increase the risk of doing business in that country. If the risk is increased, the investment has to generate more than sufficient returns as additional compensation.

THE FOREIGN CORRUPT TRADE PRACTICES ACT OF 1977

In 1977, the United States passed the Foreign Corrupt Practices Act (FCPA), the first of its kind in the world. It explicitly forbids companies to make payments to any foreign official to obtain new business or renew existing business. The law also forbids making unauthorized payments through intermediaries. Since the term "foreign official" was considered too broad, the Foreign Trade Act in 1988 clarified the category of persons that would be considered recipients of bribery. Recipients are defined as government officials that may directly or indirectly influence the outcome of a business order. The law excludes payments to facilitate or expedite routine government actions such as obtaining permits and licenses, providing power and water supply, expediting mail services, or providing police protection. In other words, it allows "grease" payments considered essential to maintain the continuity of business as a result of economic rigidities in the local country.

For financial managers, deciding whether payments do or do not constitute bribery will always remain a delicate issue. This issue becomes important when multinationals acquire foreign companies. Multinational managers need to ensure that the FCPA is included in their due diligence when they acquire companies, especially from countries with weak corporate governance. The U.S. Department of Justice will allow a time extension for complying with FCPA due diligence if a company does not have time to conduct such diligence prior to making a bid, especially if there is competition to acquire the target company.[14]

THE FINANCIAL CRISIS OF 2008

The financial crisis of 2008 affected the global financial markets throughout the world. It began with the low interest rate environment fostered by the U.S. Federal Reserve Board (the Fed) after the crash of the Internet bubble in 2001. Financial institutions offered mortgages at very low interest rates, luring individuals to purchase homes in record numbers. As the real estate sector boomed and home prices soared, financial institutions began creating a variety of investment securities such as Mortgage-Backed Securities (MBS) and Collateralized Debt Obligations that used mortgages as collateral. When the Fed began to raise interest rates in June 2004, a trend that continued until 2007, it increased the burden of payments to mortgage holders. This eventually led to record defaults and foreclosures that affected not only the real estate market but also the holders of the newly created financial instruments. Unfortunately, these instruments were not just held by investors in the United States but throughout the world.

The financial crisis impacted companies globally as banks reduced their lending sharply, forcing the governments of many countries to step in and provide emergency credit in the market. Companies that had relied on banks to finance short-term credit found themselves paying higher interest rates. Companies that relied on letters of credit for imports were forced to offer more collateral. Many shipping companies have been hurt by the crisis as a result of banks' reluctance to issue letters of credit. The Baltic Dry Index, a measure of shipping costs for commodities, fell by 11 percent to 2,221 on October 10, 2008, which was 81 percent lower than it was five months earlier, reflecting the impact of the crisis.[15] Pascal Lamy, director-general of the World Trade Organization (WTO), reported that trade finance cost had increased to 300 basis points above LIBOR (London Interbank Offered Rate) for several developing countries, while HSBC—a large international bank—reported that the cost for guaranteeing a letter of credit had doubled since the financial crisis began[16]. Thus, a financial crisis that began in the United States had managed to affect trade patterns throughout the globe.

CHAPTER SUMMARY

This chapter focuses on the different financing issues that face a multinational manager when engaged in overseas business. In particular, an international financial manager has to be knowledgeable in exchange rates and the different foreign institutions and government agencies around the world. This chapter describes the various stages of a multinational as it progresses from a domestic company to a full-fledged multinational with multiple subsidiaries. The various institutions it will face in the course of expanding its overseas business are also explained.

Different international banks are available to a multinational manager. Commercial banks can set up subsidiaries or branches overseas to offer full-fledged services to their clients that have moved overseas. Alternatively, they can establish correspondent or representative offices to provide services indirectly. Financial managers also need to be knowledgeable about the kinds of insurance coverage they must have to protect their shipments and foreign activity abroad. The most difficult insurance to obtain is coverage for political risk. In the United States, political risk insurance is obtained from the Overseas Private Investment Corporation (OPIC), a government agency, and from the Multilateral Investment Government Agency (MIGA), an affiliate of the World Bank.

This chapter also examines the three major stock exchanges in the world and explains the role of American depository receipts, which allow U.S. investors to purchase foreign stocks in U.S. dollars. The growth in the stock markets has allowed companies to raise capital in several countries through the issue of global depository receipts. Companies can also borrow debt through the Eurocurrency markets, where they have the choice of borrowing in the currency of their choice, such as the Eurodollar or the Euroyen.

Finally, financial managers also have to deal with government authorities both in the United States and abroad. In the United States, the four major government agencies that affect international business are the Office of Foreign Assets Control and the Internal Revenue Service (in the Department of the Treasury); the International Trade Administration (in the Department of Commerce); and the U.S. Customs and Border Protection (in the U.S. Department of Homeland Security). The chapter concludes with a discussion of the Foreign Corrupt Practices Act of 1977, which forbids U.S. companies from bribing foreign government officials in order to obtain new business or renew business orders.

KEY CONCEPTS

Subsidiary vs. Branch
International Shipping
Political Risk
American Depository Receipts
Stock Exchanges
Eurodollar

DISCUSSION QUESTIONS

1. What issues face a financial manager when his or her company forays into the world of international business by exporting or importing goods and services?
2. What issues face a financial manager when his or her company establishes a subsidiary overseas?
3. What is the difference between a subsidiary and a branch?
4. What is the difference between a correspondent bank and a representative bank? What purpose do they serve for commercial banks?
5. What are international banking facilities (IBFs) and how do they operate? Why and when do multinationals prefer to use offshore banks?
6. What are the different terms of payments in international transactions? Who bears the risk when the terms require an advance payment? Who bears the risk in an open revolving account?
7. What is the difference between a letter of credit and a documentary collection?
8. What are the three methods of payment, and which is the most popular?
9. What is the difference between the SWIFT number and the routing number? How are the numbers determined?
10. What are the different modes of shipping for overseas customers? What impact do advances in Internet technology have on the mode of transportation?
11. What is political risk and how do companies protect themselves from political risk?

12. What is the Eurocurrency market and why is it advantageous for a company to borrow from this market?
13. What should international financial managers be aware of regarding the various stock exchanges in the world? How can American depository receipts help a multinational financial manager?
14. What four agencies in the United States impact the foreign operations of U.S. companies? What impact can they have on the finances of a company?

APPLICATION CASE: ICELAND 2008—CONCERN FOR EXPORTERS AND IMPORTERS

Exporters and importers have to worry about the creditworthiness of their overseas clients as well as the macroeconomic conditions of the foreign countries in which they engage in business. The case of Iceland in 2008 provides an example of how a country's economic condition can change rapidly to affect the overseas transactions of multinationals. In November 2007, Iceland was voted by the United Nations as one of the best countries to live in the world, surpassing Norway for the first time. With a population of only 313,000, the country boasted a per capita income of $54,100 in 2007 and was ranked ninth by the World Bank. S&P rated its sovereign foreign debt at A+ in 2007. Then, within a span of a year, its currency had devalued by over 100 percent and inflation increased by 10 percent. In October 2008 S&P reduced its ratings to BBB and the country was nearly bankrupt. What caused the country that was booming in 2007 to deteriorate so rapidly in a span of a year?

The problem began as early as 2003, when Iceland experienced strong economic growth. Among the industries they attracted were many aluminum producers to take advantage of the clean and plentiful energy derived from their underground steams. Aluminum and marine life together accounted for over 70 percent of total exports in 2007. Unfortunately, during the boom period, several Icelandic banks began to borrow aggressively from the international debt markets to invest in a variety of projects, including real estate in Britain and retail businesses in Europe. Local Icelanders also borrowed heavily to invest in domestic real estate and increase overall consumption. By 2008, the total debt of banks increased to 11 times the GDP of Iceland, approximately $14 billion. When the property market collapsed in Britain and the economy slowed in Europe, the market value of the assets of banks went into a downward spiral.

The banks not only borrowed overseas from the wholesale market but also from small savers, primarily from Britain. Icesave, a subsidiary of the second largest bank in Iceland, Landsbanki, became one of the fastest growing Internet banks in Northern Europe through its aggressive selling tactics. By offering attractive interest rates, it managed to draw over 300,000 small savers, primarily from Britain, and deposits grew to over $7.5 billion. When the Icelandic government announced on October 7, 2008, that it was putting Landsbanki into receivership because of its deteriorating balance sheet, the extent of the country's banking problem was revealed. Eventually, the government was forced to take over the remaining two large banks in Iceland, Kaupthing and Glitnir. The country was also forced to borrow from the IMF and other countries to prevent it from defaulting on its debt obligations.

Among the contentious issues during the crisis was the obligation of the Icelandic government to deposit holders of Landsbanki's Internet subsidiary bank, Icesave, in Britain. The Financial Services Compensation Scheme, an agency of the British government, normally guaranteed £50,000 of deposits, of which the first £16,317 would have had to come from the Icelandic government. Unfortunately, the Icelandic guarantee fund only had £88 million in total to cover over £13 billion in deposits.

A furor erupted when the Icelandic government announced it would fully repay depositors in Iceland but only the minimum amount of €16,317 to its overseas depositors. The British government took the unprecedented step of freezing Landsbanki's assets in Britain under a provision in a newly created antiterrorism law. After some acrimonious exchanges, the British government agreed to lend Iceland the sum of £3 billion, so the country could pay off the minimum €16,317 owed to British depositors. The British government also made an exception and allowed the Financial Services Compensation Scheme to fully repay all deposits held at Icesave. Unfortunately, British depositors who saved at offshore banks of Landsbanki, primarily in the Isle of Man and Channel Islands, were not included in the bailout. Approximately 2,000 depositors are expected to receive only 30 percent of their savings.

Many Icelandic importers were also affected because overseas banks refused to accept letters of credit from their banks. Even if importers were willing to pay cash, they could not find dealers to exchange their currencies because nobody wanted to hold Icelandic krona as it continued to depreciate during the crisis. Multinationals and even local governments in Britain found that their deposits held in the foreign subsidiaries of Icelandic banks remained frozen while the country searched desperately for loans.

QUESTIONS

1. What caused Icelandic banks to default in 2008?
2. What lessons does the Icelandic crisis teach multinational financial managers who have to deposit money throughout the year in several different countries?

14 International Accounting

LEARNING OBJECTIVES

- To recognize the challenges posed to multinational corporations when they integrate their overseas businesses
- To understand how exchange rates affect the valuation of a company's overseas assets and liabilities
- To appreciate the effort involved in designing a global accounting standard
- To recognize the importance of instituting strong accounting standards by studying some recent corporate scandals
- To understand the various taxes faced by multinational corporations when they undertake overseas business

All companies prepare financial statements to keep track of their business activities and the inflow and outflow of cash. Financial statements are used internally to evaluate and improve business decisions. They allow management to identify costs and revenues in detail and fine-tune the company's operations. If the company is a publicly traded entity, financial statements assist shareholders and creditors in evaluating the firm's performance. Finally, financial statements are prepared to assess the company's tax liabilities.

The methods and formats used to prepare financial statements are determined by the accounting standards board of each country. The standards vary from country to country because they are based on each nation's history of commercial activities, its political system, and its cultural and social nuances.

When a company goes global, the accounting method and the preparation of financial statements must address two additional issues:

1. Convert (or translate, in accounting terminology) the financial statements from one currency to another, and
2. Reconcile the different accounting standards and formats between the two countries.

The field of international accounting has grown steadily more complex over the years, partly due to the heavy increases in trade and foreign investments and partly due to firms engaging in creative and innovative forms of cross-border partnerships. International accountants require significantly more expertise than their domestic counterparts because they need to have a strong background and knowledge of the local customs and business culture of the countries in which their firms do business. The accounting rules of most countries have adapted over hundreds of years. Culture, more than geographic proximity, seems to play an important role in the development of accounting standards. Take, for example, the Anglo-Saxon countries of the United Kingdom, the United States, Australia, and New Zealand. Even though the countries are geographically far-flung, their accounting standards have more in common with one another than they do with those of continental Europe or Canada.

Accounting rules are complex not only for companies but also for individuals working in different countries, such as global executives and staff. Most companies prefer to send their own executives and staff to work at their overseas subsidiaries. A foreign executive or staff member, termed an expatriate, usually earns income that falls under the jurisdiction of two or more taxing authorities. An executive of a Dutch company may be transferred in the middle of the year from a subsidiary in Accra, Ghana, to another in Sydney, Australia. He or she may have to files taxes in three countries for that year: the Netherlands, Ghana, and Australia. An international accountant will have to determine how to apportion the income, deductions, and exemptions among the three countries. This will depend on the accounting standards of the three countries. Accountants specializing in expatriate personal taxes have to be knowledgeable in the accounting laws of several countries and must be able to reconcile them in a manner that satisfies the various taxing authorities.

In this chapter we ignore personal taxes and focus only on accounting issues as they relate to multinational corporations. For our purposes, the multinational parent company is assumed to be located in the United States (unless otherwise specified) and has subsidiaries located in several countries that manufacture goods and provide services. As noted in earlier chapters, a subsidiary is a fully incorporated company located in another country. It may or may not be 100 percent owned, but we assume the parent has managerial control over its activities.

BASICS OF INTERNATIONAL ACCOUNTING

International accounting differs from domestic accounting primarily in two areas: (1) it has to take into account the impact of exchange rates, and (2) it has to reconcile the different formats used in different countries.

RECORDING FOREIGN EXCHANGE TRANSACTIONS

We begin with an introduction on how firms record foreign exchange transactions, both for the purchase and sale of goods and services. The procedure applies to all companies, whether they are domestic companies or multinationals with multiple subsidiaries. This is because all transactions at the end of the year are recorded, consolidated, and reconciled in the home country, and the rules for recording are based on domestic accounting standards.

When a company places an order to sell or purchase a good from another country, it has the option of invoicing the bill in the local currency or in the foreign currency.

If it is invoiced in the local currency, the transaction is no different than a domestic transaction. However, if the bill is invoiced in a foreign currency, it is still necessary to record the transaction in the home currency after converting it from the foreign currency. If there is a time lag between the order date and payment date, the company will have to account for foreign exchange differences when the payment is settled.

Assume a U.S. company imports A$1 million worth of merchandise from an Australian company, to be paid in 90 days. By U.S. generally accepted accounting principles (GAAP), the order will be recorded in U.S. dollars on the date of the order. The company will have to first convert the value of the order from Australian dollars to U.S. dollars. That amount depends on the prevailing exchange rate on the order date.

Assume the exchange rate on the order date is A$1.25/US$1. The U.S. company will record the order as A$1,000,000/US$1.25 = US$800,000, and this amount will be credited to accounts payable.

The next stage is to record the payment 90 days later. Assume the exchange rate on the date of payment is A$1/US$1. The U.S. company will need US$1,000,000 to purchase A$1,000,000, an increase of US$200,000 from the date of order. The accounting rules in the United States require a payment of US$800,000 be recorded to offset the US$800,000 in accounts payable. Separately, the company will have to record US$200,000 as an exchange loss. If the exchange rate was A$1.50/US$1 on the date of payment, the U.S. company needs only US$666,666.67 to make the payment of A$1,000,000. The company will continue to record a payment of $800,000 to offset the accounts payable but will separately record an exchange gain of US$133,333.33.

An alternative approach is to record a foreign sale or purchase in one transaction by waiting for the payment to be completed. The company can then record the activity based on the actual value of the payment. Although this one-step procedure is simpler than the two-step procedure described above, it does have one drawback. If a company is engaged in multiple foreign sales and purchases, it will find itself with many transactions valued at different exchange rates. This becomes problematic when the company has to consolidate transactions at the end of each month, quarter, or year.

The two-step procedure also has an advantage in that it provides a clear picture of whether the company's profits or losses are the result of exchange-rate movements. If they are due to exchange-rate changes, management is better off spending time managing exchange-rate risks. Accounting rules in most countries require companies to follow the two-step procedure when recording overseas sales and purchases.

BALANCE SHEET

A company's balance sheet provides information about its total assets and liabilities. If a company has several subsidiaries, the assets and liabilities of the various subsidiaries have to be consolidated at the end of the fiscal year into the parent's balance sheet. Most countries use December 31 as the year-end closing of their books. However, this date is not uniform across the globe. Some countries use March 31, while others use June 30 as their year-ends. Although year-ends are usually not mandated by country, it is normal for companies to choose dates that are common across firms in their industry. Table 14.1 (p. 358) provides the year-ends that are popular in most countries.

RECORDING TRANSLATION GAINS OR LOSSES

For a company with overseas subsidiaries, the act of consolidation becomes problematic as a result of fluctuations in exchange rates. Although the mechanics of converting or translating overseas assets and liabilities to U.S. dollars is an easy process, the impact on the financial performance of the overall firm is not clear. An example (below) highlights the issue.

Assume that Company A is a parent company located in the United States and Company B is its subsidiary located in the United Kingdom. Both parent and subsidiary are 100 percent equity financed, that is, the firms have no debt, and the spot exchange rate is US$2/£1. The balance sheets of both companies are shown below.

Company A (parent)		Company B (subsidiary)	
Assets	Equity	Assets	Equity
US$100 million	US$100 million	£50 million	£50 million
In dollars, the balance sheet of Company B will be converted at the spot exchange rate of US$2.00/£1.		US$100 million	US$100 million

The consolidated balance sheet of the parent and subsidiary will be:

Consolidated AB	
Assets	Equity
US$200 million	US$200 million

Assume that the exchange rate changes overnight from US$2/£1 to US$1.50/£1. What impact does it have on the consolidated balance sheet? First, the value of the assets and equity of the overseas subsidiary will decrease to US$75 million instead of US$100 million.

As a result, the consolidated balance sheet of the parent and subsidiary will now be:

Consolidated AB	
Assets	Equity
US$175 million	US$175 million

What does this decline in the value of the overseas assets mean to the parent company? Is it a loss that affects shareholders of the parent company? The answer depends on whether the parent company intends to sell or liquidate the subsidiary. If it plans to sell the subsidiary, then it is a real loss to the parent. If it intends to continue the firm's operations, it may not be a real loss. The exchange rate could go back to US$2/£1 the following period, and the value of the subsidiary will go back up to US$100 million. Accounting bodies used to treat such changes as real gains or losses. Today they are treated as unrealized gains and losses, as explained in the next section.

Table 14.1

Fiscal Year-ends in Selected Countries

Country	Year-end	Comments
New Zealand	March 31	Public companies use June 30 to match Australia
Japan	March 31	
India	March 31	
Australia	June 30	Mandatory
United States	December 31	
Europe	December 31	
China	December 31	For companies with foreign investments
United Kingdom	Mixed	Based on month of setup, majority use December 31

CURRENCY TRANSLATION

In the United States, the standards for financial accounting and reporting are determined by the Financial Accounting Standard Boards (FASB), an independent organization that represents the industry and the public.[1] The Securities and Exchange Commission (SEC), which regulates all publicly traded companies in the United States, has usually accepted the guidelines established by the FASB. In the United Kingdom, the Accounting Standards Board (ASB) of the Financial Reporting Council (FRC) took over the tasks from the Accounting Standards Committee in 1990, and sets the standards for UK companies.[2] Similarly, other countries have their own accounting standards boards that define the reporting standards for companies operating within their jurisdictions.[3]

For American companies with international operations, the change in the value of the asset or liability of a subsidiary used to be treated as a real gain or loss under FASB #8. In the earlier example, the company would have had to report a real loss of US$25 million the year when the exchange rate moved to US$1.50/£1. If in the following year the exchange rate moved back to US$2/£1, the company would report a real gain of US$25 million.

A number of companies complained that this rule was not only unfair but it did not make economic sense. If a business is an ongoing entity and the overall business operations are unaffected by exchange-rate changes, it is inappropriate to claim them as real losses or gains. Exchange-rate volatility rarely affects the day-to-day operations of most companies.

After several hearings, FASB #8 was replaced by FASB #52, which allowed companies to record changes in the balance sheet of their subsidiaries as unrealized losses or gains. They are recorded as real gains or losses only when the subsidiary is sold. The unrealized losses and gains are instead adjusted in a separate equity account. Outside investors can see the amount of unrealized losses or gains by examining the "Adjustments for Currency Translation" in the equity account.

Many countries had laws similar to FASB #8 but have now changed them to allow companies to record the gains and losses as unrealized on their balance sheets. The new global accounting standards, known as the International Financial Reporting Standards (IFRS), also consider gains and losses related to exchange-rate changes as unrealized till the company is sold.

CHOICE OF EXCHANGE RATE: CURRENT VS. TEMPORAL

Another issue related to the translation of the income statement and balance sheet of a subsidiary is whether market or historical exchange rates should be used. Most companies acquire assets and liabilities at different dates. Assume that a U.S. company purchased equipment for 1 million reals at the beginning of the year in Brazil, when the exchange rate was 2 reals/US$1. In dollars, the value of the purchase was US$500,000. At the end of the year, assume the exchange rate comes down to 1.25 reals/US$1 (appreciation of the Brazilian real). The value of the asset using this exchange rate became US$800,000. Should the assets be translated at the old or new rate? Does the parent company have the right to claim that it made an instant US$300,000 gain, or should it translate the value of the asset at the rate in effect at the time of the purchase?

The accounting standards have generally used either of the following two methods.

Current Method

Under the current method, all assets and liabilities are translated at the exchange rates on the date of translation. For the above example, the parent will value the assets at US$800,000 at year-end. One problem with this approach is that it may be incompatible with the parent company's balance sheet because the parent company is more than likely to value its assets at historical cost. Most accounting standards allow domestic assets and liabilities to be translated at historical costs. It is too cumbersome for a domestic company to change the value of its assets every year.

Assume that a company purchases a car valued at US$10,000 and plans to use it for five years. One way of reporting the value of its assets each year is to depreciate it by US$2,000 per year over five years. The value of the car will be US$8,000 at the end of year one, US$6,000 at the end of year two, and so on. At the end of year five, the book value of the car will be zero. This assumes that the historical price of US$10,000 remains the same over the five years. If the current method is used, the company must revalue the car and report the market value of the car at the end of each year—a cumbersome process.

Temporal Method

Under the temporal method, monetary accounts such as cash, accounts receivables, and debt are translated at the current exchange rate. Longer-term assets such as plant and equipment are translated at historical rates. Long-term assets are translated at historical rates, making the process both compatible to domestic accounting standards as well as less cumbersome.

The new IFRS has also adopted the temporal approach. Before we examine the IFRS, a brief history of the evolution of accounting standards is discussed.

HISTORY OF ACCOUNTING

It is now generally accepted that the double-entry system of bookkeeping was used extensively by the Italians in Genoa around 1400 C.E. A few scholars have claimed

Table 14.2

The "Big Four": Revenues and Number of Employees

Company	Revenues	Date	Employees	Countries/Offices
PricewaterhouseCoopers	US$25.2 billion	June 30, 2007	146,000	150 countries
Deloitte Touche Tohmatsu	US$23.1 billion	May 31, 2007	150,000	142 countries
Ernst and Young	US$21.1 billion	2007	130,000	140 offices
KPMG	US$19.81 billion	September 30, 2007	146,000	146 countries

that the double-entry system was developed even earlier. For example, B.M. Lall Nigam asserts that the double-entry system existed in India thousands of years earlier.[4] This claim is not accepted universally and has been refuted by several new studies.[5] Similarly, Omar Abdullah Zaid argues that Muslim societies engaged in double-entry bookkeeping systems well before the Italians, although clear evidence is still lacking.[6] The first major book credited to the description of double-entry bookkeeping is Luca Pacioli's *Summa de Arithmetica, Geometria, Proportioni et Proportionalita* in 1494 C.E.

The earliest book published in England that refers to accountants and bookkeeping is by Hugh Oldcastle: "A Profitable Treatyce Called the Instrument or Boke to Learn to Know the Good Order of the Keepying of the Famouse Reconynge Called in Latyn, Dare and Habdare, and in English, Debitor and Creditor." In Modern English it is translated as "A Profitable Treatise Called the Instrument or Book to Learn to Know the Good Order of the Keeping of the Famous Reconciliation called in Latin, Dare and Habdare, and in English, Debtor and Creditor."

The oldest continuously functioning accounting firm can be traced to Josiah Wade in 1780 in Bristol, England, who specialized in auditing the accounting of merchants. The company became Tribe, Clark and Company in 1871 and finally merged with Deloitte in 1969.[7]

In 1989, there were eight large accounting firms, but this number has gradually been reduced to four, which today are referred to as the "Big Four": PricewaterhouseCoopers, Deloitte Touche Tohmatsu, Ernst and Young, and KPMG. Three of the "Big Eight" merged, while the fourth, Arthur Anderson, was disbanded as a result of a major accounting scandal in 2002 involving an energy company, Enron, and will be discussed later. The remaining four firms are truly global firms because they operate in nearly all countries, mostly through local affiliates. Their revenues and total number of employees for 2007 are listed in Table 14.2.

TOWARD A GLOBAL ACCOUNTING SYSTEM

INTERNATIONAL ACCOUNTING STANDARDS BOARD

As discussed previously, operating a business in another country requires the integration of the local accounting system. This can be a cumbersome, unwieldy, and sometimes impossible process. The recent spurt in globalization of commerce and trade has forced many countries to seriously coordinate their accounting systems and to cooperate with other governing bodies. The work toward integrating global accounting standards began as early as June 1973, when the International Accounting Standards Committee (IASC) was formed. Its mission was to create international standards that are "capable of rapid acceptance and implementation world-wide."[8]

Unfortunately, the IASC struggled for many years to deal with the intransigence of various accounting boards to relinquish their authority to a global body. In the end, globalization has forced the issue to the forefront, and the new global standards are finally being adopted through the offices of the International Accounting Standards Board (IASB), an independent, privately funded accounting-standard setter based in London. Its parent organization is the International Accounting Standards Committee Foundation, formed in March 2001 and incorporated in Delaware.

The big boost for the adoption of IFRS came from the European Union, when it announced on June 2, 2002, that all companies within its jurisdiction would have to adopt IFRS as of January 1, 2005. In September 2002, a further boost was given when the U.S. FASB and IASB announced the Norwalk Agreement, whereby they pledged their best efforts to reconcile the two standards and reach common platforms. Today, more than 100 countries either have adopted IFRS or are changing their local standards to be compatible with IFRS standards. The future for IFRS seems very promising and is coming at an appropriate time, as cross-border business is expected to continue its rapid growth for the foreseeable future.

ACCOUNTING SCANDALS

The push for a common accounting standard has been partly spurred by a number of corporate scandals at the turn of this century. Top-rated companies such as Enron, Parmalat, WorldCom, Royal Ahold, Computer Associates, and Tyco International, to name a few, were caught in what have been termed "creative accounting" manipulations. These events have cast doubt on the ability of accounting firms to certify the books of corporations, especially those of multinationals. The lack of coordination among various accounting boards may have also contributed to some of the abuses. We begin with a review of some of the more notable scandals.

Enron

Enron started as the Northern Natural Gas Company and after a series of mergers became a multifaceted energy company in 2001 with over 20,000 employees. It specialized in electricity and gas transmission, pipelines, power plants, refineries, and energy trading. In August 2000, Enron's stock was trading at $90, and it was one of the most admired companies among investors. Fortune magazine named it the "most innovative company" six years in a row, while *CEO* magazine named its board one of the top five in the country. Unfortunately, very few analysts bothered to examine in detail the dramatic increases in reported revenues, from $40 billion in 1999 to more than $100 billion in 2000.[9] When they began to scrutinize them in earnest in early 2001, it became apparent that the company was not honest in their claims. By

December 2, 2001, the company had declared bankruptcy, leaving all its employees without jobs and with losses on their retirement portfolios. In addition, investors in Enron lost billions of dollars.

When the truth emerged, it showed a company that was engaged in the classic fraud of overstating revenues and profits and understating losses. In the case of Enron, the company also managed to show an amazingly upbeat and positive face to the public. In reality, many officers were involved in creating shell companies to hide their bad debts and loss-making units.

An important question that always arises in cases of corporate fraud is the role of accounting firms. Did Arthur Anderson, then one of the Big Five accounting firms, know of these phony accounts set up by Enron? After an investigation, several Arthur Anderson employees were indicted for destroying documents. On June 15, 2002, the company itself was indicted for obstruction of justice related to the shredding of the documents. This indictment was overturned by the U.S. Supreme Court in 2005, but by then the damage had been done and the company had only 200 employees left. The original Big Eight had been reduced to the Big Four. The question of whether the accounting firm was complicit in the fraud was never established.

The Enron episode is still considered one of the most notable accounting scandals for this period, although there were many that followed with even greater losses. One reason for its prominence is the high-profile approach used by management to dazzle and woo the media and investors, even when they knew their revenues were far below their claims. A numbers of executives were convicted, including CEO Jeffrey Skilling, sentenced to 25 years in prison, and CFO Andrew Fastow, sentenced to six years in prison. The case also gained notoriety because it dragged a major accounting company down with it. Finally, the company's demise was instrumental in Congress passing the Sarbanes-Oxley Act (commonly termed SOX), which significantly tightened corporate governance standards in the United States. The SOX has also generated much criticism because some if its provisions are deemed too burdensome by corporate executives.

WorldCom

An equally large scandal that erupted soon after the Enron episode was the declaration of bankruptcy by WorldCom on July 21, 2002, with assets of $107 billion. The company had accumulated a total debt of $41 billion. WorldCom was founded by Bernie Ebbers in 1983 as LDDS, a provider of long-distance telephone and data services. In 1998, Ebbers acquired MCI for $37 billion, making it the second largest telephone operator in the company. In 2000, Ebbers tried to take over another large long-distance phone company, Sprint, and failed. Although the telecommunications industry was entering one of its most competitive periods, the company continued to report significant increases in revenues, $7.6 billion in 1998, $17.6 billion in 1998, and $35.9 billion in 1999. Neither investors nor the board of directors took the time to examine WorldCom's claims of revenue growth.

It was later revealed that WorldCom had also engaged in the traditional fraud of overstating revenues and understating expenses. In this case, the fraud was discovered in 2002 by the company's internal auditors. When the accounts were rectified, the discrepancy in revenues was estimated at $3.8 billion, and the assets were overstated by $11 billion. Bernie Ebbers was convicted in July 2005 and sentenced to 25 years in prison for accounting fraud along with several other executives.

Parmalat

The accounting scandals of the late 1990s and early 2000s were taking place not only in the United States but also across the globe. The boom in the U.S. stock market of the 1980s led to massive investments in Europe and Asia. In response, financial markets were liberalized in many countries, and firms worldwide were engaging in significant expansions and mergers and acquisitions. It was inevitable that some companies would also end up committing fraud.

In Europe, the biggest scandal took place at Parmalat, a large food company from Italy, which was ranked fourth in Europe at that time. Parmalat's troubles began in 1999, when the company went on an acquisition spree in North and South America; some of these purchases turned out to be less-than-profitable ventures. In addition, founder and CEO Calisto Tanzi bought the local soccer club, Parma, and also created Parmatour, a tourism company, both of which ran into heavy losses. With the aid of several major international banks, Parmalat set up several shell companies to engage in risky derivatives trading and issue bonds using fake collateral as guarantees; ultimately, Parma released false financial statements.

On December 9, 2003, the company temporarily defaulted on a US$150 million bond, which sent the first signal to the market that something was amiss. This was followed by an announcement on December 15 by Bank of America that the company did not hold liquid assets worth US$3.9 billion, as claimed by Parmalat.[10] The price of its stock immediately tumbled, and investors' estimated loss after the dust settled was approximately €18 billion. Once again, it was the same fraudulent scheme of overstating revenues, understating costs, and falsifying documents while keeping a positive public face.

In the case of Parmalat, the company still exists and has now recovered from liquidation. However, the civil cases that followed the scandal continue today (2008) because Parmalat countersued the banks. The company claims that the banks were equally involved in helping them set up the false accounts. In some instances, the banks have been found guilty of complicity.

Several more scandals were to follow, and the period between 1997 and 2005 may be recorded as one of the worst in recent corporate history, with cases including Royal Ahold (2003), Tyco International (2002), and more recently AIG (2005). It is and will continue to be difficult to detect fraud, especially when committed by insiders. If insiders choose to engage in creative accounting, they can evade the scrutiny of both the accountants and the analysts who follow their stocks. When a company has subsidiaries overseas, it makes it even more complicated to detect fraud.

Will the adoption of the IFRS reduce this problem? It is interesting to note that for most of the fraud cases described above, managers had to create overseas shell companies to hide their losses. IFRS is expected to make it simpler to integrate the various overseas units and make it more transparent. Perhaps this is the first step in curtailing global fraudulent activities.

How Different Are the IFRS and GAAP?

The accounting standards in each country can have a big impact on the way financial figures are reported. For example, on May 2, 2008, United Microelectronics Corporation (UMC) from Taiwan announced that it had to restate its net profits of T$16.96 billion, using Taiwanese accounting standards, to a loss of T$9.06 billion (or US$304 million) when using U.S. GAAP accounting standards.[11]

Similarly, OmniVision, based in Sunnyvale, California, makers of imaging sensors, provided two sets of statements for the year 2007. Net income using U.S. GAAP for the fourth quarter of 2007 was US$9.1 million. However, when non-GAAP methodology was used, the reported net income for the fourth quarter of 2007 was US$14.3 million.[12]

A study by Citigroup found that when comparing 73 European companies that used both U.S. GAAP and IFRS standards, 82 percent using IFRS had higher net income and 70 percent had lower book values, implying a higher return on equity.[13] Profits under IFRS were on average 23 percent higher for the sampled companies, with a median of 6 percent higher than under U.S. GAAP accounting. For example, Bayer, a major German chemical company, saw its profits under IFRS go up by 525 percent compared to its profits under U.S. GAAP. Similarly, a major UK bank, Lloyds TSB, reported profits that were 54.4 percent higher when it used IFRS than when it used U.S. GAAP.

In the Citigroup study, the discrepancies arose because of differences in the treatment of taxes (60 companies), pensions (55 companies), goodwill and intangible assets (53 companies), and financial instruments (40 companies). The data for the study were for the periods 2005 and 2006.

The major difference between the two standards can be summarized as follows: IFRS is more principles based, while U.S. GAAP is more rules based. A principles-based approach is more conceptual in that it expects companies to provide reliable and accurate reports based on specific objectives and intent of the disclosure. The methods to achieve the objectives can vary, and hence different rules can be applied. In a rules-based approach, although the objectives may be the same, the procedures and methodology are rigidly defined. A problem with such an approach is that companies can always find loopholes enabling them to follow the rules but not meet the intended objective.

Even FASB usually begins as a principles-based system. The problem occurs when the FASB issues guidelines and provides examples on how to treat each principle or objective. Due to litigation worries, U.S. accountants request numerous clarifications, and as a result, the FASB ends up issuing more guidelines, pronouncements, and clarifications, making it more like a rules-based approach.[14]

For example, take the case of royalty payments sent from subsidiaries to their parent companies. Under a new bilateral treaty agreed to on December 28, 2007, between the United States and Finland, cross-border royalty payments are no longer subject to withholding taxes. Withholding taxes are additional taxes imposed by countries when subsidiaries repatriate money to their parent companies. Both countries still charge 5 percent withholding tax on any dividend income sent back to the parent, as long as the parent has less than 80 percent ownership. With 80 percent ownership or above, there are no withholding taxes on dividend payments.

A problem with the above taxation structure is that subsidiaries may be tempted to send more money as royalties rather than as dividends. In the rules-based approach used by U.S. GAAP, it is easier to use this loophole than in the principles-based approach used by IFRS.

Appendix 14.1 (see pp. 377–379) lists some of the differences between IFRS and U.S. GAAP, as published by PricewaterhouseCoopers in October 2007. It shows that several of the principles are compatible with existing rules-based guidelines, although there is still much work required for full convergence between the two systems.

TRANSITION TO IFRS

More than 100 countries have already made plans to move toward the IFRS, and there is optimism that a single global accounting standard can be achieved within the next decade. With the agreement by the United States to conform to IFRS, a major stumbling block has been removed. Following are examples of some other countries that are taking steps to implement IFRS directly or indirectly.

China

In 2007, China took a big step in its evolution of modernizing its financial markets by announcing a new set of accounting standards. For China, this is a significant transition. Until 1993, it had been using the old Soviet-style centrally planned accounting system. Then it moved on to a very rules-based approach. The new standards, termed the Accounting Standards for Business Enterprises, are in many ways similar to the principles-based approach of the IFRS. These new standards will mean a bigger change for the domestic companies in China. Although surveys have found that Chinese companies are looking forward to these new standards, it will still be challenging for a large country such as China to move away from the old and rigid accounting mind-set. The biggest change will be in reporting fair or market values for assets. This will be very difficult because most of China's industries still lack free market prices to make effective comparisons.[15]

India

In March 2007, the Institute of Chartered Accountants of India announced the convergence of Indian accounting standards to IFRS by April 1, 2010. In the beginning, the standards will be adopted by listed companies and other large entities, including banking and insurance firms. Thereafter, separate guidelines will be issued for small and medium-sized enterprises, with attempts to follow the principles of the IFRS as closely as possible.

This news was well received by many of the Indian companies that were listed on overseas stock markets, particularly in the United States and Europe. The European Union is currently investigating whether the Indian accounting standards are comparable to the IFRS, since the EU requires their own companies to adopt IFRS standards. There are currently about 80 Indian companies listed in the European markets. If the EU finds there is no likelihood of convergence taking place between the Indian accounting standards and IFRS before 2011, then all Indian companies listed in Europe will be mandated to adopt IFRS as of 2009.[16]

Russia

Russia, like China, had to dramatically change its accounting standards as it moved from a centrally planned economy to a free and open market system. In the late 1990s, the country was somewhat in a chaos as it moved to deregulate prices and sell many of its government-owned entities. The Russian Duma (or parliament; duma is the Russian word for "deliberation") passed a bill in 1997 approving the transition to a new accounting system that was based on the principles of the IFRS. It was expected to be adopted by most of the country's large enterprises. Unfortunately, however, Russia experienced a ruble crisis in 1998, when investors sold the Russian currency in a panic. The value of the ruble plummeted from R6/US$1 in August to about R22/US$1 by the end of December. It was apparent that the transition to a free market economy was not going to be successful unless major structural reforms took place in the corporate and legal environment, with enhanced corporate governance and accounting standards.

The crisis forced the Duma to attempt on many occasions to make IFRS mandatory for Russian firms. As of 2008, this change had not yet been implemented. In the meantime, Russian accounting standards have been modified to meet the principles of IFRS. A December 2007 survey by the European Union of more than 2,300 accounting professionals in Russia yielded the following results[17]:

1. Sixteen percent of the respondents stated that their company used IFRS. A majority of the firms were in the financial sector. Excluding firms in the financial sector, the percentage was not much lower: 12 percent.
2. Thirty-two percent of the organizations reported using accounting standards that are in compliance with IFRS, suggesting the transition is slowly but surely taking place.
3. Sixty-seven percent of those using IFRS said it was beneficial, while 20 percent said it was not beneficial.
4. Thirty-two percent responded that the major barrier to the implementation of IFRS is lack of a mandate by the government requiring firms to adopt it.
5. However, nearly 75 percent expect that most firms will be reporting according to IFRS standards by 2010.

The three countries profiled above illustrate the slow but steady acceptance of IFRS. Most countries are either adopting IFRS fully or modifying their accounting standards to comply with its principles. Clearly, there are benefits associated with

Table 14.3

Benefits Countries Would Gain by Adopting IFRS

Benefits for Companies
- Improved management information for decision making
- Better access to capital, including from foreign sources
- Reduced cost of capital
- Ease of using one consistent reporting standard in subsidiaries from different countries
- Facilitated mergers and acquisitions
- Enhanced competitiveness

Benefits for Investors
- Better information for decision making
- More confidence in the information presented
- Better understanding of risk and return
- Companies can be compared to a peer group of companies

Benefits for Policy Makers
- Strengthened and more effective Russian [and emerging market countries] capital market
- Better access to the global capital markets
- Promotion of cross-border investment

Benefits for National Regulatory Bodies
- Improved regulatory oversight and enforcement
- A higher standard of financial disclosure
- Better information for market participants to underpin disclosure-based regulation
- Better ability to attract and monitor listings by foreign companies

Benefits for Other Stakeholders
- Greater credibility and improved economic prospects for the accounting profession
- Enhanced transparency of companies through better reporting
- Better reporting and information on new and different aspects of the business

Source: Directorate for Financial and Enterprise Affairs, OECD, "Implementing International Financial Reporting Standards (IFRS) in Russia: The Russian Corporate Governance Roundtable," May 2005. Available at http://www.oecd.org/document/22/0,3343,fr_2649_34795_35686358_1_1_1_1,00.html (accessed July 23, 2008).

the establishment of a single accounting standard globally. The Organisation for Economic Co-operation and Development (OECD), an influential public group in Europe comprised of 30 country representatives, released a list of benefits a country like Russia would gain by adopting IFRS. This list, as shown in Table 14.3, can be extended to firms in all countries, especially those in emerging markets.

INTERNATIONAL ACCOUNTING AND TAXES

Multinationals are faced with the daunting problem of managing cash flows between subsidiaries and between a parent and a subsidiary. Taxes play an important role in international accounting since the transfer of cash flows usually overlaps two, if not more, taxing authorities. The taxation of cash flows between countries is typically governed by bilateral treaties between countries. These treaties enable multinationals to reduce some of the disparities in the taxing systems between countries.

There are two kinds of direct taxes that affect business operating across borders: corporate taxes and withholding taxes. Another is the indirect tax, which can also have an impact on cash flows across borders, and all three taxes are discussed next.

CORPORATE TAXES

With the exception of a few tax-haven countries such as the Cayman Islands or Bahrain, most countries impose corporate taxes on companies' profits, whether they are domestic or foreign owned. As long as business is being conducted in a country, the taxing authority reserves its right to impose taxes on profits generated by the firm. The issue for most multinationals is not the taxes they have to pay in the foreign country; the issue is whether the income will be taxed again when the profits are repatriated back to the home country, a phenomenon known as double taxation.

Corporations do not conduct business overseas for tax benefits alone. They have to consider various other factors including transportation, the level of skilled workers in the host country, and availability of materials, among others. Whenever a company conducts business overseas, there is an impact on the domestic economy, most notably a loss in jobs. Home-country governments cannot change the conditions in foreign countries that draw companies overseas (the low wages, favorable tax rates, and lower labor standards); however, they do have the ability to tax the profits that will eventually be repatriated back to the home country.

By and large, most countries have avoided the double taxation of profits from companies that conduct business overseas. Still, many countries have rules that ensure companies that have gone abroad will pay taxes at least equal to those of their domestic counterparts. Other countries have taken a more liberal approach and do not tax any of the profits that are repatriated to the home country.

No Additional Taxes

The approach in which no additional taxes are levied on repatriated corporate profits recognizes that capital should flow to regions where owners can maximize their returns. Different tax rates in another country should not be a factor in taxing a company's profits. This approach accepts the right of regions to use taxes as incentives for businesses. Just as the different states in the United States have different tax rates, some of which are enacted deliberately to attract businesses, national borders should not be a factor when locating plants or services abroad.

Playing-Field Taxes

The approach known as "playing-field taxes" adopts the stance that all businesses in a country, whether they operate domestically or overseas, should face the same level of minimum taxation. If a business chooses to go overseas to a lower tax environment, its profits will be subject to additional taxes up to the amount that would be paid by their domestic counterparts. If the business pays more taxes overseas than its domestic counterparts, it should receive a tax credit when its profits are repatriated to the home country. This approach essentially states that location is not a relevant factor; tax rates should be uniform.

The United States taxes the dividends of companies that have gone overseas on the principle of leveling the playing field. The European Union had similar taxation laws but 10 years ago abolished the tax equalization law. Its corporations are now allowed to repatriate dividends free of income tax. Some multinationals have complained that this gives the European companies an advantage over U.S. companies in locating their plants overseas. The United States taxes dividends only when they are actually repatriated to the United States. If a U.S. corporation chooses to leave its money overseas in the form of retained earnings, they will not be subject to additional U.S. taxes.

WITHHOLDING TAXES

Whenever a company repatriates income to its home country, the foreign country usually imposes an additional tax, termed the "withholding tax." The income may consist of the following:

1. Dividends, which are profits distributed to the shareholders. In the case of multinationals, the dividends are sent back to cover the original investment made by the parent company.
2. Interest income, usually paid for loans and bonds. In the case of multinationals, the interest is for loans made by the parent to their subsidiaries.
3. Royalties, which are payments made by subsidiaries to their parent for use of a particular technology or process that is owned by the parent company.

Withholding tax rates are usually determined by bilateral treaties signed between countries. Over the years, withholding taxes have been reduced among countries. For example, the United States does not levy any withholding taxes on the interest income of foreign investors, but it continues to impose withholding taxes on royalties and dividends. On March 13, 2003, the U.S. Senate ratified a treaty with Australia that agreed to the following:

- A zero rate of dividend withholding tax on dividends paid to an eligible entity holding 80 percent or more of the voting shares
- A 5 percent rate of dividend withholding tax on dividends paid to an eligible entity holding at least 10 percent of the voting shares
- Interest withholding tax would not be levied on interest paid to eligible financial institutions
- The withholding tax rate on royalties would be reduced from 10 percent to 5 percent

EXAMPLE OF IMPACT OF CORPORATE AND WITHHOLDING TAX

Assume that a company has a subsidiary in Brazil and at the end of the year it reports the following profits in Brazilian reals. It will repatriate all the profits to the parent company. Assume that the corporate tax rate in Brazil is 20 percent and the withholding tax is 5 percent.

Sales	10,000 reals
Variable cost	4,000 reals
Profits before taxes	6,000 reals
Taxes of 20 percent	1,200 reals
Profits after taxes	4,800 reals
Withholding tax of 5 percent	240 reals
Net profits repatriated to parent	4,560 reals

How much tax will have to be paid by the parent company when it receives the 4,560 reals? This will depend on the whether the home country exempts overseas remittances from taxes or whether it applies taxes to level the playing field with domestic companies.

If a Country Requires No Additional Taxes

In this case, the amount available to shareholders of the parent company is the full amount of 4,560 reals. If the parent company is located in an EU country and the exchange rate is 3 reals/€1, the amount available on the date of payment is €1,520.

If a Country Applies Playing-Field Taxes

It will depend on the tax rate of the home country. Assume the parent company is in the United States and the corporate tax rate is 34 percent. Also assume that the current exchange rate is 2 reals/US$1. Since the Brazilian corporate tax rate is 20 percent, the money sent back to the parent will be subject to additional taxes. The Internal Revenue Service (IRS) will first estimate the grossed-up income in order to determine the equivalent taxes that will paid by a domestic company. Grossed-up income is defined as the net dividends received plus the taxes paid on the income. In this case:

Grossed-Up Income		
Amount repatriated	4,560 reals	
Corporate taxes paid in Brazil	1,200 reals	
Withholding taxes paid	240 reals	
Total	6,000 reals	
At an exchange rate of 6,000 reals/US$2	US$3,000	

A U.S. company would pay corporate taxes of US$3,000 × 0.34	US$1020	
The company has already paid corporate taxes in Brazil	US$600	(1,200 reals/2)
The company already paid withholding taxes	US$120	(240 reals/2)
Balance to be paid to the IRS	US$300	

When the company pays US$300 in taxes to the IRS, the amount available to U.S. shareholders is 4,560 reals/2 = US$2,280–US$300 = US$1,980.

VALUE ADDED TAX AND GENERAL SALES TAX

Another tax that most companies face overseas is the value added tax (VAT) or the sales tax, both of which are termed indirect taxes. While VATs are usually imposed at the federal level, sales tax is usually imposed at the state and county levels. In some countries, such as Canada, sales tax is collected by both the federal and state governments. The biggest difference between the two forms of indirect taxation is the way they are collected.

A sales tax is collected at the end of the product cycle or at the final stage of delivery of the goods or services. When an item is purchased at a retail store, it represents a final purchase by the consumer, and a one-time tax is imposed on the purchase. In the United States, sales tax is collected at the state and county levels. During the production of the goods, no taxes are collected. At each stage of the production process, the seller is exempt from collecting taxes as long as it is clear that the purchases are intended for resale. In the United States, this can be achieved by requesting a resale certificate from the purchaser.

In the case of VAT, taxes are collected at every stage of the production process as well as from the final customer. The amount of tax collected depends on the net added value at each stage of production. The amount of tax collected at the end under both tax systems, VAT and sales tax, is the same. An example below highlights the differences in these two taxes.

Example

Assume that the manufacture and sale of a small toaster oven passes through three stages.

1. Stage 1 occurs at a steel fabricator that sells steel sheets to a toaster manufacturer at a price of US$5 per toaster.
2. Stage 2 is the assembly of the toaster using the steel sheets and other materials; the toaster is then shipped to Wal-Mart at a price of US$15.
3. Wal-Mart sells the toaster to a customer at a price of US$20.

Assume one country imposes a VAT at the rate of 5 percent and another country imposes a sales tax of 5 percent.

In the case of the country with sales tax:

1. The steel fabricator invoices US$5 to the toaster manufacturer and does not charge any tax but requests a resale certificate.
2. The toaster manufacturer charges Wal-Mart US$15 and does not charge any sales tax but requests a resale certificate. The net profit for the toaster manufacturer is US$10.
3. Wal-Mart charges the customer US$20 plus a sales tax of 5 percent. The customer pays a total of US$20 + US$1 tax. Wal-Mart remits US$1 to the state taxing authority. The net profit for Wal-Mart is US$5 (US$20–US$15).

In the case of the country with VAT:

1. The steel fabricator charges US\$5 to the toaster manufacturer and 5 percent VAT equal to US\$0.25, and remits US\$0.25 to federal taxing authority. The net proceeds for the steel fabricator are US\$5, while the cost to the toaster manufacturer is US\$5.25.
2. The toaster manufacturer charges Wal-Mart US\$15 plus VAT of US\$15 × .05 = US\$0.75. The toaster manufacturer remits only US\$0.50 (US\$0.75–US\$0.25 paid earlier) to the federal taxing authority. The net proceeds for the toaster manufacturer are US\$10 (US\$15.75–US\$5.25–US\$0.50). The cost to Wal-Mart is US\$15.75.
3. Wal-Mart charges the customer US\$20 plus VAT of US\$20 × .05 = US\$21. Wal-Mart remits US\$0.25 (US\$1.00–US\$0.75) to the federal taxing authority. The net proceeds for Wal-Mart are US\$5 (US\$21–US\$15.75–US\$0.25).

As shown above, the total proceeds under the VAT and sales tax regimes are the same. The total proceeds received by the taxing authority are also the same. The only difference is in the collection process, where every manufacturer at each stage of the production process has to make payments to the taxing authority.

GLOBAL TAXES

The assorted taxes described above—corporate, withholding, and indirect—vary significantly around the globe. The trend toward globalization has led to significant changes in taxation policies around the world.

The biggest change has been the lowering of taxes throughout the world. One reason for the decline has been the desire of many countries to lure foreign direct investment. This is especially true for emerging market countries.

Within countries in a regional bloc, there has been a tendency toward convergence and harmonization of taxes. An example is the European Union, where directives are being issued to level the playing field and work toward a common taxation policy. The Andean pact countries of Bolivia, Columbia, Ecuador, and Peru agreed in 2004 to a common VAT, but it has yet to be implemented.[18] The Mercosur bloc countries of Argentina, Brazil, Paraguay, and Uruguay are also attempting to harmonize their taxation policies.

One concern that was highlighted in a 2007 KPMG report is that countries may lower corporate taxes to lure businesses but increase indirect taxes to offset the loss in revenues. Critics point out that this amounts to a consumption tax, which affects the poor more than the rich. Unfortunately, it is difficult to measure the costs and benefits of such an approach; attracting business does increase employment, which in turn generates more jobs and tax revenue, and this has to be evaluated against the burdens imposed by the increases in indirect taxes.

Appendix 14.2 lists the corporate taxes for 2005 to 2007 and indirect taxes for 2007 for 103 countries, as compiled by KPMG.[19] Europe as a bloc in 2008 has one of the lowest corporate tax rates, averaging about 24 percent, with Bulgaria having the lowest at 10 percent, followed by Romania and Hungary at 16 percent. The highest tax rate in Europe is Germany's, at 38.36 percent. In contrast the U.S. corporate tax averages 40 percent, and Japan's averages 40.69 percent, making them the two highest in the world.

As Appendix 14.2 (pp. 380–381) shows, corporate taxes in Asia have also been reduced in the recent past. India has reduced its taxes to 34 percent, South Korea to 27.4 percent, and Fiji to 31 percent. Singapore and Taiwan continue to offer the lowest corporate taxes at 20 percent and 25 percent, respectively. Bahrain and the Cayman Islands have no corporate or personal taxes, although Bahrain imposes some taxes for those engaged in the mining and extraction industries. The next lowest are in Paraguay, Bulgaria, and Cyprus at 10 percent, followed by Macau and Oman at 12 percent.

CHAPTER SUMMARY

A country's accounting rules determine how its financial reports are prepared for record keeping, for internal management, and to satisfy the tax authorities. For companies that are publicly traded, financial reports have to be accurate, transparent, and meaningful for outside shareholders and creditors so they can evaluate the company's performance. When a company conducts business internationally, the record-keeping procedure has to include transactions that are denominated in another currency. If a company has subsidiaries abroad, the complexities increase because income statements and balance sheets denominated in several currencies have to be consolidated into one grand income statement and balance sheet.

The most challenging aspect of international accounting is consolidating the income statements and balance sheets of the various overseas subsidiaries. Not only do accountants have to worry about incorporating exchange rates but they must also reconcile the various accounting standards. The problem with reconciliation is that there are many approaches to consolidating balance sheets. Among the more common approaches are the temporal method and the current method. Most countries now use the temporal approach when consolidating the balance sheets of various subsidiaries.

The trend toward globalization has led to the creation of International Financial Reporting Standards (IFRS), coordinated by the International Accounting Standards Board. Although the first push for a global accounting standard began as early as 1973, it was not until 2002, when the European Union mandated that companies adopt IFRS, that the movement started gathering steam. It has also been helped by the announcement from the Financial Accounting Standards Board (FASB), an independent body that helps sets U.S. standards, that they too will attempt to converge toward IFRS standards. More than 100 countries have now signed on to move to the IFRS standards.

International accounting is further complicated by the various taxes imposed by countries on the profits of firms. Three of the most common taxes are corporate taxes, withholding taxes, and indirect taxes such as value added tax (VAT) and sales tax. Multinationals are not concerned about paying taxes on profits they have earned. However, they are concerned about double taxation. One example of double taxation is when a U.S. subsidiary pays taxes on the profits it repatriates to the United States. Most countries have bilateral treaties that eliminate double taxation. They either do not tax any of the repatriated profits or they tax them only if the multinational companies pay lower taxes than a comparable domestic company. This additional tax levels the playing field so companies conducting business overseas do not have an advantage over domestic firms.

KEY CONCEPTS

Translation Gain and Losses
International Financial Reporting Standards (IFRS)
Generally Accepted Accounting Principles (GAAP)
Value Added Taxes

DISCUSSION QUESTIONS

1. Why is international accounting more challenging than domestic accounting?
2. Explain how and why accounting for personal taxes of global executives and staff can become complicated.
3. Assume a U.S. company purchases goods worth €1,500,000 from a German company and has to make payment in 60 days. The exchange rate is US$1.50/€1. When the payment is made 60 days later, the exchange rate is US$1.25/€1. How would the company record the transaction on the order date and the payment date?
4. Why is the two-step procedure to record foreign exchange transactions better than the one-step procedure?
5. The balance sheet of a U.S. company has US$200 million in assets and US$200 million in equity. Its subsidiary in Belgium has assets and equity valued at €100 million. The exchange rate today is US$1.50/€1. At the end of the year, the exchange rate changes to US$1.25/€1. Do they report an unrealized loss or gain, and how much?
6. Explain the current and temporal methods of translating the asset and liabilities of a subsidiary.
7. What common theme runs through the scandals of Enron, WorldCom, and Parmalat?
8. Compare principles-based versus rules-based accounting standards for financial reporting.
9. What is major difference between IFRS and U.S. GAAP? Under which system is it easier to use loopholes?
10. What benefits may a company obtain if it adopts the IFRS, according to the OECD report?
11. Distinguish between corporate taxes, withholding taxes, and indirect taxes.
12. What approaches have countries used when taxing the repatriated profits of companies that conduct business overseas?
13. An aluminum manufacturer sells the equivalent of US$5 per sheet to a manufacturer of aluminum trays. The aluminum-tray manufacturer in turn delivers finished trays to a major retailer for US$10 per tray. The retailer sells it to a final

customer for US$15. If the VAT and sales tax is 6 percent, show how the total taxes paid to the taxing authorities are the same under both indirect taxes.

APPLICATION CASE: THE FANNIE MAE ACCOUNTING SCANDAL

The gap between the average salary of a chief executive officer (CEO) and that of a rank-and-file worker in the United States has been increasing steadily over the years. A study by the Institute of Policy Studies in Washington, D.C., estimated that the gap in total compensation increased from 40 times in 1980 to 364 times in 2007. In Europe, the gap is estimated at 32 times higher; in Japan, it is 17 times higher. Studies have also shown that CEO compensation in the United States is unrelated to performance; they continue to increase even when profits and share prices decline. One such executive recently in the news was Rick Wagoner, CEO of General Motors (GM), who was paid millions of dollars in bonuses beginning in 2000. His compensation in 2006 alone was in excess of $9 million. Two years later, GM was near bankruptcy and was pleading with the U.S. Congress for a bridge loan. (Wagoner later agreed to a $1 salary during GM's restructuring.) What is astonishing is that during the same period, the top executives of Japanese car companies earned less than $1 million per year, even as they outperformed GM throughout the globe.

A major portion of executive compensation in the United States is in the form of stock options. From a shareholder's point of view, offering stock options is an effective way to align the interests of the CEO with that of the shareholders; both will benefit when stock prices are maximized. Unfortunately, a weakness in the model is that it also encourages CEOs to focus on short-term profits. This is particularly true when one considers that the average tenure of CEOs in the United States is just five years. This provides strong incentives to CEOs to postpone critical decisions that can benefit the company in the long run, such as retooling, replacing, or repairing essential equipment to accommodate new technology and foster employee productivity.

In some cases, it also encourages CEOs to engage in accounting manipulations. A large number of corporate scandals in recent years have been the result of accounting manipulations that inflate earnings in order to boost share prices. A recent example was the case of Fannie Mae, one of the institutions that played a major role in the collapse of the financial markets in 2008. Fannie Mae was created in 1938 as the Federal National Mortgage Association by the U.S. government. Its mission was two-fold: to encourage home ownership by making funds available to mortgage lenders, and to purchase mortgages from banks. Privatized in 1968 with an implicit backing from the U.S. government, it increased lending successfully over the years to become one of the largest mortgage institutions in the United States. Fannie Mae's efforts allowed U.S. home ownership to reach a record 69 percent of households in 2004, the highest in the world.

Fannie Mae also generated significant profits during this growth period and awarded large bonuses to their top executives. Franklin Raines, the CEO of Fannie Mae, earned over $90 million between 1998 and 2003. In 2003, federal regulators began to question some of the accounting practices used by Fannie Mae to report their earnings. An investigation by the accounting firm of PWC (PricewaterhouseCoopers) led to a restatement of earnings by about $6.3 billion. A criminal investigation initiated by the U.S. Department of Justice in 2004 did not find evidence of willful manipulation of earnings. However, federal regulators decided to press civil charges against the top management.

In 2008, the top management reached a settlement with the regulators. Franklin Raines, by this time Fannie Mae's former CEO, agreed to pay a total of $24.7 million back, including $2 million in fines; J. Timothy Howard, former chief financial officer, agreed to pay back $6.4 million; and Leanne Spencer, former controller, agreed to pay back $645,000. Fannie Mae also paid $400 million in fines as part of the settlement for misstating the revenues.

Financial misreporting was one issue, but the other was the quality of decisions made by the executives to deserve such large bonuses. In the third quarter of 2008, Fannie Mae reported losses of $29.1 billion. This single quarter loss exceeded the total profits of $28.1 billion earned between 2002 and 2006. It is now apparent that the millions of dollars earned in bonuses between 1995 and 2006 ignored the high risks incurred by Fannie Mae. These risks were finally realized in 2007 and 2008, when loan after loan began to default in a cascading manner. This is yet another example of executives making decisions that trigger far-reaching, catastrophic effects on a company well after their tenure is over.

How did Fannie Mae underestimate the risks and quality of the mortgages they purchased from the various banks? Mortgages are originally written by banks, but they are supposed to follow the strict guidelines issued by Fannie Mae. If Fannie Mae had checked the documents carefully prior to their purchase, they would have found evidence of paperwork that indicated incorrect or forged statements. Did the executives foster a culture that ignored their own strict risk management guidelines? These are questions yet to be answered. What we do know is that, in the end, the lack of effective oversight led Fannie and its sister institution, Freddie Mac, to become insolvent, forcing the U.S. government to nationalize both institutions. Taxpayers ended up paying for the mismanagement of executives who had left the company years earlier.

QUESTIONS

1. What are some of the unique characteristics of executive compensation in the United States?
2. What suggestions can you offer to ensure that CEOs who collect multimillion-dollar bonuses make the right long-term decisions for a company?

Appendix 14.1

Summary of Some Similarities and Differences between IFRS and U.S. GAAP

Subject	IFRS	US GAAP
Accounting framework		
Historical cost or valuation	Generally uses historical cost, but intangible assets, property, plant and equipment (PPE) and investment property may be revalued to fair value. Derivatives, certain other financial instruments and biological assets are revalued to fair value.	No revaluations except for certain types of financial instrument.
Financial statements		
Components of financial statements	Two years' balance sheets, income statements, cash flow statements, changes in equity and accounting policies and notes.	Similar to IFRS, except three years required for SEC registrants for all statements except balance sheet. Specific accommodations in certain circumstances for foreign private issuers that may offer relief from the three-year requirement.
Balance sheet	Does not prescribe a particular format. A current/non-current presentation of assets and liabilities is used unless a liquidity presentation provides more relevant and reliable information. Certain minimum items are presented on the face of the balance sheet.	Entities may present either a classified or nonclassified balance sheet. Items on the face of the balance sheet are generally presented in decreasing order of liquidity. SEC registrants should follow SEC regulations.
Income statement	Does not prescribe a standard format, although expenditure is presented in one of two formats (function or nature). Certain minimum items are presented on the face of the income statement.	Present as either a single-step or multiple-step format. Expenditures are presented by function. SEC registrants should follow SEC regulations.
Consolidated financial statements		
Consolidation model	Based on control, which is the power to govern the financial, and operating policies. Control is presumed to exist when parent owns, directly or indirectly through subsidiaries, more than one half of an entity's voting power. Control also exists when the parent owns half or less of the voting power but has legal or contractual rights to control, or de facto control (rare circumstances). The existence of currently exercisable potential voting rights is also taken into consideration.	A bipolar consolidation model is used, which distinguishes between a variable interest model and a voting interest model. The variable interest model is discussed below. Under the voting interest model, control can be direct or indirect and may exist with less than 50% ownership. "Effective control," which is a similar notion to de facto control under IFRS, is very rare if ever employed in practice.
Presentation of jointly controlled entities (joint ventures)	Both proportional consolidation and equity method permitted.	Equity method required except in specific circumstances.

(continued)

Appendix 14.1 *(continued)*

Subject	IFRS	US GAAP
Business combinations		
Types: Acquisitions or mergers	All business combinations are acquisitions; thus the purchase method is the only method of accounting that is allowed.	Similar to IFRS.
Purchase method—fair values on acquisition	Assets, liabilities, and contingent liabilities of acquired entity are fair valued. Goodwill is recognized as the residual between the consideration paid and the percentage of the fair value of the business acquired. In-process research and development is generally capitalized. Liabilities for restructuring activities are recognized only when acquiree has an existing liability at acquisition date. Liabilities for future losses or other costs expected to be incurred as a result of the business combination cannot be recognized.	There are specific differences to IFRS. Contingent liabilities of the acquiree are recognized if, by the end of the allocation period: • their fair value can be determined, or • they are probable and can be reasonably estimated. Specific rules exist for acquired in-process research and development (generally expensed). Some restructuring liabilities relating solely to the acquired entity may be recognized if specific criteria about restructuring plans are met.
Purchase method—intangible assets with indefinite useful lives and goodwill	Capitalized but not amortized. Goodwill and indefinite-lived intangible assets are tested for impairment at least annually at either the cash-generating unit (CGU) level or groups of CGUs, as applicable.	Similar to IFRS, although the level of impairment testing and the impairment test itself are different.
Business combinations involving entities under common control	Not specifically addressed. Entities elect and consistently apply either purchase or pooling-of-interest accounting for all such transactions.	Generally recorded at predecessor cost; the use of predecessor cost or fair value depends on a number of criteria.
Revenue recognition		
Revenue recognition	Based on several criteria, which require the recognition of revenue when risks and rewards and control have been transferred and the revenue can be measured reliably.	Similar to IFRS in principle, although there is extensive detailed guidance for specific types of transactions that may lead to differences in practice.
Expense recognition		
Interest expense	Recognized on an accruals basis using the effective interest method.	Similar to IFRS.
	Interest incurred on borrowings to construct an asset over a substantial period of time are capitalized as part of the cost of the asset.	Similar to IFRS with some differences in the detailed application.
Assets		
Property, plant and equipment	Historical cost or revalued amounts are used. Regular valuations of entire classes of assets are required when revaluation option is chosen.	Historical cost is used; revaluations are not permitted.

Inventories	Carried at lower of cost and net realizable value. FIFO or weighted average method is used to determine cost. LIFO prohibited. Reversal is required for subsequent increase in value of previous write-downs.	Similar to IFRS; however, use of LIFO is permitted. Reversal of write-down is prohibited.
Financial assets—measurement	Depends on classification of investment—if held to maturity or loans and receivables, they are carried at amortized cost; otherwise at fair value. Gains/losses on fair value through profit or loss classification (including trading instruments) is recognized in income statement. Gains and losses on available for-sale investments, while the investments are still held, are recognized in equity.	Similar accounting model to IFRS, with some detailed differences in application.

Liabilities

Provisions—general	Liabilities relating to present obligations from past events recorded if outflow of resources is probable (defined as more likely than not) and can be reliably estimated.	Similar to IFRS. However, probable is a higher threshold than "more likely than not."
Financial liabilities versus equity classification	Capital instruments are classified, depending on substance of issuer's contractual obligations, as either liability or equity. Mandatory redeemable preference shares are classified as liabilities.	Application of the U.S. GAAP guidance may result in significant differences to IFRS, for example, certain redeemable instruments are permitted to be classified as "mezzanine equity" (i.e., outside of permanent equity but also separate from debt).

Equity instruments

Capital instruments—purchase of own shares	Show as deduction from equity.	Similar to IFRS.

Derivatives and hedging

Derivatives	Derivatives not qualifying for hedge accounting are measured at fair value with changes in fair value recognized in the income statement. Hedge accounting is permitted provided that certain stringent qualifying criteria are met.	Similar to IFRS. However, differences can arise in the detailed application.

Other accounting and reporting topics

Functional currency definition	Currency of primary economic environment in which entity operates.	Similar to IFRS.

Source: Published by PriceWaterhouseCoopers, October 2007.

Appendix 14.2

Global Corporate and Indirect Taxes, 2007 (in percent)

Country	Corporate Tax			VAT or GST
	Jan. 1, 2005	Jan. 1, 2006	Jan. 1, 2007	Jan. 1, 2007
Albania	23	20	20	20
Argentina			33	21
Aruba	35	35	28	3
Australia	30	30	30	10
Austria	25	25	25	20
Bahrain		0	0	
Bangladesh	30	30	30	15
Barbados	30	25	25	15
Belgium	33.99	33.99	33.99	21
Belize				
Bolivia	25	25	25	13
Bosnia & Herzegovina				17
Botswana	25	25	25	10
Brazil	34	34	34	Vary
Bulgaria	15	15	10	20
Canada	36.1	36.1	36.1	6
Cayman Islands		0	0	0
Chile	17	17	17	19
China	33	33	33	17
Colombia	35	35	34	16
Costa Rica	30	30	30	13
Croatia	20.32	20.32	20	22
Cyprus	10	10	10	15
Czech Republic	26	24	24	19
Denmark	28	28	28	25
Dominican Republic	25	30	29	16
Ecuador	25	25	25	12
Egypt		20	20	10
El Salvador				
Estonia	24	23	22	18
Fiji	31	31	31	12.5
Finland	26	26	26	22
France	33.83	33.33	33.33	19.6
Germany	38.31	38.34	38.36	19
Greece	32	29	25	19
Guatemala				12
Honduras	30	30	30	12
Hong Kong	17.5	17.5	17.5	0
Hungary	16	16	16	20
Iceland	18	18	18	24.5
India	36.5925	33.66	33.99	12.5
Indonesia	30	30	30	10
Ireland	12.5	12.5	12.5	21
Israel	34	31	29	15.5
Italy	37.25	37.25	37.25	20
Jamaica	33.33	33.33	33.33	16.5
Japan	40.69	40.69	40.69	5
Kazakhstan	30	30	30	14
Korea, Republic of	27.5	27.5	27.4	10

(continued)

Appendix 14.2 *(continued)*

Country	Corporate Tax			VAT or GST
	Jan. 1, 2005	Jan. 1, 2006	Jan. 1, 2007	Jan. 1, 2007
Kuwait			55	
Latvia	15	15	15	18
Lithuania	15	15	15	18
Luxembourg	30.38	29.63	29.63	15
Macau	12	12	12	0
Malaysia	28	28	27	10
Malta	35	35	35	18
Mauritius	25	25	22.5	15
Mexico	30	29	28	15
Montenegro				17
Mozambique	32	32	32	17
Netherlands	31.5	29.6	25.5	19
Netherlands Antilles	34.5	34.5	34.5	3–5
New Zealand	33	33	33	12.5
Norway	28	28	28	25
Oman	12	12	12	0
Pakistan	35	35	35	15
Panama	30	30	30	5
Papua New Guinea	30	30	30	10
Paraguay			10	10
Peru	30	30	30	17
Philippines	32	35	35	12
Poland	19	19	19	22
Portugal	27.5	27.5	25	21
Qatar			35	
Romania	16	16	16	19
Russia	24	24	24	18
Saudi Arabia		20	20	0
Serbia				18
Singapore	20	20	20	5
Slovak Republic	19	19	19	
Slovenia	25	25	23	20
South Africa	37.8	36.9	36.9	14
Spain	35	35	32.5	16
Sri Lanka	32.5	32.5	35	15
Sweden	28	28	28	25
Switzerland	21.3	21.3	21.3	7.6
Taiwan	25	25	25	5
Thailand	30	30	30	7
Tunisia	35	35	30	18
Turkey	30	30	20	18
Ukraine	25	25	25	20
United Arab Emirates	55	55	55	0
United Kingdom	30	30	30	17.5
United States	40	40	40	Vary by state
Uruguay	30	30	30	23
Venezuela	34	34	34	11
Vietnam	28	28	28	10
Zambia	35	35	35	17.5

Source: KPMG.

Appendix 1
Regional Economic Integrations

Regional economic integrations are efforts by groups of countries to assist one another in attaining economic and political stability. Most regional economic integrations are formed among countries that are geographically close (within the same region). Geographic proximity is a sound basis for these agreements for the following reasons: the people in these countries may have similar consumption habits; they may share a common history; and because of their proximity, they may also benefit from shorter distances traveled in the distribution of goods and services. The impetus to form economic cooperation among countries came about after the devastation of World War II, which economically crippled most of the Asian and European countries. Basically, regional economic integration is a political and economic agreement among countries that give preferences in trade and economic cooperation to member countries with the aim to assist one another through cooperation and collective efforts. For international and global companies, these regional agreements provide an opportunity to serve a large market base. For example, the European Union is made up of 500 million consumers, whereas the number of consumers in a single country in Europe does not exceed 83 million.

Regional economic integrations vary in scope, and each type of integration focuses on specific economic and trade aspects of the member countries. The four forms of integrations are:

1. Free trade area
2. Customs union
3. Common market
4. Economic union

Table A1.1 presents the four different types of integrations and their key differences. As evident from the table, forming a free trade area is much simpler than forming an economic union. As countries move from free trade agreements to an economic union, the level of integration becomes progressively more comprehensive and complete. In a free trade area, the member countries agree on just one condition—removal of internal tariffs. In contrast, in an economic union, in addition to removing tariffs, member countries also agree on common tariffs with the rest of the world, permit free mobility of production factors, and harmonize their economies, including agreeing to

Table A1.1

Distinctions among Types of Economic Integration

Type of Integration	Conditions	Examples
Free trade area	Free trade among member countries Each country has individual trade arrangements with the rest of the world	North American Free Trade Agreement (NAFTA); member countries include Canada, Mexico, and the United States
Customs union	Free trade among member countries Member countries have common external tariffs with the rest of the world	Mercosur; member countries include Argentina, Brazil, Paraguay, and Uruguay; a common external tariff has been adopted, and Mercosur is on its way to becoming a customs union
Common market	Free trade among member countries Member countries have common external tariffs with the rest of the world Free mobility of production factors such as labor and capital	Although there are many unions with the term "common market" in them, such as the Common Market for Eastern and Southern Africa (COMESA) and the Common Market of the South (Mercosur), these organizations have yet to attain the goals of a common market. The only successful common market was the European Common Market, the predecessor of the European Union (EU)
Economic union	Free trade among member countries Member countries have common external tariffs with the rest of the world Free mobility of production factors such as labor and capital Adoption of common economic policies including common currency and the establishment of a common central bank	European Union (EU); member countries include Austria, Belgium, Britain, Cyprus, Czech Republic, Denmark, Estonia, Finland, France, Germany, Greece, Hungary, Ireland, Italy, Latvia, Lithuania, Luxembourg, Malta, Netherlands, Poland, Portugal, Slovakia, Slovenia, Spain, and Sweden

have a single currency. It is much easier to form a free trade area than an economic union; hence, there is only one economic union in existence.

BENEFITS OF INTEGRATION

Theoretically, regional integrations benefit member countries through improved exchanges in cultural and social activities, a better understanding of each member's political system, and achievement of economic growth. From an economic standpoint, the three benefits of integration are: (1) trade creation, (2) trade diversion, and (3) economies of scale. Trade creation and trade diversion are called the "static effects" of integration, and economies of scale are referred to as the "dynamic effects" of integration.

TRADE CREATION

Regional integration forces the shifting of resources from inefficient companies to companies that are more efficient. Efficient companies, with their cost advantage, are able to market goods and services at much lower prices than unproductive ones.

As more and more consumers buy goods and services from efficient companies, the inefficient companies lose market share and are either forced to improve or leave the industry. Because of the removal of trade barriers, efficient companies from other countries that could not have competed before the integration are able to export goods and services and compete for market share.

TRADE DIVERSION

Because of regional integration, trade shifts from nonmember countries to member countries. This shift helps member countries to have more trade between them than they did before integration.

ECONOMIES OF SCALE

Because of trade creation and trade diversion, the size of the market within the member countries grows substantially, reducing the cost of production for companies within the group through economies of scale.

ACTIVITIES AND OPERATIONS OF NAFTA AND THE EUROPEAN UNION

Two of the most successful regional integrations are NAFTA, a free trade agreement among Canada, Mexico, and the United States, and the European Union (EU) made up of 25 European countries. Following is a brief description of the activities and operations of NAFTA and the European Union.

THE NORTH AMERICAN FREE TRADE AGREEMENT

The North American Free Trade Agreement (NAFTA) is a regional agreement among the governments of Canada, Mexico, and the United States. The objectives of this agreement are stated in Article 102 of the agreement, as follows:

1. Eliminate barriers to trade in, and facilitate the cross-border movement of goods and services between, the territories of the Parties.
2. Promote conditions of fair competition in the free trade area.
3. Increase substantially investment opportunities in the territories of the Parties.
4. Provide adequate and effective protection and enforcement of intellectual property rights in each Party's territory.
5. Create effective procedures for the implementation and application of this Agreement, for its joint administration and for the resolution of disputes; and
6. Establish a framework for further trilateral, regional, and multilateral cooperation to expand and enhance the benefits of this Agreement.

In June 1990, President Carlos Salinas de Gortari of Mexico and President George Bush of the United States announced their intention to negotiate a free trade agreement between their countries. The next year, Canada joined the process, and in June

1991, formal negotiations began among the three countries on a North American Free Trade Agreement.[1] The proposed agreement was negotiated in the midst of a recession in the United States. The initial reaction from some sectors of the U.S. economy, including labor organizations and the environmentalist movement, was very negative to the proposed agreement. Organized labor argued that NAFTA would result in hundreds of U.S. companies relocating to Mexico to take advantage of cheap labor, which would result in a loss of jobs in the United States. At the same time, corporate America and its leaders supported the agreement because of the potential lower production costs that would be derived through the agreement. After a lengthy debate, the U.S Congress approved the treaty in November 1993. On January 1, 1994, the North American Free Trade Agreement was activated by Canada, Mexico, and the United States.

After the inauguration of U.S. president Bill Clinton, he proposed side arrangements to the NAFTA which resulted in the formation of the North American Agreement on Environmental Cooperation (NAAEC), the North American Development Bank (NADB), the Border Environmental Cooperation Commission (BECC), and the North American Agreement on Labor Cooperation (NAALC). Through its Commission for Environmental Cooperation, the NAAEC was formed in response to environmentalists' concerns that the United States would lower its pollution and emissions standards if the three countries did not achieve consistent environmental regulation. The NADB was organized for financing investments to reduce pollution in the region. The BECC and the NADB are programs for funding specific projects that elevate environmental problems, especially those affecting water resources. The North American Agreement on Labor Cooperation (NAALC) was formed to resolve labor problems and to foster greater cooperation among labor unions within the member countries.

NAFTA went into effect on January 1, 1994. The implementation of NAFTA superseded the U.S.–Canada Free Trade Agreement (FTA), signed by the two countries on January 1, 1989. Since its implementation, NAFTA has been examined many times to determine whether it has achieved its stated objectives. Research on the success of NAFTA has focused on four critical issues: economic growth, employment rates, FDI flows, and impact on the environment.

Many researchers who have studied NAFTA feel that the overall results of the agreement have been positive.[2] Economic growth has been achieved by the intensified competition in domestic markets and at the same time the agreement has promoted investment from both domestic and foreign sources. The increased competition has led U.S. companies to operate more efficiently. Prior to the recession of 2008, the economies of Canada and the United States have performed well during the NAFTA era, growing by an average annual rate of 3.3 percent and 3.6 percent, respectively.[3] However, Mexico's economy grew at an annual rate of only 2.7 percent between 1994 and 2003. This rate is considered to be well below Mexico's potential growth, despite its sharp recession after the 1995 peso crisis.

In the area of trade, NAFTA seems to have benefited the member countries. U.S. trade with Mexico substantially increased after NAFTA, especially in vehicles, machinery, and steel and iron. The agreement has also increased trade between the countries more rapidly than between these two countries and the rest of the world.

In terms of the volume of trade, Mexico seems to have gained more than the United States has.[4] In 1998, Mexico replaced Japan as America's second-largest trading partner. The U.S.–Mexico Chamber of Commerce reported that trade between the two countries doubled between 1993 and 1997, increasing from US$80 billion to US$160 billion a year. NAFTA seems to have had positive results on the flows of goods, capital, and labor.[5]

According to the Office of the U.S. Trade Representative web site, in the first decade of NAFTA, U.S. manufacturing output soared, U.S. employment grew, and U.S. manufacturing wages increased dramatically. Income gains and tax cuts from NAFTA were worth up to US$930 each year for the average U.S. household of four. Wages in export-related industries of Mexico were 37 percent higher than in the rest of its economy. Mexican wages and employment tend to be higher in states with higher foreign investment and trade, and migration from those states is lower. Wages are also higher in sectors with more exposure to imports or exports. Two-way agricultural trade between the United States and Mexico increased more than 125 percent since NAFTA went into effect, reaching US$14.2 billion in 2003 compared to US$6.2 billion in 1993. Merchandise exports from Canada to the United States increased by 250 percent since 1989 and account for 87.2 percent of Canada's total merchandise exports. Foreign direct investment (FDI) from Canada into Mexico has also shown dramatic increases, especially in the financial sector, accounting for 36 percent of Canadian FDI in Mexico in 2001, compared to no measurable investments in this sector just a few years back. This trend continued until early 2007, just before the economic crisis.

NAFTA has also had some negative effects on the three countries.[6] Although NAFTA succeeded in its core goal of removing trade and investment barriers, it was not as successful in decreasing unemployment and increasing wages. Although the figures for all three countries improved in the initial post-NAFTA years, they did not reach the levels that were forecast when the agreement was first proposed. Also, it is not clear whether these increases were the result of the agreement or simply time-related growth. Between 1993 and 2007, U.S. employment rose from 110 million to 137 million,[7] in Canada it grew from 12.9 million to 16.9 million,[8] and in Mexico, jobs increased from 32.8 million to 40.6 million.[9] However, some researchers have argued that NAFTA has had only a small impact on these numbers, since this growth was the normal growth expected over time.

The member countries are also concerned about environmental issues. The Mexican government estimates that pollution damages since the mid-1990s have exceeded $36 billion per year.[10] According to some estimates, NAFTA might have directly contributed to about a 2 percent increase in annual gross emissions of carbon monoxide and sulfur dioxide. In addition, the free trade agreement has increased the air pollution levels at the border between Mexico and the United States because of the increased truck traffic used for hauling goods from Mexico to countries up north. NAFTA has not affected the friendly relationship between Canada and the United States. Although from time to time there have been some disagreements on specific issues, in general they have been settled quickly. For example, the Canada–U.S. softwood lumber dispute has been raised on and off for about a quarter century.[11] It has gone through four rounds, the last two with the FTA/NAFTA in place. When the U.S. Congress demanded a 15 percent duty on Canadian lumber exports, Canada challenged them at the multilateral trade body, GATT. However, the pressure of negatively affecting the free trade relations pushed Canada into opting for a settlement that replaced the U.S. duty with a 15 percent Canadian lumber export tax.

Through the efforts of the NAAEC, all three countries have benefited from coordination and cooperation, which is increasing the effectiveness of North American conservation efforts by:

- Developing common priorities for the protection of certain species
- Developing North American Conservation Action Plans for three shared marine species
- Providing tools, such as a map of terrestrial ecoregions, which management agencies are using in their programs
- Setting out common mechanisms for planning and monitoring bird conservation programs

In conclusion, the primary focus of NAFTA was to reduce barriers to investment and trade, and it has succeeded in that goal. The agreement brought the continent closer to a free trade, which improved the quality of life in North America. Although the objectives have not all been reached, the agreement has worked for all three countries in terms of being a building block for future agreements.

THE EUROPEAN UNION

The largest and most comprehensive of the regional integrations is the European Union.[12] Although the EU was formed in January 1993, its creation was preceded by modest integration efforts among some of the European countries dating back to the 1950s.

In 1950, Robert Schuman—the chief architect of the European Unity and then-French foreign minister—proposed integrating the coal and steel industries of Western Europe. Schuman's idea was inspired by the work of French-born European integrationist Jean Monnet. Because energy and steel production were two components essential for economic success, Schuman reasoned that it was important to establish a mechanism of collective cooperation among countries to solve some of the endemic problems associated with these industries. As a result, in 1951, the European Coal and Steel Community (ECSC) was set up to include Belgium, West Germany, Luxembourg, France, Italy, and the Netherlands. The power to make decisions about the coal and steel industry in these countries was placed in the hands of an independent, supranational body called the High Authority. Monnet was its first president.

Building on the success of ECSC, these same six countries decided to go further and integrate other sectors of their economies. In 1957, they signed the Treaty of Rome, creating the European Atomic Energy Community (EURATOM) and the European Economic Community (EEC). The member states agreed to first remove trade barriers among them and at a later date to form a common market. In 1967, the institutions of the three European communities—ECSC, EURATOM, and EEC—were merged, establishing a single commission and a single Council of Ministers as well as the European Parliament. The European Economic Community was made up of 12 countries—Austria, Belgium, Denmark, France, Ireland, Italy, Luxembourg, Norway, Portugal, Spain, Sweden, and the United Kingdom. The EEC member countries agreed to:

- Eliminate all trade barriers between members
- Establish a common external tariff
- Introduce a common agricultural and transport policy
- Create a European Social Fund
- Establish a European Investment Bank
- Develop closer relations between member countries

The Treaty of Maastricht (1992) creating the European Union added new forms of cooperation among the member states, including the introduction of a single European currency managed by a European Central Bank. The single currency—the euro—became a reality on January 1, 2002, when euro notes and coins replaced national currencies in 12 of the 15 countries of the European Union: Belgium, Germany, Greece, Spain, France, Ireland, Italy, Luxembourg, the Netherlands, Austria, Portugal, and Finland.

The European Union has grown in size from its first attempt at a regional integration with six European countries to its present membership of 25 countries. Denmark, Ireland, and the United Kingdom joined the original six countries in 1973, followed by Greece in 1981, Spain and Portugal in 1986, and Austria, Finland, and Sweden in 1995. The membership totaled 25 after 10 new countries joined the European Union in 2004: these 10 new countries include Cyprus, the Czech Republic, Estonia, Hungary, Latvia, Lithuania, Malta, Poland, Slovakia, and Slovenia. Bulgaria and Romania followed in 2007. Croatia and Turkey are in the process of becoming member states, but they have yet to be approved by the European Parliament. To ensure that the expanded European Union can continue to function efficiently, it needs a more streamlined system for making decisions. That is why the Treaty of Nice lays down new rules governing the size of the EU institutions and the ways in which they work. The treaty went into effect on February 1, 2003, but was replaced three years later by the new EU Constitution.

The countries that make up the European Union (its "member states") remain independent sovereign nations, but they pool their sovereignty in order to gain a strength and world influence none of them could have on their own. Pooling sovereignty means, in practice, that the member states delegate some of their decision-making powers to shared institutions they have created, so that decisions on specific matters of joint interest can be made democratically at the European level.

The European Union is composed of the European Parliament, the Council of the European Union, and the European Commission as the decision-making bodies; the Court of Justice and the Court of Auditors as the other main institutions; the European Economic and Social Committee and the Committee of the Regions

Figure A1.1 **The European Union**

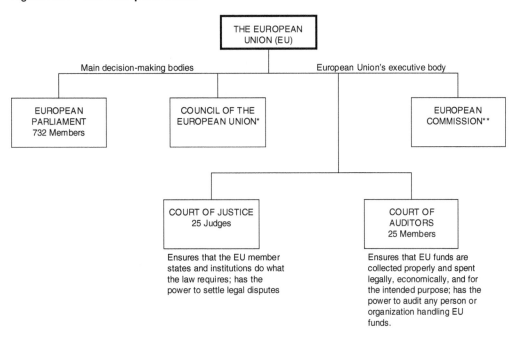

*The council is made up of the ministers of the member states.
**The commission is independent of national governments. It represents and upholds the interests of the European Union as a whole.

as the consultative bodies; and the European Central Bank and the European Investment Bank as the financial bodies. (See Figure A1.1). In addition, specific institutions have the responsibility for managing some of the key agencies, including the European Ombudsman, the European Data Protection Supervisor, the Office for Official Publications of the European Communities, and the European Communities Personnel Selection Office.

The European Parliament

The European Parliament (EP) is elected every five years by the citizens of the European Union to represent their interests. Its origins go back to the 1950s and the founding treaties, and since 1979 its members have been directly elected by the people they represent. The present parliament, elected in June 2004, has 732 members from all 25 EU countries. Nearly one-third of the members (222) are women. Members of the European Parliament (MEPs) do not sit in national blocs, but in seven European-wide political groups. Among them, they represent all views on European integration, from the strongly pro-Federalist to the openly Eurosceptic. In 2007, Hans-Gert Pöttering was elected president of the European Parliament.

The European Parliament has its offices in Brussels, Belgium; Luxembourg; and Strasbourg, France. Luxembourg is home to the administrative offices, the

General Secretariat. Parliamentary meetings, called "plenary sessions," take place in Strasbourg and sometimes in Brussels. Committee meetings are also held in Brussels.

The European Parliament has three main roles:

1. *Passing Laws.* The most common procedure for adopting (that is, passing) EU legislation is codecision. This procedure places the European Parliament and the Council of the European Union on equal footing and applies to legislation in a wide range of fields. In some fields, including agriculture, economic policy, visas, and immigration, the council alone legislates through consultations with the parliament. However, the parliament's assent is required for certain important decisions, such as allowing new countries to join the European Union. The parliament also initiates new legislation for the European Union.

2. *Democratic Supervision.* The parliament exercises democratic supervision over the other European institutions in several ways. When a new commission takes office, its members are nominated by the EU member-state governments, but they cannot be appointed without the parliament's approval. The parliament interviews each nominee individually, including the prospective commission president, and then votes on whether to approve the commission as a whole. Throughout its term of office, the commission remains politically accountable to the parliament, which can pass a "motion of censure" calling for the commission's mass resignation.

   More generally, the parliament exercises control by regularly examining reports sent to it by the commission. These reports include the annual general report and reports on the implementation of the budget. Moreover, MEPs regularly ask the commission questions about their operations that the commissioners are legally required to answer.

   The parliament also monitors the work of the council: MEPs frequently ask questions of the council, and the president of the council attends the parliament's plenary sessions and takes part in important debates. The parliament can exercise further democratic control by examining petitions from citizens and setting up committees of inquiry.

   Finally, the parliament provides input at every EU summit (the European Council meetings). At the opening of each summit, the president of the parliament is invited to express the parliament's views and concerns about topical issues and the items on the European Council's agenda.

3. *The Power of the Purse.* The European Union's annual budget is decided jointly by the parliament and the Council of the European Union. The parliament debates the budget in two successive readings, and the budget does not come into force until it has been signed by the president of the parliament. The parliament's Committee on Budgetary Control (COCOBU) monitors how the budget is spent, and each year the parliament decides whether to approve the commission's handling of the budget for the previous financial year. This approval process is technically known as "granting a discharge."

The Organization of the European Parliament. The parliament's work is divided into two main stages:

- *Preparing for the plenary session.* Preparing for the plenary session is done by the MEPs in the various parliamentary committees that specialize in particular areas of EU activity. The issues for debate are also discussed by the political groups.
- *The plenary session itself.* Plenary sessions are normally held in Strasbourg (one week per month) and sometimes in Brussels (two days only). At these sessions, the parliament examines proposed legislation and votes on amendments before coming to a decision on the text as a whole.

Other items on the agenda may include council or commission "communications," or questions about what is going on in the European Union or the wider world.

The Council of the European Union

The council is the European Union's main decision-making body. Like the European Parliament, the council was set up by the founding treaties in the 1950s. It represents the member states, and its meetings are attended by one minister from each of the EU's national governments.

The EU's relations with the rest of the world are dealt with by the General Affairs and External Relations Council (GAERC). The GAERC is responsible for general policy issues, so its meetings are attended by whichever minister or state secretary each government chooses. There are nine different GAERC subcommittees or configurations:

1. General Affairs and External Relations
2. Economic and Financial Affairs (ECOFIN)
3. Justice and Home Affairs (JHA)
4. Employment, Social Policy, Health, and Consumer Affairs
5. Competitiveness
6. Transport, Telecommunications, and Energy
7. Agriculture and Fisheries
8. Environment
9. Education, Youth, and Culture

Each minister in the council is empowered to commit his or her government. Moreover, each minister in the council is answerable to his or her national parliament and to the citizens that the parliament represents. This ensures the democratic legitimacy of the council's decisions.

Up to four times a year, the presidents and/or prime ministers of the member states, together with the president of the European Commission, meet as the "European Council." These summit meetings set overall EU policy and resolve issues that could not be settled at a lower level, that is, by the ministers at normal council meetings.

The European Council has six key responsibilities:

1. *Legislation.* Much of EU legislation is adopted jointly by the council and the parliament. As a rule, the council acts only on a proposal from the commission, and the commission normally has responsibility for ensuring that EU legislation, once adopted, is correctly applied.

2. *Coordination of the policies of member states.* The EU countries have decided that they want an overall economic policy based on close coordination of their national economic policies. Such coordination is carried out by the economics and finance ministers, who collectively form the Economic and Financial Affairs (ECOFIN) Council.

   This council also wants to create more jobs and to improve the European Union's education, health, and social protection systems. Although each EU country is responsible for its own policies in these areas, the member states can agree on common goals and learn from one another's experience what works best. This process is called the "open method of coordination," and it takes place within the council.

3. *Concluding international agreements.* Each year the council "concludes" a number of agreements between the EU and non-EU countries, as well as with international organizations.

4. *Approving the EU budget.* The EU's annual budget is decided jointly by the council and the European Parliament.

5. *Common Foreign and Security Policy.* The member states of the European Union are working to develop a Common Foreign and Security Policy (CFSP). But foreign policy, security, and defense are matters over which the individual national governments retain independent control. Hence, the parliament and the European Commission play only a limited role in this area. However, the EU countries have much to gain by working together on these issues, and the council is the main forum in which this intergovernmental cooperation takes place. To enable it to respond more effectively to international crises, the European Union has created a Rapid Reaction Force. This is not a European army: the personnel remain members of their national armed forces and under national command, and their role is limited to carrying out humanitarian, rescue, peacekeeping, and other crisis-management tasks. In 2003, for example, the EU conducted a military operation (code named Artemis) in the Democratic Republic of Congo, and in 2004 it began a peacekeeping operation (code named Althea) in Bosnia and Herzegovina.

6. *Freedom, security, and justice.* EU citizens are free to live and work in whichever EU country they choose, so they should have equal access to civil justice everywhere in the European Union. Freedom of movement within the European Union is of great benefit to law-abiding citizens, but it is also exploited by international criminals and terrorists. To tackle cross-border crime requires cross-border cooperation among the national courts, police forces, customs officers, and immigration services of all EU countries. These security and justice issues are dealt with by the Justice and Home Affairs Council, that is, the ministers for justice and of the interior. The aim of this council is to create a unified and uniform approach to freedom, security, and justice within the European Union's borders.

The Organization of the Council of the European Union

Permanent Representatives Committee (COREPER). In Brussels, each EU member state has a permanent team, called a Permanent Representatives Committee (COREPER), that represents it and defends its national interest at the EU level. The head of each representative committee is, in effect, his or her country's ambassador to the European Union. These ambassadors (known as "permanent representatives") meet weekly within the COREPER. The role of this committee is to prepare the work of the council, with the exception of most agricultural issues, which are handled by the Special Committee on Agriculture. The COREPER is assisted by a number of working groups, made up of officials from the national administrations.

Council Presidency. The presidency of the council rotates every six months: each EU country in turn takes charge of the council agenda and chairs all the meetings for a six-month period, promoting collaborative legislative and political decisions and brokering compromises among the member states.

General Secretariat. The president is assisted by the General Secretariat, which prepares and ensures the smooth functioning of the council's work at all levels. Javier Solana is the current secretary-general of the council. He is also high representative for the Common Foreign and Security Policy (CFSP), and in this capacity helps coordinate the European Union's actions on the world stage. Under the new constitutional treaty, the high representative would be replaced by an EU foreign affairs minister. The secretary-general is assisted by a deputy secretary-general in charge of managing the General Secretariat.

Qualified Majority Voting. Decisions in the council are taken by vote. The number of votes allotted to each country is based on its population, but the numbers are also weighted in favor of the less populous countries. In some particularly sensitive areas such as Common Foreign and Security Policy, taxation, asylum, and immigration policy, council decisions have to be unanimous. In other words, each member state has the power of veto in these areas. In addition, a member state may ask for confirmation that the votes in favor represent at least 62 percent of the total population of the European Union. If this is found not to be the case, the decision will not be adopted.

The European Commission

The commission is independent of national governments. Its job is to represent and uphold the interests of the European Union as a whole. It drafts proposals for new European laws, which it presents to the parliament and the council. It is also the European Union's executive arm, responsible for implementing the decisions of the parliament and the council.

Like the parliament and council, the European Commission was set up in the 1950s under the European Union's founding treaties. The term "commission" is used in two senses. First, it refers to the team of men and women—one from each EU country—appointed to run the institution and make its decisions. Second, the term "commission" refers to the institution itself and to its staff. Informally, the appointed members of the commission are known as "commissioners." They have all held political positions in their countries of origin, and many have been government ministers, but as members of the commission they are committed to acting in the interests of the European Union as a whole and not taking instructions from national governments.

A new commission is appointed every five years, within six months of the elections to the European Parliament. The present commission's term of office runs until October 31, 2009. Its president is José Manuel Barroso, from Portugal. The commission remains politically accountable to the parliament, which has the power to dismiss the whole commission by adopting a motion of censure. Individual members of the commission must resign if asked to do so by the president, provided the other commissioners approve.

The commission attends all the sessions of the parliament, where it must clarify and justify its policies. It also replies regularly to written and oral questions posed by MEPs.

The day-to-day running of the commission is done by its administrative officials, experts, translators, interpreters, and secretarial staff. There are approximately 25,000 staff members and civil servants. The "seat" of the commission is in Brussels, Belgium, but it also has offices in Luxembourg, representatives from all EU countries, and delegations in many capital cities around the world.

The European Commission has four main roles:

1. *Proposing new legislation.* The commission has the "right of initiative." In other words, the commission alone is responsible for drawing up proposals for new European legislation, which it presents to the parliament and the council. These proposals must aim to defend the interests of the European Union and its citizens, not those of specific countries or industries.

Before making any proposals, the commission must be aware of new situations and problems developing in Europe, and it must consider whether EU legislation is the best way to deal with them. That is why the commission is in constant touch with a wide range of interest groups and with two advisory bodies—the Economic and Social Committee and the Committee of the Regions. It also seeks the opinions of national parliaments and governments.

2. *Implementing EU policies and the budget.* As the European Union's executive body, the commission is responsible for managing and implementing the EU budget. Most of the actual spending is done by national and local authorities, but the commission is responsible for supervising it—under the watchful eye of the Court of Auditors. Both institutions aim to ensure good financial management. Only if it is satisfied with the Court of Auditors' annual report does the European Parliament grant the commission discharge for implementing the budget. The commission also has to manage the policies adopted by the parliament and the council, such as the Common Agricultural Policy.

3. *Enforcing European law.* The commission acts as "guardian of the treaties." This means that, together with the Court of Justice, the commission is responsible

for making sure EU law is properly applied to all the member states. If it finds that an EU country is not applying an EU law, and therefore not meeting its legal obligations, the commission takes steps to put the situation right.

4. *Representing the European Union on the international stage.* The European Commission is an important mouthpiece for the European Union on the international stage. It enables the member states to speak "with one voice" in international forums such as the World Trade Organization.

The Organization of the European Commission. It is up to the commission president to decide which commissioner will be responsible for which policy area, and to reshuffle these responsibilities during the commission's term of office. The commission meets once each week, usually on Wednesdays, in Brussels. Each item on the agenda is presented by the commissioner responsible for that policy area, and the whole team then makes a collective decision on it.

The commission's staff is organized into departments, known as "directorates-general" (DGs) and "services" (such as the Legal Service). Each DG is responsible for a particular policy area and is headed by a director-general who is answerable to one of the commissioners. Overall coordination is provided by the secretariat-general, which also manages the weekly commission meetings. It is headed by the secretary-general, who is answerable directly to the president. The DGs actually devise and draft legislative proposals, but these proposals become official only when adopted by the commission at its weekly meeting. If at least 13 of the 25 commissioners approve the proposal, the commission will adopt it, and it will have the whole team's unconditional support. The document will then be sent to council and the European Parliament for their consideration.

The Court of Justice. The Court of Justice of the European Communities, often referred to simply as "the court," was set up under the ECSC Treaty in 1952. Its job is to make sure that EU legislation is interpreted and applied uniformly in all EU countries. Based in Luxembourg, the court ensures that national courts do not give different rulings on the same issue. It also makes sure that EU member states and institutions do what the law requires. The court has the power to settle legal disputes between EU member states, EU institutions, businesses, and individuals.

The court is composed of one judge per member state, so that all 25 of the European Union's national legal systems are represented. For the sake of efficiency, however, the court rarely sits as the full court. It usually sits as a "grand chamber" of just 13 judges, or in chambers of five or three judges. The court is assisted by eight advocates-general. Their role is to present reasoned opinions on the cases brought before the court. They must do so publicly and impartially.

The judges and advocates-general are people whose impartiality is beyond doubt. They have the qualifications or competence needed for appointment to the highest judicial positions in their home countries. They are appointed to the Court of Justice by joint agreement between the governments of the EU member states. Each is appointed for a term of six years, which may be renewed.

To help the Court of Justice cope with the large number of cases brought before it, and to offer citizens better legal protection, a Court of First Instance was created in 1989. This court is responsible for giving rulings on certain kinds of cases, particularly actions brought by private individuals, companies, and some organizations, and cases relating to competition law.

The Court of Justice and the Court of First Instance each have a president, chosen by their fellow judges to serve for a renewable term of three years. Vassilios Skouris, from Greece, is the president of the Court of Justice and Bo Vesterdorf, from Denmark, is president of the Court of First Instance.

A new judicial body, the European Civil Service Tribunal, has been set up to adjudicate disputes between the European Union and its civil service. This tribunal is composed of seven judges and is attached to the Court of First Instance.

The Court of Auditors. The Court of Auditors was set up in 1975. It is based in Luxembourg. The court's job is to check that EU funds, which come from the taxpayers, are properly collected and that they are spent legally, economically, and for their intended purpose. Its aim is to ensure that the taxpayers get maximum value for their money, and it has the right to audit any person or organization handling EU funds. The court has one member from each EU country, appointed by the council for a renewable term of six years. The members elect the president for a renewable term of three years. Hubert Weber, from Austria, was elected president in January 2005.

The Court of Auditors has approximately 800 staff members, including translators, administrators, and auditors. The auditors are divided into audit groups. They prepare draft reports on which the court makes decisions. To carry out its tasks, the court frequently carries out on-the-spot checks, investigating the paperwork of any person or organization handling EU income or expenditures. Its findings are written up in reports that bring any problems to the attention of the commission and EU member-state governments. To do its job effectively, the Court of Auditors must remain completely independent of the other institutions but at the same time stay in constant touch with them.

One of the court's key functions is to help the European Parliament and the council by presenting them with an annual audit report on the previous financial year. The parliament examines the court's report in detail before deciding whether or not to approve the commission's handling of the budget.

Finally, the Court of Auditors gives its opinion on proposals for EU financial legislation and for EU action to fight fraud. The court itself has no legal powers of its own. If auditors discover fraud or irregularities, they inform the European Anti-Fraud Office.

The European Economic and Social Committee. Founded in 1957 under the Treaty of Rome, the European Economic and Social Committee (EESC) is an advisory body representing employers, trade unions, farmers, consumers, and the other interest groups that collectively make up the organized civil society. It presents their views and defends their interests in policy discussions with the commission, the council and the European Parliament. The EESC is a bridge between the European Union and its citizens, promoting a more participatory, more inclusive, and therefore more democratic society in Europe.

The EESC is an integral part of the European Union's decision-making process. It must be consulted before decisions are made on economic and social policies. On its own initiative, or at the request of another EU institution, it may also give its opinion on other matters. The EESC has 317 members—the number from each EU country roughly reflecting the size of its population. The members are nominated by the EU governments, but they work in complete political independence. They are appointed to four-year terms and may serve more than once.

The European Economic and Social Committee meets in Plenary Assembly, and its discussions are prepared by six subcommittees known as sections. Each of these sections deals with a particular policy area. It elects its president and two vice presidents for two-year terms. Anne-Marie Sigmund, from Austria, became president of the EESC in October 2004.

The EESC has three main roles:

1. To advise the council, commission, and European Parliament, either at their request or on the committee's own initiative;
2. To encourage civil society to become more involved in EU policy making; and
3. To bolster the role of civil society in non-EU countries and to help set up advisory structures.

The Committee of the Regions. Set up in 1994 under the Treaty on European Union, the Committee of the Regions (CoR) is an advisory body composed of representatives of Europe's regional and local authorities. The CoR has to be consulted before EU decisions are taken on matters such as regional policy, the environment, education, and transportation, all of which concern local and regional governments.

The CoR has 317 members. The number from each member state approximately reflects its population size. The members of the CoR are elected municipal or regional politicians, often leaders of regional governments or city mayors. They are nominated by the EU governments but they work in complete political independence. The Council of the European Union appoints them for four years, and they may be reappointed. They must also have a mandate from the authorities they represent or be politically accountable to them. The CoR chooses a president from among its members, for a term of two years. Peter Straub, from Germany, was elected president in February 2004.

The role of the CoR is to put forward the local and regional points of view on EU legislation. It does so by issuing opinions on commission proposals.

The commission and the council must consult the CoR on topics of direct relevance to local and regional authorities, but they can also consult the CoR whenever they wish. For its part, the CoR can adopt opinions on its own initiative and present them to the commission, the council, and the parliament.

The European Central Bank. The European Central Bank (ECB) was set up in 1998, under the Treaty on the European Union, and it is based in Frankfurt, Germany. Its job is to manage the euro, the European Union's single currency. The ECB is also responsible for framing and implementing the European Union's economic and monetary policy.

To carry out its role, the ECB works with the European System of Central Banks (ESCB), which covers all 27 EU countries. However, only 12 of these countries have so far adopted the euro. The 12 collectively make up the euro area/region, and their central banks, together with the European Central Bank, make up what is called the Eurosystem.

The ECB works in complete independence. Neither the ECB, nor the national central banks of the Eurosystem, nor any member of their decision-making bodies can ask for or accept instructions from any other body. The EU institutions and member-state governments must respect this principle and not seek to influence the ECB or the national central banks.

The ECB, working closely with the national central banks, prepares and implements the resolutions made by the Eurosystem's decision-making bodies—the Governing Council, the Executive Board, and the General Council. Jean-Claude Trichet, from France, became president of the ECB in November 2003.

One of the ECB's main tasks is to maintain price stability in the euro region, so that the euro's purchasing power is not eroded by inflation. The ECB aims to ensure that the year-on-year increase in consumer prices is less than 2 percent. It does this in two ways:

1. By controlling the money supply. If the money supply is excessive compared to the supply of goods and services, inflation will result. Controlling the money supply involves, among other things, setting interest rates throughout the euro region.
2. By monitoring price trends and assessing the risk they pose to price stability in the euro area.

The European Investment Bank. The European Investment Bank (EIB) was set up in 1958 by the Treaty of Rome. Its job is to lend money for major infrastructure projects, such as rail and road links, airports, and environmental schemes. The EIB undertakes projects particularly in the less developed regions within member countries as well as the developing world. It also provides credit for small businesses. Philippe Maystadt, from Belgium, is the president of the EIB.

The EIB is nonprofit organization and gets no money from savings or current accounts, nor does it use any funds from the EU budget. Instead, the EIB is financed through borrowing on the financial markets and by the bank's shareholders, that is, the member states of the European Union. The EU countries subscribe jointly to its capital, each country's contribution reflecting its economic weight within the union. This backing by the member states gives the EIB the highest possible credit rating (AAA) on the money markets, where it can therefore raise very large amounts of capital on very competitive terms. This in turn enables the EIB to invest in projects of public interest that would otherwise not get the money or would have to borrow it more expensively.

The projects the EIB invests in are carefully selected according to the following criteria:

- Projects must help achieve EU objectives, such as making European industries and small businesses more competitive; creating trans-European networks (transport, telecommunications, and energy); boosting the information technology sector; protecting the natural and urban environments; and improving health and education services.
- Projects must chiefly benefit the most disadvantaged regions.
- Projects must help attract other sources of funding.

The EIB also supports sustainable development in countries of Africa, Asia, the Caribbean, and Latin America. An autonomous institution, it makes its own borrowing and lending decisions purely on the merits of each project and the opportunities offered by the financial markets.

The European Ombudsman. The position of European Ombudsman was created by the Treaty on the European Union. The ombudsman acts as an intermediary between the citizens and the EU authorities. He or she is entitled to receive and investigate complaints from EU citizens, businesses, and organizations, and from anyone residing in or having their registered office in an EU country. The ombudsman is elected by the European Parliament for a renewable term of five years, which corresponds to the parliament's legislative term. Nikiforos Diamandouros, the former national ombudsman of Greece, took up the post of European Ombudsman in April 2003 and was reelected in January 2005 for a five-year term.

The ombudsman helps to uncover "maladministration" in the European Union's institutions and bodies. Maladministration, or failed administration, occurs "when an institution fails to act in accordance with the law, or fails to respect the principles of good administration, or violates human rights." Some examples of maladministration are unfairness, discrimination, abuse of power, lack of or refusal to provide information, unnecessary delay, and incorrect procedures. The ombudsman carries out investigations in response to a complaint or based on his or her own initiative. Operating independently and impartially, the ombudsman does not request or accept instructions from any government or organization.

The European Data Protection Supervisor. The position of European Data Protection Supervisor (EDPS) was created in 2001. The responsibility of the EDPS is to make sure that all EU institutions and bodies respect people's right to privacy when processing their personal data.

"Processing" covers many activities, including collecting information, recording and storing it, retrieving it for consultation, making it available to other people, and also blocking, erasing, or destroying data. Strict privacy rules govern these activities. For example, EU institutions and bodies are not allowed to process personal data that reveals racial or ethnic origin, political opinions, religious or philosophical beliefs, or trade-union membership, nor may they process data on a citizen's health or sex life, unless the data is needed for health care purposes. Even then, the data must be processed by a health professional or another person who is sworn to professional secrecy. The EDPS works with the Data Protection Officers in each EU institution or body to ensure that the date privacy rules are applied. In 2004, Peter Johan Hustinx was appointed European data protection supervisor with Joaquin Bayo Delgado as the assistant supervisor.

The Office for Official Publications of the European Communities. The Office for Official Publications of the European Communities acts as the publishing house for the EU institutions, producing and distributing all official EU publications on paper and in digital form.

The European Personnel Selection Office. The European Personnel Selection Office (EPSO) became operational in January 2003. Its task is to set competitive examinations for recruiting staff to work in all the EU institutions. The office was established to be efficient and cost saving. Previously, all recruiting was handled by individual institutions. The EPSO, with an annual budget of roughly €21 million, spends 11 percent less than the individual institutions used to spend on recruitment.

The European Union: Success or Failure

The European Union was formed as the European Economic Community (EEC) in 1958 and known as such until 1992. The people who drafted the Treaty of Rome set the following task for the European Economic Community: "By establishing a common market and progressively approximating the economic policies of member states, to promote throughout the Community a harmonious development of economic activities, a continuous and balanced expansion, an increase in stability, an accelerated raising of the standard of living and closer relations between the States belonging to it." There have been many debates about whether the EU has achieved its goals. In general, it has achieved most of its goals—if not fully then at least partially.[13] The EU has brought stability, modernization, and prosperity to old as well as new members. It has also benefited from an integrated market of the kind that can be found in the United States. As a group, the EU has encouraged world trade and has been a force behind the formation of the WTO. These initiatives have provided great benefits to the European Union's member countries.

The introduction of a single European currency, the euro, is another major achievement of the European Union; it has been a positive force throughout the region.[14] From an economic standpoint, the European Union has helped its member countries to weather the financial problems in Asia and has also successfully fought off inflationary pressures. The European Central Bank has acted forcefully to maintain price stability without having to build any additional uncertainty premium into interest rates.

The introduction of the euro had its own set of challenges. The success of the euro depended on how well the European Union's leaders were able to settle their differences in political philosophies, economic principles, and sovereignty concerns.[15] However, the real challenge appeared to be in having the general population accept the new currency. The people in countries with strong currencies, such as Germany and the United Kingdom, were uneasy about giving up their known, low-inflation currencies for an unknown and untested euro. In the early years, the euro did fall in value against some of the major currencies, especially the U.S. dollar, and this decline caused economic problems for some of the European countries.[16]

One of the goals of the EU was to be competitive in the knowledge-based industries by the year 2010. Although the EU has achieved some measure of success in this area, it has been more successful in providing a system of rules and guidelines through the union's competition authorities, thereby helping European companies compete in the world markets.[17]

On the negative side, the defeat of the proposed EU Constitution in referendums in France and the Netherlands in mid-2005 not only brought to a halt plans to strengthen the European Union through the creation of more coherent institutions, procedures, and rules, but also exposed a severe division within the union on economic, social, and external trade policies.[18] The constitutional treaty's defeat was largely motivated by worries that welfare achievements of the French social model were threatened by an EU policy impetus toward the removal of market barriers, both within the European Union and with the outside world. The rejection by two founding members of the union has almost certainly ended not only the constitution, but also the entire drive toward deeper European integration. For decades, this process has proceeded through a succession of treaties, most of which handed over more power from national to European institutions. Now, and for the foreseeable future, new treaties will have to be put to voters.

Appendix 2
Worldwide Organizations and International Agencies

Worldwide organizations, also called international agencies, were established to serve as intermediaries among nations to promote peace, resolve disputes, build economies, aid countries in financial crisis, and so on. Organizations such as the United Nations, the International Bank for Reconstruction and Development, also called the World Bank, the International Monetary Fund, and others have evolved over the years in scope and practices paralleling the internationalization process. Following is a brief description of a few of these organizations: the International Monetary Fund, the Organisation for Economic Co-operation and Development, the United Nations, and the World Bank.[1]

THE INTERNATIONAL MONETARY FUND

The International Monetary Fund, also known as the IMF, was conceived at a United Nations conference convened in Bretton Woods, New Hampshire, in July 1944. The 45 governments represented at that conference sought to build a framework for economic cooperation that would avoid a repetition of the disastrous economic policies that had contributed to the Great Depression of the 1930s. Headquartered in Washington, D.C., the IMF is governed by its almost global membership of 184 countries.

The IMF's main responsibilities include:

- Promoting international monetary cooperation
- Facilitating the expansion and balanced growth of international trade
- Promoting exchange stability
- Assisting in the establishment of a multilateral system of payments
- Making its resources available (under adequate safeguards) to members experiencing balance-of-payments difficulties

More generally, the IMF is responsible for ensuring the stability of the international monetary and financial system, which is the system of international payments and exchange rates among national currencies that enables trade to take place between countries. The IMF seeks to promote economic stability and prevent crises; to help resolve crises when they do occur; and to promote growth and alleviate poverty. It employs three main tactics to meet these objectives: surveillance, technical assistance, and lending.

Surveillance

Surveillance is the regular dialogue and policy advice that the IMF offers to each of its members. Generally once a year, the IMF conducts in-depth appraisals of each member country's economic situation. It discusses with the country's authorities the policies that are most conducive to stable exchange rates and a growing and prosperous economy. Members have the option to publish the IMF's assessment, and the overwhelming majority of countries opt for transparency, making extensive information on bilateral surveillance available to the public. The IMF also combines information from individual consultations to form assessments of global and regional developments and prospects.

Technical Assistance

Technical assistance and training are offered (mostly free of charge) to help member countries strengthen their capacity to design and implement effective policies. Technical assistance is offered in several areas, including fiscal policy, monetary and exchange-rate policies, banking and financial system supervision and regulation, and statistics.

In the event that member countries do experience difficulties financing their balance of payments, the IMF is also a fund that can be tapped for help in recovery.

Lending

Financial assistance is available to give member countries the breathing room they need to correct balance-of-payments problems. A policy program supported by IMF financing is designed by the national authorities in close cooperation with the IMF, and continued financial support is conditional on effective implementation of this program.

The IMF is also actively working to reduce poverty in countries around the globe, independently and in collaboration with the World Bank and other organizations.

The IMF's resources are provided by its member countries, primarily through payment of quotas that broadly reflect each country's economic size. The total amount of the quotas is the most important factor determining the IMF's lending capacity. The annual expenses of running the IMF are met mainly by the difference between interest receipts (on outstanding loans) and interest payments (on quota "deposits").

The IMF is accountable to the governments of its member countries. At the apex of its organizational structure is its Board of Governors, which consists of one governor from each of the IMF's 184 member countries. All governors meet once each year at the IMF–World Bank Annual Meetings; 24 of the governors sit on the International Monetary and Finance Committee (IMFC) and meet twice each year. The day-to-day work of the IMF is conducted at its Washington, D.C., headquarters by its 24-member Executive Board; this work is guided by the IMFC and supported by the IMF's professional staff. The managing director is head of the IMF staff and chairman of the Executive Board, and is assisted by three deputy managing directors.

The Board of Governors

The Board of Governors, the highest decision-making body of the IMF, consists of one governor and one alternate governor for each member country. It usually meets once a year at the annual meetings of the IMF and the World Bank. The governor is appointed by the member countries and is usually the minister of finance or the governor of the central bank. All powers of the IMF are vested in the Board of Governors, which may delegate to the Executive Board all except certain reserved powers.

Key policy issues relating to the international monetary system are considered twice-yearly in the IMFC (known until September 1999 as the Interim Committee). A joint committee of the Boards of Governors of the IMF and World Bank—called the Development Committee—advises and reports to the governors on development policy and other matters of concern to developing countries.

The Executive Board

The Executive Board consists of 24 executive directors, with the managing director as chairman. The Executive Board usually meets three times a week, in full-day sessions, and more often if needed, at the organization's headquarters in Washington, D.C. The IMF's five largest shareholders (the United States, Japan, Germany, France, and the United Kingdom), along with China, Russia, and Saudi Arabia, have their own seats on the board. The other 16 executive directors are elected for two-year terms by groups of countries known as constituencies.

The documents that provide the basis for the board's deliberations are prepared mainly by IMF staff, sometimes in collaboration with the World Bank, and presented to the board with management approval, but some documents are presented by executive directors themselves.

Unlike some international organizations that operate under a one-country, one-vote principle (such as the United Nations General Assembly), the IMF has a weighted voting system: the larger a country's quota in the IMF (determined broadly by its economic size), the more votes it has. But the board rarely makes decisions based on formal voting; rather, most decisions are based on consensus among its members and are supported unanimously.

The Executive Board selects the managing director, who besides serving as the chairman of the board is the chief of the IMF staff and conducts the business of the IMF under the direction of the board. Appointed for a renewable five-year term, the managing director is assisted by a first deputy managing director and two other deputy managing directors.

IMF employees are international civil servants whose responsibility is to the IMF, not to national authorities. The organization has about 2,800 employees recruited from 141 countries. About two-thirds of its professional staff are economists. The IMF's 26 departments and offices are headed by directors who report to the managing director. Most staff work in Washington, although about 90 resident representatives are posted in member countries to advise on economic policy. The IMF maintains offices in Paris, France, and Tokyo, Japan, for liaison with other international and regional institutions,

Figure A2.1 **The International Monetary Fund**

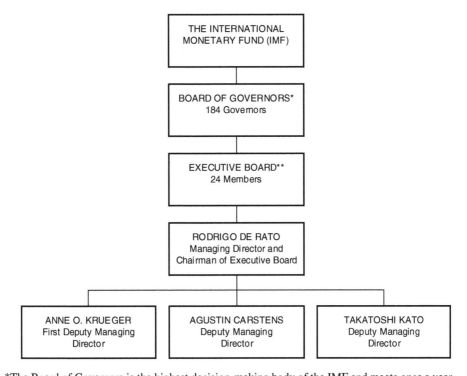

*The Board of Governors is the highest decision-making body of the IMF and meets once a year.
**The Executive Board carries out the day-to-day work of the IMF and usually meets three times a week.

and with organizations of civil society; it also has offices in New York City and Geneva, Switzerland, mainly for liaison with other institutions in the UN system. Figure A2.1 presents the IMF's organizational structure.

Resources of the IMF

The IMF's resources come mainly from the quota (or capital) subscriptions that countries pay when they join the IMF, or following periodic reviews in which quotas are increased. Countries pay 25 percent of their quota subscriptions in Special Drawing Rights (SDRs), or major currencies, such as U.S. dollars or Japanese yen; the IMF can call on the remainder, payable in the member's own currency, to be made available for lending as needed. Quotas determine not only a country's subscription payments, but also the amount of financing that it can receive from the IMF and its share in SDR allocations. Quotas also are the main determinant of countries' voting power in the IMF.

Quotas are intended broadly to reflect members' relative size in the world economy: the larger a country's economy in terms of output, and the larger and more variable its trade, the higher its quota tends to be. The United States, the world's largest economy, contributes most to the IMF, 17.5 percent of total quotas; Palau, the world's smallest economy, contributes 0.001 percent. The most recent (eleventh) quota review came into effect in January 1999, raising IMF quotas (for the first time since 1990) by about 45 percent to SDR 212 billion (about US$300 billion).

If necessary, the IMF may borrow to supplement the resources available from its quotas. The IMF has two sets of standing arrangements to borrow if needed to cope with any threat to the international monetary system:

- General Arrangements to Borrow (GAB), set up in 1962, which has 11 participants (the governments or central banks of the Group of Ten industrialized countries and Switzerland)
- New Arrangements to Borrow (NAB), introduced in 1997, with 25 participating countries and institutions

Under the two arrangements combined, the IMF has up to SDR 34 billion (about US$50 billion) available to borrow.

The IMF holds 103.4 million ounces of gold at designated depositories. Its total gold holdings are valued on its balance sheet at SDR 5.9 billion (about US$9 billion) on the basis of historical cost. As of February 2008, the IMF's resources amounted to US$362 billion. The IMF acquired virtually all its gold holdings through four main types of transactions under the original Articles of Agreement. First, the original articles prescribed that 25 percent of initial quota subscriptions and subsequent quota increases were to be paid in gold. This represented the largest source of the IMF's gold. Second, all payments of charges (that is, interest on members' use of IMF credit) were normally made in gold. Third, a member wishing to purchase the currency of another member could acquire it by selling gold to the IMF. The major use of this provision was sales of gold to the IMF by South Africa in 1970–71. And finally, members could use gold to repay the IMF for credit previously extended.

THE IMF: SUCCESS OR FAILURE

The International Monetary Fund has been assisting the governments of many countries in their recovery from poor economic conditions. Although the IMF applies the same programs of economic recovery to all countries it helps, the results have not been the same in all situations. In some cases, its efforts have resulted in full recovery of the economy; in other cases, they have led to marginal results. Following are a few examples of the successes and failures of the economic recovery programs initiated by the IMF.

In Bangladesh, the IMF's efforts led to a decrease in the country's poverty levels. In addition, the country was able to maintain economic stability through the assistance of the IMF.[2] It has been argued that although the country's growth rate is below 6 percent, the original target of the recovery program, this can still be considered an achievement under admittedly difficult circumstances.

In recent surveys of the Bosnian economy, the IMF has highlighted the hazards that arise from the country's complex fiscal architecture.[3] The country has achieved some success in the field of indirect taxation with the establishment of shared administration. However, IMF proposals for further unification may be politically unacceptable.

Timothy Adams, former undersecretary for international affairs of the U.S. Treasury, pushed the IMF to play a bigger role in monitoring the US$1.9 trillion-per-day currency market.[4] Adams criticized the IMF's failure to push China to make its currency, the yuan, more flexible and was quoted as saying that the IMF was "asleep at the wheel" on currencies. The Bush administration opened this new front in its campaign to pressure China to raise the value of its currency, demanding that the IMF crack down on countries that engage in currency manipulation.[5] Adams, who issued this demand, criticized the IMF for failing to enforce its own rules that bar member nations from maintaining artificially cheap currencies.

Between 2001 and 2003, the Dominican Republic's growth rate dropped by about 5 percent annually. The main reason for the decline was poor performance in two of the key sectors of the economy—tourism and agriculture.[6] But the economy picked up after it began its IMF austerity program.

Reports on the outlook of the economy in Peru show signs that the government is succeeding in meeting and even exceeding the fiscal targets set by the IMF under the terms of its "stand-by arrangement" with the country.[7] Continued growth in international mining prices will allow the government to use the tax revenues for additional debt repayments.

In 2001, Turkey faced a severe economic downturn. The IMF had to intervene to stabilize the economy and maintain a steady currency.[8] Turkey has successfully rebounded from its economic problems: inflation has fallen, the economy has maintained a steady growth rate, and the Turkish currency has appreciated for the first time in decades. In addition, Turkey's privatization program had a remarkably successful 2005.[9] Revenue from sales within the privatization program have reached around US$9.7 billion since January 2005, with a further US$3 billion coming from sales outside the program. This belated success is a tribute to the determination of Turkey's Justice and Development Party government to meet targets agreed to with the IMF and the World Bank.

At the urging of the IMF, the Ukrainian parliament approved the government's revised 2005 budget, cutting the deficit target to 1.6 percent of GDP from the 2.2 percent set by the outgoing administration. As recommended by the IMF, the Ukrainian parliament removed tax breaks that were frequently criticized by the IMF.[10] The easy parliamentary passage of the financial plan represents a key success for the government in its relations with the traditionally recalcitrant chamber.

Serbia's economic progress, with guidance from the IMF, has been impressive in recent years.[11] According to Business Monitor International (BMI), tight fiscal discipline and strong export growth are two success stories so far for the year 2005. However, it is also important for the country to successfully complete the IMF loan deal to implement further reforms to pensions and the energy sector, which are highly vulnerable to political interference.

According to an article by Graham Bird in *World Economy,* one way of assessing the impact of IMF programs is to see whether performance and policy targets are achieved.[12] In the article, Bird asked whether "a *failure* to hit targets mean that the programs have been unsuccessful, or could it be that targets have been too ambitious?" He analyzed political-economic factors that stymie government efforts. Some of the under-achievement of the IMF initiatives might be due to the high goals (overoptimism) set by the agency. Bird concludes that if the IMF eliminates overoptimism in its targets, the agency's psychology of *failure* surrounding its programs could be significantly reduced or even broken.

There is also concern among some economists that the IMF follows outdated economic models that do not take into account current economic realities.[13] These economists think that the IMF's intervention in economic crises in Latin America, East Asia, and Russia worsened their situations.

THE ORGANISATION FOR ECONOMIC CO-OPERATION AND DEVELOPMENT

The Organisation for Economic Co-operation and Development (OECD) is a unique forum where the governments of 30 market democracies work together to address the economic, social, and governance challenges of globalization as well as to exploit its opportunities. The OECD provides a setting where governments can compare policy experiences, seek answers to common problems, identify good practice, and coordinate domestic and international policies.

The OECD grew out of the Organisation for European Economic Cooperation (OEEC), which was set up in 1947 with support from the United States and Canada to coordinate the Marshall Plan for the reconstruction of Europe after World War II. Created as an economic counterpart to the North Atlantic Treaty Organization (NATO), the OECD took over from the OEEC in 1961. The OECD's mission has been to help governments achieve sustainable economic growth and employment and raise standards of living in member countries. At the same time, the OECD tries to maintain financial stability among member countries so as to contribute to the development of the world economy. Its founding convention also calls on the OECD to assist sound economic expansion in member countries and other countries that would lead to growth in world trade on a multilateral, nondiscriminatory basis. In recent years, the OECD has moved beyond a focus on its 30 member countries to offer its analytical expertise and accumulated experience to more than 70 developing and emerging market economies.

Globalization has seen the scope of the OECD's work move from examining each policy area within each member country to analyzing how various policy areas interact with one another, between countries, and beyond the OECD area. This is reflected in its work on issues such as sustainable development, bringing together environmental, economic, and social concerns across national frontiers for a better understanding of the problems and the best way to tackle them together.

The OECD provides a setting for reflection and discussion, based on policy research and analysis, that helps governments shape their own internal policies. The goal is for these discussions to eventually lead to formal agreements among member governments or to be acted on in domestic or other international arenas. Unlike the World Bank or the International Monetary Fund, the OECD does not dispense money.

The OECD's way of working consists of a highly effective process that begins with data collection and analysis and moves on to a collective discussion of policy, then decision making and implementation. Mutual examination by governments, multilateral surveillance, and peer pressure to conform or reform are at the heart of OECD effectiveness. The OECD has achieved success in areas such bribery, technology, and trade. Through its efforts, many formal agreements and policy initiatives have been reached, including the Convention on Combating Bribery in International Business Transactions, a resolution to use technology as a means for economic growth, the introduction of programs to reduce unemployment, and agreements to increase multilateral trade.

Discussions at the OECD sometimes evolve into negotiations during which OECD countries agree on the rules of the game for international cooperation. They can culminate in formal agreements, for example on combating bribery, on export credits, or on capital movements; or they may produce standards and models for international taxation or recommendations and guidelines covering corporate governance or environmental practices.

ORGANIZATIONAL STRUCTURE

The staff of the OECD Secretariat in Paris carries out research and analysis at the request of the OECD's 30 member countries. Representatives of member countries meet and exchange information in committees devoted to key issues. Decision-making power lies with the OECD Council.

The OECD Council

The OECD Council is made up of one representative from each member country, plus a representative from the European Commission. The council meets regularly at the level of ambassadors to the OECD, and decisions are taken by consensus. The council meets at the ministerial level once a year to discuss key issues and set priorities for OECD work. The work mandated by the council is carried out by the OECD Secretariat.

Committees

Representatives of the 30 member countries meet in specialized committees to advance ideas and review progress in specific policy areas such as economics, trade, science, employment, education, or financial markets. There are about 200 committees, working groups, and expert groups in all.

Some 40,000 senior officials from national administrations come to OECD committee meetings each year to request, review, and contribute to work undertaken by the OECD Secretariat. Once they return home, the national officials have online access to OECD documents and can exchange information through a special network (OLISnet).

The OECD Secretariat

Some 2,000 OECD Secretariat staff members in Paris work to support the activities of the committees. They include about 700 economists, lawyers, scientists, and other professionals, mainly based in a dozen substantive directorates, who provide research and analysis.

The secretariat is headed by a secretary-general, who is assisted by four deputy secretaries-general. The secretary-general also chairs the council, providing the crucial link between national delegations and the secretariat.

The OECD works in two official languages: English and French. Staff members are citizens of OECD member countries but serve as international civil servants with no national affiliation during their OECD posting. There is no quota system for national representation; there is simply an equal opportunity policy of employing highly qualified men and women with a cross-section of experience and nationalities.

The work of the secretariat parallels the work of the committees, with each directorate servicing one or more committees, as well as committee working parties and subgroups. Increasingly, however, OECD work is cross-disciplinary.

The OECD's work on sustainable development, and its International Futures Program, which aims at identifying emerging policy issues at an early stage, are multidisciplinary. Work on population aging has brought together macroeconomic specialists with experts on taxes, enterprises, health, the labor market, and social policy analysis.

The environment and economic issues can no longer be examined in isolation. Trade and investment are inextricably linked. Biotechnology concerns affect policy issues in agriculture, industry, science, the environment, and economic development. The overall effects of globalization draw in virtually every field in developing policies.

The 30 member countries of the OECD are Australia, Austria, Belgium, Canada, the Czech Republic, Denmark, Finland, France, Germany, Greece, Hungary, Iceland, Ireland, Italy, Japan, Korea, Luxembourg, Mexico, the Netherlands, New Zealand, Norway, Poland, Portugal, the Slovak Republic, Spain, Sweden, Switzerland, Turkey, the United Kingdom, and the United States. Figure A2.2 presents OECD's organizational structure.

THE OECD: SUCCESS OR FAILURE

Under Article 1 of the convention that was signed in Paris on December 14, 1960, and took effect on September 30, 1961, the OECD policies are designed for the following purposes:

- To achieve the highest sustainable economic growth and employment and a rising standard of living in member countries, while maintaining financial stability, and thus contributing to the development of the world economy
- To contribute to sound economic expansion in member as well as nonmember countries in the process of economic development
- To contribute to the expansion of world trade on a multilateral, nondiscriminatory basis in accordance with international obligations

In many areas outlined in its charter, the OECD has achieved success, including in advancing multilateral trade, in reducing unemployment among OECD countries, and in its attempts to standardize tax policies across countries. In a few other areas such as helping nations of the world to achieve economic growth and in dealing with tax haven countries, the OECD did not fully achieve its goals.

In the area of trade, efforts by the OECD to liberalize multilateral trade have been

Figure A2.2 **The Organisation for Economic Co-operation and Development**

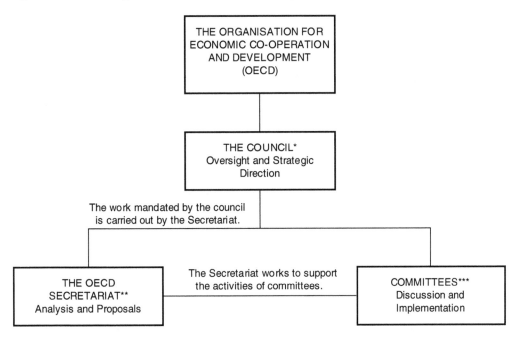

*The council is made up of one representative per member country, plus a representative from the European Commission.

**The secretariat is headed by the secretary-general, who also chairs the council and is assisted by four deputy secretaries-general.

***Representatives of member countries and countries with "observer" status meet in specialized committees.

successful. According to a study comparing the effects of three multilateral organizations—the World Trade Organization (WTO), the International Monetary Fund, and the OECD—on the international trade levels of the member countries, the results indicate that the OECD membership has had a consistently large positive effect on trade, while accession to the WTO also increases trade.[14] Similarly, in bringing nations together to draw up a policy on tax to facilitate globalization, the OECD has achieved reasonable results. The OECD committee on fiscal affairs has been able to harmonize transfer pricing guidelines and the model tax convention on income and on capital.[15] In the area of the economy, specifically as it relates to achieving stable growth rates among the OECD's member countries, the organization has partially succeeded in attaining reasonable growth rates, at the same time achieving full employment. This growth has been realized under some adverse conditions, including rising energy costs and spiraling inflation.[16] Finally, in the area of labor reform, the OECD did take a leadership role in creating and disseminating liberal welfare reform and labor market policy proposals between 1994 and 2001. These attempts resulted in the European Union adopting some of the guidelines in its European Employment Strategy.[17]

The OECD has not succeeded in its efforts to stimulate the world's economy through policy initiatives that direct its member countries to work with poorer nations of the world. In spite of its efforts, the OECD has not evenly affected economic growth among nations of the world and, in some instances, even among its members.[18] Similarly, in dealing with tax haven countries, the OECD has had no consequential effects. A study reported on the failure of the OECD to satisfy tax haven countries when it released the progress report on harmful tax practices in December 2001.[19] In this area, the OECD is in a no-win situation. If it comes on strong on this issue, it is accused of being overbearing and not listening, but when it does make changes in response to criticism, it is accused of compromising its principles.

Finally, the OECD seems to have little influence when it comes to controlling its relief efforts when disasters strike. Through its member countries, the OECD is able to quickly raise funds and supplies for relief efforts, but once it sends this aid to stricken areas, it does not seem to be able to distribute it efficiently or effectively. A case in point is in the aftermath of the Indian Ocean tsunami: the European Commission and 22 OECD countries pledged US$5 billion in humanitarian aid.[20] But as of September 2005, an OECD study says, only 41 percent of the money had been spent.

THE UNITED NATIONS

In 1945, representatives of 50 countries met in San Francisco at the United Nations Conference on International Organization to draw up the UN Charter. The organization officially came into existence on October 24, 1945, when the charter had been ratified by China, France, the Soviet Union, the United Kingdom, the United States, and a majority of other signatories. United Nations Day is celebrated each year on October 24. Today, nearly every nation, 191 in all, belongs to the United Nations. The UN Charter is the constituting instrument of the United Nations, setting out the rights and obligations of member states and establishing the organization's organs and procedures.

The purposes of the United Nations, as set forth in the charter, are to maintain international peace and security; to develop friendly relations among nations; to cooperate in solving international economic, social, cultural, and humanitarian problems and in promoting respect for human rights and fundamental freedoms; and to be a center for harmonizing the actions of nations in attaining these ends.

The six principal organs of the United Nations are the General Assembly, the Security Council, the Economic and Social Council, the Trusteeship Council, the International Court of Justice, and the Secretariat.

THE GENERAL ASSEMBLY

The General Assembly is the main deliberative organ of the United Nations. It is composed of representatives of all member states, each of which has one vote. Decisions on important questions—peace and security, admission of new members, and budgetary matters, for instance—require a two-thirds majority. Decisions on other questions are by simple majority.

Under the charter, the functions and powers of the General Assembly include:

- Considering and making recommendations on the principles of cooperation in the maintenance of international peace and security, including the principles governing disarmament and arms regulation
- Discussing any question relating to international peace and security and, except where a dispute or situation is being discussed by the Security Council, making recommendations on it
- Discussing and, with the same exception as above, making recommendations on any question within the scope of the charter or affecting the powers and functions of any organ of the United Nations
- Initiating studies and making recommendations to promote international political cooperation, the development and codification of international law, the realization of human rights and fundamental freedoms for all, and international collaboration in economic, social, cultural, educational, and health fields
- Making recommendations for the peaceful settlement of any situation, regardless of origin, that might impair friendly relations among nations
- Receiving and considering reports from the Security Council and other United Nations organs
- Considering and approving the UN budget and apportioning the contributions among members
- Electing the nonpermanent members of the Security Council, the members of the Economic and Social Council, and additional members of the Trusteeship Council (when necessary); electing jointly with the Security Council the judges of the International Court of Justice; and, on the recommendation of the Security Council, appointing the secretary-general

The General Assembly's regular session usually begins each year in September and ends in December. Beginning with its sixty-first regular session (2006–2007), the assembly opens on Tuesday of the third week in September, counting from the first week that contains at least one working day. The election of the president of the assembly, as well as its 21 vice presidents and the chairpersons of the assembly's six main committees, take place at least three months before the start of the regular session. To ensure equitable geographical representation, the presidency of the assembly rotates each year among five groups of states: African, Asian, Eastern European, Latin American and Caribbean, and Western European and other states.

In addition, the assembly may meet in special sessions at the request of the Security Council, a majority of member states, or one member if the majority of members concur. Emergency special sessions may be called within 24 hours of a request by the Security Council on the vote of any nine council members, or by a majority of the United Nations members, or by one member if the majority of members concur.

At the beginning of each regular session, the assembly holds a general debate, often addressed by heads of state and government, in which member states express their views on the most pressing international issues.

When the assembly is not meeting, its work is carried out by its six main committees, other subsidiary bodies, and the UN Secretariat. The UN's committees are as follows:

- Disarmament and International Security
- Economic and Financial
- Social, Humanitarian, and Cultural
- Special Political and Decolonization
- Administrative and Budgetary
- Legal

Some issues are considered only in plenary meetings, while others are allocated to one of the six main committees. All issues are voted on through resolutions passed in plenary meetings, usually toward the end of the regular session, after the committees have completed their consideration of them; these draft resolutions are then submitted to the plenary assembly. Voting in committees is by a simple majority. In plenary meetings, resolutions may be adopted by acclamation, without objection or without a vote, or the vote may be recorded or taken by roll call. While the decisions of the Assembly have no legally binding force for governments, they carry the weight of world opinion, as well as the moral authority of the world community.

The work of the United Nations during a given year derives largely from the decisions of the General Assembly—that is to say, the will of the majority of the members as expressed in resolutions adopted by the assembly. That work is carried out:

- by committees and other bodies established by the assembly to study and report on specific issues, such as disarmament, peacekeeping, development, and human rights
- in international conferences called for by the assembly
- by the Secretariat of the United Nations—the secretary-general and his staff of international civil servants

THE SECURITY COUNCIL

The UN Charter gives the Security Council primary responsibility for maintaining international peace and security. It is organized so as to be able to function continuously, and a representative of each of its members must be present at all times at UN headquarters.

When a complaint concerning a threat to peace is brought before it, the council's first action is usually a recommendation that the parties to try to reach an agreement by peaceful means. In some cases, the council itself undertakes investigation and mediation. It may appoint special representatives or request that the secretary-general do so; it may also set forth principles for a peaceful settlement.

When a dispute leads to a war, the council's first concern is to bring it to an end as soon as possible. On many occasions, the council has issued cease-fire directives, which have been instrumental in preventing wider hostilities. It also sends UN peacekeeping forces to help reduce tensions in troubled areas, keep opposing forces apart, and create conditions of calm in which peaceful settlements may be sought. The council may decide on enforcement measures, economic sanctions (such as trade embargoes), or collective military action.

In the case of a member state against which preventive or enforcement action has been taken by the Security Council, the General Assembly (on the recommendation of the Security Council) may suspend the member country's exercise of the rights and privileges of membership in the UN. A member state that has persistently violated the principles of the charter may be expelled from the United Nations by the assembly on the council's recommendation.

A state that is a member of the United Nations but not of the Security Council may participate, without a vote, in its discussions when the council considers that the interests of that particular country are affected. Members of the United Nations and nonmembers—if they are parties to a dispute being considered by the council—are invited to take part, without a vote, in the council's discussions; the council sets the conditions for participation by a nonmember state.

The Security Council has 15 members: five permanent members and 10 elected by the General Assembly for two-year terms. The presidency of the council rotates monthly, according to the English alphabetical listing of its member states. Each council member has one vote. Decisions on procedural matters are made by an affirmative vote of at least nine of the 15 members. Decisions on substantive matters require nine votes, including the concurring votes of all five permanent members. This is the rule of "great power unanimity," often referred to as the "veto" power.

Under the charter, all members of the United Nations agree to accept and carry out the decisions of the Security Council. While other organs of the United Nations make recommendations to governments, the council alone has the power to take decisions that member states are obligated under the charter to carry out.

Under the charter, the functions and powers of the Security Council are:

- To maintain international peace and security in accordance with the principles and purposes of the United Nations
- To investigate any dispute or situation that might lead to international friction
- To recommend methods of adjusting such disputes or the terms of settlement
- To formulate plans for the establishment of a system to regulate armaments
- To determine the existence of a threat to the peace or act of aggression and to recommend what action should be taken
- To call on members to apply economic sanctions and other measures not involving the use of force to prevent or stop aggression
- To take military action against an aggressor
- To recommend the admission of new members
- To exercise the trusteeship functions of the United Nations in "strategic areas"
- To recommend to the General Assembly the appointment of the secretary-general and, together with the assembly, to elect the judges of the International Court of Justice

ECONOMIC AND SOCIAL COUNCIL

The UN Charter established the Economic and Social Council (ECOSOC) as the principal organ to coordinate the economic, social, and related work of the 14 UN specialized agencies, 10 functional commissions, and five regional commissions. ECOSOC also receives reports from 11 UN funds and programs, and it serves as the central forum for discussing international economic and social issues, and for formulating policy recommendations addressed to member states and the United Nations system. It is responsible for promoting higher standards of living, full employment, and economic and social progress; identifying solutions to international economic, social, and health problems; facilitating international cultural and educational cooperation; and encouraging universal respect for human rights and fundamental freedoms. ECOSOC has the power to make or initiate studies and reports on these issues. It also has the power to assist in the preparation and organization of major international conferences in the economic and social and related fields and to facilitate a coordinated follow up to these conferences. With its broad mandate, ECOSOC's purview extends to more than 70 percent of the human and financial resources of the entire UN system.

In the Millennium Declaration, heads of state and government declared their resolve to further strengthen ECOSOC, building on its recent achievements, to help it fulfill the role ascribed to it in the UN Charter. In carrying out its mandate, ECOSOC consults with academics, business sector representatives, and more than 2,100 registered nongovernmental organizations. ECOSOC holds a four-week substantive session each July, alternating between New York and Geneva. The session includes a high-level segment, at which national cabinet ministers, chiefs of international agencies, and other high officials focus their attention on a selected theme of global significance. In 2005, a high-level segment took place in New York to address the following theme: "Achieving the internationally agreed development goals, including those contained in the Millennium Declaration, as well as implementing the outcomes of the major United Nations conferences and summits: progress made, challenges and opportunities." ECOSOC is expected to adopt a ministerial declaration on the theme of the high-level segment, which will provide policy guidance and recommendations for action. The ministerial declaration, together with the outcome of the discussions of the coordination segment addressing the theme of "achieving internationally agreed development goals, including those contained in the Millennium Declaration," provided an important input to the 2005 General Assembly plenary event.

ECOSOC has taken a lead role in key policy areas in recent years. Its 1999 high-level segment issued a "Manifesto on Poverty," which in many respects anticipated the formulation of the Millennium Development Goals that were approved at the UN Millennium Summit in New York. The ministerial declaration of the high-level segment in 2000 proposed specific actions to address the digital divide, leading directly to the formation in 2001 of the Information and Communication Technologies (ICT) Task Force. The consideration of African development at the 2001 high-level segment resulted in the first formal international endorsement of the New Partnership for Africa's Development (NEPAD). In 2002, the high-level segment adopted an innovative resolution on the contribution of human resources to development, particularly in the areas of health and education. The 2003 high-level segment focused on the promotion of an integrated approach to rural development in developing countries; the segment helped concentrate attention on the issues of poverty eradication and sustainability and led to the launch of a related initiative on Madagascar. In 2004, the high-level segment focused on least developed countries (LDCs) and resources mobilization and an enabling environment for poverty eradication. The high-level dialogue of the council helped to highlight the specific problems of LDCs. It also led to the launch of a rural initiative in Benin.

Outside of the substantive sessions, ECOSOC initiated in 1998 a tradition of meeting each April with finance ministers heading key committees of the Bretton Woods institutions (the World Bank and IMF). These consultations initiated interinstitutional cooperation that paved the way for the success of the International Conference on Financing for Development, which was held in March 2002 in Monterrey, Mexico, and which adopted the Monterrey Consensus. At that conference, ECOSOC was assigned a primary role in monitoring and assessing follow up to the Monterrey Consensus. These ECOSOC meetings have been considered important for deepening the dialogue between the United Nations and the Bretton Woods institutions, and for strengthening their partnership for achieving the development goals agreed upon at the global conferences of the 1990s. Participation in the meetings has broadened since the initial meeting in 1998. In addition to the chair of the Development Committee of the World Bank and the chair of the International Monetary and Financial Committee of the International Monetary Fund, the General Council of the World Trade Organization and the Trade and Development Board of UNCTAD are now also participating in the meeting.

The council's 54 member governments are elected by the General Assembly for overlapping three-year terms. Seats on the council are allotted based on geographical representation, with 14 allocated to African states, 11 to Asian states, six to Eastern European states, 10 to Latin American and Caribbean states, and 13 to Western European and other states.

The Bureau of the Economic and Social Council is elected by the council at large at the beginning of each annual session. The bureau's main functions are to propose the agenda, draw up a program of work, and organize the session with the support of the United Nations Secretariat.

THE TRUSTEESHIP COUNCIL

The Trusteeship Council was established to provide international supervision for 11 trust territories administered by seven member states and ensure that adequate steps were taken to prepare the territories for self-government or independence. It suspended operation on November 1, 1994, with the independence of Palau, the last remaining United Nations trust territory, on October 1, 1994. By a resolution adopted on May 25, 1994, the council amended its rules of procedure to drop the obligation to meet annually and agreed to meet as occasion required, by its decision or the decision of its president, or at the request of a majority of its members or the General Assembly or the Security Council.

In setting up an International Trusteeship System, the charter established the Trusteeship Council as one of the main organs of the United Nations and assigned to it the task of supervising the administration of trust territories placed under the system. Major goals of the system were to promote the advancement of the inhabitants of trust territories and their progressive development toward self-government or independence. The Trusteeship Council is made up of the five permanent members of the Security Council: China, France, the Russian Federation, the United Kingdom, and the United States.

The aims of the Trusteeship System have been fulfilled to the extent that all trust territories have attained self-government or independence, either as separate states or by joining neighboring independent countries.

Under the charter, the Trusteeship Council is authorized to examine and discuss reports from the administering authority on the political, economic, social, and educational advancement of the peoples of trust territories and, in consultation with the administering authority, to examine petitions from and undertake periodic and other special missions to trust territories.

THE INTERNATIONAL COURT OF JUSTICE

The International Court of Justice, also known as the World Court, is the principal judicial organ of the United Nations. Its seat is at the Peace Palace in The Hague (Netherlands). The World Court began work in 1946, when it replaced the Permanent Court of International Justice, which had functioned in the Peace Palace since 1922. It operates under a statute similar to that of its predecessor, which is an integral part of the Charter of the United Nations. The court has a dual role: to settle in accordance with international law the legal disputes submitted to it by states, and to give advisory opinions on legal questions referred to it by duly authorized international organs and agencies.

The court is composed of 15 judges elected to nine-year terms of office by the UN General Assembly and Security Council sitting independently of each other. It may not include more than one judge of any nationality. Elections are held every three years for one-third of the seats, and retiring judges may be reelected. The members of the court do not represent their governments but are independent magistrates.

The judges must possess the qualifications required in their respective countries for appointment to the highest judicial offices or be jurists of recognized competence in international law. In addition, the composition of the court must reflect the main forms of civilization and the principal legal systems of the world. When the court does not include a judge possessing the nationality of a state that has a case in the court, that state may appoint a person to sit as a judge on an ad hoc basis for the purpose of the specific case.

THE SECRETARIAT

The Secretariat is the arm of the UN that carries out the day-to-day work of the organization. It is made up of an international staff working in duty stations around the world. It services the other principal organs of the United Nations and administers the programs and policies laid down by them. At its head is the secretary-general, who is appointed by the General Assembly on the recommendation of the Security Council for a five-year renewable term. The current secretary-general is Ban Ki Moon of South Korea.

The duties carried out by the Secretariat are as varied as the problems dealt with by the United Nations. These range from administering peacekeeping operations to mediating international disputes, from surveying economic and social trends and problems to preparing studies on human rights and sustainable development. Secretariat staff also inform the world's communications media about the work of the United Nations; organize international conferences on issues of worldwide concern; and interpret speeches and translate documents into the organization's official languages.

The Secretariat has a staff of about 8,900 under the regular budget drawn from some 170 countries. As international civil servants, the staff members and the secretary-general answer to the United Nations alone for their activities, and they take an oath not to seek or receive instructions from any government or outside authority. Under the charter, each member state undertakes to respect the exclusively international character of the responsibilities of the secretary-general and the staff and to refrain from seeking to influence them improperly in the discharge of their duties.

The United Nations, while headquartered in New York, maintains a significant presence in Addis Ababa, Bangkok, Beirut, Geneva, Nairobi, Santiago, and Vienna, and has offices all over the world.

Some of the issues on the UN agenda in 2008 included climate change, human rights abuses, terrorism, HIV/AIDS and other deadly diseases, and the importance of stimulating economic development. Figure A2.3 presents the UN's organizational structure.

THE UNITED NATIONS: SUCCESS OR FAILURE

The UN, whose primary purpose is maintaining international peace and security, has profound effects on many aspects of global life. With its six main bodies and all the commissions connected to them, the organization works to promote respect for human rights, protect the environment, fight disease, and reduce poverty. Over the years, the UN has played a major role in helping to defuse international crises and resolve protracted conflicts. It has undertaken complex operations involving peacemaking, peacekeeping, and humanitarian assistance in Africa, Serbia, Kosovo, Cambodia, Vietnam, Algeria, Palestine, and the Middle East. After a conflict, it has increasingly undertaken action to address the root causes of war and lay the foundation for durable peace.

However, like many other international organizations, the UN has also been criticized for some of the actions it has taken. Ralph Greer, writing in the *Vancouver Sun,* stated that both the failures and the successes of the UN belong to its most powerful members, as they constitute the majority of the Security Council, which makes all important decisions.[21] Also, UN officials talked about the successes and failures of the UN during the fiftieth-anniversary commemoration of the signing of the UN Charter. The officials pointed out that, despite the failures, the organization had 16 active

420

Figure A2.3 **The United Nations**

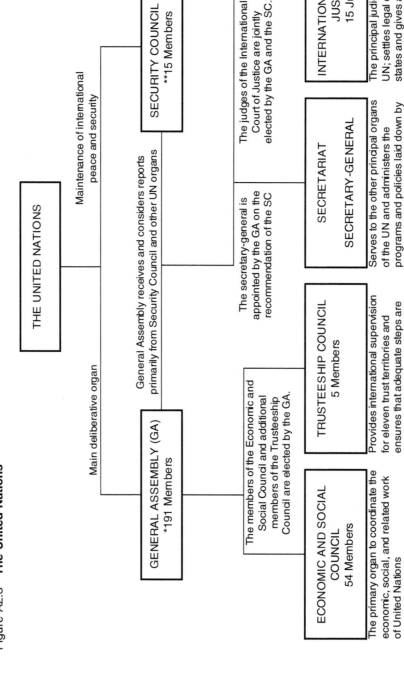

THE UNITED NATIONS

Main deliberative organ

Maintenance of international peace and security

GENERAL ASSEMBLY (GA)
*191 Members

SECURITY COUNCIL (SC)
**15 Members

General Assembly receives and considers reports primarily from Security Council and other UN organs

The secretary-general is appointed by the GA on the recommendation of the SC

The judges of the International Court of Justice are jointly elected by the GA and the SC.

ECONOMIC AND SOCIAL COUNCIL
54 Members

The primary organ to coordinate the economic, social, and related work of United Nations

TRUSTEESHIP COUNCIL
5 Members

Provides international supervision for eleven trust territories and ensures that adequate steps are taken to prepare the territories for self-governance or independence

The members of the Economic and Social Council and additional members of the Trusteeship Council are elected by the GA.

SECRETARIAT

SECRETARY-GENERAL

Serves to the other principal organs of the UN and administers the programs and policies laid down by them. The secretary-general is the "chief administrative officer" of the organization

INTERNATIONAL COURT OF JUSTICE
15 Judges

The principal judicial organ of the UN; settles legal disputes between states and gives advisory opinions to the UN and its agencies

*The General Assembly is composed of representatives of all member states, each of which has one vote.
**The Security Council has five permanent members (China, France, Russia, the United Kingdom, and the United States); the other ten members are elected by the General Assembly for two-year terms.

peacekeeping operations and had helped negotiate settlements in at least 172 regional conflicts from the Iran-Iraq war to the civil war in El Salvador. Further, they added that the United Nations had played a role in supervising elections, promoting human rights, curbing nuclear proliferation, fighting epidemics, and promoting development. Boutros Boutros-Ghali, a former secretary-general of the UN, said he believed the main accomplishments of the organization in its first half century were the roles it played in decolonizing the third world, promoting international cooperation between rich and poor countries, and increasing awareness of environmental problems. However, the UN has had limited success in its efforts in the human rights area. Unfortunately for the UN Commission on Human Rights (CHR), six of its human rights commission members—China, Cuba, Eritrea, Saudi Arabia, Sudan, and Zimbabwe—were among the most repressive regimes in the world as of 2005.[22]

Settling disputes between warring parties is another area in which the UN has had very little success. For example, the UN failed to settle the disputes between Croatia and Serbia. After waiting for the UN to help Serbia get back the disputed Krajina, Serbia took matters into its own hands. Similarly, the UN was not initially successful in bringing the Iran-Iraq war to an end. Only after the intervention of Sir John Thompson, the United Kingdom's representative to the UN, did the peace settlement between the two countries end in a peace accord.[23] Thompson's initiative marked a turning point in the Security Council's approach to conflict resolution. The change was underscored when Mikhail Gorbachev, in a departure from previous Soviet positions, called in 1987 for broader uses of UN peacekeeping forces.[24]

Charles W. Yost, who was the U.S. ambassador to the United Nations in 1970, described the UN's inability to keep the peace as "the central and critical failure" of the world organization. He said, "It was created to keep the peace and if it can't keep the peace, any other successes it may have are likely to be overshadowed and neglected." He also stated that new kinds of international peacekeeping efforts were needed for any Middle East settlement.

On the urging of some Security Council members, former Secretary-General Kofi Annan embarked on reforming the UN to be more sensitive to some of the critical world issues. While in office, he proposed and implemented numerous changes to bring the organization's management in line with best international practices. His initiatives include the Brahimi recommendations for comprehensive changes to United Nations peace operations, the 2002 Agenda for Further Change, the 2004 overhaul of the staff security system, improved coordination of humanitarian assistance, as well as a host of important budget, personnel, and management reforms. The current phase of reform comes at a particularly crucial time for the UN. The organization has faced an unprecedented series of challenges to meet the demands of member states, and yet its operations continue to need updating to be able to handle these tasks.

As UN secretary-general, Kofi Annan assumed direct responsibility for implementing reforms in a short time frame, as elaborated in his Implementation Report (A/60/430). This update provided a status report on specific reforms agreed to by the member states at the summit, as well as the ongoing reform measures previously initiated under the secretary-general's own authority. The task of continuing this reform was then passed on to Ban Ki Moon.

"The United Nations is the only hope of the world," said Winston Churchill back in 1944. Now, with the UN in crisis, attention should be given to his words and all possible support from each member country should be given to the UN rather than watching hope die.

THE WORLD BANK

The World Bank is a vital source of financial and technical assistance to developing countries around the world. It is not a bank in the common sense. It is made up of two unique development institutions owned by 184 member countries: the International Bank for Reconstruction and Development (IBRD) and the International Development Association (IDA). Each institution plays a different but supportive role in the bank's mission of global poverty reduction and the improvement of living standards. The IBRD focuses on middle-income and creditworthy poor countries, while the IDA focuses on the poorest countries in the world. Together, they provide low-interest loans, interest-free credit, and grants to developing countries for education, health, infrastructure, communications, and many other purposes.

Organized after the Bretton Woods, New Hampshire, meetings in July 1944, the World Bank has expanded from a single institution to a closely associated group of five development institutions. Their mission evolved from the IBRD as facilitator of postwar reconstruction and development to the present-day mandate of worldwide poverty alleviation in conjunction with their affiliate, the IDA.

The World Bank Group is made up of the following five organizations:

1. *International Bank for Reconstruction and Development.* The International Bank for Reconstruction and Development provides loans and development assistance to middle-income countries in Latin America, Asia, Africa, and Eastern Europe. The IBRD gets most of its funds by selling bonds in international capital markets.

2. *International Development Association.* The International Development Association plays an important role in the World Bank's mission to reduce poverty. Its support is focused on the poorest countries, to which it provides interest-free loans and grants. The IDA depends on contributions from its wealthier member countries for most of its financial resources.

3. *International Finance Corporation.* The International Finance Corporation (IFC) promotes growth in the developing world by financing private sector investments and providing technical support and advice to governments and businesses. In partnership with private investors, the IFC provides loans and equity finance for business ventures in developing countries.

4. *Multilateral Investment Guarantee Agency.* The Multilateral Investment Guarantee Agency (MIGA) encourages foreign investment in developing countries by providing guarantees to foreign investors against loss caused by noncommercial risks. The MIGA also provides technical support to help developing countries promote investment opportunities and uses its legal services to reduce possible barriers to investment.

5. *International Centre for the Settlement of Investment Disputes.* The International Centre for the Settlement of Investment Disputes (ICSID) provides facilities for settling investment disputes between foreign investors and their host countries.

The World Bank is like a cooperative, where its 184 member countries are shareholders. The shareholders are represented by the Board of Governors, which is the ultimate policy maker at the World Bank. Generally, the governors are member countries' ministers of finance or ministers of development. They meet once a year at the Annual Meetings of the Boards of Governors of the World Bank Group and the International Monetary Fund. Because the governors meet only annually, they delegate specific duties to 24 executive directors, who work onsite at the bank. The five largest shareholders—France, Germany, Japan, the United Kingdom, and the United States—appoint an executive director, while other member countries are represented by 19 executive directors.

The Board of Governors

One governor and one alternate governor in accordance with the Bank's Articles of Agreement are appointed for the Board of Governors by each member country. The governor and alternate each serve a five-year term and may be reappointed. If the member of the bank is also a member of the IFC or IDA, the appointed governor of the bank and his or her alternate also serve as ex-officio governor and alternate on the IFC and IDA Boards of Governors. MIGA governors and alternates are appointed separately. Generally, these governors are government officials, such as ministers of finance or ministers of development.

Under the articles, all powers of the bank are vested in the Board of Governors. Pursuant to the bank's bylaws adopted by the Board of Governors, the governors have delegated to the executive directors all the powers that are not expressly reserved to the governors under the articles.

The governors admit or suspend members, increase or decrease the authorized capital stock, determine the distribution of net income, review financial statements and budgets, and exercise other powers that they have not delegated to the executive directors. The Board of Governors meets once a year at the bank's annual meetings. The meetings are traditionally held in Washington two years out of three and, in order to reflect the international character of the institutions, every third year in a different member country.

The Executive Directors

The executive directors are responsible for the conduct of the general operations of the bank and exercise all the powers delegated to them by the Board of Governors. Regular elections of executive directors are held every two years, normally in connection with the bank's annual meetings. Over the years, it has been customary for election rules to ensure that wide geographical and balanced representation be maintained on the

Board of Executive Directors. Increases in the number of elected executive directors require a decision of the Board of Governors by an 80 percent majority of the total voting power. Before November 1, 1992, there were 22 executive directors, 17 of whom were elected. In 1992, in view of the large number of new members that had joined the bank, the number of elected executive directors was increased to 19. The two new seats, Russia and a new group around Switzerland, brought the total number of executive directors to its present level of 24.

The executive directors function in continuous sessions at the bank and meet as often as the bank's business requires. Executive directors consider and decide on IBRD loan and guarantee proposals and IDA credit, they grant and guarantee proposals made by the president, and they decide on policies that guide the bank's general operations. They are also responsible for presenting to the Board of Governors, at the annual meetings, an audit of accounts, an administrative budget, and an annual report on the bank's operations and policies, as well as other matters. In shaping bank policy, the Board of Executive Directors takes into account the evolving perspectives of member countries on the role of the bank group as well as the bank's operational experience. In addition to attending regular board meetings twice a week, the executive directors also serve on one or more of five standing committees: the Audit Committee, Budget Committee, Committee on Development Effectiveness (CODE), Personnel Committee, and Committee on Governance and Executive Directors' Administrative Matters. The committees help the board discharge its oversight responsibilities through in-depth examinations of policies and practices. Figure A2.4 presents the World Bank's organizational structure.

THE WORLD BANK: SUCCESS OR FAILURE?

The World Bank, in its role as one of the world's leading development lending agencies, has had some successes as well as some failures. An area where the World Bank has done quite well is in pursuing privatization policies, especially among the less developed countries. Privatization seems to encourage local investments and that, in turn, stimulates the economy. A case in point is the success of the privatization policies in Bangladesh.[25] Research has shown that when countries undertake deregulation and liberalization of formerly state-run industries, they can improve economic performance.[26] Recently, the World Bank has played a role in forcing the Group of Eight to agree on aid and debt relief to low-income countries and middle-income countries.[27]

The influence of the World Bank and its affiliates in shaping the economy of South Africa is considered a success story.[28] Survey findings from Asian executives on the achievements of the World Bank and the IMF in Asia show that the institutions are believed to have adequately responded to financial crises in Thailand and the Philippines and had influence in improving the region's environmental conditions.[29]

In 2002, the World Bank issued a US$300 million loan to Mexico to finance an education reform project.[30] The loan was the second phase of a three-part Adaptable Program Loan (APL). These loans have influenced the Mexican government to take

Figure A2.4 **The World Bank Group**

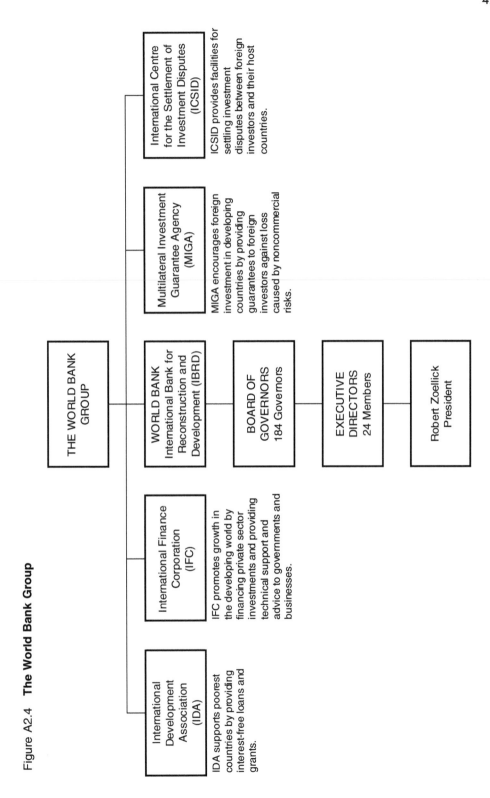

steps toward modernization, decentralization, and democratization. The project is considered a success for the World Bank as long as it takes the cultural needs of the indigenous peoples into account.

In its efforts to reduce income inequality within and among countries, it appears that the World Bank has not succeeded.[31] The main causes of the rise in world income inequality are attributed to the failure of the World Bank and the IMF to deal effectively with the broader economic structural issues.[32] One of the UN reports criticizes the World Bank for failing to foster diversification. More than half of the countries in Africa still depend on one or two commodities for 70 percent or more of their export earnings.

Appendix 3
The Internet in International Business

THE INTERNET AND BUSINESS

The Internet has revolutionized the way businesses operate in the twenty-first century. Beginning in 1990, Internet technology began to be used not only in production processes but also in marketing, finance, human resources, and nearly all other administrative functions. Today, few businesses can survive without a Web page of their company that prominently provides detailed information for consumers and investors. All companies recognize that they will be at a competitive disadvantage if they do not keep up with the latest technological advances at both the back and front room operations. These include the ability to implement automatic ordering processes for raw materials, maintain lean inventory, and run back-office services cost effectively. The term to describe the use of Internet technology in business functions is defined as e-commerce, a word that did not exist two decades ago.

E-commerce can be defined as business activity that usually involves trading a service or product between two parties through the use of computers. The process can be categorized into the following:

1. Electronic retailing or e-tailing, where online catalogs or a virtual mall with multiple online catalogs are made available to customers to purchase goods and services. This form of e-retailing is also called B2C or business-to-consumer services.
2. B2B or business-to-business electronic transactions form another major component of e-commerce and cover all activities between businesses over the Internet. Activities include procurement and supply chain management, delivery and sales of business information, and portals for exchange of goods.
3. B2G is a new term to denote the business-to-business electronic transactions that take place between businesses and government. Most governments account for a significant proportion of spending in an economy, roughly 20 percent of GDP for the United States, and therefore B2G is an important component for growth in technological applications in the future.

The Internet and International Business

This appendix highlights the role of the Internet as it relates to business applications and functions in the course of international activity. The use of the Internet continues to evolve in the marketplace as innovations improve productivity and efficiency in the workplace. We examine the innovations in technology in the three major areas of finance, marketing, and production in international business.

International Finance

The use of computers in banking goes back a far as 1959, when Bank of America ordered 32 ERMA (Electronic Recording Method of Accounting) computing machines from General Electric to perform their accounting functions and checking handling. It was based on the Magnetic Ink Character Reading (MICR) technology that is still used today in checks.[1] Similarly, the Automated Teller Machine (ATM) was originally designed by Luther Simjian in 1939 and field tested by a bank that later became Citibank. However, they discontinued the use citing a lack of demand. It was not until 1967 that Barclays Bank installed the first machine in London.[2]

The progress in electronic transactions was already in motion by the 1990s, with the use of telex that transmitted text messages across telephone lines. The advent of fax transmission further increased the speed of sending instruction for cross-border transactions. However, these were only messaging systems; the actual transfer of funds was usually done by another set of staff of the banks in both countries. Today, with Internet technology, the complete transaction of transferring funds can be executed from one location. As a result, depositing money at a teller of a local bank is a real-time transaction: it updates the client's account as well as all other departments that require notification of the transaction. At the end of the day, the total cash inflows and outflows for the whole bank is available to senior management.

Transactions among financial institutions in 2008 exceeded a quadrillion trades per year, and the speed of processing is now measured in milliseconds. The major institutions that process these trades are the Fedwire Funds Services, TARGET, Automated Clearing House (ACH), and the Depository Trust and Clearing Corporation (DTCC).

Real-Time Gross Settlement System (Fedwire and TARGET)

The Federal Reserve Board (the Fed) in the United States adopted the use of the Internet in its payments system early on by developing the Fedwire and the ACH systems. All banks in the United States use the Fedwire to transmit large value payments among themselves by having an account with the Fed. When Citibank decides to send $10 million on behalf of a client to Wachovia Bank, it sends instructions via the Internet, and the Fed debits the $10 million to Citibank's deposit and credits the same amount to Wachovia's account. The payment is in real-time, irrevocable, and final.[3] In Europe, the same system is called TARGET (Trans-European Automated Real-Time Gross Settlement Express Transfer system); it has recently been upgraded to TARGET2 and went live on November 19, 2007.

Automated Clearing Houses

The Federal Reserve also developed the Automated Clearing House in the 1970s, enabling the transfer of small payments between private groups and generating significant savings by reducing the flow of paper checks. ACH payments enable direct deposits of payroll and payments related to social security, insurance, mortgages, loans, federal and state taxes, business-to-business payments, and other entitlements of the U.S. government. Over the years, several private clearing houses have also been established that provide the same services as ACHs. They work under the rules developed by the National Automated Clearing House Association (NACHA), which are similar to those established by the Fed. Among the largest is the Electronic Payments Network that operates mainly in the Northeast sector of the United States. NACHA has recently developed rules for cross-border payments to comply with the requirements of the Office of Foreign Assets Control of the Department of the Treasury. Named the International ACH Transaction (IAT), it must be implemented by all financial institutions by March 2009, and will provide more information on the originator and receiver of payments, especially when it goes through correspondent banks.

Depository Trust and Clearing Corporation

When an individual purchases a stock or bond today, there is rarely physical delivery of the stock or bond certificates. Instead a book-entry takes place where the seller receives payment directly into his or her bank account and the stock certificate number is transferred from the seller to the buyer electronically. The U.S. government was the first to issue government bonds and notes in paperless form ("dematerialized"). Today, many companies also issue stocks or bonds in electronic form and it is expected to become the norm throughout the world. All trades are then channeled through the Depository Trust and Clearing Corporation (DTCC), which handles nearly all of the securities trading in the United States. The DTCC is a not-for-profit organization that is owned and controlled by all member institutions that provide trading services such as the large commercial banks, investment banks, and mutual funds. The company was started in the 1970s by the New York Stock Exchange (NYSE), American Stock Exchange (AMEX), and other exchanges looking for ways to reduce the paperwork associated with the sales of stocks.

As early as 1961, the NYSE with 15 member banks had begun book-entry trading for 31 securities. This format then led to the creation of seven clearing and settlement groups by the rest of the stock exchanges in the country. The two largest were the National Securities Clearing Corporation (NSCC) and the Depository Trust Corporation (DTC), owned by the NYSE, AMEX, and NASDAQ. Eventually the rest were merged into the NSCC and DTC, and they in turn merged in 1999 to form the DTCC.[4]

Reuters and Bloomberg

All traders around the globe have either a Reuters or Bloomberg terminal on their desk. These terminals receive a large volume of information from financial markets worldwide and are processed via algorithms to provide meaningful charts and analysis to the traders. Reuters was providing such data even before Bloomberg began its services, but Bloomberg managed to capture a larger market share in the United States by providing data that was deemed relevant to traders and more user friendly than their competitors. Although Reuters has an overall edge globally, both companies are tied neck and neck in the supply of financial information to global markets.

INTERNATIONAL MARKETING

In the field of marketing, Internet technology has been useful to companies in two areas, advertising and sales.

Advertising

The Internet has changed the world of advertising by slowly replacing print, radio, and television advertisements as the dominant media to reach customers worldwide. As mentioned earlier, it is necessary today for all companies to have a Web site that effectively displays information about the company and their products and services. Research shows that consumers with Internet access research products online even if they intend to purchase them in stores. A Web site alone, however, is not sufficient for a company to improve its sales, domestic or international. It has to ensure that traffic on the Internet is directed to their Web site, which is difficult when one considers that in 2008 there were more than 250 billion pages available on the World Wide Web. The two keys ways to ensure the flow of traffic to a company's Web site are discussed next.

Paid Advertisements (Pay per Click)

Companies can pay to have their Web sites appear on the pages of major search engines, which include Google, Yahoo, and MSN. The terms of payments are "pay per click" (PPC), and the cost depends on the number of clicks made by potential clients when visiting the Web pages. Companies may contract directly with the search engines or deal with advertising companies that specialize in placing ads online around the globe.

As an example, Google will display a company's advertisement as a sponsored link on key search words. If a company in Indonesia provides tourism packages, and a U.S. customer types "travel and Indonesia" in Google, the company's advertisement will appear as part of a sponsored link. Google also offers what is called "contextual targeting technology," in which companies can place their advertisements in sites related to their business. A company that writes blogs on travel, for instance, can have travel advertisements directed to their site. The payments are usually based on the number of clicks on the advertisement.

Search Engine Optimization (SEO)

The other method is for the company to ensure through the development of its Web site that online traffic is maximized to its page. All major search engines keep their policy of selecting pages to display in response to keywords a carefully guarded secret. However, some minimum requirements must be met in the design of Web pages in order to have them selected for front page display. Professional companies or search engine optimization (SEO) programmers must continuously monitor the traffic and tweak the meta tags (words that are searched by search engines to determine content) used in a Web page to increase its chances of being selected for the first few pages of browsing. Research has shown that most users do not go past a few pages when searching on the Internet.

Companies that optimize their Web pages (defined as organic search Web sites) are generally trusted more than companies using paid advertisements. Customers are somewhat skeptical of sponsored Web sites. Organic Web sites are cheaper because advertisement are free; however, these sites require effort and finesse to ensure they end up on the front pages of the top search engines. For international business, this will require interacting with the local search engines in the relevant countries.

Sales

The Internet has proved to be a major tool for companies to boost their international sales. The ability to contact firms globally via the Web has created a new industry that specializes in packaging global data for companies planning their global marketing strategy. Most companies have also set up Web pages for orders to be placed directly to their portal for delivery of goods through their international sales offices.

INTERNATIONAL PRODUCTION AND OPERATIONS

Perhaps the biggest benefits of Internet technology are those related to improving efficiency in international production and operations. The two most important productivity advances involve:

1. The use of Internet technology to design efficient allocation of resources between subsidiaries and the parent. The integration of workflow processes between subsidiaries and the parent has to be fully optimized in order to achieve efficiency throughout the company. This requires software that can evaluate the inventory levels and requirements of all subsidiaries and provide the information to one central location, thereby assisting in the procurement of resources as well as the allocation of the output from the various subsidiaries.
2. The use of Internet technology to design efficient allocation of resources between companies and external stakeholders. External stakeholders include (1) the clients whose success hinges on an efficient delivery method, and (2) the suppliers whose costs decrease when the most efficient method of procurement is used.

The major improvements in the efficiency of these services have taken place through the implementation of software for managing information effectively between the various stakeholders and their respective units. The three popular software programs that support these activities include Oracle, SAP, and Sage Software. These programs usually cover different functional areas and different phases of the workflow process of an organization. They include the following areas:

1. Product life cycle (PLC) management
2. Enterprise resource planning
3. Supply-chain management
4. Human resource management
5. Customer relationship management
6. Electronic commerce
7. Real estate management
8. Environment, health, safety, and other regulatory issues

Electronic Data Interchange (EDI)

Electronic Data Interchange is the delivery of standardized forms of messages between companies, mostly in the area of sales and purchase management. This was among the earliest vehicles used by companies to automate the purchase and sales processes. EDI is a subset of e-commerce in that it only pertains to the transmission of information between two business entities. The information allows for Company A to purchase from Company B by inputting just the information relevant to the sale, which then can be transmitted electronically; the order recording, shipment information, and confirmation of payment can all be accomplished electronically. Wal-Mart, for example, expects its suppliers to be fully compliant with their EDI requirements. Goods have to be shipped and confirmed within very tight schedules. If goods do not reach the central docks on time, suppliers miss their opportunity to transport them to the various stores; suppliers will then end up paying for the missed deliveries.

There are currently three standards in place for designing EDI protocols.

1. ISO/IEC 14662:1997 was established by the International Organization of Standardization (ISO), along with the International Electrotechnical Commission, to make EDI standards uniform across the world. It uses an open-edi approach to make it much simpler for companies to develop protocols for interacting with diverse companies.
2. ANSI ASC X12 (American National Standards X12) is the standard used in the United States and is applicable to all kinds of business documents, including invoices and purchase orders. The Accredited Standards Committee X12 was given the task of designing the standards that initially began with the Transportation Data Coordination Committee in 1975, followed by the implementation in other industries, such as financial services, in 1986, and the insurance and health care industries in 1991.[5]
3. UN/EDIFACT or United Nations/Electronic Data Interchange for Administration Commerce and Transport was adopted by the United Nations and is still used in Europe. The Accredited Standards Committee of the United States is attempting to makes its standards converge toward the EDIFACT design.

There are many companies that offer global EDI packages that make it easy to communicate between different industries in different countries. The programs are basically written to make them compatible across the three standards.

APPENDIX 3 SUMMARY

Internet technology has greatly impacted the way business is conducted globally. As in domestic business, it has changed the mode of operations in all areas of business, including finance, marketing, production, and administration.

In finance, the biggest impact has been on the way payments are transferred between companies and financial institutions in different countries. They have reached an efficiency level where payments across countries can be cleared and settled in one day. In additional, financial information is available instantly across the globe via computer for traders, eliminating price discrepancies and opportunities to arbitrage.

In marketing, the biggest change has taken place in the world of advertising, where the Internet is expected to replace print, TV, and radio as the dominant media. Companies have the option of paying to have their Web pages accessible to potential customers, or they can optimize their Web sites to ensure their pages are selected when specific words are keyed in by customers. The latter is termed an "organic search," and customers usually trust organic search results over paid or sponsored links. In international marketing, companies have to be aware of not only targeting globally recognized search engines such as Google, MSN and Yahoo but also the local search engines popular in each country or region.

In production, there have been rapid advances in the use of Internet technology to improve efficiency and speed in the global operations of companies. Internet technology has reduced the distances between subsidiaries and the parent company. Software by SAP and Oracle, for example, can link the production and operation schedules of many factories into a single database and coordinate activities simultaneously.

Notes

NOTES TO CHAPTER 1

1. "International Merchandise Trade," *UNCTAD Handbook of Statistics,* 2007, Table 1.1.

2. "Economic Statistics," June 2008. Available at http://www.cia.gov/.

3. Matt Richtel, "As U.S. Cools, World Demand Helps HP Outpace Rivals," *New York Times,* November 19, 2007, pp. C1, C4.

4. Peter S. Goodman, "Companies Bolster Sales Abroad to Offset Weakness at Home," *New York Times,* November 20, 2007, pp. A1, A18.

5. Louise Story, "Seeking Leaders, U.S. Companies Think Globally," *New York Times,* December 12, 2007, pp. A1, A12.

6. "Minimum Monthly Wage Standards in Selected Provinces/Municipalities/Cities in China," *China Labor Watch,* July 24, 2006, pp. 1–4.

7. Dan Keeler, "Global Business in the New Millennium," *Global Finance* 14, no. 1 (2000): 104–5.

8. Keith Bradsher, "With First Car, a New Life in China," *New York Times,* April 24, 2008, pp. C1, C4.

9. Barbara Kiviat, "Sewn in the U.S.A.," *Business Week,* April 28, 2008, pp. global 1–2.

10. "Intel Goes Volume with 65nm Fab in Ireland," *Electronic Weekly,* June 28, 2006, p. 1.

11. Fara Warner, "Marketing Army Hits China: Researchers Track the Changing Patterns and Tastes of Chinese Consumers," *Asia Wall Street Journal,* March 1, 1997, p. 1.

12. Barton Lee, Tony Zhao, and David Tatterson, "Emerging Trends in China's Marketing Research Industry," *Quirk's Marketing Research Review,* November 1998, p. 1.

13. "International Market Research," June 5, 2008. Available at http://www.asiamarketresearch.com.

14. Liz Brooks, "Inspiring the C-Level Audience," *Adweek,* February 2002, p. 17.

15. David A. Ricks, *Big Business Blunders* (Homewood, IL: Irwin, 1983).

16. Sheila Reily, "Using Market Research to Survive and Thrive in Financial Service," *Marketing Review,* December 1996, pp. 7–8.

17. Kevin Daniels, Leslie De Chernatony, and Gary Johnson, "Validating a Method for Mapping Managers' Mental Models of Competitive Industry Structures," *Human Relations,* September 1995, pp. 975–91.

18. The Client/Market Research Group, JPMorgan, "The Do's and Don'ts of International Market Research," *Marketing Review,* December 1996, pp. 18–20.

19. Kathleen Morris, "The Town Watcher," *Financial World,* July 19, 1994, pp. 42–44.

20. Paula Kephart, "Think Globally," *American Demographics,* November/December 1994, p. 76.

21. Abdalla F. HaYajneh and Sammy G. Amin, "The Utilization of International Information for Global Marketing Competitiveness: An Empirical Investigation," *Journal of Applied Research* 11, no. 2 (1995): 29–37.

22. Susan J. Hart, John R. Webb, and Marian V. Jones, "Export Marketing Research and the Effects of Export Experience in Industrial SME's," *International Marketing Review* 11, no. 6 (1994): 4–22.

23. Archie B. Carroll, "A Three-Dimensional Conceptual Model of Corporate Performance," *Academy of Management Review* 4, no. 4 (1979): 497–505.

24. Mark S. Schwartz and Archie B. Carroll, "Corporate Social Responsibility: A Three-Domain Approach," *Business Ethics Quarterly* 13, no. 4 (2003): 503–30.

25. Jeff H. Smith, "The Shareholders vs. Stakeholders Debate," *Sloan Management Review* 44, no. 4 (2003): 85–90.

26. Roger L. Martin, "The Virtue Matrix: Calculating the Return on Corporate Responsibility," *Harvard Business Review* 80, no. 3 (2002): 68–75.

27. "Doing the Right Thing Is Good for Business," *New Statesman,* September 4, 2006, pp. 20–30.

28. Esther M.J. Schouten and Remm Joop, "Making Sense of Corporate Social Responsibilities in International Business: Experiences from Shell," *Business Ethics: A European Review* 15, no. 4 (2006): 365–79.

29. "Corporate Social Responsibility: The Collaboration Paradigm; Strategic Partnerships for Business," *New York Times,* November 8, 2006, pp. ZR1–ZR8.

30. Paul F. Buller, John J. Kohls, and Kenneth S. Anderson, "When Ethics Collide: Managing Conflicts across Cultures," *Organizational Dynamics* 28, no. 4 (2000): 52–66.

31. Thomas Donaldson, "Values in Tension: Ethics Away from Home," *Harvard Business Review* 74, no. 5 (1996): 48–62.

32. Ruth Alas, "Ethics in Countries with Different Cultural Dimensions," *Journal of Business Ethics* 69, no. 3 (2006): 237–47.

33. Steven F. Messner and Richard Rosenfeld, *Crime and the American Dream* (Belmont, CA: Wadsworth, 2006).

34. William D. Ross, *The Right and the Good,* ed. Philip Stratton-Lake (Oxford, UK: Oxford University Press, 1930).

35. Oliver F. Williams, "Business Ethics: A Trojan Horse?" *California Management Review* 24, no. 4 (1982): 14–24.

36. Thomas Donaldson, "The Language of International Corporate Ethics," *Business Ethics Quarterly* 2, no. 3 (1992): 271–81.

37. Philip Pattberg, "The Influence of Global Business Regulation: Beyond Good Corporate Conduct," *Business & Society Review* 111, no. 3 (2006): 241–68.

38. "Corporate Social Responsibility as a New Paradigm in the European Policy: How CSR Comes to Legitimate the European Regulation Process," *Corporate Governance: The International Journal of Effective Board Performance* 6, no. 4 (2006): 358–68.

39. Bodo B. Schlegelmilch and Diana C. Robertson, "The Influence of Country and Industry on Ethical Perceptions of Senior Executives in the U.S. and Europe," *Journal of International Business Studies* 26, no. 4 (1995): 859–81.

40. E. Merrick Dodd, Jr., "For Whom Are Corporate Managers Trustees?" *Harvard Law Review* 45, no. 7 (1932): 1145–63.

41. Andrew Friedman and Samantha Miles, "Developing Stakeholder Theory," *Journal of Management Studies* 39, no. 1 (2002): 1–21.

42. William R. Dill, "Environment as an Influence on Managerial Autonomy," *Administrative Science Quarterly* 2, no. 4 (1958): 409–43.

43. Edward R. Freeman, *Strategic Management: A Stakeholder Approach* (Boston, MA: Pitman, 1984), p. 31.

44. James D. Thompson, *Organizations in Action* (New York, NY: McGraw-Hill, 1967) pp. 27–28.

45. Anthony A. Atkinson, John J. Waterhouse, and Robert B. Wells, "A Stakeholder Approach to Strategic Performance Measurement," *Sloan Management Review* 38, no. 3 (1997): 25–38.

46. Klement Podnar and Janicic Zlatko, "Towards a Categorization of Stakeholder Groups: An Empirical Verification of a Three Level Model," *Journal of Marketing Communications* 12, no. 4 (2006): 297–308.

47. Rosabeth Moss Kanter, "Transcending Business Boundaries: 12,000 World Managers View Change," *Harvard Business Review* 69, no. 3 (1991): 151–64.

48. Pedro Lorca and Julita Garcia-Diez, "The Relation between Firm Survival and the Achievement of Balance among Its Stakeholders: An Analysis," *International Journal of Management* 21, no. 1 (2004): 93–99.

49. "Stakeholder Symbiosis," *Fortune,* March 30, 1998, p. S2.

50. James E. Post, Lee E. Preston, and Sybille Sachs, "Managing the Extended Enterprise: The New Stakeholder View," *California Management Review* 45, no. 1 (2002): 6–28.

51. Anthony J. Rucci, Steven P. Kirn, and Richard T. Quinn, "The Employee-Customer-Profit Choices at Sears, *Harvard Business Review* 76, no. 1 (1998): 82–97.

52. Jeremy Galbreath, "Does Primary Stakeholder Management Positively Affect the Bottom Line? Some Evidence from Australia," *Management Decision* 44, no. 8 (2006): 1106–21.

53. Muriel Cozier, "DuPont Widens Goals," *ICIS Chemical Business,* October 16, 2006, p. 35.

54. Lee E. Preston and Harry J. Sapienza, "Stakeholder Management and Corporate Performance," *Journal of Behavioral Economics* 19, no. 4 (1990): 361–75.

55. Philip Kotler, *Marketing Management* (Upper Saddle River, NJ: Prentice Hall, 2000), p. 41.

56. Mette Morsing and Majken Schultz, "Corporate Social Responsibility Communication: Stakeholder Information, Response, and Involvement Strategies," *Business Ethics: A European Review* 15, no. 4 (2006): 323–38.

57. Robert S. Kaplan and David P. Norton, *The Balanced Scorecard: Translating Strategy into Action* (Cambridge, MA: Harvard Business School Press, 1996).

58. Kimberly Elliott, "Corruption as an International Policy Problem: Overview and Recommendations," in *Corruption and the Global Economy,* ed. Kimberly Elliot (Washington, DC: Institute for International Economics, 1997), p. 177.

59. Robert Klitgaard, *Controlling Corruption* (Berkley, CA: University of California Press, 1991).

60. Andres M. Claros, "Corruption in International Business," Unpublished Honors Essay (Hempstead, NY: Hofstra University, 2002), pp. 6–10.

61. Tom Hall and Glenn Yago, "Policy Briefing" (Washington, DC: Milken Institute, 1999), pp. 1–10.

62. Edgardo Buscaglia, "An Analysis of Judicial Corruption and Its Causes: An Objective Governing-Based Approach," *International Review of Law and Economics* 21, no. 2 (2001): 233–49.

63. Paul Mauro, "Corruption and Growth," *Quarterly Journal of Economics* 110, no. 3 (1995): 681–712.

64. G.R. Weaver, L.K. Trevino, and P.L. Cochran, "Corporate Ethics Practices in the Mid-1990s: An Empirical Study of the Fortune 1000," *Journal of Business Ethics* 18, no. 2 (1999): 283–94.

NOTES TO CHAPTER 2

1. Teresa C. Morrison, Wayne A. Conway, and Joseph J. Douress, *Dun & Bradstreet's Guide to Doing Business around the World* (Upper Saddle River, NJ: Prentice Hall, 1997).

2. Carl A. Rodrigues, "Cultural Classifications of Societies and How They Affect Cultural Management," *Journal of Cross-Cultural Management* 5, no. 3 (1998): 31–41.

3. Runja Jing and John L. Graham, "Values versus Regulations: How Culture Plays Its Role," *Journal of Business Ethics* 80, no. 3/4 (2008): 791–806.

4. Petra Bohnke, "Does Society Matter? Life Satisfaction in Enlarged Europe," *Social Indicators Research* 87, no. 2 (2008): 189–210.

5. Malte Brettel, Andreas Engelen, Florian Heinemann, and Pakpachong Vadhanasindhu, "Ante-

cedents of Market Orientation: A Cross-Cultural Comparison," *Journal of International Marketing,* 16, no. 2 (2008): 84–119.

6. Scot Shane, "The Effect of National Culture on the Choice between Licensing and Foreign Direct Investment," *Strategic Management Journal* 15, no. 8 (1994): 627–43.

7. Gupta Vipin, "Cultural Dimension and International Marketing," *IIM Bangalore Management Review* 15, no. 3 (2003): 69–74.

8. Jae H. Pae, Saeed Samiee, and Susan Tai, "Global Advertising Strategy," *International Marketing Review* 19, no. 2/3 (2002): 176–80.

9. Simcha Ronen, *Comparative and Multinational Management* (Hoboken, NJ: John Wiley & Sons, 1986).

10. Harm J. de Blij and Alexander B. Murphy, *Human Geography* (Hoboken, NJ: John Wiley & Sons, 1999).

11. Kylie Hansen, "Business Lost in Transition," *Australian CPA* 7, no. 44 (2004): 46–49.

12. David A. Ricks, M.Y.C. Fu, and Jeffrey S. Arpan, *International Business Blunders* (Columbus, OH: Grid Publishing, 1974).

13. William Whitely and George W. England, "Managerial Values as a Reflection of Culture and the Process of Industrialization," *Academy of Management Journal* 20, no. 3 (1977): 439–53.

14. "Turning toward Mecca," *Economist,* May 10, 2008, pp. 83–84.

15. Nancy J. Adler, "Asian Women in Management," *International Studies of Management & Organizations* 23, no. 4 (1993–94): 3.

16. Jared Wade, "The Pitfalls of Cross-Cultural Business," *Risk Management* 51, no. 3 (2004): 38–43.

17. Gert Hofstede, *Culture's Consequences* (Beverly Hills, CA: Sage Publications, 1980).

18. P.W. Dorfman and J.P. Howell, "Dimensions of National Culture and Effective Leadership Patterns," *Advances in International Comparative Management,* Vol. 3 (1988): 127–50.

19. Christopher P. Earley and Cristina B. Gibson, "Taking Stock in Our Progress on Individualism-Collectivism: 100 Years of Solidarity and Community," *Journal of Management* 24, no. 3(1998): 265–305.

20. Senguin Yeniyurt and Janiel D. Townsend, "Does Culture Explain Acceptance of New Products in a Country?" *International Marketing Review* 20, no. 4 (2003): 377–97.

21. Elke U. Weber, William P. Bottom, and Robert N. Bontempo, "Cross-Cultural Differences in Risk Perception: A Model-Based Approach," *Risk Analysis: An International Journal* 17, no. 4 (1997): 479.

22. Huang Chih-Wen and Ai-Ping Tai, "Different Cultural Values Reflected in Customer Value Perceptions of Products: A Comparative Study of Chinese and Americans," *Journal of International Marketing & Marketing Research* 28, no. 1 (2003): 37–57.

23. M. Sondergraad, "Hofstede's Consequences: A Study of Reviews, Citations and Replications," *Organizational Studies* 15, no. 3 (1994): 447–56.

24. M.H. Hoppe, "Validating the Masculinity/Femininity Dimension on Elites from 19 Countries," in *Masculinity and Femininity: The Taboo Dimension of National Cultures,* ed. Gert Hofstede and W. Arrindell (Beverly Hills, CA: Sage Publications, 1998).

25. James Neelankavil, Anil Mathur, and Yong Zhang, "Determinants of Managerial Performance: A Cross-Cultural Comparison of the Perceptions of Middle-Level Managers in Four Countries," *Journal of International Business Studies* 40, no. 1 (2000): 121–40.

26. Nitish Singh, "From Cultural Models to Cultural Categories: A Framework for Cultural Analysis," *Journal of American Academy of Business* 5, no. 1/2 (2004): 95–102.

27. Michele J. Gelfand, Lisa M. Leslie, and Ryan Fehr, "To Prosper, Organizational Psychology Should . . . Adopt a Global Perspective," *Journal of Organizational Behavior* 29, no. 4 (2008): 493–517.

28. Florence Kluckhohn and Fred Strodtbeck, *Variations in Value Orientations* (Westport, CT: Greenwood Press, 1961).

29. Ka Wain Chan, Huang Xu, and Man Ng Peng, "Managing CMS and Employee Cultural Outcomes: The Mediating Role of Trust," *Asia Pacific Journal of Management,* 25, no. 2 (2008): 277–95.

30. Edward T. Hall and Mildred R. Hall, *Understanding Cultural Differences* (Yarmouth, ME: Intercultural Press, 1990); Edward T. Hall, "How Cultures Collide," *Psychology Today,* July 1976, pp. 67–74.

31. Simcha Ronen and Oded Shenkar, "Clustering Countries on Attitudinal Dimensions: A Review and Synthesis," *Academy of Management Review* 10, no. 3 (1985): 435–54.

32. S.H. Schwartz, "A Theory of Cultural Values and Some Implications for Work," *Applied Psychology: An International Review* 48, no. 1 (1999): 23–47.

33. Charles Hampden-Turner and Fons Trompenaars, *Building Cross-Cultural Competence: How to Create Wealth from Conflicting Values* (New Haven, CT: Yale University Press, 2000), pp. 1–2.

34. A.G. Cant, "Internationalizing the Business Curriculum: Developing Intercultural Competence," *Journal of American Academy of Business* 5, no. 1/2 (2004): 177–83.

35. Xiaodong Deng, William J. Doll, Said S. Al-Gahtani, Tor J. Larsen, John Michael Pearson, and T.S. Raghunathan, "A Cross-Cultural Analysis of the End-User Computing Satisfaction Instrument: A Multi-Group Invariance Analysis," *Information & Management* 45, no. 4 (2008): 211–20.

36. Michael Wynne, "Shake, Hug, or Kiss," *Global Cosmetic Industry* 172, no. 5 (2004): 26–28.

37. Chun-ju Flora Hung, "Cultural Influence on Relationship Cultivation Strategies: Multinational Companies in China," *Journal of Communication Management* 8, no. 3 (2004): 264–82.

NOTES TO CHAPTER 3

1. Cowen Tyler, "The Global Show Must Go On," *New York Times,* June 8, 2008, p. BU 5.

2. For a detailed review of economic variables, refer to Karl E. Case and Ray C. Fair, *Principles of Economics,* 6th ed. (Upper Saddle River, NJ: Prentice Hall, 2004).

3. The World Bank, "World Economic Statistics," June 10, 2008. Available at http://www.world-bank.WBSITE/EXTERNAL/DATASTATISTICS/ (accessed June 10, 2008).

4. Alphonso O. Ogbuehi, "Pricing Strategies in High-Inflation Markets: Implications for the Multinational Corporation," *Journal of Applied Business Research* 9, no. 1 (1990): 44–49.

5. "China's Trade Surplus Soars," CNN.com/World Business (accessed January 11, 2008).

6. Paul J.H. Schoemaker, "Scenario Planning: A Tool for Strategic Thinking," *Sloan Management Review* 36, no. 2 (Winter 1995): 25–40.

7. For an extensive discussion of scenario planning, see Mats Lindgren and Hans Bandhold, *Scenario Planning: The Link between Future and Strategy* (New York: Palgrave/Macmillan, 2003).

8. Elizabeth Becker, "Nordic Countries Come Out near Top in Two Business Surveys," *New York Times,* October 14, 2004, p. C3.

9. "Light on the Shadows," *Economist,* May 3, 1997, pp. 63–64.

10. Friedrich Schneider and Dominik Enste, *Hiding in the Shadows: The Growth of the Underground Economy* (Washington, DC: International Monetary Fund, 2002).

11. Michael E. Porter, *The Competitive Advantage of Nations* (New York: Free Press, 1990), p. 1.

12. "Seto Ohashi Bridge," *Japan Atlas: Architecture,* Winter 2004, p. 1.

13. Jack Baranson, *Technology and Multinationals* (Lexington, MA: D.C. Heath, 1978).

NOTES TO CHAPTER 4

1. Martin William, "Africa's Future: From North-South to East-South?" *Third World Quarterly* 29, no. 2 (2008): 339–51.

2. Simon Romero and Clifford Krauss, "Venezuelan Plan Shakes Investors," *New York Times,* January 10, 2007 pp. 1, C5.

3. Enrico Giovannini, "Statistics and Politics in a 'Knowledge Society,'" *Social Indicators Research* 86, no. 2 (2008): 177–200.

4. Paul M. Vaaler, "How Do MNCs Vote in Developing Country Elections," *Academy of Management Journal* 51, no. 1 (2008): 21–43.

5. R.J. Rummel and David A. Heenan, "How Multinationals Analyze Political Risk," *Harvard Business Review* 56, no. 1 (178): 67–76.

6. R.T. Lenz and Jack L. Engledow, "Environmental Analysis Units and Strategic Decision-Making: A Field Study of Selected 'Leading Edge' Corporations," *Strategic Management Journal* 7, no. 1 (1985): 69–89.

7. Fredrick Stapenhurst, "The Rise and Fall of Political Risk Assessment," *Management Decision* 30, no. 5 (1992): 54–57.

8. John F. Preble, Pradeep A. Rau, and A. Reichel, "The Environmental Scanning Practices of Multinational Firms—An Assessment," *International Journal of Management* 6, no. 1 (1989): 18–28.

9. Jean J. Boddewyn and Thomas L. Brewer, "International Business Political Behavior: New Theoretical Direction," *Academy of Management Review* 19 no. 1 (1994): 119–43.

10. Benjamin Weiner, "What Executives Should Know about Political Risk," *Management Review,* January 1992, pp. 19–22.

11. Thomas L. Brewer, "An Issue Area Approach to the Analysis of MNE-Government Relations," *Journal of International Business Studies* 23, no. 2 (1992): 295–309.

12. Jack N. Behrman, *U.S. International Business and Governments* (New York: McGraw-Hill, 1971).

13. Ivar Kolstad and Espen Villanger, "Determinants of FDI in Services," *European Journal of Political Economy* 24, no. 2 (2008): 518–33.

14. John D. Daniels, Lee H. Radebaugh, and Daniel P. Sullivan, *International Business: Environments and Operations,* 11th ed. (Upper Saddle River, NJ: Prentice Hall, 2007), p. 91.

15. Gabriel A. Almond and G. Bingham Powell, Jr., eds., *Comparative Politics Today: A World View,* 3rd ed. (Boston: Little, Brown, 1984), pp. 1–9.

16. Stephen B. Tallman, "Home Country Political Risk and Foreign Direct Investment in the United States," *Journal of International Business Studies* 19, no. 2 (1988): 219–34.

17. Gardiner Morse, "Doing Business in a Dangerous World," *Harvard Business Review* 80, no. 4 (2002): 22–24.

18. Weiner, "What Executives Should Know about Political Risk."

19. Stefan H. Robock and Kenneth Simmonds, *International Business and Multinational Enterprises* (Homewood, IL: Richard D. Irwin, 1989), chap. 15.

20. Jerry Rodgers, ed., *Global Risk Assessments: Issues, Concepts, and Applications* (Riverside, CA: GRA Publications, 1986).

21. Stephen J. Kobrin, John Basek, Stephen Blank, and Joseph LaPalombara, "The Assessment and Evaluation of Non-Economic Environments by American Firms: A Preliminary Report," *Journal of International Business Studies* 11, no. 1 (1980): 32–47.

22. Rodgers, ed., *Global Risk Assessments.*

23. Andrea Glodstein, "A Latin American Global Player Goes to Asia: Embraer in China," *International Journal of Technology & Globalization* 4, no. 1 (2008): 4.

24. Frederick Stapenhurst, "Political Risk Analysis in North American Multinationals: An Empirical Review and Assessment," *The International Executive* 37, no. 2 (1995): 127–45.

25. Lee Ann Gjertsen, "Different Strategies for Managing Political Risk," *American Banker* 169, no. 128 (2004): 6.

26. Clark Ephraim, "Valuing Political Risk," *Journal of International Money and Finance* 16, no. 3 (1997): 477–91.

27. Elena Iankova and Jan Katz, "Strategies for Political Risk Mediation by International Firms in Transition Economies: The Case of Bulgaria," *Journal of World Business* 38, no. 3 (2003): 182–203.

28. Jean-Claude Cosset and Jean-Marc Suret, "Political Risk and the Benefits of International Portfolio Diversification," *Journal of International Business Studies* 26, no. 2 (1995): 301–19.

29. Joseph A. Cherian and Enrico Perotti, "Option Pricing and Foreign Investment under Political Risk," *Journal of International Economics* 55, no. 2 (2001): 359–78.

30. David P. Baron, *Business and Its Environment* (Upper Saddle River, NJ: Prentice Hall, 1993), pp. 177–79.

31. Donald Ball and Wendell H. McCulloch, Jr., *International Business: Introduction and Essentials,* 5th ed. (Homewood, IL: Richard Irwin, 1993), p. 368.

32. Kirk T. Albrecht, "Turning the Prophet's Words into Profits," *Business Week,* March 16, 1998, p. 14.

NOTES TO CHAPTER 5

1. Business Roundtable, "NAFTA: A Decade of Growth," White Paper (Washington, DC: The Trade Partnership, February 2004). Available at http://www.tradepartnership.com/pdf_files/NAFTA_Decade_of_Growth.pdf (accessed July 7, 2008).

2. Tarini J. Carr, "The Harappan Civilization," *Archeology Online.* Available at http://www.archaeologyonline.net/artifacts/harappa-mohenjodaro.html (accessed July 07, 2008).

3. Raymond Vernon, "International Investment and International Trade in the Product Life Cycle," *Quarterly Journal of Economics* 80 (1966): 190–207.

4. Directorate for Financial and Enterprise Affairs, OECD, "Foreign Direct Investment for Development; Maximising Benefits, Minimising Costs," OECD Report (Paris: OECD Publishing, 2002). Available at http://www.oecd.org/document/33/0,3343,en_2649_34893_1960161_1_1_1_1,00.html (accessed July 07, 2008).

5. John Dunning, "The Eclectic (OLI) Paradigm of International Production: Past, Present, and Future," *International Journal of the Economics of Business* 8, no. 2 (July 2001): 173–90.

6. ALCOA, "Alcoa Announces Cooperation Agreement with Vietnam on Development of Bauxite Mining and Alumina Refineries," news release, June 24, 2008. Available at http://www.alcoa.com/global/en/news/news_detail.asp?pageID=20080624006033en&newsYear=2008 (accessed July 08, 2008).

7. Theo Eicher and Jong Woo Kang, "Trade, Foreign Direct Investment, or Acquisition: Optimal Entry Modes for Multinationals," Working Paper CESIFO 1174, May 2004. Available at www.ssrn.com (accessed July 08, 2008).

8. David Barboza, "U.S. Group Accuses Chinese Toy Factories of Labor Abuses," *New York Times,* August 22, 2007.

9. Food and Agricultural Organization, *The State of Agricultural Commodity Markets 2004,* Biennial Report, Rome, Italy, p. 22. Available at www.fao.org.

10. United Nations Conference on Trade and Development, "Foreign Direct Investment Reached New Record in 2007," news release, January 8, 2008. Available at www.unctad.org.

11. David E. Sanger, "Worries about Reaction in U.S., Japanese Assess Investment Policy," *New York Times,* November 24, 1989.

12. The Computer Science and Technology Board, National Research Council, "Keeping the U.S. Computer Industry Competitive: Defining the Agenda," (Washington, DC: CSTB, 1990). Available at http://www7.nationalacademies.org/cstb/.

13. Joshua Aizenman and Ilan Noy, "FDI and Trade—Two Way Linkages," Working Paper 05–09, University of California, Santa Cruz, May 2005; and J. Peter Neary, "Trade Costs and Foreign Direct Investment," CEPR Discussion Paper 5933, University of Ireland, University College, Dublin, November 2006. Available at www.ssrn.com (accessed July 10, 2008).

14. Courtney Fingar, "A Tangled Web That Is Courting Chaos," *FDI Magazine,* October 6, 2008. Available online through Financial Times Ltd., London, at http://www.fdimagazine.com/news/printpage.php/aid/2529/Editor_s_note:_A_tangled_web_that_is_courting_chaos.html (accessed November 14, 2008).

NOTES TO CHAPTER 6

1. Richard Harris and Qian Cher Li, "Evaluating the Contribution of Exporting to U.K. Productivity Growth: Some Microeconomic Evidence," *World Economy* 31, no. 2 (2008): 212–35.

2. Luis Filipe Lages, Sandy D. Jap, and David A. Griffin, "The Role of Past Performance in Export Ventures: A Short-Term Reactive Approach," *Journal of International Business Studies* 39, no. 2 (2008): 304–25.

3. Ven Sriram, James P. Neelankavil, and Russell Moore, "Export Policy and Strategy Implications for Small-to-Medium-Sized Firms," *Journal of Global Marketing* 3, no. 2 (1989): 43–61.

4. T.K. Das and Bing-Sheng Teng, "A Resource-Based Theory of Strategic Alliances," *Journal of Management* 26, no. 1 (2000): 31–61.

5. Richard C. Hoffman and John F. Preble, "Global Diffusion of Franchising: A Country Level Examination," *Multinational Business Review* 9, no. 1 (2001): 66–76.

6. John Tozzi, "Is It Time to Buy a Franchise?" *Business Week,* March 10, 2008, p. 12.

7. "Merck Signs Licensing Agreement with Sol-Gel," *Soap, Perfumery & Cosmetics,* February 2008, p. 8.

8. Kyuho Lee, Mahmood A. Khan, and Jae-Youn Ko, "Outback Steakhouse in Korea," *Administration Quarterly* 49, no. 1 (2008): 62–72.

9. Tony Dignam, "Franchising a Structured Plan Is the Key to Success," *Accountancy Ireland* 40, no. 1 (2008): 54–55.

10. Destan Kandemir and G. Tomas Hult, "A Conceptualization of an Organizational Learning Culture in International Joint Ventures," *Industrial Marketing Management* 34, no. 5 (2005): 440–46.

11. Mike W. Peng and Oded Shenkar, "Joint Venture Dissolution as Corporate Divorce," *Academy of Management Executive* 16, no. 2 (2002): 92–105.

12. Arvind Parkhe, "Building Trust in International Alliances," *Journal of World Business* 33, no. 4 (1998): 417–37.

13. "Motorola Joins Two India Joint Ventures," United Press International (UPI) News Brief, July 25, 2006.

14. Anne-Wil Harzing, "Acquisitions versus Greenfield Investments: International Strategy and Management of Entry Modes," *Strategic Management Journal* 23, no. 3 (2002): 211–27.

15. Charles W.L. Hill, Peter Hwang, and Chan W. Kim, "An Eclectic Theory of the Choice on International Entry Mode," *Strategic Management Journal* 11, no. 2 (1990): 117–28.

16. Ashish Arora and Andrea Fosfuri, "Wholly Owned Subsidiary versus Technology Licensing in the Worldwide Chemical Industry," *Journal of International Business Studies* 31, no. 4 (2000): 555–72.

Notes to Chapter 7

1. Tim Brown, "Design Thinking," *Harvard Business Review* 89, no. 6 (2008): 84–92.

2. Jay R. Galbraith, *Designing Organizations: An Executive Guide to Strategy Structure and Process* (San Francisco: Jossey-Bass, 2002).

3. Cliff Edwards, "Shaking Up Intel's Insides," *Business Week,* January 31, 2005, p. 35.

4. Danny Miller, Russell Eisenstat, and Nathaniel Foote, "Strategy from the Inside Out: Building Capability-Creating Organizations," *California Management Review* 44, no. 3 (2002): 37–54.

5. Mohanbir Sawhney, "Don't Homogenize, Synchronize," *Harvard Business Review* 79, no. 7 (2001): 100–108.

6. Julian Birkinshaw, Neil Hood, and Stefan Jonsson, "Building Firm-Specific Advantages in Multinational Corporations," *Strategic Management Journal* 19, no. 3 (1998): 221–41.

7. Sergio Olavarrieta and Roberto Friedmann, "Market Orientation, Knowledge-Related Resources and Firm Performance," *Journal of Business Research* 61, no. 6 (2008): 623–30.

8. Claudio Carpano and Manzur Rahman, "Information Technology, International Marketing and Foreign Subsidiaries Market Share," *Multinational Business Review* 6, no. 1 (1998): 36–43.

9. David Cray, "Control and Coordination in Multinational Corporations," *Journal of International Business Studies* 15, no. 2 (1984): 85–98.

10. Peter Drucker, *The Practice of Management* (New York: Harper & Row, 1954).

11. Paul Evans, Vladimir Pucik, and Jean-Louis Barsoux, *The Global Challenge: Frameworks for International Human Resource Management* (Boston: McGraw-Hill, 2002).

12. John Child and Rita Gunther McGrath, "Organizations Unfettered: Organizational Form in an Information-Intensive Economy," *Academy of Management Journal* 44, no. 6 (2001): 1135–48.

13. Ting-Ping Liang and Mohan Tanniru, "Customer-Centric Information Systems," *Journal of Management Information Systems* 23, no. 3 (Winter 2007): 9–15.

14. Indranil Bardhan, Jonathan Whitaker, and Sunil Mithas, "Information Technology, Production Process Outsourcing, and Manufacturing Plant Performance," *Journal of Management Information Systems* 23, no. 2 (Fall 2006): 13–40.

15. Jules Duga and Tim Studt, "Globalization Distributes More of the R&D Wealth, *R&D Magazine* 49, no. 9 (2007): G3–18.

16. Barry Jaruzelski, Kevin Dehoff, and Rakesh Bordia, "A Select Set of Companies Sustain Superior Financial Performance While Spending Less on R&D Than Their Competitors," *Booz Allen Hamilton's Annual Study of the World's 1,000 Largest Corporations R&D Budgets,* November 13, 2006, pp. 1–21.

17. "Spending by Semiconductors," *Electronic News* 52, no. 30 (2006): 29.

18. Jaruzelski, Dehoff, and Bordia, "A Select Set of Companies Sustain Superior Financial Performance While Spending Less on R&D Than Their Competitors."

19. K. Kim, J-H Park, and J.E. Prescott, "The Global Integration of Business Functions: A Study of Multinational Business in Integrated Global Industries," *Journal of International Business Studies* 34, no. 4 (2003): 327–44.

20. Paul Larson, "An Empirical Study of Inter-organizational Functional Integration and Total Costs," *Journal of Business Logistics* 15, no. 1 (1994): 153–69.

21. George S. Day, "Aligning the Organization with the Market," *Sloan Management Review* 48, no. 1 (2006): 41–49.

22. Vijay Govindrajan, "A Contingency Approach to Strategy Implementation at the Business-Unit Level: Integrating Administrative Mechanisms with Strategy," *Academy of Management Journal* 31, no. 4 (1988): 828–53.

NOTES TO CHAPTER 8

1. Xiaofeng Ma and Marcel Dissel, "Rapid Renovation of Operational Capabilities by ERP Implementation: Lessons from Four Chinese Manufacturers," *International Journal of Manufacturing Technology and Management* 14, no. 3–4 (2008): 431–47.

2. David A. Aaker, "Creating a Sustainable Competitive Advantage," *California Management Review,* Winter 1989, pp. 91–106.

3. Theodore Levitt, "Marketing Intangible Products and Product Intangibles," *Harvard Business Review,* May–June 1981, pp. 94–102.

4. M. Bachlaus, M.K. Tiwari, and R. Shankar, "Cost Management and Time Management in Lean Manufacturing," *International Journal of Production Research* 46, no. 12 (2008): 3387–413.

5. Matthias Zimmermann, Lars Zschom, Joachim Kaschel, and Tobia Teich, "A Conceptual Model and an Information Tool for the Establishment of Production Networks Based on Small and Smallest Enterprises," *International Journal of Manufacturing Technology and Management* 14, no. 3–4 (2008): 342–58.

6. Shawnee K. Vickery, Cornelia Droge, and Robert E. Markland, "Production Competence and Business Strategy: Do They Affect Business Performance?" *Decision Sciences* 24, no. 2 (1993): 435–55.

7. Robert N. Mefford, "Determinants of Productivity Differences in International Manufacturing," *Journal of International Business Studies,* Spring 1986, pp. 63–82.

8. David Woodruff, "Why Mercedes Is Alabama Bound," *Business Week,* October 11, 1993, pp. 138–39.

9. City Mayors, "The World's Top Cities Offering the Best Quality of Life," March 7, 2009. Available at http://www.citymayors.com/features/quality_survey.html; "The World's Most Expensive Big Cities," March 7, 2009. Available at http://www.citymayors.com/features/cost_survey.html.

10. Richard Chacon, "Managing the Crisis BankBoston Sticks to Latin Expansion Strategy; Despite Global Breakdown and Investor Jitters," *Boston Globe,* September 30, 1998, p. E1.

11. Grit Walther, Thomas Spengler, and Dolores Queiruga, "Facility Location Planning for Treatment of Large Household Appliances in Spain," *International Journal of Environmental Technologies and Management* 8, no. 4 (2008): 405–25.

12. Paul M. Swamidass, "A Comparison of the Plant Location Strategies of Foreign and Domestic Manufacturers in the U.S.," *Journal of International Business Studies* 21, no. 2 (1990): 301–17.

13. For a detailed discussion of these two methods, refer to Jay Heizer and Barry Render, *Production and Operations Management* (Upper Saddle River, NJ: Prentice Hall, 1996), pp. 352–53.

14. Manoj K. Malhotra and Larry P. Ritzman, "Resource Flexibility Issues in Multistage Manufacturing," *Decision Sciences* 21, no. 4 (1990): 673–90.

15. Steven C. Wheelwright and Robert H. Hayes, "Competing through Manufacturing, *Harvard Business Review,* January–February 1985, pp. 99–109.

16. K.R. Harrigan, *Strategies for Vertical Integration* (Lexington, MA: D.C. Heath, 1983).

17. S.K.M. Ho, "TQM and Organizational Change," *International Journal of Organizational Analysis* 7, no. 2 (1999): 169–81.

18. "How Manufacturers Drive Improvement," *Industrial Engineer* 36, no. 3 (2004): 1. For additional information on TQM, see E.A. Anderson and Adams A. Dennis, "Evaluating the Success of TQM Implementations: Lessons from Employees," *Production and Inventory Management Journal* 38, no. 4 (1997): 1–6; A.M.Y. Chan, Fangus Wai-Wa Chu, and Chi Kwong Yuen, "A Successful TQM Project in China," *International Journal of Commerce & Management* 11, no. 1 (2000): 75–90; Z. Zhang, "Developing a Model of Quality Management Methods and Evaluating Their Effects on Business Performance," *Total Quality Management* 11, no. 1 (2000): 129–37.

19. Dennis Sester, "Motorola: A Tradition of Quality," *Quality* 40, no. 10 (2001): 30–34.

20. General Electric, "Making Customers Feel Six Sigma Quality." Available at http://www.ge.com/sixsigma/makingcustomers.html (accessed August 5, 2004).

21. "How Manufacturers Drive Improvement," *Industrial Engineer* 36, no. 3 (2004): 1.

22. Fataneh Taghaboni-Dutta and Keith Moreland, "Using Six-Sigma to Improve Loan Portfolio Performance," *Journal of American Academy of Business, Cambridge* 5, no. 1–2 (2004): 15–21.

23. iSixSigma, "Ask the Expert. The Topic: Six Sigma and Business Strategy." Interview with Joe Valasquez, Senior Vice President, Bank of America. Available at http://www.isixsigma.com/library/content/a040823a.asp (accessed June 2008).

24. Will Wade, "The Tech Scene: B of A Touts Six Sigma's Bottom-Line Benefits," *American Banker* 169, 144 (July 28, 2004): 1–2.

25. John P. Shewchuk, "Worker Allocation in Lean U-Shaped Production Lines," *International Journal of Production Research* 46, no. 13 (2008): 3485–502.

26. Gerald R. Aase, John R. Olson, and Marc J. Schniederjans, "U-Shaped Assembly Layouts and Their Impact on Labor Productivity: An Experimental Study," *European Journal of Operations Research* 156, no. 3 (2004): 698–712.

27. E.P. Hibbert, "Global Make-or-Buy Decisions," *Industrial Marketing Management* 22, no. 2 (1993): 67–77.

28. Song Huang, Yujin Hu, and Chenggang Li, "A TCPN Based Approach to Model the Coordination in Virtual Manufacturing Organizations," *Computers and Industrial Engineering* 47, no. 1 (2004): 61–77.

29. Jamie Flinchbaugh and James J. Benes, "In Search of Waste," *American Machinist* 148, no. 6 (2004): 56–58.

30. Drew Lathin and Ron Mitchell, "Learning from Mistakes," *Quality Progress* 34, no. 6 (2001): 39–45.

31. "How Manufacturers Drive Improvement," *Industrial Engineer* 36, no. 3 (2004): 1.

32. Scott McMurray, "Ford's F-150: Have It Your Way," *Business Week,* March 2004, pp. 53–55.

33. Shigeo Shingo, *Non-Stock Production: The Shingo System for Continuous Improvement* (Cambridge, MA: Productivity Press, 1988), p. 36.

34. Robert D'Avanzo, "The Reward of Supply Chain Excellence," *Optimize,* December 2003, p. 68.

35. Timothy Aeppel, "Manufacturers Cope with Costs of Strained Global Supply Lines," *New York Times,* December 8, 2004, p. 1A.

36. D. Hunter, "How Dell Keeps from Stumbling," *Business Week,* May 14, 2001, pp. 38–40.

37. "E. China City Becomes Auto Part Export Giant," *Xinhua,* May 26, 2004, p. 1.

38. Masaaki Kotabe and Glenn S. Omura, "Sourcing Strategies of European and Japanese Multinationals: A Comparison," *Journal of International Business Studies,* Spring 1989, pp. 113–30.

39. George S. Day, *Understand CRM* (London: Financial Times, 2000), pp. 10–13.

NOTES TO CHAPTER 9

1. "Sourcing Global Talent: Europe's Place in a Globalised Economy—Interview with Mark Spelman, Chairman of the American Chamber of Commerce's Executive Committee in Brussels," *New Europe,* June 16, 2008. Available at http://www.neurope.eu/articles/87848.php (accessed August 28, 2008).

2. U.S. Department of Labor, Bureau of Labor Statistics, Table of Civilian Unemployment Rate, 1974–2007. Available at http://www.federalreserve.gov/boarddocs/hh/2007/february/figure34.htm (accessed August 28, 2008).

3. Cédric Tille and Kei-Mu Yi, "Curbing Unemployment in Europe: Are There Lessons from Ireland and the Netherlands?" *Current Issues in Economics and Finance* 7, no. 5 (May 2001).

4. Neil Shister, "Executive Overview: Near-Sourcing," *World Trade,* January 3, 2008. Available at http://www.worldtrademag.com/Articles/Column/BNP_GUID_9-5-2006_A_10000000000000226880 (accessed August 28, 2008).

5. "Big 6 'Switch' to Bigger Deals, Corner 2.4% of Global Work," *Economic Times,* June 13, 2008. Available at http://economictimes.indiatimes.com/articleshow/msid-3124559,prtpage-1.cms (accessed August 28, 2008).

6. E-Business Strategies (EBS), "Offshore Outsourcing Failure Case Studies." Available at http://www.ebstrategy.com/Outsourcing/cases/failures.htm (accessed August 28, 2008).

7. Dell, "Dell Commences Manufacturing in India for Large, Growing Number of Indian Customers," July 30, 2007. Available at http://www.dell.com/content/topics/global.aspx/corp/pressoffice/en/2007/2007_07_30_in_000?c=us&1 =en&s=corp.

8. NASSCOM, "NASSCOM-McKinsey Report 2005: Extending India's Leadership in the Global IT and BPO Industries," news release, December 13, 2007. Available at http://www.nasscom.in/Nasscom/templates/NormalPage.aspx?id=2599.

9. Denise Dubie, "Gartner: Top 30 Offshore Locations for 2008," *Network World,* May 20, 2008. Available at http://www.networkworld.com/news/2008/052008-gartner-top-offshore-locations.html?page=1.

10. Rachelle Jackson, "Wage Rates—China's Rising Costs Make Buyers Think Twice," Ethical Corporation, March 10, 2008. Available at http://www.ethicalcorp.com/content.asp?ContentID=5768.

11. Enrico Benni and Alex Peng, "China's Opportunity in Offshore Services," *McKinsey Quarterly,* May 2008.

12. Government Accountability Office, "Offshoring of Services: An Overview of the Issues," Report to Congressional Committees, December 29, 2005. Available at http://www.gao.gov/new.items/d065.pdf (accessed August 28, 2008).

13. Wal-Mart Watch, "That Was Then, This Is Now." Available at http://walmartwatch.com/pages/that_was_then_this_is_now.

14. D. Monga and C. Chakravarty, "Barclays to Set Up Captive BPO in India," *Economic Times,* May 10, 2008. Available at http://economictimes.indiatimes.com/articleshow/msid-3026165,prtpage-1.cms.

15. Sudin Apte, "Shattering the Offshore Captive Center Myth," Forrester Research, April 30, 2007. Available at http://www.forrester.com/Research/Document/Excerpt/0,7211,42059,00.html.

16. "Captive BPO Centres Begin to Pay Off," *Economic Times,* September 26, 2007. Available at http://economictimes.indiatimes.com/Infotech/ITeS/Captive_BPO_centres_begin_to_pay_off/articleshow/2402877.cms.

17. Marianne Kolbasuk McGee, "Vast Majority of U.S. Companies Don't Offshore IT Work," *InformationWeek,* January 23, 2008. Available at http://www.informationweek.com/news/management/outsourcing/showArticle.jhtml?articleID=205917099.

18. "Off-Shoring: How Big Is It?" A Report of the Panel of the National Academy of Public Administration for the U.S. Congress and the Bureau of Economic Analysis, October 2006. Available at http://www.bea.gov/papers/pdf/NAPASecondOff-ShoringReport10–31–06.pdf.

19. Procurement Leaders Network, "European Offshoring Spend Set to Soar in 2008," December 17, 2007. Available at http://www.procurementleaders.com/learninggroups/global-sourcing/global-sourcing-news/european-offshoring-soar-2008/.

20. Alice Lipowicz, "Most States Offshore Human Services Tech Support," *Government Computer News,* March 3, 2006. Available at http://www.gcn.com/online/v011_n01/40274–1.html#.

21. Linda Tucci, "PWC Study: Majority of Top Executives Bullish on Outsourcing," *CIO News,* May 24, 2007. Available at http://searchcio.techtarget.com/news/article/0,289142,sid182_gci1256272,00.html.

22. "KPO sector to be worth $10 billion by 2012," *Economic Times,* June 17, 1008. Available at http://economictimes.indiatimes.com/Infotech/ITeS/KPO_sector_to_be_worth_10_billion_by_2012_Assocham/articleshow/3137959.cms (accessed November 21, 2008).

23. Jamie Liddell, "Sourcing Superstars: Alok Aggarwal & Marc Vollenweider, Evalueserve," Articlebase, September 26, 2008, available at http://www.articlesbase.com/outsourcing-articles/sourcing-superstars-alok-aggarwal-marc-vollenweider-evalueserve-579083.html (accessed November 21, 2008).

NOTES TO CHAPTER 10

1. Testimony of Chairman Alan Greenspan before the Committee on Financial Services, U.S. House of Representatives, February 11, 2004, Federal Reserve Board's semiannual Monetary Policy Report to Congress. Available at http://www.federalreserve.gov/boarddocs/hh/2004/february/testimony.htm (accessed July 18, 2008).

2. China may have begun to mint coins even prior to 600 B.C., although they were made of base metals as opposed to silver or gold. See Glyn-Davies, *History of Money from Ancient Times to the Present Day,* 3rd ed. (Cardiff: University of Wales Press, 2002). Excerpts available at http://www.ex.ac.uk/~RDavies/arian/amser/chrono.html (access May 18, 2008).

3. Bank of England, "History and Timeline." Available at www.bankofengland.co.uk (accessed July 18, 2008).

4. Triennial Central Bank Survey, "Foreign Exchange and Derivatives Market Activity in 2007," December 2007, p. 9. Available at www.bis.org (accessed June 16, 2008).

NOTES TO CHAPTER 11

1. Philip M. Parker and Nader T. Tavassoli, "Homeostasis and Consumer Behavior across Cultures," *International Journal of Research in Marketing* 17, no. 1 (2000): 33–53.

2. C. Samuel Craig, William H. Greene, and Susan P. Douglas, "Culture Matters: Consumer Acceptance of U.S. Firms in Foreign Markets," *Journal of International Marketing* 13, no. 4 (2005): 80–103.

3. Musa Pinar and Paul S. Trapp, "Creating Competitive Advantage through Ingredient Branding and Brand Ecosystem: The Case of Turkish Cotton and Textiles," *Journal of International Food and Agribusiness Marketing* 20, no. 1 (2008): 29–56.

4. Lenita Davis, Sijun Wang, and Andrew Lindridge, "Culture Influences on Emotional Response to On-Line Store Atmospheric Cues," *Journal of Business Research* 61, no. 8 (2008): 806–12.

5. Wagner A. Kamakura, "Lifestyle Segmentation with Tailored Interviewing," *Journal of Marketing Research* 32, no. 3 (1995): 308–17.

6. Miriam Jordan, "In India, Luxury Is within Reach of Many," *Wall Street Journal,* October 17, 1995, p. A15.

7. Svein Ottar Olsen and Ulf H. Olsson, "Multientity Scaling and the Consistency of Country-of-Origin Attitudes," *Journal of International Business Studies* 33, no. 1 (2002): 149–67.

8. Zeynep Gurhan-Canli and Durairaj Maheswaran, "Cultural Variations in Country of Origin Effects," *Journal of Marketing Research,* August 2000, pp. 309–17.

9. Terrence Witkowski and Mary Wolfinbarger, "Comparative Service Quality: German and American Ratings of Five Different Service Settings," *Journal of Business Research,* November 2002, 875–81.

10. Theodore Levitt, "The Globalization of Markets," *Harvard Business Review* 61, no. 3 (1983): 92–101.

11. Levitt, "The Globalization of Markets."

12. Henry F.L. Chung, "An Investigation of Cross-Market Standardization Strategies: Experiences in the European Union," *European Journal of Marketing* 39, no. 11–12 (2005): 1345–71.

13. W. Chan Kim and Renée Mauborgne, "Creating New Market Space," *Harvard Business Review,* January–February 1999, pp. 83–93.

14. Chris Barnham, "Instantiation," *International Journal of Market Research* 50, no. 2 (2008): 203–20.

15. Susan P. Douglas, C. Samuel Craig, and Edwin J. Nijssen, "Integrating Branding Strategy across Markets: Building International Brand Architecture," *Journal of International Marketing* 9, no. 2 (2001): 97–114.

16. Shirley Leitch and Sally Davenport, "Corporate Brands and Social Brands," *International Studies of Management and Organization* 37, no. 4 (2008): 45–63.

17. "The 100 Top Brands," *Business Week,* August 6, 2007, pp. 59–63.

18. J. Lynch and L. Whicker, "Do Logistics and Marketing Understand Each Other? An Empirical Investigation of the Interface Activities between Logistics and Marketing," *International Journal of Logistics Research and Applications* 11, no. 3 (2008): 167–78.

19. "Unshackling the Chain Stores," *Economist,* May 31, 2008, pp. 69–70.

20. Ralf W. Seifert, Ulrich W. Thonemann, and Marcel A. Sieke, "Integrating Direct and Indirect Sales Channels under Decentralized Decision-Making," *International Journal of Production Economics* 103, no. 1 (2006): 209–29.

21. Francis Bassolino and Sean Leow, "FICE and the Liberalization of Distribution in China," *China Business Review* 33, no. 4 (2006): 16–30.

22. "Establish New Channels of Distribution to Reduce Our Export Costs," *Controller's Report,* March 2006, p. 10.

23. Patrick Bryne, "Supply Chain Mastery: One Key Success in China," *Logistics Management* 45, no. 7 (2006): 30–32.

24. Yoshinobu Sato, "Some Reasons Why Foreign Retailers Have Difficulty in Succeeding in the Japanese Market," *Journal of Global Marketing* 18, no. 1–2 (2004): 21–44.

25. Alex Rialp, Catherine Axinn, and Sharon Thach, "Exploring Channel Internationalization among Spanish Exporters," *International Marketing Review* 19, no. 2–3 (2002): 133–55.

26. Jerry Kliatchko, "Towards a New Definition of Integrated Marketing Communications," *International Journal of Advertising* 24, no. 1 (2005): 7–34.

27. Claudia Penteado, "InBev Aggressive Marketer with a Diverse Portfolio," *Advertising Age,* June 2, 2008, p. 45.

28. Gillian Rice and Mohammed Al-Mossawi, "The Implications for Islam for Advertising Messages: The Middle Eastern Context," *Journal of Euro-Marketing* 11, no. 3 (2002): 71–96.

29. Charles R. Taylor and Shintaro Okazaki, "Comparison of U.S. and Japanese Subsidiaries'

Advertising Practices in the European Union," *Journal of International Marketing* 14, no. 1 (2006): 98–120.

30. "Leading National Advertisers," *Advertising Age,* June 5, 2008, p. 8.

31. Erica Riebe and John Dawes, "Recall of Radio Advertising in Low-Clutter and High-Clutter Formats," *International Journal of Advertising* 25, no. 1 (2006): 71–86.

32. Sunil Erevelles, Fred Morgan, Ilkim Burke, and Rachel Nguyen, "Advertising Strategy in China: An Analysis of Cultural and Regulatory Factors," *Journal of International Consumer Marketing* 15, no. 1 (2002): 91–123; Suzanne Bidlake, "Survey Results Used in Fight to Resist Restrictions on Ads," *Advertising Age International,* June 2000, pp. 1–2.

33. Yi-Zheng Shi, Ka-Man Cheung, and Gerard Prendergast, "Behavioral Response to Sales Promotions Tools," *International Journal of Advertising* 24, no. 4 (2005): 467–86.

34. "Doing Business in Europe," *European Business Journal* 14, no. 1 (2002): 54–56.

35. Leo Y.M. Sin, Alan C.B. Tse, and Frederick H.K. Yim, "CRM: Conceptualization and Scale Development," *European Journal of Marketing* 39, no. 11–12 (2005): 1264–90.

36. Lynette Ryals and Adrian Payne, "Using IT in Implementing Relationship Marketing Strategies," *Journal of Strategic Management* 9, no. 1 (2001): 3–27.

NOTES TO CHAPTER 12

1. C.K. Prahalad and Jan P. Oosterveld, "Transforming Internal Governance: The Challenge for Multinationals," *Sloan Management Review,* Spring 1999, pp. 31–41.

2. Alan Clardy, "The Strategic Role of Human Resource Development in Managing Core Competencies," *Human Resource Development International* 11, no. 2 (2008): 183–97.

3. Mark A. Royal and Melvyn J. Stark, "Why Some Companies Excel at Conducting Business Globally," *Journal of Organizational Excellence* 25, no. 4 (2006): 3–10.

4. Cristina McEachey, "A Revolutionary Renovation," *Wall Street and Technology,* June 2008, pp. 32–37.

5. Carol A. Rusaw and Michael F. Rusaw, "The Role of Human Resource Development in Integrated Crisis Management: A Public Sector Approach," *Advances in Developing Human Resources* 10, no. 3 (2008): 380–96.

6. Paul R. Sparrow, "Globalisation of HR at Function Level: Four UK-Based Case Studies of the International Recruitment and Selection Process," *International Journal of Human Resource Management* 18, no. 5 (2008): 845–67.

7. Randall S. Schuler, John R. Fulkerson, and Peter J. Dowling, "Strategic Performance Measurement and Management in Multinational Corporations," *Human Resource Management* 30, no. 3 (1991): 365–92; Catherine Truss and Lynda Gratton, "Strategic Human Resource Management: A Conceptual Approach," *International Journal of Human Resource Management* 5, no. 3 (1994): 663–86.

8. Christopher A. Bartlett and Sumantra Ghoshal, "What Is a Global Manager?" *Harvard Business Review,* August 2003, pp. 101–8.

9. Valeria Pulignano, "The Diffusion of Employment Practices of U.S.-Based Multinationals in Europe: A Case Study Comparison of British and Italian-Based Subsidiaries," *British Journal of Industrial Relations* 44, no. 3 (2006): 497–518.

10. Michael Dickman and Noeleen Doherty, "Exploring the Career Capital Impact of International Assignments within Distinct Organizational Contexts," *British Journal of Management* 19, no. 2 (2008): 145–61.

11. Michael Goold, "Strategic Control in the Decentralized Firm," *Sloan Management Review* 32, no. 2 (1991): 69–81.

12. Kevin DeSouza and Yukika Awazu, "Emerging Tensions of Knowledge Management Control," *Singapore Management Review* 28, no. 1 (2006): 1–13.

13. Richard F. Meyer, "N.V. Philips Electronics: Currency Hedging Policies," *Harvard Business Review Interactive Case Study,* October 13, 1994, p. 1. Available at http://harvardbusinessonline.hbsp.

harvard.edu/b02/en/common/item_detail.jhtml;jsessionid=Y4N341PRGZB5WAKRGWCB5VQBKE
0YOISW?id=295055&referral=2340 (accessed December 7, 2008).

14. Bob Lewis, "Send the Right People to the Right Places," *People Management* 12, no. 14 (2006): 85–86.

15. Hung-Wen Lee and Ching-Hsiang Liu, "Determinants of the Adjustment of Expatriate Managers to Foreign Countries: An Empirical Study," *International Journal of Management* 23, no. 2 (2006): 302–11.

16. Ramudu Bhanugopan and Alan Fish, "An Empirical Investigation of Job Burnout among Expatriates," *Personnel Review* 35, no. 4 (2006): 449–68.

17. Steven D. Maurer and Shaomin Li, "Understanding Expatriate Managers' Performance: Effects of Governance Environment on Work Relationships in Relation-Based Economies," *Human Resource Management Review* 16, no. 1 (2006): 29–46.

18. Hal B. Gregersen, "The Right Way to Manage Expats," *Harvard Business Review,* March–April 1999, pp. 52–61.

19. Phyllis Tharenou and Michael Harvey, "Examining the Overseas Staffing Options Utilized by Australian Headquartered Multinational Corporation," *International Journal of Human Resource Management* 17, no. 6 (2006): 1095–1114.

20. Ma. Evelina Ascalon, Deidra J. Schleicher, and Marise Ph. Born, "Cross-Cultural Social Intelligence: An Assessment for Employees Working in Cross-National Contexts," *Cross-Cultural Management* 15, no. 2 (2008): 109–30.

21. Robert Taylor, "Companies Cut Back Overseas Transfer Benefits," *Financial Times,* July 18, 1996, p. 1.

22. Karen Dawn Stuart, "Teens Play a Role in Moves Overseas," *Personnel Journal,* March 1992, pp. 72–78.

23. Charles M. Vance and Yongsun Paik, "Forms of Host-Country National Learning for Enhanced MNC Absorptive Capacity," *Journal of Management Psychology* 20, no. 7 (2005): 590–606.

24. Anil K. Gupta and Vijay Govindarajan, "Knowledge Flows within Multinational Corporations," *Strategic Management Journal* 21, no. 4 (2000): 473–96.

25. "Building a Competitive Organization for the 1990s," *Business International,* June 11, 1990, p. 190.

26. Tarun Khanna and Krishna Palepu, "The Right Way to Restructure Conglomerates in Emerging Markets," *Harvard Business Review,* July–August 1999, pp.125–34.

27. Sarah Ellison "Kimberly-Clark to Reorganize: High-Ranking Official to Retire," *Wall Street Journal,* January 20, 2004, p. A3.

28. Marlynn L. May and Ricardo B. Contreras, "Promotor(a)s, the Organizations in Which They Work, and an Emerging Paradox: How Organizational Structure and Scope Impact Promotor(a)s' Work," *Health Policy* 82, no. 2 (2007): 153–66.

29. John W. Hunt, "Is Matrix Management a Recipe for Chaos?" *Wall Street Journal,* January 12, 1998, p. 10.

30. Christopher A. Bartlett and Sumantra Ghoshal, "Matrix Management: Not a Structure, a Frame of Mind," *Harvard Business Review,* July–August 1990, pp. 138–45.

31. Irja Hyväri, "Project Management Effectiveness in Project-Oriented Business Organizations," *International Journal of Project Management* 24, no. 3 (2006): 216–25.

32. "Corporate Networking Increases Organizational Choices," *Business International,* July 9, 1990, p. 225.

Notes to Chapter 13

1. Peter Bachman, "Former Managers Threaten SAP with Legal Action," *China Business News,* August 20, 2008. Available at http://www.bizchina-update.com/content/view/1239/2/.

2. As a result of the financial crisis of 2008, Congress has temporarily increased the deposit insurance from $100,000 to $250,000 until December 31, 2009.

3. For more about the International Standards Organization, see http://www.iso.org.

4. For more about the SWIFT organization, see http://www.swift.com.

5. "Global Air Freight Forecast to Return to Strong Growth, says OAG," Official Airline Guide press release, May 21, 2008. Available at http://www.oag.com/oagcorporate/pressreleases/08+OAG+Air+Freight+Forecast+May08.html (accessed July 14, 2008).

6. For more about the Ex-Im bank, see http://www.exim.gov.

7. For more about the Overseas Private Investment Corporation, see http://www.opic.gov.

8. For more about the Multilateral Investment Guarantee Agency, see http://www.miga.org.

9. For more about the New York Stock Exchange, see http://www.nyse.com/.

10. For more about the London Stock Exchange, see http://www.londonstockexchange.com.

11. JPMorgan, *Global Depository Receipts: Reference Guide* (New York: JPMorgan Chase & Co., 2008). Available at http://www.adr.com/pdf/ADR_Reference_Guide.pdf (accessed July 16, 2008).

12. Patrick McGuire, "A Shift in London's Eurodollar Market," *BIS Quarterly Review,* September 2004, pp. 67–77. Available at http://econpapers.repec.org/article/bisbisqtr/0409g.htm (accessed July 16, 2008).

13. For more about the Office of Foreign Assets Control, see http://www.cbp.gov.

14. Gibson, Dunn, & Crutcher LLP, "FCPA Opinion Procedure Release 2008–02," in *2008 Mid-Year FCPA Update,* July 7, 2008. Available at http://www.gibsondunn.com/Publications/Pages/2008Mid-YearFCPAUpdate.aspx (accessed July 17, 2008).

15. Robin Wright and Alan Beattie, "Shipping Suffers as Credit Dries Up," *Financial Times,* October 13, 2008.

16. Carl Mortished, "Commerce Becalmed over Letters of Credit," *London Times,* November 3, 2008. Available at http://business.timesonline.co.uk/tol/business/industry_sectors/banking_and_finance/article5069065.ece (accessed November 11, 2008).

NOTES TO CHAPTER 14

1. For more about the Financial Accounting Standards Board, see http://www.fasb.org (accessed March 18, 2008).

2. For more about the Financial Reporting Council, see http://www.frc.org.uk/ (accessed March 18, 2008).

3. For more details about other countries' accounting boards, see http://www.asb.or.jp/ for Japan; http://www.minefi.gouv.fr/directions_services/CNCompta/ for France; http://www.acsbcanada.org/ for Canada; http://www.standardsetter.de/drsc/news/news.php for Germany; and http://www.aasb.com.au/ for Australia.

4. B.M. Lall Nigam, "Bahi-Khata: The Pre-Pacioli Indian Double-Entry System of Bookkeeping," *Abacus* 22, no. 2 (September 1986): 148–61.

5. See Michael Scorgie, "Indian Imitation or Invention of Cash-Book and Algebraic Double-Entry," *Abacus* 26, no. 1 (March 1990): 63–70; and Christopher Nobes and Edward Elgar, *International Accounting and Comparative Financial Reporting: Selected Essays of Christopher Nobes* (Cheltenham, UK: Edward Elgar, 1999).

6. Omar Abdullah Zaid, "Accounting Systems and Recording Procedures in the Early Islamic State," *Accounting Historians Journal* 31, no. 2 (December 2004).

7. Peter Boys, "What's in a Name: Firms' Simplified Family Trees on the Web," Institute of Chartered Accountants in England and Wales (ICAEW) Online. Available at http://www.icaew.com/index.cfm?AUB=TB2I_36747 (accessed July 20, 2008).

8. See www.iasb.org/ for additional details.

9. The income in the prior years was $31 billion in 1998, $20 billion in 1997, and $13 billion in 1996. Source: Annual reports, Enron.

10. Claudio Celani, "The Story behind Parmalat's Bankruptcy," *Executive Intelligence Review,*

January 16, 2004. Available at http://www.larouchepub.com/other/2004/3102parmalat_invest.html (accessed July 23, 2008).

11. "UMC Has \$304 Million Net Loss in 2007 on U.S. Standard," *Reuters,* May 2, 2008. Available at http://www.reuters.com/articlePrint?articleId=USTP6654220080502 (accessed July 23, 2008).

12. "OmniVision Reports Financial Results for Fourth Quarter and Fiscal 2008," *Barron's,* May 29, 2008. Available at http://online.barrons.com/article/PR-CO-20080529–906291.html (accessed July 23, 2008).

13. See David Jetuah, "Citigroup Lays Out IFRS-US GAAP Gulf," *Accountancy Age,* August 30, 2007.

14. Rebecca Toppe and Mark Myring, "Defining Principles-Based Accounting Standards," *CPA Journal,* August 2004. Available at http://www.nysscpa.org/cpajournal/2004/804/essentials/p34.htm (accessed July 10, 2008).

15. Don Durfee, "The Great Experiment: China Is Attempting Its Biggest Accounting Change since the Abandonment of Soviet-Style Bookkeeping," *CFOAsia.com,* May 2007. Available at http://www.cfoasia.com/archives/200705–02.htm (accessed July 23, 2008).

16. "Indian Firms Listed in Europe May Have to Adopt IFRS Standards," *The Economic Times,* April 20, 2008. Available at http://economictimes.indiatimes.com/News/News_By_Industry/Services/Consultancy__Audit/Indian_firms_listed_in_Europe_may_have_to_adopt_IFRS_standards/rssarticleshow/2965694.cms (accessed July 23, 2008).

17. Romir Monitoring Group, "Accounting Reform IFRS Survey Results," survey, September–October 2007. Available at http://www.accountingreform.ru/en/about/view (accessed July 23, 2008).

18. Daniel Drosdoff, "Andean Countries Forge Historic Tax Pact," *IDB America,* May 2005. Available at http://www.iadb.org/idbamerica/index.cfm?thisid=3517 (accessed July 23, 2008).

19. KMPG International, "KMPG's Corporate and Indirect Tax Rate Survey 2007." Available at http://www.kpmg.com/PDF/KPMG%27s%20Corporate%20&%20Indirect%20Tax%20rate%20survey%202007.pdf (accessed July 23, 2008).

Notes to Appendix 1

1. Maxwell A. Cameron, "North American Free Trade Agreement Negotiations: Liberalization Games between Asymmetric Players," *European Journal of International Relations* 3, no. 1 (1997): 105–39.

2. Office of the U.S. Trade Representative, "NAFTA: A Strong Record of Successes," March 2006. Available at http://www.ustr.gov/assets/Document_Library/Fact_Sheets/2006/asset_upload_file242_9156.pdf (accessed June 2008).

3. National Center for Policy Analysis, "Economic Benefits of NAFTA," June 2008. Available at http://www.ncpa.org/pd/trade/pdtrade/pdtrade1.html.

4. S. Sarkar and H.Y. Park, "Impact of the North American Free Trade Agreement on the U.S. Trade with Mexico," *International Trade Journal* 15, no. 3 (Fall 2001): 269–92.

5. Raymond Robertson, "Wage Shocks and North American Labor-Market Integration," *American Economic Review* 90, no. 4 (September 2000): 742–64.

6. Office of the U.S. Trade Representative, "NAFTA: A Strong Record of Successes."

7. U.S. Department of Labor, Bureau of Labor Statistics, "Current Employment Statistics," 2007. Available at http://www.bls.gov/ces.

8. Statistics Canada, "Employment by Industry and Sex," 2007. Available at http://www40.statcan.ca/l01/cst01/labor10a.htm.

9. Secretaria del Trabajo y Prevision Social, "Encuesta Nacional de Empleo," 2004. Available at http://www.stps.gob.mx/.

10. Scott Vaughan, "How Green Is NAFTA? Measuring the Impacts of Agricultural Trade," *Environment* 46 (March 2004): 26–42.

11. Bruce Campbell, "Time to Draw a Line in the Sand: NAFTA and the Softwood Lumber Dispute," *Briefing Paper* 6, no. 1 (March 2005).

12. Tristan Garel-Jones, "Anatomy of a Good Deal," *New Statesman,* October 29, 2007, p. 12.

13. "A Few More Smiles Wouldn't Hurt," *Economist* 377, no. 8447 (October 2005): 64.

14. Hans-Eckart Scharrer, "The Euro's Start-Up Phase Is a Success," *Intereconomics* 35, no. 1 (January 2000): 1.

15. Jerome Sheridan, "The Consequences of the Euro," *Challenge* 42, no. 1 (January–February 1999): 43–54.

16. Jörg Bibow, "The Euro: Market Failure or Central Bank Failure?" *Challenge* 45, no. 3 (May–June 2002): 83–99.

17. "1992 Going on 2010," *European Business Forum,* no. 12 (Winter 2002): 1.

18. "Economic Policy Outlook," *Country Report, European Union,* no. 4 (December 2005): 10–11.

NOTES TO APPENDIX 2

1. The basic information on the workings and organizational structures of the four international agencies was obtained from their individual Web sites: http://www.imf.org; http://www.oecd.org; http://www.un.org; and http://www.worldbank.org (all accessed December 27, 2007).

2. "Bangladesh: Progress, Yes, Substantial *Success,* No," *Market: Asia Pacific* 14, no. 12, (December 2005): 1–2.

3. "Risk Summary: Bosnia-Herzegovina," *Emerging Europe Monitor: South East Europe Monitor* 12, no. 9 (September 2005): 11.

4. "Citigroup Economist Moving to Treasury; Shakers; Marketplace by Bloomberg," *International Herald Tribune,* February 13, 2006, p. 17.

5. Curtis J. Hoxter, "U.S. Raps China's Yuan Exchange Rate as Far Out of Line with Market Levels," *Caribbean Business* 33, no. 39 (October 2005): 8.

6. "Layoffs of Government Workers (DOMINICA)," *Caribbean Update* 22, no. 1 (February 2006): 1.

7. "A Success Story," *Latin America Monitor: Andean Group Monitor* 22, no. 9 (September 2005): 6.

8. Jon Gorvett, "Turkey Turns a Corner," *Middle East,* no. 345 (May 2004): 54–55.

9. "Going, Going, Gone," *Business Middle East* 13, no. 16 (January 2005): 6–7.

10. "Risk Summary: Ukraine," *Emerging Europe Monitor: Russia & CIS* 9, no. 5 (May 2005): 5.

11. "On the Right Path," *Emerging Europe Monitor: South East Europe Monitor* 12, no. 9 (September 2005): 1–10.

12. Graham Bird, "Over-optimism and the IMF," *World Economy* 28, no. 9 (September 2005): 1355–73.

13. Joseph Stiglitz, "The Insider," *New Republic* 222, no. 16–17 (April 2000): 56–59.

14. Andrew Rose, "Which International Institutions Promote International Trade?" *Review of International Economics* 13, no. 4 (September 2005): 682–98.

15. Robert Couzin, "Fighting for Harmony, Not Balance," *International Tax Review* 11, no. 6 (June 2000): 17.

16. W.W. Rostow, "Working Agenda for a Disheveled World Economy," *Challenge* 24, no. 1 (March–April 1981): 5.

17. Jörg Michael Dostal, "Campaigning on Expertise: How the OECD Framed EU Welfare and Labor Market Policies—and Why Success Could Trigger Failure," *Journal of European Public Policy* 11, no. 3 (June 2004): 440–60.

18. Jean-Philippe Cotis, "Statistics-Knowledge and Policy," *OECD World Forum on Key Indicators,* November 2004, p. 1.

19. "OECD Compromises Fail to Satisfy Havens," *International Tax Review* 13, no. 1 (December 2001–January 2002): 4.

20. Matthew Swibel, "Watch What's Done, Not Said," *Forbes,* January 2006, p. 32.

21. Ralph Greer, "UN Is Only as Effective as Biggest Members Want It to Be," *Vancouver Sun* (British Columbia), editorial, March 16, 2004, p. A13.

22. Arnold Beichman, "UN Human Rights and Wrongs," *Washington Post,* May 8, 2005, p. 1.

23. Paul Lewis, "Security Council Pursuing Its Broader World Peace Mission," *New York Times,* January 21, 1990, p. 1.

24. Mikhail S. Gorbachev, "Secure World," *Foreign Broadcast Information Service—Soviet Union,* September 17, 1987, pp. 23–28.

25. Shahzad Uddin and Trevor Hopper, "Accounting for Privatization in Bangladesh: Testing World Bank Claims," *Critical Perspectives on Accounting* 14, no. 7 (October 2003): 739.

26. Zoë Chafe, "World Bank Involvement in Economic Reform: 'A Warning Flag'?" *World Watch* 18, no. 6 (November–December 2005): 9.

27. Tom Buerkle, "Who's Afraid of the Big, Bad Wolfowitz?" *Institutional Investor* 39, no. 9 (September 2005): 52–62.

28. David Wessel, "South Africa Is a Success Story at World Bank," *Wall Street Journal,* Eastern ed., October 6, 1994, p. A15.

29. "Asian Executives Poll," *Far Eastern Economic Review* 160, no. 40 (October 1997): 34.

30. Jayson W. Richardson, "Toward Democracy: A Critique of a World Bank Loan to the United Mexican States," *Review of Policy Research* 22, no. 4 (July 2005): 473–82.

31. Robert Hunter Wade, "The Rising Inequality of World Income Distribution," *Finance and Development* 38, no. 4 (December 2001): 37.

32. "Whose Land Reform?" *Multinational Monitor* 22, no. 6 (June 2001): 7; "Remembering Africa," *Economist* 320, no. 7722 (August 1991): 33.

NOTES TO APPENDIX 3

1. Both technologies were developed by SRI International. See SRI International, "ERMA and MICR: The Origins of Electronic Banking." Available at http://www.sri.com/about/timeline/erma-micr.html (accessed July 30, 2008).

2. Mary Bellis, "Automatic Teller Machines—ATM. The ATM Machine of Luther George Simjian," About.com: Inventors. Available at http://inventors.about.com/od/astartinventions/a/atm.htm (accessed July 30, 2008).

3. The Fed offers three services: Fedwire Fund Services for cash payments, Fedwire Securities Services for transfer of securities, and National Settlement Services for private clearing houses to settle payments at the end of the day. See http://www.federalreserve.gov/paymentsystems/ for more details.

4. Depository Trust and Clearing Corporation, "An Introduction to DTCC: Services and Capabilities," April 2008. Available at http://www.dtcc.com/about/business/index.php (accessed July 28, 2008).

5. More information is available from "The Creation of ASC X12," available at http://www.x12.0rg/x120rg/about/X12History.cfm (accessed August 28, 2008).

Glossary

Absolute advantage: A theory proposed by Adam Smith which states that because some countries can produce certain goods more efficiently than others, they should specialize in and produce enough of these goods for their own consumption and for exports, and they should import certain goods from other countries that might have more efficient production factors.

Accounting: The process of identifying, recording, and interpreting cost and financial data.

Acquisition: The purchase of a company by a group of investors or another company.

American Depository Receipt (ADR): A negotiable certificate issued by a U.S bank. in the United States to represent the underlying shares of a foreign corporation's stock held in trust at a custodian bank in the foreign country.

Arbitrage: Buying and selling currencies or other commodities at a profit by making use of price discrepancies between markets.

Balance of payments: A statement that summarizes all trade and economic transactions between a given country and the rest of the world.

Bank for International Settlements: A bank in Basel, Switzerland, that facilitates financial transactions among central banks.

Bill of lading: A document that is issued to a shipper by a carrier, listing the goods received for shipment.

Black market: Market for goods and services that lies outside the official market.

Brand: A product that is identified with a company by means of a name, symbol, or logo.

Business ethics: The accepted principles of right or wrong governing the conduct of businesses and the people running them.

Capital account: Transactions involving previously existing assets.

Capitalism: An economic system based on the free market approach.

Central bank: A government bank responsible for a country's money supply.

Centralization: An organizational structure in which all decisions are made at a company's headquarters.

Certificate of origin: A shipping document that determines the origin of products and is validated by an external source.

Command economy: An economic system in which resources are allocated and controlled by the government.

Commercial invoice: A bill of goods from the buyer to the seller.

Comparative advantage: A trade theory suggesting that there may still be global efficiency gains from trade if a country specializes in those products that it can produce more efficiently than other products.

Copyright: A legal concept giving the creator of an original work exclusive rights to it, usually for a limited time. It can also be defined as the legal right to reproduce, publish, distribute, and license an original work exclusively.

Corporate social responsibility (CSR): The idea that businesspeople should consider the social consequences of economic actions when making business decisions, and that there should be a presumption in favor of decisions that have both good economic and social consequences.

Country-of-origin effect: The positive effects gained by the quality and reputation of products originating from one country.

Cross-border trade: If countries trade freely, consumers benefit from cheaper goods and services and higher quality goods because of allocation of the most efficient resources and competition.

Cross rate: An exchange rate between two currencies computed from the exchange rate of each currency in relation to the U.S. dollar.

Cultural influences: The forces that affect the communication and interaction patterns of various groups. For instance, the media can be viewed as a cultural influence on members of society.

Culture: The value system of a society that guides its beliefs, customs, knowledge, and morals.

Culture shock: The negative feelings and/or anxiety that an individual feels when relocating to another culture or country. This may manifest itself as a sense of disgust for every aspect of the new society. Many people suffer from reverse culture shock— the feeling of culture shock upon return to their home culture.

Customization (or local adaptation): Adapting a global marketer's products/brands so that they are best suited to the culture and consumer demands of a single target country.

Decentralization: The opposite of centralization; decisions are made at the lower levels of the management.

Democracy: A political system in which the people of the country elect officials to govern the affairs of the nation.

Devaluation: A reduction in the value of one currency in relation to another currency.

Downstream: Management of the supply of finished goods and services to the market.

Dumping: The selling of goods in a foreign market at a price below their cost of production or "fair" market value, using profits from a company's home market to subsidize prices. This is often done to unload excess production or to drive out existing competition in a market.

Economic factors: All of the factors that contribute to the growth/decline of an economy. These include *gross domestic product* (GDP) = the total of all domestic economic activity of a country; *inflation* = a condition where consumer prices are rising; *balance of payments* (BOP) = a statement that summarizes all economic transactions between one country and the rest of the world; and *external debt* = the amount of money borrowed by one country from all banks.

Economic integration: The removal of all trade barriers and factor mobility between countries to facilitate growth. NAFTA is an example of a free trade agreement, which is one form of economic integration.

Economies of scale: The effect of optimal production capacities that reduces total cost by lowering unit cost as output increases through reduction in fixed costs.

Ethnocentric behavior: The belief that one's own culture is superior to that of other cultures. A related concept called consumer ethnocentrism is the belief that one should purchase domestically produced goods, not imported ones.

Ethnocentrism: A belief that one's own values are superior to others.

Exchange market: The system through which transactions in various currencies take place.

Exchange rate: The price of one currency against another currency.

Expatriates: A citizen of one country who is working abroad in a firm's subsidiary.

First-mover advantage: Advantages gained by moving into a foreign market ahead of competitors.

Foreign Corrupt Practices Act (FCPA): A U.S. law that penalizes American companies who engage in bribery.

Foreign direct investments (FDI): The flow of investments from overseas companies that enable them to control operations in a foreign country or a company. FDI flows are influenced by opportunities offered by foreign operations.

Forward rate: A foreign exchange rate quoted today for future delivery (typically 30, 60, or 90 days ahead).

Franchising: Similar to licensing, except it requires a longer commitment. In franchising, the franchiser not only sells intangible property to the franchisee, but also insists that the franchisee abide by the rules of the business. In some cases, the franchiser also assists the franchisee in running the business. The franchiser receives a royalty payment that is usually a percentage of the franchisee's revenues.

GAAP: Generally accepted accounting principles. The accounting standard followed by U.S. companies and set by the Financial Accounting Standards Board (FASB).

Globalization: The process or trend toward a more integrated and interdependent world economy. Through this process, companies are more likely to compete anywhere, source their raw material or R&D anywhere, and produce their products anywhere.

Gray market: The selling of goods through unofficial distributors.

Greenfield investments: Starting foreign operations from scratch. Greenfield investments give the foreign firm a greater ability to build the kind of subsidiary it wants in terms of operations and management philosophy. However, these ventures are slower to establish than acquisitions; therefore, the firm has the possibility of being preempted by other competitors in the market.

Gross domestic product (GDP): The total output of all economic activity in a country.

Gross national income (GNI): New name for GNP.

Gross national product (GNP): The total incomes earned by residents of a country.

Home country: The country in which an international company is headquartered.

Horizontal integration: Entry by a firm into other businesses.

Host country: Any foreign country in which an international company operates.

Intellectual property rights: Ownership rights to intangible assets.

International agencies (World Trade Organization [WTO], United Nations [UN], International Monetary Fund [IMF], World Bank): Significant players or organizations in the global economy.

International business: Any firm that engages in international trade or investment.

International companies: International companies are identified by various names depending on the extent of their operations. In general terms, an *international company* is any company operating in at least one country; a *multinational enterprise* (MNE)/ *multinational corporation* (MNC) is a company that operates in many countries and is involved in all types of international operations; a *transnational company* (TNC) is a company owned by and managed by nationals in different countries (TNC is also a term used by the United Nations to refer to an MNE/MNC); and a *global company* is a company that integrates its operations and has a vast network of operations in many parts of the world.

International Financial Reporting Standards (IFRS): New global standards in accounting that are being adopted throughout the world and replacing existing local standards.

International Monetary Fund (IMF): An international agency created to promote international monetary cooperation after World War II.

Inventory management: A management function critical to the continuous flow of supplies and goods that minimizes the cost of maintaining a safe volume of stock. In international business, because of distances between suppliers and markets, this function takes on an added importance.

Joint ventures: Contractual agreements that require direct investments in which two or more companies share the ownership. Joint ventures can take the form of a minority partnership, a 50/50 partnership, or a majority partnership, where each firms owns a percentage of the business and its corresponding profits.

Just-in-time: An inventory system in which deliveries of inputs are made as they are needed.

Legal systems: Legal systems are often characterized as being based on common law (tradition, precedent, and custom-based), civil law (highly organized into codes with less flexibility than common law), and theocratic law (based upon a religion).

Letter of credit: A guarantee to the exporter that the importer's bank will make payment for the goods upon presentation of the bill of lading.

Licensing: An arrangement whereby a company (licensor) grants the rights to intangible property like patents, inventions, formulas, processes, designs, copyrights, and trademarks to another company (licensee) for a specified period of time. The licensor receives a royalty fee from the licensee.

London Inter-Bank Offered Rate (LIBOR): The interest rate for large interbank loans of Eurocurrencies.

Mixed economy: An economic system characterized by a mix of market and command economies.

Nationalization: The transfer of ownership to the state.

Nontariff barriers: Trade barriers other than tariffs such as quotas and administrative controls.

Offshoring: The process of shifting production to a foreign country.

Outsourcing: The practice of using outside suppliers to perform functions that are executed more efficiently by the outside firms.

Political risk: Exposure of losses to an international company due to changes in the political environment of a host country.

Political systems: Can be characterized as either democratic or totalitarian. Democratic systems have elected officials and typically guarantee individuals various freedoms (speech, media, religion, etc.); totalitarian systems are characterized by one group or political party having power over the society and citizenry.

Polycentrism: Accepting differences in cultural systems.

Purchasing-power parity (PPP): An equalization process in incomes, exchange rates, and household spending based on differences in purchasing power.

Quality: Meeting or exceeding the expectations of a customer.

Quota: A limit on the quantity of a product allowed to be imported or exported.

Services: Nongoods and intangible items that are bought and sold.

Six Sigma: A sophisticated system of quality control that uses data and statistical analysis to achieve close to zero defects.

Special drawing rights (SDR): A unit of account issued to countries by the IMF to help them to manage their reserves.

Spot rate: An exchange rate quoted for immediate delivery on a transaction that occurs within two business days.

Standardization: A strategy adopted by international companies; standardization offers similar products using a similar marketing mix to a similar target market across multiple target countries.

Strategic alliances: Cooperative agreements between potential or actual competitors that can range from formal joint ventures to short-run contractual agreements.

Strategy: Actions by companies to achieve objectives.

Subsidiary: Individual operations of companies in foreign countries.

Supply chain: The management of materials, semifinished goods, and finished goods from supplier to the marketplace.

Target market: Refers to the selection of a homogeneous segment within a single country, or alternatively across multiple countries.

Tariff: Tax levied on imported goods.

Total quality management: A system of quality control that checks quality at every step of the process and is customer driven.

Trade creation: Shifting of production to more efficient countries because of comparative advantage.

Trade diversion: In trade diversion, exports shift to a less efficient country because of trade barriers.

United Nations: An international organization whose goals are to promote world peace and security.

Value added tax: A tax that is a percentage of the value added to a product at each stage of the process.

Vertical integration: Entry by a firm into a different stage of productions in its own industry.

Wholly owned subsidiaries: In a wholly owned subsidiary, the firm owns 100% of the stock of the subsidiary. Wholly owned subsidiaries can be established in a foreign country in two ways. A firm can set up new operations in the foreign country from the ground up (greenfield) or it can acquire a firm and promote its products through that firm (acquisition).

World Bank: A multilateral lending institution that aids developing countries through loans and investment capital.

World Trade Organization (WTO): A voluntary organization through which groups of countries negotiate trading agreements.

Name Index

Italic page references indicate charts and graphs.

Subject Index

About the Authors

James P. Neelankavil is the Robert E. Brockway Distinguished Professor of Marketing and International Business at the Zarb School of Business at Hofstra University. He received his doctoral degree in international business from the Stern School of Business at New York University (NYU) and his MBA with distinction from the Asian Institute of Management in Manila, the Philippines. Prior to joining the Zarb School of Business, Dr. Neelankavil taught at NYU's Stern School of Business.

Recently, Dr. Neelankavil was awarded a Fulbright Senior Specialist fellowship to the Philippines. He has held visiting professorships at Rotterdam School of Management in the Netherlands; at Bocconi University in Milan, Italy; and at NYU's Stern School of Management. His teaching interests include corporate strategy, global business strategy, and international marketing.

Dr. Neelankavil has published over 25 articles and seven books in the area of international business, corporate strategy, and cross-cultural studies. His research has appeared in many leading business journals, including the *Journal of International Business Studies* and the *Journal of Business Research.* His primary research interests are in the areas of cross-cultural management, strategic management, and R&D and innovation.

Anoop Rai received his Ph.D. from Indiana University. He is a professor of finance at the Zarb School of Business at Hofstra University. His current research focuses on international financial markets and institutions, and he has published papers in the *Journal of Banking and Finance,* the *Journal of Economics and Business,* the *Journal of Risk and Insurance,* the *Journal of Futures Markets,* and the *Journal of International Financial Markets.* Professor Rai has taught at several other institutions as a visiting or adjunct professor, including the Rotterdam School of Management in the Netherlands, the University of Catania in Sicily, Italy, and Rutgers University in Singapore. He has also conducted seminars on risk management for bankers from Russia and its newly independent states and for the Netherlands Antilles.

For Product Safety Concerns and Information please contact our EU
representative GPSR@taylorandfrancis.com
Taylor & Francis Verlag GmbH, Kaufingerstraße 24, 80331 München, Germany

www.ingramcontent.com/pod-product-compliance
Ingram Content Group UK Ltd.
Pitfield, Milton Keynes, MK11 3LW, UK
UKHW011455240425
457818UK00021B/847